APPLIED MICROECONOMICS

APPLIED MICROECONOMICS

by
Stephen Hope

JOHN WILEY & SONS LTD

Chichester • New York • Weinheim • Brisbane • Singapore • Toronto

National 01243 779777
International (+44) 1243 779777
e-mail (for orders and customer service enquiries): cs-books@wiley.co.uk
Visit our Home Page on http://www.wiley.co.uk or http://www.wiley.com

Other Wiley Editorial Offices

John Wiley & Sons, Inc., 605 Third Avenue,
New York, NY 10158-0012, USA

WILEY-VCH Verlag GmbH, Pappelallee 3,
D-69469 Weinheim, Germany

Jacaranda Wiley Ltd, 33 Park Road, Milton,
Queensland 4064, Australia

John Wiley & Sons (Asia) Pte Ltd, 2 Clementi Loop #02-01,
Jin Xing Distripark, Singapore 129809

John Wiley & Sons (Canada) Ltd, 22 Worcester Road,
Rexdale, Ontario M9W 1L1, Canada

British Library Cataloguing in Publication Data

A catalogue record for this book is available from the British Library

ISBN 0-471-97914-7

Designed by Mark and Sally Spedding, Salisbury, Wiltshire
Typeset in 10/14pt Times by Mayhew Typesetting, Rhayader, Powys
Printed and bound in Great Britain by Cambrian Press, Aberystwyth, Wales
This book is printed on acid-free paper responsibly manufactured from sustainable forestry, in which at least two trees are planted for each one used for paper production.

Contents

Contents

Preface

This text has been written for students of economics on a single or a combined honours programme. It is aimed at the intermediate courses in microeconomics that are given in many UK universities, although much of the discussion should be accessible to those who have at least some background in the subject.

The explanation of the core theory is almost entirely in words and diagrams. The theory is viewed, at times rather critically, in the light of empirical evidence. Given the importance of the iteration between theory and evidence in many economic problems, the approach of this book is to take selected applications, study them in some depth and then point to the need for further analysis, or additional data, as appropriate.

The main features of the book are

(I) Analysis

This book is divided into four parts covering (I) household decision-making, (II) the firm and market structures, (III) factor markets and (IV) general equilibrium analysis and social welfare. It could therefore be used on both one and two-semester courses. Each part starts with a straightforward discussion of analytical tools, which could be read by way of review by those with more background. Subsequent chapters in each part go on to consider refinements of the analysis. Risk and uncertainty are introduced in Chapter 5, which discusses the demand for insurance by households. The role of asymmetric information is brought in several places, but particularly in analyses of the labour market and the market for investment finance.

(II) Discussion of Equity Issues

The mainstream neo-classical approach emphasises the importance of economic efficiency and it is arguable that equity issues tend to be neglected. This book addresses matters of equity directly in a number of places. For example, the importance of housing tenure in the asset-accumulation of individuals is discussed more than once in Part 1. The role of work incentives is analysed in relation to those on low incomes in Chapter 3 and to those on high incomes in Chapter 8. The changes to the structure of the earnings distribution that took place in some countries in the 1980s and 1990s are taken up in Part 3 of the book. Chapter 12 discusses the role regulation and the introduction of competition in the utility industries; and also draws together evidence on executive remuneration and the distribution of gains between households from falling prices after privatisation. Chapter 18 is devoted to the distribution of household income and introduces the important subject of income dynamics.

(III) A European Orientation

There are a number of very good texts that cover the analytical material, but give a US perspective on the applications and institutional context. The applied material and empirical evidence in this book is intended to be of greater relevance to a UK and a European audience. Against a background of moves towards a common monetary policy, the applications in Part 1 variously discuss the important practical subject of harmonising measures of inflation, and also the large differences in housing finance in EU countries. The operation of the Common Agricultural Policy of the EU, and the reforms that have taken place in the 1980s and 1990s, are discussed in some detail in Chapter 9. Alternative theories of the firm are considered in Chapter 8. This leads to contrasting the corporate governance arrangements in large corporations in the so-called Anglo-Saxon economies with those of continental Europe. Differences in corporate governance are returned to in Chapter 15, which looks at the cost of capital to firms and alternative systems of finance.

Pedagogy

The mathematical background necessary to read this text is kept to a minimum. There are questions in the main body of the text, which are there to help break up the amount of reading. Answering some of them may take a moment's thought, but others will take longer. Some of the questions at the end of each chapter are there to reinforce understanding by asking about variations of the analysis, while others relate the discussion to problems of data analysis or put the discussion in a wider context by asking about policy issues.

Supplementaries

There is an Instructor's Manual available to adopters of this text. This contains full solutions to the exercises and suggestions on approaches to answering all the questions. There is also a Microsoft PowerPoint disk accompanying the guide, which contains a selection of the figures from the text to ease the workload of classroom presentations.

Acknowledgements

My thanks go to Paul Bishop, University of Plymouth, Dave Brewster, Thames Valley University, John Chard, University of Exeter, Andy Dunnett, Thames Valley University, David Glen, London Guildhall University, Han van Ees, University of Groningen, Stephen Heasell, Nottingham Trent University, Seamus Heslin, University College Dublin, James Nugent, Kingston University and two anonymous reviewers for providing their comments on draft chapters of this book.

Thanks are also due to John Crowley for his appreciation of economic problems in a wider context and to Howard Tribe for his enduring sense of humour. Alba Silletti of Avventura provided some technical advice about coffee. At Wiley, Steve Hardman and See Hanson were a co-operative team and Dawn Booth enlivened the production process no end.

Household Decision-Making

1 Consumer Theory and Demand

Key ideas and material

Indifference maps and budget constraints, income and substitution effects, demand functions and elasticities

Introduction

This chapter starts our discussion of consumer decision-making. The scope of the discussion is wide and includes analysis of more than just decisions about how consumers allocate their income between particular goods and services. In subsequent chapters, we will look at a range of issues concerning labour supply and discuss in detail decisions about individual borrowing and saving.

Decisions made at an individual level are important in a wider context. How much consumers spend on certain goods and services is of prime interest to business planners who want to anticipate future demand levels, but also to governments considering the imposition of a new tax, or increasing the rate of an existing one. Whether individuals decide to work is of obvious importance for the allocation of resources within a household, but it is also important for government decisions about the structure of social security payments. The collective decisions made by millions of individuals whether to save or spend is important to them as individuals, but is also important to financial institutions, and the government's finances, which depend on the level and the pattern of expenditures by consumers.

These are large and important matters and all of them involve elements of choice by individuals. This leads us to ask how economists represent, or model, the decision-making made by households, and how the decisions made are affected by changes in the economic circumstances that individuals face. This is the subject matter of Part 1 of this book.

It should be appreciated at the outset that in the UK, as in other countries, there is a wide range of different types of household decision-making units, whether classified by size, family

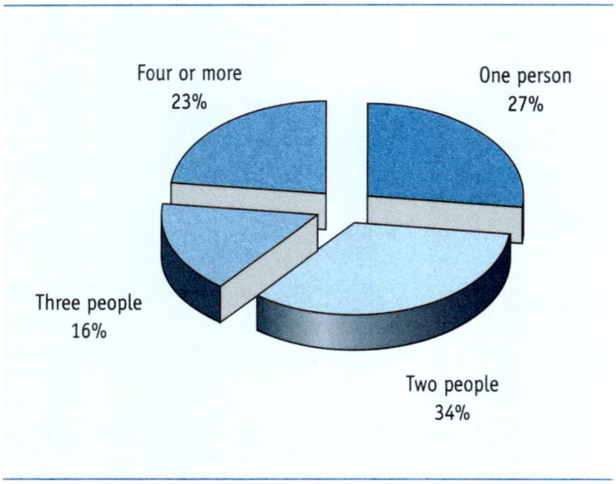

Chart 1.1 Size of households in the UK 1995–96
Source: Economic Trends 1997.

1995–6	
One person	27%
Two unrelated adults	6%
Married couple – no children	25%
– with children	31%
Lone parent	10%
Two or more familes	1%

Table 1.1 Household breakdown by family type
Source: Economic Trends 1997.

type or in some other way. Chart 1.1 gives a breakdown of household sizes in the UK and Table 1.1 gives some idea of the variation by family type.

The discussion of consumer theory that follows will start simply by treating the individual as the relevant decision-making unit, and introduce some important interdependencies in household decision-making in later chapters. What the material of this chapter does allow us to do is develop a framework for analysing the decisions of all individuals: high-earners and low-earners, students and pensioners and so on.

The approach taken in the discussion that follows will mainly use the neo-classical framework. This assumes that individuals are utility maximisers, something that is often criticised for being unrealistic. The theory is not meant to be an accurate description of every situation that an individual faces. What it does provide is an approach that can be used to make predictions when individual circumstances change. This first chapter is therefore largely about analytical tools, indifference curves to represent the preferences of individuals and 'budget' lines to represent the constraint of a given amount of income.[1]

1.1 Consumer theory

Consumer preferences and indifference maps: an introduction

We will start with a simple way in which we can represent the preferences of individuals between different combinations of goods that they might buy. It is simple because we will limit

1 These basic constructs appear repeatedly in later chapters and a familiarity with them is important.

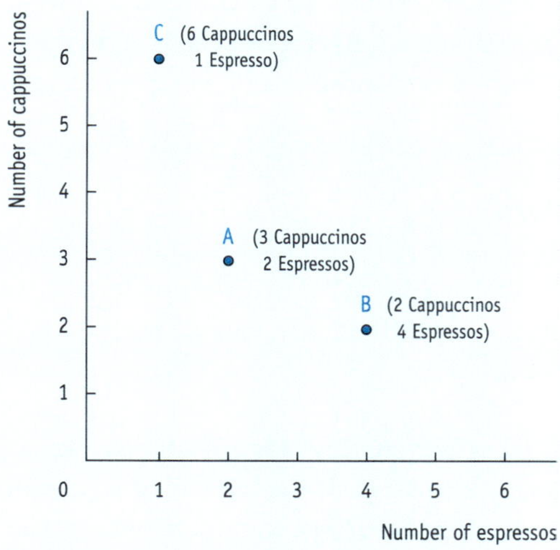

Figure 1.1A **Alternative combinations of two drinks**

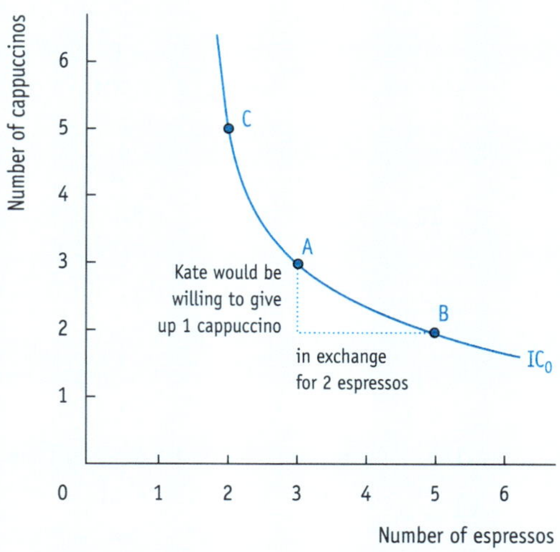

Figure 1.1B **An indifference curve**

ourselves to looking at decisions concerning only two goods.[2] Suppose we imagine one particular individual, Kate, who spends her time drinking coffee. She likes both cappuccino and espresso, both of which give her satisfaction or, in the language of economics, utility. Figure 1.1A shows alternative combinations that she might drink over a particular period of time, say each week. Point A shows three cups of cappuccino and two cups of espresso, points B and C show other possible combinations.

The preferences she has in relation to cappuccino and espresso can be represented by an indifference curve. This is a graphical way of showing alternative combinations of two goods that yield a particular level of utility, or satisfaction, to an individual. Figure 1.1B shows one particular indifference curve, labelled IC_0, which illustrates the different combinations of the two drinks that gives Kate a particular level of utility. Point A on the indifference curve represents three cups of cappuccino and three cups of espresso, which gives her the same satisfaction as five cups of one drink and two cups of the other, as shown by points B and C. The rate at which she would be willing to give up one drink for the other will depend on her tastes. Starting at point A, the indifference curve is drawn on the assumption that Kate would be willing to give up one cappuccino for two espressos. This gives us what is known as the marginal rate of substitution between, in this case, the two drinks. As drawn in Figure 1.1B the marginal rate of substitution itself varies as the quantity of the two goods varies along the indifference curve.

An indifference curve represents just one level of utility; different levels of utility can be represented by a set of indifference curves, or an indifference map. This is illustrated in Figure

2 The analysis can be extended in a straightforward fashion to many goods.

1.2. In principle, to completely illustrate an individual's preferences we would need to draw one indifference curve for each level of utility or satisfaction. Intuitively, indifference curves that are further away from the origin involve larger quantities of both drinks, and so represent higher levels of utility to the individual.

The assumptions of indifference curve analysis

We will now look at the indifference curves drawn in Figure 1.2 in a more formal way. Downward-sloping indifference curves such as those drawn there are based on a number of assumptions and these are listed as (I) – (IV) below.

(I) **The completeness assumption**. The consumer has preferences between all possible combinations of goods, and these preferences may be ordered. If the individual is presented with two alternative combinations of goods then he or she can state which one is preferred (or whether he or she is indifferent between them).

(II) **The assumption of transitivity**. The assumption that consumers' preferences are transitive. This means that consumers are taken to be rational in the sense that their preferences are consistent. For example, in Figure 1.2, if the individual prefers the combination of goods associated with point E to that at point D, and also prefers (the combination associated with) point D to that at point C, then we can say that point E is preferred to point C.

(III) **The assumption of non-satiation**. The wants of the consumer are insatiable. Intuitively the consumer is assumed to prefer more of a good to less of it. It follows that indifference curves that are further away from the origin represent a higher level of satisfaction or utility. To see why look at Figure 1.3 where points A, B, C have been marked on the two indifference curves. By comparison with point A on IC_0 points B and C on IC_1 involve either more espresso (and no less cappuccino) or alternatively more cappuccino (and no less espresso). Points between B and C mean more of both. The utility associated with IC_1 is therefore greater than that associated with IC_0. Starting from point A on IC_0, to maintain a given level of utility means less cappuccino when the number of espresso drinks increases and vice versa.[3]

(IV) **The assumption of a diminishing marginal rate of substitution**. The rate at which the consumer is willing to exchange one good for another decreases the more the individual has of the second good. In terms of our example, the more cappuccino drunk, the greater the willingness to exchange a cup for an espresso drink. This is illustrated in Figure 1.4 where the changing slope of the indifference curve shows the diminishing marginal rate of substitution.

3 This line of argument could be put into reverse for an indifference curve drawn below IC_0.

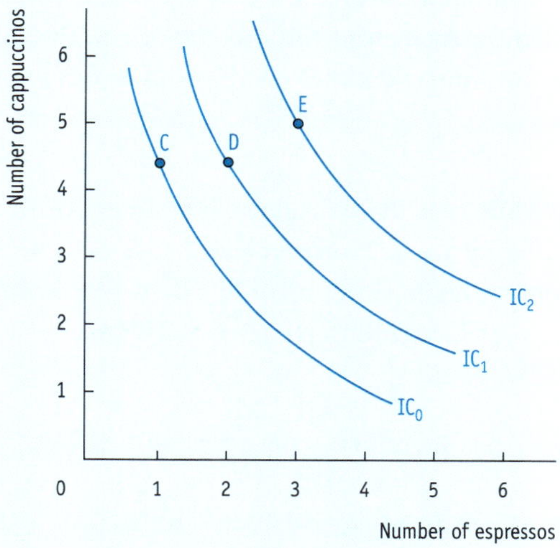

Figure 1.2 **An indifference map**

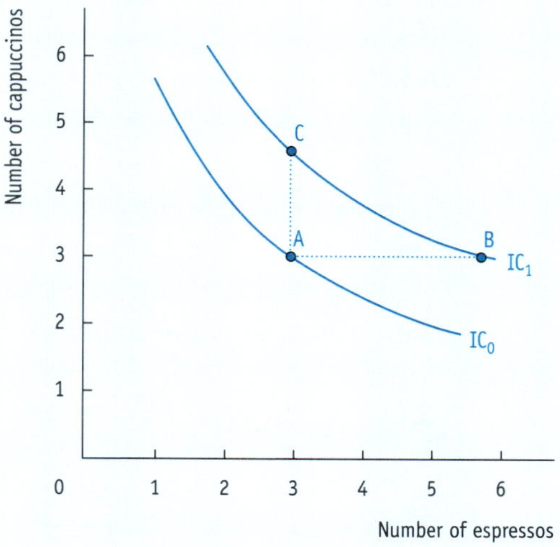

Figure 1.3 **The assumption of non-satiation**

The two key assumptions for analysing consumer preferences are (I) and (II), the completeness assumption and the assumption that preferences are transitive. In order for the representation of preferences to be consistent, we should note that given assumption (III) indifference curves do not intersect. Referring to Figure 1.5, we have drawn two indifference curves which we take to represent combinations of any two goods, X and Y. Point A is on both indifference curves,

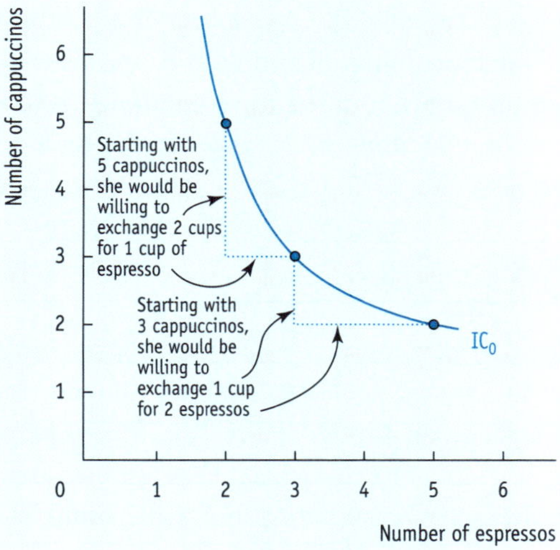

Figure 1.4 **The assumption of a diminishing marginal rate of substitution**

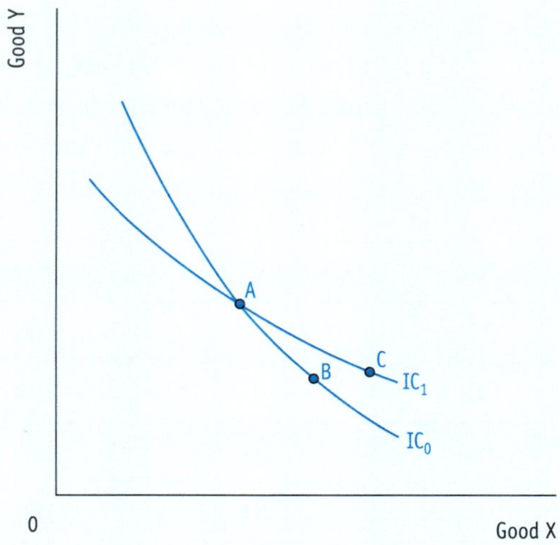

Figure 1.5 **Indifference curves do not intersect**

IC_0 and IC_1, where it represents one particular combination of the two goods, and hence a given level of utility. From our definition of an indifference curve any two points on the same curve yield the same utility level. This is the case for points A and B on IC_0, and as drawn, for points A and C on IC_1 as well.

The assumption that preferences are transitive means that the consumer would be indifferent between point B and C, since they are both indifferent to A. However point C is on a higher indifference curve, which we have noted represents a higher level of utility than is associated with point B. Given assumptions (I)–(III) we cannot have indifference curves that intersect.

Utility functions

Another way of representing consumer preferences is with utility functions. In the case where the consumer buys just two goods a utility function can be written as

$$U = U(X,Y)$$

where U stands for utility, X and Y represent the quantities of the two goods.

The utility associated with any particular indifference curve can therefore have a number attached to it. What that number is will depend on the particular function; for example, the function $U = XY$ assigns the number that is the product of the quantities of X and Y that are consumed.

The first two columns of Table 1.2A give five possible combinations of the two goods that lie on a particular indifference curve. The associated utility given in the third column is 100. For example, the individual is indifferent between having 25 units of X and 4 units of Y, and

X	Y	U = XY	X	Y	U = XY
25	4	100	50	8	400
20	5	100	40	10	400
10	10	100	20	20	400
5	20	100	10	40	400
4	25	100	8	50	400

Table 1.2A **An example of a utility function**

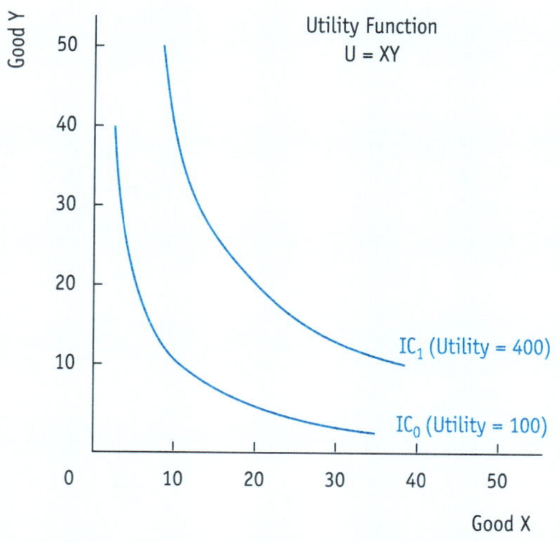

Figure 1.6A Illustration of a utility function

X	Y	U = XY	U = 10XY	U = 3XY–100
25	4	100	1000	200
20	5	100	1000	200
10	10	100	1000	200
5	20	100	1000	200
4	25	100	1000	200

Table 1.2B Alternative utility functions

having 5 units of X and 20 units of Y. A doubling of the amounts of X and Y consumed would give $U = 400$ which is shown in columns four to six in the table. The utility number assigned to any particular indifference curve has no meaningful interpretation; what is important is that larger numbers are associated with higher levels of utility. This is what happens here, when the combinations of X and Y increase, the utility number associated with these combinations increases as well. Figure 1.6A illustrates the particular preferences represented by the utility function in Table 1.2A.

In addition to $U = XY$, the functions $U = 3XY - 100$ and $U = 10XY$ would do equally well in representing this individual's preferences. Both these functions represent the combinations of X and Y in the first two columns in Table 1.2A on a particular indifference curve. This is shown in Table 1.2B. Although the number assigned to a particular utility level differs between the functions, for each function higher utility levels will again be associated with larger numbers.

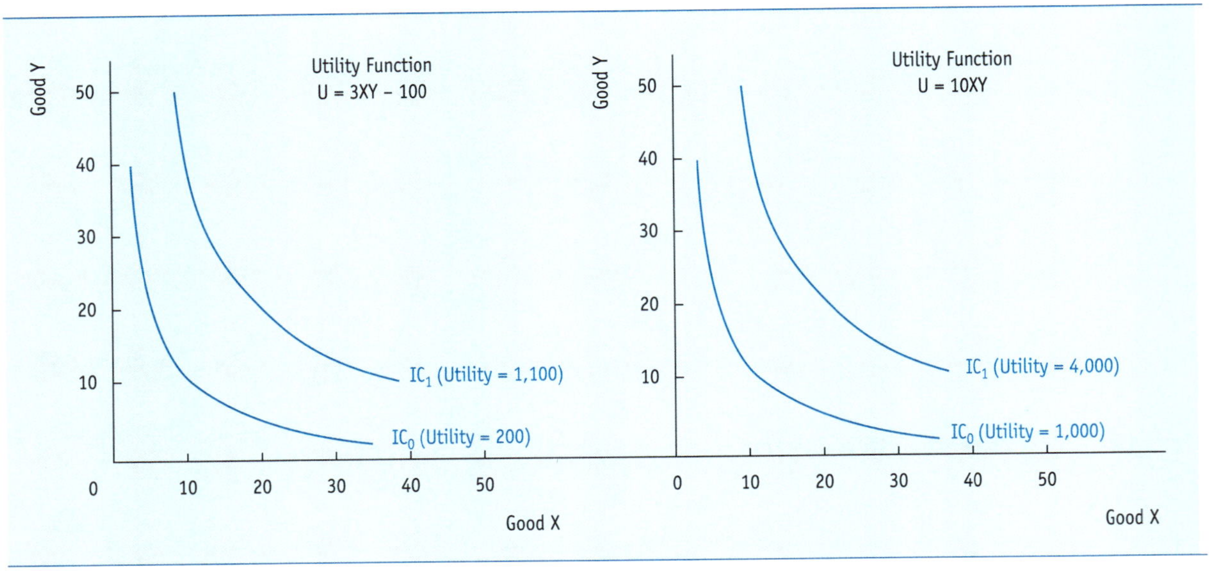

Figure 1.6B Other utility functions that represent the same preferences

A doubling of the amounts of X and Y consumed would again be represented by a larger number whether the utility function was $U = 3XY - 100$ or $U = 10XY$. This point is illustrated in Figure 1.6B.[4]

Representation of other relationships between goods

We have so far dealt with the conventionally shaped indifference curve, which is concerned with two goods that are substitutes. There are, of course, other types of relationships between goods and these can be represented by indifference curves that have different shapes. When, for example, the individual would exchange one good for another at a fixed rate no matter how much of either is consumed, we have the extreme case of the two goods being perfect substitutes. Figure 1.7A illustrates the case when the individual would exchange them on a one-for-one basis: all of either good and none of the other yields the same utility as any other point on the indifference 'curve'. The representation of two goods that are (perfect) complements is drawn in Figure 1.7B. This depicts a situation where a particular combination of the two goods generates a certain level of utility and any amount of additional X, without any additional Y (and vice versa) will not increase utility. A standard example of two goods that leads to an indifference map of this sort are left and right shoes.

4 We are concerned here with ordinal utility functions, that is functions that preserve the order of an individual's preferences. A monotonic transformation of a particular function will preserve the ordering of an individual's preferences. Examples of this are multiplication of the original function by a positive number, or adding/subtracting a constant. There are, therefore, many other examples of utility functions that would also represent this individual's preferences.

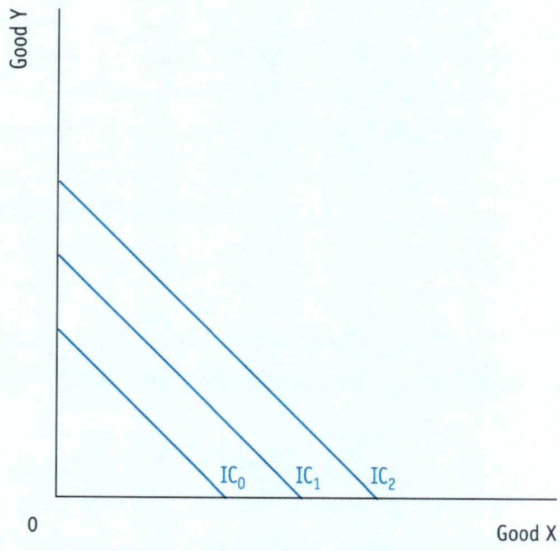

Figure 1.7A **Indifference curves when the two goods are perfect substitutes**

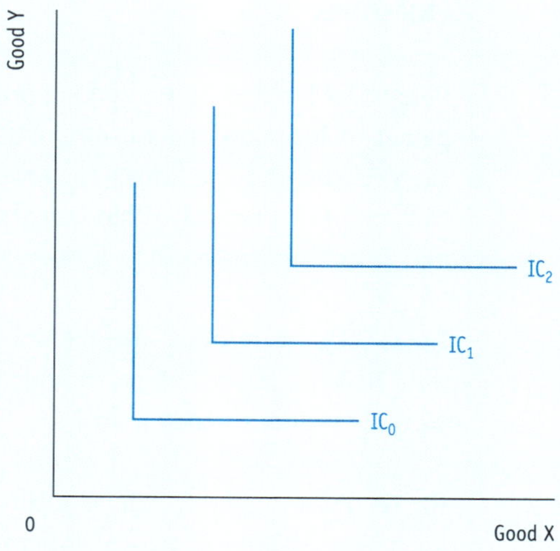

Figure 1.7B **Goods which are perfect complements**

We have so far shown consumers in relation to only two goods. A straightforward adaptation of the existing structure of indifference curves will generalise the two-good example to an analysis of all goods. All that is needed is to define one of the two goods as a composite good, or the expenditure on all goods bar one. Each indifference curve shows a combination of one good and expenditure level on all other goods that yields a given level of utility. This is shown in Figure 1.8. We will use this kind of indifference curve in the analysis of housing subsidies in Chapter 2.

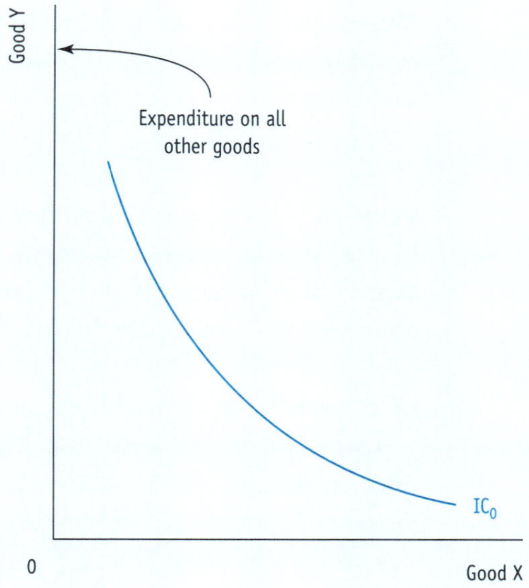

Figure 1.8 **An indifference curve to represent more than two goods**

Questions

Q1 Pete is a Manchester United supporter and derives utility from only two goods: attending the games of his team and eating portions of chips. He takes great pride in attending every match each season and the longer he goes without missing a game, the more determined he becomes to keep up his record. What can you say about his marginal rate of substitution between chips and watching football?

Q2 Liz is very aware of environmental issues and cycles to work. Assume that her utility is derived only from eating baked pasta and the level of air pollution she breathes while out riding. What would her indifference map look like?

Q3 Reg is a couch potato whose utility only depends on watching ballgames on TV and drinking lager that he buys in a local supermarket in 4-packs. His sense of self-esteem requires that one pack is consumed in the course of watching a game, but a sense of self-preservation tells him he has nothing to gain from drinking anything more. What shape would you draw indifference curves to represent his preferences?

Q4 Karen is a teetotal with a sweet tooth, and derives utility from drinking glasses of water and eating pieces of shortbread. Would you expect the assumption of non-satiation to hold for these two goods? What shape would you expect her indifference curves to be if it didn't?

The budget constraint

The second aspect of individual decision-making that we need to consider is the financial constraint the individual faces. In this context we can think of this as simply the weekly (or monthly or annual) income of an individual. In algebraic form

$$M = P_X X + P_Y Y$$

where M is the consumer's money income, and as before, X and Y are the two goods, P_X and P_Y are the prices of the two goods. In words, the consumer's income can be broken down into expenditure on each of the two goods. We will assume here, for simplicity, that all income is spent and that the prices that he or she faces are fixed.

In diagrammatic terms, a budget line as illustrated in Figure 1.9 shows this financial constraint. The position of the budget line depends on both the income of the consumer and the price of the two goods. If the consumer spends all of his or her income on one good, the maximum amount that can be consumed will be either M/P_X for good X, or M/P_Y for good Y. The straight line that joins up these two points reflects the alternative combinations of X and Y that can be bought.

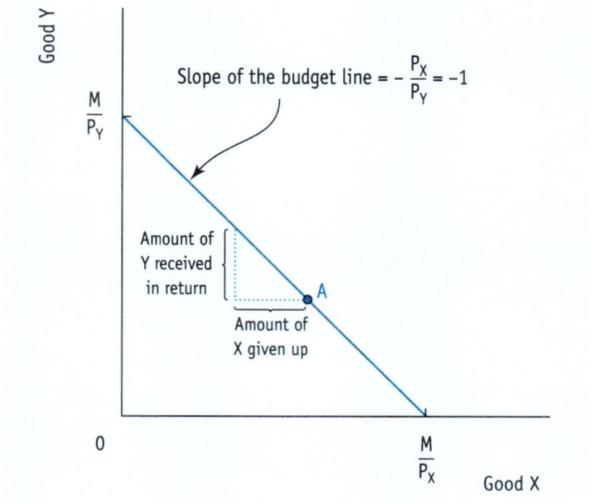

Figure 1.9 **The consumer's budget line**

To see why, suppose we take a particular point on the budget line such as that marked as point A in Figure 1.9. If the consumer wants to increase the consumption of good Y then he or she will have to give up some of good X. The amount of extra Y that can be purchased will depend on the amount of income to be reallocated and also on the price of Y. For example, if the consumer decides to switch ten pounds from good X to good Y, and the price of Y is five pounds then two extra units of Y are available. How much of a sacrifice of X is needed depends on the price of X. If the price of X happens to be five pounds, then two units of X must be given up and so on.

Given that a certain sum is reallocated from buying X to buy Y, the rate of exchange of one good for the other simply depends on the prices of the two goods. The slope of the budget line is (minus) P_X/P_Y and this is a constant given our earlier assumption of fixed prices. In Figure 1.9, we have assumed that the two prices are equal and so the slope of the budget line is therefore –1.[5]

A higher income level will increase the ratios of M/P_X and M/P_Y, and this will lead to a parallel shift out of the budget constraint further from the origin, since the price ratio is unchanged. If the price of both goods drop by the same percentage, and the consumer's money income is unchanged, the budget line will again be further away from the origin, parallel to its original position. On the other hand, if the price of one of the goods falls but nothing else changes the budget line will rotate outwards along the axis of the good concerned. If the price of the good rises it will rotate inwards. If this paragraph seems confusing try Q5 now.

5 It is the negative of this ratio given that the budget line is sloping downwards. The derivation of the price ratio from the budget line is given in the mathematical appendix at the end of the chapter.

The consumer's equilibrium

At the beginning of this chapter, it was stated that neo-classical theory assumes that consumers are maximisers of utility. In order to model this behaviour we need to bring together our representation of the individual's preferences and the financial constraint faced. The utility maximising consumer will attain the highest utility possible given his or her budget constraint. Figure 1.10A shows this as a point of tangency between the indifference curve, IC_0, and the budget line, B_0, marked as point E_0. At the optimum point, the individual consumes the quantity X_0 of good X, and the quantity Y_0 of good Y. The point E_0 represents the highest possible level of utility for the individual given the income available, and the prices of the two goods that he or she faces. Higher indifference curves would yield higher utility levels, but are not within the individual's budget. Lower indifference curves are within budget but simply do not maximise utility.

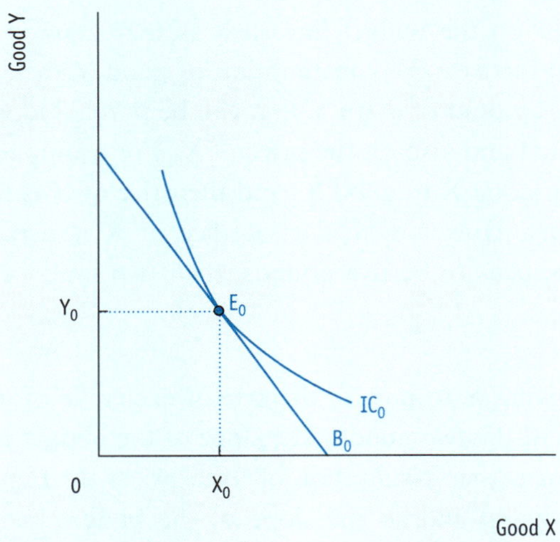

Figure 1.10A The consumer's equilibrium

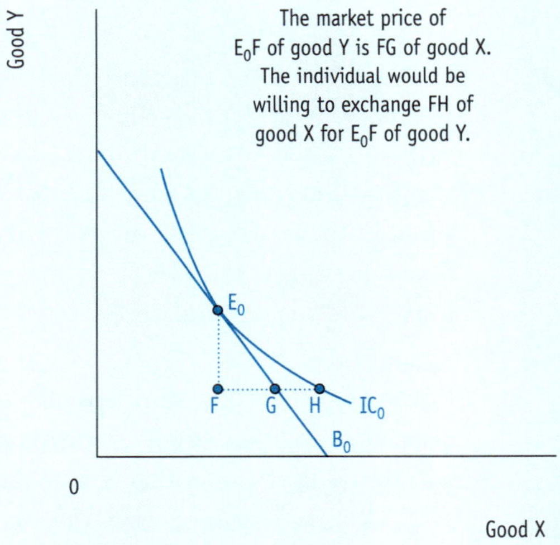

Figure 1.10B MRS and the price ratio when not in equilibrium

The point of tangency has the analytical property that the marginal rate of substitution between the two goods, MRS_{YX}, is equal to the price ratio P_X/P_Y. The rate at which the individual is prepared to substitute (small) amounts of Y for X is just equal to the rate at which the prices of the two goods allows substitution of one for the other. At points to the right of E_0 along the consumer's indifference curve, the individual would be willing to exchange good X for Y at a greater rate than that given by the market price ratio. As shown in Figure 1.10B the individual can move from point H to point E_0 along IC_0 by exchanging X for Y. Point H involves a combination of the two goods that the individual could not afford, but by moving to point E_0 the level of utility associated with both points is affordable.

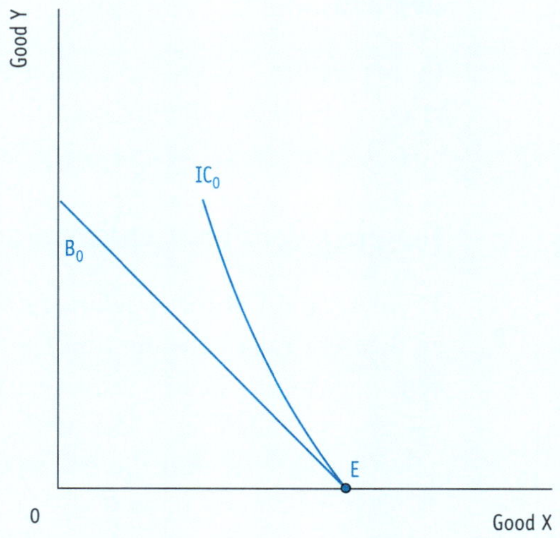

Figure 1.11 A corner solution

It is not necessarily the case that the consumer's equilibrium will involve consumption of both X and Y. The shape of the consumer's indifference curves could produce a utility maximising outcome which involves consumption of only X or Y, known a corner solution. This possibility is illustrated in Figure 1.11 and will be discussed further in Chapter 3 when we analyse labour supply.

Questions

Q5 Ray has a money income of £160 per week that he spends on two goods: cinema tickets and rail journeys. Suppose the admission price to the cinema is £4 and the price of his train journey is £8. Taking the price of cinema tickets as good X and railway journeys as good Y draw the budget constraint and show which combinations of the two goods are available and which are not. What is the slope of the budget line?

What happens to Ray's budget line if

(I) his income rises to £200
(II) the price of his train trip rises to £10
(III) the price of both cinema tickets and train journeys double
(IV) the price of both goods double and his income rises to £320 at the same time?

Q6 Referring to Figure 1.10B, what is the relationship between the individual's marginal rate of substitution of Y for X, and the price ratio above and to the left of point E_0? Starting at a point above E_0 along IC_0 explain why it is advantageous to the individual to exchange Y for X.

1.2 Demand

In this section, we will be looking at the relation between the demand for a good, its price, the price(s) of related good(s) and the income that the consumer receives. We can then analyse how demand might change as prices and income levels change.

The price consumption curve and individual demand

The derivation of the individual's demand curve comes from the indifference map via what is known as a price consumption curve. Figure 1.12A shows the initial position for the individual consumer as E_0; a point of tangency between the indifference curve, IC_0, and the budget line B_0. Suppose there is a fall in the price of good X, then the budget line rotates outwards reflecting the fact that the price ratio P_X/P_Y has fallen. The lower price for the good means that the maximum amount of it that an individual could buy has risen and we get a second equilibrium point where the indifference curve IC_1 is tangential to the new budget line B_1 at point E_1.

This can be repeated for another fall in the price of good X, giving a third point of equilibrium at E_2. These falls in price of good X have been associated with a rise in the consumption of X, from X_0 to X_1 to X_2 as marked in the Figure. In principle, we could, of course, decrease the price of X by a greater or lesser amount (or increase it from the initial level) and this would produce other changes in the consumption of X. The price-consumption curve is simply formed by joining up all the points of equilibrium as we vary the price of the good.

Figure 1.12A has shown the change in the price of good X implicitly (through the change in the budget line), and the change in the quantity of X demanded explicitly. The demand curve simply makes this relationship between price and quantity explicit, by replacing the quantity of Y on the vertical axis with the price of good X. In Figure 1.12B the three prices for good X, P_0, P_1 and P_2 are shown on the vertical axis, and the associated demands X_0, X_1 and X_2 are brought down from the price consumption curve.

In looking at the effect on demand of a change in price we need to take care in distinguishing between demand curves which hold real income constant, and demand curves which are drawn for a constant money income. This distinction made by economists gives what are known as compensated and uncompensated demand curves. To appreciate this distinction we will first break down the effect of a price change into income and substitution effects, which is an important conceptual distinction to be able to make.[6]

(I) **The income effect**. There is an effect on a consumer's income when there is a change in the price of one or other of the goods. For example, suppose the consumer only bought good X and the price of it fell. The maximum amount that he or she could buy is given

6 The distinction will re-appear in several of the chapters that follow.

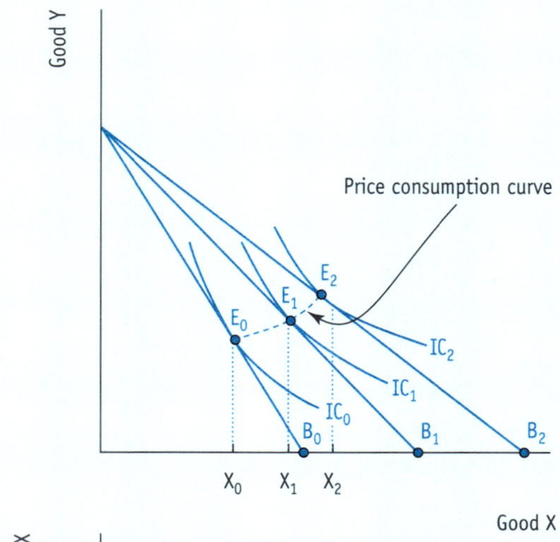

Figure 1.12A The price consumption curve

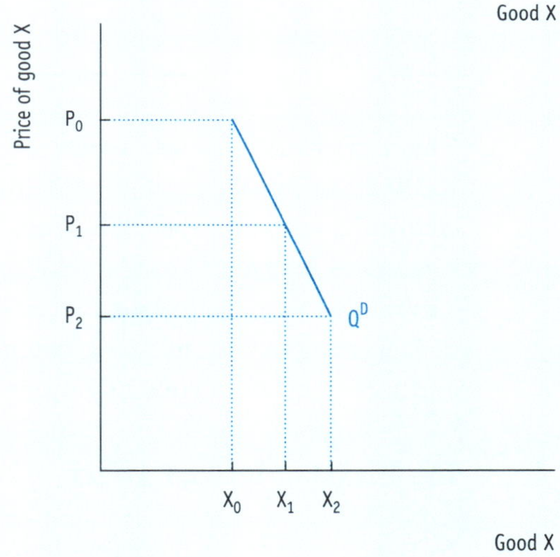

Figure 1.12B An individual's demand curve

by the ratio of money income to the price of X, M/P_X, which will rise giving an increase in purchasing power or real income. This income effect can lead to an increase, decrease or no change in the demand for the good.[7]

(II) **The substitution effect**. This is the effect of a change in the relative price ratio on the demand for a good. For example, a fall in the price of X lowers the price ratio and this will increase the demand for X, for a given a level of purchasing power available to the individual.[8]

7 More generally, the extent of the rise in real income arising from a fall in the price of X is clearly affected by the proportion of the budget spent on X.

8 The substitution effect is often referred to as being 'negative' since the change in the price ratio and the effect on the demand for X move in opposite directions.

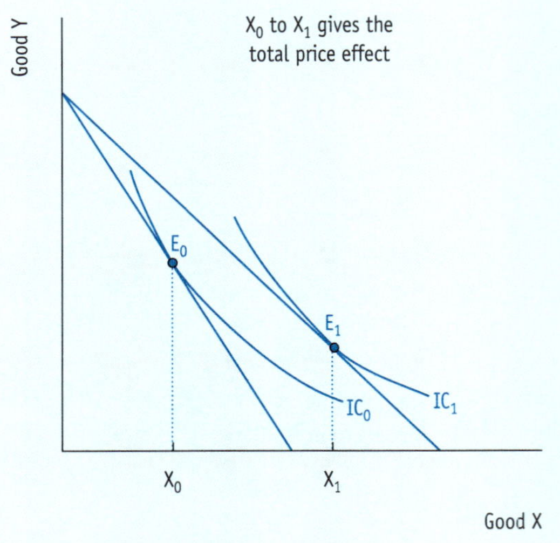

Figure 1.13 The total price effect

The combined effects are shown diagrammatically in Figure 1.13. The initial equilibrium is at E_0, with X_0 consumed of good X; the new equilibrium point is at E_1, with X_1 demanded. This change in consumption of X from X_0 to X_1 includes both income and substitution effects, sometimes referred to as the total price effect. To identify the income and substitution effects separately raises the question of exactly what we mean by a change in real income. There are, in fact, two possible answers, one associated with the work of the economist Sir John Hicks and the other with work of Eugene Slutsky.

The Hicksian income effect

In Figure 1.14A, we have reproduced the previous figure and drawn a third budget line, B_2, parallel to the budget constraint after the price change, but tangential to the original indifference curve. The difference between the budget lines B_1 and B_2 gives the Hicksian measure of a change in real income. It is the change in income necessary to keep the individual on the original indifference curve after a change in relative prices. The point of tangency between the budget constraint B_2 and IC_0, marked as point E_2, gives the consumption of the X good as X_2. This shows the new demand for good X following the change in relative prices. The distance X_2 to X_1 gives the income effect of the price fall and X_0 to X_2 gives the substitution effect.

As we have drawn the figure the good in question is a normal good, that is to say as income rises demand for the good rises. This need not always be, the equilibrium point E_1 could be to the left of E_2, reflecting a negative income effect. Such a good is known as an inferior good; if the negative income effect is sufficiently large so that the equilibrium point is to the left of E_0, then it is called a Giffen good.

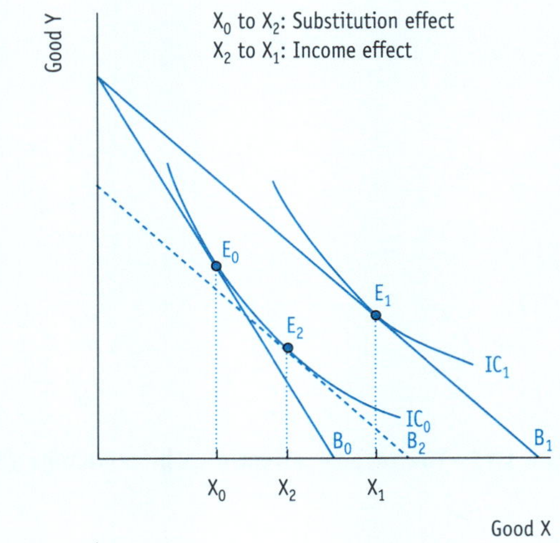

Figure 1.14A The income and substitution effects of a price change (Hicks)

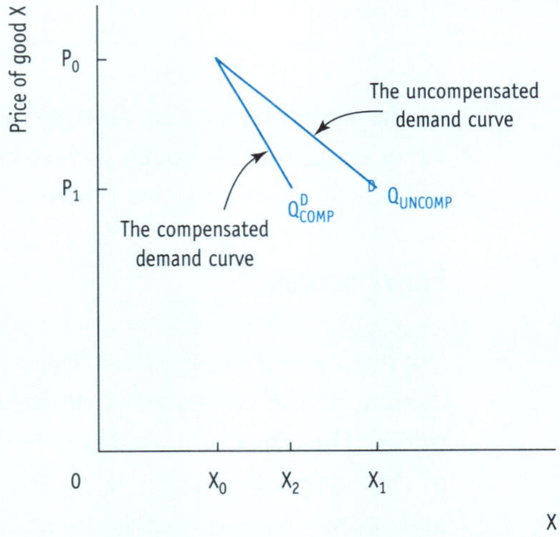

Figure 1.14B Compensated or real income demand curve

It is a straightforward step to derive the demand curve for a given real income level from our indifference map in the same way that we did for a constant money income. This is shown in Figure 1.14B. For a normal good the real income (compensated) demand curve will be steeper than it was with a constant money income (uncompensated) demand curve.

The Slutsky income effect

The Slutsky real income effect of a price change is drawn in Figure 1.15. This is the change in income that would just allow the individual to purchase the original combination of X and Y prior to the change in relative prices. The budget line B_2 is now drawn through the point E_0, although it is still parallel to the budget line B_1 (and that drawn for the Hicksian income effect). The substitution effect will leave the consumer on a higher indifference curve than he

Figure 1.15 **The income effect of a price change (Slutsky)**

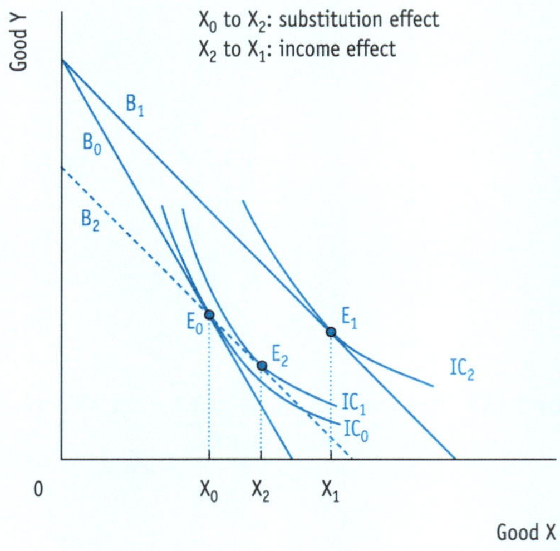

or she would have been on if we had used the Hicksian definition. The compensated demand curve using this approach to measuring the income effect of a price change will be flatter than the one shown in Figure 1.14B.

Engel curves

We have so far shown the relation between demand and the price of the good itself given the income of the consumer. Consumer demand does, of course, depend on incomes as well as prices. The effect of an increase in income is shown in Figure 1.16A by a parallel shift outward in the budget line, from B_0 to B_1. The resulting equilibrium point moves out from E_0 to E_1 and, as we have drawn it, there is an increase in the consumption of X from X_0 to X_1. A further increase in income is shown to lead to a further increase in demand for the good. In a similar fashion to our analysis of a change in price of X, we can, in principle, vary the amounts by which income increases, or allow it to fall, and this will give us the associated level of demand for X.

The relationship between the level of demand for a good and the level of income is represented by what is known as an Engel curve. On the vertical axis of Figure 1.16B we have the income levels implicit in the budget constraint, and on the horizontal axis we have the level of demand brought down from the income-consumption curve in Figure 1.16A. For a normal good, such as the one drawn in Figure 1.16B, the relationship between the two will be positive though not necessarily linear.[9]

9 The shape of the Engel curve in Figure 1.16B is the conventional shape for a normal good. In some applied studies, the fraction of a good's expenditure is used and so the curve may slope downwards.

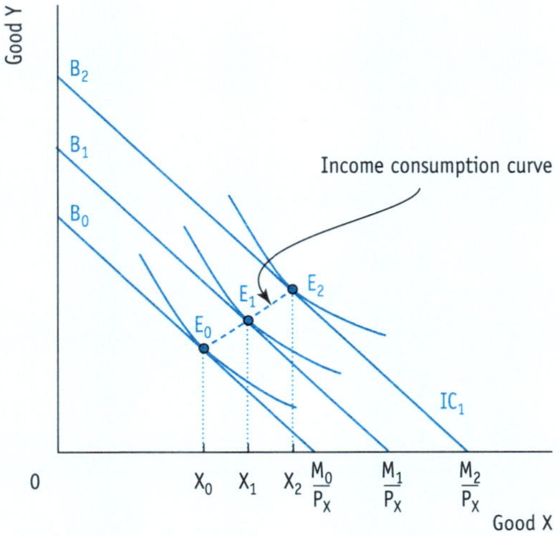

Figure 1.16A Income consumption curve

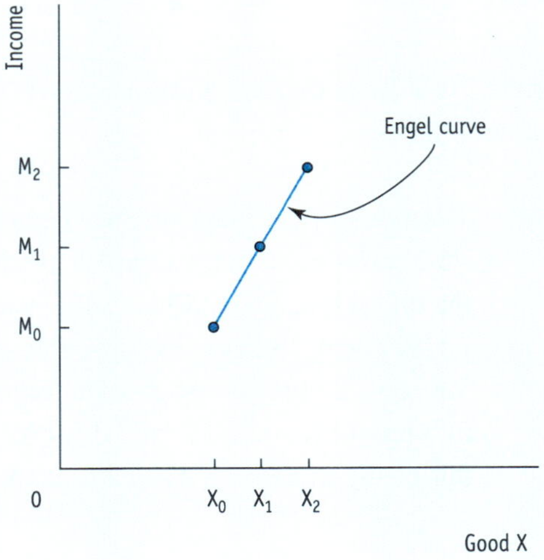

Figure 1.16B Engel curve

1.3 Comparative statics

You may have been wondering in some of the discussion so far what it is that determines the points of equilibrium in Figures such as 1.16. Why isn't the point E_0 further up to the left along the budget constraint B_0, or further down to the right for that matter? A general answer is that the analysis of this chapter has been mainly developing structures that can be used to make predictions about the effects of changes to prices and incomes. This brings us to comparative static analysis. What this involves is

(I) Defining an initial equilibrium.
(II) Allowing a variable that affects the equilibrium to change.[10]
(III) Observing the result.

10 In a mathematical model, we would be observing the effect of a change in an exogenous variable or one of the parameters of the model.

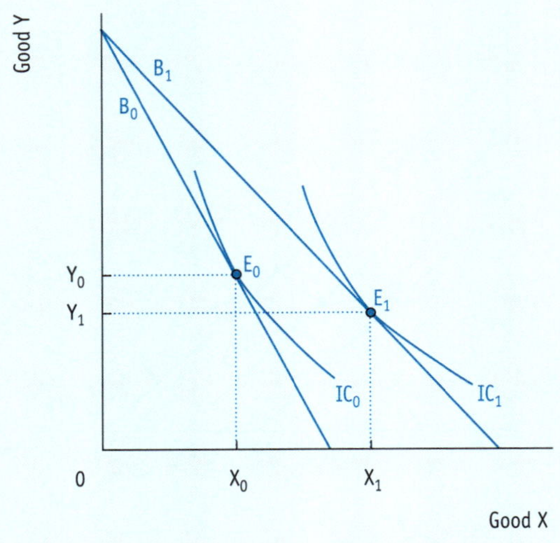

Figure 1.17A **Two goods that are gross substitutes**

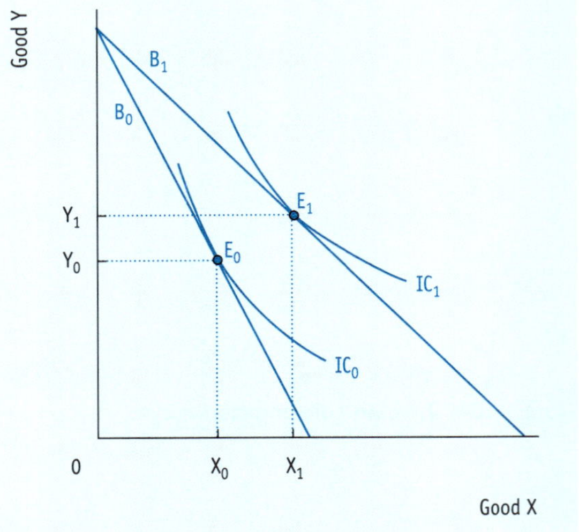

Figure 1.17B **Two goods that are gross complements**

The total price effect on the demand for good X is therefore one example of a comparative static exercise. Other examples of comparative statics include cross-price effects. These relate to the effect that the change in the price of a good has on the demand for another good. Figures 1.17A and 1.7B show two possible outcomes of a change in the price of good X on the demand for good Y. In the first case the two goods are gross substitutes, a fall in the price of X has lead to a reduction in the demand for Y. In Figure 1.17B the two goods are gross complements as a fall in the price of X has lead to the opposite effect on the demand for good Y.

Questions

Q7 Is the compensated demand curve for an inferior good steeper or flatter than the uncompensated demand? Would it make any difference if it were a Giffen good?

Q8 Suppose the price of good Y was to increase, draw a figure showing the income and substitution effects similar to Figure 1.14A. Where would the new point of equilibrium be if the two goods were (I) gross substitutes or (II) gross complements?

1.4 Market demand and demand functions

We have so far concentrated on the demand at the level of the individual. It is a straightforward step, in principle, to aggregate the demand by individuals to obtain the total demand for a commodity. There is of course no reason to think that all individual demand curves will

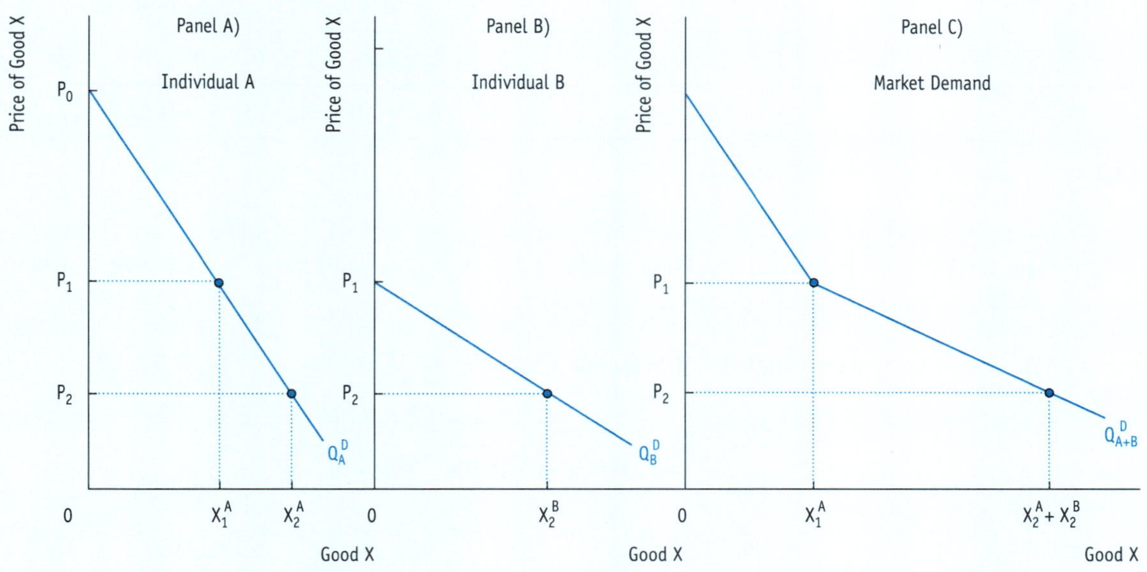

Figure 1.18 **Market demand from individual demand curves**

be identical. Figure 1.18 illustrates a simple case where there are just two individuals whose demands are shown in the first two panels. The horizontal summation of these two demand curves gives the market demand curve. At prices between P_0 and P_1 there is only the demand of individual A. When the market price falls below P_1, adding the demand of individual B gives a kink in the market demand curve in panel C. At prices below P_1 the market demand curve then becomes flatter.

A demand function is a mathematical relation between the level of demand and the variables that determine the level of demand. Given our analysis we can write a simple example of a demand function as

$$Q^d = F(M, P_X P_{Y,})$$

where Q^d is quantity demanded, M is money income and P_X and P_Y are the prices of the two goods. This is a convenient way of analysing how demand changes as prices and incomes change. Suppose, for example, a demand function is estimated to be

$$Q^d = 20 + 0.2M - 0.5P_X + 0.1P_Y$$

then given information on (or estimates of) the prices of the two goods and the incomes of consumers we can obtain an estimate of demand. Table 1.3 gives a numerical illustration. Given the particular values for money income, the price of X and the price of Y, substitution into the function gives the level of demand shown in the fourth column.

M	P_X	P_Y	$Q^d = 20 + 0.2M - 0.5P_X + 0.1P_Y$
200	50	100	$20 + 0.2(200) - 0.5(50) + 0.1(100) = 45$
100	70	80	$20 + 0.2(100) - 0.5(70) + 0.1(80) = 13$

Table 1.3 **An example of a demand function**

The relationship between the quantity demanded of a good and each individual variable that affects it can be summarised by an elasticity.

(I) **The own price elasticity of demand**. This is

$$\frac{\text{The percentage change in change in quantity demanded}}{\text{The percentage change in price}}$$

The own price elasticity measures the responsiveness of demand to changes in the price of the good itself. It could indicate a high degree of sensitivity between demand and price changes, or a relationship in which demand is completely insensitive to price. Economists distinguish between elastic demand, where the percentage change in demand is greater than the percentage change in price, and inelastic demand where the relation is the other way around. Unit elasticity of demand occurs when the percentage change in demand is equal to the percentage change in price.

(II) **The income elasticity of demand**. This is

$$\frac{\text{The percentage change in quantity demanded}}{\text{The percentage change in income}}$$

Whether the elasticity is positive or negative indicates the general nature of the relationship. If we have a normal good then as income rises, the level of demand rises, and the income elasticity is positive. If it is an inferior good, then the income elasticity will be negative as demand and income move in opposite directions. The strength of the relationship is shown by its numerical magnitude, the larger the number the stronger the relation.

(III) **The cross-price elasticity of demand**. This is

$$\frac{\text{The percentage change in the quantity demanded for one good}}{\text{The percentage change in the price of another good}}$$

Whether this is positive or negative will again provide us with information about the nature of the relationship. In the case of two substitute goods, an increase in the price of one will lead to an increase in the demand for the other as consumers switch between the two goods. The percentage change in the price of the one good, and the percentage change in the demand for the other, will therefore both be positive. The greater the degree of substitutability the greater the value of the elasticity.

If the two goods are complements, an increase in the price of one good will lead to a reduction in the demand of the other. The cross-price elasticity of demand measure will be negative. The smaller the number (the greater the negativity) the greater the degree of complementarity between the two goods. Finally, if there is no relationship between the two goods, then a change in the price of one good will have no effect on the level of demand for the other. The cross-price elasticity will be zero.

An example: the demand for English league football

Finally, in this chapter, a short look at an example of the price elasticity of demand and why it may be useful. The own price elasticity of demand for football is something of interest to both the administrators and the supporters of football clubs. If the price of admission goes up by 25% how much do gates drop? The demand for league football at a particular club varies, of course, with a club's success on the pitch, their tradition and image, and the incomes of their supporters as well. So to obtain an estimate of the responsiveness of demand to ticket prices alone requires an estimate (by regression methods) of a demand function.

In the context of a study of the demand for football an overwhelming majority of those who attend a game are supporters ('fans') of one or other team. This points to the need for data at the level of the individual club, including information on attendances and admission prices. There is a distinction to be made between attendances that include season-ticket holders, and those that count only those who pay at the gate. An estimate of the price elasticity of demand that excluded season-ticket holders would be greater than if they were included. As far as admission prices are concerned this may vary considerably according to what part of the ground the seat is located (and before the implementation of all-seater stadiums in the English Premiership whether the spectator was sitting or standing). The price data may therefore involve considerable averaging depending on which club is involved and what the time period happens to be.

Table 1.4 below gives summary estimates of the price elasticity of demand for a number of clubs taken from a study by Simmons (1996) covering the period 1962–91.[11]

---

11 This study was based on a relatively sophisticated modelling procedure that requires some knowledge of econometric methods.

Club	Price elasticity of demand
Chelsea	–0.40
Everton	–0.97
Manchester United	–0.12
Newcastle	–0.39
Nottingham Forest	–0.57
Tottenham Hotspur	–0.44

Table 1.4 **Estimated price elasticities of demand for football clubs in England**

Source: Simmons (1996) Estimates refer to attendance including season-ticket holders.

Questions

Q9 How would you have expected the price-elasticity of demand to have changed at individual clubs since the introduction of the English Premiership? More generally, do changing consumer preferences over time invalidate indifference curve analysis?

Q10 What would you expect the income-elasticity of demand for football to be in general? Would you expect there to be much difference between the clubs and, if so, why?

Concluding comment

The analysis of consumer preferences in this chapter relies heavily on indifference curves, which are of course not directly observable. This approach to consumer theory is often criticised for its lack of realism and it is sometimes argued that individuals are nothing like sufficiently well-informed to maximise utility by choosing some particular combination of goods and services.

As was stated earlier, the purpose of the theory introduced here is to provide a basis for explaining the behaviour of what individuals do and to analyse how they will react to changing circumstances. While the theory is built on assumptions that are unrealistic, it does provide a way of thinking about the decision-making of households that can prove useful, as we shall see in the chapters that follow.

Mathematical appendix

Given the assumption of utility-maximisation, in the two good model the problem the individual consumer faces is to maximise

$$U = U(X,Y)$$

subject to a budget constraint

$$M = P_X X + P_Y Y$$

where X,Y are two goods and P_X, P_Y are their respective prices. The Lagrangian for this constrained optimisation problem can be written as

$$V = U(X,Y) + \lambda(M - P_X X - P_Y Y)$$

Setting the derivatives equal to zero gives the first-order conditions for a maximum

$$V_X = U_X - \lambda P_X = 0 \qquad \text{(I)}$$
$$V_Y = U_Y - \lambda P_Y = 0 \qquad \text{(II)}$$
$$V_\lambda = M - P_X X - P_Y Y = 0 \qquad \text{(III)}$$

Dividing (I) by (II) and re-arranging gives

$$\frac{Ux}{Uy} = \frac{P_x}{P_y}$$

This is the equilibrium condition when there is a tangency solution: the marginal rate of substitution (the ratio of the marginal utilities of the two goods) is equal to the price ratio. The price ratio is equal to the slope of the budget constraint. To see this, start with

$$M = P_X X + P_Y Y$$

which can be re-arranged as

$$P_Y Y = M - P_X X$$

And so

$$Y = \frac{M}{P_Y} - \frac{P_X X}{P_Y}$$

Differentiating gives

$$\frac{dY}{dX} = \frac{-P_X}{P_Y}$$

Demand functions

We know that in equilibrium the budget constraint will bind since all income is spent, which will enable us to the obtain (uncompensated) demand functions for the two goods

$$Q_x^d = F(M, P_X, P_Y)$$
$$Q_Y^d = F(M, P_X, P_Y)$$

An example

Suppose

$$U = X^{0.5}Y^{0.5} \text{ and } M = 100, P_X = 5, P_Y = 10$$

The Lagrangian is

$$V = X^{0.5}\ Y^{0.5} + \lambda(100 - 5X - 10Y)$$

and the first-order conditions are

$$V_X = 0.5X^{-0.5}Y^{0.5} - 5\lambda = 0$$
$$V_Y = 0.5X^{0.5}Y^{-0.5} - 10\lambda = 0$$
$$V_\lambda = 100 - 5X - 10Y = 0$$

from which

$$\frac{0.5X^{-0.5}Y^{0.5}}{0.5X^{0.5}Y^{-0.5}} = \frac{5}{10} \Rightarrow \frac{Y}{X} = \frac{5}{10}$$

Substituting $5X = 10Y$ into the budget constraint gives the optimal X and Y values as 10 and 5 respectively.

To derive the demand functions, re-arrange the budget constraint as

$$P_Y Y = M - P_X X$$

from which

$$Y = \frac{M}{P_y} - \frac{P_x}{P_y}X$$

We know from finding the optimal X and Y values that

$$\frac{Y}{X} = \frac{P_x}{P_y}$$

which can be re-written as $X = \frac{P_y}{P_x} Y$. This can then be substituted into the budget constraint

$$Y = \frac{M}{P_y} - \frac{P_x}{P_y}\frac{P_y}{P_x} Y$$

Giving $2Y = \frac{M}{P_y}$

Dividing both sides by 2 we obtain the demand function for Y. In terms of the general notation for demand functions we have $Q_Y^d = M/2P_y$. Following this procedure will also give the demand function for good X: $Q_X^d = M/2P_X$.

The Slutsky equation

This provides us with a way of separating the income and substitution effects of a price change. The actual change in the demand for a good following a price change is represented on the left-hand side in the expression below; the right-hand side gives the substitution effect (the compensated response) and the income effect separately.

$$\frac{\Delta X}{\Delta P_X} = \left.\frac{\Delta X}{\Delta P_X}\right|_{Comp} + \frac{\Delta X}{\Delta M}\frac{\Delta M}{\Delta P_X}$$

The income effect is the second term on the right-hand side. From the budget constraint

$$\frac{\Delta M}{\Delta P_X} = X$$

So if we deal with the situation when the price of good X rises we get

$$\frac{\Delta X}{\Delta P_X} = \left.\frac{\Delta X}{\Delta P_X}\right|_{Comp} - X\frac{\Delta X}{\Delta M}$$

We have in our example $M = 100$, $P_X = 5$, $P_Y = 10$ from which

$$Q_X^d = \frac{M}{2P_X}$$

To identify income and substitution effects, suppose P_X rises to 6, then the demand for X falls from 10 to 8.33. The income change necessary so that the original combination of the two goods could be bought is

$$\begin{aligned} \Delta M &= X\Delta P_X \\ &= 10(1) = 10 \end{aligned}$$

If the consumer had money income of 110 then the demand for X is 9.17 (by substituting $M = 110$ into the demand function). Given that the individual has enough income to buy the original combination at the new relative prices, it is the substitution effect that reduces demand from 10 to 9.17. The income effect of the price change further reduces demand for X to 8.33.

Summary

1 Consumer decision-making can be interpreted widely so as to include decisions about labour supply and whether to borrow or save as well as decisions about what goods and services to buy. The analysis of consumer decision-making is usually discussed in terms of one individual, although many households in the UK (and elsewhere) have two or more individuals.

2 Economists use indifference curves to represent consumer preferences. An indifference curve represents different combinations of two goods, which yield a given level of utility, or satisfaction, to an individual.

3 It is assumed that preferences are complete, that is consumers can rank any two combinations of goods and it is also assumed that consumers are consistent in that their preferences are transitive. The conventionally-shaped downward-sloping indifference curves such as those drawn in Figure 1.2 also assume the non-satiation of individual wants and a diminishing marginal rate of substitution.

4 A utility function is a mathematical representation of consumer preferences. This means we can associate numbers with particular indifference curves but all that is meaningful is the relation between the numbers on different indifference curves. A higher indifference curve is associated with higher utility levels and the number associated with it should be higher. There are many functions that will satisfy this requirement.

5 It is assumed that individuals maximise their utility given the level of income available to them. The income of the individual can be represented by a budget line, which shows different combinations of the two goods that the individual can afford to buy if he or she was to spend all the income available.

6 Given a conventionally-shaped set of indifference curves the utility-maximising outcome for the individual is often represented by a point of tangency between the budget line and the highest possible indifference curve. It is however not necessarily the case that the equilibrium involves the consumption of both goods. The equilibrium could result in a corner solution, for example.

7 By changing the price of one of the goods we can trace a series of points where the individual maximises utility. This allows us to draw a price consumption curve. An individual consumer's demand curve relates the optimal consumption levels of a good to different prices for that good, and is derived from the price consumption curve. Similarly changing the consumer's income allows us to draw an income consumption curve.

8 The distinction between the income and the substitution effect of a price change is conceptually important. There are two alternative definitions of the substitution effect, known as the Hicksian effect and the Slutsky effect. The first gives the change in income necessary after a relative price change to restore the individual to his or her original utility level; the second gives the individual just enough income to buy the original combination of goods.

9 The substitution effect of a price change refers to the change in demand from a change in relative prices. The effect on demand of a price increase is typically negative. The income effect on demand could be positive, negative or zero.

10 A demand function relates the quantity demanded to the price of a good, related goods and consumers' income. It is important to appreciate the distinction between the compensated demand curve, which measures just the substitution effect of a price change, and the uncompensated demand curve, which measures both income and substitution effects.

11 A demand curve provides us with a convenient way of analysing what happens to demand when prices and incomes change. The idea of an elasticity is a useful way of summarising this information. The own price elasticity of demand is defined as the ratio of the percentage change in the quantity demanded to the percentage change in price of the good. The income elasticity is defined in the same way in relation to incomes. The cross-price elasticity of demand is defined as the percentage in the quantity demanded of one good when the price of another good changes.

End of chapter questions

Q11 An individual's preferences between two goods can be represented by the utility function $U = X + Y$. What shape would you expect the indifference curves to be? What is the marginal rate of substitution between the two goods? What difference would it make to your answers if the function were $U = 2X + Y$ or $U = 2X + 3Y$?

Q12 Suppose an individual had preferences which could be represented by the utility function $U = X \times Y$. Which of the following functions could also represent the individual's preferences: (I) $U = 5XY$, (II) $U = -5XY$, (III) $U = (-5XY)^2$, (IV) $U = (-5XY)^3$?

Q13 A consumer has a utility function of the form

$$U = X^{0.25} Y^{0.75}$$

where X and Y are two goods. The price of good X is 2 and the price of good Y is 6, the consumer's money income is 300. What are the consumption levels of X and Y in equilibrium? Obtain the individual's demand functions for the two goods. What is the own price elasticity of demand for good X?

Q14 An individual has a utility function of the form

$$U = X^{0.5} + Y^{0.5}$$

What is the relationship between the two goods? What are the demand functions for the two goods, given prices P_x, P_y and income M for the consumer?

Q15 Explain what is meant by $MRS_{yx} = P_x/P_y$. Is it possible for the consumer to be in a utility-maximising equilibrium and this condition not to hold?

Q16 Given a conventionally shaped set of indifference curves what happens to the MRS as you move down a demand curve derived from the price consumption curve?

Q17 What do you understand by the distinction between gross and net substitutes and gross and net complements?

Q18 A government is trying to help those who are in low-paid employment. It has to decide between increasing the general level of benefit or spending an equivalent sum in reducing the level of rent paid by those living in social housing. What would you advise it to do?

References and suggested further reading

The material in this chapter is often presented in more than one chapter in other texts. A strong theoretical foundation is given in Nicholson. Varian covers similar ground. Blaug gives a critical view on the progress made by economists in developing consumer theory from a historical perspective. Earl, Chapter 3.1–3.4, gives a thorough and also generally rather critical discussion of the material covered in this chapter.

The article written by Simmons gives more background on the demand for league football, but the methodological details requires a knowledge of econometric methods.

Blaug, M. (1992), *The Methodology of Economics*, 2nd edition, Cambridge University Press.

Earl, P.E. (1995), *Microeconomics for Business and Marketing*, Edward Elgar.

Estrin, S. and Laidler, D. (1995), *Introduction to Microeconomics*, 4th edition, Harvester Wheatsheaf.

Nicholson, W. (1995), *Microeconomic Theory, Basic Principles and Extensions*, 6th edition, The Dryden Press.

Office for National Statistics (1997), *Economic Trends*.

Simmons, R. (1996), 'The Demand for English League Football: A Club Level Analysis', *Applied Economics* **28**, 139–55.

Varian, H.R. (1996), *Intermediate Microeconomics, A Modern Approach*, 4th edition, W.W. Norton & Co.

2 Price Changes and Consumer Welfare

Key ideas and material

Monetary measures of price changes, cost-of-living indices, the RPI, the characteristics approach, The Halifax index

Introduction

This chapter looks at the relation between price changes and consumer welfare in some detail. Large changes in the price of housing, for example, can dramatically affect the welfare of the individuals. Much of the work of economists is, in practice, concerned with matters of measurement, and in this chapter we will discuss the construction of price indices and how they relate to changes in consumer welfare.

How a price index is constructed affects the price movements that are measured and this, in turn, will impact on pay negotiations, impact on how much social security payments are increased and affect government macroeconomic policy generally. What measure is used can make a sizeable difference to the living standards of individuals and to policy-making. In practical terms, the subject matter of this chapter is of big importance.

The outline of this chapter is as follows. In Section 1 we look at two alternative ways of measuring the effect of a price change. The use of these measures is then applied to give us a first look at the effect of a change in the price of housing on individual welfare. Section 2 introduces cost-of-living indices and alternative ways in which they may be constructed. Section 3 presents some detail on the construction of the main measure of retail price inflation in the UK, the RPI. In addition, this section also discusses the reliability of inflation measures and the moves to harmonise the construction of price indices between European Union member states. This is of obvious importance given the moves toward a common monetary policy in the EU, and the discussion brings out the importance of adjustment for quality changes and the introduction of new goods in constructing indices of price changes.

Section 4 introduces an alternative approach to consumer demand known as the characteristics approach. Individual demands are seen in terms of the attributes or characteristics that goods possess rather than for the goods themselves. This discussion will lead us to one application of an hedonic price index, The Halifax house price series. There is very great variation in the type of properties that are sold in terms of their age, location, size and other characteristics in any one year and what the hedonic index does is measure price changes allowing for changes in the characteristics of properties traded. The importance of this is brought out when we look at the timing of record price changes, and the chapter finishes with an exercise to look at the effect on price movements on the cost of housing.

2.1 Price changes and welfare analysis

We saw in Chapter 1 that a (relative) price change has two distinct effects: an income effect and a substitution effect. Suppose we now consider the effect of an increase in the price of a good and ask how much worse off the consumer becomes in monetary terms. There are two different measures of this: the compensating variation and the equivalent variation.[1]

The first of these measures, the compensating variation, is illustrated in Figure 2.1. The initial point of equilibrium is E_0; let us suppose the price of good X was to rise, then the budget line B_0 would pivot round the vertical axis, and the new constraint the individual faces would be B_1. The compensating variation is simply the amount of income that would return the individual to the original level of utility. This is the additional income necessary after the change in relative prices, so in Figure 2.1 we can measure this amount by the parallel shift in the budget constraint from B_1 to B_2.[2]

The equivalent variation is shown in Figure 2.2. After the price change we have drawn another budget constraint B_2, parallel to the original constraint B_0, and tangential to the new indifference curve, IC_1. The equivalent variation is the amount of income that would shift the budget constraint from B_0 to B_2, and gives the reduction in the amount of money income that is equivalent to an increase in the price of one of the goods. These two measures of the change in the welfare of the consumer give different answers to different questions. The compensating variation evaluates the welfare loss at the new relative prices, the equivalent variation at those before the price change. We will now see how we can use the idea of equivalent variation in relation to changes in the price of housing.

Housing subsidies and welfare analysis

In the UK and in many other parts of the world the cost of housing is subsidised both for those that rent housing and for those who are buying their own property. The policy of

1 The effect of a price change can also be approached by consumers' surplus. This we take up in Chapter 9.

2 The compensating variation associated with a price fall was, in effect, shown in Figure 1.14A.

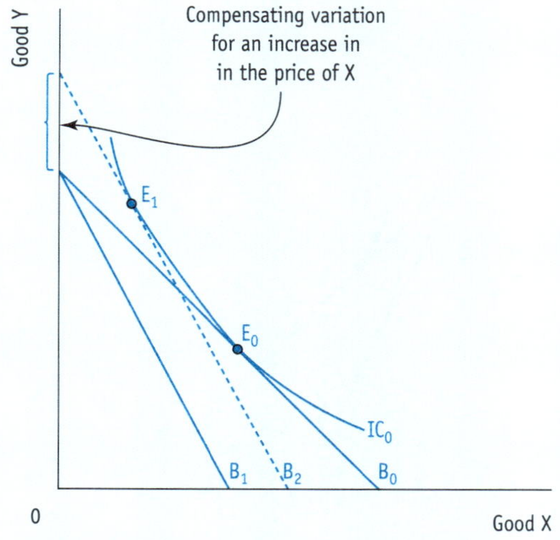

Figure 2.1 **The compensating variation of a price change**

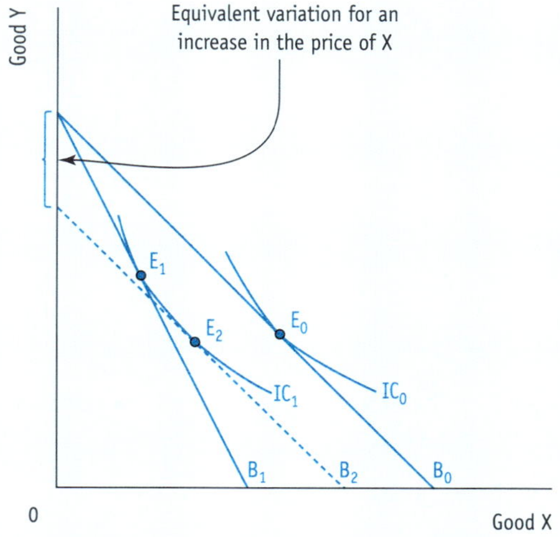

Figure 2.2 **The equivalent variation of a price change**

governments in relation to housing is a big subject, partly because of the large percentage of individual incomes that are spent on housing and partly because of the extent of government involvement in providing housing directly or to subsidising owner-occupation. We will start by looking at the welfare effects of providing a subsidy to those that rent.

Figure 2.3 measures an individual's consumption of housing services on the horizontal axis and the consumption of all other goods on the vertical axis. For the sake of simplicity, we can think of the amount of housing services in terms of floor space. The initial point of equilibrium is given by point E_0, where the consumer obtains utility associated with the indifference curve IC_0. Suppose the government was to introduce a subsidy on housing, or to increase the size of an existing subsidy, then the effect would be to rotate the budget constraint out along the horizontal axis. As drawn, we have assumed a 50% price subsidy, so the new budget line intersects the horizontal axis twice the distance from the origin. This enables the individual to move onto a higher indifference curve, which in the figure is shown as point E_1 on IC_1 where the quantity of housing for the individual has increased, as has consumption of the composite good. The new level of housing consumption is OH_1 and the consumption of all other goods increases to OG_1 units.

The vertical distance between the budget lines B_0 and B_1 measures the cost of providing the subsidy to the individual. In the extreme case of the individual not buying any housing at all, there is no subsidy and so the two budget lines intersect the vertical axis at the same point. As the quantity of housing purchased increases, the effect of the per unit subsidy increases as shown by the increasing vertical distance between B_0 and B_1. Given that the individual has

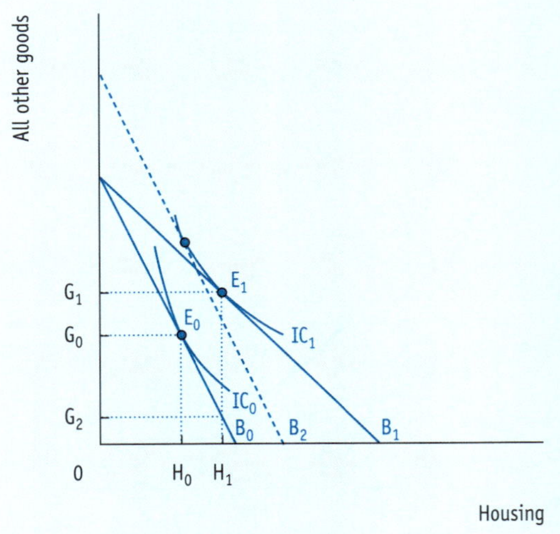

Figure 2.3 **The effect of a subsidy on the rented housing sector**

chosen the amount OH_1 of housing, the vertical distance between the budget constraints gives the additional amount of all other goods that the individual can obtain as a result of the subsidy. If we measure the cost of units of all other goods as £1 per unit then this distance gives us the cost to the government as £$(G_1 - G_2)$.

How much has the individual benefited from the introduction of the subsidy? This is measured by the equivalent variation in income moving from B_0 to B_2. This is less than the cost to the government in providing the subsidy to the individual. Generally, in this kind of analysis a per unit subsidy is worth less to the individual than a lump-sum income transfer of the same cost.

In most EU countries the majority of the population are owner-occupiers.[3] There has been a long-term trend towards home-ownership which national governments have supported by tax concessions in some form over a period of several decades. This has enabled those who have a taken out a mortgage to finance house purchase to claim tax relief on the interest payments. To understand the nature of the advantage this has given some individuals we need to briefly look at the way income tax operates.

We can think of a simple income tax system in terms of a tax allowance and two rates of tax. Suppose, for example, there was a tax allowance of £5,000 pounds per annum and a basic tax rate of 25% payable on the first £25,000 of taxable income (income less the tax allowance). We will also suppose that there is a single higher rate of 40% paid on taxable income in excess of £25,000. An individual who earns £5,000 and has no other income would therefore pay no tax. Someone earning £15,000 would pay a 25% rate on their taxable income, which in this case is

3 In 1995 the exceptions were Germany, the Netherlands, Austria and Sweden. The details are shown in Chart 6.2 in Chapter 6.

Country	Main tax relief	Direction of policy
Belgium	MITR	
Denmark	MITR	Cut
Germany	Depreciation allowance	Maintained. Costs have risen
Spain	MITR	Maintained
France	MITR	Mixed
Netherlands	MITR	Maintained
UK	MITR	Cut
Finland	MITR	Mixed
Sweden	MITR	Cut

Table 2.1 **Tax relief for owner-occupiers**
Source: Maclennan and Stephens (1997).

25% of £15,000–£5,000, i.e. £2,500. Their income after tax would be £12,500. For someone earning £50,000 they would pay 25% of £30,000–£5,000 and 40% of £50,000–£30,000, which is £14,250. Their net of tax income would be £35,750.

The principal form of tax relief that has been given in EU countries is Mortgage Interest Tax Relief, or MITR. This has much the same effect as would an additional tax allowance. For example, someone with a mortgage of £30,000 paying interest at 8% per annum would pay £2,400 in interest each year. For the basic rate taxpayer in the above regime this interest cost can be offset against tax, reducing the payments by £600. If the system allowed individuals with incomes above £30,000 to claim at 40%, then their payment would be reduced by £960. Table 2.1 shows how widespread this form of tax concession has been throughout Western Europe.

When the tax concession was introduced (the 1960s in the UK for example) those who were mortgagors at that time would have benefited from a lower cost of housing. A simple analysis of the kind illustrated in Figure 2.3 would have been appropriate. Over time as owner-occupation became the preferred form of tenure for a growing proportion of the population, demand and property prices rose partly as a result of this and other tax advantages. This gave a second benefit to members of the generation who bought at the time the concession was introduced, although it diminished the benefit to those who bought later at higher prices. Finally, as the general direction of policy in the UK and in some other countries has changed, those who have bought when prices have risen on a long-term view have seen the cost of mortgage debt rise. Overall the impact on individuals has therefore been very mixed, a subject we will return to.

Questions

Q1 Anna lives in social housing and following a new government policy now receives a 50% subsidy from the government for her housing costs. Assuming that Anna has a diminishing marginal rate of substitution between all other goods and housing

(I) What would the relationship be between the benefit of the subsidy to her and the cost of the subsidy to government if she cannot move?

(II) In what other circumstances would the answer be as in (I)?

Q2 Lucky Sue bought her home for £3,000 in 1965 with a mortgage of £2,000. For simplicity, assume she lived in a land without inflation and paid off her outstanding debt at a constant interest rate of 6%.

(I) What was her saving in interest payments each year if she paid income tax at a rate of 30% and was entitled to MITR?

In another world 25 years later, the general rise in prices had been 1000%. Unlucky Sid bought a flat in this kingdom for £60,000 with a mortgage of £57,000. The interest rate he paid was fixed at 10%, but at least he had the benefit of paying a tax rate of only 20%.

(II) What would be the reduction in interest paid if MITR was available on the full amount of his mortgage?

(III) Suppose the government decided to reduce tax concessions to owner-occupation, by limiting the relief to the first £30,000 of the sum borrowed, and only giving the concession at a rate of 15p in the £. How does the interest saving differ from (II)?

2.2 Cost-of-living indices

The cost-of-living can be thought of as the expenditure level necessary to maintain a particular level of utility. A cost-of-living index measures the change in the cost-of-living between two points in time. Suppose, for example, that consumers bought only two goods, bread and wine, and let us also suppose that between 1990 and 1998 the price of bread rose from 60p to 65p, and the price of a bottle of wine rose from £4.00 to £5.00. How much has the cost-of-living changed over this period of time? To answer this question we need a way of representing the change in the cost-of-living to all consumers. In general terms, this varies between individuals because they buy different quantities of the two goods because of differences in income or differences in tastes. An index is one way of taking these variations into account.

For the moment, we will simplify and assume that consumers buy one loaf of bread with each bottle of wine.[4] A cost-of-living index weights the percentage change in the price of each good by the share of total expenditure that goes on each good. To calculate a cost-of-living index in our example we require

(I) The percentage increase in the price of bread

$$((65p/60p) - 1) * 100 = 8.33\%$$

(II) The percentage increase in the price of a bottle of wine

$$((£5.00/£4) - 1) * 100 = 25\%$$

(III) The weights for the two goods

$$60p/£4.60 = 0.13 \text{ for bread and } £4/£4.60 = 0.87 \text{ for wine.}$$

This gives us an increase in the cost-of-living of

$$(0.13 * 8.33\% + 0.87 * 25\%) = 22.83\%.$$

The above is an example of a Laspeyres, or base-weighted, index. The percentage increase in the price of the two goods is weighted by the expenditure shares of the two goods in the base (or reference) year of 1990.

There is, however, more than one way of calculating a cost-of-living index. We could equally have taken the weights from the 1998 expenditure shares, which in our example would give (65p/£5.65) = 0.12 for the bread and (£5/£5.65) = 0.88 for the wine. Given the increases in the price of the two goods, the increase in the cost-of-living on a current-weighted, or Paasche, index is 23.1%.

In the case where consumers buy just two goods, the Laspeyres index can be written as

$$\frac{P_1^X X_0 + P_1^y Y_0}{P_0^X X_0 + P_0^y Y_0}$$

X_0, Y_0 refer to the quantities of each good bought in period 0, the base year. P_0^x is the price of X in the base period, P_1^x is the price of X in the current period, period 1. Likewise for P_0^y and P_1^y. The counterpart for the Paasche index is

$$\frac{P_1^x X_1 + P_1^y Y_1}{P_0^x X_1 + P_0^y Y_1}$$

where the current period quantities X_1, Y_1 are used to form the weights.

4 We are, in effect, assuming here that bread and wine are perfect complements. It is a big simplification as will become apparent.

The Laspeyres index gives the change in the cost of obtaining the goods bought in the base year. The Paasche index gives the change in the cost of obtaining the bundle of goods bought in the current year. There is, therefore, no single answer in principle to the question asking how much the cost-of-living has risen (or fallen) as it can, and does, depend on which index is used. It is also possible that one index gives a rise in the cost-of-living while the other shows a fall. In practice, the RPI, and other indices, are usually calculated with base weights and the details of its construction are taken up in the next section.

In our example, if the individual bought ten loaves of bread and ten bottles of wine in each year, expenditure in the base year would be £46 and in 1998 it would be £56.50. The percentage increase in the expenditure of the individual is the same as the increase in the cost of living index. The welfare of the individual is unchanged as the same amount of bread and wine is consumed in each year and our measures above reflect this.[5] However, when the prices of goods rise (or fall) by differing amounts, which typically they do, we would in general expect there to be some substitution effects. In our example, wine became more expensive relative to bread and this may lead the individual to purchase more bread and less wine. Suppose we have a situation in which

$$P_1^x X_0 + P_1^y Y_0 < Exp_1$$

On the left hand side, we have the combinations of the two goods purchased in year 0 and the prices of the two goods in year 1; on the right hand side, we have expenditure in year 1. Here, an individual could have bought the base year combination of goods in the current year, but chose not to do so (if he or she had done so the two sides of the expression would be equal). It follows that the person is better off in year 1 than in year 0. Generally, an individual will be better off if the Laspeyres index rises by less than the ratio of current to base year expenditures. Algebraically, if we divide both sides by the expenditure in year 0, by $P_0^x X_0 + P_0^y Y_0$ we get

$$L < \frac{Exp_1}{Exp_0}$$

where L is the Laspeyres index.

There is, therefore, a difference between a cost-of-living index and an index of price changes; ignoring substitution effects will overstate changes in the cost-of-living. In Figure 2.4, the initial (base-year) equilibrium is given by point E_0 at the point of tangency of indifference curve, IC_0, and the budget constraint, B_0. The change in the budget line is drawn on the basis of a fall in the price of Y relative to that of X, hence the budget constraint at the new relative prices will be steeper. As drawn, the new budget line, B_1, gives the consumer just enough income to purchase the base-year bundle of goods at the new prices. Hence B_1 passes through the point E_0. The individual could have bought the combination X_0 Y_0 but chose not to do so,

5 We are effectively assuming here that the consumer's income rose in the same proportion as the price rises.

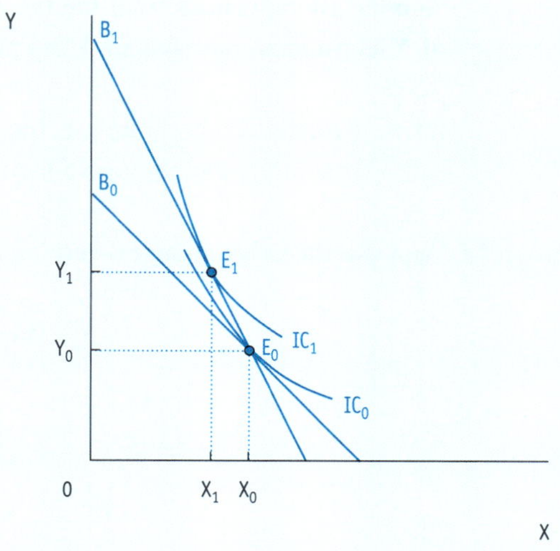

Figure 2.4 **Price indices and the substitution effect**

because by substituting Y for X the individual can attain a higher level of utility. This is shown by the higher indifference curve IC_1, where the combination X_1 Y_1 is chosen.[6]

We have kept the discussion relatively simple so far. In practice, individuals purchase many goods and services and when aggregating over all individuals it makes sense to think in terms of categories of expenditure rather than purchase of individual items. There are also large variations in the patterns of expenditure between different groups of individuals, e.g. those with very high and very low incomes, or the retired and the non-retired. Additionally, changes in the cost of housing in particular raise awkward questions of measurement for price indices. In the next section, we will look at construction of the Retail Price Index in the UK and how it addresses these issues.

Question

Q3

Year	Price of	Price of
	X	Y
0	£10	£20
1	£20	£10

6 An example of a Slutsky substitution effect.

Assume all individuals treat the two goods, X and Y, as perfect complements, so that for each unit of X consumed, one unit of Y is consumed as well.

(I) Calculate the change in the cost-of-living according to the Laspeyres and the Paasche formulas. Do they give sensible results?

Suppose the price changes were

Year	Price of	Price of
	X	Y
0	£12	£10
1	£10	£20

(II) What changes in the cost-of-living does the Laspeyres index give? Suppose the two goods were perfect substitutes what would be the increase in the cost of living?

2.3 The Retail Price Index

The Retail Price Index, known as the RPI, is the main measure of retail price changes in the UK. The index is compiled using a large sample of information on the prices of goods and services purchased by individuals each month. In all, there are around 130–150,000 individual prices collected. In the case of bread, for example, there are five price indicators to cover different varieties, and these indicators are then used to estimate the overall change in the price of bread. The individual price items are combined into some 600 separate indicators used in compiling the RPI.

This level of detailed information is then summarised into 14 more general classifications, which are shown in Table 2.2. These classifications cover virtually all types of household spending and the table gives the weights attached to each classification in 1998. These are mainly taken from the Family Expenditure Survey (FES), which is a household budget survey.[7]

The weights are expressed as parts per 1,000, so for example food expenditure got a weight of 13.0% in the calculation of the RPI in 1998, catering a weight of 4.8% and so on. The pattern of expenditure varies over time to some degree and so the weights are changed annually to reflect these changes. This makes the RPI a 'chained' Laspeyres index rather than a fixed

7 The FES is a survey conducted by the government of the spending patterns of around 7,000 households in the UK. The National Food Survey is used to provide the weights for some prices.

	(Parts per 1,000)
Food	130
Catering	48
Alcoholic drink	71
Tobacco	34
Housing	197
Fuel and light	36
Household goods	72
Household services	54
Clothing and footwear	55
Personal goods/services	40
Motoring expenditure	136
Fares and other travel costs	20
Leisure goods	46
Leisure service	61

Table 2.2 RPI commodity classification and their weights 1998
Source: Economy (1998).

weight index as discussed in the previous section. In practice, the changes to the weights on a year-on-year basis are not dramatic: over the five year period from 1993 to 1998 the largest change was in the area of housing costs where the weight increased from 16.4 to 19.7%.

The pattern of expenditure shown in Table 2.2 is not typical of everyone. For example, those without a car would probably have a much higher weight than 20 parts per 1,000 for fares and other travel costs. The weights are based on expenditure patterns of diverse groups of individuals, although there are two groups whose pattern of expenditure is sufficiently different from the rest that they are excluded. These are people in households with incomes in the top 4% and pensioners who are on low incomes.

The nature of these variations between individuals also changes over time, sometimes as a result of changes in policy by government. For example, when the UK joined the (then) European Economic Community in 1973, the operation of the Common Agricultural Policy (CAP) pushed up the price of food. Some low income households, who spend a higher proportion on food than the weight given in the RPI, would have experienced a faster increase in the price of what they buy than was shown by the index. A more recent study by Crawford (1996) into UK household cost-of-living indices over the period 1979–92, found some fall in the relative price of necessities and a corresponding increase in the price of luxuries. Consequently, cost-of-living indices rose faster for richer households than it did for poorer ones during this period.

The treatment of housing costs

We have noted that housing costs in 1998 received the largest weight within the RPI. The breakdown of the weight is as follows.

	(Parts per 1,000)
Housing	197
— Rent	47
— Mortgage interest	45
— Depreciation	32
— Council tax and rates	30
— Water and other charges	12
— Repairs and maintenance	10
— DIY materials	14
— Dwelling insurance/ground rent	7

Table 2.3 **Housing costs in the RPI 1998**
Source: Economy (1998).

This is a problematic area for calculating changes in the cost of living. The approach adopted in the RPI for those owner-occupiers with a mortgage is to use mortgage interest payments as the cost of 'shelter'. The average outstanding mortgage debt forms the weight and the rate of interest is the 'price'. Changes in the capital values of housing only enter the RPI via the effect on the size of the average mortgage outstanding. This raises a number of problems, one of which is the high degree of sensitivity between movements in mortgage interest payments and the RPI. A 1% increase in mortgage interest payments from say 8% to 9% would therefore increase the overall RPI by $0.045 * 12.5\% = 0.56\%$.[8]

8 This creates a problem in macroeconomic policy in that a 1% increase in interest rates raises the inflation rate in the short-term by around 0.5%.

The rise and fall of the capital values of houses can greatly reduce the cost of housing in the case of price rises, or greatly increase it in the case of price falls. In the UK, there have been large price fluctuations since the beginning of the 1970s and to take no account at all of these can and does at times give a very misleading impression.[9] This aspect of the cost of housing is taken up at the end of the chapter.

The reliability of the RPI

The Boskin Report

This report cast serious doubts about the reliability of the main measure of price inflation in the US, the Consumer Price Index (CPI). The main criticism of the report was that inflation in the US had been overstated by around 1.3% over the period 1978–96, although modifications to the CPI by 1998 reduced this figure to 1.1%. The effect of bias of this order of magnitude for this length is time is large. Given the methodology applied to construct the index is broadly in line with the RPI in the UK, this report has raised questions about the reliability of the RPI and other indices of price changes used in Europe.

Table 2.4 provides a breakdown of the sources of bias as estimated by the Boskin Commission.

Source of bias	Estimate % per annum
Substitution effect	0.4
New products/quality change	0.6
New outlets	0.1
Total	**1.1**
Plausible range	(0.8–1.6)

Table 2.4 Boskin estimates of CPI bias in US
Source: Oulton (1998).

The view of the Commission was that the CPI is a cost-of-living index and the estimated bias is relative to the ideal measure. The estimates given by the Commission therefore included a breakdown into substitution bias (both between commodity groupings when relative prices change, and also from changes in relative prices within a commodity group). The largest single

9 Chart 2.1 and Table 2.7 gives some idea of the movement of house prices.

source of bias in the report was that attributed to the introduction of new products and quality changes; a problem that can occur when it is not possible to accurately measure the quality change in a good between two periods and deduct its effect from the increase in price. Finally, outlet bias refers to effects from changes in the structure of retailing such as the introduction of large cost-cutting stores in particular which may not be fully reflected in the index.

In the UK, the RPI does not include the substitution effects of price changes and, as we saw in Section 2, this will lead a price index to overstate the rise in the cost-of-living. The importance of this in the UK, where the weights are changed annually, is likely to be less than in the US, and some other European countries, where the weights are only changed periodically.

There are a number of possible approaches to allow for quality changes and the introduction of new goods. One way is to track the price of a given item, a particular type of washing-machine or a car of a given specification, for example, and if there are no changes to it over a period of time then the problem is solved for that item. This is known as the matched models method. It does, of course, leave open what to do when the specification changes or the model is no longer available.

In the construction of the RPI, decisions about changes of this sort are often left to the discretion of the individual data collectors. There are a number of practical alternatives that they can follow. Small changes may simply be ignored. When there are larger changes which lead to an upgraded model sold at the same time as one of a lesser specification, the differences in the two prices at a given date gives an estimate of the effect of the quality changes, and this can be used. In some cases, a new product or model is included with an estimate of the quality adjustment with data from the producer.

The introduction of a new good or service can be dealt with conceptually by what is known as the reservation price approach. This involves treating a new good as if it already exists, but that its price is just at the level where there is no demand for it. The reservation price is just the price at which demand becomes zero. The appearance of a new good can then be taken to indicate that its price has fallen below its reservation level. It follows that ignoring new goods

Period	Bread price	Quantity	Wine price	Quantity	Laspeyres index
0	£0.50	20	£6	0	100
1	£0.50	20	£5	1	100
2	£0.50	20	£4	2	93.3

Table 2.5 An example of the reservation price approach

will mean that price rises will be overstated. Table 2.5 modifies the earlier example involving just bread and wine.

In period 0, there are 20 loaves of bread consumed and the price of wine is at its reservation level. The Laspeyres index for the base period is 100. In period 1, the price of wine falls below its reservation level but, given that the Laspeyres index is base-weighted, this fall in price has no effect on the index. Using a chain-weighted Laspeyres index we get a fall in prices of 6.7% by the end of period 2. Clearly, if there is a time delay in introducing the new good into the index, then it will take that much longer to record its effect. Such an approach is not easy to implement in practice given the need to estimate the reservation price: although if new goods, particularly durables, tend to be expensive initially the weighting for the good may be small and the size of the bias not large.

European harmonisation

The measurement of inflation in a European context is obviously important given the moves toward monetary union and a common monetary policy. There is also the issue of how inflation is to be measured in those countries which are not in the first wave of member states joining a single currency, but who may wish to do so at a later date. The price indices that are used at a national level, the RPI in the UK and CPI's in other European countries vary in the way they are constructed, particularly in relation to the treatment of owner-occupied housing, educational and health goods. This has necessitated the development of Harmonised Indices of Consumer Prices (HICPs), which will be used at both a national and European level in an effort to measure inflation in member states on a comparable basis.

The harmonised indices are a Laspeyres-type index. For HICPs the expenditure pattern is based on the whole of the population. The European Commission does not require budget surveys to be conducted more frequently than every five years (although in addition to the UK, France, the Netherlands and Sweden also revise the weights for their indices annually). The coverage of the HICPs differs from the UK RPI in that it does not include owner-occupied housing costs. On the other hand they do include prices indices for airfares and personal computers. For new cars and personal computers there are explicit quality adjustments using what is called the option cost approach. In effect, this simply entails the cost of buying an individual component as an option, a half of which is allowed against the increase in price between two models.

HICPs use the geometric mean to aggregate the raw price data, whereas the RPI uses the arithmetic mean. This last point can be a matter of important detail. There is no information on the weights of consumer expenditure at the most elementary level so using the arithmetic mean to calculate price changes, in effect, gives each individual item an equal weight. For example, given the following data on the price of bread.

Time period	Local open all hours	Local bakery	Supermarket chain	Supermarket chain
0	60p	59p	63p	62p
1	75p	72p	67p	68p

Table 2.6 **Aggregating raw price data**

Using the arithmetic mean we get an increase in the price of bread of 15.76%. This procedure gives equal weights to each of the outlets; so if the price of bread in a supermarket chain rises by less than it does in a local retail shop, it is effectively assumed that individuals continue to buy the same amounts of bread from the same retail outlets. There is no substitution between outlets.

Clearly, individuals may switch from one outlet to another when (relative) prices change between outlets. The geometric mean effectively assumes that the proportion of total expenditure in each shop is constant. This corresponds to preferences which can be represented by a Cobb-Douglas utility function, examples of which we introduced in Chapter 1. The geometric mean is calculated by multiplying the ratio price changes together and then taking nth root of the resulting product[10] Using the numbers in Table 2.6 we get

$$(1.25 * 1.220 * 1.063 * 1.097)^{0.25}$$

giving an increase of 15.49% in this example.

According to O'Donoghue and Wilkie (1998) the effect of using the geometric mean was to reduce the HICP for the UK by about 0.5 percentage points below the RPI, which is a sizeable effect given the overall rates of inflation.

Questions

Q4 Suppose there were just two goods consumed with associated quantities as given below

Period	Price of Good 1	Quantity of Good 1	Price of Good 2	Quantity of Good 2
0	£10	10	£20	0
1	£10	10	£15	2
2	£10	10	£10	5

10 The formula for the geometric mean is given in the appendix.

(I) What is the Laspeyres base-weighted inflation index for the three periods?
(II) What is the chain-weighted index and how does it compare with your answer to (I)?

Q5 Suppose the changes in bread prices at the four different outlets were as follows

Time period	Local open all hours	Local bakery	Supermarket chain	Supermarket chain
0	70p	50p	50p	60p
1	77p	55p	55p	66p

(I) What is the difference in the increase in prices using the arithmetic mean of price relatives and the geometric mean?
(II) When would it make sense to use the arithmetic mean and when to use the geometric mean?

2.4 The characteristics approach

An alternative way of looking at consumer demand is given by the characteristics approach, which is a way of analysing the demand for goods in terms of their attributes. For example, in the decision to rent or buy a house, the attributes or characteristics that would typically interest the consumer are its location, distance from a town centre for example, the number of bedrooms it has, the size of its garden and so on.

Figure 2.5 illustrates this in the case of the demand for rented property. For simplicity, we will assume that there are just two characteristics which interest prospective renters: space (measured in square feet) and the number of facilities of interest within say a one mile radius (the number of public houses, coffee shops, etc.). These two characteristics are measured on the vertical and horizontal axis respectively in the figure.

There are two rays drawn out of the origin in the Figure, R_1 and R_2. These show different proportions of the two characteristics; properties that are further out of a town or city centre may be bigger, but may offer less in the way of some amenities. Properties represented by the ray R_1 could be taken as being an out-of-town area, those along R_2 as being in a more central location.

The budget line is drawn for a given level of expenditure by the individual and the figure shows the quantity of housing the individual could buy given the rents charged. At point E, an individual can afford to rent a property with 800 square feet of floor space but only has, say,

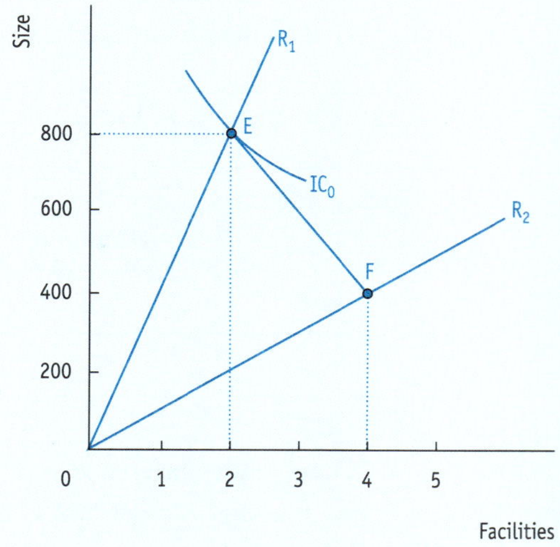

Figure 2.5 **The characteristics approach**

two public houses within a mile. At point F, we represent the possibility that an individual can afford to rent a flat half that size but with twice the number of amenities within easy reach.

The individual's preferences are again represented by indifference curves, but here they refer to different combinations of the two characteristics that yield a given level of utility. Indifference curves further away from the origin will again yield higher utility levels and the optimal position of the consumer will be on the highest indifference curve attainable given the budget available. In Figure 2.5 this is shown as point E.

In this context, a change in the rent for a property will shift the budget constraint in a similar fashion to that considered before in Chapter 1. For example, a fall in rent for the property represented by the ray R_1 will move the point E further away from the origin. An increase in income will shift the budget line EF further away from the origin. The equilibrium position will therefore vary as the rent paid and the budget of the consumer varies. What this analysis shows is that for a given budget, the demand for rented property, and other goods, can be broken down into the characteristics or attributes that it possesses.

Question

Q6 Suppose in Figure 2.5 that the individual had the choice of only two alternative places to rent.

(I) Would it be possible to obtain a demand curve for an individual?
(II) What would you expect the shape of the market demand curve to be?

2.5 The Halifax House Price Index

The stock of owner-occupied housing in the UK consists of around sixteen million properties that vary enormously from small flats to country mansions. Generally, property prices vary hugely with location, size, age and other characteristics and this is reflected in the types of property traded over time. A simple average of price changes will therefore reflect both the change in price of properties of a given type, and also the changes in the mix or types of property traded.

To measure house price inflation there is a need to control for the changing type of properties traded and an hedonic price index is one way of doing this. The main idea is to relate the price of a house to the attributes it has in detail: the factors mentioned above together with the amenities it provides — the number of habitable rooms it has, whether or not it has a garage and so on. The implicit valuation of each characteristic is then estimated with a regression equation of the form

$$P_i = b_0 + b_1X_{1i} + b_2X_{2i} + \ldots + b_KX_{Ki} + u_i$$

The i subscript refers to each individual property. P is the price of a particular property, $X_1 \ldots X_K$ are the variables used to represent the characteristics, and $b_0 \ldots b_k$ are the regression coefficients. Table 2.7 lists the right hand side variables used in the regression for The Halifax index.

This requires a lot of data on the physical nature of the property and a representative sample of properties. The Halifax does have a large database, which includes around one mortgagor in five in the UK and so the number of transactions each month means that such a model can be estimated with some confidence. Some of the variables associated with a particular characteristic are mutually exclusive: for example, in the case of property type it is detached or semi-detached or one of the three others. This gives five variables only one of which is relevant for any particular property. Likewise with location, only one variable will be relevant.[11]

The coefficients give the (implicit) price for each characteristic. If, for example, the X_1 variable is a detached property and the b_1 coefficient is 12,000, then the characteristic of being a detached house contributes £12,000 * 1 to the price of a property. If the variable X_6 is the number of habitable rooms and the coefficient b_6 is 1,500, then £1,500 is the implicit valuation placed on each room.

To construct the index a regression of the above form is estimated for the base year, 1983, and subsequent years. The change in coefficients therefore gives the change in the price of the

11 The dataset, therefore, consists mainly of 0,1 dummy variables together with those that record the actual age of the property, the number of habitable rooms and so on.

Characteristic	Variables
— House type	Detached, semi-detached, terrace, bungalow, flat
— Size	Number of habitable rooms in total, number of bathrooms, separate toilets, garages, and garage spaces. Also whether the property has a garden, and whether the property exceeds one acre
— Central heating	Full, none or partial
— Freehold	
— Location	Twelve economic planning regions — North, Yorks & Humberside, North-West, East Midlands, West Midlands, East Anglia, Wales, South-West, South-East, Greater London, Northern Ireland, Scotland
Road charge liability	
— Age	Number of years since construction

Table 2.7 Characteristics for The Halifax House Price Index
Source: Flemming and Nellis (1984).

characteristics over time. The Halifax index is a based-weighted Laspeyres index: the weights come from the properties that were traded in 1983. The weight for the characteristic price of being a detached house is the proportion of detached properties that were traded in that year. The weight for the characteristic price of a habitable room comes from the average number of habitable rooms in properties traded in the base year. The price changes in The Halifax index are therefore relative to the particular type, or mix, of properties that were traded in 1983.[12]

Table 2.8 gives The Halifax house price series on a mix-adjusted basis and also on the basis of simple averages of price changes. Chart 2.1 gives the annual rates of change of prices from both series. Broadly, the two series move in line with each other over longer periods of time. However, a key feature of the owner-occupied housing market is the apparent cyclical pattern of price rises and price falls. Looking at the year-on-year changes, there have been some sharp differences between the two series; so adjusting for the different types of property traded in a particular year is important for the timing of recorded price changes. For example, in 1989 the standardised price rose by nearly 21%, the simple average by less than a third of this figure. In 1996 the relative movements in the two series were the other way around; the standardised price rose by less than 5%, the simple average by over 15%. The perception about the state of the housing market is to some extent dependent on the price series chosen, although given our discussion here, clearly the standardised price series should be taken as the more reliable guide.

12 A year determined by data availability.

Year	Standardised price £	Simple average £
1983	30,898	30,898
1984	33,117	30,952
1985	36,145	32,953
1986	40,126	38,693
1987	46,315	47,482
1988	57,087	57,594
1989	68,946	61,163
1990	68,950	64,729
1991	68,130	65,377
1992	64,309	63,163
1993	62,455	62,811
1994	62,750	62,013
1995	61,666	61,343
1996	64,441	70,898
1997	68,504	74,475

Table 2.8 **The Halifax house price series**
Source: The Halifax.

Question

Q7 Trevor bought a house in 1985 for the average (standardised) price of £36,145. Assume that the price of his house moved in line with property prices generally.

(I) If Trevor had a mortgage of £30,000 on which he paid an interest rate of 10% per annum, what would be the effective rate of interest if he was given tax relief on all his mortgage and the tax rate was 27p in the £?

(II) Suppose that the deposit he paid on his house would otherwise have been left in a bank account where it would have earned 6% interest. What is the opportunity cost of the downpayment on his house?

(III) What is the cost of housing to Trevor in the years from 1985 to 1989 given the interest paid, the opportunity cost of his deposit and the capital gain on his house? (For simplicity ignore capital repayments on his mortgage).

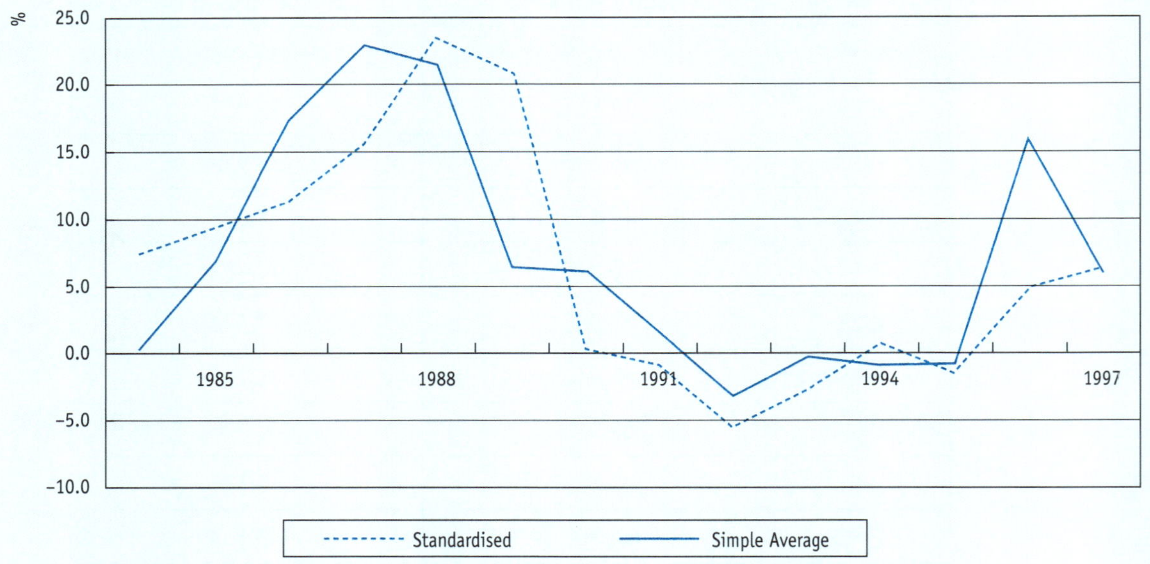

Chart 2.1 **% change in UK house prices**
Source: The Halifax.

(IV) If Trevor had delayed purchasing his house for four years and now had a deposit of 10%, how would your answers to the above change over the period to 1993? Assume (to keep matters simple) that the mortgage rate, the bank deposit rate and the terms of the tax relief were the same.

Concluding comment

This chapter has been concerned with the practical issues of price measurement, which is an important component of the work of economists in industry and government. It is worth remembering that there is unavoidable ambiguity in questions about changes in the cost-of-living. There is also uncertainty arising from data limitations and statistical problems, when measuring changes in the prices of goods and services when there are wide variations in quality.

The fundamental distinction between real and nominal price changes is made in many of the chapters that follow, and an understanding of the material discussed here should help reinforce the distinction. The particular issue of the cost of housing and European integration is returned to in Chapter 6. An alternative way of looking at the effect on consumer welfare is presented in Chapter 9, and the CV and EV measures are used again when we discuss the consumer benefits of introducing competition into the utility industries in Chapter 12.

Mathematical appendix

There are three formulae in use to aggregate raw price data, i.e. to construct the elementary price indices: the ratio of averages, the arithmetic mean of price relatives and the geometric mean of price relatives.

(I) For the ratio of the averages

$$\text{RA:} \quad I_t = \frac{\sum_{l=i}^{n} P_{it}/n}{\sum_{l=i}^{n} P_{io}/n}$$

(II) For the arithmetic mean of price relatives

$$\text{AR:} \quad I_t = \frac{1}{n}\sum_{l=i}^{n} \frac{P_{it}}{P_{io}}$$

(III) For the geometric mean of price relatives

$$\text{G:} \quad I_t = \left(\prod_{i} \frac{P_{it}}{P_{io}}\right)^{1/n}$$

The ONS for the most part uses the first formula but sometimes the second (when changes in quality are involved). Eurostat uses the third for the construction of the HICPs.

Summary

1 Compensating variation and equivalent variation are two alternative measures of the effect of a price increase on consumer welfare. The first measures the amount of income we would have to give the consumer after the change in relative prices to compensate the individual for the price increase. The second gives how much income we would have to take away from him or her at the original relative prices that would result in an equivalent welfare loss.

2 One application of the analysis of consumer choice is to cost-of-living indices. We distinguished between the Laspeyres or 'base-weighted' index, and the Paasche or current-weighted index. In practice, nearly all indices are of the former, base-weighted types.

3 The Retail Price Index is the main measure of changes in consumer prices in the UK. It is based on a monthly survey of many thousands of individual prices. The weights for the RPI come mainly from consumer expenditure information collected by the government in the Family Expenditure Survey (FES).

4 There is an important conceptual distinction between an index of price changes and a cost-of-living index. When relative prices change a price index will not take account of substitution effects and will overstate changes in the cost-of-living.

5 There are a number of important issues relating to the reliability of the RPI (and other consumer price indices). These include the way in which quality changes and the introduction of new products are incorporated. The RPI is not representative of all households and a separate measure is published for pensioners. There is a difficult problem with measuring the changes in the costs of owner-occupied housing when the owner has a mortgage.

6 Monetary union in Europe has led to moves to harmonise price indices in EU member states with the construction of Harmonised Indices of Consumer Prices (HICPs). Work on harmonisation has involved a number of areas of methodological detail, including the formula used to aggregate raw price data on individual items. The use of the geometric mean may be more appropriate than the arithmetic mean.

7 The characteristics approach is alternative way of analysing consumer demand. Consumers are viewed as wanting goods for the attributes that they possess rather than for the good itself. This approach provides background to understanding hedonic price indices, which attempt to measure price changes when there are quality variations. One important index of this type in the UK is The Halifax House Price Index.

End of chapter questions

Q8 Given price information on the price of a coffee at four different retail outlets

Time period	Railway station	Chic café	Lorry-drivers pull-in	Public house
0	80p	£1.10	50p	£1
1	95p	£1.45	55p	£1.10

(I) Calculate three indices for the rate of inflation for the price of coffee as measured by the ratio of arithmetic means, arithmetic mean of price relatives and the geometric mean of price relatives between period 0 and period 1.

(II) What does the ratio of arithmetic means assume about substitution between outlets when prices change? What does the geometric mean of price relatives assume?

(III) Suppose that the prices in period 1 and period 0 were changed over, which of the methods give price indices that are the reciprocal of your answer to (II)?

Q9 Suppose that an individual consumer has a utility function of the form

$$U = XY$$

Where X and Y are two goods, $P_X = 8$ and $P_Y = 8$ in the base period.

(I) Given an income of 100 what are the expenditures on the two goods?

(II) Suppose the following year $P_Y = 10$, while there is no change to P_X. What is the increase in the Laspeyres price index?

(III) What is the increase in expenditure necessary for the individual to maintain a given level of utility?

Q10 What is the difference between the RPI, the RPIX and the RPIY? If you were in charge of producing the Retail Price Index what kinds of data would you collect and why? Do the problems of measuring price changes justify the publication of more than one index?

Q11 A rail user buys a network card that gives a discount of one-third on journeys undertaken. Does it follow that the individual will be better off with the card than without it? What assumptions are necessary for this to be true?

Q12 In 1980, the UK government decided to increase state National Insurance retirement pensions in line with inflation. What difference would it have made if it had used the all-items retail price index rather than a pensioner index? What difference would it have made had they increased pensions in line with average earnings? (Hint: You will find this data in Economic Trends Annual Supplement, Labour Market Trends and other publications.)

References and suggested further reading

The treatment of this topic tends to be fairly brief in texts that are primarily concerned with principles. Varian, for example, covers the subject as a subsection in a Chapter on Revealed Preference. There is also a similarly brief treatment in Estrin and Laidler, although it does have a chapter devoted to the analysis of the characteristics approach to consumer demand. Crawford provides an accessible read on the problems associated with the treatment of housing costs in the RPI. Oulton discusses the reliability of the RPI more generally.

Bank of England Quarterly Bulletin (1994), 'Inflation over three hundred years' **34**, (2).

Borooah, V.K., McGregor, P.P.L., McKee, P.M. and Mulholland, G.E. (1996), 'Cost-of-living differences between the regions of the United Kingdom' in Hills, J. (ed.), *New Inequalities*, Cambridge University Press.

Crawford, I. (1996), 'UK household cost-of-living indices, 1979-92' in Hills, J. (ed.), *New Inequalities*, Cambridge University Press.

Estrin, S. and Laidler, D. (1995), *Introduction to Microeconomics*, 4th edition, Harvester Wheatsheaf.

Flemming, M.C. and Nellis, J.G. (1984), '*The Halifax House Price Index Technical Details*', The Halifax.

Freemans, A.J.M., Holmans, A.E. and Whitehead, C.M.E. (1996), '*Is the UK Different? International Comparisons of Tenure Patterns*', Council of Mortgage Lenders.

Maclennan, D. and Stephens, M. (1997), '*EMU and the UK Housing and Mortgage Markets*', Council of Mortgage Lenders.

O'Donoghue, J. and Wilkie, C. (1998), 'Harmonised indices of consumer prices', *Economic Trends*, No. 532.

Oulton, N. (1995), 'Do UK Price Indices Overstate Inflation?', *National Institute Economic Review*, No. 2.

Oulton, N. (1998), 'The implications of the Boskin Report', *National Institute Economic Review*, No. 3.

Office for National Statistics (1996), '*Retail Price Index: A brief guide to the RPI*'.

Office for National Statistics (1998), '*Economy*'.

Robinson, B. and Skinner, T. (1989), 'Reforming the RPI: A Better Treatment of Housing Costs', *IFS Commentary*, **15**.

The Halifax (various issues), '*House Price Index*'.

Varian, H.R. (1996), *Intermediate Microeconomics: A Modern Approach*, 4th edition, W.W. Norton & Co.

3 Labour Supply

Key ideas and material

Income-leisure trade-off model, labour supply functions, analysis of individual labour supply, estimates of labour supply elasticities

Introduction

There have been large changes to the nature and pattern of work towards the end of the 20th century in many countries with an increasing need for skilled workers, a decline in the demand for those with few skills and, in some countries, a growing proportion of women in the labour force. This changing environment raises important issues for household labour supply and in this chapter we will examine the role of work incentives and how they affect diverse groups of individuals.

The question of individual work incentives is for many individuals closely tied up with the operation of the tax-benefit system. This leads to controversial policy questions about the effects of tax on the decision to work, and to the importance of detail in analysing the impact of social security provision. Do high tax rates discourage work effect? What is the effect of paying benefits to those on low earnings? These are the kind of questions that are addressed in the discussion that follows.

The outline of this chapter is as follows. Section 1 adapts the indifference curve analysis of Chapter 1 to provide a simplified framework for analysing labour supply decisions. We go on to show in more realistic analysis the restricted choice many individuals face about the number of hours they work, and whether to work at all. The basic analysis is built around a 'representative' individual. Section 2 develops this by looking at the position of some particular groups of individuals — students, single parents, those earning low incomes and those earning high incomes. This is a far from complete breakdown of the labour force, but it will illustrate the range of circumstances which people find themselves in, and we will see how the use of the basic structures can still be of relevance. It also paves the way for Section 3 by showing the varied response to different government policies by different groups in the workforce. Section 3 summarises some empirical findings on the responsiveness of hours worked to changes in wages, and also the incentive effects of different tax measures.

3.1 The income-leisure trade-off

Figure 3.1 illustrates the basic income-leisure trade-off model. The structure that we used to analyse decisions about the consumption of two goods, indifference maps and budget constraints, can be adapted to the analysis of decisions that an individual makes about labour supply. In this application, the two goods are income and leisure. Leisure here means time not spent in paid work: it is time that might be used for pleasure but also for other purposes as well such as studying, or household work.

In Figure 3.1, the horizontal axis measures leisure time, so if we consider the decision process within, say, a weekly time frame, this has a literal maximum of 168 hours. On the vertical axis we measure total income. This is both labour and non-labour income (such as benefit income and income from investments). We can therefore use an indifference curve to show different combinations of income and leisure that yield the same level of utility to an individual. The indifference curve IC_0 represents one such set of combinations. Given that we are treating both income and leisure as goods, higher indifference curves — those that are further away from the origin — represent higher levels of utility. IC_1 and IC_2 therefore represent higher levels of utility than does IC_0.

The slope of an indifference curve drawn in Figure 3.1 reflects the marginal rate of substitution between income and leisure for the individual, MRS_{YL}. In other words, this is the rate at

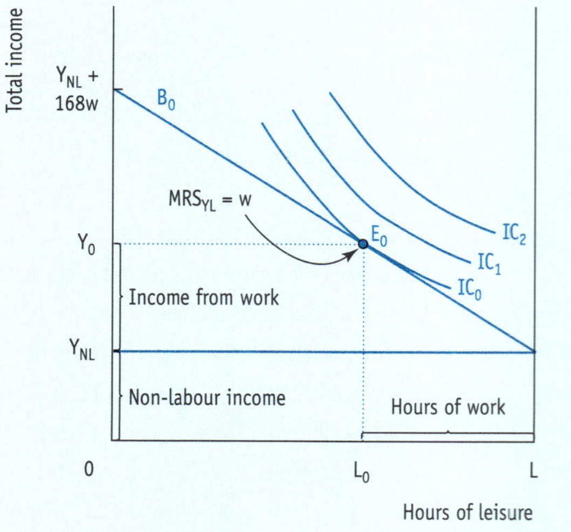

Figure 3.1 The income-leisure trade-off model

which the individual is prepared to exchange income for leisure without diminishing his or her utility. The indifference curves we have drawn are conventionally shaped, convex to the origin, reflecting a diminishing marginal rate of substitution. This means that the more leisure time the individual has the lower is the wage rate necessary to persuade him, or her, to sacrifice a given amount of leisure.

As to the constraint facing the individual, we will assume initially that the amount of non-labour income does not affect, and is not affected by, the level of earnings from work. On the vertical axis, Y_{NL} represents non-labour income, which is the income the individual receives if no work is done (leisure time is 168 hours per week). The budget line B_0 is drawn for a particular wage rate, so the income from work will simply be the number of hours worked times the wage rate. This gives a maximum income level of $Y_{NL} + 168w$ where w is the hourly wage rate. The higher the wage rate the steeper the budget constraint will be. More realistically, the intersection of the budget constraint and vertical axis can be re-interpreted as the maximum feasible working week, which might be taken to be around a half the literal maximum.

The optimum position for the individual is, as you might expect, given by the point of tangency between the highest indifference curve attainable and the budget constraint. This is E_0 in Figure 3.1 where the indifference curve, IC_0, is tangential to the budget line, B_0. The individual has an income level of Y_0, made up of Y_{NL} nonlabour income and $Y_0–Y_{NL}$ earned income, from a working week of length $L–L_0$.

At the point E_0 the individual's marginal rate of substitution between income and leisure is equal to the wage rate. To the left of point E_0, further up the indifference curve, IC_0, the MRS_{YL} is greater than the wage rate. This represents the situation where the individual would be prepared to sacrifice greater amounts of income for extra leisure than is necessary at the wage rate he or she is being offered. The optimum choice of income and leisure therefore involves more leisure and less income. To the right of point E_0 the MRS_{YL} is less than the wage rate, so the individual is being paid more than is necessary to get him or her to work at the margin. Hence, the individual will continue to substitute leisure for work until the equilibrium point at E_0 is reached.

The effect of a fixed working week

The above assumed that individuals can freely vary the amount of work that they do. Clearly some groups of people do have some choice or discretion about the amount of time spent at work. For example, those working part-time and, at the top end of the earnings spectrum, some self-employed professional groups such as accountants and solicitors. However, for large numbers there is a working week of fixed length and the decision the individual faces is whether to work for this given number of hours, or not to work at all.

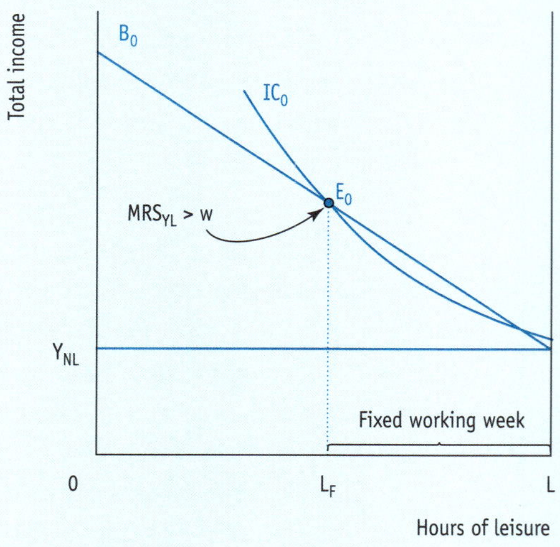

Figure 3.2 **A fixed working week**

Figure 3.2 introduces the effect of this constraint into the income-leisure trade-off model. Here we represent a given working week of fixed length by $L-L_F$. As drawn in the Figure, the individual is on a higher indifference curve when the decision to work is taken. The indifference curve IC_0 intersects the budget constraint at point E_0; the MRS_{YL} is greater than the wage rate and the individual is working for a longer number of hours than would be the case if they were chosen freely. If leisure could be substituted for income at the margin the individual could move onto a higher indifference curve.

The precise shape of the indifference curve drawn in Figure 3.2 is, of course, arbitrary. There is nothing a priori to say the MRS_{YL} has to be greater than the wage rate at the point E_0. If it were less, the individual could move onto a higher indifference curve by working more hours rather than less. It also possible that the highest indifference curve attainable would lead the individual to work no hours at all, in which case we would have a corner solution. In this situation the MRS_{YL} is greater than the wage rate over the entire range of hours between L and L_F. This differs from the case drawn in Figure 3.2 where at low levels of work hours the indifference curve is drawn flatter than the budget constraint.

The number of hours that individuals work varies for a number of reasons some of which we will come to. The broad variation between full-time workers in a number of EU countries is shown in Table 3.1.

There is also some evidence for the UK in the 1990s that individuals were working for longer hours than they wanted to given the wage rate they were offered. Stewart and Swaffield (1997) using data from the British Household Panel Survey found around one-third of the male workforce in this position.

1996	Full-time men	Full-time women
UK	45.8	40.6
France	40.5	38.8
Germany	40.4	39.3
Sweden	40.1	39.9
Netherlands	39.5	39.0
Denmark	39.4	37.6
EU average	41.3	39.0

Table 3.1 **Average hours usually worked in EU countries**
Source: Social Trends (1998).

One factor affecting the length of the working week is overtime. This may involve payments at a premium rate to encourage individuals to work longer hours than they would freely choose. In terms of indifference map analysis, the effect of this is to produce a kink in the budget constraint facing the individual, since beyond a certain number of hours worked he or she receives a higher wage rate. This is illustrated in Figure 3.3 at point H along the budget constraint marked B_0. At E_0 the higher hourly rate for overtime equates the individual's MRS_{YL} and wage rate, giving $L-L_1$ hours of work, a higher figure than the basic working week shown as $L-L_F$.

The effect of an income tax

We have so far not taken any account of income tax. As we saw in Chapter 2, the UK personal income tax system consists of two main components: a tax allowance and a number of different rates of tax. An important distinction is between the average and the marginal rate of tax that an individual pays. The first of these, the average rate, is simply the total amount of tax paid divided by the individual's income and is relevant in discussions about equity between individuals. The marginal rate of tax is the change in tax paid divided by the change in the (pre-tax) income and it is this that is relevant in discussion about work incentives.

Diagrammatically, the introduction of a tax threshold also produces a kink in the budget constraint that the individual faces. The position is shown in Figure 3.4, where the gross income budget constraint is marked as B_0.[1] At earnings up to the level of the tax threshold, Y_{T0}, gross and net (or after-tax) earnings are the same. When income rises above the threshold

1 This is drawn coming out of the bottom right corner, since we are ignoring nonlabour income for simplicity.

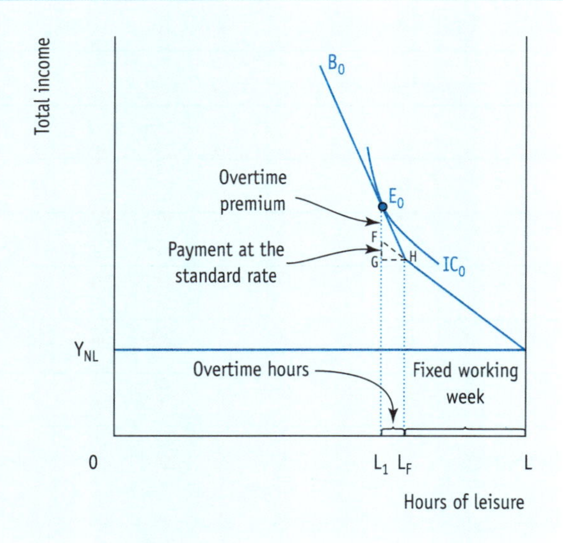

Figure 3.3 **The effect of overtime payments**

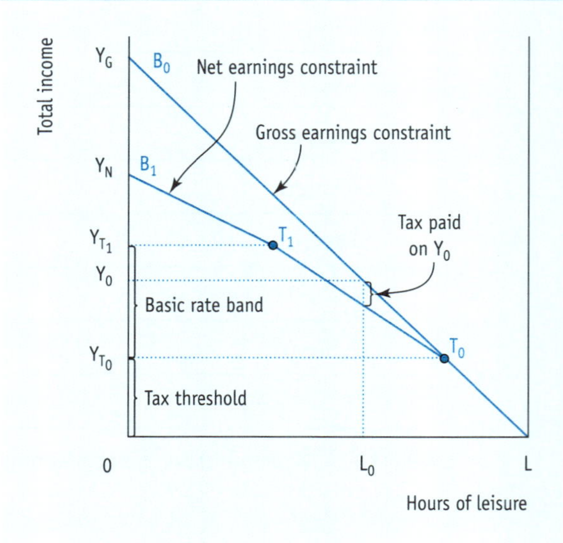

Figure 3.4 **The effect of an income tax**

the individual will start paying tax and it is the net earnings constraint, B_1, that is then relevant to the individual's labour supply decision. The slope of the individual's budget constraint varies with the marginal rate of tax: the higher the rate of tax the flatter the net earnings budget constraint, and the greater the difference between gross and net income.

As the individual's earnings rise the rate of tax paid on the additional income rises, so creating a second kink in the net earnings budget constraint. In Figure 3.4, this is shown at income level Y_{T_1}, with the threshold point marked T_1. The budget constraint therefore gets progressively flatter as the individual's earnings rise. Clearly relative to the position in the absence of an income tax, the individual will be on a lower indifference curve, as he or she will receive a lower level of net earnings given the number of hours worked.[2]

The effects of changing tax

In the 1980s and 1990s an area that attracted interest in policy making was the effect of a reduction in income tax on labour supply decisions. Tax reforms to lower the amount of tax an individual pays can come in the form of a higher tax allowance for all, or a higher tax threshold for those paying higher rates of tax. This would eliminate the tax bill altogether for some or lower the rate of tax paid by others. Alternatively, a tax reduction could simply involve a cut in tax rates, which would lower the amount of tax paid by all those who pay tax.

2 We are concerned here with partial equilibrium analysis. The tax paid by individuals may lead to more or better public services, which is not taken into account.

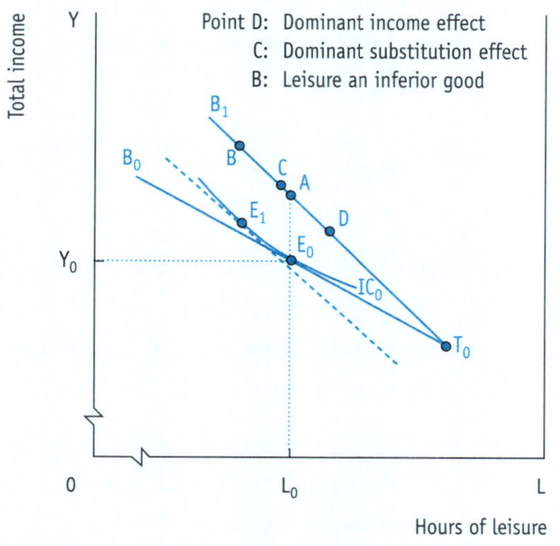

Figure 3.5 **The income and substitution effects of a cut income tax**

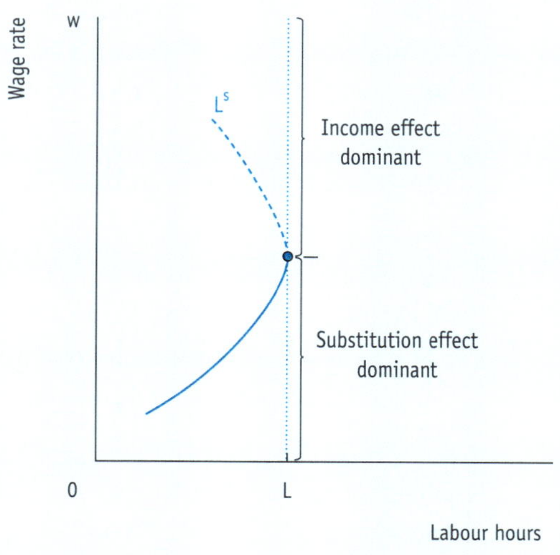

Figure 3.6 **The labour supply function**

These types of changes can be analysed using the model developed, although it is not possible to make definite predictions about labour supply responses on the basis of analysis alone. A tax cut may or may not lead the individual to work longer hours; the outcome depends on his/her preferences, represented by the indifference map. In Figure 3.5, we have illustrated the case where the marginal rate of tax paid by basic rate taxpayers has been cut. The initial equilibrium position is at E_0, where we have a tangency between the indifference curve IC_0, and the budget constraint B_0. The individual works $L-L_0$ hours. The cut in the rate of tax (with an unchanged tax threshold) pivots the net earnings constraint upward around the threshold, point T_0, to create a second net earnings constraint labelled B_1. Four points on the new constraint have been marked. The point A represents no change in hours worked, points B and C show more hours worked and point D fewer hours. Clearly, if there is a fixed working week then the individual simply moves to point A.

If the individual can determine the amount of hours worked, the decision is the outcome of two forces working in opposite directions, the income effect and the substitution effect. This is shown in the diagram by drawing another budget line parallel to the net income constraint B_1, but tangential to the original indifference curve, IC_0. The movement around the indifference curve gives the substitution effect, from point E_0 to E_1, reflecting the fact that the relative price of leisure has gone up. The individual has to forego more pay in order to take time as leisure, and this will encourage the individual to work more hours. However, the cut in income tax will also increase the individual's net earnings and given that leisure is a normal good, the individual will want more leisure. This could lead the individual to work fewer hours overall, point D in Figure 3.5, or more hours overall such as at point C. In the event that leisure is an inferior good, then the income effect in this context would result in the individual moving to a point such as B in Figure 3.5 where the two effects reinforce one another. In overall terms however, the outcome depends on the preferences of the individual.

The labour supply function

The preceding analysis allows us to develop a labour supply function that relates the number of hours of labour supplied to the wage rate received. Starting at E_0 in Figure 3.5 we can, in principle, vary the wage rate received by the individual, and obtain new equilibrium points of tangency between the indifference curves in the indifference map and the budget line.

Whether labour supply rises or falls as the wage rate rises depends on the balance of income and substitution effects. This, of course, is simply a generalisation of the analysis of a cut in tax to allow for changes in the wage rate arising for other reasons. As the wage rate rises, diagrammatically as the budget line swivels upwards, the effect on the decision to supply labour effort may be positive or negative. The analysis is the same as that for the income and substitution effects of a tax change. Figure 3.6 shows a labour supply function where the substitution effect is dominant up to OL hours of work, after which the income effect dominates.

We can also make a distinction between what are called compensated and uncompensated supply curves. The former relates to just the substitution effect of a wage increase, the latter to both income and substitution effects. The first of these supply functions will have a positive slope; a rise in wages will lead to a rise in the hours supplied, if only the substitution effect is considered. The second could be either positive or negative just depending on which of the income and substitution effects is stronger.

Also of interest here is the wage elasticity, which is simply defined as the percentage change in labour supplied divided by the percentage change in the wage rate. The greater the value of the elasticity the more sensitive the hours supplied are to changes in wages paid. A wage elasticity of 1.5, for example, would mean that a 1% change in the wage rate would lead to 1.5% increase in the number of hours worked.[3]

Generally, the question of how sensitive labour supply is to changes in wages is a difficult one and the answer depends on which group of the labour force is being considered. To take this discussion further we will look at a number of empirical studies in Section 3, where it is important to appreciate the distinction between the compensated and uncompensated supply functions.

---

3 It is conventionally assumed that the elasticity applies equally to increases and decreases in the wage rate, although in some circumstances this need not be as we shall see in Section 2.

Questions

Q1 What would you expect the marginal rate of substitution between income and leisure to be for (I) workaholics and (II) the workshy? What would you expect their indifference maps to look like?

Q2 In a question in Chapter 1, we saw that if the income of the individual doubles, there is a parallel shift outwards twice the distance from the origin of the budget constraint. If an individual's income from all sources doubles what happens to the budget constraint in the income-leisure trade-off model?

Q3 Suppose an individual had no choice but to work a fixed amount of overtime. Is it possible to say whether the individual will end up on a higher or lower indifference curve than if he or she had been allowed to freely determine the number of hours worked?

Q4 Are there any circumstances when a change in either the tax threshold or the rate of tax has no effect on the utility of the individual?

Q5 Draw a diagram showing the Slutsky income and substitution effects of a wage increase. Can you say anything about the relative size of the substitution effect by comparison with the Hicksian analysis?

3.2 Labour supply decisions of different groups

Conventionally neo-classical consumer choice theory deals with a 'representative' individual. In practice, however, individual circumstances and preferences vary widely. What we are going to do here is adapt the basic analysis of Section 1 to consider some of the main factors that affect the labour supply decisions of students, single parents, low-earning families and also high-earners. Clearly, these particular groups do not constitute an exhaustive breakdown of the UK workforce, but they will allow us to analyse a wide range of personal circumstances.

The analysis covered in Section 1 was based at an individual rather than a household level. We will see that for some groups, such as students and single parents this is reasonable, though for families it will often not be. For students and single parents we will see that it is important to be clear about the nature of leisure, as this clearly does not mean time wholly devoted to the pursuit of pleasure. For low-earning families we will see that there are important interactions between various sources of income, and who it is that receives it, that need to be considered in analysing their decisions. Finally, the fourth group, those paying the top rate of income tax may face a very different set of considerations from the others.

The labour market opportunities of these groups vary widely and as a consequence their labour supply responses when wage rates change can be expected to differ sharply. It will become clearer that it is sensible to think in terms of a range of wage elasticities depending on which group is being considered. However, the analytical structure developed above is sufficiently flexible that it will still be useful.

Labour supply decisions of students

The changing financial circumstances facing students has led to a large increase in the numbers undertaking some form of paid work. Chart 3.1A shows the percentage of students in the labour force in the mid-1990s in the EU, Chart 3.1B shows the changes over time in the UK and includes a projection to 2006.[4] In broad terms, this increase in labour market involvement is a consequence of the decline in student funding from grants and other forms of state support, that have taken place over a period of time. Some idea of the scale of the change is given in Table 3.2 which gives the (maximum) student grant that was payable in various years in terms of 1997/8 prices.

1963 was the year of the Robbins Committee, a period of expansion with the objective that '. . . higher education should be made available to all those who are qualified by ability and attainment . . .'. The commitment of governments to find this ideal waned as the size of the student body expanded and the real value of the maximum grant payable declined until 1989/90, which was the last year before loans were phased in to replace grants.[5]

This change in the value of grant income and its effect on labour force participation, that is the decision to enter the labour force or not, is represented in Figure 3.7. For simplicity, we have assumed the initial position to be given by a corner solution, where the level of non-labour income in the form of grant is given by Y_0.[6] At this grant level no paid work is done. The effect of reducing the level of maintenance income available to students is shown by a parallel shift downwards of the line representing nonlabour income. The new budget constraint is B_1. If the individual sets out to replace the grant income with income from work then the new equilibrium point will be at E_1.[7]

This change forces the individual student onto a lower indifference curve as he or she has in effect been forced into working part-time hours to maintain a given income level. The reduction in 'leisure' time is in practice is likely to lead to a reduction in time for recreational

4 The data refers to full-time students only as defined by the Labour Force Survey.

5 There were a number of other related changes made in the 1980s to withdraw the entitlement of full-time students to social security benefits.

6 Y_0 is representing both grants and social security benefits.

7 This ignores the tax system and the outcome is again subject to the comments about individuals being able to freely choose the number of hours they work.

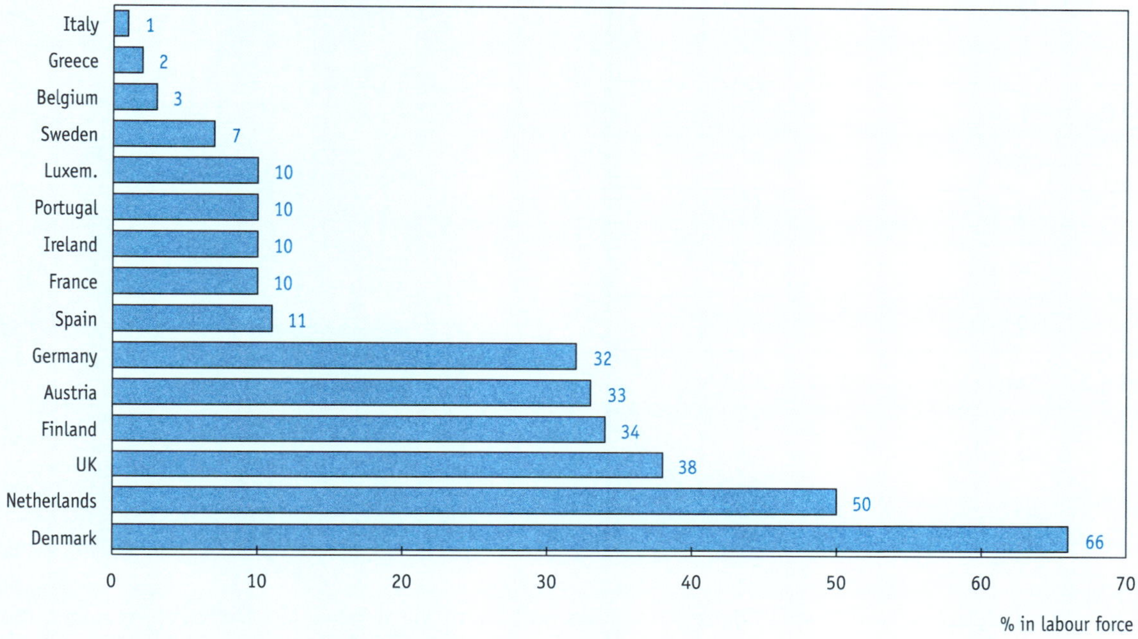

Chart 3.1A **Students in the European labour force 1995**
Source: TUC (1997).

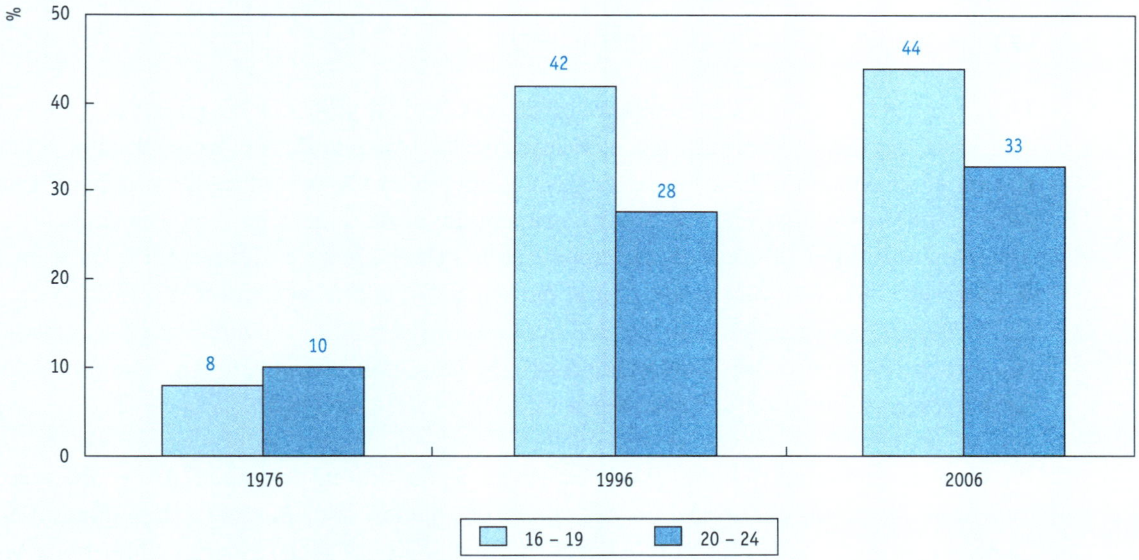

Chart 3.1B **Student labour force participation in UK**
Source: TUC (1997).

(1997/8 Prices)	
1962/63	£3812
1969/70	£3250
1979/80	£3096
1989/90	£2906

Table 3.2 **Student grants 1962/63–1989/90**
Figures given are for those studying away from home outside London.
Source: Adapted from NUS (1995)

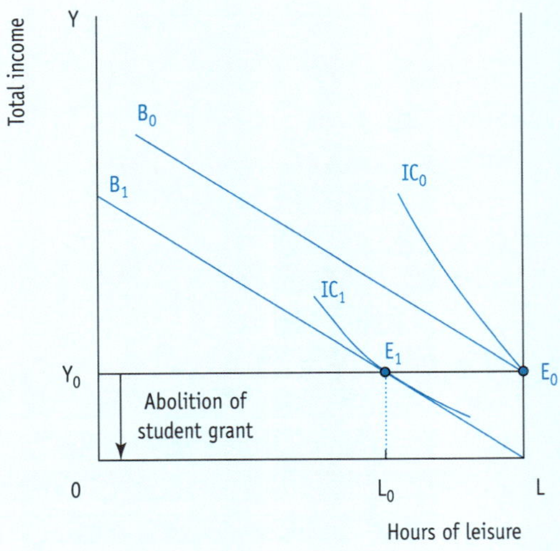

Figure 3.7 **The effect of abolishing student grants**

pursuits, or time for studying, or some combination of both. In the circumstances facing students, decisions about labour supply are likely to be sensitive to government policy, particularly in relation to the income tax threshold and the wage rate received by those in relatively routine employment. For students, the analysis predicts the likely nature of the responses at an individual level.

Labour supply decisions of single parents

There are over a million single-parents in the UK and we now come to analyse the circumstances facing them. A key feature of this particular group is the existence of what is called household production. This means the availability of work on which there is a (financial) return, although it does not involve any paid employment. The most obvious example of this is staying at home to look after children although there are several other forms of domestic production. The decisions made about participation in the workforce by this group are therefore likely to be sensitive to the interaction of household production with the availability of (part or full-time) work. This group is also generally sensitive to the operation of the tax-benefit system in relation to work incentives.

We have incorporated the impact of household production into Figure 3.8A by the line hh. The slope represents the return on household production and, as drawn, this diminishes as more time is given to this type of activity. The availability of social security payments to meet housing costs and provide income for maintenance is shown as nonlabour income, marked as the point Y_{NL_0}. An equilibrium point such as E_0 represents an outcome where the single parent takes up no paid employment, but engages in $L-L_0$ hours per week of household production.

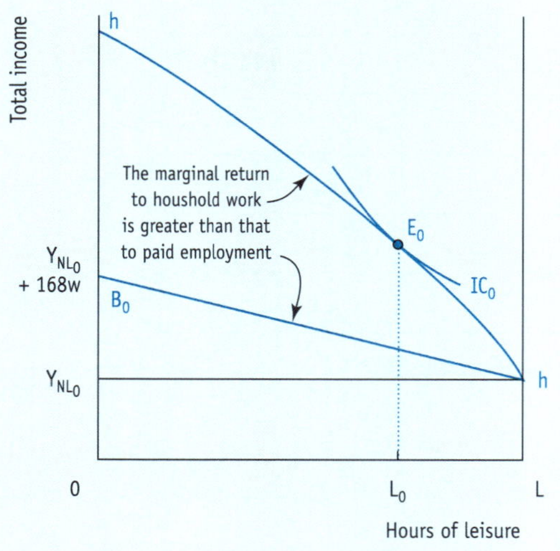

Figure 3.8A Household production and single parents

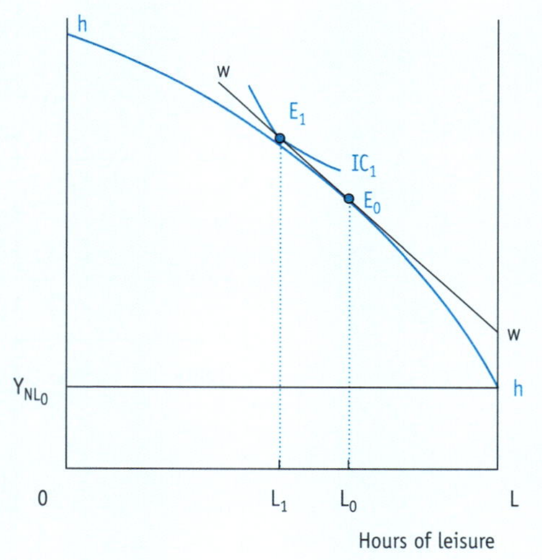

Figure 3.8B Labour market activity, household production and single parents

Such an outcome would be the consequence of there being no work available with a return greater than that available from household production. For example, it would not be make sense to work for an hourly wage below the hourly rate paid for child-care costs.

In Figure 3.8A, the budget line, B_0, arising from labour income has a flatter slope than does the line representing household production, hence the equilibrium point involving no earned income. Clearly, if the net wage from work was higher than the return to household production beyond a certain point, then the equilibrium outcome would involve a combination of both paid work and household work. If the individual can choose freely how much time is given to household production and how much is given to paid employment, then the equilibrium will lie to the left of point E_0. This is what is shown in Figure 3.8B at E_1 where the individual has $L–L_0$ hours of household production and $L_0–L_1$ hours of paid labour market activity.

Single parent families are often in the position of deciding whether it is worthwhile taking up low paid employment. They are a significant minority of a larger group of families on low incomes for whom the net wage is closely tied up with the structure of social security benefits, and the way that benefits interact with the tax system. The UK benefit system provides two main types of benefit: means-tested benefits and contingent benefits. Means-tested benefits are paid to individuals with incomes from work (or other sources) below a certain level. Contingent benefits are paid to individuals in particular circumstances, such as those who are sick or disabled. A single-parent who did no paid work would have zero earnings and so non-labour income would consist of benefit paid to meet housing costs and maintenance needs. If

(1998/9)	
Single parent + family premium	£50.35 + £11.05
Child additions	
— Under age 11	£19.80
— Aged 11–15	£25.35
— Aged 16–18	£30.30

Table 3.3 Needs allowances for housing benefit
Source: CPAG (1998).

this person then decided to go out to work, a percentage of the benefit paid is withdrawn as the level of income from work rises.

The actual operation of the social security system consists of a large of amount of detail. To start simply with the lone-parent's entitlement to Housing Benefit when they rent property. The formula for calculating benefit entitlement is

$$\text{HB} = \text{Rent} - (\text{Taper} * \text{Excess Income})$$

where HB is the amount of Housing Benefit and the individual's 'excess income' is the difference between his, or usually her, earnings and income from other sources, less what the benefit system allows for a person's needs. The taper we will come to. The amount allowed to cover needs varies with individual circumstances, the detail for single parent families in 1998/99 is shown in Table 3.3.

For example, for a single parent family with one child aged 6 the needs allowance was £81.20. A single parent with an income equal to the needs allowance would have no 'excess income' and would therefore have all their rent covered by Housing Benefit. If the individual had an income of £100, the excess income would £18.80 (£100–£81.20) and benefit paid would be reduced by a fraction of this amount, 'the taper'. This was 65p in the £ in 1998/9 and so the amount of Housing Benefit paid would be £12.22 (£18.80 * 0.65) less than the amount of rent the individual was paying. Plainly, as the individual's income rises the marginal rate of benefit withdrawal can adversely affect the return from paid employment.

Labour supply decisions of low-earning families

The effect of the withdrawal of means-tested benefits is shown in Figure 3.9. The income from benefits when not in work is given by Y_{NL_0}. However, as the level of earnings rises, benefit income is withdrawn and this is represented the parallel shift down of the nonlabour income line to Y_{NL_1}. By working $L-L_0$ number of hours the individuals income will rise to Y_1. The

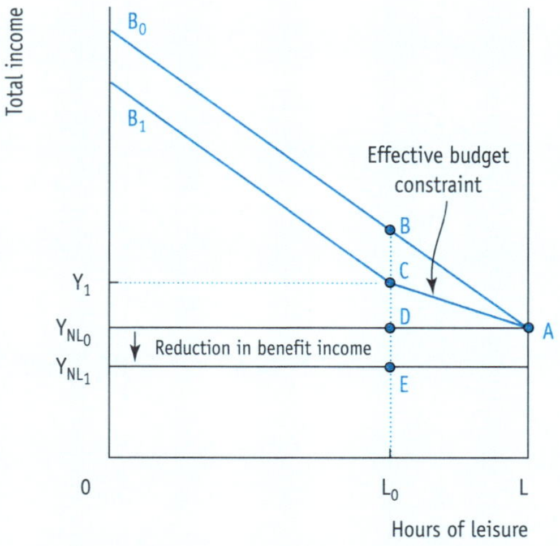

Figure 3.9 **The effect of withdrawing social security benefits on the individual's budget constraint**

distance DE (or equivalently that of BC) shows the reduction in benefit income. The line AC in Figure 3.9 shows that the budget constraint faced by individuals when entering low paid employment can be rather flat.[8]

In a two-parent family, the level of benefit received by one individual may include an element for his or her partner. Whether or not it is financially advantageous to work may then depend on (I) benefit withdrawn from the individual concerned as earnings from work rises, (II) the level of earnings from work after tax of a partner and also (III) benefit that may be withdrawn from the partner.

In the UK system, if one partner in a household goes out to work for more than 16 hours a week, the family entitlement to the income maintenance benefit, Income Support, is withdrawn. Until 1999 it was replaced by an in-work benefit, Family Credit. In terms of work incentives this is clearly desirable: the income from a low paid job, plus the in-work benefit should encourage individuals to enter employment. The amount paid was again closely tied to particular circumstances. Table 3.4 gives some details.

In calculating benefit entitlement, the first step is to compare the family's weekly income with the 'Applicable Amount'. If it is less than the 'Applicable Amount' the amount of benefit paid is given by the sum of whatever applies from Table 3.4. For example, suppose a household consisted of a couple with two children aged 10 and 12, whose only source of income is £60 per week from a part-time job. Their income is below the 'applicable amount' and they would have been entitled to Family Credit of £48.80 + £14.85 + £20.45 = £84.10.

8 In the past it has been negatively sloped for some individuals over certain ranges of income.

(1998/99)	
Applicable amount	£79.00
Family Credit amounts: adult	£48.80
— Each child under the age of 11	£14.85
— Each child between the age of 11 and 15	£20.45
— Aged 16–18	£25.40

Table 3.4 Family Credit amounts
Source: CPAG (1998).

As income levels exceed the figure of £79.00 the level of benefit was withdrawn at the rate of 70p in the £. The same family with an income of £160 per week would receive £84.10 less 70% of the difference between their earnings and the applicable amount. In this case, they would get £27.40.

The operation of Family Credit was in some respects a success. The number of families receiving the benefit more than doubled in the decade after its introduction in 1988 to around 470,000 in the late 1990s. It may partly explain the decline in the unemployment rate among mothers of young children from 27.2% in 1984 to 9.8% in 1996. Although as a means-tested benefit the 'take-up' (the percentage of those eligible to claim who do claim) was less than 100%. There was also a high rate of benefit withdrawal. Family Credit is due to be replaced in 1999 by the introduction of the Working Family Tax Credit, WFTC.

Some details of this scheme are set out in Table 3.5

(1998/99 Prices)	
Basic tax credit (one per family)	£48.80
Tax credits for each child — aged 0–11	£14.85
— aged 11–16	£20.45
— aged 16–18	£25.40
30 hours tax credit	£10.80
Taper	55%

Table 3.5 Structure of WFTC
Source: Taylor (1998).

Earnings (father)	£200.00
— less National Insurance	£13.60
— less Income Tax	£21.31
Earnings (mother)	£100.00
— less National Insurance	£3.60
— less income tax	£3.86
Net family income	£257.63
WFTC £48.80 + £29.70 + £10.80 (from Table 3.5)	£89.30
Add 70% of childcare costs of £60	+£42.00
Subtract 55% of the excess of net family income over £90	–£92.20
WFTC entitlement	£39.10
Child benefit	£23.25
Total income	£319.38

Table 3.6 **An example of the operation of WFTC**
Source: Taylor (1998).

The tax credit is withdrawn when the net income of the family exceeds £90 per week. The intention of the new benefit is to be more generous in terms of the amounts paid and the numbers of low-income families that are affected. The 30 hours tax credit is intended to encourage individuals to move from part-time to full-time work. The system also includes a childcare tax credit worth 70% of eligible childcare costs (subject to an overall limit).

As an example of the proposed WFTC structure on the income of a low paid family and the incentives that they face, Table 3.6 shows the case of one particular family, with two children aged under 11 and childcare costs of £60.

We have not so far discussed the operation of National Insurance Contributions, NICs, although in general terms they can be thought of as an income tax by another name.[9] The net family income after the payment of income tax/NICs is £257.63. The effect of the WFTC on the family's net income almost entirely offsets the tax paid: the operation of the tax credit will mean that instead of the household paying £25.17 in income tax, it will receive a tax credit of £39.10 so its net income tax paid is –(minus) £13.93. Once Child Benefit (a universal benefit paid for bringing up children) is included the net family income exceeds the household's gross

9 The figures in the Table assume that the NIC paid is 10% of the excess of £64 per week.

earnings. In general terms, it is evident that in-work benefits do provide an incentive to take up low paid employment, although the household faces a withdrawal of benefit at the rate of 55p in the £1 on their net income.

Labour supply decisions of higher rate taxpayers

This is a relatively small group of individuals whose incentive to work is sometimes considered to be particularly sensitive to the rate of income tax paid and also to the thresholds at which the tax rates are set. A feature of government policy over a period of almost twenty years has been the general reduction in the rates of income tax and increases in the real value of tax thresholds. Chart 3.2 shows the extent to which the tax rates facing individuals have changed.[10]

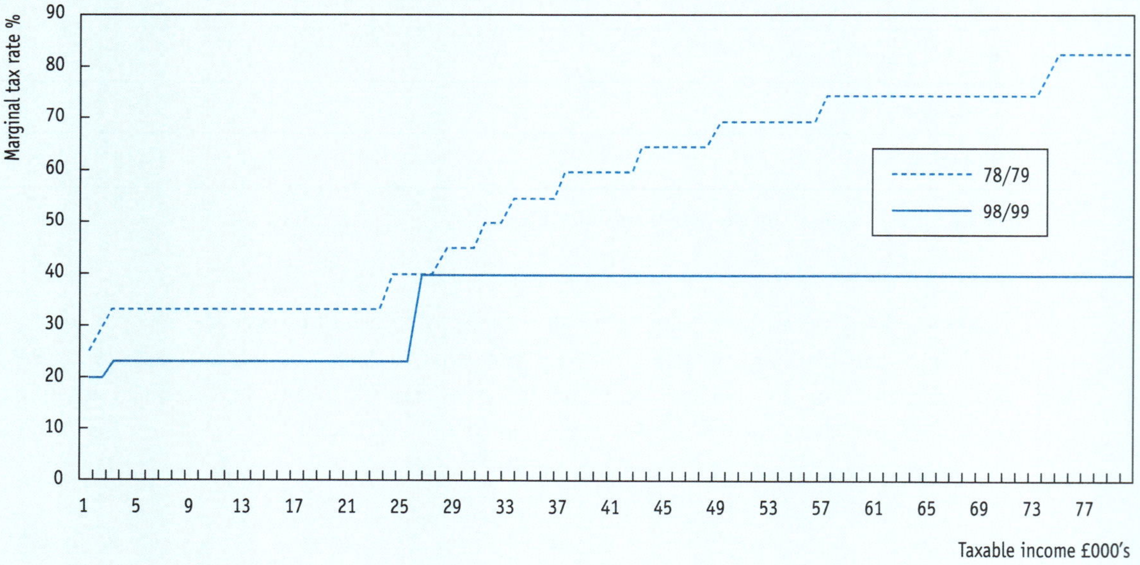

Chart 3.2 Marginal tax rates in 1978/79 and 1998/99
Source: Annual Abstract of Statistics.

The case for the beneficial effects of tax reform is sometimes put in terms of a broad change in the economic environment facing those earning high incomes. The chart shows the detailed changes that have been made to those taxpayers who pay income tax above the basic rate (33p in 1978/79 and 23p in 1998/99). In terms of the income-leisure model, in 1978/79 an individual paying the highest marginal rate of tax would have a budget line with some eleven kinks in it.

10 This refers to income from earnings only; income from investments attracted tax at a further 10 or 15% depending on the amount of income in 1978/79.

A feature of the general reduction in the rates of tax since then has been the simultaneous simplification of the structure, reducing the number of marginal rates of income tax to just three.

Whether or not these changes have resulted in significant incentive effects is taken up in Section 3. This is a difficult question to answer but we can note in passing that the simple income-leisure trade-off model may not be an appropriate structure at all for analysing this group. The model assumes that the individual's net earnings depends directly on the number of hours worked and this type of payment system simply does not reflect the 'remuneration packages' of many higher-earners. The simple model also treats the supply of labour as being homogeneous, that is a unit of labour supplied by one person is freely interchangeable with that from another. This may be a reasonable approximation for some types of routine work, but for many higher-paid employees (and self-employed people) it is the quality of the work done which is more important. There are also other influences on decisions about labour supply, such as the desire for power and prestige, or the role of moral obligation, which may be the prime motivating forces for some individuals.[11]

Questions

Q6 Pat is a full-time university student given £40 per week by her parents as a contribution to her maintenance. She decides to work part-time rather than take out a loan. A local fast-food outlet will employ her for as many hours as she can stand at £3.25 per hour.

(I) Draw her budget constraint.
(II) If she requires an income of £100 per week for her needs and she intensely dislikes the work, how many hours a week will she work? What would the slope of her indifference curve be at that point?
(III) Suppose a minimum wage of £3.60 per hour was introduced, what would you expect the income and substitution effects to be of an increase in the wage rate in her case?

Q7 Howard is an impoverished mature student who has a background in motorcycle maintenance. He can earn £8 per hour working part-time in his former occupation, but has no other sources of income with which to support himself. He needs £120 per week for his needs. Assume that the single person's tax allowance is £4,160 per annum and that the basic rate of tax is 20p in the £.

(I) How many hours per week will he have to work?

11 This is a subject that we will return to when we come to discuss the objectives of the firm in Chapter 8.

(II) What would be the effect of increasing the tax allowance to £5,200 for a single person and introducing a basic rate of 10p in the £ payable for the £3,000 of taxable income? Illustrate the effect in the income-leisure trade-off model

(III) In what circumstances is the introduction of the 10p basic rate of tax more advantageous?

Q8 Penny is a single parent and has earnings of £120 per week. She has one child aged 4, and pays rent of £50 per week to her Local Authority. How much Housing Benefit is she entitled to given the figures in Table 3.3?

(I) If her earnings increase by £40 per week, by how much does her HB fall?

(II) Ignoring all other taxes and benefits, what is the marginal rate of benefit withdrawal on an extra £10 of earnings? What is it on an extra £100?

(III) What does the slope of her effective budget constraint look like?

(IV) Suppose the government decides to raise rents by 20% and that her earnings remain unchanged at £120. What effect does this have on the incentive to increase the number of hours spent working?

Q9 For the family whose details are given in Table 3.6, what is the effect on the incentive to work of

(I) The children passing the age of 11 and there being no need for the family to pay for childcare.

(II) The family's net income rising to £300?

Q10 A single parent earns £90 per week, receives child benefit of £13.95 per week for her son aged 10, pays no income tax but has to pay National Insurance Contributions at the rate of 10% when her earnings exceed £64 per week. Assume that she has no childcare costs.

(I) What is the effect of WFTC on her net income?

(II) If she continues to pay no income tax, what is the increase in her net income if she earns another £20 per week?

3.3 Empirical evidence on labour supply

In this section we will draw on studies by economists that attempt to quantify the sensitivity of hours worked to changes in wage rates and tax rates. We will look at two kinds of empirical evidence, firstly econometric modelling that gives estimates of labour supply elasticities and secondly survey evidence about the effects of tax changes on labour supply decisions. The first kind of evidence, econometric research by economists into labour supply decisions, uses large cross-section datasets of UK households.[12] These datasets contain a great deal of detailed information about the number of hours worked and income from various sources, for thousands of individuals. Estimates of the size of labour supply elasticities are then obtained using regression analysis.[13]

Table 3.7 below presents some estimates of wage elasticities drawn from a number of different studies. Empirical work tends to make a distinction between the labour supply for married women, for single parent mothers and for husbands in the UK.

	Uncompensated	Compensated
Married women		
— No children	0.37	0.44
— Young children	0.29	0.50
— Old children	0.71	0.82
Lone mothers	0.76	1.28
Husbands	–0.23	0.13

Table 3.7 Labour supply elasticities
Source: Blundell (1994).

The interpretation of the elasticities is quite straightforward. For example, the uncompensated wage elasticity for lone mothers is 0.76 so that a 1% increase in the wage leads to a 0.76% increase in the number of hours worked. The uncompensated elasticity includes both the income and substitution effects of the change in wages. The compensated elasticity, simply the substitution effect, is noticeably larger at 1.28. The negative income effect, which is what our theoretical analysis predicts, is apparent from the differences between the compensated and uncompensated elasticities.

There are some quite sizeable differences between the respective groups and it is clear that women are more sensitive to the financial incentives they face than are men. In particular the estimates for single parents, the great majority of whom are women, differ very markedly from those for husbands. For married women three separate elasticities are given depending whether there are children or not, and what age they are. The responsiveness of married mothers with young children is less than that of those whose children are older. The married men uncompensated wage elasticity is negative, which may be due to the different employment

12 Such as the Family Expenditure Survey (FES) or the Labour Force Survey (LFS).

13 The details concerning the statistical method lie beyond the scope of this book.

circumstances that men face; that is a working week which is often of fixed length and also the fact that their earnings are generally higher may also be a factor.

Tax and labour supply

Assessing the impact of tax cuts on labour supply is difficult. One possible approach is to conduct a survey of high-earning individuals to elicit information about their responses. Studies of this type date as far back as those done by Break (1957) and Fields and Stanbury (1971), well before the changes that were noted in Chart 3.2. These were studies of solicitors and accountants, individuals who are likely to appreciate the significance of tax changes on their incomes, and whose working practices would allow them some discretion over the numbers of hours worked. Careful analysis showed a relatively small percentage of individuals plausibly claiming to have either an incentive or disincentive effect. The results were not startling; the Break study commented that 'the net effect was not large enough to be of great economic or sociological significance'.

The conclusions of these studies, conducted between 25–40 years ago, shows that this is not a new debate. A more recent survey along similar lines by Brown and Sandford (1990) looked into the reactions of 300 accountants to the large tax cuts of the late 1980s in the UK. This survey found that the cuts in higher rate tax, reducing the highest rate down to 40p from 60p, had little discernible effect on the numbers of hours worked, although it did suggest that less time was spent on tax avoidance measures.

A different approach was taken by Dilnot and Kell (1988) who used another large dataset, the Survey of Personal Incomes, the SPI, to analyse the factors behind the changing level and distribution of tax payments between 1978/79 and 1985/86. They concluded that the evidence was consistent with (though not proof of) moderate incentive effects arising from tax cuts for those paying top rate tax. A feature of this study is that it looked at the effect of tax changes over a period of six years, unlike the survey evidence referred to above which was asking questions about the short-run (one-year) effects. This may partly account for the different emphasis in the conclusions. At the outset of the programme of tax reform introduced in the 1970s its proponents argued that a cut in income tax rates would produce large incentive effects for both basic rate and higher rate taxpayers. The research done by economists since then has narrowed this down to questions about those high-earners paying higher rates of tax, for whom there may be some incentive effect.

Concluding comment

In this chapter, we have confined our economic analysis to a simple, one-period model, of decisions about labour supply. This provides a background, but examining the important questions about the sensitivity of labour supply to wage rate, and to government tax-benefit policy, has taken us in the direction of looking at empirical evidence.

We return to some of the issues raised in this chapter later in the book. The role of work incentives and executive remuneration is discussed when we consider alternative theories of the firm in Chapter 8. The discussion of factor markets in Chapter 14 focuses on the effects of introducing a National Minimum Wage on employment levels and work incentives for low-income working families. The final chapter of this book looks at the role of low pay in accounting for the numbers who live in a state of poverty.

Summary

1 The indifference curve analysis presented in Chapter 1 can be adapted to present the income-leisure trade-off model. Indifference curves now represent different combinations of income and leisure that yield the same level of utility to an individual. The position of the budget constraint depends on whether the individual has any nonlabour income. The slope of the individual's budget line is determined by the wage rate received.

2 The simple version of this model assumes that an individual can freely choose how much time to spend working and how much time to give to other pursuits (leisure). Where the individual decides to do some work, the equilibrium point for the individual is where the marginal rate of substitution between income and leisure is equal to the wage rate. In practice, many individuals have a fixed working week (which may include overtime). The actual hours worked may therefore mean that the individual could obtain a higher level of utility by working either a larger or smaller number of hours.

3 A simple tax system can be described in terms of a personal tax allowance and the tax rates on particular bands of taxable income. The average rate of tax is the tax an individual pays divided by the income he or she receives. The marginal rate of tax is the additional amount of tax paid divided by the amount of additional earnings.

4 One subject that has attracted a lot of interest is the relation between changes in the rate of income tax and labour supply. In principle, the effect of a cut in income tax is indeterminate. The income effect of a tax cut will usually reduce labour supplied, although if leisure is an inferior good it will increase it. The substitution effect will increase labour supply as the opportunity cost of leisure increases.

5 The income-leisure trade-off model can be adapted to analyse a range of individual circumstances. The model can, for example, predict the likely labour market response of students to changing financial circumstances. The financial position of many students is likely to be sensitive to the tax threshold and government policy that affects the wages of those in part-time employment.

6 The position of single parents can be examined with the introduction of household production. The interaction of social security benefits and labour market income can be accommodated to analyse the circumstances of other low-income families. In practice, the operation of the benefit system is very detailed and individuals can face very high marginal rates of tax as benefit is withdrawn as income from work rises.

7 Labour supply elasticities are a measure of the responsiveness of labour supplied to a change in the wage rate. Empirical evidence suggests that they differ to an important extent between

men and women, with the elasticities of married women being higher than those of married men. Single parents tend to have relatively high wage elasticities.

8 The empirical evidence concerning the incentive effects of tax cuts suggests that the impact may not have been large in the UK.

End of chapter questions

Q11 Suppose an individual's optimum outcome was a tangency solution at the point of the income tax threshold (such as point T_o in Figure 3.4). What would the effect be on the budget constraint if the government decided to raise the tax threshold? Would an increase in the number of hours worked necessarily leave the individual on a lower indifference curve?

Q12 Eric is a utility-maximising individual who finds that his MRS_{YL} is greater than the wage rate paid at zero hours of work. Assume that he is entitled to benefit income, draw his budget constraint and optimum position.

(I) Is it possible that simply reducing his benefit income could encourage him to work? If so, how?

(II) Suppose a government wants to encourage individuals into work and offers to pay an extra 20% benefit to those prepared to participate in the voluntary sector, or work for an environmental task force for a certain period of time. Is it possible that this could raise Eric's utility?

Q13 The utility-maximising chairman of a utility company receives £200,000 annually gross. Additional benefits include a travel allowance of £30,000 (chauffeur-driven company car, foreign trips and so on). Other benefits are worth £70,000 (profit-taking from share options, free health insurance). Additionally the chairman has investment income yielding £25,000 from private sources. Is the income-leisure trade-off model relevant in the circumstances of this individual?

Q14 National Insurance Contributions have been described as a tax on income by another name. The tax rates for in the financial year 1998/9 for employees are given in the table below.

Taxable income band	Income tax rate	Income bands £	NIC rate
0–£4,300	20%	0–£3,828	0%
£4,301–£27,100	23%	£3,329–£25,220	10%
£27,101–	40%	£25,221–	0% plus 2% on first £3328

How many different marginal rates of tax were there? Is it any different in the financial year in which you are reading this book?

Q15 This question deals with housing benefits, HB, for a family on low income. The basic principle for calculating HB is as in the main text. The need allowances are given below for the year 1998/9.

Family type	**£ Allowance per week**
Couple	75.20
Child additions: each child under 11	16.45
— aged 11–15	24.10
— aged 16–17	28.85
Premiums: family	10.55

(I) For a family of three with children aged 9,10 and 12 what is the needs allowance? Suppose that family earnings are £160 per week, what is the excess income of this household? If the family unit pays £55 in rent what is the entitlement to HB? If earnings for this family rise to £200 what is the reduction in HB?

(II) The government decides that it wants to encourage the amount of work done. One way it can do this is by what are known as earnings disregards. This is an amount that can be earned without affecting the entitlement to benefit. Suppose the government disregarded the first £25 of earnings each week. What is the entitlement to HB for the family in the circumstances in part (I)? What does the effective budget constraint look like?

References and suggested further reading

Blundell (1994) is an accessible discussion. The other articles in Bryson and McKay include a range of perspectives on questions of household labour supply. HM Treasury has an excellent website *http://www.hm-treasury.gov.uk* from which you can download papers of policy relevance, as does the Institute for Fiscal Studies, *http://www.ifs.org.uk*, where you can take the opportunity to be your own Chancellor.

Blundell, R.W. (1994), 'Work incentives and labour supply in the UK' in Bryson, A. and McKay, S. (eds), 'Is it worth working?', *PSI Research Report* 766.

Break, G.F. (1957), 'Income taxes and incentives to work: an empirical study', *American Economic Review*, **47**.

Brown, C.V. and Sandford, C.T. (1990), 'Taxes and Incentives: the effects of the 1988 cuts in the higher rates of income tax', *IPPR Economic Study* No 7.

Bryson, A. and McKay, S. (eds) (1994), 'Is it Worth Working?', *PSI Research Report* 766.

Child Poverty Action Group (1998), '*National Welfare Benefits Handbook*'.

Dilnot, A. and Kell, M. (1988), 'Top-rate tax cuts and incentives: some empirical evidence', *Fiscal Studies*, **9**.

Fields, D.B. and Stanbury, W.T. (1971), 'Income taxes and incentives to work: some additional empirical evidence', *American Economic Review*, **41**.

National Union of Students (1995), '*Student Financial Support Press Pack*'.

Office for National Statistics (1998), *Social Trends*.

Office for National Statistics (various issues) Annual Abstract of Statistics.

Stewart, M.B. and Swaffield, J.K. (1997), 'Constraints on the Desired Hours of Men', *Economic Journal*, **107**.

Taylor, M. (1998), '*The Modernisation of Britain's Tax and Benefit System*' **3**, HM Treasury.

Trade Union Congress (1997), '*Students at Work*', TUC labour market report.

4

Savings and Asset Accumulation

Key ideas and material

Intertemporal preferences and the wealth constraint, the life-cycle hypothesis, evidence on the level of saving and the distribution of wealth

Introduction

This chapter is concerned with the decisions that individuals make about spending, saving and borrowing over time; what is known as intertemporal decision-making. The principles involved are again an application of the theory of consumer choice that was introduced in Chapter 1. The analysis presented there was restricted to looking at decisions within a single period of time and it was assumed that all income was spent. As a result, the possibilities that individuals might either save part of the income they receive in the present or, alternatively, borrow against the income they will receive in the future were not considered.

In practice, of course, many people make repeated decisions about how much of their income they are going to spend per week, per month, or over some other period of time. This leads us to important questions about what motivates individuals to save or borrow and, what form the saving and borrowing takes. The questions that arise about the amounts involved and timing of these decisions are important in understanding the decision-making of individuals as consumers.

The level of individual saving, and the stock of individual wealth-holdings is also very relevant to the policy debate over the balance of public and private sector welfare provision. The decisions reached on the future levels of state pensions, social security payments to the unemployed, the sick and those in need of nursing care will depend on the existing patterns of saving, and how far governments can expect to influence the decisions made by individuals. A first step in looking at questions of these sorts is simply to describe the position at present and so empirical evidence is clearly important in this context.

The outline of this chapter is as follows. We start in Section 1 by developing the theoretical framework. In Section 2, we analyse the interaction of decisions about education and training, what economists call human capital, with saving and consumption decisions. We then put these decisions into the context of a life-cycle model. As we have seen in earlier chapters, the neo-classical analysis involves examining the position of a 'representative' individual. The empirical evidence in Section 3 discusses the variation in saving between individuals and gives some idea how much support the theoretical predictions of the lifecycle model receives.

4.1 The two-period model of consumption and savings

The two-period model is a framework that allows us to analyse decisions about consumption over time, and with it the decision whether to borrow or to save. In the lifetime of most people these decisions are repeated often. There are periods when people borrow heavily and other times when they save substantial sums. The reduction of this down to just two periods and the one decision whether to borrow, save or do neither will, however, still allow us to analyse the nature of these decisions.

We will refer to the two periods as period 0, the current period, and period 1 the next period. They might simply be thought of as the present and the future. It is not necessary that these two periods be of equal duration. Period 0 could be, for example, time spent receiving a University education and period 1 the rest of a person's working life. Or period 0 could be an individual's working life and period 1 his or her retirement. We can, therefore, think of the time frame as covering the (adult) lifetime of an individual. For simplicity, we will assume that the individual spends all of his or her income by the end of period 1.

We will follow the analysis of the earlier chapters and, again, assume that the individual's objective is to maximise his or her utility subject to a budget constraint. An indifference curve for the model is shown in Figure 4.1A. On the horizontal axis, we now have consumption in period 0, on the vertical axis we measure consumption in period 1. To be clear, this differs from the two good model where each axis refers to the quantity of two goods consumed. Here we are referring to total expenditure on all goods in the two time periods. Indifference curves, such as IC_0, represent different combinations of consumption levels in the current and future periods that yield the same level of utility to an individual. Points A and B on IC_0 represent two such possible combinations; point A represents a higher level of consumption in period 1 than period 0, point B represents the opposite. As before, indifference curves further away from the origin would represent higher levels of utility.

We have again drawn the indifference curve as convex to the origin, assuming a diminishing marginal rate of substitution between consumption in period 1 and period 0. The higher the level of current consumption, the less the individual will be willing to sacrifice in the way of future consumption for an extra unit of current consumption. The slope of the indifference curve drawn in this context shows the marginal rate of substitution between consumption in

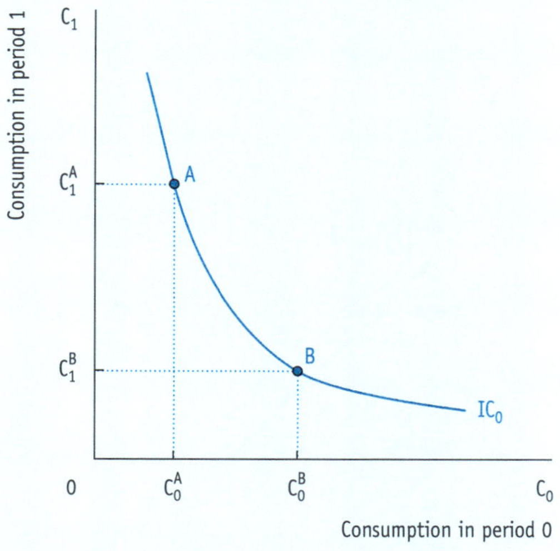

Figure 4.1A **The consumer's indifference curve in the intertemporal model**

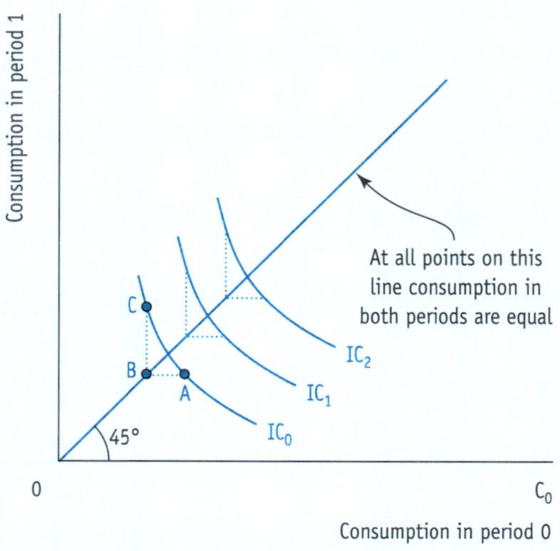

Figure 4.1B **The individual's rate of time preference**

the future and consumption in the present, $MRSc_1c_0$. This can be expressed as $-(1 + \rho)$, where ρ is known as the rate of time preference.[1]

When $\rho = 0$ the individual is willing to exchange one unit of consumption in the future for the same amount in the present. Generally, the slope of the indifference curve reflects the individual's willingness to exchange consumption between the two periods and also the level of consumption in a particular period. When the individual has equal amounts of consumption in each period, we are controlling for this latter effect, and simply reflecting his or her preferences over time (known as the rate of time preference proper).

Figure 4.1B shows the preferences of an individual who values current consumption more highly than that in the future when he or she has equal amounts of both. Along the indifference curve IC_0, the individual requires an additional CB in period 1 for giving up the amount AB of consumption in period 0. The rate of time preference is clearly positive and so the slope of the indifference curve is greater than one.[2]

The wealth constraint

The budget constraint in this context is referred to as a wealth constraint, for reasons that will become apparent. An example of a wealth constraint is drawn in Figure 4.2A. Where each

1 Negative because the indifference curve slopes downwards.

2 The slope is greater than one in absolute terms, numerically $-(1+\rho)$ is less than minus one.

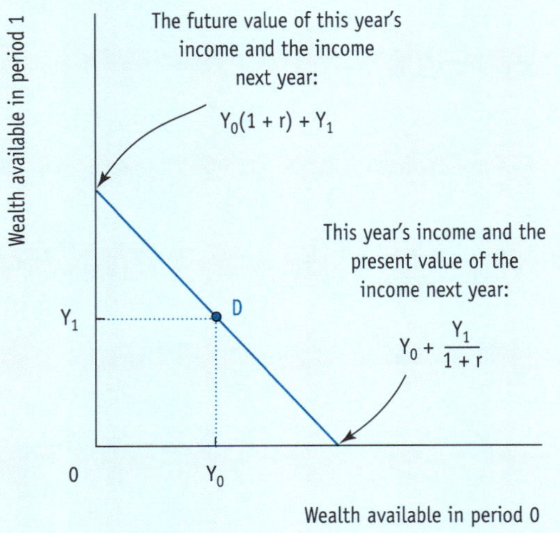

Figure 4.2A **The wealth constraint**

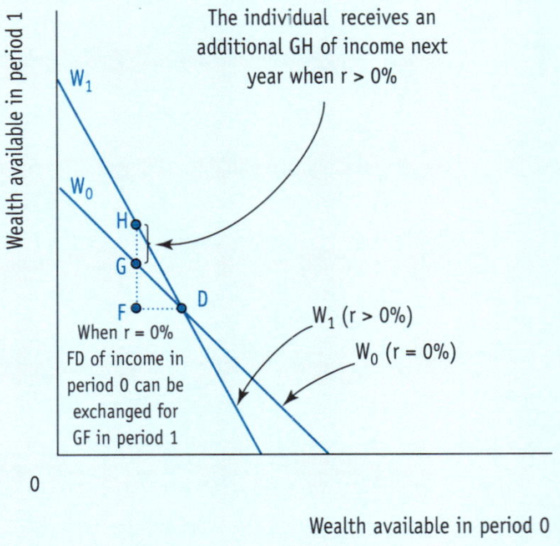

Figure 4.2B **The effect of varying the interest rate on the wealth constraint**

point on the constraint represents the sum of the incomes the individual receives in period 0 and period 1. Looked at in this way, it represents a 'stock' and hence it is referred to as a wealth constraint.[3] We do however need to be careful about the way in which we value the sum of the incomes in the two periods.

We will initially assume a perfect capital market, so that an individual can save or borrow at a given rate of interest. The intersection of the wealth constraint with the horizontal axis gives the maximum level of consumption available to the individual if all present and future income were spent in the current period. This is equal to the present value, PV, of the income stream. At the other end of the constraint we have the point which represents the consumption level possible if the individual's wealth was all spent in the future period. At this point the level of consumption would equal the future value, FV, of the same cash stream of income.

In general, the present and future values of a stream of income will not be the same. On a two-year time horizon, the FV of an income stream available to an individual is the sum of this year's income, plus the interest that can be earned on it, together with next year's income. Suppose that an individual received an income of £10,000 this year, which we will refer to as Y_0, and £20,000 next year, referred to as Y_1. To calculate the FV of income of £10,000 when the interest rate is 10%, simply multiply the sum by $1 + r$; in this case multiply £10,000 by 1.1, giving £11,000. Table 4.1 below shows the relationship between the rate of interest and the

3 We are assuming here that the individual receives income in both periods (though it is not necessary that the amount received in the two periods be equal).

Interest rate	FV (Y_0)	FV (Y_1)	FV(Y_0+Y_1)
0%	£10,000	£20,000	£30,000
10%	£11,000	£20,000	£31,000
20%	£12,000	£20,000	£32,000

Table 4.1 **Future value (FV) of an income stream**

future value of the income stream for three different interest rates. The FV of the income stream is given in the final column.

The FV of a particular income stream gives us the intersection point on the vertical axis in Figure 4.2A. The higher the rate of interest, the greater the FV of the current period's income and the further away from the origin the point will be.

Turning to the PV of the same income stream, this is the sum available to an individual from whatever this year's income happens to be plus the discounted value of next year's income. The cash value of these two amounts is £30,000 in our example and this is the PV of the income stream when the rate of interest is 0%. Given a rate of discount of 10%, to obtain the PV of the £20,000 income next year divide by $1 + r$, where r is the discount rate. In this case, we get a PV of £18,181; the FV of this sum when the interest rate is 10% is, of course, just £20,000. The PV of the income stream is clearly £28,181.

The PV of an income stream also varies as the rate of interest varies. Table 4.2 shows that as the rate of discount increases, the value of a given sum of income received in the future will decrease, as shown in the second column. So overall the PV of the income stream will decrease as the discount rate rises.

In Figure 4.2A, the PV of the income stream gives the point of intersection with the horizontal axis. This shows the wealth available to the individual to spend in period 0. The higher the rate of discount, the closer to the origin is the point of intersection.

Discount rate	PV (Y_0)	PV (Y_1)	PV(Y_0+Y_1)
0%	£10,000	£20,000	£30,000
10%	£10,000	£18,181	£28,181
20%	£10,000	£16,667	£26,667

Table 4.2 **Present value (PV) of an income stream**

The line joining the two endpoints gives us the wealth constraint. The individual receives income Y_0 and Y_1 in the two periods, marked as point D in Figure 4.2A, giving us what is known as the endowment point. As drawn in the figure the individual receives the same (cash) income in both years. The slope of the line, which gives the rate at which income this year can be exchanged for income next year, is dependent on the discount rate. If the rate of discount was zero, the two endpoints would be an equal distance from the origin as the present and future values of the income stream would be the same. This is how it is drawn in Figure 4.2A.

However, if the rate of interest was positive we have to discount future income and the wealth constraint pivots around point D. It becomes steeper as the PV of a given stream becomes less, the FV becomes greater. At the endowment point, however, the individual is not exchanging present income for future income and so a change in the rate of discount will not affect it. This is what is shown in Figure 4.2B.

It should be noted that the rate of interest or discount referred to above is the real rate of interest. This gives how much additional purchasing power the individual receives from a given amount of income not spent. Suppose, for example, the (nominal) rate of interest was 10% then £100 saved this year would give £110 next year. If the rate of inflation was 5% then purchasing power of the £100 saved this year rises to £110/£105. The real rate of interest in this example is then (110/105)–1, which is 4.8%. When the rate of interest and the rate of inflation are both 'low', the real rate of interest can be approximated by taking the difference between them.

Questions

Q1 What kind of preferences in the two-period model are represented by indifference curves that are I) very steep and II) very flat?

Q2 In the two period model draw the wealth constraint if a person's income is £15,000 in the first period and £20,000 in the second and the rate of interest is (I) 5% and (II) 25%. What is the maximum amount that could be spent in the first and second periods if there is a perfect capital market and the interest rate is 5%? How does it differ if the interest rate is 25%? What is the slope of the wealth constraint at each of the rates of interest? How much additional consumption in the present is available in the individual borrows £2,500 at a rate of interest of 25%?

Q3 Given the following rates of interest and rates of inflation, what is the real rate of interest approximately? What is it exactly?

Interest rate	Inflation rate
5%	3%
16%	6%
15%	25%
60%	200%

What happens to the individual's wealth constraint when there is a negative real rate of interest?

The equilibrium

In Figure 4.3A, the indifference curve representing the individual's preferences and the wealth constraint are put together. The point of tangency between the indifference curve IC_0 and the wealth constraint, W_0, shown in the figure gives the equilibrium for the individual. As we have drawn it the individual has an income level Y_0 in period 0 and Y_1 in period 1. The point of tangency is directly above the Y_0 income level, so that $C_0^E = Y_0^E$ and $C_1^E = Y_1^E$ (the subscripts refer to the period, the superscripts to particular levels of consumption and income).[4] All this year's income is spent on consumption this year, and all next year's income is spent next year. There is neither borrowing nor saving. The indifference curve, IC_0, represents the highest level of utility an individual could attain in making decisions about consumption over two periods of time, given the wealth constraint. At this point of equilibrium the individual's rate of time preference is equal to the market rate of interest.

The simplifying assumption of a perfect capital market is a key part of the equilibrium outcome in Figure 4.3A. Suppose, for example, the individual was faced with the same wealth constraint but that he or she only received income in period 0. The endowment point would then be where the wealth constraint intersects the horizontal axis. Given the shape of the individual's indifference map, this would mean a lower level of utility. The individual would only be able to attain the utility associated with IC_0 by saving to the point where consumption is C_0^E in Figure 4.3A.

The outcome we have drawn in Figure 4.3A is, of course, simply the consequence of a particular set of preferences assumed in this diagram. The point of tangency could be to the right of the endowment point, which is what has been drawn in Figure 4.3B. In this case, consumption is greater than income in the first period, which would involve borrowing on the part of the consumer.

4 In this case, the endowment point and the equilibrium point coincide.

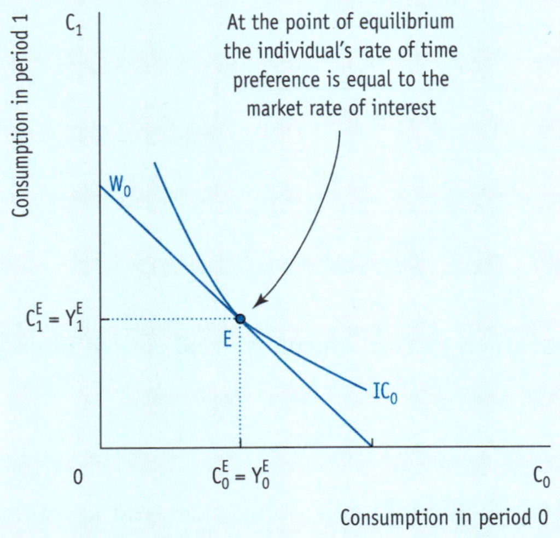

Figure 4.3A **The consumer's equilibrium**

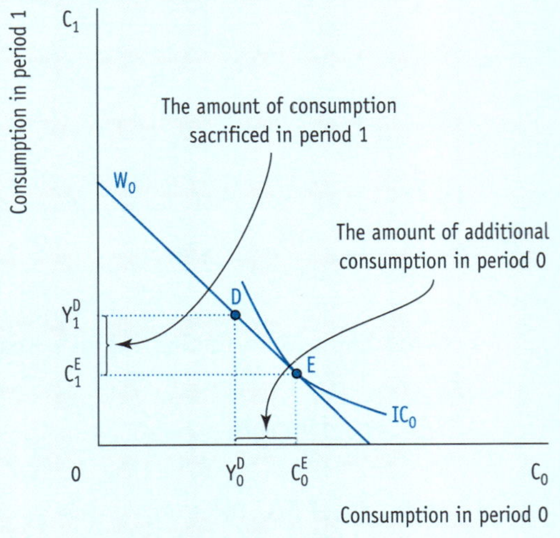

Figure 4.3B **The consumer's equilibrium when there is borrowing**

The decision of the consumer to borrow, save or do neither depends on his or her preferences, represented by the indifference map, and the income stream, represented by the wealth constraint. This neo-classical analysis of intertemporal decision-making is, therefore, similar to other analysis already encountered. It provides a structure for analysing decisions but it does not directly explain the initial point of equilibrium the individual chooses, and so it does not tell us whether a particular individual will borrow or save.

What the model does allow us to look at directly is the effect of changes in circumstances. The questions that arise in the comparative static analysis of this model concern the effect of a change in income, and a change in the rate of interest, on the decision of the individual to borrow or save. Additionally, we assumed that there was a perfect capital market so that the individual could borrow or save freely at the same rate of interest. In practice, interest rates differ widely, with borrowers often paying a much greater rate of interest than is received by savers. There are also limits to the amount that can be borrowed. These aspects can be incorporated into the model, and are taken up below, but first we will go through some comparative static analysis.

Comparative static analysis: (I) the effect of varying the level of income

The effect of an increase in income is to shift out the wealth constraint further away from the origin as illustrated in Figure 4.4. This is true whether there is an increase in income in period 0 or period 1, or both. To see why this is we will continue with the earlier numerical example.

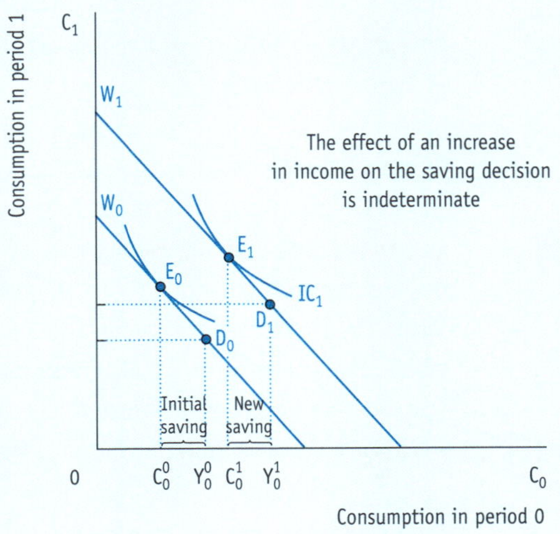

Figure 4.4 **The effect of an increase in income (savers)**

Given incomes in period (year) 0 and 1 of £10,000 and £20,000 respectively and a rate of interest of 10%, then the PV of the income stream is £28,181 and the FV is £31,000, as was shown before. This is now the first line in Table 4.3.

Suppose now that the individual receives a further £10,000, the second, third and fourth rows show the effect on the present and future values when the extra £10,000 is all received in period 0, all received in period 1, and half in both periods.

How far the wealth constraint shifts out depends on the timing of the additional income. An additional £10,000 coming in the first period adds most to both the PV and the FV of the income stream, receiving it all in period 1 adds the least. The receipt of the extra £10,000 in period 0 will raise the FV by the £1,000 interest in addition to the sum itself. The receipt of an extra £10,000 in period 1 has to be discounted to obtain the PV of the income stream. Hence,

(Interest rate = 10%)			
Y_0	Y_1	$PV(Y_0+Y_1)$	$FV(Y_0+Y_1)$
£10,000	£20,000	£28,181	£31,000
£20,000	£20,000	£38,181	£42,000
£10,000	£30,000	£37,273	£41,000
£15,000	£25,000	£37,727	£41,500

Table 4.3 **Effect of income changes on the wealth constraint**

the PV and the FV of the income stream in row 2 are greater than those in row 3. The fourth row gives an intermediate case. However, the slope of the wealth constraint for each payment stream is the same.

Figure 4.4 shows the general effect of an increase in income on consumption levels on the basis of a reasonable assumption that consumption in both periods is a normal good. Here, this simply means consumption rises as income rises; the opposite is implausible given that we are considering consumption of all goods in a particular period. The equilibrium point moves from E_0 to E_1 as drawn in the figure. While the level of consumption in both periods has risen (by assumption), the effect on saving is theoretically indeterminate. If the rise in consumption in period 0 is less than the rise in income, then saving will rise; if it is greater, the savings level will fall.

Comparative static analysis: (II) the effect of varying the interest rate

Next, suppose the rate of interest rises, but that income levels are unchanged in both periods. The FV of the income stream will be higher as the interest earned on this year's income will be greater, hence the point of intersection of the wealth constraint along the vertical axis, in Figure 4.5A, is further from the origin. A rise in the rate of interest increases the opportunity cost of current consumption in terms of consumption in the future. In this respect, a higher interest rate is analogous to a price change introduced in Chapter 1.

We therefore can use the breakdown into income, or in this case wealth, and substitution effects in order to analyse the effect on saving of a rise in interest rates. A higher interest rate rotates the wealth constraint around point D, the endowment point. Suppose the individual is a saver at the outset, as the FV of the income saved from period 0 has gone up the individual will be able to move onto a higher indifference curve. In Figure 4.5A, the wealth constraint facing the saver moves out from W_0 to W_1, but on the reasonable assumption that consumption levels in both periods rise the net effect on saving is ambiguous.

The explanation for this, perhaps surprising, conclusion lies with the balance of the wealth and substitution effects. The substitution effect of higher rate of interest works in the direction of encouraging a higher level of saving, as there is a greater incentive to defer consumption from period 0 to period 1. However, the wealth effect increases consumption in both periods, so the total level of consumption may or may not rise in period 0. In turn, we cannot predict the exact nature of the effect on saving.[5] In Figure 4.5A, we have expanded the area to the north-west of the endowment point D for clarity. The (Hicksian) substitution effect is shown by the move round IC_0. from point E_0 to E_1. The wealth effect on consumption could mean that

5 This is the same indeterminate result that we came across in studying demand and the effect of a tax cut on labour supply.

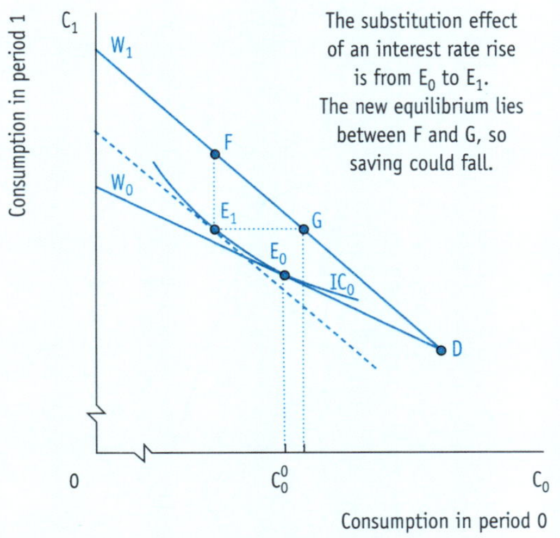

Figure 4.5A **The effect on savers of an increase in the rate of interest**

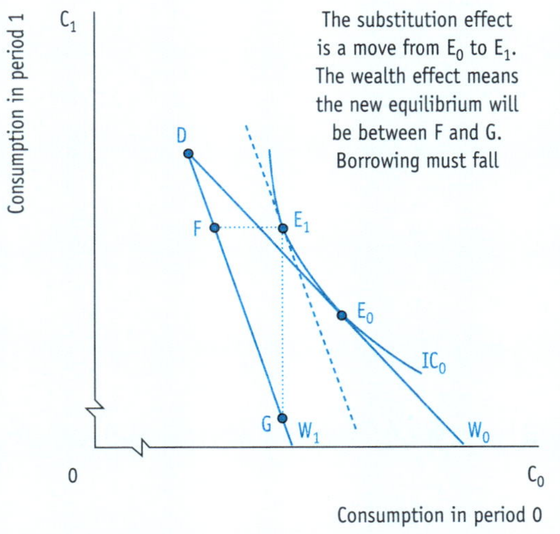

Figure 4.5B **The effect of an increase in interest rates (borrowers)**

consumption increases in period 0 by enough to reduce saving; in the figure this would mean the new equilibrium for the consumer would be at (or near) point G.

The case of the borrower is shown in Figure 4.5B. The increase in interest rates moves the wealth constraint inwards and for a borrower the wealth effect reinforces the substitution effect, given our assumption that consumption is a normal good. The substitution effect of an increase in the price of borrowing is to move the individual around IC_0 from point E_0 to E_1. Given that the wealth effect means that consumption in both periods will decrease, the new equilibrium will lie at a point on the new wealth constraint to the left of E_0. The effect is to reduce the amount of borrowing given the endowment point D.

An imperfect capital market

The linear wealth constraint we have shown so far is predicated on the assumption of a perfect capital market. Figure 4.6 illustrates the case where the rate of interest paid to savers, and that paid by borrowers, is different. In circumstances where borrowers pay a higher rate it follows that the wealth constraint will be steeper to the right of endowment point D than it is to the left of it.

There are several factors that can lead to such a kink in the wealth constraint. Firstly, there is the margin that is taken by financial intermediaries. Secondly, the measure of income above has not been made explicit, but if we interpret it as net income, then the interest paid to lenders may be taxed, while that for borrowers may not be. A higher level of saving, for

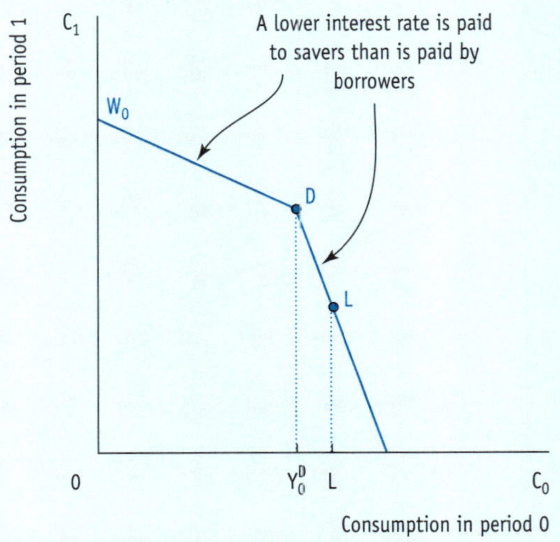

Figure 4.6 **A capital market with borrowing limits**

example, may also involve a higher rate of interest within a graduated structure, which raises the possibility of several kinks. The nature of the wealth constraint an individual faces will therefore generally depend on institutional details and government policy.

In practice, there are also (negotiable) limits on the extent of an individual's borrowings. For example, a mortgage is often the largest single loan that an individual will take out. With a repayment period of twenty-five years, a lender might typically lend up to three times one individual's annual income. For an individual who works for 30 years and earns £25,000 per annum a mortgage loan of £75,000 constitutes 10% of the income over the period.[6] The model's structure may therefore need to be adapted to allow for limits on the amount that individuals are able to borrow. Suppose in Figure 4.6 that the individual can borrow only $L - Y_0^D$, then the only part of the wealth constraint that is relevant to the individual's decision-making is that above this point. Equally, there will be practical limits on the ability of individuals to save their income, so that only a part of the budget constraint to the left of point D is relevant.

Question

Q4 A government decides that it wants to encourage individual savings and to this end introduces a tax-exempt savings scheme. In the two-period model, given an imperfect capital market, what is the effect of this on the budget constraint of the individual? Can you say, in principle, whether a saver would save more as a result of the tax concession? What if the individual neither borrowed nor saved before the introduction of the scheme?

6 This is a very simple example. It assumes a constant rate of discount among other things.

4.2 Human capital and the life-cycle hypothesis

The analysis of Section 1 was based on the assumption that the wealth of the individual was a given. Since we were using the two periods to cover potentially a major part of an individual's life, this was unrealistic. The decisions made about, for example, how much education and training to receive, are an important determinant of future income levels for a growing number of individuals; Table 4.4 gives details of the rising number of enrolments in further and higher education in the UK.

Economists refer to investment in education and training as investment in human capital, and a straightforward analogy can be drawn between capital goods and humans in terms of the effect on productive potential. The effect of investment in human capital on the individual's wealth constraint is shown in Figure 4.7. To keep the picture clear, we have drawn a linear wealth constraint, and, for simplicity, we again assume the individual has Y_0^D income period 0 and Y_1^D in period 1. The wealth constraint W_0 gives the opportunities open to the individual in the absence of acquiring any additional human capital.

In practice, individuals may vary their investment levels; for example taking part-time or full-time courses, going from further education on to higher education and so on. This raises the possibility of a series of investment levels and with it will be associated a series of steps in the wealth constraint. Suppose an individual gives up an amount of consumption in period 0 given by the amount Y_0^D–T. The additional human capital will increase the future income stream of

('000's)		
	1970–71	**1995–96**
Further Education		
— Full time	211	768
— Part time	1,521	1,839
Higher Education		
— Full time undergraduate	414	1,048
— Part time "	146	531
— Full time postgraduate	43	136
— Part time "	18	187
Total full time/part time	**668/1,685**	**1,952/2,557**

Table 4.4 **UK enrolments in further and higher education**
Source: Social Trends (1998).

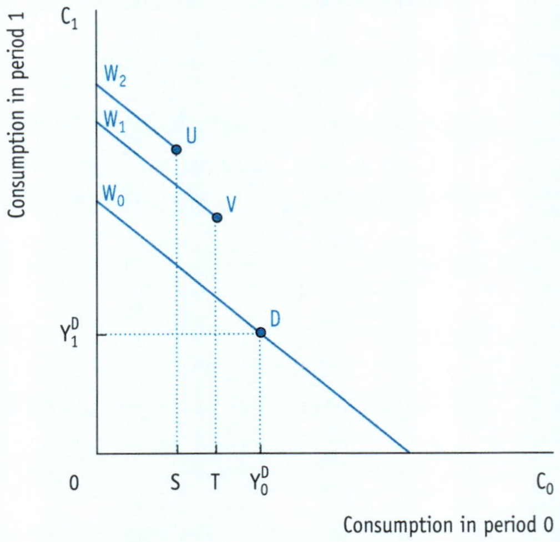

Figure 4.7 **The impact of investment in human capital on the wealth constraint**

the individual to a level higher than it would have been had the money not been spent on education and/or training.[7] Diagrammatically, this is the extent of the shift in the wealth constraint above the point T, from W_0 to W_1. By extending the period of education an training, represented by giving up T–S the individual can move up to point U on the wealth constraint W_2.

In principle, the decision rule for the individual is to invest up to the point where the marginal return on the last unit is equal to the opportunity cost of investing in education (which is given by the rate of discount).[8] If there were other forms of saving undertaken as well, then the range from U along the wealth constraint W_2 becomes relevant. The decision whether or not to forego some present consumption for a higher future income will depend on how much additional income a particular individual will generate. It will, of course, also depend on the individual's preferences, those represented by steep indifference curves, have a high willingness to forego future consumption for the present and are likely to invest less in education, other things being equal.

The life-cycle hypothesis

This analysis brings us to the more complete life-cycle model developed originally over forty years ago by Modigliani and Brumberg. The model suggests that the individuals take account of lifetime income when planning for consumption and saving decisions. The most important

7 This, of course, assumes that the individual takes a more highly paid job after the period of education and training than he or she would have been able to without the investment in human capital. Empirical evidence on the returns to education is a subject that we return to in Chapter 14.

8 This discussion of human capital anticipates the material presented in Chapter 7.

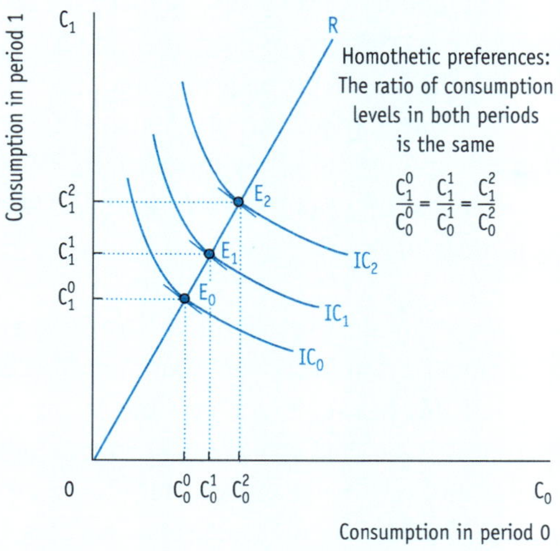

Figure 4.8 **Homothetic preferences**

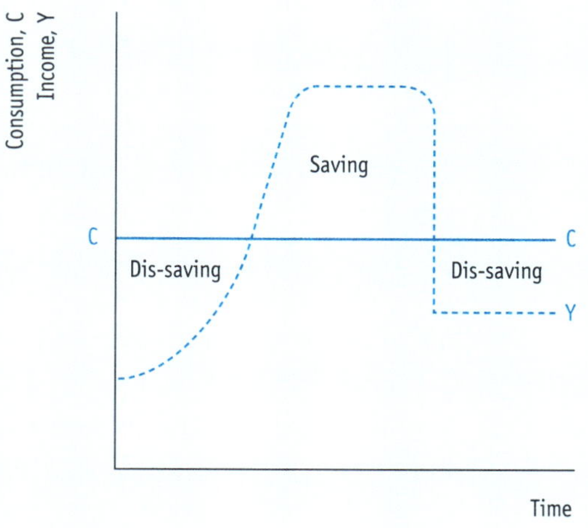

Figure 4.9 **A time profile of consumption and income**

implication is that individuals will maximise their utility by smoothing out the pattern of consumption over their lifetime. We can illustrate how this might be so with Figure 4.8, where we have drawn the indifference map of an individual whose preferences are homothetic. What this means is that the marginal rate of substitution between two goods depends only on the ratio of the two goods consumed but not the total quantities of either.

Diagrammatically, the slope of each indifference curve is identical when a straight line out of the origin passes through it. As the individual's income increases over a period of time and the wealth constraint shifts out, the ratio of consumption in period 0 to that in period 1 will stay the same.[9] A consumption pattern suggested by the life-cycle hypotheses is shown in Figure 4.9 where we have the consumption and income pattern of an individual over time. Assuming the individual enters the labour force at time $t = 0$, we have the time profile of income as initially rising, then stable and falling sharply at the point of retirement. Consumption expenditure is constant and so is a horizontal line, indicating periods of dis-saving at either end of the life-cycle and a period of saving during the middle.

In the early part of adult life, consumption levels exceed income and the individual has negative wealth at the end of this period. This might be due to any one (or a combination of) educational expenses, the costs of raising a family or those of buying a home. During the subsequent period until retirement, there is a period of sustained saving and asset accumulation. These savings are then used to finance the period of retirement when the individual's assets are run down to zero at the end of a lifetime.

9 When $r=\rho$ the individual will consume equal amounts in both periods.

We should note that the basis for the life-cycle is an individual passing through various stages of his or her life. A comparison of different individuals at different points in their respective life-cycles is not what is meant. It should be said that this profile of consumption and saving over a period of time is clearly a stylised example. While it may portray the essential features of individual households, not all households could be expected to follow this pattern. What it does do is add another factor that may explain the savings pattern of some particular individuals, namely the point they have reached in their life-cycle.

The analysis presented here and in Section 1 is more of an aid to thinking about the factors which can influence the level of savings (and borrowings) by an individual than anything else. We have set the analysis within a life-cycle model, and this has suggested that the savings rate should vary with the age (or the age-range) of the individual. The comparative static analysis has pointed to the likely importance of interest rates and income levels in determining saving and wealth levels. At this stage, we are still in the dark as to the pattern of savings and borrowings between individuals and the particular form that they may take. This leaves us with much that we might learn from the empirical evidence, which is what we come to in Section 3.

Questions

Q5 Dave, a student of economics, borrows £12,000 over three years to study for a degree, after which he lives happily for ten years earning £30,000 a year as a business analyst. Assuming that the real rate of interest is 0%, use the two-period model to show his wealth constraint when period 0 is his time as a student and period 1 is his first ten years at work. Where is his endowment point? How much of the constraint is relevant given the availability of loans for individuals when they are students?

Q6 Beth is saving to take a degree. She earns £15,000 this year but knows now she will earn nothing next year. She needs to save £5,000. Suppose that the interest rate is 10%, draw her wealth constraint. What would you expect the wealth and substitution effects to be of an increase in the rate of interest for her? Suppose the government gave tax concessions for those saving to take a university degree, what would be the effect in the model? Does your answer seem plausible?

4.3 Empirical evidence on household savings and asset accumulation

We need to be careful to distinguish between savings per period, essentially a flow concept, and assets or wealth-holdings, a stock. We will start this section by looking at the pattern of saving in households. A simple way of thinking about the savings rate is presented in Table 4.5, which summarises the breakdown of the average propensity to save by households by the

DEMOGRAPHIC GROUPS			
Head's age	**Marital status**	**Children**	**Saving rate**
20–34	Single	No	0.03
35–49	Single	No	0.04
50–64	Single	No	0.06
20–34	Married	No	0.05
35–49	Married	No	0.18
50–64	Married	No	0.10
20–34	Single	Yes	–0.21
35–49	Single	Yes	–0.16
20–34	Married	Yes	0.00
35–49	Married	Yes	0.04
50–64	Married	Yes	–0.05
Retired	Single	Yes	0.08
Retired	Married		0.03
Multiple tax unit			0.09
All			0.06

Table 4.5 **Household savings in the UK 1995/96**
Source: Banks, Dilnot and Tanner (1997).

age of the head of household. These figures are based on FES data on household weekly incomes and expenditure levels. The saving rate here is simply taken to be the difference between the two, divided by the level of household income.

This gives us a starting point for a critical look back at the simple version of the life-cycle model considered in the previous section. The peak saving period, according to the theory, is during an individual's working life; in retirement the savings accumulated are run down. Table 4.5 does not show such a pattern. What is evident from the table are the differences between single person and two-person (married) households and those with and without children. Single parent households who have large negative savings rate on this definition of saving also stand out. This leads to the question whether we need to modify the theory presented, or whether the data in Table 4.5 is misleading, or whether it is some combination of the two.

Age range	Housing wealth	Financial wealth
20–34	57%	75%
35–49	75%	81%
50–64	74%	84%
65+	62%	84%
Average	**67%**	**80%**

Table 4.6 Ownership of wealth in the UK 1994/95
Source: Adapted from Banks and Tanner (1996).

A part of the explanation may lie in the assumptions of the simple version of the model. It is assumed that individual motives for saving are to level out their lifetime consumption around a fluctuating income. In practice, there are other potentially powerful motives for saving; for instance, there may be precautionary motives for saving later in the life-cycle to cover possible medical expenses, or long-term nursing care. Individuals may also continue saving into their retirement in order to leave bequests, or assist relatives who may be passing through a period of heavy borrowing.

Household weekly expenditure includes spending on durable goods (cars, electrical goods and so on) and also expenditure on housing. This measure of saving therefore excludes, or disguises, what are important components of saving from a conceptual viewpoint. The analysis of Section 1 gave the idea of savings as the difference between the level of current income and current consumption. Both consumer durables and housing provide a flow of future services and in this way a part of the current weekly expenditure is providing for future consumption. The amount of expenditure on these types of goods is likely to vary systematically with the age of the individual. For example, most expenditure on housing occurs when servicing a mortgage and this typically takes place during an individual's working life. The measure of savings in Table 4.5 may well systematically understate the provision for future consumption being made by those below retirement age.

The data in Table 4.6 gives detail on the nature and the extent of individual wealth-holdings, showing the percentage within each age range that has as at least some amount of the type of wealth listed. To be clear this is the stock of individual assets, not a savings flow. The decisions involved here are of a long-term nature and this form of data reflects the accumulation of past and present saving decisions by the individuals concerned.[10] It has been broken down into what are called housing wealth and financial wealth. Housing wealth relates to those who own their home, whether outright or with a mortgage. Financial wealth relates to those who own at least one of the following: an interest-bearing bank or building society account, National

10 It also reflects sums from gifts, inheritances and other windfalls.

Savings account, gilt-edged securities, unit trusts, stocks, shares and bonds. It is therefore a broad measure of those who own at least some financial wealth.

As far as housing wealth is concerned the average figure is a simple reflection of the tenure pattern within the UK. The age-range with the lowest percentage is the youngest. This may reflect changing preferences and a move away from owner-occupation, but we can note here that the survey data relates to a time of recession in the housing market. The breakdown of the age profile for housing wealth in the other cohorts reflects the growth of owner-occupation over a period of decades. There is therefore a higher proportion with housing wealth between the ages of 35 and 65, than there is among those who have retired.

The initial impression from Table 4.5, that those in the middle part of the life-cycle were typically saving less, may not be valid. The age structure of those with financial wealth holdings is more even in terms of the number of people with some form of savings account, or other form of asset. It is also worth noting that one in five did not have any financial wealth at all at the time of the survey.

As far as the data is concerned, the FES is a cross-section dataset and so the information in Tables 4.5 and 4.6 relates to different individual households at different ages rather than to particular individuals progressing through their lives. To provide a proper test of the life-cycle hypothesis requires data that would let researchers control for variations between cohorts, and also allow for particular variations over time.

The comparison here between the saving rate of the retired population and those of working age therefore takes no account of differences in lifetime resources available to those of different generations. The figures from one survey may also be heavily influenced by the state of the macroeconomic environment. For example, a period of high interest rates would increase the mortgage repayments of those buying a house and would depress their saving rate given the way the measure is constructed in Table 4.5.

More recent studies have begun to make use of panel data in analysing questions relating to the life-cycle model, which is a step forward.[11] This kind of information has been available in the US since a biennial survey of those (then) aged 58–63 was started in 1969. In Europe, data of this sort has not been available until recently, although with the advent of the Retirement Survey in the UK this is now changing. The first set of interviews, that is the first 'wave' of the survey was carried out in 1988, with a follow up in 1994.

Disney, Johnson and Stears used this data to study the extent of the decumulation of assets between the two waves of the survey. They found that a typical value for asset holdings at retirement was around £200,000 (valued at 1996 prices), and that wealth-holdings increased up

---

11 A panel dataset is a large household survey where the same individuals are re-interviewed at various points in time.

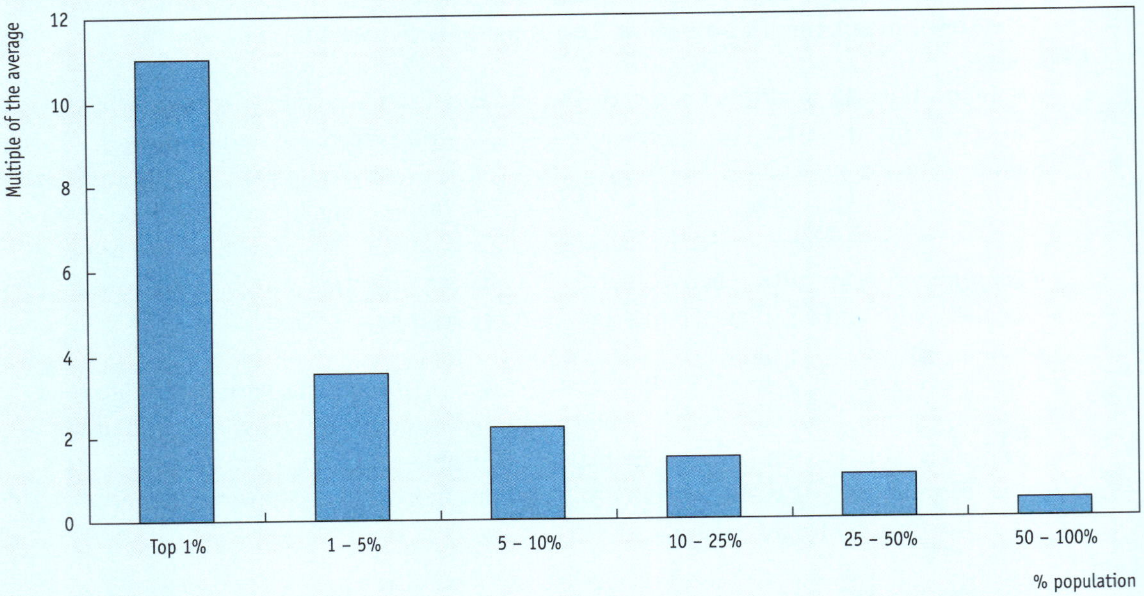

Chart 4.1 **Distribution of wealth in the UK 1994**
Source: Inland Revenue Statistics (1997).

to the age of 60, but declined thereafter. However with only two waves of the survey, it is an open question as to how far the pattern in the data reflects individual behaviour conforming to the life-cycle model, and how much can be attributed to the macroeconomic environment.

We have gone some way into the issues that arise when examining whether or not the life-cycle hypothesis provides an adequate basis for understanding individual decisions about savings. A simple life-cycle model provides a starting point, but the available data suggests than the actual patterns of saving will, not surprisingly, vary with individual or household needs at different points in the cycle. We have also seen the extent and some detail on the form of individual asset-holdings, but there remains the important matter of what the level of saving and wealth-holdings are, and also how they are distributed between individuals.

We will conclude this chapter with a first look at the distribution of wealth between individuals. The focus of the life-cycle model presented was the decision-making of the individual. It is silent on questions relating to the distribution of asset-holdings between individuals. Table 4.6 gave the first indication that there might be large differences between households, and Chart 4.1 gives a more general picture of the distribution of wealth in the UK.[12] On the vertical axis we have the multiple of the average wealth-holding. The chart shows that the top

12 Wealth defined as marketable wealth — housing and financial assets that can quite readily be sold on the market, together with wealth-holdings in the form of pension rights, which cannot. The latter, whether in the form of a state pension or occupational pension scheme, also provides a future income stream.

1% hold 11% of the total wealth (11 times the average). At the other end of the scale, half the population have around one-third of the average wealth-holding. Given our discussion above, variations in incomes and savings between cohorts will be one factor that accounts for the unequal distribution of wealth. However, the data shown in Chart 4.1 raises a number of important issues relating to the design of government policy in relation to both individual savings and asset-holdings, and these are taken up in the chapters that follow.

Concluding comment

This chapter has applied the conventional theory of household choice to individual decisions to save and build-up holdings of wealth. We have seen that a simple version of the life-cycle model gives us some guidance as to the decisions made by individual households. A careful consideration of the data has helped inform us further about the decisions made and pointed out the need for re-examining some of the assumptions of the life-cycle hypothesis. There are issues relating to the way uncertainty affects individual decision-making and also the distribution of assets between individuals that we have yet to address.

Summary

1 The neo-classical theory of consumer choice can be used to analyse decisions by individuals as to whether to borrow or save or do neither. An indifference curve in this context is defined as different combinations of consumption levels in two different periods of time that yield the same level of utility. The slope of the indifference curve gives the individual's marginal rate of substitution between consumption in the two periods.

2 In the two-period model, the individual's income stream is represented by a wealth constraint. The wealth constraint reflects both the present value, PV, and future value, FV, of a given income stream. The slope of the wealth constraint depends on the market rate of interest.

3 When utility maximisation for the individual occurs at a tangency point between an indifference curve and wealth constraint, the rate of time preference is equal to the market rate of interest.

4 In practice, there are many capital market imperfections which mean that individuals who save receive a different rate of interest from those who borrow. Many borrowers will face some upper limit in terms of the amount that can be borrowed.

5 The comparative statics of the two-period model show that an increase in income will increase consumption in both periods (assuming that consumption is a normal good). The effect on saving or borrowing could go either way.

6 The effect of an increase in the rate of interest on the decisions of savers is also uncertain. This rather surprising conclusion comes about because the overall effect is a combination of both wealth and substitution effects. The effect of an increase in interest rates on borrowers is to decrease borrowing.

7 The life-cycle hypothesis suggests that individuals try to smooth their consumption levels over their lifetime. This may involve a period of borrowing, for example to pay for educational expenses, and a period of saving while working for retirement.

8 Empirical evidence provides limited support for this model. Saving rates — the percentage of income saved — rise on average during the time of people's working lives. They also vary with individual circumstances, and in particular with whether they are married or have children. The evidence suggests that those who have retired still save a fraction of their income.

9 It is important to be careful with data definitions. One of the simplest definitions of savings is the difference between weekly (or annual) income and expenditure. However, some items of expenditure, payments on a mortgage for example, will involve an element of both current consumption and providing for future consumption.

End of chapter questions

Q7 Can you say with certainty what the effect on the level of individual saving is when the rate of interest falls? Would it matter if the individual were a borrower or saver?

Q8 Suppose that an individual receives an income of £30,000 in period 0 and £40,000 in period 1 and that the rate of interest is 10%, if payments of interest income are subsequently taxed at a rate of 20%, what happens to the wealth constraint? How would this affect the level of saving?

Q9 Rob graduates from university and has a working life of 30 years during which his income is £25,000 on average. After he retires, assume that he lives for another 30 years, and that for simplicity his income is £0. Using the two-period model diagram, draw his wealth constraint. Where is his endowment point?

Q10 Suppose that an individual receives an income of £10,000 in Period 0 and £10,000 in period 1 and the real rate of interest was −10%, how would the wealth constraint differ from when it is +10%? In what circumstances would you expect there to be a negative real rate of interest?

Q11 Louise is a well-funded student who can take out an interest-free loan that she does not need. She can also obtain a rate of interest of 4% on the savings account at her bank. Is she acting irrationally if she decides not take out a loan? Why or why not?

References and suggested further reading

An alternative presentation of the two-period model is given in a number of intermediate microeconomics texts including those by Estrin and Laidler, and by Varian. The applied material by Banks, Dilnot and Tanner, and that by Banks and Tanner is accessible and again indicates the importance of household survey datasets in work in this area.

Banks, J., Dilnot, A. and Tanner, S. (1997), '*Taxing household saving: What role for the new individual savings account?*, IFS Commentary No 66.

Banks, J. and Tanner, S. (1996), 'Savings and wealth in the UK: evidence from micro-data', *Fiscal Studies*, **17**.

Disney, R., Johnson, P. and Stears, G. (1998), 'Asset wealth and asset decumulation among households in the Retirement Survey', *Fiscal Studies*, **19**.

Estrin, S. and Laidler, D. (1995), *Introduction to Microeconomics*, Harvester Wheatsheaf.

Hamnett, C. and Seavers, J. (1996), 'Home-ownership, housing wealth and wealth distribution in Britain' in Hills, J. (ed.), *New Inequalities*, Cambridge University Press.

HMSO (1997), Inland Revenue Statistics.

Modigliani, F. and Brumberg, R. (1954), 'Utility analysis and the consumption function: an interpretation of cross-section data', in Kurihara, K. (ed.), *Post-Keynesian Economics*, Rutgers University Press.

Office for National Statistics (1998), Social Trends.

Rosen, S. (1997), 'Human Capital' in Eatwell, J., Milgate, M. and Newman, P., (eds) *The New Palgrave: A Dictionary of Economics*, Macmillan.

Varian, H.R. (1996), *Intermediate Microeconomics, A Modern Approach*, 4th edition, W.W. Norton & Co.

5

Risk, Uncertainty and Insurance

Key ideas and material

Risk and uncertainty, state-preference model, demand for insurance, adverse selection and moral hazard, social insurance

Introduction

In the analysis of consumer choice we have so far have been assuming that individuals operate in a world of certainty. For example, when they purchased goods we assumed that they knew exactly what they were getting and what utility the purchases would generate. When we analysed the decisions made about how much to save or borrow in the last chapter, we assumed both a known rate of interest and known incomes in the present and the future.

This assumption of a certain environment is a very great simplification. In practice, many goods and services are not standardised, and uncertainty arises from the lack of prior information available to the consumer. Individuals do not know what the rate of interest will be in the future nor do they know their lifetime incomes; partly because they face the possibility of adverse experiences such as being made unemployed at some point. This will lead us to analyse circumstances where individuals can pool or share such risks and, in turn, to the policy debate about what the role of private firms and what the role of the government should be in providing insurance.

We will begin this chapter by discussing ideas of how we can represent decision-making when the individual faces uncertainty. To this end, we will start by clarifying what we mean by the terms risk and uncertainty. We will then introduce the state preference model that will allow us to analyse preferences towards risk with the familiar structures of budget lines and indifference maps. In Section 2 we analyse problems associated with asymmetries of information in the insurance market and the difficulties that they can create for private sector firms. We return to this subject in Section 3, where we discuss whether the private sector is able to provide forms of social insurance such as unemployment compensation and retirement pensions.

5.1 Risk and uncertainty

In this section, we want to consider events that might occur in an individual's life where he or she has no control over what happens. For example, a person may be unfortunate enough to have their car stolen, or they may work for a company for twenty-five years and then have to retire through ill-health. These are examples of what economists refer to as different 'states of nature' or different 'states of the world'. We shall refer to the first state as state 0, the second state as state 1. You may suffer the experience of a car burglary, one state of nature, or you may not, a second state. Likewise, with the second example, there are two states of nature: that you are and that you are not forced to retire.

These different states of the world can be associated with very different levels of consumption, referred to as state dependent consumption levels. For example, in the case of car theft we can take state 0 to be when the individual is without the use of his or her car, state 1 as when the individual does have it. We also need to take account of the likelihood or probability of each particular state of the world occurring. If the probability of a car theft is 0.02 this gives us the probability of state 0 occurring; the probability of state 1 is then 0.98.

There is, therefore, a probability distribution of different levels of consumption associated with each state of the world. Suppose that an individual has an income of £10,000 per annum, all of which is spent, including the purchase of a car costing £6,000.[1] There is a probability of 0.02 that the individual will have (the utility from) £4,000 of consumption in state 0 and a 0.98 probability that he or she will have (the utility from) £10,000 of consumption in state 1.

The example of car theft illustrates what is often called risk, where all the possible states of the world are known and the probability of each state occurring is also known. The term uncertainty is often used when the probabilities associated with each state of the world are not known, or where it is not possible to determine all the possible states that might occur.

Risk and uncertainty

Individual attitudes to risk can be characterised by how a person approaches what is called a fair gamble. This is a gamble in which the stake is equal to the expected value of the bet. For example, a bet in which there is a 5% probability of winning £100 and a 95% probability of winning nothing has an expected value (or expected return) of $0.05 * £100 + 0.95 * £0$, which is £5. In this case, a payment of £5 to take the bet would make it a fair gamble and someone who would pay just this sum is characterised as risk-neutral. They are indifferent between having the certain sum of £5 and a gamble with the same expected value. Those who are not prepared to pay as much as £5 are considered to have risk-averse preferences; they would have to be

1 We are assuming that the car is written off at the end of the year with a scrap value of £0.

paid to take the bet because they prefer the certainty of having £5. The third category consists of those who are risk-loving; these individuals would be prepared to pay something for the risk associated with the gamble. An individual with this kind of attitude to risk would be prepared to pay more than a £5 stake in this example.

Figures 5.1A–C show the different types of preference toward risk. In each case, we measure the total utility of the individual on the vertical axis, and his or her wealth-holdings on the horizontal axis. The individual's utility increases as his or her wealth increases, so the total utility curve slopes upward. The use of wealth-holdings here is a rather general term: in the example it can be thought of as the return on the bet. In Figure 5.1A, we have drawn the relation between the individual's total utility and wealth-holdings based on the assumption of a diminishing marginal utility of wealth. Successive additions to the individual's wealth add less additional utility; diagrammatically, the slope of the total utility curve becomes flatter as the individual's wealth increases.

Suppose we now consider the following alternatives: firstly, that the individual has an equal chance of two wealth levels W_0 or W_1, with associated expected value, $\bar{W}$ and, secondly, that the individual has the wealth-holding of $\bar{W}$ for sure. This is a similar situation to that we considered earlier where we looked at whether the individual preferred the expected value in the uncertain situation to the certainty of the sum equal to the expected value.

The risk-averse person will prefer the certain situation to the uncertain one. Figure 5.1A depicts this preference by showing a higher utility associated with the certain situation. The utility associated with the expected value of $\bar{W}$ is $U[E\bar{W}]$. The utility associated with the certain sum is $U(\bar{W})$, and the additional utility is measured by the vertical distance between points A and B. The distance from C to B indicates the sum the risk-averse person would be prepared to sacrifice to move from the uncertain situation to the certain one.

Figures 5.1B and 5.1C deal with the other types of attitude to risk. In Figure 5.1B, the total utility curve is linear, reflecting a constant marginal utility of wealth. Successive additions to wealth add the same amount to total utility, and in this case, the individual gets the same level of utility from having the expected value, $\bar{W}$ and having the identical sum for sure. By comparison with Figure 5.1A, points A and B coincide. The amount the individual would be willing to pay for the certain sum is zero, so points C and B also coincide.

Finally, there is the case of the individual with risk-loving preferences which is depicted in Figure 5.1C. For this person the marginal utility of wealth is positive, successive additions to wealth-holding add greater amounts to his or her total utility. Therefore, total utility rises disproportionately when wealth rises. In Figure 5.1C the individual's utility from the expected value, $\bar{W}$ is greater than that from having the same sum for certain. The distance between points A and B shows the additional utility to the individual from taking the fair gamble with

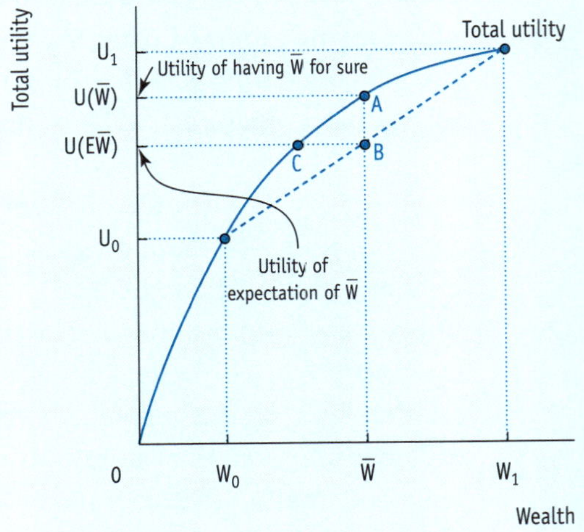

Figure 5.1A **Utility and wealth-holdings (diminishing marginal utility of wealth)**

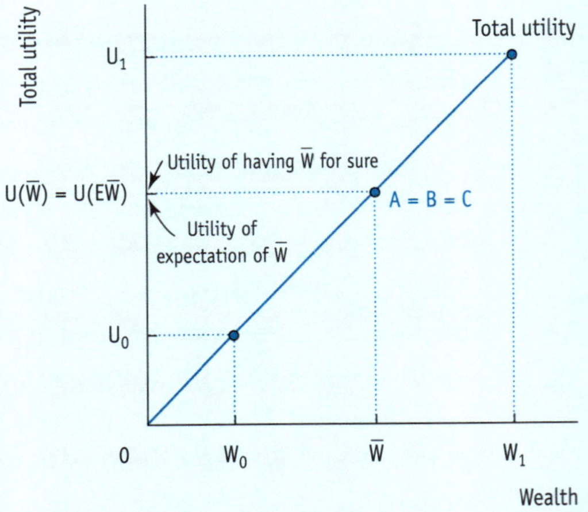

Figure 5.1B **Utility and wealth-holdings (constant marginal utility of wealth)**

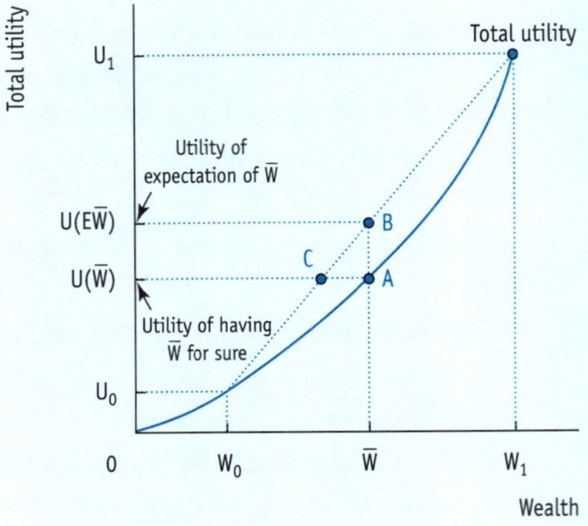

Figure 5.1C **Utility and wealth-holdings (increasing marginal utility of wealth)**

expected value $\bar{W}$. The distance from point A to point C shows how much the individual would be prepared to pay to take the fair gamble.

The state-preference model

The analysis of individual attitudes to risk can be helpfully recast in the indifference curve framework, which in this context is referred to as the state-preference model. To understand the model, it will be easier to start with the individual's budget constraint and then go on to examine ways of representing individual preferences towards risk.

The budget constraint

In Figure 5.2A, we have drawn part of an individual's budget line for consumption levels in two different states of the world. To see the intuition behind it, we will use another gambling example. Suppose an individual had £100 and was offered a bet on the toss of a penny coin: win £1 for every £1 stake if the penny comes up heads, but lose the stake if it is tails. The two states of the world are winning and losing the bet; the part of the budget line shown in Figure 5.2A gives the alternative consumption levels open to the individual when presented with the bet. On the horizontal axis is the level of consumption if the penny comes down tails, on the vertical axis consumption if it is heads. One option open to the individual is of course to refuse the bet, so he or she would have £100 in both states of the world. This is the endowment point, marked as point D in the figure.

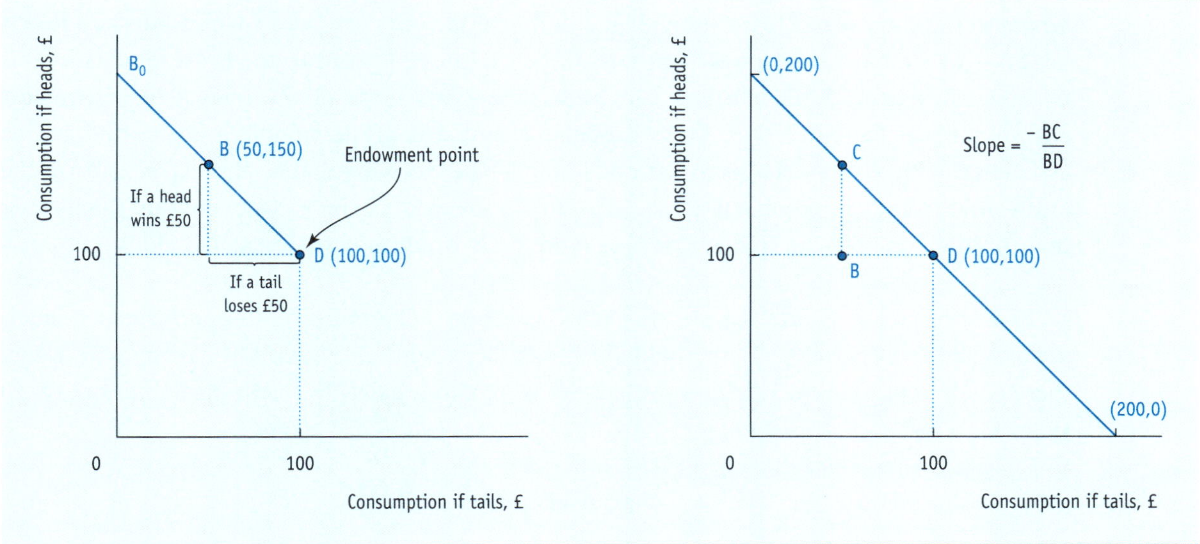

Figure 5.2A Budget line for consumption in different states of the world

Figure 5.2B Slope of budget line for consumption in different states of the world

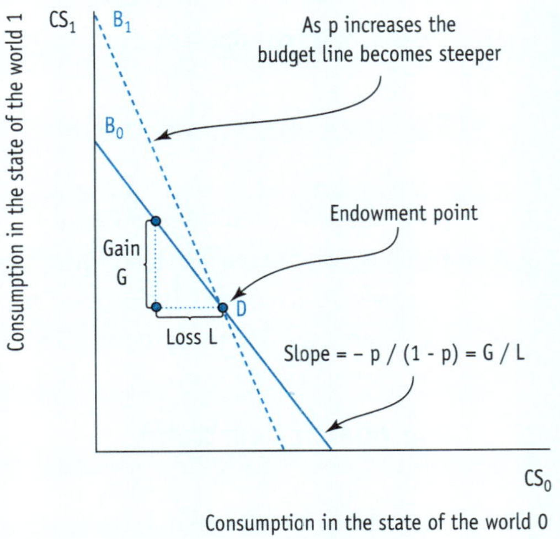

Figure 5.3 **Fair odds budget lines**

Suppose the individual decides to bet £50 on the outcome of the coin toss, then the consumption level available when it comes down tails would be £50, when heads it would rise to £150. This gives us point B on the budget line. Points between D and B represent the situation when the individual bets sums between £0 and £50 on the terms offered. If he or she was to bet more than £50 then it would involve moving to a point further up the budget constraint beyond point B. The most that could be staked, obviously, is £100, and this gives us the point of intersection on the vertical axis.

Figure 5.2A only covers points to the north-west of the endowment point D. What about points to the south-east? If the individual could take the opposite bet — win if tails and lose if heads — by similar reasoning we can extend the budget constraint to the horizontal axis. This is shown in Figure 5.2B, where it can be seen that the slope of the budget line is, in this example, equal to minus one. This particular example is a fair gamble and the budget line associated with it is known as a fair odds line. The expected value of the bet is zero on the terms offered and the gamble is actuarially fair. In the example here, a slope of anything other than (minus) one for the budget line in Figure 5.2B would not represent fair odds.

In Figure 5.3 we illustrate the position more generally. The individual's endowment point is again marked as point D. If the individual was faced with an actuarially fair gamble where there is a loss of amount L with a probability of p, and a gain of G with probability of (1–p) then

$$pL + (1-p)G = 0$$

by definition. The slope of the fair odds budget line is the height of the distance that measures the gain divided by the length of the distance that measures the loss. Rearranging the above expression we get $G/L = -p/(1-p)$.[2] All the points along a given fair odds line represent the same expected value of consumption. An increase in the probability of making a loss would mean that for a gamble to remain fair, the amount of the gain, G, would have to increase. This is shown in Figure 5.3 by the dashed line representing the budget constraint.

Preferences toward risk

We can again use indifference curves to represent a consumer's preferences where in this context, the two goods are the consumption levels in the two states of the world, states 0 and 1. Indifference curves therefore represent different combinations of state-dependent consumption levels that yield the same level of utility to the individual. The shape of the indifference curves will depend on the individual's attitude to risk.

In Figure 5.4A, we have drawn a certainty line, OC, that represents equal amounts of consumption in the two states of the world and the individual's fair odds budget constraint. The individual's endowment point is at D. We have seen earlier that a person with risk-averse preferences will refuse a fair gamble: he or she would not accept a bet with an expected value of zero. Given the alternatives of a certain sum and an uncertain one with the same expected value, the individual would prefer to keep the certain sum. In terms of Figure 5.4A, the individual would prefer point D on the fair odds line to other points such as B and C. Starting at points such as B and C, the individual would require a higher level of consumption in one or other states of the world, or both, to obtain the same utility level as at D.

An individual who has risk-averse preferences will therefore have indifference curves that are convex to the origin, similarly shaped to those we have seen in previous chapters. The indifference curve will be tangential to the fair odds line when it passes through the certainty line. At this point, the slope of the indifference curve is also equal to $-p/(1-p)$. As before, indifference curves that are further away from the origin represent higher levels of utility. The slope of the indifference curve away from point D will, however, differ between individuals whose preferences can be characterised as risk-averse.

A person with risk-neutral preferences is indifferent between different combinations of consumption with the same expected value. In Figure 5.4B, points such as B, C and D all yield the same level of utility. In this case the indifference curves coincide with the fair odds line. The case of individuals with risk-loving preferences is shown in Figure 5.4C. Moving from point D on the budget line B_0, to points B and C represent a higher level of utility to the individual. The general shape of the indifference curve is therefore bowed outward from the origin. The degree of curvature for the difference curves away from point D will again vary between

2 If the state in which the individual loses is on the vertical axis then the slope is $-(1-p)/p$.

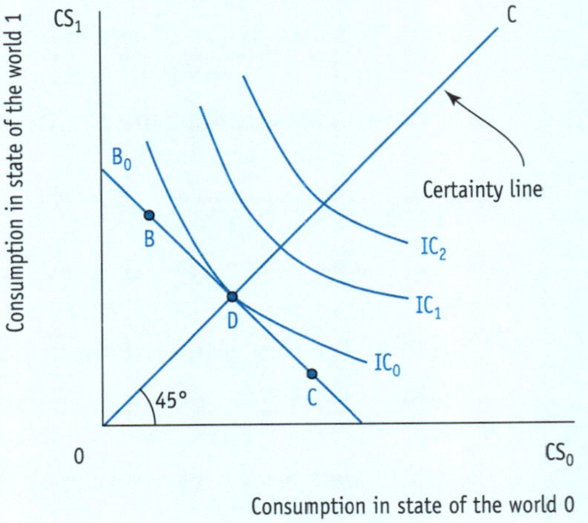

Figure 5.4A **Indifference map reflecting risk-averse preferences**

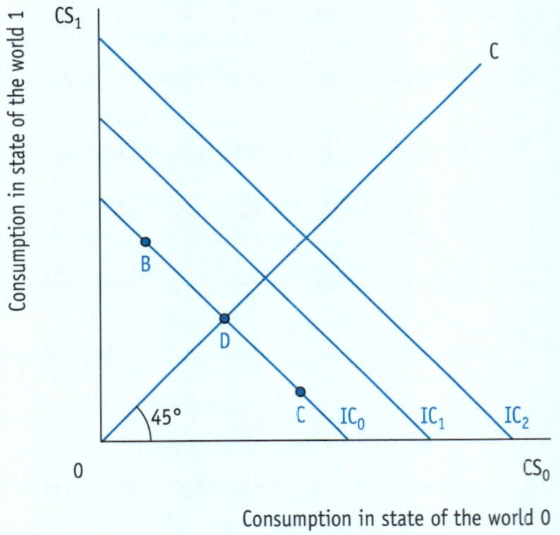

Figure 5.4B **Indifference map reflecting risk-neutral preferences**

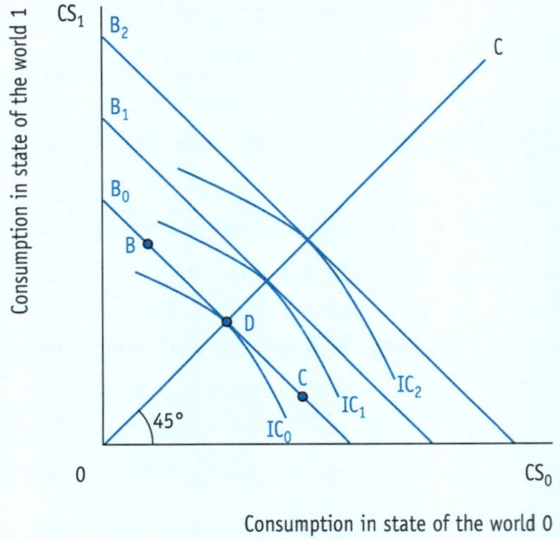

Figure 5.4C **Indifference map reflecting risk-loving preferences**

individuals. Again, indifference curves that are further away from the origin represent a higher level of utility.

The widespread availability of insurance, provided by profit-making private sector companies suggests that most individuals have risk-averse preferences in relation to many alternative states of the world. In the next section, we look more closely at insurance markets and particularly the role that information plays in their operation. First, though, we will discuss the idea of an expected utility function.

Expected utility

In Chapter 1, when we first encountered utility functions, we gave examples where the utility level depended on two goods. In the current context, utility depends on the two state dependent consumption levels. A simple and convenient way of expressing this is with an expected utility function, which is of the form

$$EU = PS_0 * U(CS_0) + PS_1 * U(CS_1)$$

Where EU is expected utility, PS_0 is the probability of state 0 occurring and CS_0 is consumption in state 0, PS_1 and CS_1 are the probability of state 1 occurring and the consumption level in that state. In words, expected utility is a weighted average of the utility associated with the consumption levels, with the weights being given by the probabilities associated with each state.

A utility function of this form is known as a von-Neumann-Morgenstern utility function. For example, suppose an individual had a 50–50 chance of consumption of £1,000 and £3,000, then his or her expected utility would be

$$EU = 0.5U(£1{,}000) + 0.5U(£3{,}000).$$

The utility of having the same expected wealth for sure is U(£2,000). For those with risk-averse preferences the utility function will be such that U > EU and so as utility-maximisers they would not gamble.

To illustrate the use of expected utility, suppose that someone faces two states of health, 'good' and 'bad', which affects the amount of time they can spend in work. In good health, earnings are £24,000 per annum, when unable to work through sickness the individual's income falls to £6,000. Assume the probability of being in work is 0.9 and so the probability of being sick is 0.1. We will also assume that this person's utility function is

$$U = Y^{0.5}$$

In this case the individual's expected utility is

$$EU = 0.9(£24{,}000)^{0.5} + 0.1(£6{,}000)^{0.5} = 147.17.$$

For this particular individual, expected income is £22,200 and so a fair insurance premium would be £1,800. If the individual buys full insurance, so that income in both states of the world is the same, expected utility would be

$$EU = 0.5(£22{,}200)^{0.5} + 0.5(£22{,}200)^{0.5} = 149.00$$

so that he or she would be better off when fair insurance is purchased. If fully insured the individual would be as well off with an income of $(147.17)^2$ = £21,659 as he or she would be without any insurance at all. The maximum amount that this individual would be willing to pay for the costs of supplying insurance is therefore (£22,200 – £21,659) = £541.

Questions

Q1 Gary earns £20,000 per annum and has no other sources of income. He faces a 50% probability of being made unemployed for a year, which would mean his income falling to £8,000. What is the expected value of his income over the year? Assume that Gary has risk-averse preferences, show in a utility-of-wealth diagram that he would be worse off without unemployment insurance. What would be the cost of actuarially fair insurance? What would the cost of fair insurance be to individuals with probabilities of unemployment equal to 5%, 75% with the same income prospects?

Q2 Bert is a landscape gardener with a back problem. In a year when he manages to work full-time, his income is £18,000 per year but there is an 80% chance he will be off work some of the time, when his income falls to £12,000. What is the expected value of his income and what would be the cost of fair insurance to him? Suppose that he could obtain only £2,000 of insurance for when he was unable to work. If actuarially fair insurance were not available would he take out a policy? What does your answer depend on?

Q3 Aileen has an endowment of £1,000 and is offered a fair bet where the probability of making a loss is 0.3. Draw her budget constraint. What happens to the slope of the budget constraint when the probability of a loss in the fair gamble rises to 0.6?

Q4 Lucinda is offered a gamble involving the toss of a coin where she wins 50p for a £1 stake if she calls correctly. If she has an endowment of £500,000 what is her budget line? What is its relation to the fair odds line?

5.2 Insurance markets and the role of information

The range of insurance products that households takes out is wide and Table 5.1 below gives some indication extent of insurance for major risks faced.[3]

Insurance	Households
Home: building	63.5%
Home: contents	74.5%
Motor	64.0%
Medical	8.8%
Life insurance	65.7%
Personal pension	21.3%

Table 5.1 **% UK households with insurance 1993**
Source: Association of British Insurers (1993).

The risks which households insure against on an individual basis are broadly in line with what might be expected. The number of policies that cover the first three risks will have risen over time as the home-ownership rates and the proportion owning cars have risen. Life insurance, a policy that pays out to family dependants if an individual dies, is now less widespread than 20 years ago when the proportion holding a policy was around 80%.[4] This may be rather surprising, but could be attributed to the changing structure of households, and in particular the growing number with only one adult.

The number of households with a personal pension has grown throughout the 1990s. This raises a number of points about public and private sector provision, which we will come to in Section 3. Before that, we will develop our analysis of insurance markets and examine two aspects that attract a lot of attention in economic analysis. These are the problems of moral hazard and adverse selection, both of which emphasise the role of information in the operation of markets.

The analysis of demand for insurance can build directly on the state-preference model of Section 1. The examples used before involved gambles such as a coin toss to generate different combinations of consumption possibilities. In this section, we will adapt the framework to

3 The number of households with buildings insurance looks surprisingly low, although it should be seen in relation to the number of owner-occupiers. Those in the rented sector are (or should be) covered by the landlord.

4 Banks and Tanner (1996).

consider risk more generally in relation to burglary, ill-health and so on. Different amounts of luck in relation to being burgled also generate different consumption levels, different states of health generate different income and consumption levels. With the gambling example, the individual had the option of walking away from it; considered widely, individuals face risks that cannot be avoided and the analysis of this is what we come to now.

To start, we will assume for simplicity, that the supply of insurance is a costless activity and that insurance policies are provided on actuarially fair terms. In the adverse state of the world the policy pays out, in the favourable state the individual receives nothing. The level of the insurance premium is simply the probability of a loss multiplied by the amount of the loss. For example, in the case of a car theft insurance policy, suppose there is £6,000 of cover and a probability of 0.1 that the car will be stolen in the course of a year. An actuarially fair premium will be £600 per year; for each £1 of cover the premium will be 10p, or 0.1 of the cover, which is just the probability of there being a theft.

Figure 5.5 illustrates the equilibrium position of individuals when they can buy fair insurance. Point D is the individual's endowment point with associated consumption levels as marked on the axes. Suppose the individual wanted to take out full insurance so that he or she had the same consumption level, whatever the state of the world. This would involve moving along the budget line at fair odds to the point E_0 on the certainty equivalent (or full insurance) line OC. The distance DF gives the insurance premium necessary to obtain the payout FE_0. As drawn in the figure the individual has risk-averse preferences and attains a higher level of utility by moving from point D to E_0. In general an individual with risk-averse preferences will purchase full insurance if it is offered at fair odds.[5]

In practice, the supply of insurance is obviously not costless. This means that there is a difference between the insurance premium paid for any particular policy and the expected payout from the policy for an individual. This may be due to the cost of administration and it may also be due the fact that risks differ between individuals. When insurance is available at unfair odds, the budget constraint is steeper than before as a larger premium is now charged for any given expected payout, or alternatively the cover will be less for a premium of a given amount. This does not affect the endowment point so the effect of changing the odds is to pivot the budget line through point D, as shown in Figure 5.6.

When insurance is available on terms that are not actuarially fair, those with risk-averse preferences will take out partial insurance. Intuitively, it makes sense even for those with risk-averse preference to accept some of the risk when the premium paid for insurance is greater than the expected loss. This outcome is shown in Figure 5.6 by the move along the new,

5 There is a direct counterpart here to the analysis of Chapter 5. A perfect capital market allowed individuals to spread consumption over time. A fair insurance policy allows consumption to be evened out across different states of the world.

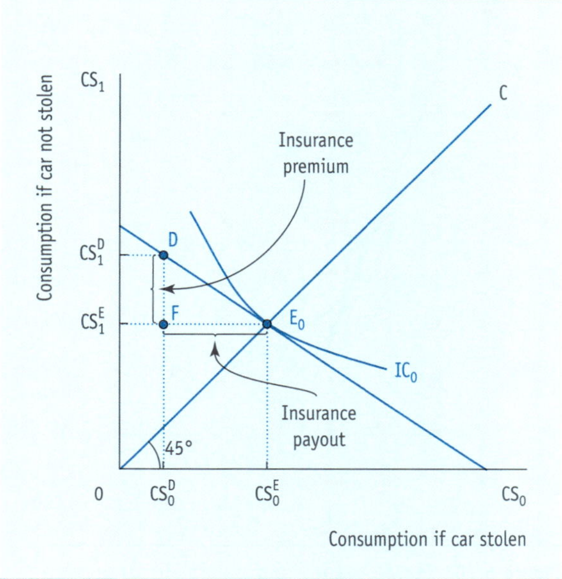

Figure 5.5 **Those with risk-averse preferences buy full insurance at fair odds**

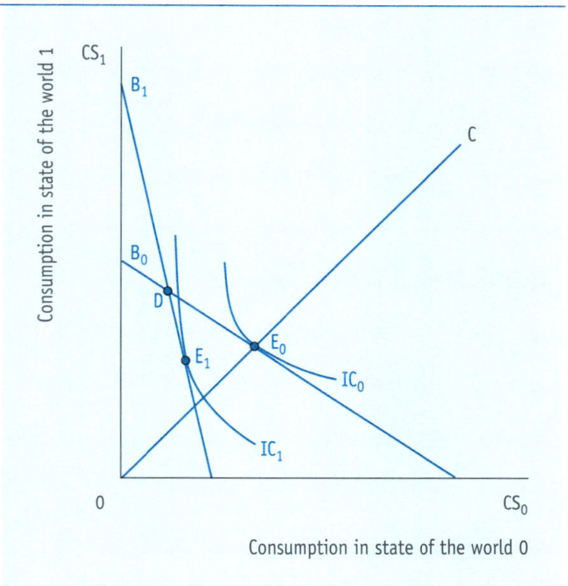

Figure 5.6 **Those with risk-averse preferences take out partial insurance at unfair odds**

steeper, budget constraint from point D to the equilibrium at point E_1. In equilibrium, the individual's marginal rate of substitution between state dependent consumption levels will again be equal to the slope of the budget constraint, B_1, though in this case the consumption levels will obviously differ in the two states of the world.

Moral hazard

It is possible that if an individual is fully covered against a loss in a particular state of the world then there may be a problem known as moral hazard. To return to the car theft example, if the individual receives exactly the same consumption levels in both states of the world then there is no financial incentive to take adequate precaution against the possibility of theft. In general, moral hazard refers to situations when the probability of the outcome against which the individual is insuring can be affected by the behaviour of the individual.

The premium, P, charged by an insurance company can be expressed as

$$P = pL + A$$

Where p: is the probability of a loss occurring
L: loss occurring in a particular state of nature
A: administrative cost.

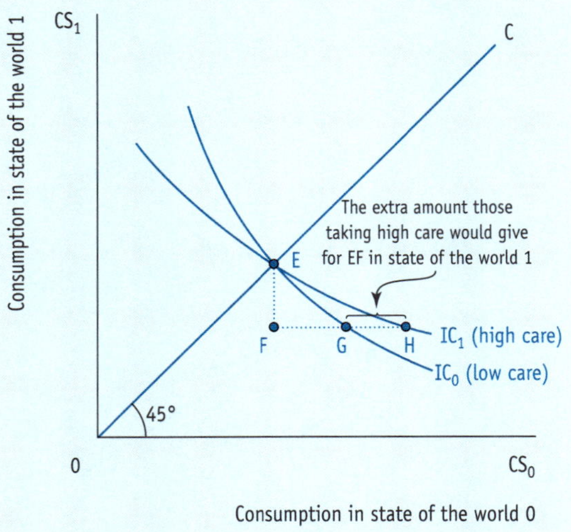

Figure 5.7A The slope of the indifference curve depends on the level of care taken

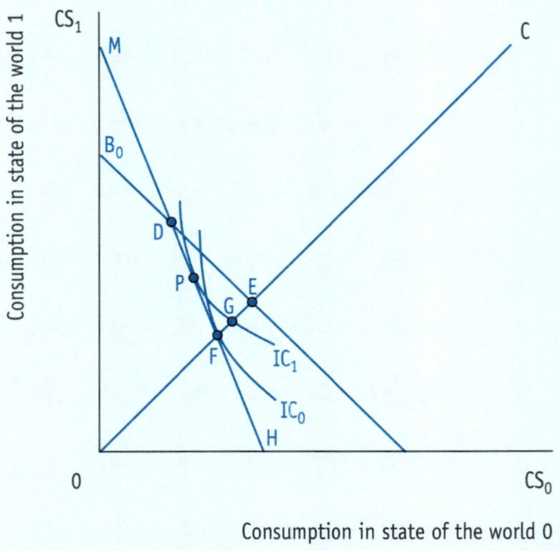

Figure 5.7B Moral hazard and partial insurance

Moral hazard refers to the situation in which the individual taking out the insurance can determine the value of p. If those taking out the policy can set $p = 1$, an insurance company will not offer a policy against car theft. Intuitively, individuals are in effect trying to exchange an insurance premium for a new car, so the insurance premium would have to be the same as the price of new car (in a world without administrative costs).

The problem of moral hazard arises in circumstances where the insurer does not know the probability of an individual claim (or cannot estimate it). To this extent, moral hazard can be seen as a problem of asymmetric information in that the insured is better informed than the insurer about the level of care taken in trying to avoid having to make a claim. It is, therefore, sometimes referred to as a hidden action problem.

In Figure 5.7A, the amount of care an individual takes to avoid the possibility of a loss is reflected in the shape of the indifference curves. We have drawn a pair of indifference curves that pass through point E on the certainty line to reflect different levels of care by the individual. Suppose, for simplicity, there are just two levels of care that an individual could take: high and low. The indifference curve labelled IC_1 reflects the case when the individual takes a high level of care. To see why, we can ask how much an individual would be willing to give up in the adverse state of the world in exchange for a given amount of additional consumption in the favourable state, CS_1.

This answer to this will depend on how likely the individual is to experience the adverse state and, in turn, therefore depends on his or her own actions. In Figure 5.7A, for an amount of extra consumption measured by the distance EF in the favourable state, the individual who takes a high level of care would be prepared to give up more in the adverse state than would an individual who did not. This is because the probability of the adverse state occurring is lower given the high level of care he or she takes. The additional amount is shown as the distance GH in the figure and the indifference curve IC_1 therefore reflects the behaviour of those individuals who take a high level of care.

In Figure 5.7B, we have drawn the individual's endowment at point D and the budget line representing fair odds is B_0. If the insured can increase the probability of making a claim by his or her actions (by taking less care) then the fair odds line reflecting this behaviour will become steeper rotating through point D. In the figure, it is drawn as the line MH.[6] Point E on the fair odds budget line cannot now be an equilibrium point when there is a moral hazard problem (no insurance company would offer such a payout for the premium, given the behaviour of the individual).

This raises the possibility that the equilibrium point would be at F, which given the individual's behaviour would be along the fair odds line, MH, associated with a low level of care. However, if the individual was offered insurance anywhere along the MH line, then he or she might obtain a higher level of utility by exercising a high level of care and choosing partial insurance. This is shown in Figure 5.7B at point P. Because of the individual's claim minimising behaviour the indifference curve IC_1 passes through the certainty line above point F. The individual will be better off providing the distance between F and G does not represent a cost greater than that associated with modifying his or her behaviour.[7]

Adverse selection

This is a problem that arises when there are individuals in different risk categories seeking insurance and it is not possible for an insurance company to distinguish between them. Suppose, for simplicity, there are just two groups of individuals, one with a low probability of making a claim and a second group with a high probability. One response from an insurance company would be to charge a premium that is based on a weighted average of the premiums they would charge to the two groups separately.

As a numerical example, suppose that there are 50 individuals in an area with a probability, $p = 0.1$ of having their car stolen at a loss of £6,000, and 50 individuals with a probability

---

6 As we discussed in relation to Figure 5.3, the larger the value of p the greater the (absolute) value of the expression and the steeper the slope.

7 In a competitive market, the insurance companies will then be making supernormal profits. A fuller analysis of this would involve competition between insurance companies leading to a reduction in the per unit price of insurance and an increase in the quantity of insurance bought. The equilibrium in a competitive market would involve the individual purchasing partial insurance at fair odds.

Figure 5.8 **The market average fair odds line**

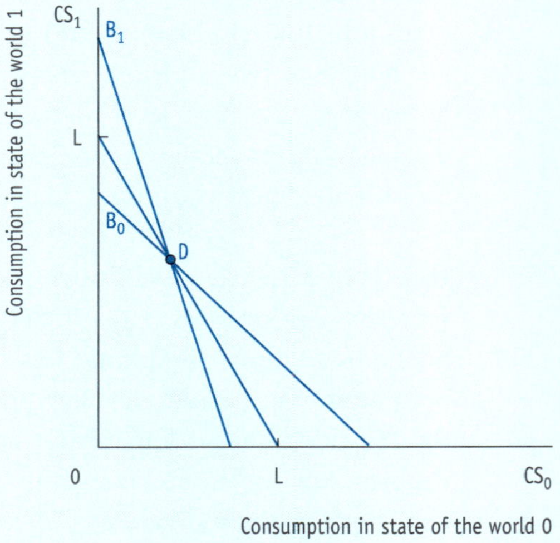

which is ten times less, that is p = 0.01. The first group taken together would have five cars stolen on average every year, the second group would have a car stolen once every other year. The individual premium to cover the first group alone would be £600 per annum (at fair odds); the premium to cover the second group would be £60. If the insurance company does not know who belongs in each group, then basing the premium on the average risk would mean setting it at £330.

This may seem like an excessive premium to some of those in the low risk group in which case they may withdraw from the market. Suppose only 25 of the low-risk individuals decide to take up the insurance available, this will have the effect of increasing premiums given the changing pool of those seeking insurance. The weights are now two-thirds high-risk, one-third low-risk and the average premium rises to £420. The process may continue until only the most risk-averse (if any) of the low-risk group are prepared to take out the insurance.

In terms of the state-preference model, in Figure 5.8 we have the fair odds lines of two different groups of individuals, one high-risk and one low-risk. All individuals are given the same endowment point D. The low risk individuals face the budget constraint marked B_0, the high risk individuals the constraint B_1. The market average line is shown by the constraint LL and assumes equal numbers in each group.[8]

The different risks that individuals face are again reflected by the slope of the indifference curves. Because they are less likely to make a claim, those at low risk of a loss will require a higher degree of compensation for a given reduction in consumption in the favourable state.

8 It is worth noting that the slope of the LL line is not equal to half the difference between B_0 and B_1.

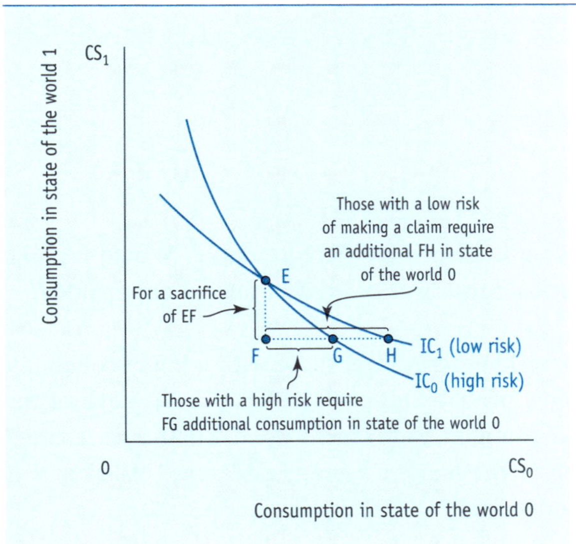

Figure 5.9 **The slope of the indifference curve depends on whether the individual is high or low-risk**

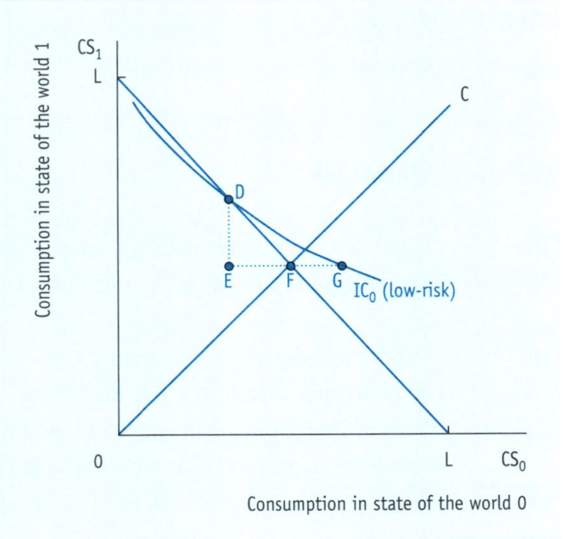

Figure 5.10 **Adverse selection: low-risk individuals choose no insurance**

This is point is illustrated in Figure 5.9, where the indifference curve of the low-risk individual is drawn more flatly and marked as IC_1.

The adverse selection problem is illustrated in Figure 5.10 where we have drawn a low-risk individual's indifference curve marked as IC_0. The slope of the indifference curve is flatter than that of the market average odds line at the endowment point D. Given this the individual cannot move onto a higher indifference curve to the right of point D. In exchange for DE of consumption in the favourable state of the world, the individual could only obtain EF of cover in the adverse state. However, to be as well off as he or she would be at point D, the individual requires an additional EG of consumption in the adverse state. The individual would be better off not taking out any insurance.

In general terms, adverse selection is more likely to be a problem if there are a large proportion of high risk individuals. In analytical terms, this has the effect of moving the market odds line closing to the budget line B_1 in Figure 5.8. It is also more likely to be a problem if there is a large difference in the risks associated with the two groups. Finally, there are the preferences of the individual to consider. Adverse selection is less likely if some individuals are very risk-averse.

In practice, there are differential premiums paid just depending on what and who is being insured. Premiums depend on the individual's age, occupation and area of home address for car insurance and also household insurance. This brings us to the wider subject of what risks can be insured by a private company and what the role for government might be, which we take up in the next section.

Questions

Q5 What sort of preferences are characterised by an L-shaped indifference curve? Would it make any difference to such an individual whether insurance was offered at fair or unfair odds?

Q6 Suppose there were two groups of consumers seeking insurance: those with a high probability of making a claim, $p = 0.8$ and those with a low probability, $p = 0.2$. What is the slope of the budget lines that each group face? (Assume a common endowment point.) If there are equal numbers in the two groups what is the slope of the market average odds line? What is it if there are 75% or 90% in the first group of individuals?

5.3 Public policy and the provision of insurance

Introduction

In this section, we turn our attention to what the role of government might be in providing insurance against certain types of risk. Hitherto in this chapter, we have restricted our analysis to two alternative states of the world. In practice, there are several risks that an individual might want to insure against and a number of the associated states of the world may be linked over time. For example, some individuals may be more likely to face repeated spells of unemployment or sickness than others. There are potentially a large number of risks that an individual may wish to insure against and complexities arise from such linkages. This leads to the question where the boundaries should be between private and public sector provision of insurance.

Since the Second World War, what is called 'social insurance' has been provided in the main by the government in the UK.[9] A minimum level of cover against the contingencies of unemployment, sickness and long-term disability has been a part of general social security provision. This traditional role has, however, come under challenge partly on the grounds of its impact on the level of public expenditure, but also in part because private insurance companies may offer individuals greater discretion in deciding what level of insurance to choose, and what risks to insure against. The question whether the state or the private sector is better suited to providing insurance also involves judgements about equity; with state provision the cost of

9 Institutional practice varies between countries in Europe. Some Scandanavian countries, for example, have in the past relied to a greater extent on the role played by Trade Unions in respect of unemployment compensation.

(Men)			
Quartile	**Within 6 months**	**Within 12 months**	**Within 30 months**
Bottom	14.4%	18.8%	29.9%
2nd	5.6%	11.7%	19.2%
3rd	3.6%	8.4%	15.3%
Top	2.8%	6.7%	12.1%

Table 5.2 **Probability of moving out of work, by wage quartile in UK, 1991**
Source: Gosling et al. (1997).

insurance is ultimately met through the tax system, and as a result depends on the ability of an individual to pay. With private sector provision it is premium-based, and hence determined by an individual's risk status.[10]

Social insurance: (I) unemployment

For there to be a market in unemployment insurance the premium charged to the individual has to meet a number of conditions. It cannot be affected by the risk of anyone else making a claim, that is the probability of one person making a claim has to be independent of anyone else making a claim. The probability of the individual making a claim has to be less than 100% and this is something the insurance provider has to know or can estimate. Finally, there cannot be the informational problems of moral hazard and adverse selection.

The risk of being made unemployed differs between individuals. The probability of becoming unemployed by wage level is shown in Table 5.2. It is greater for those in the bottom quarter of the wage distribution than it is further those further up. On a six-month time horizon this particular study found that, for men, the probability of moving out of work was around five times higher for those in the bottom quarter compared to those in the top quarter. This difference varies over the length of the time horizon into the future, but it is clear enough that those at the bottom are bigger risks.[11]

The differential risk of being made unemployed would not prevent a private company from offering unemployment insurance, provided that the risks were stable over time and could be estimated with some degree of accuracy.

10 This section starts our discussion of these issues, we return to them in Chapter 18 where the discussion is focussed on the distribution of income.

11 The picture for women is broadly similar over a 30 month time horizon, with the percentage leaving work in the top quartile being around twice that of those in the bottom quintile.

Wave 1991	Unemployed	Employment	Self-employment	Other
1992	55.6%	26.5%	8.0%	8.4%
1993	39.4%	25.6%	5.6%	6.3%
1994	25.9%	22.8%		

Table 5.3 **Labour market experience of unemployed men in the UK in 1991**
Source: Gosling et al. (1997).

The duration of unemployment spells is also important and Table 5.3 provides some data on this.

This table shows the experience of all those men who were unemployed in 1991. The following year over a half of them were still in that state, while around a quarter had returned to employment. The table also shows those who remain unemployed, or employed or self-employed over the period to 1994.[12] About a quarter of those who were unemployed in 1991 were still unemployed in 1994.

The distribution of unemployment risk and the variation in the length of unemployment spells point to the possible need for government unemployment compensation schemes. Private provision of unemployment insurance is made difficult by changing macroeconomic circumstances which may affect the risk of individual unemployment and the length of unemployment spell differentially over time.[13] Additionally, some groups of the workforce may have probabilities of entering into unemployment that that are so high that they are effectively uninsurable risks. There will also be other groups without an employment record on which to estimate a probability of becoming unemployed.

To some extent, the private sector has become involved with unemployment insurance through mortgage protection policies.[14] These schemes cover expenditure rather than replace income although they clearly overlap in purpose. However, they are far from an open-ended commitment, often being restricted to owner-occupiers, who typically have a lower risk of entering into unemployment than the population as a whole. The period of payment is typically limited to twelve months. This may limit the problems that arise from adverse selection and moral hazard, but it also limits the proportion of the population who are eligible for coverage.

12 It follows that the sum of the percentages in the third and fourth rows will not sum to 100%. For example, some of those who were employed in 1992 might become unemployed in 1993 or 1994 and they are not included in the table.

13 There is an analogy here between the impact of macroeconomic fluctuations and risks that insurance companies treat as 'Acts of God' and offer no cover against (wars, for example).

14 Or if individuals are unable to work because of accident and sickness.

The case for compulsory (state-provided) insurance also lies partly with the costs of non-insurance, which would be borne not only by the individual who did not pay for insurance cover, but also potentially by his or her dependants. This cost imposed on others might again be compared with the compulsory nature of third party car insurance; individuals have to insure themselves against the costs they impose on others. In terms of broad principle, state provision also overcomes the problems that arise with adverse selection. All individuals are insured at the level set by the UK government: those individuals with low-risk status, or those who are risk lovers, cannot opt out.

Social insurance: (II) retirement

This is another area where the boundaries of public and private provision of insurance have been the subject of policy debate. In terms of our discussion of intertemporal decision-making in Chapter 4, the essential function of a retirement pension is to provide an income transfer from one period of an individual's life to another. Can the private sector be the providers of pensions? The conditions that need to be met for an insurance market to operate discussed above are fulfilled here. To provide an income stream in retirement an insurance company would have to know, or be able to estimate how long a period this would be. This it can estimate readily, and the age at which one person dies does not depend on the age at which another person dies. The problems associated with asymmetries of information do not arise here; the insurance company is as well informed about life-expectancy as are policy holders, and moral hazard is not a problem in this instance.

There is, however, a more general problem with the private provision of pensions and that concerns the risks associated with inflation that is not anticipated. Our two-period model of Chapter 5 is concerned with the transfer of consumption over time defined in real terms. A private sector insurance scheme would work in providing an income stream to purchase consumption in nominal terms, and also in real terms if there was a world without inflation. A private sector scheme would also work if inflation was anticipated; if, for example, it was known that inflation was 2% per year and that it was to continue at that rate. The difficulty is that nobody knows whether this will be the case over the lifetime of an individual. This then raises the question as to whether it is possible, in principle, for a private sector scheme to insure against unanticipated inflation. There is a problem here as plainly the probability of unanticipated inflation affecting one individual is clearly not independent of the risk faced by others.

Questions

Q7 What is the effect of an increase in the level of unemployment compensation in (I) the state preference model (II) the income-leisure trade-off model of Chapter 3? Why might the conclusions of partial equilibrium analysis be misleading?

Q8 A supporter of free market provision of unemployment insurance argues that the data in Table 5.3 is evidence of the problem of moral hazard that arises with state-run unemployment insurance. Do you agree? What kinds of other evidence would you look for to support or refute the argument?

Concluding comment

The question of what is the most appropriate way of providing insurance and, hence, who should provide it, is not a straightforward one to answer. This is partly because it involves questions of redistributing the income of an individual across his or her lifetime, but also because it raises questions about how far some groups of individuals are prepared to go to transfer income to others. The distributional aspect of preferring premium based finance to tax based finance or vice versa, is fundamental to understanding the arguments. There is agreement that the private insurance industry cannot run insurance policies against contingencies that involve major cross-subsidisation of one group by another. There is also agreement that when there are joint risks private insurance cannot operate. The provision of unemployment insurance may be taken as an example of this.

However, there are large areas where, in principle, it would be feasible for insurance to be provided by private firms or by the public sector. In the discussion of principle, adverse selection and moral hazard traditionally receive much attention. In practice, insurance policies have introduced elements of coinsurance (such as disregarding the first part of a claim) to restrict the size of the problems. Additionally, we can note that the failure of the market to provide insurance in some cases does not necessarily mean the government would be able to perform any better. The reverse, of course, may also be true.

Summary

1 Economists distinguish between risk and uncertainty. Risk refers to situations in which individuals face a known range of outcomes with known probabilities. Uncertainty refers to situations in which the range of outcomes is not known, or cannot be enumerated.

2 A fair bet or gamble is where the expected value of the bet is the same as the certain alternative. The individual with risk averse preferences would not take a fair bet, those with risk-loving preferences would. Somebody with risk-neutral preferences would be indifferent between a certain sum for sure and a gamble with the same expected value.

3 Expected utility functions are a convenient way of characterising different individual attitudes towards risk.

4 Individuals face a wide range of risks, and insurance markets are established to pool or share risks between individuals. Individual households spend significant sums on household, medical and motor insurance, as well as in a number of other areas.

5 Information can play an important role in insurance. If potential buyers of insurance are better informed about risks than potential sellers, then it might not be possible for the market to provide insurance at all.

6 Moral hazard refers to the situation in which the buyer of insurance can affect the probability of making a claim. Insurance policies, in practice, therefore usually involve an element of coinsurance.

7 Adverse selection refers to a situation in which there are different risks among the buyers of insurance that are unknown to the seller. If premiums paid reflect the average risk, this may discourage the low risk individuals from buying insurance and a private company may not provide insurance.

8 The government in the UK has traditionally provided certain forms of social insurance, for example unemployment insurance and retirement pensions. This role has come under challenge because of the growing level of government expenditure.

9 Whether the government provides social insurance or not is an important question. The level and pattern of cover will vary between individuals depending on whether there is state or private sector provision. Broadly, a shift from tax-financed state provision to premium-based private provision is likely to benefit the better-off at the expense of the less well-off.

End of chapter questions

Q9 'Private insurers can only pool risks between similar individuals. If cross-subsidisation is required then the state must provide.' Do you agree? Would it make any difference if insurance was provided by a mutual society or a friendly society, rather than profit-maximising insurance company?

Q10 Suppose Gary who we met in Question 1 had a utility function of the form

$$U(W) = Ln(W).$$

What would be the most he would be prepared to pay for unemployment insurance, given his circumstances?

Q11 Paul is supporter of Liverpool Football Club and is offered odds of 3/1 against his team winning the FA Cup, when he believes that the odds on them winning it is 50–50. Assume that he has a utility function of the form

$$U = W^{0.5}$$

how much should he bet if his wealth-holding without the bet is £4,000?

Q12 Suppose there are 100 householders living on the same estate and there is a 1 in a million chance of each of them having their property destroyed by fire at a loss of £50,000. What would the actuarially fair insurance premium be to cover this loss? Are there likely to be any problems with private insurance?

Q13 If a large number of people in a particular country expected to be abducted by aliens, would you expect a private insurance company to be able to offer insurance against such a risk? Would the necessary conditions for a private sector outcome be met?

Q14 A large number of people choose the same lottery numbers each week and the thought of not winning if their numbers come up keeps them playing. Would it be possible to offer an insurance policy against the risk of *not* winning?

References and suggested further reading

An alternative treatment of risk and uncertainty is covered in both Nicholson and Varian. The text by Hillier gives a more formal treatment of the analysis. The conference proceedings edited by Silburn gives a range of perspectives on issues relating to social insurance. Burchardt and Hills look at the boundaries between the role of public and provision of insurance via three case studies, which are (I) mortgage payments for the unemployed, sick and disabled (II) permanent health insurance, and (III) health care costs in old-age.

Association of British Insurers (1993), '*Insurance Statistics Yearbook 1983–93*.

Banks, J. and Tanner, S. (1996), '*Savings and wealth in the UK: Evidence from micro-data*', Fiscal Studies, **17**.

Barr, N. (1992), 'Economic Theory and the Welfare State: A Survey and Interpretation', *Journal of Economic Literature*, **30**.

Burchardt, T. and Hills, J. (1997), '*Private welfare insurance and social security*', Joseph Rowntree Foundation.

Fenn, P. (1994), 'Conclusion' in Silburn, R. (ed.) '*Social Insurance — The Way Forward*', Benefits Research Unit.

Gosling, A., Johnson, P., McCrae, J. and Paull, G. (1997), *The Dynamics of Low Pay and Unemployment in Early 1990s Britain*, Institute for Fiscal Studies.

Hillier, B. (1997), *The Economics of Asymmetric Information*, Macmillan.

Kessler, D. (1994), 'Social Insurance in Europe: contrasts and similarities' in Silburn, R. (ed.), *Social Insurance — The Way Forward*, Benefits Research Unit.

Nicholson, W. (1995), *Microeconomic Theory: Basic Principles and Extensions*, 6th edition, The Dryden Press.

Silburn, R. (1994), 'Social insurance: key themes and issues from the first phase' in Silburn, R. (ed.), *Social Insurance — The Way Forward*, Benefits Research Unit.

Varian, H.R. (1996), *Intermediate Microeconomics, A Modern Approach*, 4th edition, W.W. Norton & Co.

6

Risk, Uncertainty and Household Assets

Key ideas and material

Demand for financial assets, risk and diversification, evidence of household wealth-holdings, the housing market

Introduction

In Chapter 4, we took a first look at the savings decisions of individuals and the broad pattern of wealth-holding. We saw there the breakdown of household assets into financial and housing wealth, and with it looked at the pattern of ownership over the life-cycle. In Chapter 5, we introduced the ideas of risk and uncertainty, and analysed the demand for insurance. This chapter develops the discussion by looking at the demand by individuals for risky assets, which is another aspect of household decision-making and a part of the explanation of the pattern of wealth-holdings between households.

In Section 1 below, we will develop a relatively simple model of the demand for risky assets, once again adapting the indifference curve framework to analyse decisions. Section 2 presents information on the pattern of financial asset-holding to give us a first look at the relevance of the theoretical ideas of Section 1. In Section 3, we look at the important area of housing in an European context. The nature of the housing market in the UK has some particular features and this is of interest given the increasing economic integration in Europe and the introduction of a common monetary policy. In this section, we will also look at the alternative systems of mortgage finance in EU countries and consider some of the particular risks that individuals face from the move to the euro.

6.1 The demand for financial assets

Introduction

We are concerned in this chapter with returns to two types of assets: financial assets such as bank deposits and shares, and housing assets in the form of ownership of residential property.

In the case of a financial asset, the return comes in the form of a flow of money paid to the owner. The return may come in the form of regular payments such as interest paid on a bank deposit. For some assets the return may also come in the form of a capital appreciation, equities being an obvious example. The rate of return on an asset can therefore be expressed simply as the flow of monetary payments in a particular time period, plus the capital appreciation, divided by the purchase price of the asset. A share costing £10 that paid a dividend of 75 pence per annum would give a rate of return of 7.5%, if the share value rose by £1 over the year then the return would be 17.5% and so on.[1]

The return in the case of housing is the flow of consumption services that householders get from owning their home. This may seem like a rather strange idea, but suppose an owner was to let his or her property, then there would be a series of rental payments for the services it provides. We can think of owner-occupiers as effectively renting the property to themselves. Housing is in part a financial investment, as there may be a monetary return in the form of an increase in the price of the property, as well as being a consumption good. Overall, the return on housing will come from the sum of the consumption services it provides, together with the change in its capital value.

If assets differed only in terms of their monetary return, then in equilibrium the rate of return on all assets will be the same. If they were not, individuals would want to trade those with a lower return for those whose return was higher, bidding up the price of the latter and so reducing the return. In practice, the returns on assets will differ for a number of reasons, as we shall see. One reason is that the degree of risk attached to a particular asset varies: National Savings Accounts have very little risk attached to them and correspondingly earn a relatively low return. Other investments such as 'Penny-Shares' are much more risky, but offer the prospect of a much higher return. A house is generally less liquid than financial wealth in the form of, say, a bank deposit and as a result this may reduce the return to owning property. Government policy toward the taxation of different types of asset may also partly explain the different returns paid. In the rest of this section, we will be concerned with an analysis of assets with different levels of risk and return.

Risk and return of an asset

We will start with a numerical example of what we mean by risk and return. Assume that there are four possible states of the world, which generate four outcomes in terms of the monetary returns on three different assets. These assets we will refer to here as A, B and C.

---

1 We are concerned here with real returns.

State of the world	Probability	Return on asset A	Return on asset B	Return on asset C
1	0.25	3%	4%	12%
2	0.25	3%	6%	11%
3	0.25	3%	8%	3%
4	0.25	3%	10%	2%
Expected return		3%	7%	7%
Risk (standard deviation)		0	2.24	4.53

Table 6.1 Risk and return on assets: an illustration

The expected return on the asset is the sum of each possible return multiplied by the probability of obtaining that particular return. For example, in the case of asset B the expected return is

$$E(R_B) = (0.25 * 4\%) + (0.25 * 6\%) + (0.25 * 8\%) + (0.25 * 10\%) = 7\%.$$

This does not necessarily have to be equal to one of the actual returns, although it can be as in the case of asset A for instance.[2] The riskiness of an asset is concerned with the variation around its expected return and will be measured here by the standard deviation of the asset's return. This is one particular statistical measure of variation. In the case of asset B again we have

$$SD_B = (((4-7)^2 * 0.25) + ((6-7)^2 * 0.25) + ((8-7)^2 * 0.25) + ((10-7)^2 * 0.25))^{0.5}$$
$$= 2.236^3$$

The standard deviation measure of risk for the other two assets is shown in the bottom row of Table 6.1. Asset A is an example of a risk-free asset as the return in each of the states of the world is the same. There is no situation in which the asset owner gets a return that is anything other than 3%. The two other assets have the same expected return, but asset C has a greater spread of returns around the expected value of 7%.[4] Consequently, the standard deviation of its returns is greater than that for asset B.

Representing preferences

In the previous chapter, we characterised individual preferences towards risk using the state preference model. We distinguished between preferences that were risk-averse, those that were

2 It is not necessary that all possible returns are the same for this to be so.

3 In words take the difference between each possible outcome and its expected value, and square it, weight each term by its probability, add them and finally take the square root of the resulting sum.

4 The two assets also have a different pattern of returns, the importance of which we will come to.

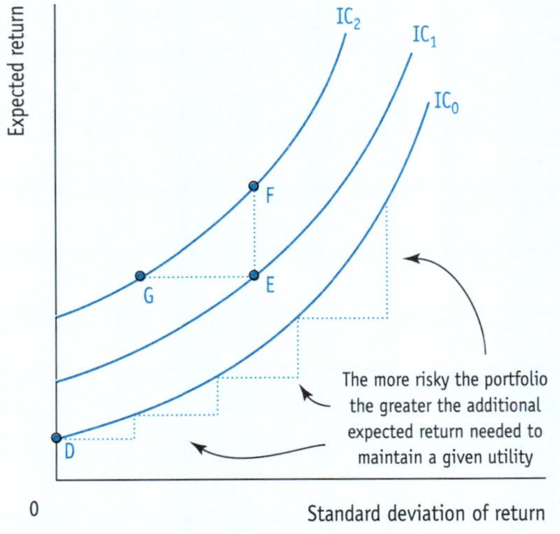

Figure 6.1 **An indifference map for an individual with risk-averse preferences**

risk-neutral and those that were risk-loving. Preferences were characterised in terms of the willingness to accept a fair bet. As a reminder, this is a bet in which an individual is presented with a certain sum for sure or a sum with the same expected value. For example, the offer of a 50–50 chance of winning and losing £50 is a fair bet. A risk-averse person is someone who declines it or alternatively has to be paid to take it. Risk is therefore a 'bad' for individuals who are risk-averse, and given the prevalence of insurance companies it is often taken that most people hold risk-averse preferences, particularly in relation to large and important risks.

We can again use indifference curve analysis to represent the preferences of an individual, this time over combinations of risk and return that yield a given utility. In Figure 6.1, we have an indifference map for the risk-averse individual. Indifference curves in this figure slope up because the individual is ranking different combinations of a good (the expected monetary return of an asset) and a bad (the risk associated with it). As drawn, the greater the level of risk associated with an asset, the greater the additional expected return needs to be to persuade the individual with risk-averse preferences to hold it. This is shown in Figure 6.1 by the increasing height of the steps as we move up and along IC_0.

Figure 6.1 shows three indifference curves, those that intersect the vertical axis further away from the origin represent a higher level of utility. This follows from the fact that there is a higher level of expected return for the (zero) level of risk associated with each point. That a higher indifference curve represents a higher utility can also be seen by comparing points F and G on IC_2 with point E on IC_1. By comparison with point E, point F represents a higher expected return for a given level of risk and point G a lower level of risk for a given expected return.

The budget line

In Figure 6.2, we have drawn the market opportunities available to the individual in terms of the different combinations of a risky and risk-free asset that he or she could hold. Here, the budget line gives the 'price' of risk expressed in terms of the additional expected return. Suppose that an individual has an endowment point at D, where he or she receives a risk-free rate of return of ER_0. In order to obtain a higher expected return the individual has to accept a certain amount of risk. In moving from point D to F, the additional expected return is EF when moving along B_0; the amount of risk is measured by the distance DE.

The slope of the budget line is therefore the difference between the expected return on the risky asset and that from the return on the risk-free asset, divided by the standard deviation of the risky asset. A steeper slope indicates a greater additional expected return for any given level of additional risk, a flatter slope the opposite. For example, with the budget line B_1 in Figure 6.2 the additional expected return is given by the distance EG, given the same level of (additional) risk as before.

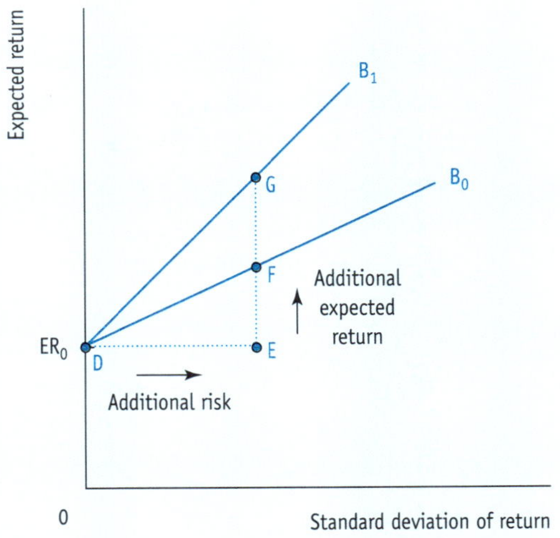

Figure 6.2 The budget line

The equilibrium

Figure 6.3A shows an equilibrium outcome for an individual with risk-averse preferences: a tangency solution between the indifference curve IC_0 and the budget line B_0, with equilibrium point E_0. At this point, the individual chooses a combination of risk and return that maximises utility given the budget constraint faced. This type of equilibrium outcome is analytically similar to the equilibrium analysis in other applications. At point E_0, the slope of the indifference curve is equal to that of the budget constraint. The individual's marginal rate of substitution between return and risk is equal to the market price of risk.

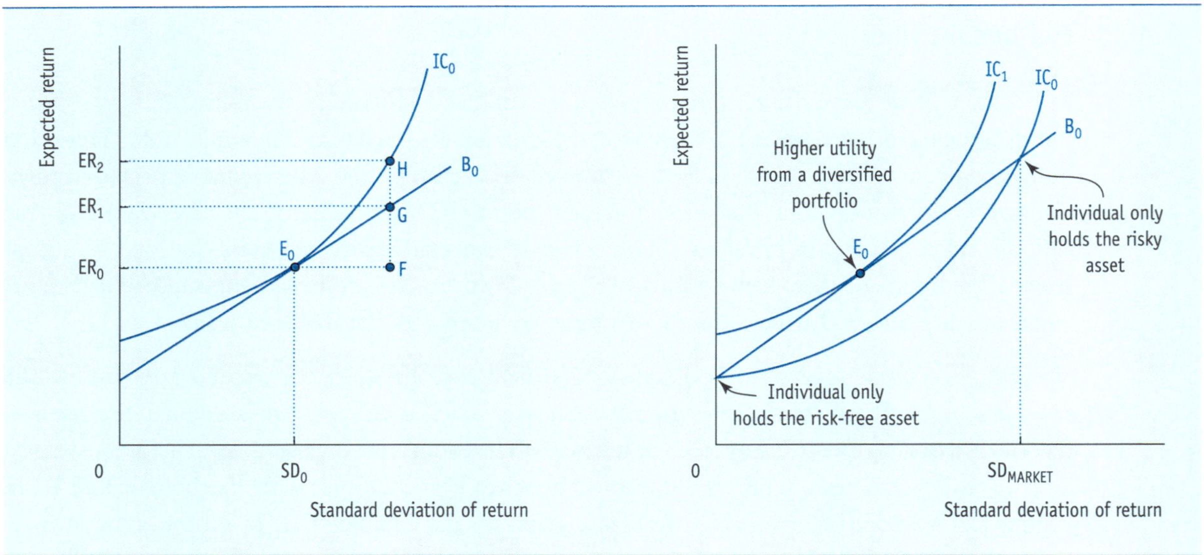

Figure 6.3A An equilibrium outcome for an individual with risk-averse preferences

Figure 6.3B A diversified portfolio

There are combinations of asset-holdings that have a higher expected return, but the individual would prefer not to choose them. For example, in Figure 6.3A, to accept the additional risk as measured by the distance E_0F, the individual would require an expected return of ER_2 associated with point H on the indifference curve. Given the market price of risk, the individual would only be able to obtain the expected return ER_1 and so prefers point E_0 to H along the indifference curve IC_0.

In the equilibrium shown in Figure 6.3A, the individual is holding a combination of both the risk-free and the risky asset. Suppose that the individual held some combination of assets A and B given in Table 6.1. The expected return from the combination of asset holdings, or the portfolio, can be expressed as

$$E(R) = kE(R_A) + (1 - k)E(R_B)$$

where k is the percentage of the portfolio in the risk-free asset, and (1 – k) is that given to the risky asset. The expected return from holding some combination of both assets is simply a weighted average of the expected return of the individual assets. In this example, the return will vary between 3% and 7% just depending on what the proportion held in each asset happens to be as Table 6.2A shows. In this particular example the overall risk is a straight proportion of the risk associated with asset B, given that the other asset is risk-free.

Figure 6.3B shows the benefit of a diversified portfolio; if the individual held only or other asset then it would put him or her on IC_0. However, by varying the proportions that are

k	0	0.25	0.75	1
Expected return	3%	4%	6%	7%
Risk (standard deviation)	0	0.56	1.68	2.24

Table 6.2 Expected return from a portfolio

invested in the two assets, the individual can move onto a higher indifference curve than that associated with either of the two assets if invested in alone. This is marked as E_0 in the figure.

Risk and diversification

The analysis above has had the obvious simplification that there has only been one risky asset. When there are several risky assets the individual's utility will be dependent on the risk associated with all the assets he or she holds. In order to determine the risk overall we need to take account of the way the returns of different assets interact. To continue with the example, suppose we now include asset C. This asset is more risky than B, as shown by the standard deviations of both assets in Table 6.1. A question that arises is whether the individual should hold one asset or the other or a combination of both.

When considered together, the standard deviation of an asset's return is no longer an appropriate measure of risk. To see why, suppose that in the example an individual held equal proportions of the two assets B and C. The expected return in each state of the world is in this case the average of the returns for the two assets as shown in Table 6.3.

State of the World	1	2	3	4	
Expected return	8%	8.5%	5.5%	6%	Standard deviation = 1.27

Table 6.3 Risk and portfolio diversification

The standard deviation of the expected return from this holding is less than either of the standard deviations from holding assets B or C alone. What this example shows is that if asset returns move in opposite directions in different states of the world then risk can be reduced. In the extreme case, if the returns on B and C had been the mirror images of each other then the risk would have been eliminated altogether.

We can distinguish between diversifiable and non-diversifiable risk. In general, by holding many different assets it is possible to eliminate 'diversifiable risk'; the reduction in risk from holding two assets in the above example illustrates this. Non-diversifiable risk cannot be eliminated by holding a broad portfolio of assets (we did not eliminate risk in the example).

This kind of risk arises because the profitability of firms is generally dependent on the overall state of the economy.

What we need is a way of measuring the risk of one particular asset in relation to the risk in all other assets, i.e. in relation to the market risk. One way of doing this is shown in Figure 6.4, where on the vertical axis we measure the (expected) return to a particular asset, and on the horizontal axis we have the (expected) market return. A line such as OB, which comes out of the origin at a 45 degree angle, represents the case where the asset's expected return moves in exactly the same way as does the market as a whole. A 1% increase in expected market returns from 4% to 5% would be associated with the same expected increase in the return for this particular asset.

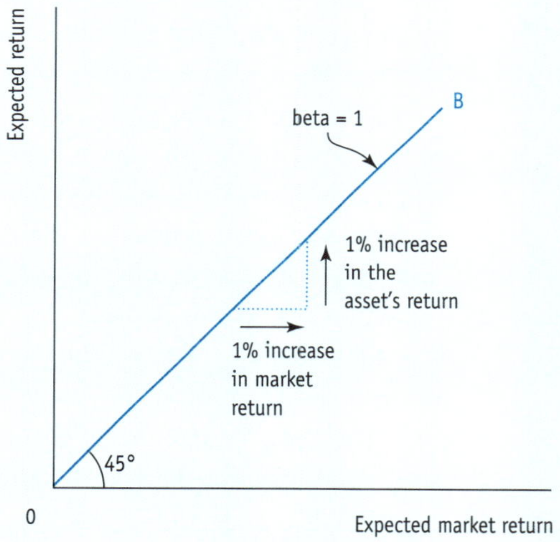

Figure 6.4 **The beta of an asset**

The slope of this line is known as the beta of an asset, which is simply the additional expected return to a particular asset relative to the market as a whole. A steeper slope would mean a higher beta value. A beta value of 1.5, for example, would mean that if market returns rose by 10% the return on the asset would rise by 15%.

Capital asset pricing model (CAPM)

At the beginning of this section, we said that if assets only differed in terms of their monetary return, in equilibrium the return on different assets would then be equal. Plainly, in a world where assets differ in terms of their riskiness this conclusion needs to be modified. The equilibrium condition now, according to the capital asset pricing model (CAPM), is that all assets should have the same rate of return after allowing for an adjustment for their differing risk levels. In other words the risk-adjusted rates of return should be the same.

This can be expressed as

$$R_i = R_{RF} + \beta(R_M - R_{RF})$$

Where R_i is the return on one particular asset, β is the beta of the asset, R_M is the expected return on the stock market and R_{RF} is the expected return on the risk-free asset.

In words, the return on the asset is equal to the return on a risk-free asset, plus the risk adjustment factor. The risk adjustment is equal to the beta of an asset multiplied by the difference in the return on the asset and that on a risk-free asset. For example, if the expected return on an asset was 10% and the return on the risk-free asset was 6%, then the risk premium (the adjustment) is 4%. In the particular case of an asset with a beta value of 1, the risk adjustment is simply equal to the difference between the market return and that on a risk-free asset. A simple rearrangement of the above gives

$$R_i - R_{RF} = \beta(R_M - R_{RF})$$

The left-hand side gives the risk premium on a particular asset — the difference between its expected return and the return on the risk-free asset. The right-hand side gives the risk premium on the market, β as discussed above measures the asset's non-diversifiable risk. The larger the value of beta, the greater the risk premium because the non-diversifiable risk of the asset is greater.

Questions

Q1 Given the following range of returns for three financial assets calculate their respective expected values and the associated degree of risk as measured by the standard deviation.

Probability	Asset D	Asset E	Asset F
0.25	10	25	0
0.25	10	10	0
0.25	10	5	0
0.25	10	0	40

(I) Is the standard deviation a good measure of riskiness? What is the expected return from holding a portfolio of assets D and E in 50–50 proportions? How does it vary if the proportions are 25–75 or 75–25 between the two assets?

(II) If you were to put equal amounts into assets E and F, what would the riskiness of the portfolio be? How does this compare with the level of riskiness calculated for the two assets separately?

Q2 What shape are the indifference curves of risk-neutral and risk-loving individuals?

6.2 Household asset-holdings

In this section, we turn our attention to the pattern of household asset-holding. Chart 6.1 shows the broad picture of asset-holdings by type of asset, where we can see that life insurance and pensions account for around one-half of the financial assets held by the personal sector.[6] This broad pattern raises a number of issues about the nature of individual saving decisions, although here we will be primarily concerned with individual household decision-making, rather than decisions made by a financial intermediary.[7]

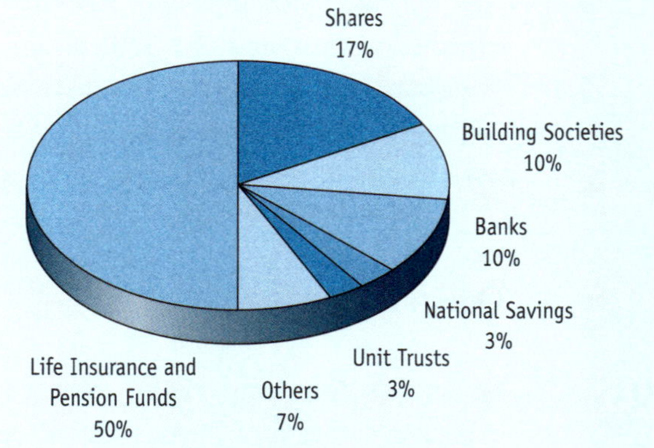

Chart 6.1 **Financial assets of personal sector 1996**
Source: Financial Statistics (1997).

To start by looking at the percentage of households in the UK that hold a portfolio of assets. A breakdown is given in Table 6.4 by different types of household.

What the table shows is the percentage of each household type with both a savings account (for example a bank or building society interest account) and also holdings of stock and

6 The personal sector and the household sector are not identical: the personal sector includes unincorporated businesses.

7 Many individuals have occupational pension schemes where the funds will be invested in a range of financial assets, but this will typically be done by pension fund managers rather than by the individual.

DEMOGRAPHIC GROUPS			%
Head's age	**Marital status**	**Children**	**Portfolio**
20–34	Single	No	11.1
35–49	Single	No	14.7
50–64	Single	No	13.4
20–34	Married	No	14.5
35–49	Married	No	24.0
50–64	Married	No	33.6
20–34	Single	Yes	0.4
35–49	Single	Yes	7.6
20–34	Married	Yes	9.7
35–49	Married	Yes	19.9
50–64	Married	Yes	19.5
Retired	Single		20.9
Retired	Married		35.2
Multiple tax unit			23.4
All			20.6

Table 6.4 Asset ownership by household type in UK 1995–96
Source: Adapted from Banks, Dilnot and Tanner (1997).

shares. This gives us some indication of the numbers who are directly involved with some form of more sophisticated savings activity. Around one household in five overall hold both a savings account and some stocks and shares. This kind of savings pattern tends to increase with the age of the head of the household, which may in part reflect rising saving levels over the life-cycle of the individual.[8] What also stands out from the table is the small percentage of single-parent households with this savings profile. It is also worth noting that the household type with the largest percentage is retired married couples, something that cannot be straightforwardly reconciled with the (simple) life-cycle model.

8 The comments made in Chapter 4 about datasets and their relation to the lifecycle model still apply here. The data in Table 6.4 come from the FES, a cross-section dataset.

Year	1973	1978	1983	1988	1993
Financial assets	50%	55%	67%	73%	66%
— Share-holdings	9%	8%	8%	22%	22%
— Housing assets	49%	52%	59%	65%	67%

Table 6.5 **Financial and housing wealth in UK households 1973–93**
Source: Banks and Tanner (1996).

The data from one particular year may of course be rather sensitive to the macroeconomic situation in that year. Table 6.5 shows the long-term trend of a growing number of households having at least some financial and housing wealth.[9]

The table also shows the growth in the number of share-owning households following the programme of privatisation, which started in the 1980s. What is equally clear from looking at the table is how important the decision taken by households concerning their housing wealth is in the UK.

Taxation

One subject that receives prominence in policy-making is the question of whether the level of household saving is too low and what the role of government might be in promoting individual saving. It is a question that forms a part of wider debate about the level of investment in the UK.[10] Here, we will confine our attention to the tax treatment of household savings.

Looked at broadly, governments can tax saving at three main points: on the initial sum saved, on the interest income that is earned and at the point that income is withdrawn. For example, suppose that an individual earns £5,000 in a year and is in a position to save all of it in a deposit account. In one year's time we assume the sum will be withdrawn. If the rate of interest is 6% and the rate of inflation is 0%, the individual will earn £300 in interest, giving the individual an asset worth £5,300.

Suppose now there is a single rate of tax of 20% payable on all income. If tax is levied on the original earnings of the individual then he or she will be left with £4,240 in one year's time after tax; if it is levied on the sum when it is withdrawn from the savings account the amount

9 It also raises the question as to why the figure for financial wealth in 1993 is below that for 1988. A part of the explanation is likely to be that the two years corresponded to two different points in the macroeconomic cycle, 1988 was a year of the 'Lawson Boom', in 1993 the economy was in recession. It should also be remembered that survey data would be subject to some sampling fluctuation between years.

10 It is something we will discuss in Chapter 15 as well.

will be the same. Plainly, if the individual is taxed on both the earnings from which the saving is made and the interest income, then he or she will be left with a smaller sum; in this example it is £4,192.

The tax treatment of savings in the UK varies between assets. Interest-bearing savings accounts are more heavily taxed than some other forms of saving because individuals are taxed on both the interest-income as well as the income from which savings are made. Other assets such as pensions and housing have been more favourably treated. In principle, the tax treatment of savings should not distort individual decision-making about the appropriate level of savings, although there are some tricky issues involved as the questions below ask you to examine.

Questions

Q3 An individual can put money into a risky asset or alternatively into one that is risk-free. The returns in two possible states of the world are shown in the table below. There is a 50–50 chance of a boom which is shown as state of the world 1 and a slump, state 0

	Asset X		Asset Y	
	State of the world 0	State of the world 1	State of the world 0	State of the world 1
No tax	500	1,500	1,000	1,000
25% tax	375	1,125	750	750

(I) What is the standard deviation of the return to asset X before and after the tax of 25% is introduced?

(II) Would the imposition of the tax make those with risk-averse preferences more likely to hold asset X?

Q4 An individual has earnings of £100 all of which will be to saved for the period of one year, after which it will be spent.

(I) If the rate of interest is 5% in a world without inflation and the tax rate is 25% does it matter whether the government taxes income at source (i.e. when earned) or when it is withdrawn?

(II) Suppose that the rate of inflation is 3% does the point of taxation above make any difference to the return paid to the individual?

(III) If the government taxed interest income from savings as well what difference does it make by comparison with (I) and (II)?

6.3 Housing in UK and Europe

The model of decision-making we looked at in Section 1 was concerned with risky assets, by which we meant assets for which there was a known range of possible returns, together with associated probabilities of each outcome happening. We saw in Table 6.5 that housing wealth is one major component of the asset holdings of individuals, with around two-thirds of the population in the UK now being in some form of owner-occupation. The decisions made by individuals whether or not to move into home ownership, and more particularly the timing of the decision is a key factor in the distribution of household wealth-holding generally; a point we first made at the end of Chapter 2.

We will start this section looking at the pattern of owner-occupation and the volatility of property prices in the EU. Chart 6.2 shows the tenure pattern of the EU member states in 1995. It is clear that there is no straightforward linkage between income levels and the percentage of the population who own their home. Broadly tenure patterns throughout Europe are influenced by the policy of governments towards the cost of housing, the type of housing and the general macroeconomic environment.

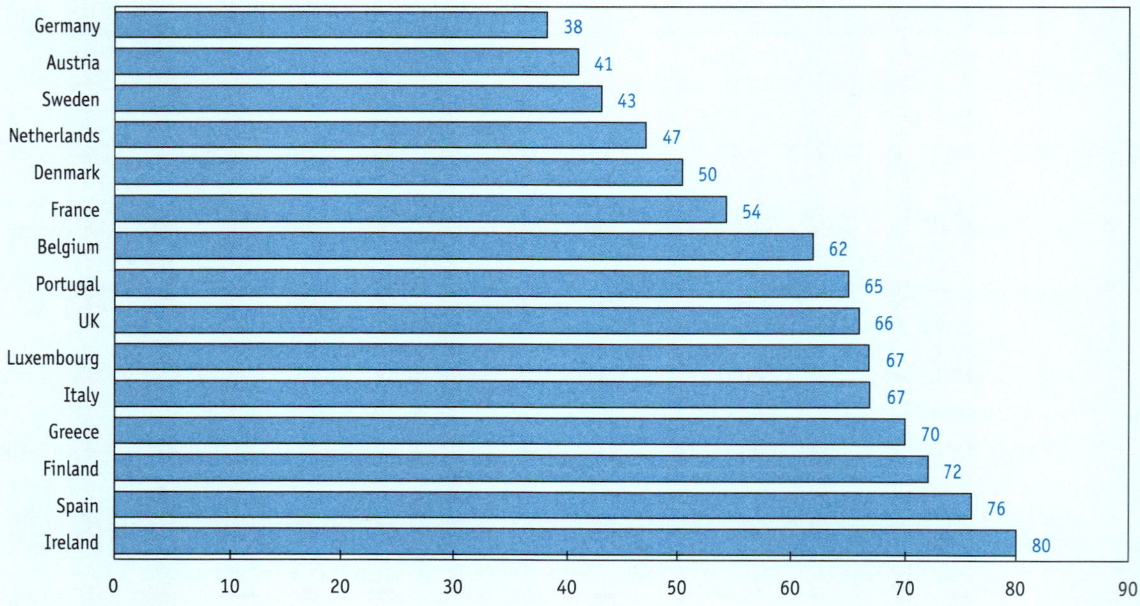

Chart 6.2 Owner-occupation rates in Europe 1995

Source: Maclennan and Stephens (1997).

Government policies in Europe have involved a number of detailed tax reliefs and subsidies to owner-occupation and the rented sector. The type of housing stock has been a factor in some countries in that flats can be more difficult than houses to arrange legal title to owner-occupation. The rate of inflation is also important in terms of its effects on the outstanding debt-holding of households, a point that is taken up below.

The growth of owner-occupation in the UK has been on a long view a major influence in widening the ownership of wealth. At the beginning of the twentieth century, the overwhelming majority of the population rented a property from a landlord. By the middle of the twentieth century, the numbers had risen to the point where there were around 4.3 million owner-occupiers, around 30% of the total housing stock. As Chart 6.2 shows, by 1995 this figure had risen to some 66%; around sixteen million owner-occupiers in a housing stock of approximately twenty-four million dwellings.

A characteristic of the housing market in some EU countries is a high level of price volatility; in the UK, Spain and some of the Scandanavian countries, for example. Chart 6.3 shows the real and nominal price movements in average house prices in the UK over the period 1983–97. Real price rises have been less than nominal increases due to periods of inflation, although when there are nominal price falls the real price falls are greater. The impact of this can be brought out with a particular example. Table 6.6 gives the average house price bought with a Halifax mortgage in 1983, 1989 and 1997, the second column adjusts the price data to allow for inflation.

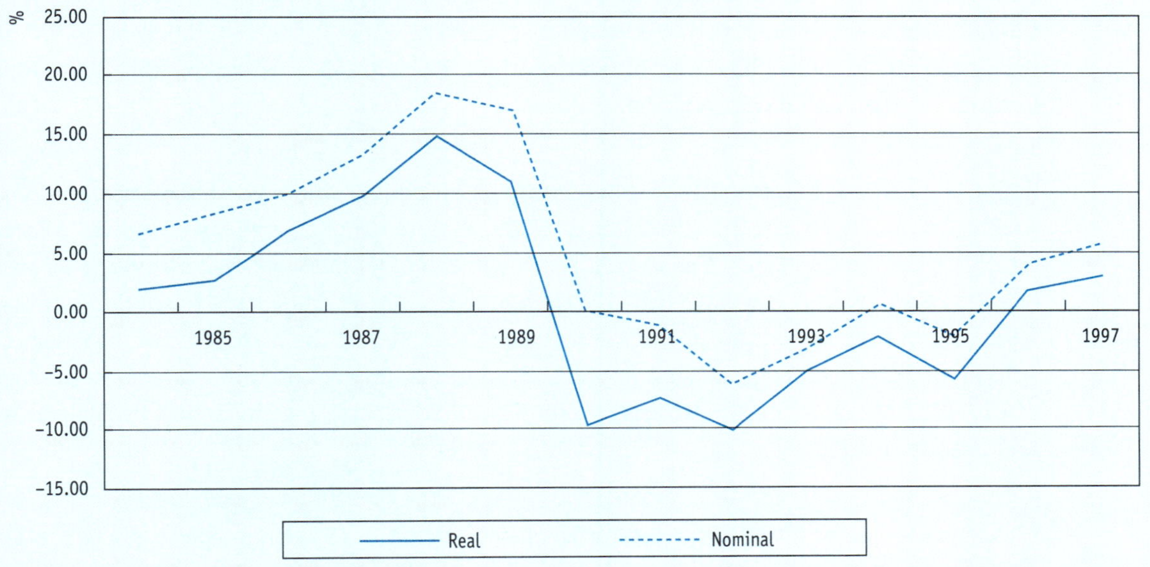

Chart 6.3 **% change in UK house prices 1984–97**
Source: The Halifax.

Year	Price	Constant 1997 prices
1983	£30,898	£57,248
1989	£68,946	£94,183
1997	£68,504	£68,504

Table 6.6 **Average UK house prices 1983–97**
Source: The Halifax.

On the relatively short time-span (in housing terms) covered by Table 6.6, a large gain could have been made by buying in 1983 and selling in 1989, and similarly a large loss through buying in 1989 and selling in 1997. In broad terms, looking at Chart 6.3 suggests the numbers in the table take us through one boom-bust cycle. The table refers to average house prices, the variation in housing wealth for those who bought more expensive properties could easily be much greater than in the example. As it could be for those who bought in earlier decades. In short, the emphasis on housing wealth has to some extent equalised wealth-holding looked at in the aggregate. At the level of the individual, the impact has been rather arbitrary depending as much on the timing of entry into the market and also what part of the UK the person happened to live in.

It should be appreciated that the percentage change in the property price above relates to the capital value, not the equity of the owner. The change in the owner's equity is potentially much greater. For example, suppose an individual bought a house in 1983 at a price of say £30,000 and saw the price rise to £50,000 in 1989. The capital gain is £20,000 or 66.6% over the period. If the house has been bought outright, i.e. without a mortgage, this is the return in terms of the capital appreciation.

Suppose, however, the property was bought by an individual who made a deposit of 50%, and took out a mortgage for the remaining £15,000, then the capital appreciation gives a rate of return that is much greater. The overall return for the individual will therefore depend on the balance of equity and mortgage debt. Those who are entering the market for the first time will typically have the highest proportion of mortgage to equity — the highest Loan-to-Value ratio — a figure 90% not being unusual in the UK. In our example, an individual with a mortgage of £27,000 buying a £30,000 property would have had a capital appreciation of £20,000 with their equity of £3,000.[11]

This process can be put into reverse for those who buy a time when property prices are high. Those individuals who bought in 1989 with say a 10% deposit on their property costing

11 This ignores any additional equity accumulated (or debt repaid) over the period.

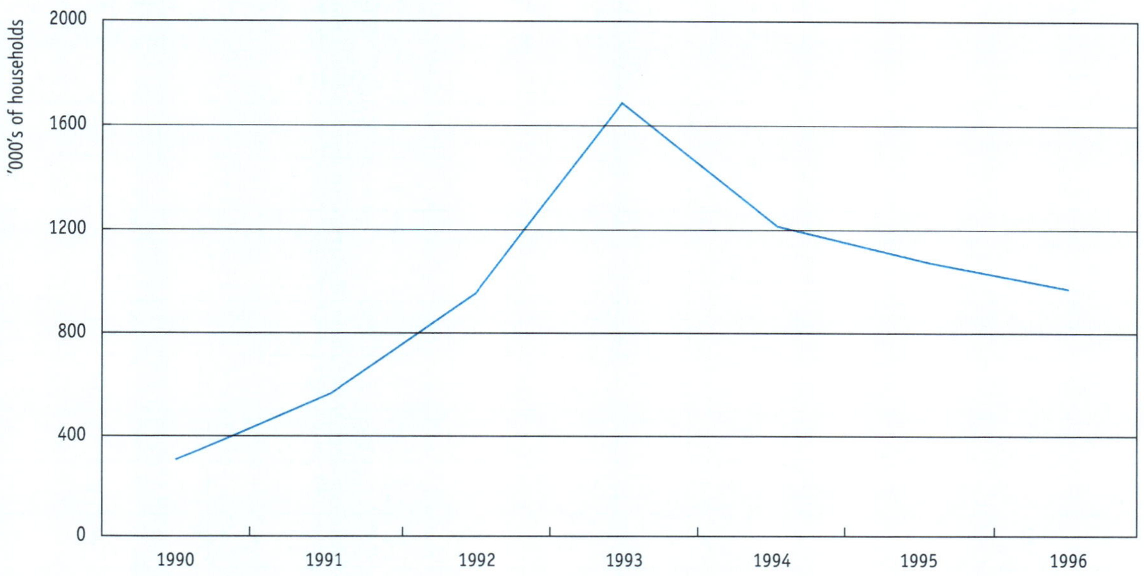

Chart 6.4 **Numbers of households with negative equity**
Source: Thomas (1996).

£50,000 would find that that their losses were magnified. For example, if the property value had dropped to £35,000 by 1997, there would be a capital loss of £15,000 associated with the equity of £5,000.

The drop in capital values of residential property gave rise in the 1990s in the UK to the phenomenon of negative equity. This refers to the situation where a household has a mortgage larger than the market value of their property. Chart 6.4 gives some indication of the scale of this phenomenon in terms of the number of households unfortunate to have had such an experience. At one point in the cycle this phenomenon affected about one mortgagor in six.

Mortgage finance

In addition to the uncertainty over property values, the costs of repaying mortgage debt are a second major area of uncertainty. In the UK, most loan finance for property purchase is of a variable rate type, although again European practice varies as is shown in Table 6.7.

The table indicates the variety of mortgage finance systems that operate in Europe. The importance of the loan-to-value ratio is evident from the discussion above, particularly for countries which may experience cyclical fluctuations. What also stands out is the predominance of fixed rate over variable rate finance. Fixed rate finance is, as its name suggests debt finance with an interest rate that does not change over the period of the loan. Variable

Country	Fixed (F) or variable (V) mortgages	Repayment period	Loan-to-value ratio (max)	Repayment (R) or endowment (E)
Belgium	F			R
Denmark	F	20–30	80	R
Germany	F, with V from savings banks	25–30, depends on type of lender.	70–80	R
Spain	V	15	80	R
France	F	20	80–90	R
Greece	F	6–15	50–75	R
Ireland	V, F short-term	20–30	80	R
Italy		30		R
Luxembourg				R
Netherlands	F		75	Both
Portugal				R
United Kingdom	V, F short-term	25	90–95	Both
Austria	Mixed	25	70–80	R
Finland	V	10–15	70	R
Sweden	Mixed	30	85	R

Table 6.7 **Mortgage systems in Europe**
Source: Maclennan and Stephens (1997).

rate mortgage finance simply means that the interest payments on a mortgage will rise and fall when interest rates rise and fall generally in the economy, so that the interest rate charged will not remain the same as the rate charged at the time the loan is taken out.

To illustrate what a difference this can make, Table 6.8 shows the average real rate of interest paid for those taking out a mortgage in 1983, 1986, 1989 and 1992 until 1996.

The average real mortgage rate over the period 1983–96 was 6.3%. Table 6.8 shows that it has fallen slightly for those who started a mortgage repayment in later years. The average rate of inflation has however dropped by around two percentage points for those who started their mortgage repayments in 1992 by comparison with those in the previous years.

Starting year	Average rate	Inflation rate
1983	6.3	4.6
1986	6.1	4.5
1989	5.7	4.6
1992	5.5	2.7

Table 6.8 **Real rates of interest on mortgages in the UK**
Source: Financial Statistics (various years).

These may appear to be relatively small differences, although the relationship between the real rate of interest and the inflation rate has a particular feature in the context of mortgage finance, known as 'the tilt'. We will explain what this means with an example, but first a reminder that the real rate of interest is the nominal rate divided by the inflation rate. When the figures are relatively small the difference may be taken as a satisfactory approximation. Hence a nominal rate of 10% and an inflation rate of 6% is (approximately) equal to a nominal rate of 7% and an inflation rate of 3%. They give the same real rate of interest of 4%, as would a nominal rate of interest of 4% in a world without inflation.

Suppose an individual borrows £30,000 to buy a property. The interest repayment in the first year assuming a real rate of 4% can vary greatly depending on what the inflation rate is. The differences are illustrated in Table 6.9.

A given real rate of interest can be associated with a large variation in mortgage interest payments depending on just what the rate of inflation is. Clearly, if the rate of inflation were to remain at 6% over the lifetime of a mortgage, typically a period of 25 years in the UK, the real value of the £3,000 interest paid will decline. If there was no inflation the interest payments would not change in real terms. Where the rate of inflation can be a big influence on the real cost of the interest paid on a mortgage loan is if there are relatively short periods of inflation that are not anticipated. In this situation, mortgage repayments rise for the period in which inflation rises. In sum, the real rate of interest and the inflation rate are both factors which will affect the cost of meeting the interest payments of a mortgage.

Mortgage	Nominal rate of interest	Rate of inflation	Real rate of interest	Interest payment
£30,000	10%	6%	4%	£3,000
£30,000	7%	3%	4%	£2,100
£30,000	4%	0%	4%	£1,200

Table 6.9 **Inflation and mortgage payments**

Concluding comment

In terms of household decision-making, we have seen the importance of housing wealth. The asset value of residential property will clearly change as the flow of consumption services changes over a period of time. If there are more people working from home, or if there is an increase in the amount of home entertainment, then property values should rise on account of such changes. However, the experience of the UK housing market in the past has been dominated by short-term instability and this, in turn, has very pronounced effects on the overall distribution of wealth-holdings between individuals. It also makes the transition to a common European monetary policy more problematic in the UK where most mortgage finance is variable rate.

Summary

1 An asset provides a flow of services to its owner. This can take the form of a monetary payment or it can come in the form of housing services in the case of housing assets. Different assets have different monetary returns depending on the level of risk (or variability) of their returns.

2 The indifference curve for the individual shows different levels of risk and expected return that yield a given level of utility. For risk-averse individuals, the curve will slope up as an additional (expected) return is needed to reward the individual for assuming additional levels of risk. The budget line shows the price of risk, which in the case of two assets (one risky, one risk-free) is the difference between their expected returns divided by the standard deviation of the portfolio.

3 As with the analysis of household choice in earlier chapters, the optimum outcome depends on the shape of the individual's indifference map. A risk-averse individual may be able to obtain a higher level of utility by holding a diversified portfolio of asset holdings.

4 Around one household in five hold both a savings account and stocks and shares in some form. The pattern varies with the type of household.

5 In the UK, housing wealth is important. The capital values of property have been subject to large fluctuations and the rate of return on housing assets at the level of the individual has been a matter of luck and judgement.

6 Most owner-occupiers have a mortgage. The real level of repayments for individuals with the same size of mortgage will again vary over time due to the effects of inflation.

End of chapter questions

Q5 You are offered the alternatives of £1 or a 1 in 14 million chance of winning £14mn which would you accept? If you were offered £100 or a 1 in 14 million chance of winning £1,400mn which would you take? What does this say about your attitude to risk?

Q6 In the two asset model what happens to the individual's budget constraint if the return on the risk-free asset goes up, but that on the risky asset does not? What happens if the return on the risky asset goes up, but that on the risk-free asset does not?

Q7 If the rate of return on a risk-free asset is 4% and the market rate of return is 6% what is an assets risk-premium if its beta value is 1, 1.5 and 2.3?

Q8 'If the government introduces a tax-free savings account for those on low incomes, those on low incomes won't be able to save but those with high-incomes will have been given a tax break.' Does this seem likely? Is it the job of governments to encourage indivduals to save? If so, why?

Q9 Suppose that the real rate of interest on a mortgage happens to be 5%. If inflation rises to 5% and the nominal mortgage rate rises to 10%, would the mortgage interest payments, rise, fall or remain unchanged? Explain.

References and suggested further reading

The principles covered in the first section are discussed a more technical way in Varian and Nicholson. The Banks and Tanner article, though largely descriptive, does provide a fund of information on household wealth-holdings. Banks, Dilnot and Tanner provides updated background to the nature of household savings and discusses the issue of government policy toward individual saving levels.

Banks, J. and Tanner, S. (1996), '*Savings and wealth in the UK: evidence from microdata*', Institute for Fiscal Studies.

Banks, J., Dilnot, A. and Tanner, S. (1997), '*Taxing household saving: What role for the new individual saving account?*', Commentary **66**, Institute for Fiscal Studies.

Maclennan, D. and Stephens, M. (1997), 'EMU and the UK Housing and Mortgage Markets', Council of Mortgage Lenders.

Nicholson, W. (1995), *Microeconomic Theory, Basic Principles and Extensions*, 6th edition, The Dryden Press.

Office for National Statistics (various issues). *Financial Statistics.*

The Halifax (various issues), The House Price Index.

Thomas, R. (1996), *Negative Equity: Outlook and Effects*, Council of Mortgage Lenders.

Varian, H.R. (1996), *Intermediate Microeconomics, A Modern Approach*, 4th edition, W.W. Norton & Co.

The Firm and Market Structures

7 The Neo-Classical Theory of the Firm

Key ideas and material

The firm, production functions, isoquant maps, average and marginal cost curves, comparative statics of factor demand

Introduction

Neo-classical analysis applied to the theory of the firm is approached in a similar way to the theory of consumer choice. The analysis is centred on a representative firm, and is very much orientated towards the external environment in which it operates. There is, of course, in practice, a range of organisations covered by 'the firm', which vary hugely in terms of size and the nature of their activity. The largest five UK firms measured by capital employed are shown in Table 7.1, four of which happen to be finance or oil companies.

At the other end of the spectrum, in terms of size, there are thousands of small (often retail) firms, some with less than a millionth of the capital of the largest five. In broad terms, the analysis covers organisations of a much greater range of size and form than was encountered with household units.

Rank	Company	Capital employed
1	HSBC Holdings	£26.9bn
2	Shell Transport and Trading	£21.0bn
3	British Petroleum	£20.6bn
4	Abbey National	£20.1bn
5	British Telecommunications	£17.5bn

Table 7.1 The UK's largest companies 1997
Source: Times 1000 (1998).

In order not to be overwhelmed by the scope of the subject matter, we will start in Section 1 with some fundamental ideas as to why firms exist at all. We will also introduce there the idea of a profit-maximising firm. Section 2 begins the analysis of the neo-classical theory, starting with the way that economists represent the state of technology that a firm faces. This section also analyses the firm's choice of production technique and paves the way for the development of the cost structures that a firm faces which is discussed in Section 3. In this chapter, we will be mainly concerned with developing analytical tools that will be used later on.

7.1 The firm

We will start with the question of why firms exist at all. One rationale was put forward by Coase (1937) who argued that firms exist to minimise transactions costs. This view sees the market-place, and the organisation of individuals into firms, as alternative means of producing goods and services. The advantage that a firm has as an organisation will, therefore, depend on its costs of production relative to those of the activity being left to the open market.

This may seem rather abstract, but the basic point is not difficult to grasp. For example, suppose we take a professional football club as one particular type of firm, which is in the business of producing one particular form of entertainment. Each player and the manager will typically have a contract of employment for a specified period of time with the club. If production of this type of entertainment was left to the open market, each player would need to know who his fellow professionals were, what position they played in, what their salary expectations were and so on. Each player would need to negotiate, on an individual basis, contracts to play with the other team members in a given place, for a specified period of time. The contracts would need to cover a number of important details including, for example, what the arrangements would be if he, or a team-mate was injured, or called up to play in an international.

The contracts drawn up would necessarily be incomplete. No one can foresee with certainty all the possible variations in a player's form and fortune, the impact of changing television coverage, the effects of possible league re-structuring that may take place and many other details. It would be prohibitively expensive to attempt to draw up contracts that covered all contingencies. If production was left to the open-market place, when some unforeseen event occurs those involved would have to renegotiate the contracts they had entered into, which would be expensive, time-consuming and may lead to a breakdown in co-operation. To try and organise a professional football club on this basis is an obvious nonsense, but it does point to the kind of transaction costs that a club, and more generally, a firm can reduce relative to the open market.[1]

1 There are other costs that may arise from using the market. For example, transactions on the open market and those within a firm may be treated differently for tax purposes.

There is also a question as to what limits there are to the size of a firm's activities. Theoretically, one firm could carry out all production, if the costs of organising it in this way were less than if left to the open market. The view put forward by Coase was that any one firm would expand until 'the costs of organising an extra transaction within the firm become equal to the costs of carrying out the same transaction by means of an exchange on the open market'.[2] The point at which this happens will vary depending on the costs of organisation in a particular firm and how costs vary as the firm size gets larger. Coase argued that this will depend on, among other things, the way factor prices vary as the size of the firm varies.

A second approach to understanding the rationale for firms stems from the work of Alchian and Demsetz who emphasise the benefits of team working. The original example they gave was of unskilled manual labour lifting boxes onto a truck. If the boxes are heavy, or large or awkward to lift in some other way then the productivity of two individuals working together may be greater than that of two individuals working separately. If it is simply not possible for one individual to lift the boxes, then the productivity of a two-person team will be infinitely greater. The idea of teamworking has obvious applicability in a number of areas, building and construction work for example, and teamworking is essential in some forms of activity. It is not always easy to identify the contribution of each team member, giving some individuals the opportunity to shirk. Again, this creates a rationale for individuals to organise as firms, which provide a monitor, or a manager, of the efforts made by the team members.

Firms with some form of internal hierarchy arise from the cost of market exchanges; particularly where there are interdependencies between the factors of production. The next question is what is it that firms are trying to do? There are a number of alternative views that are put forward. The neo-classical theory of the firm assumes that firms set out to maximise profits in the interests of the shareholders. However, most large companies are not run by the people who own them, and this divorce between ownership and control is the starting point for a number of those who suggest that firms have objectives other than maximising profits. A detailed discussion of this is the subject matter of Chapter 8.

In this chapter, we will be concerned with the profit-maximising model of the firm's decision-making. The analysis treats the firm as a 'black box' organisation that converts inputs into outputs in the interests of meeting its sole objective. We do, however, need to be clear about what we mean by profit. This is defined as

Total Revenue — Total **Economic** Cost

Profit is the difference between the total revenue that a firm receives and its total economic cost. It is the residual income for the owners of a firm after they have paid for the factors of

2 Coase (1937).

production that they hire. This much is straightforward, but there is a difference between accountants and economists in the view taken of the costs of production. For example, a newsagent that receives £115,000 per annum in revenues and has costs of £97,000 in hiring an assistant and buying stock, would make an accounting profit of £18,000. What this ignores is the opportunity cost to the shopkeeper of the time spent working in the shop. If the owner could have been employed working for the firm that does the shop accounts at a salary of £20,000, then the newsagent is making an economic loss.

However, it does not always follow that accounting cost understates the economic cost. For example, suppose a football club agrees to pay a player £200,000 per annum basic salary on a three-year contract. If, following a loss of form, the player was no longer playing in the first team after two years of the contract, what would be the cost to the club of having this player for one more year? The accounting cost is his £200,000 salary. The opportunity cost of having the player on the club's staff depends on the alternatives available. Given the decision to offer the contract was made two years before it may be £0. If the player could be loaned for three months to another club who paid his wages, the opportunity cost of keeping the player on the bench (or in the reserves) is then £50,000. The difference of £150,000 would be a sunk cost to the club. In general, sunk costs are not economic costs because firms are committed to such expenditures, no matter what action they take.

The neo-classical view is that firms set out to maximise profits in the interest of their shareholders. If the future stream of profits of a firm were known, then the present value of the firm would be equal to the present value of the profit stream; no one would pay more to buy a firm than the present worth of its future profits.[3] If a firm issued shares, its stock market value would be equal to the present value of the firm (in a world of certainty). We can therefore equate the objective of maximising profits with that of maximising the stock market value of the firm. The next section starts the neo-classical analysis of the firm in detail.

Questions

Q1 A variety performance for charity attended by VIPs generates £1mn revenue from ticket sales and has production costs of £200,000. There are five major stars on the bill who give their time for free, but all of them could have been on tour elsewhere where they each would have made £250,000. Is the variety performance economically profitable? Are there any other considerations that affect how (economically) desirable such a performance might be?

Q2 Is it desirable that firms set out to maximise profits? In what areas might it be desirable that other objectives be pursued?

---

3 Present values were introduced in Chapter 4.

7.2 The firm's production function

The short-run production function

In simple neo-classical theory, the firm is assumed to know the technology available to it. This known state of technology is represented by a production function; which is a mathematical relationship describing how a given factor input, or combination of factor inputs, produces a certain level of output. A production function is concerned with technical efficiency, that is the minimum combination of inputs to produce a given level of output. For simplicity, we will assume here that the level of output is determined by two homogeneous inputs, capital and labour[4]. We can therefore express such a relationship in general terms by

$$Q = F\ (K,L)$$

where Q is the firm's level of output, K is the level of capital input and L the level of labour input.

A short-run production function is illustrated in Figure 7.1A, where the output of the firm is measured on the vertical axis, and the labour input is measured on the horizontal axis. In the short-run one of the factor inputs, here taken to be capital, is fixed. What the relationship shows, therefore, is the highest level of output possible as the level of labour input varies, given a particular level of capital stock. Points such as A, B and C give three output levels that are produced in a technically efficient manner. The area below the production function is technically feasible, but not technically efficient since for a given combination of factor inputs, output could be higher. Point D is therefore not technically efficient. Conversely, points such as E are simply not technically feasible. Since the production function in Figure 7.1A is drawn for a particular level of capital employed, we could, of course, represent a whole series of such short-run relationships as the level of capital is varied.

The slope of the function reflects the marginal product of labour, which is how much additional output can be produced as the labour input increases. This is shown in Figure 7.1B. It is evident that the marginal product diminishes as the labour input increases; though it remains positive as drawn in the figure. A numerical example of a short-run production function is given in Table 7.2, where we have tabulated a (hypothetical) relationship between the level of output and the labour input.

L measures labour input in terms of the numbers of workers employed per period (weekly/monthly or some other period) and Q measures the corresponding number of units of output.

4 It is also taken that we can count a particular number of units of each factor.

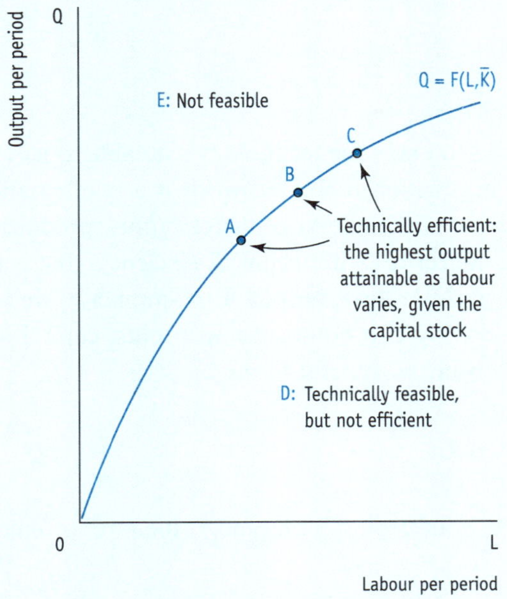

Figure 7.1A The short-run production function

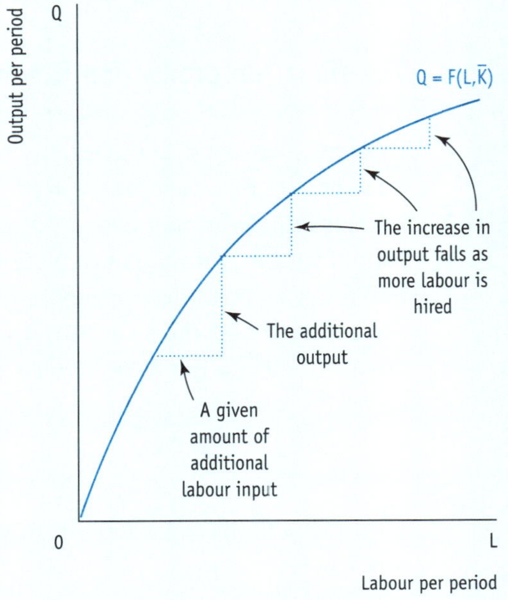

Figure 7.1B The diminishing marginal product of labour

L	Q	APL	MPL
1	6	6	6
2	13	6.5	7
3	21	7	8
4	28	7	7
5	34	6.8	6
6	39	6.5	5
7	42	6	3
8	40	5	–2

Table 7.2 An example of a short-run production function

The third and fourth columns measure the average product of labour and the marginal product of labour, APL and MPL, respectively. The average product is simply the total quantity produced divided by the amount of labour employed. For example, the fourth row in Table 7.2 shows that with four units of labour input the output is 28 units; the APL is therefore seven units of output per unit of labour input.

The marginal product is the change in output as the amount of labour employed is increased. The first individual produces six units giving the marginal product of that worker (assuming that the level of output without the use of labour would be zero). The addition of a second person increases output to thirteen, a rise of seven units, which is the marginal product of the second person. The marginal products of the remaining individuals follow straightforwardly.

The general relationships being illustrated here are (i) for a range of labour employment levels, attainable output rises with the number of employees, but (ii) the rate at which output can rise will fall and (iii) after a certain point, additional labour may actually reduce the total output attainable. Hence, the marginal product of some individuals may be negative. In other words the relationship in Table 7.2 illustrates a diminishing MPL, which is often taken to be a property of a 'typical' short-run production function.

It is also worth noting, before moving on, that there is a general relationship between the average and marginal products of labour. While the marginal product is above the average product, the average product will be rising. If the addition of one more unit of labour adds more to the level of output than the existing workforce has produced on average, then it will pull-up the average product. Conversely, if the marginal product of an extra worker adds less, it will lower the average of the existing workforce and the APL will fall. Where the marginal and average products are equal, the average product will be constant.

The production function in the long-run: isoquants and isoquant maps

In the long-run, the firm is able to vary both factor inputs. We can represent the firm's long-run production function, how much output is produced in relation to different levels of capital and labour, in two dimensions with an isoquant map. An isoquant is defined as the set of technically efficient combinations of capital and labour that produce a given level of output. In Figure 7.2A we have drawn an isoquant labelled Q_0. The vertical axis in the figure measures the amount of capital used per period and the horizontal axis measures the amount of labour. The combination of K_0 and L_0 represents a relatively capital-intensive method of production; K_1 of capital and L_1 of labour would be a more labour-intensive production technique.

An isoquant map shows a number of isoquants associated with differing levels of output; those that are further away from the origin represent higher levels of output. In Figure 7.2B,

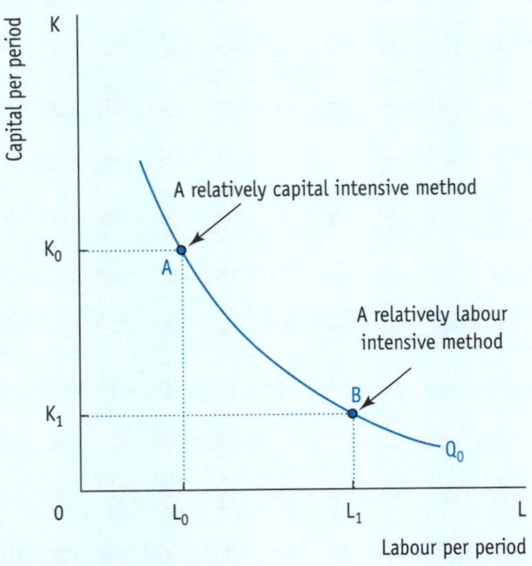

Figure 7.2A **An isoquant**

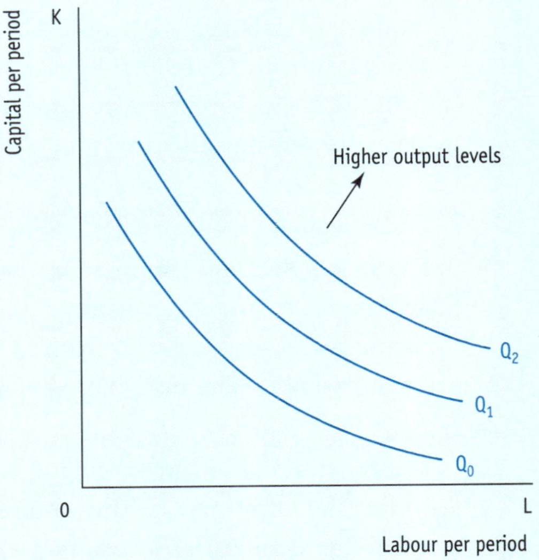

Figure 7.2B **An isoquant map**

the output associated with the isoquant labelled Q_2 is higher than that associated with Q_1, which in turn represents a higher level of output than does the isoquant labelled Q_0. Clearly, this figure is similar to the indifference map that we looked at in Chapter 2, although it should be appreciated that the firm does not set out to reach the highest isoquant attainable.[5]

A downward-sloping isoquant reflects substitutability between the factor inputs. Suppose we start at point A on the isoquant Q_0 in Figure 7.3A, and extend a horizontal line to point B. At point B more labour will be used with a given level of capital; L_1 units of labour rather than L_0 with K_0 units of capital. If we extend a vertical line from point A to C, we are representing more capital for a given amount of labour; K_1 units of capital rather than K_0 with L_0 units of labour. Assuming that the two factors both have positive marginal products, it follows that points B and C cannot be on the isoquant Q_0 as both points will be associated with a higher level of output. Starting at point A, we will remain on the same isoquant only if we reduce the capital input when the labour is increased and vice versa.

An isoquant that is convex to the origin represents a diminishing marginal rate of technical substitution, MRTS. What this means is that the rate at which capital will be substituted for labour falls, as the level of labour employed increases. This is evident in Figure 7.3B. We should also note that the slope of the isoquant depends on the ratio of the marginal products

5 By comparison with an indifference curve, the two substitute goods have been replaced with two factors of production and a given level of utility has been replaced with a given level of output.

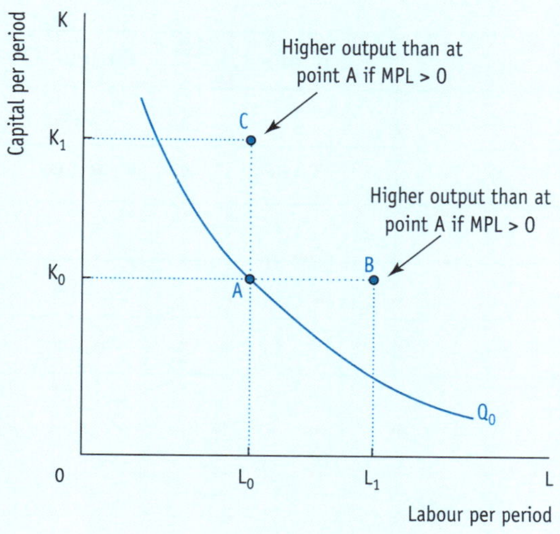

Figure 7.3A **Isoquants slope downwards**

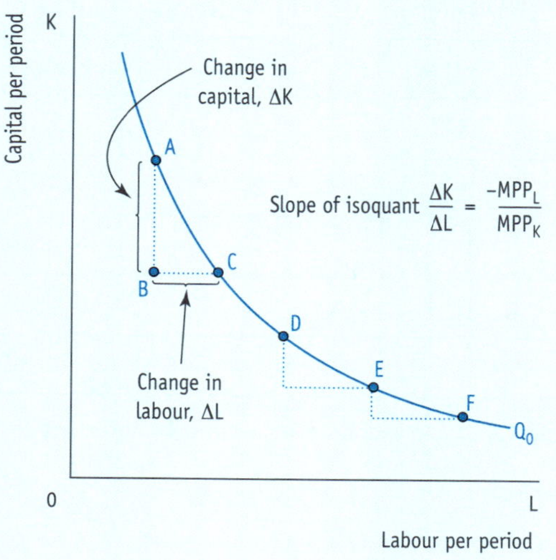

Figure 7.3B **The diminishing marginal rate of technical substitution**

of the two factors of production. To see why in Figure 7.3B, start at point B where there is the same level of labour but a lower level of capital employed than at point A. The difference in the level of output between the two points will depend on the marginal productivity of capital. The change in output in moving from point A to B can be expressed as

$$\Delta Q = \text{MPK}\,\Delta K.$$

where ΔQ is the change in output, MPK the marginal physical product of capital and ΔK is the change in capital used. The move from point B to point C gives the increase in output arising from the increase in labour used, with the level of capital employed held constant

$$\Delta Q = \text{MPL}\,\Delta L$$

where MPL, as before, is the marginal physical product of labour and ΔL is the change in labour. The total effect of moving from A to C via B is therefore

$$\Delta Q = \text{MPK}\,\Delta K + \text{MPL}\,\Delta L = 0$$

It is equal to zero since the level of output on an isoquant is the same at all points. In moving from point A to point C the change in output is therefore zero. The slope of the isoquant, $\Delta K/\Delta L$, can now be expressed in terms of the marginal products of the two factor inputs. Re-arranging the above we get

Cobb-Douglas production function Q = KL					
Capital K	Labour L	Output Q	Capital K	Labour L	Output Q
4	25	100	4	36	144
5	20	100	9	16	144
10	10	100	12	12	144
20	5	100	16	9	144
25	4	100	36	4	144

Table 7.3 **An example of a Cobb-Douglas production function**

$$\Delta K/\Delta L = -MPL/MPK$$

In words, the slope of the isoquant is (the negative of) the marginal product of labour divided by the marginal product of capital. Moving down an isoquant we are representing a higher level of labour input, and a lower input of capital. The marginal product of labour will be declining and the marginal product of capital will be rising. Moving down the isoquant will therefore involve smaller reductions in capital and increasing amounts of additional labour. This is what is shown in moving from points D to E, and from E to F, along Q_0 in Figure 7.3B.

Table 7.3 gives an example of one particular type of production function, a Cobb-Douglas function, Q = KL.[6] The table shows alternative combinations of the capital and labour inputs that produce two different levels of output, 100 and 144 units. Figure 7.4 draws the two isoquants associated with the output levels given.

Other production functions

There are, of course, many other types of production function. Figure 7.5A shows isoquant where the capital and labour inputs are perfect substitutes; a given output level could be produced with just one input, or by some combination of the two. In the example drawn in the figure, one unit of capital could be exchanged for one unit of labour in producing any given level of output. Figure 7.5B shows the opposite extreme when the two inputs are perfect complements. This is known as a fixed coefficient production function. In this case to produce a given output in a technically efficient manner there has to be a particular — fixed — combination of capital and labour. The example drawn in the figure shows that equal amounts

6 This kind of functional form we first encountered in Chapter 1 in our discussion of utility functions.

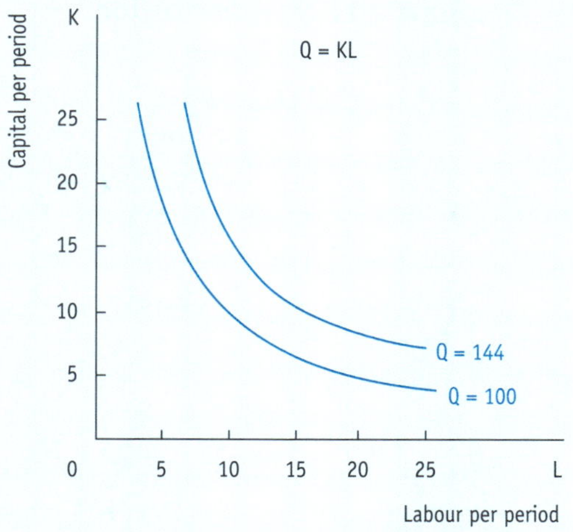

Figure 7.4 **A Cobb-Douglas production function**

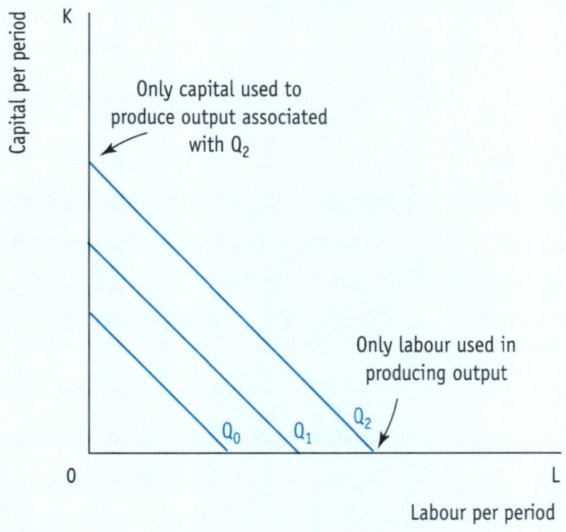

Figure 7.5A **An isoquant map when capital/labour are perfect substitutes**

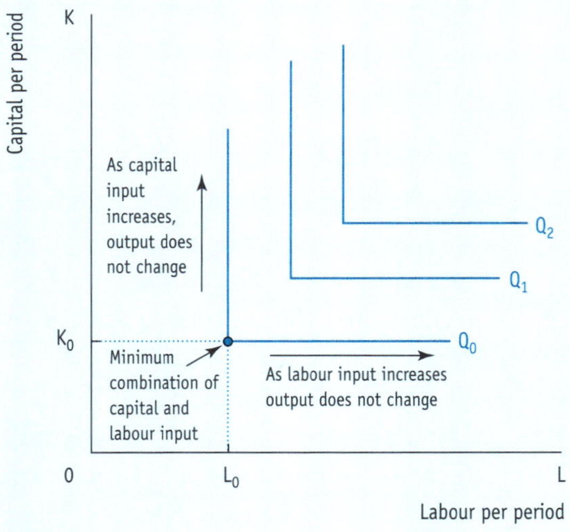

Figure 7.5B **An isoquant map when capital/labour are (perfect) complements**

of capital and labour are needed to produce a given level of output. Additional labour without the necessary increase in capital (and vice versa) adds nothing to output, hence the particular shape of the isoquants.

We now come to two ways in which the nature of a production function can be summarised. The first is concerned with substitutability between factors to produce a given level of output, the second is concerned with what happens to output when all the factor inputs are increased simultaneously.

Elasticity of substitution

The elasticity of substitution is a measure of how easily one factor input can be replaced with another while producing a given level of output. It is measured by the proportionate change in the K/L ratio relative to the proportionate change in the MRTS. Referring back to Figure 7.3B we can see that moving down the isoquant Q_0 the K/L ratio decreases as the MRTS decreases. The elasticity of substitution will therefore be positive (or in the limit zero). Symbolically, it can be expressed as

$$\sigma = \%\Delta(K/L) \; / \; \%\Delta(MRTS)$$

where σ is the elasticity of substitution. If there is a high value for the elasticity the MRTS does not change much as K/L changes so the isoquant will be relatively flat. Conversely, the slope of an isoquant will be relatively steep if the elasticity of substitution is low. Figures 7.5A and 7.5B represent the two limiting cases: where the factor inputs are perfect substitutes the elasticity is infinite, where they are perfect complements the elasticity is zero.

Returns to scale

This refers to how much the level of output increases when both the factor inputs are increased by a given proportion. It is, therefore, concerned with a physical relationship.[7] In Figure 7.6, we have drawn a ray out of the origin marked as OR. This gives a particular proportion of capital to labour all the way along it and is sometimes referred to as a particular production technology. The returns to scale a firm experiences is defined with reference to movement along a particular ray such as OR.

There are three cases to be distinguished: increasing, constant and decreasing returns to scale. Increasing returns to scale occurs when the proportionate increase in output is greater than the proportionate increase in inputs. There are constant returns when the increase in output is the same proportion as the increase in the inputs, and decreasing returns where the increase in output is less than proportionate. There is no particular reason why a production technology should be associated with the same returns to scale at all levels of factor inputs. Table 7.4 gives a numerical example.

The doubling of factor inputs from 10 units of capital and labour to 20, yields a threefold increase in output, giving a region of increasing returns to scale. A 50% increase in capital and labour from 20 units of each to 30, produces a 50% increase in output, giving a region of constant returns to scale. Finally, increasing both factors by a third from 30 units to 40,

7 An understanding of returns to scale is central to the development of the firm's cost curves later in this chapter, and is important in the analysis of competitive market structures.

Capital input	Labour input	Output
10	10	100
20	20	300
30	30	450
40	40	500

Table 7.4 **An example of returns to scale**

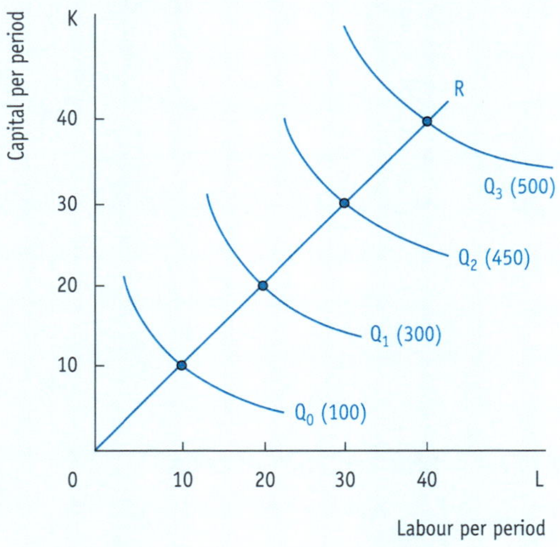

Figure 7.6 **Returns to scale**

increases output by a smaller proportion, a region of decreasing returns to scale. The production function exhibits at first increasing, then constant and eventually decreasing returns to scale. Figure 7.6 illustrates this example diagrammatically.

Representation of costs

The representation of costs for the firm is analogous to the budget line for the consumer. In the two-factor model the total cost of the firm is the sum of the expenditures on capital and labour respectively. In turn, the expenditure on each factor is simply equal to the factor price times the number of units of the factor the firm hires. We can express this as

$$TC = wL + rK$$

where TC is total cost, w is the wage rate and r is rental rate of capital. L and K are the number of units of labour and capital hired. It should be appreciated that the rental rate is not the same as the rate of interest, but rather the charge that a firm would pay if it were able to rent its capital equipment from another company

The costs of production are represented diagrammatically in Figure 7.7 by an isocost line, marked as C_0.[8] What an isocost line shows is the different combinations of the two factors that can be employed for a given total outlay by the firm.[9] Assuming that a firm can employ

8 Isocost meaning the same cost.

9 The treatment of the firm's costs is really orientated towards cost outlays, rather than opportunity costs.

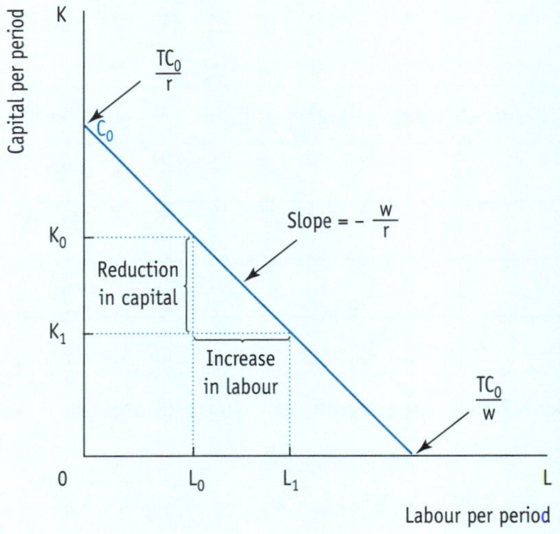

Figure 7.7 Representation of costs

all the labour that it wants to at a fixed wage rate, then the maximum amount of labour that could be hired for a given total cost is simply whatever that cost happens to be divided by the wage rate. This gives us the point of intersection of the isocost line with the horizontal axis in Figure 7.7. It shows how much labour could be employed if no capital was used. A similar line of reasoning applies to the employment of capital which then gives us the intersection point on the vertical axis.

The slope of the isocost line depends on the factor price ratio, in other words the ratio of the wage rate to the rental rate of capital. If the factor prices happened to be equal the slope of the isocost line would be (minus) one; one unit of extra capital could be exchanged for one unit of extra labour. If the rental rate for capital is twice the wage rate, then two units of the labour input could be exchanged for one unit of capital and the slope would be (minus) one-half, and so on.

Equilibrium of the profit-maximising firm

The objective of the profit-maximising firm requires minimising the cost outlay of producing a given level of output (or equivalently maximising the level of output for a given cost outlay). In Figure 7.8A, this is illustrated at the point of tangency between the isoquant, Q_0, and the isocost line, C_0, marked as point E_0. At the point of equilibrium, the slope of the isoquant equals that of the isocost line, so the MRTS is equal to the factor price ratio. It is not possible for the firm to substitute capital for labour (or vice versa) and produce the same level of output at the same total cost. To see why this is, look at Figure 7.8B. Starting at point E_0 to move to point H on the isoquant Q_0, would require an additional amount of capital represented by the distance FH. Given the reduction in labour input, with the factor prices that the firm faces, this

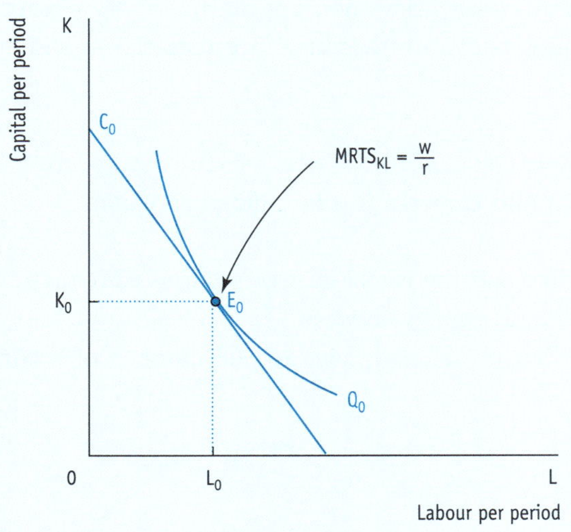

Figure 7.8A **The firm's equilibrium**

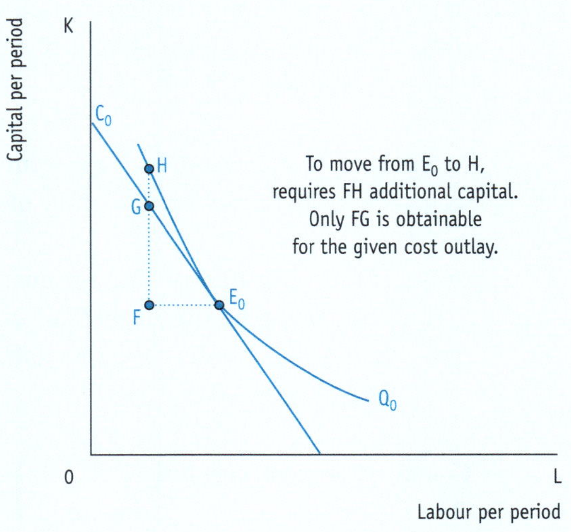

Figure 7.8B **A point of non-equilibrium**

would require an increase in total costs as point H lies outside the firm's isocost line, C_0. Point H is not the cost-minimising method of producing the output level associated with Q_0 and this line of reasoning can be repeated for points other than E_0 on the isoquant.

Questions

Q3 Suppose the production function of a toy doll is characterised by

$$Q = 100LK$$

(I) What shape would the short-run production function be if the capital input were fixed at 10 units?

(II) Obtain expressions for the (short-run) average and marginal productivity of labour. What is the relationship between them?

(III) Obtain five values of capital and labour inputs that would lie on the isoquant associated with an output of 10,000 dolls. If the firm wanted to double its output level is it necessary for it to double the level of its factor inputs? What does this tell you about the returns to scale properties of this production function?

Q4 Draw isoquants for the following

(I) A system of child road crossings requiring one adult and a stick ('lollipop') for each school in a town.

(II) The operation of a lighthouse system where each lighthouse is staffed by two keepers.
(III) The operation of a system of lighthouses where no personnel are required to staff the lighthouses.

Q5 A transport system can hire 60 security guards or install 30 security cameras to cover its security needs (or any combination of guards and cameras in the same proportion).

(I) If the wage rate of security guards is five and the rental cost of security cameras is 15, what is the least-cost method of providing security services?
(II) If the rental price of cameras falls to eight what happens to the number of security guards employed?

Comment on your conclusion.

7.3 The firm's cost curves and factor demands

The expansion path and the average and marginal cost curves

The firm's expansion path shows how its most efficient production technique changes as its level of output increases. For simplicity, the expansion path in Figure 7.9 is drawn on the assumption that the wage rate and the rental rate of capital do not change when output rises. The total cost of producing the output level associated with Q_0 is that represented by the isocost line C_0. The average cost is simply the total cost divided by the output level and, similarly, we can obtain the average cost of producing the output levels associated with the isoquants Q_1 and Q_2. In principle, it is possible to imagine a whole range of output levels, and associated costs, and hence obtain an average cost curve.

Figure 7.10 shows the expansion path for a firm in the short-run. The initial point of equilibrium is at E_0, a tangency point between the isoquant Q_0, and the isocost line, C_0. Suppose the firm experiences an increase in the demand for its product then, given the constraint that the firm cannot change the amount of capital it employs, its output decision can be represented by the movement from E_0 to E_1. The expansion path in the short-run is the horizontal line that is drawn due east from E_0. At point E_1 the firm is using the least cost method of producing output associated with Q_1 when it cannot vary its use of capital. When the firm can substitute capital for labour its equilibrium is the point E_2. The long-run average cost will therefore be less than its short-run counterpart when the firm can substitute capital for labour and reduce its total cost.

The firm's marginal cost is the change in total cost divided by the change in output (a one-unit change in output or a larger change). The short-run marginal cost is therefore the difference

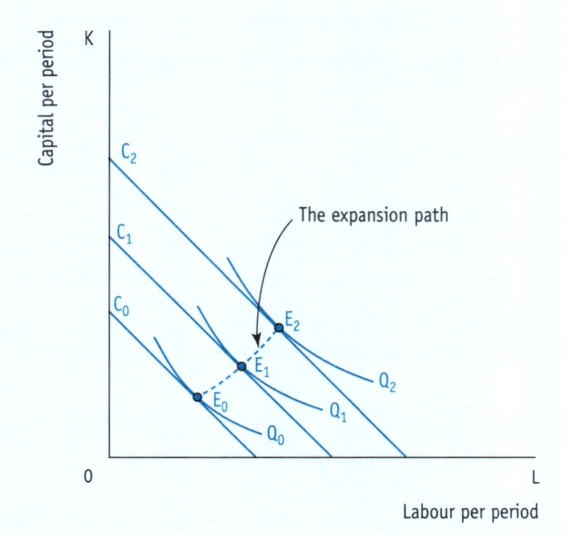

Figure 7.9 **The firm's long-run expansion path**

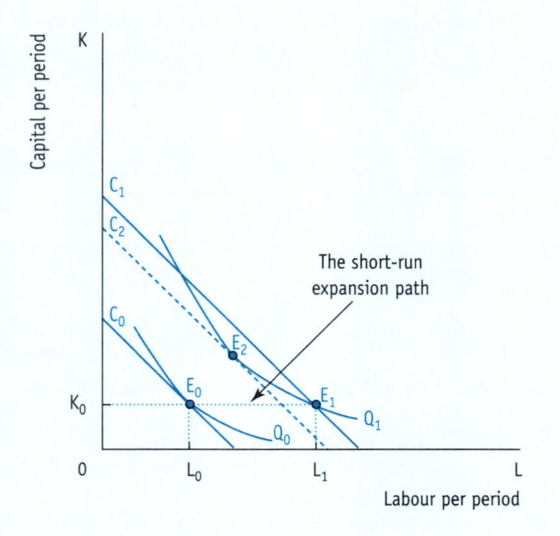

Figure 7.10 **The firm's short-run expansion path**

between the costs associated with isocost lines C_1 and C_0 in Figure 7.10, divided by the change in output associated with moving from Q_0 to Q_1. In the long-run, the change in total cost is the difference between that associated with C_2 and C_0 and so, in the long-run the marginal cost of production is less than it is in the short-run.

The shape of the average and marginal cost curves

The average and marginal cost curves of the firm relate to the entire range of possible output. The general shape of the long-run curves will depend on the returns to scale of the firm's production function, and also on what happens to factor prices as the factor input levels vary. Table 7.5 links the earlier example of returns to scale to the firm's costs for given factor input prices. It is assumed that the wage rate and the rental rate of capital are both five per unit.

The firm initially experiences increasing returns to scale, so, with given wage and capital rental rates, the cost per unit of output will fall. The average cost of producing 300 units in the example is less than the average cost of producing 100.[10] In the region where the firm experiences constant returns, the cost per unit is constant and equal to the marginal cost. This is shown in moving from producing 300 to 450 units of output. Where there are decreasing returns, the marginal cost of the extra output will rise and will pull-up the average cost, as shown in the third and fourth rows. When long-run average costs decline over a

10 In practice when a firm faces declining average costs it is difficult to know how far it can be attributed to increasing returns rather than a change in the factor input mix.

Capital input	Labour input	Output	Total cost wL + rK	Long-run average cost	Long-run marginal cost
0	0	0	0	Not defined	Not defined
10	10	100	100	1.0	1.0
20	20	300	200	0.66	0.5
30	30	450	300	0.66	0.66
40	40	500	400	0.8	2.0

Table 7.5 An example of returns to scale and the firm's costs

range of output the firm is said to be facing economies of scale, when they rise, diseconomies of scale.

In the short-run, the average cost will initially decline from a combination of a declining average fixed cost and a rising MPL. As the marginal product of labour declines, the average cost will eventually rise. The short-run marginal cost is the change in the total variable cost and this will fall and rise as the MPL rises and falls.

Short-run and long-run average cost curves are shown in Figures 7.11A and 7.11B. When there are constant returns to scale and the factor prices are constant over the entire range of output, the long-run average and marginal cost curves, LAC and LMC, are horizontal. They are therefore superimposed on one other in Figure 7.11A. Long-run costs are constant as output expands. In increasing output from Q_1 to Q_2, for example, the firm would in the short-run experience an increase in costs for the reasons discussed in relation to Figure 7.10. When the firm is able to increase its capital stock, the unit cost of producing the higher output will be the same as producing Q_1. It is sometimes assumed in presenting the theory of the firm that the long-run average cost curve facing the firm will be U-shaped, reflecting initially increasing and then decreasing returns to scale. This is shown in Figure 7.11B. The output level Q_{MIN} gives the point where long-run average costs are at a minimum. At lower levels of output there are economies of scale and the firm's long-run marginal cost is below the average cost. Conversely for output levels above Q_{MIN}.

Comparative statics and factor demands

The simple structure of the firm we have set up in this chapter is sometimes justified in terms of its usefulness in predicting the responses of a firm to changes in its external environment. For example, we can use the analysis to predict the effect of a change in the price of a factor input on factor demand. In subsequent chapters we will use the neo-classical approach to

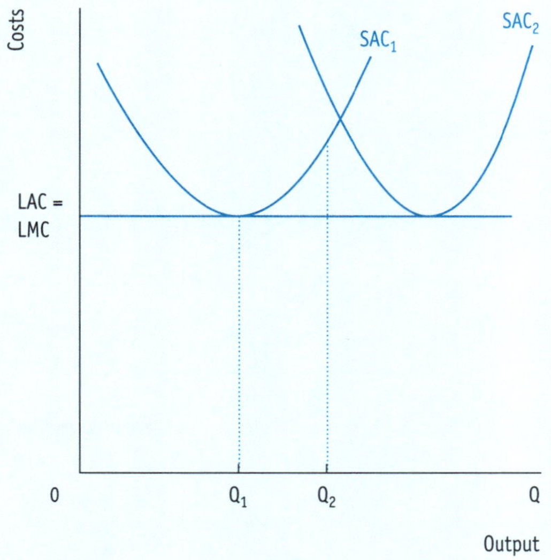

Figure 7.11A **Long-run cost curves under constant returns to scale**

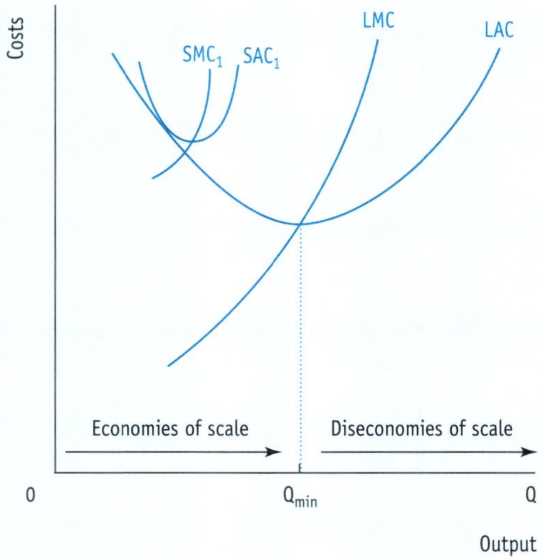

Figure 7.11B **Long-run cost curves when there are economies/diseconomies of scale**

examine the response of firms, and industries, to changes in demand more generally and also to changes in government policy.[11]

The changes to the factor prices that the firm pays are summarised by the factor price ratio. While, clearly, there only two possible changes to the factor price ratio: it either increases or decreases, there are however a number of permutations possible in terms of the changes to the wage or rental rate considered separately. The possible effects when only one of them changes are summarised in Table 7.6 below.

When both factor prices change the outcome will depend not only on the direction of the change, but also on the rate at which the respective prices change.

Factor price ratio (w/r) increasing	**Factor price ratio (w/r) decreasing**
(I) Wage rate rises, rental rate unchanged	(I) Wage rate falls, rental rate unchanged
(II) Wage rate unchanged, rental rate falling.	(II) Wage rate unchanged, rental rate rising

Table 7.6 **Changes in the factor price ratio**

11 The analysis of factor markets is covered generally in Chapters 13–15.

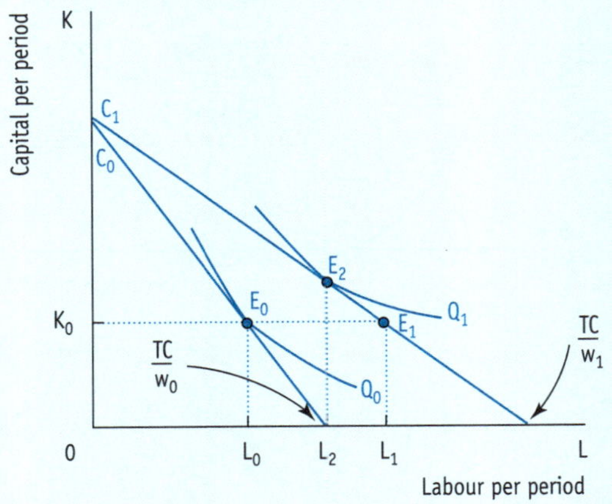

Figure 7.12A The effect of a fall in the wage rate on labour demand

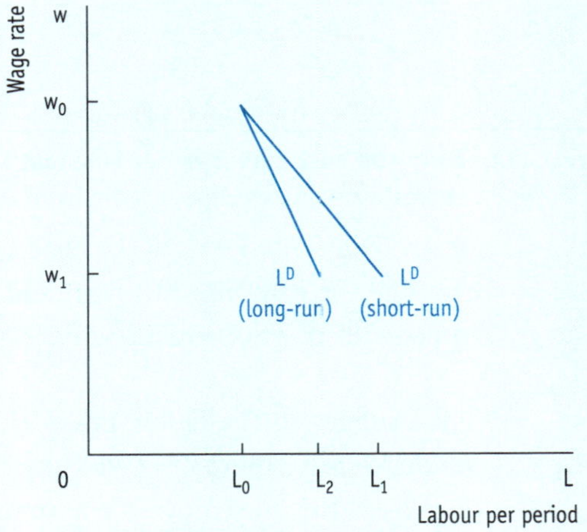

Figure 7.12B Labour demand schedules

Figure 7.12A shows the effect of a fall in the wage rate on labour demand. The original equilibrium is at point E_0, with the associated level of employment at L_0; the new long-run equilibrium is at point E_1 with a rise in employment to L_2. The firm's cost minimising output decisions therefore determine its factor demands. Figure 7.12B shows labour demand in both the short and long-run. The effect of the fall in the wage rate can also be broken down into what, in this context, are called the output and substitution effects of a change in the factor price ratio. Q8 below asks you to make this distinction.

Questions

Q6 A profit-maximising firm faces a Cobb-Douglas production function $Q = KL$ and a demand for 36 units of output. Five of the possible production techniques available to it are given in the table.

Cobb-Douglas production function: $Q = KL$ Wage rate = rental rate of capital = 5 per unit			
Capital K	**Labour L**	**Output Q**	**Total cost**
18	2	36	
9	4	36	
6	6	36	
4	9	36	
2	18	36	

(I) What is the least cost of method of producing 36 units of output?

(II) Suppose that demand rises from 36 units to 72. What is the firm's production technique and what is the associated total cost in the short-run?

(III) What is the total cost of producing 72 units in the long-run?

(IV) What happens to the unit cost of production when output doubles (assuming that factor prices remain the same)?

(V) What happens to the unit costs if the input levels treble? How many firms would you expect there to be in an industry characterised by such technology? Why?

Q7 A firm faces known technology with a production function $Q = 100K^{0.5}L^{0.5}$. Five of the possible input combinations that would yield an output level of 1,000 are shown in the table below.

Production function $Q = 100K^{0.5}L^{0.5}$ Wage rate = 2 Rental rate of capital = 25			
Capital K	**Labour L**	**Output Q**	**Total cost**
100	1	1,000	
25	4	1,000	
10	10	1,000	
4	25	1,000	
1	100	1,000	

(I) What is the minimum cost of producing 1,000 units of output?

(II) Suppose demand rises from 1,000 units to 2,000 what is the least cost of meeting the demand in the short-run?

(III) What is the firm's short-run marginal cost of increasing output from 1,000 to 2,000 units?

(IV) What are the returns to scale properties of this production function? Assuming fixed factor prices, what shape would you expect the firm's long-run cost curves to be?

Q8 Distinguish between the price and output effect of a fall in the rental rate of capital. When would a factor demand curve be upward-sloping? Is this likely in practice?

Concluding comment

The neo-classical model discussed in this chapter is a very simplified view of the firm. The theory treats all firms as being profit-maximising entities. It assumes that changes that affect the firm are reversible, and there is generally an emphasis with points of equilibrium, rather than the process of adjustment to change. The model is static in that the technological constraints are taken as known and hence treated as a given, rather than something that a firm tries to determine. The use of the short-run and long-run analysis is within this given state of technology.

We have in this chapter mentioned that the objective of the firm in the neo-classical view is to maximise profits. However, so far we have only considered the firm's costs and so our discussion of the decision of the firm has been limited to analysis of the cost-minimising output level. In the next chapter, we complete the neo-classical analysis by introducing revenues and the profit-maximising output level and also consider alternative views of the objectives of firms.

Mathematical appendix

(I) Production functions

The two-variable production function

$$Q = F(K,L)$$

can take a wide range of functional forms. The Cobb-Douglas production function is often used for analytical purposes, this takes the general form

$$Q = AK^{\sigma}L^{\beta}$$

where Q is the level of output, K and L the factor inputs. The coefficient A is a general multiplicative constant. The exponents α and β determine the returns to scale properties of each particular function. Suppose that the factor inputs were increased by a constant $k > 0$,

$$F(kK,kL) = A(kK)^{\alpha}(kL)^{\beta} = Ak^{\alpha+\beta}\, K^{\alpha}L^{\beta}$$

If $\alpha + \beta > 1$ there are increasing returns to scale, if $\alpha + \beta = 1$ there are constant returns, and if $\alpha + \beta < 1$ there are decreasing returns.

In the case where the two factor inputs are perfect substitutes the production function is

$$Q = aK + bL$$

where a and b are positive coefficients. In the fixed coefficient production function case we have

$$Q = \min(aK,bL).$$

Where again a and b are two positive coefficients.

The isocost line

The total cost of production can be written as

$$TC = wL + rK$$

and is represented by the isocost line. The slope of the isocost line is given by the ratio of the factor prices. This can be obtained by re-arrangement

$$rK = TC - wL$$

$$K = \frac{TC}{r} - \frac{w}{r}L$$

and then by differentiation

$$\frac{dk}{dL} = -\frac{w}{r}$$

Equilibrium

Assuming a convex to the origin set of indifference curves, the point of tangency with the budget constraint implies

$$(MPL/MPK) = (w/r)$$

which can be found by setting up a Lagrangian and solving as we did in the appendix to Chapter 1.

The cost functions

The total cost function gives the minimum total cost of producing any level of output. The total cost will, of course, vary as the factor prices vary so total cost is generally a function of w, r and Q. In general form, we have

$$TC = F(w,r,Q)$$

The average and marginal cost functions follow directly as

$$AC = TC/Q$$

and

$$MC = dTC/dQ$$

An example

Suppose we have a Cobb-Douglas production function

$$Q = 100L^{0.5}K^{0.5}$$

in equilibrium (MPL/MPK) = w/r, so in this case

$$K/L = w/r$$

The way to proceed from here is to use this condition by substituting it into the production function to eliminate the terms in K and L. First, divide the production function by L giving

$$\frac{Q}{L} = 100\left(\frac{K}{L}\right)^{0.5}$$

Using the equilibrium condition, we get

$$\frac{Q}{L} = 100\left(\frac{w}{r}\right)^{0.5}$$

Re-arranging

$$L = \frac{Q}{100}\left(\frac{r}{w}\right)^{0.5}$$

so

$$wL = \frac{Q}{100}\, w^{0.5}\, r^{0.5}$$

Similarly for K produces

$$rK = \frac{Q}{100}\, w^{0.5}\, r^{0.5}$$

Since

$$TC = wL + rK$$

We find that

$$TC = \frac{Q}{50}\, w^{0.5}\, r^{0.5}$$

Given factor prices we have the relation between TC and output. If, for example, $w = r = 5$, then

$$TC = 0.1Q$$

Then in this case

$$AC = MC = 0.1$$

As discussed in the text, a production function with constant returns to scale, and fixed factor prices, generates constant average and marginal costs in the long-run.

Summary

1 The existence of firms can be explained in terms of the transactions costs associated with organising production on the open market. Another view is that firms exist to take advantage of teamworking.

2 The neo-classical theory assumes that the objective of firms is to maximise profit. The state of technology a firm faces is assumed to be known and is represented by a production function. This shows the technically efficient combinations of factor inputs to produce any level of output.

3 An isoquant is a way of graphing a relation between the alternative (technically efficient) ways of combining capital and labour to produce a given level of output. Isoquants representing different levels of output are shown in an isoquant map.

4 The level of capital and labour input that a firm can purchase for a given total outlay is represented by an isocost line. This is analogous to the budget constraint that the consumer faced in the analysis of household decision-making.

5 The profit-maximising firm will produce a given level of output at the lowest possible cost. The marginal rate of technical substitution will be equal to the factor price ratio when this occurs at a tangency point.

6 The returns to scale that a firm faces shows how much output rises for a given percentage rise in both factor inputs. If the firm faces increasing returns, the rise in output is greater than proportionate; if the rise in output is equiproportionate then there are constant returns to scale, and if the resulting rise in output is less than proportionate there are decreasing returns.

7 In the long-run, the returns to scale will determine the shape of the average and marginal cost curves, if factor prices are fixed. In the short-run, the U-shaped average cost curve can be thought of in terms of a combination of declining average fixed costs and eventually diminishing marginal returns to a variable factor which causes average costs to rise.

8 The analytical structures of the neo-classical theory of the firm can be used to predict the response of a firm to some change in its external environment. The response to a change in the price of a factor of production is one simple example.

End of chapter questions

Q9 The combinations of capital and labour in the table are all points on two particular isoquants. Draw them. What is the degree of substitutability between the factor inputs in each case?

Isoquant 1		Isoquant 2	
Capital input K	Labour input L	Capital input K	Labour input L
100	0	100	200
75	25	100	150
50	50	100	100
25	75	150	100
0	100	200	100

Q10 A firm operates with a production function where two factor inputs, capital and labour are perfect substitutes. Its production function is $Q = 2K + 8L$, the wage rate is £10 per unit of labour and the rental rate of capital is £5

(I) What is the least-cost production technique for making 100 units? What is the relation between the MRTS and the factor price ratio at the equilibrium point?

(II) Suppose the wage rate rose to £20 and the rental rate of capital fell to £4 where is the new equilibrium? How much capital and how much labour does the firm now use?

Q11 Suppose the production of a particular type of bicycle is characterised by

$$Q = 100K^{0.5}L^{0.5}$$

(I) Obtain an expression for the average and marginal productivity of labour.

(II) Graph the average productivity of labour curve, for a capital stock of 10 units.

(III) What happens to the level of output as the amount of capital and labour input rises from 16 units to 25?

(IV) If following the development of new technology the production function becomes $Q = 100K^{0.5}L^{1.5}$ how would it affect your answers to (I) and (II)?

Q12 Suppose the effort of 10 workers produced exactly the same amount of output as did one machine on a farm.

(I) What would the production function be?

(II) Suppose the wage rate = £2 per unit and the rental rate £10 what would the equilibrium employment levels of labour and capital be? If the rental rate rose to £25 per unit what difference would it make?

Q13 Given a fixed coefficient production function

$$Q = \min(K,L)$$

(I) What are the technically efficient levels of capital and labour inputs that produce output levels of 10, 50 and 100?
(II) If the factor prices are w = r = £5 what are the minimum costs of producing the output levels in (I)? What happens to the minimum costs of output if the factor prices rise to w = £10 and r = £15?
(III) If the production function was $Q = \min(2K,4L)$ how would the answers above differ?

Q14 Given the Cobb-Douglas production function

$$Q = 100K^{0.75} L^{0.25}$$

Obtain expressions for the total cost, average and marginal cost functions if the wage rate and rental rate of capital were 10 per period.

Q15 A firm has the production function

$$Q = 7K^{0.5} L^{0.5}$$

Where Q is the quantity produced, K and L are the labour and capital inputs. The price of the labour input is 1 per unit and that of the capital input is 4.

(I) Find the maximum output attainable for a budget of 200.
(II) Find the minimum cost of producing an output of 100 units.
(III) Obtain the firm's factor demands.

(Hint: follow the constrained optimisation procedure in the mathematical appendix to Chapter 1.)

Q16 How would you go about constructing an index for the costs of production? Do you think that it would be any more straightforward than the construction of a retail price index?

References and suggested further reading

The material of this chapter is covered in depth in other textbooks. Nicholson and Varian have separate chapters devoted to discussing the role of technology, costs and the profit-maximising firm. On the rationale for the existence of firms, Coase (1937) is an important article, although the language now appears rather stilted. Eaton and Eaton give detailed coverage to several aspects of the firm including teamworking. Moschandreas, Chapter 3 gives a good summary on the nature of the firm. Conn gives a critical account of the role of the profit motive in the world of football.

Alchian, A. and Demsetz, H. (1972), 'Production, Information Costs and Economic Organization', *American Economic Review*, **62**, 777–95.

Coase, R.H. (1937), 'The Nature of the Firm', *Economica*, **4**, 386–405.

Conn, D. (1997), '*The Football Business*', Mainstream Publishing Projects.

Eaton, B.C. and Eaton, D.F. (1995), *Microeconomics*, Prentice Hall.

Moschandreas, M. (1994), *Business Economics*, Routledge.

Nicholson, W. (1995), *Microeconomic Theory, Basic Principles and Extensions*, 6th edition, The Dryden Press.

Times 1000 (1998), Times Books, London.

Varian, H.R. (1996), *Intermediate Microeconomics, A Modern Approach*, 4th edition, W.W. Norton & Co.

8

Alternative Theories of the Firm

Key ideas and material

The divorce between ownership and control, managerial theories, the principal-agent relationship, evidence on executive remuneration

Introduction

Do firms set out to maximise profits and does it matter if they do not? In this chapter, we will examine alternative views about the objectives that firms pursue. The neo-classical idea of profit maximisation has been much criticised by those who point to the growth of large firms, and with it the separation of effective control from formal ownership. This is a development that has led to a number of managerial theories of the firm suggesting self-interested behaviour on the part of management.

In this context, the controversial subject of pay for top executives, particularly in relation to company performance is of interest. The starting point for our discussion of this subject will be the principal-agent model, which provides a framework for analysing the work incentives of company executives. This is then used to examine the role of stock (or share) options paid to some individuals. These schemes are seen by some as a way of aligning the interests of shareholders and management and are seen by others as a vehicle for executive abuse. In this chapter, we take a look at the evidence on this issue and open the discussion out to consider corporate governance questions more widely.

The outline of this chapter is as follows. In Section 1, we start simply with the price and output decisions of the profit-maximising firm. This is a point of comparison for the analysis of managerial models that suggest revenue (or growth) maximisation as the firm's objective. We also take a first look at data on the concentration of shareholdings and questionnaire evidence on the objectives of firms.

Section 2 approaches the split between ownership and management with the analysis of the principal-agent problem. We will look at alternative institutional mechanisms that might align the actions of management with the interests of shareholders, although the main focus is with contract design as a way of resolving the conflicts of interest that may arise.

In Section 3, there is a review of empirical evidence that bears on the relationship between executive pay and company performance. Executive share option schemes have a longer history in the US than the UK and we summarise findings from both countries. This is another area where the details of measurement may be important, although the empirical research is suggestive rather than definitive. We conclude this chapter with some criticisms of the principal-agent model itself.

8.1 Alternative objectives for the firm

The neo-classical view

In Chapter 7, we characterised a firm as an organisation that converts inputs into outputs via a known technology represented by a production function. We discussed the development of the firm's cost structures from this known technology via an isoquant map. We saw there that the equilibrium output for the firm was given by the lowest cost of producing a given level of output (or equivalently the highest output for a given cost outlay).

We did, however, defer the discussion of demand and the profit-maximising output level until this chapter. To identify this level of output, we need to introduce revenues into the picture, which, in turn, depend on the exact nature of the demand that a firm faces. Here, we will assume that the firm faces a downward-sloping demand curve for its product.[1] Table 8.1 gives a numerical example of a tea bar's demand for its product and the associated revenues and costs.

The demand relationship is given in the first two columns. The firm's total revenue is simply the price (or average revenue) multiplied by the number of cups it sells. Marginal revenue is the change in total revenue when output changes; as with marginal cost this can be a one-unit change in output or a greater change. In the table, the figures are for the marginal revenue per cup when the bar sells the additional number of cups in the second column. We assume that the tea bar has a fixed cost of £150 and that the marginal cost of making a cup of tea is constant.

The decision rule for the firm is simply to maximise the difference between total revenue and total cost. In this example, the point at which this occurs is when it sells 900 cups of tea at a

1 We will discuss the case of a perfectly elastic demand curve in Chapter 9.

Demand for tea		Revenues		Costs	
Price £	Quantity (cups per week)	Total revenue £	Marginal revenue	Total costs £	Marginal costs per cup £
0	0			150	
0.50	600	300	0.50	210	0.10
0.45	750	337.50	0.25	225	0.10
0.40	900	360	0.15	240	0.10
0.35	950	332.50	–0.55	245	0.10
0.30	1,000	300	–0.65	250	0.10

Table 8.1 **Example of demand, revenues and costs for a tea bar**

price of 40 pence. An increase in price would reduce demand, and total revenue would fall by more than would the total cost of selling fewer cups. A decrease in price would not raise demand sufficiently to increase the firm's revenue. The largest profit the tea bar can make is therefore £120 per week, given the information in the table.[2]

Figures 8.1 and 8.2 illustrate this type of demand relationship more generally. In Figure 8.1 we have drawn a demand curve for the firm's product and the associated marginal revenue curve.[3] At the top of the demand curve, a decrease in price will lead to a greater than proportionate increase in demand, and hence the firm's total revenue rises with output. In other words demand is price elastic. At the output when marginal revenue ceases to be positive there are no further additions to total revenue. Total revenue is therefore at a maximum at that point and the price elasticity of demand is unity. In the region where demand is price inelastic, a price decrease will lead to a less than proportionate increase in demand and so total revenue falls. The shape of the total revenue curve drawn in Figure 8.2 therefore shows a rise, a peak and then a fall as the output of the firm increases.

The vertical distance between the total revenue and total cost curves gives the profit of the firm at each level of output. When this vertical distance is maximised profits are maximised. In Figure 8.3, this is at the output level marked Q_{Π}. At this point, the slopes of the total revenue and total cost curves are also equal to one another, so that marginal revenue is equal to marginal cost at the profit-maximising output.

2 Clearly, at a price of 40 pence, marginal revenue is greater than marginal cost and profits could be increased if the tea bar knew exactly how many more cups to sell.

3 The marginal revenue schedule lies half way between the firm's demand curve and the horizontal axis. Why this is so is demonstrated in the mathematical appendix.

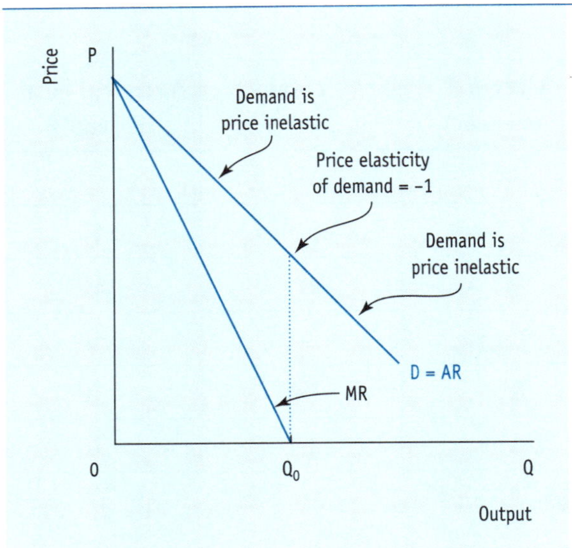

Figure 8.1 **The firm's demand curve**

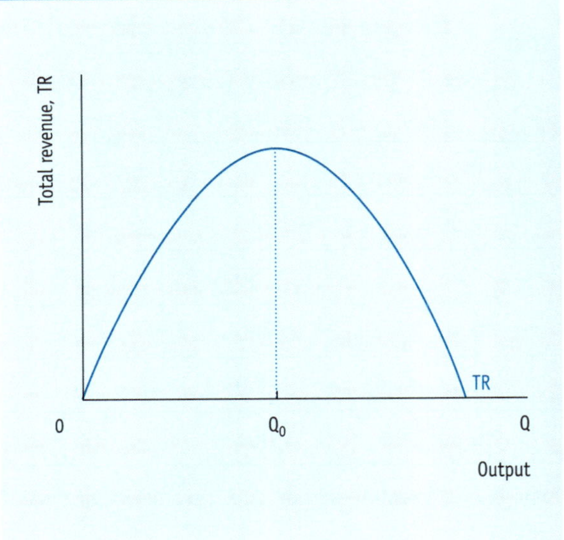

Figure 8.2 **The firm's total revenue curve**

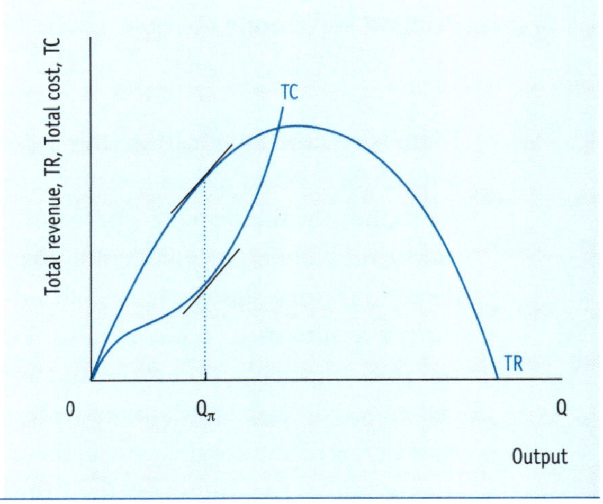

Figure 8.3 **The profit maximising level of output**

The divorce between ownership and control

The neo-classical model has its origins relating to the small scale owner-managed firms of the 19th century. The changing size and structure of many firms in the 20th century has led to the development of managerialist theories which build on the separation between the 'owners' of a firm, and those in control of the firm' s strategic decision-making. The increasing dispersion of share ownership, and the growing proportion of shareholdings held by financial institutions on behalf of others, is a part of the background to the management control of many large firms. Chart 8.1 highlights this by showing the changing pattern of shareholdings over the period 1963–93 in the UK.

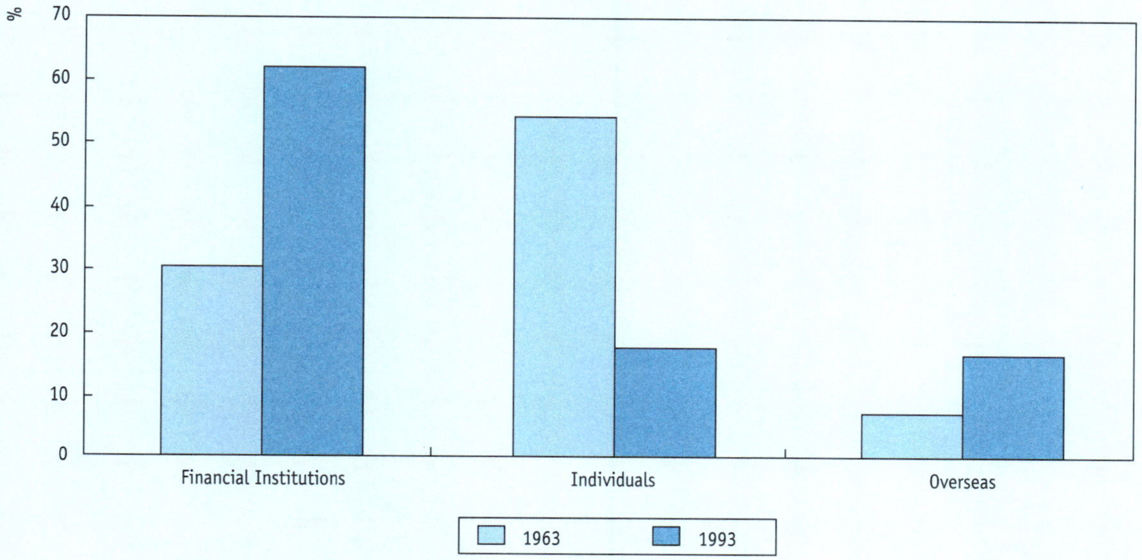

Chart 8.1 UK pattern of share ownership
Source: Financial Statistics (1996).

There is still the awkward question of how we would know whether a particular firm is owner-controlled or not. The concentration of shareholdings by individual is one approach to this question, and studies by Franks and Mayer (1990) and by Leech and Leahy (1991) point to the small number of large companies in the UK with a majority shareholding. Chart 8.2 gives the percentage of shares owned by the largest shareholder from the Franks and Mayer study and Table 8.2 gives evidence from the study by Leech and Leahy.

The two studies give a similar picture as far as the number of companies with a majority shareholding is concerned. In practice, a holding of more than 50% may not be necessary to exert control over a firm, particularly if there are a large number of small shareholders. Pragmatically, a lower threshold figure could be set, although the choice of the percentage is, of course, rather arbitrary. The number of firms classified as owner-controlled would then rise straightforwardly as the threshold figure is lowered.

Sales revenue maximisation

We will now turn to the managerial models of the firm. Broadly, these assume that managers seek to maximise their utility, which is taken to depend on their power, prestige and other benefits. Baumol's model (1959) relegates the role of profit from being the firm's objective to simply that of a constraint on managerial discretion. He suggests that the variables affecting management behaviour are directly related to (and can therefore be summarised by) the total

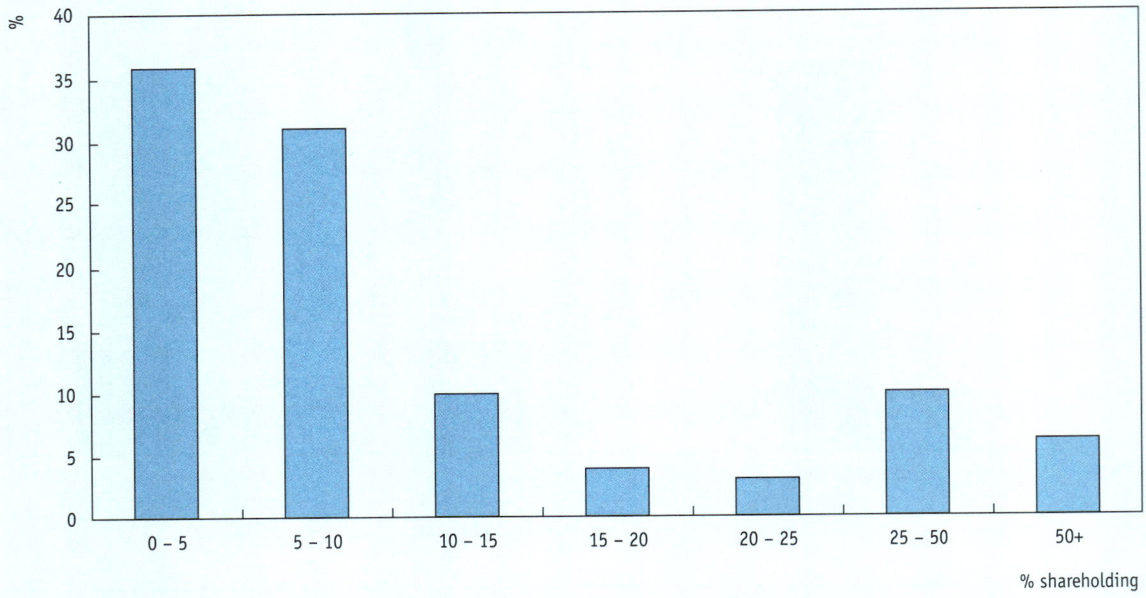

Chart 8.2 **Largest shareholding in UK top 200 in 1990**
Source: Franks and Mayer (1990).

1983–5		
Size of largest shareholding (%)	**Number**	**Percentage**
> 50	25	5.3
20–50	135	28.8
10–20	125	26.6
5–10	144	30.6
< 5	41	8.7
Total	**470**	**100**

Table 8.2 **Leading firm shareholding by size in the UK**
Source: Leech and Leahy (1991).

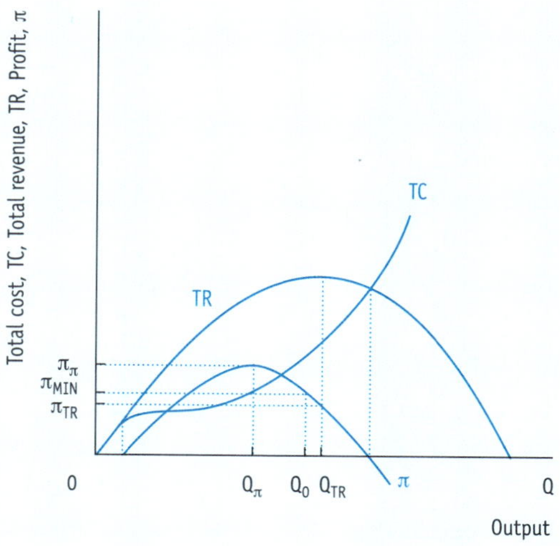

Figure 8.4 **Sales revenue maximisation**

sales revenue of the firm. This, it is argued, stems from the salary structure of senior management and its linkage to sales revenue.

The decision-making of the firm that maximises sales revenue is illustrated in Figure 8.4. The firm's total revenue and total cost curves, TR and TC, together with the profit level, Π, are plotted in relation to the output of the firm.[4] The profit-maximising firm would produce an output of Q_Π, and the revenue maximising firm would produce Q_{TR}. The profits at the revenue maximising level of output are clearly not as high as they could be. A profit-maximising firm would make a profit level of Π_Π, the revenue maximising firm a profit of Π_{TR}. The model makes clear the divergence of management performance and the interests of shareholders.

Suppose we now introduce a profit constraint, that is a minimum level of profit that the management of a firm feels the firm must make to 'keep the shareholders happy'. The precise impact of this will clearly depend on the particular level at which it is set. In Figure 8.4 it is shown as π_{MIN}. The output level of the firm will now be where total revenue is maximised given the constraint. This is marked as Q_0 in the figure, but clearly such an outcome still points to the management not fully pursuing the interests of the shareholders.

Growth maximisation

A second model due to Marris relates the motivation of managers to the growth rate of firms, given that this is one way in which managers achieve status and acquire power. Managers are

4 The shape of the firm's total cost curve reflects economies then diseconomies of scale as its output expands.

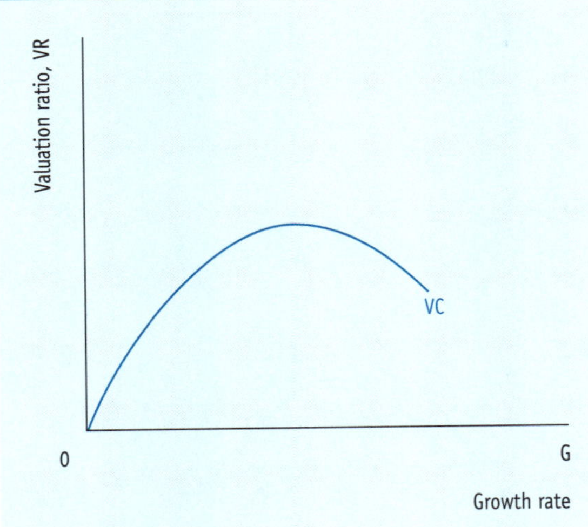

Figure 8.5A A valuation curve

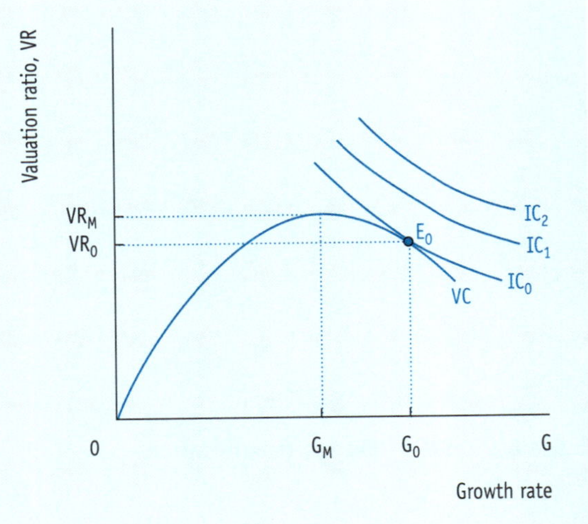

Figure 8.5B Equilibrium in the Marris model

also assumed to desire (job) security and this is captured by the idea of a firm's valuation ratio, which is the ratio of the stock market value of the firm to its highest possible value. This clearly has a maximum value of 1. The importance of this ratio is that it gives some idea of how likely the firm is to be taken over and how likely is a shareholders revolt against the incumbent management. The higher the value of this ratio the more secure the incumbent management will feel, and this provides an incentive for managers to make profits in order to pay high dividend levels.

In Figure 8.5A, we have drawn the relation between the valuation ratio and the growth rate of a firm. This is called the valuation curve, VC. As drawn, it shows that a faster growth rate will lead initially to increases in the firm's valuation ratio, after which it falls. The shape of the curve assumes that the investment opportunities the firm engages in first will be the most profitable ones; the higher the profitability of the firm, the higher will be the valuation ratio as the demand for equity in the firm increases. Beyond a certain point, growth can only be achieved by undertaking less profitable activities and this will discourage individuals from holding equity in the firm.

The preferences of management in this model are represented by indifference curves which show combinations of growth and security available to utility-maximising managers. The constraint that is imposed on them is the firm's valuation curve. In Figure 8.5B, we have drawn a point of tangency at E_0, where the firm's growth rate is G_0, which is higher than the rate which maximises the stock market value of the firm, shown by G_M. In this outcome, the firm's management is choosing a faster growth rate to give themselves more power and prestige, at the expense of the asset values held by shareholders.

Management perquisites

Figure 8.6 illustrates the effect of what is known as expense-preference behaviour by management. This refers to expenditure on perquisites ('perks'): corporate hospitality at Wimbledon, Twickenham and the Grand Prix circuit is the more high profile end of such practice, but the prevalence of perks in management positions is widespread. In the Figure, profits per period are measured on the vertical axis, and expenditure on management benefits is measured on the horizontal axis. In the case of an owner-managed firm, the budget constraint, B_0, shows the combinations of profits and benefits that the owner could choose. If, for simplicity, we ignore tax considerations, then expenditure on benefits reduces profits £ for £, and the slope of the budget line is minus one. The equilibrium for the owner-manager illustrated in Figure 8.6 is at point E_0.

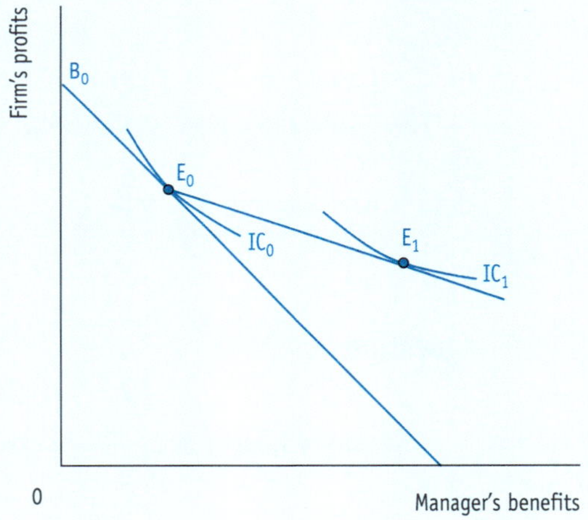

Figure 8.6 Expense-preference behaviour

Now suppose that the firm is under management control and that the manager has a 33% equity stake in the firm. A £1 spent on personal benefits, for example, will only reduce the share of the profit received by the manager by 33p. The budget constraint the manager faces will now have a slope of –0.33. The utility-maximising outcome for the manager is at point E_1 where expenditure on benefits is higher and the firm's profits are lower.[5]

Questionnaire evidence

The managerialist models suggest that firms may have multiple objectives. One source of evidence about the general validity of such models is questionnaires directed to senior

5 In principle at least, it may be possible for prospective investors in a firm to anticipate the divergence of interests between the owners and the management and lower the share price they pay.

Objective of company	% of companies
No single objective	29.9
Profit maximisation	28.6
Sales revenue maximisation	1.3
Increasing value	14.3
Other	26

Table 8.3 Objectives of Scottish companies 1993
Source: Hornby (1995).

management of firms that asks directly about the objectives of their companies. A study by Shipley (1981) of 728 UK companies found that just under a half (48%) of the firms classified themselves as profit-maximisers, while the remainder were aiming to achieve a 'satisfactory' level of profits. The figure of 48% was reduced to only 16% who stated that profit-maximisation was their over-riding objective. A more recent study by Hornby (1995) looked at the objectives of a sample of top companies in Scotland with broadly similar findings. The details are given in Table 8.3.

Questions

Q1 A company whose average total costs are $(16/Q) + 4Q$ has the following demand for its output

$$Q = 12 - (1/2)P$$

(I) What is its price-quantity decision if it sets out to maximise profit? What are the profit level and the associated total revenue?

(II) If its objective changes to maximising total revenue given a profit constraint of 2, what is its price and output level?

Q2 Suppose that a manager of a firm happened also to be its sole owner.

(I) Draw a budget constraint to show the trade-off between the profits and the perquisites that the individual could take if profits are taxed at 25%. What is the slope of the budget line?

(II) If the owner hires a manager who has 9.5% equity interest in the firm, what is the budget constraint that this individual faces? Is it possible that both the owner and manager would choose the same combination of profits and perks in equilibrium?

8.2 The principal–agent relationship and work incentives

In this section, we will cast the relationship between the owners and management of a firm in terms of the principal-agent problem. In general terms, a principal engages an agent to act on his or her behalf, but problems can arise when the principal is not able to observe directly what the agent does or does not do. The problems may be compounded when the agent also has some particular area of knowledge or expertise that the principal does not share.

The profits that firms make will often depend on the wider state of the world and when the profitability of a firm declines, it is not unknown for its management to attribute the fall in profits to a changing external environment. The explanations given may relate to macro-economic fluctuations, but they may they also relate to special factors and one-off events. For example, in 1998 several companies attributed falling sales in the summer to the effect of the World Cup. Fallen leaves and the wrong type of snow on the track have, in the past, been put forward as factors affecting the railways in the UK; although clearly there are industries that are sensitive to the weather, agriculture being an obvious example.

Some explanations for why a firm is making poor (or no) profits may be more plausible than others and there are a number of alternative ways that shareholders can attempt to assert their interests. The presence of non-executive directors on boards of companies who (in legal terms) are decision-makers, and who can also monitor the performance of the executive decision-makers is one such way. Although, in practice, the role of non-executive directors may be hampered by difficulties in getting access to detailed information, given that it is the Chief Executive Officer of a company who determines the agenda of boardroom meetings. Another development has been the establishment of remuneration committees, whose role is to determine the terms of executive reward in relation to corporate performance. Although again such committees tend to face the same difficulties that affect non-executive directors.

An alternative way of raising the shareholders' 'voice' is to encourage groups of large shareholders ('active investors') to participate in the strategic decisions made at boardroom level. The role of external shareholders varies between countries, but in the UK the financial institutions are not generally seen as a part of the governance of the company they have holdings in.[6] This picture is not repeated everywhere. Table 8.4A shows the pattern of ownership and agency relationships in the US, the UK, Japan and Germany taken from a comparative study by Prowse (1994), which highlighted international differences.[7] In the UK and the US, there was a general tendency for financial institutions to hold relatively small shareholdings in a large number of companies.

6 Financial institutions themselves have limited room to exercise discretion, given that criticism could adversely affect the share price of their holdings or make the disposal of the shares problematic.

7 This study drew together data from a number of sources covering the period from the 1970s through to the 1990s.

	United States	United Kingdom	Japan	Germany
Individuals	30–35	22.4	22.4	3.0
Financial institutions — agents	55–62	57.8	9.5	3.0
Financial institutions — owners	2.0	0.7	38.5	33.0
Non-financial corporations	7.0	10.1	24.9	42.0
Foreign	5.4	6.5	4.0	14.0
Government	0	2.5	0.7	5.0

Table 8.4A Estimated comparative pattern of ownership and agency relationships

Source: Prowse (1994).

Note: 'Financial institutions — agents' are pensions funds, mutual funds who hold equity as agents for other individuals. 'Financial institutions — owners' hold equity for their own accounts.

	United States	United Kingdom	Japan	Germany
Frequency of majority ownership %	10.8	9.8	8.4	25.1
Identity of owner — individual	5.1	6.7	2.1	6.4
— Financial institution — Non-financial institution — Other (foreign and government-owned)	5.7	3.1	5.3	18.8

Table 8.4B Majority ownership and identity of shareholder

Source: Prowse (1994).

By contrast, in Germany and Japan the financial institutions that owned shares on their own account, together with the non-financial institutions, held a much higher percentage of the shares in a company. A related point is the identity of the majority shareholding. This may have implications for corporate governance if the monitoring skills and incentives differ between individual owners and those firms owned by institutions. Table 8.4B provides further details from the Prowse study, which suggests that there is certainly scope for more shareholder monitoring in Germany than in the other three countries. Whether there is more monitoring in practice is taken up again in the discussion in Section 3.

The concentration of share ownership, and the identity of the large shareholders, are clearly an important part of the background in looking at how effectively shareholders are able to assert their interests. Institutional forms of control mechanism in UK-US companies have been criticised as being ineffective, and the development of the executive stock (or share) option can be seen as another attempt to align the interests of management and shareholders. We will start by analysing how these schemes might work in principle.

Contracts and symmetric information

In analytical terms, the principal (the owners of the firm) pays the agent (its management) and takes the profits arising from the agent's action. The higher is the level of profit for a given payment to the agent, the greater will be the sum that goes to the principal. To the extent that the profits of a firm depend directly on the effort level of the agent, there is a divergence of interest between the principal and agent assuming that the agent dislikes work effort. This divergence of interest gives rise to what are known as agency costs.

To begin with, we will assume that the same information is available to both principal and agent. Suppose that the firm's profit level depends on two variables: the effort of the firm's management and alternative states of the world (reflecting variations in company tax levels, the level of demand and so on). We can express this as

$$\Pi = F(WE, SW)$$

where Π is profits, WE is work effort and SW is the state of the world.

The work effort and the different states of the world could, in principle, interact in many different ways. To simplify, we will assume that there are just two alternative levels of work effort, high and low, and that there are three states of the world, favourable, neutral and adverse. These are referred to as WE_1 and WE_2 and SW_1, SW_2 and SW_3 in Table 8.5, which gives a numerical example for a particular firm.

In two out of three of the states of the world, the profits of the firm do not depend on the efforts of the management. In the favourable state profits are £40mn and in the unfavourable state £20mn, regardless of management performance. The middle column, a neutral external environment, is where the role of management is assumed to make a difference. The firm's

Work effort/ state of world	Favourable state, SW_1	Neutral state, SW_2	Adverse state, SW_3
High effort, WE_1	£40mn	£40mn	£20mn
Low effort, WE_2	£40mn	£20mn	£20mn

Table 8.5 Profits under different work effort and states of the world: an example

profits are the same as SW_1, the favourable state, with a high work effort and the same as SW_3, the adverse state, when work effort is low. If the alternative states of the world are known to both principal and agent, then a contract can be drawn up that specifies work effort level WE_1, in state of the world SW_2, and WE_2 in the two other states of the world.

This leaves open the question of what remuneration level the agent should receive, which is difficult to determine partly because of the risk involved. If the agent's remuneration was a fixed sum, it would mean that all the risk was borne by the principal; if remuneration levels varied with the state of the world there would be some sharing of risks between the two parties.

It may be reasonable to think of the agent as having risk-averse preferences, particularly if all, or most, of his or her income came from employment with the one firm. The principal may be considered to have risk-neutral preferences, particularly if the equity holding was one part of a portfolio of financial assets. In these circumstances it would be to the benefit of both parties if the principal assumed all the risk.

This is an outcome we can analyse with the indifference curve framework we covered in Chapter 5.[8] To simplify, we will begin with only the first and third columns of Table 8.5, so that the profit level of the firm depends only on the state of the world. In Figure 8.7, we measure the profit level in the favourable environment on the vertical axis, and, the profit level in the adverse environment on the horizontal axis. Any point marked in the figure represents a combination of payments to the agent in the two states of the world. Points along the 45 degree line represent a certain payment to the agent in either state. Clearly point C as marked in panel A represents a higher level of payment in the favourable state of the world than does point A. Point D represents a higher payment in the adverse state, SW_3, than does point A but a lower payment than point B in SW_1.

An indifference curve in this context shows alternative combinations of reward, or remuneration payments, in the two states of the world that gives the same expected utility to the individual agent. For the agent with risk-averse preferences, the indifference curves will be convex to the origin as illustrated in panel B of the figure.

As we saw in Section 5.2, the utility-maximising outcome for the risk-averse individual will occur at a point on the certainty line. An individual with risk-neutral preferences will have indifference curves that are straight lines and this is illustrated in panel C. The expected utility of the principal depends only on the expected profit level and points A, B and C on IC_2, for example, all give the individual the same expected utility.

8 This analysis proceeds is discussed in terms of individuals, although what we have in mind is potentially large groups.

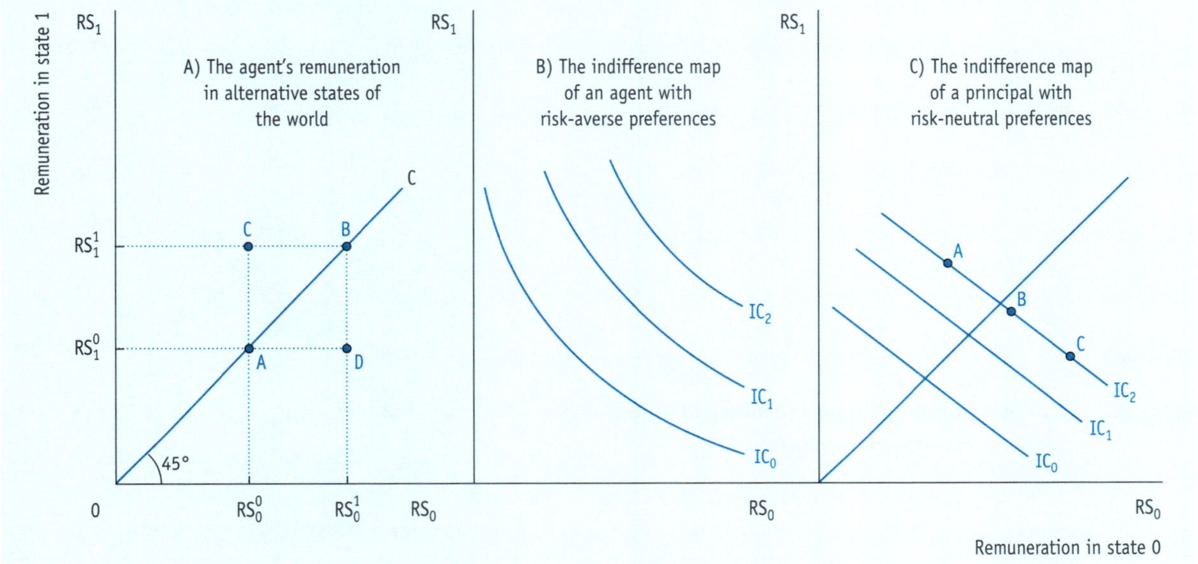

Figure 8.7 **The preferences of the risk-averse agent and the risk-neutral principal**

The next step in this piece of analysis is to bring the preferences of the agent and principal together and this is done in the box diagram Figure 8.8. This shows the preferences of the agent with respect to the south-west corner, those of the principal with respect to the north-east. The height of the vertical axis measures the profit in the favourable state of the world, the horizontal axis measures profits in the adverse state. In terms of our numerical example, these would be £40mn and £20mn respectively.

Each point within the box represents a particular contractual outcome: it tells us how much each party in a contract between principal and agent will receive. In the figure, we have marked 3 possible outcomes at points B, C and D. The outcome at point D gives the agent RS_0^A when profits are low, RS_1^A when they are high. The two subscripts relate to the two states of the world: state 0 is the adverse state, the favourable state is state 1 as was the case with the analysis in Chapter 5. The principle receives the residual in the two alternative states. This contract, however, is not optimal in the sense that it would be possible to raise the utility of one of the individuals, without lowering that of the other.[9] In Figure 8.8, a move from point D to point B would move the agent onto a higher indifference curve, while keeping the principal on the same indifference curve. A move to point C from point D would do the opposite.

At points B and C, it is not possible to make one party better off without making the other one worse off. Both these points represent what are called Pareto-optimal outcomes: moving

9 This is known as a Pareto-improvement and is an idea that is covered more thoroughly in Chapter 16.

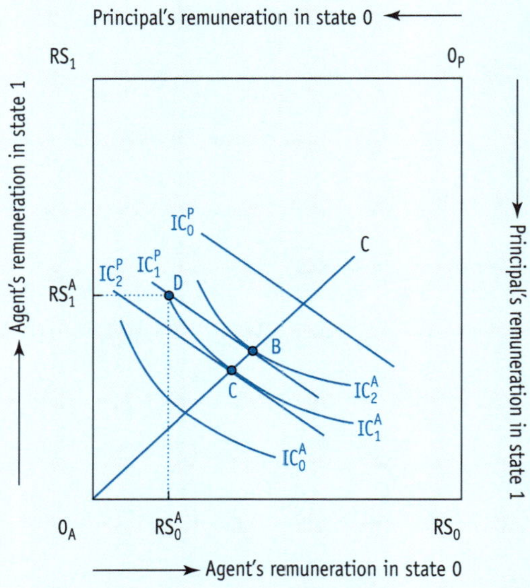

Figure 8.8 **Pareto-optimal outcome for principal agent problem (symmetric information)**

from point B to C would make the agent better off at the expense of the principal, the move from C to B does the opposite. An optimal contract will therefore lie somewhere along the agent's certainty line between these two points, given that we start at point D.[10]

When there is symmetric information it is therefore possible, in principle, to design a contract that overcomes the problem of inducing appropriate effort levels on the part of the risk-averse agent. The agent gets a fixed salary and the principal accepts all the risk concerning the profit level. Exactly what point on the certainty line of the agent this negotiated outcome will be depends on the degree of risk aversion of the agent.

Contracts and asymmetric information

When there are information asymmetries, designing contracts to encourage work incentives is more problematic. In our numerical example in Table 8.5, if the state of the world is not known to the principal, the agent can represent a low profit figure as a result of an adverse environment when it may be as a result of low work effort. The agent is in a position to take advantage of the lack of information available to the principal.[11]

We therefore have a problem in which there is both an asymmetry of information and risk, given that alternative states of the world may occur. The question is can the principal design a

10 Point D is the endowment or initial position.

11 In practice, the principal may have an idea about the general state of the economy, but it often remains difficult to know the effect on a particular company.

contract that will makes the agent's interest consistent with his or her own interest? Can the principal offer the agent an additional sum in the favourable state of the world that would encourage a high level of work effort? In answering this, we will assume that by more work effort the agent can increase the probability of there being a high level of profit. For example, if the three states of the world in Table 8.5 have the same probability of occurring, then the probability of a profit level of £40mn is increased to 0.67 when the agent's work effort is high.

In Figure 8.9A, we show the effect of work effort on the agent's indifference map. Whereas previously the remuneration of the agent in state of the world 1 did not depend on his or her effort level, now it does and to reflect this we have two differently sloped indifference curves. The indifference curve IC_0 is drawn on the assumption of a high effort, WE_1, and IC_1 is drawn on the basis of a low work effort, WE_2.

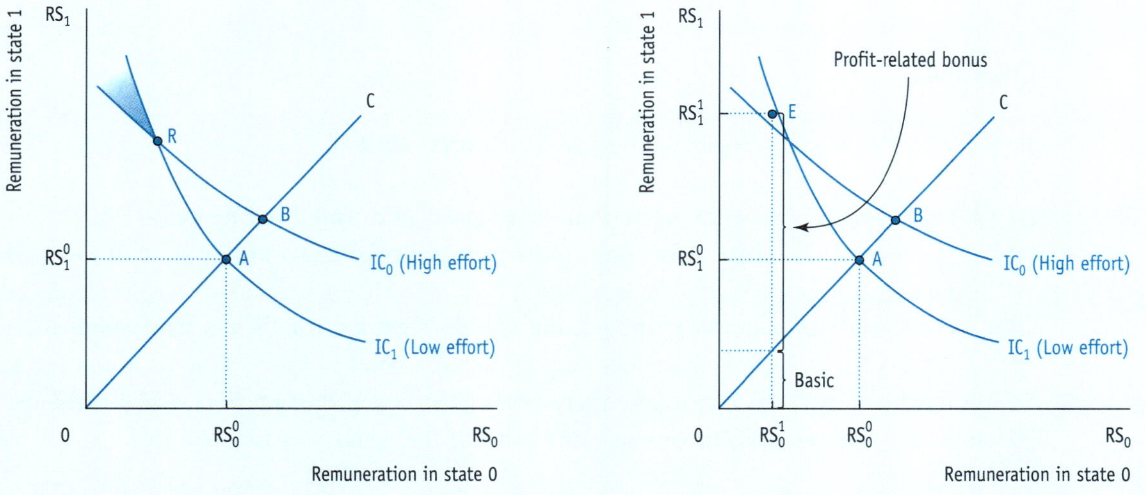

Figure 8.9A Agent's indifference curves (alternative work effort levels)

Figure 8.9B Work incentives for the risk-averse agent

To see why this is, start at point A on the certainty line. This gives the agent the same level of consumption in both states of the world. The extra work effort necessary with WE_1 means that point A represents a lower level of (expected) utility than it does with WE_2. To compensate the individual, a higher level of reward is necessary, as shown at point B. The distance AB, therefore, gives the extra remuneration required for the agent to obtain the same level of utility, when the work effort involved is WE_1.

The slope of the individual's indifference curve through point B is flatter than that through point A because the probability of a high profit level occurring has risen. The willingness to exchange remuneration in state 0 for that in state 1 has risen, because state 1 is more likely to occur when the work effort rises. At the point of intersection marked R, the additional reward the individual receives when profits are high, leaves him or her indifferent between making the additional work effort and not making it.

With remuneration levels in the alternative states at points to the north-west of R, the individual is better off by making the high level of effort. In the region bounded by ABR the agent receives more than when making a low effort but is not offered enough remuneration to induce a high work effort. If the agent with risk-averse preferences initially has a contract at point A, on the certainty line and is paid RS_0^0 RS_1^0 in the two states of the world, the principal can induce additional work effort by offering RS_0^1 RS_1^1 to the agent marked as point E, as shown in Figure 8.9B. The remuneration for the agent can then be broken down into a basic payment and a bonus scheme as shown.

Questions

Q3 In Figure 8.9A, what happens to the size of the area ABR if

(I) The agent is more risk-averse than is assumed in drawing the figure.
(II) The impact that work effort has on the probability of a favourable state of the world is greater.
(III) The agent's aversion to making a high level of work effort is less than assumed?

Q4 Suppose the principal has risk-averse preferences as well as the agent, how would it change the conclusions of the analysis in this section? What if the agent was risk-neutral?

8.3 Evidence on executive reward and corporate governance

In this section, we will focus on the effectiveness of executive share option schemes, ESOs, in aligning the interests of management and shareholders. In broad terms, the operation of executive rewards can be broken down into three component parts. Firstly, there is base pay such as fees and salaries. Additionally, there are a range of benefits or perquisites and compensation agreements that may need to be taken into account. Finally, there are share option schemes, which are intended to link the pay of senior executives to the future long-term performance of the firm. It is worth noting at the outset that share options are generally awarded only to a small number of top executives.

An ESO gives the executive the right to buy at some future date a share in the company at a particular price. The price is known as the exercise price. The worth of the share option to the executive increases as the firm's share price rises over a period of time, and hence the link between executive remuneration and company performance. Until 1995, in the UK, the Inland Revenue 'approved' schemes, and these had certain limits placed on them.[12] The executive had to wait for a period of three years before he or she had the option of buying shares at the exercise price. The option of purchasing the shares expired after a period of ten years. ESO schemes also had other limits placed on them: approval was limited to schemes with a value of £100,000 or four times the executive's emoluments.

If the share price rises and the executive exercises the option then he or she will receive the difference between the market price and exercise price (less the transaction costs) on selling the shares. The individual, for obvious reasons, is said to be 'in the money'. Should however the market price of the firm's shares fall below the exercise price, the executive suffers no direct financial loss, as he or she has the option to not buy shares in the company. In which case the share price, rather than the individual, is 'under water'.

Option schemes have a long history, particularly in the US. In the UK, the number of schemes has expanded rapidly growing by a factor of five in the 1980s, and as Main, Bruce and Buck note 'British directors have been enthusiastic providers and consumers of executive share options . . .'.[13] Table 8.6 below summarises the main findings of a number of studies that have investigated the executive compensation-firm performance relationship.

The conclusions summarised in the notes show differences in the importance attached to the pay-performance relationship. It should be appreciated that the relationship might simply vary over time, and also between countries as economic, cultural and political circumstances change. There may also be methodological differences that affected the conclusions reached and we will now discuss some of these.

Four of the bottom five studies listed in Table 8.6 offer critical findings about the absence of a systematic link between pay and performance in the UK. The standard approach to investigating the pay-performance relationship is by regression analysis, estimating a single-equation model of the form

$$\text{Comp} = b_0 + b_1\text{Perf} + \text{other variables} + u_i$$

On the left hand side is a measure of compensation and (one of) the right hand side variables is a measure of company performance. The coefficient b_1 is taken as a measure of the

12 At one point, there were considerable tax advantages to an executive if the ESO was an 'approved' scheme.

13 Main, Bruce and Buck (1996, p. 1632).

Author(s) date	Nature of sample	Results
Lewellen and Huntsman (1970)	50 US companies 1942–63	Including long-term elements has little effect on reward-performance
Cosh (1975)	1,601 UK companies 1969–71	Size more important than profitability in determining narrowly defined pay
Meek and Whittington (1975)	1,008 UK companies 1969–71	Sales the best determinant of pay but profits significance reaffirmed
Murphy (1985)	73 US companies 1964–81	Performance more significant than size in explaining executive reward
Deckop (1988)	108 US companies 1977–81	Profit-sales ratio most important determinant
Szymanski (1992)	51 UK companies 1981–91	Weak pay-performance link
Gregg, Machin and Szymanski (1993)	288 UK companies 1983–91	Weak pay-performance link. No ESOs
Conyon and Gregg (1994)	170 highest-paid UK directors 1985–90	Sales growth more important than performance. No ESOs
Conyon and Leach (1994)	294 highest-paid UK directors 1983–86	Weak pay-performance link. No ESOs
Main, Bruce and Buck (1996)	59 UK companies, aggregate board and highest paid directors 1982–89	Inclusion of ESOs significantly increases pay-performance link.

Table 8.6 **The compensation-performance relationship**
Source: Adapted from Bruce and Buck (1997).[14]

sensitivity of pay to performance; the larger its value the stronger the relationship between pay and performance. The overall conclusion from the more recent empirical work in the UK is that when there was a link, its size was estimated to be very small. For example, the Gregg *et al.* study of 1993 investigated the relationship in a number of companies over the period 1983–91 and found that the weak link that existed until the late 1980s had disappeared by the early 1990s.

14 This study gives the references for the studies mentioned in the table.

However, these studies are suggestive not definitive, partly arising from difficulties of measurement. For example, what should the definition of the dependent variable be? Much research has used time-series data at a company level, taking observations on the highest-paid director, but the postholder not the pay of a particular individual. This may conflate the variations in remuneration for an individual over time with changes that might be due to the recruitment of a new individual. A number of studies were also based on data series that excluded the deferred benefits of ESOs.

The study by Main *et al.* (1996) found that by changing the definition of the left-hand side variable to include share options the sensitivity of the pay-performance relationship increased markedly. On a broader definition of pay they estimated that a 10% increase in shareholder wealth had the effect of (immediately) increasing the pay of the highest paid director by 8.94%.[15] The defenders of share option schemes suggest that ESOs are a way of reducing agency problems. Attempts by institutional investors, such the Association of British Insurers and the National Association of Pension Funds, to place ceilings on the scope of option schemes are therefore viewed as being counter-productive.

Critics of the schemes suggest that they only increase agency costs.[16] Certainly, there are a number of more general methodological issues to be aware of in considering the evidence, including that of Main, Bruce and Buck. One is the possibility of reverse causation: it may be that changes to executive work incentives are made in anticipation of improved company performance. It should be appreciated that the dependent variable is based on share prices to determine the value of ESOs, and that the independent variable is also based on market measures of company performance.

More fundamental are the objections raised to the principal-agent model by, among others, Kay and Silberston (1995), who criticise the basic premise that a corporation is owned by its shareholders and that managers exert power and responsibility on their behalf. What does ownership mean in this context? If you own a car, you have the right to use it when you want, to re-spray it in whatever colour you fancy and to sell it as and when you please. Share ownership is essentially different: ten shares in British Airways does not entitle you to free use of the Concorde lounge. On the other hand, senior executives in large corporations do typically enjoy the opportunity to re-carpet their offices, travel first-class and in some respects tend to act in a manner befitting the owners of the firm.

15 There are also questions that arise about the measurement of the company performance variables, which can be measured in terms of total shareholder's returns (the dividend paid plus the capital appreciation or depreciation), or by accounting profits (measured by earnings per share, or by return on capital employed).

16 This is a subject that we return to in Chapter 12 when we discuss the remuneration of the top executives in privatised utility companies.

Kay and Silberston contend that the statement that a company is owned by its shareholders 'makes little sense'.[17] This raises the question whether this apparently indeterminate state of non-ownership is important, and if so, why? They point to those outside the Anglo-American tradition who conceive of large companies as social organisations. Major examples are the practices in Japan, Germany and elsewhere in continental Europe where managers see their company's development as depending on the interests of a number of stakeholders — suppliers, employees, shareholder, and customers — rather than with the single objective of profit-maximisation (or making statements to that effect). Looked at in this way it can be argued that corporate governance is about more fundamental matters than the issue of pay for top executives alone. Some further issues on this subject are taken up in the question that follows.

Question

Before thinking about this question you should read Kay and Silberston (1995).

Q5 The authors propose a New Companies Act to address a number of issues of corporate governance, including

(I) The establishment of a PLC board, comprising a (financially) independent Chair and independent directors.
(II) Fixing the term of appointment for the Chief Executive Officer of corporations for a period of four years, with a maximum of one period of renewal (akin to the US Presidency).
(III) Determining in advance the salary and bonuses to be paid to the CEO.

Would it be advantageous to adopt these proposals?

Concluding comment

In this chapter and the previous one we have reviewed a number of alternative models of the firm. It should be clear that no single, unified theory of the firm exists which commands agreement amongst economists; rather there have been a number of different approaches emphasising different aspects of a firm's operation.

The traditional neo-classical theory provides a clear, simple and intuitively plausible summary of the objectives of small firms, and remains influential among economists, at least as a point of departure in analysis. We have seen from some survey evidence that a majority of the firms

17 Kay and Silberston (1995) p. 87.

sampled did not see themselves as profit maximisers. The managerial theories which point to a divergence between the interests of the owners of firms and their managers, have broadly been supported by the limited degree of linkage between pay and performance in the boardroom of companies (at least for certain periods). What kind of policy response is appropriate to this perceived failure of managerial accountability produces a wide spectrum of opinion. In this text we will return to this issue when in Chapter 12 when we discuss the costs of agency in relation to utility regulation, and in Chapter 15 when we discuss the cost of capital.

Mathematical appendix

Linear demand curves and marginal revenue

Given a downward-sloping linear demand curve

$$P = a - bQ$$

Total revenue is

$$TR = PQ = aQ - bQ^2$$

Marginal revenue is

$$MR = \frac{dTR}{dQ} = a - 2bQ$$

The slope of which is twice that of the demand function.

For example, if $P = 60–4Q$, $TR = 60Q - 4Q^2$ and $MR = (dTR/dQ) = 60–8Q$.

The profit-maximising firm

The profit-maximising firm maximises the difference between total revenue and total cost, which can be written as

$$\pi(Q) = TR(Q) - TC(Q)$$

The first-order condition for maximisation is

$$\frac{d\pi}{dQ} = \frac{dTR}{dQ} - \frac{dTC}{dQ} = 0$$

So that

$$MR = \frac{dTR}{dQ} = MC = \frac{dTC}{dQ}$$

with the second-order condition that

$$\frac{d^2\pi}{dQ^2} < 0$$

Summary

1 The profit-maximising firm will maximise the difference between total revenue and total cost. An equivalent decision rule for the firm is to equate marginal revenue with marginal cost.

2 Managerial theories of the firm point to the separation of ownership and control over decision-making in large companies. Managers are seen as individuals who exercise discretion over the decisions made and this leads to objectives other than profit-maximisation being pursued.

3 There are a number of different managerial theories that emphasise different aspects of the objectives of management. Baumol's analysis summarises these objectives in terms of sales maximisation, other analysis points to the role of the growth of firm size.

4 The principal-agent model analyses the divergence of interest between the management and shareholders of a firm, when it is difficult to monitor the behaviour of the agent, i.e. when there is a problem of asymmetric information. When there is risk concerning the firm's profitability, the management may have the opportunity to explain their poor work effort in terms of an adverse state of the world.

5 When there is a risk-neutral principal and a risk-averse agent, performance-related pay can, in principle, help to align the interests of management and shareholders.

6 It is not straightforward to establish whether there is a link between pay and company performance. Several studies of companies in the 1980s and 1990s suggest that the rewards of the top directors are closely linked to the size of the operation that they manage, but that links to company performance are not strong. However, data definitions may be important and studies that include long-term rewards such as executive stock options suggest that the links are stronger.

End of chapter questions

Q6 A firm faces the following demand for its product

$$Q = 6 - 0.25P$$

has Average Total Costs, $ATC = 4Q + 9Q^{-1}$

Q = Quantity produced and sold, at Price P.

(I) What are the price and output levels that maximise total revenue? What is the firm's profit level at this output?
(II) What is the firm's profit-maximising price and output level? What are the profits?
(III) Suppose that the firm maximizes total revenue within a profit constraint of 7. What is the firm's price and output level?

Q7 Alba runs a small company importing exotic fruit, Papaws'R'us. The Table below gives the profits in three alternative states of the world, which reflect the weather in South Florida. The profits also depend on whether the firm's manager, Steve, works for five days a week or six.

Work effort\state of world	Favourable state, SW_1	Neutral state, SW_2	Adverse state, SW_3
High effort, E = 6	£50,000	£50,000	£25,000
Low effort, E = 5	£50,000	£25,000	£25,000

Both agree that each state of the world is equally likely to occur. Alba's utility function is

$$U_A = P - S$$

Where P is the profit of the firm and S is Steve's salary. His utility function is

$$U_S = S^{0.5} - E^2$$

Where E is the effort level expended.

(I) Given the alternatives of an equal chance of £36 and £64 and the certainty of receiving £49 how would Steve rank them? What do you conclude about the preferences towards risk from the utility function for the manager?

(II) What is the marginal utility of profit income from the utility function of the firm's owner? What kind of preferences towards risk does this utility function represent?
(III) Suppose Steve can earn a salary of £18,000 working elsewhere making an effort level of 5. What is the value of his utility index?
(IV) If the firm's owner was offering a basic salary of £15,000 what incentive bonus would have to be offered to Steve to persuade him to work for the firm?
(V) If the salary that Steve can command working elsewhere rises to £23,000, what is the minimum incentive payment necessary to keep him working for the firm?

Q8 According to Llewellyn (1997)

> 'there are two fundamental differences between firms in, say the manufacturing sector of the economy, and those providing financial intermediation services — financial intermediaries:

(1) One of the major inputs of the financial intermediary is money which is the same commodity that companies requires as capital.
(2) In the case of the financial intermediary, its customers provide money and stand at both ends of the value process: customers provide the basic input (money) but also demand the service being supplied.'

Given this, why do you think some building societies have converted from mutual organisations to PLC status?

Q9 You should read Chapter 11 of 'Corporate Governance', by Clarke and Bostock (editors Keasey, Thompson and Wright) before thinking about this question. The authors conclude that

> '. . . the German governance system, with its supervisory board, with both shareholder and employee representations on it, is in many ways a superior governance system to that in the Anglo-Saxon world . . .'

Do you agree with them?

References and suggested further reading

In this chapter, we have not discussed behavioural approaches to the firm. This emphasises the institutional aspects of a firm's structure and its actual decision-making to understand the behaviour of a firm. Earl provides a good introductory source. The text edited by Keasey *et al.* (1997) provides accessible introductions to a number of aspects of the Corporate Governance debate. A number of the empirical studies require some understanding of econometrics to appreciate the analysis presented (and its limitations). The questionnaire evidence of Shipley (1981) and Hornby (1995) do not.

Baumol, W.J. (1959), *Business Behaviour, Value and Growth*, Macmillan.

Bruce, A. and Buck, T. (1997), 'Executive Reward and Corporate Governance'. In Keasey, K., Thompson, S. and Wright, M. (eds), '*Corporate Governance*', Oxford University Press.

Clarke, T. and Bostock, R. (1997), 'Governance in Germany: The Foundations of Corporate Structure?'. In Keasey, K., Thompson, S. and Wright, M. (eds), '*Corporate Governance*', Oxford University Press.

Conyon, M.J., Gregg, P. and Machin, S. (1995), 'Taking Care of Business: Executive Compensation in the UK', *Economic Journal*, **105**, 704–14.

Earl, P.E. (1995), *Microeconomics for Business and Marketing*, Edward Elgar.

Franks, J. and Mayer, C. (1990), 'Corporate Ownership and Corporate Control: A Study of France, Germany and the UK', *Economic Policy*.

Gregg, P., Machin, S. and Syzmanski, S. (1993), 'The Disappearing Relationship Between Directors' Pay and Corporate Performance', *British Journal of Industrial Review*, **31**, 1–10.

Hornby, W. (1995), 'The Theory of the Firm Revisited: A Scottish Perspective', *Management Decision*, **33**.

Jensen, M.C. and Meckling, W.H. (1976), 'Theory of the Firm: Managerial Behaviour, Agency Costs and Ownership Structure', *Journal of Financial Economics*, **3**.

Kay, J. and Silberston, A. (1995), 'Corporate Governance', *National Institute Economic Review*, **84** (Aug), 84–97.

Keasey, K., Thompson, S. and Wright S. (1997), *Corporate Governance: Economic, Management and Financial Issues*, Oxford University Press.

Leech, D. and Leahy, J. (1991), 'Ownership Structure, Control Type Classifications and the Performance of Large British Companies', *Economic Journal*, **409**, 1418–1437.

Llewellyn, D.T. (1997) '*The Mutuality-Conversion Debate*', Loughborough University Banking Centre — Building Society Association Project Papers, Project Paper No 2.

Main, B.G.M., Bruce, A. and Buck, T. (1996), 'Total Board Remuneration and Company Performance', *Economic Journal*, **106/439**, 1627–1644.

Office for National Statistics (1996) Financial Statistics.

Prowse, S. (1994) '*Corporate Governance in an International Perspective*', BIS Economic Papers, Basle.

Shipley, D.D. (1981), 'Primary Objectives of British Manufacturing Industry', *Journal of Industrial Economics*, **29**.

9

Competition

Key ideas and material

Perfect competition, comparative static analysis, European and UK agriculture

Introduction

This chapter begins our discussion of alternative market structures. We will start with a simple model of a perfectly competitive market in which the product bought and sold is identical, and where there is free entry and exit by firms into and out of the industry. While it is obvious that this does not describe actual markets in the UK, or anywhere else, the analytical framework that we will develop can be used to examine the effect of government intervention and policy-making in a number of areas.

The main application in this chapter is the intervention by EU governments in agriculture via the Common Agricultural Policy (the CAP). Since its formation, the operation of the CAP has dominated budgetary expenditure within the EU, and the implementation of the support for farmers has raised controversial questions about how policy affects the interests of producers and consumers. The analysis of this chapter will help us to evaluate the impact of the CAP, and the reform process that started in the 1980s with production quotas for dairy farmers and which now extends more widely following the Uruguay round of GATT negotiations.

The outline of this chapter is as follows. In Section 1, we develop the industry supply curve in a competitive market, starting with the decision-making of the individual firm. The nature of industry supply in the long-run is shown to depend on the firm's production technology and what happens to the prices of the firm's factor inputs when demand for them rises. Putting together industry supply and demand, which we discussed in Chapter 1, allows us to explain the price and output decisions of firms in a competitive industry.

In Section 2, we analyse the effect that different types of taxes have on a firm's decision-making and we also examine the important subject of tax incidence. The government may impose a tax on producers, but how much of the tax is shifted forward on to consumers in the form of higher prices, is something that will depend on the elasticity of the supply and demand. Finally, in Section 3, we analyse the welfare impact of price supports that are given to European agriculture via the CAP.

9.1 Perfect competition

A perfectly competitive market is one in which there are a very large number of buyers and sellers of an identical good (or service) none of whom have any influence on the market price. The firm in such a market faces a horizontal, or perfectly elastic, demand curve so that it can sell as much as it wants to at the going market price. Since its output is a perfect substitute for the output of every other firm, if it were to raise its price above the market level, demand for its product will fall to zero. Conversely, it has no financial incentive to lower its price.[1] Such a market is also characterised by the free entry and exit of firms; which is important as it is the ability of new firms to compete with those already in the industry that determines the profit levels made in the long-run.

The firm in the short-run

The profit maximising output level of the firm is represented in Figure 9.1, where we have drawn the total revenue and total cost curves. A perfectly elastic demand curve means that total revenue is simply a multiple of the quantity sold, and so is drawn as a straight line out of the origin.[2] The shape of the firm's total cost curve reflects the assumption that it eventually faces decreasing returns to scale. As before, profits are again maximised where the difference between total revenue and total cost is at a maximum. This is shown diagrammatically in Figure 9.1 at the output level Q_{Π}.

The short-run adjustment by the firm to variations in demand is shown in Figure 9.2. A perfectly elastic demand curve means that the firm's average revenue will be equal to its marginal revenue.[3] Suppose we start with the level of demand marked Q_0^D, then the response of the profit maximising firm is to equate marginal revenue with marginal cost, resulting in an output level of Q_0 for the firm. The firm is in equilibrium at this point.

1 The industry demand curve is based on the analysis of household choice and is therefore is downward sloping. The perfectly elastic demand curve facing the firm is, in effect, subject to it remaining one of a large number of firms in the industry.

2 The shape of the total revenue is therefore different to that drawn in Chapter 8 where we assumed a downward-sloping demand curve.

3 As can also be noted from the slope of the total revenue curve in Figure 9.1.

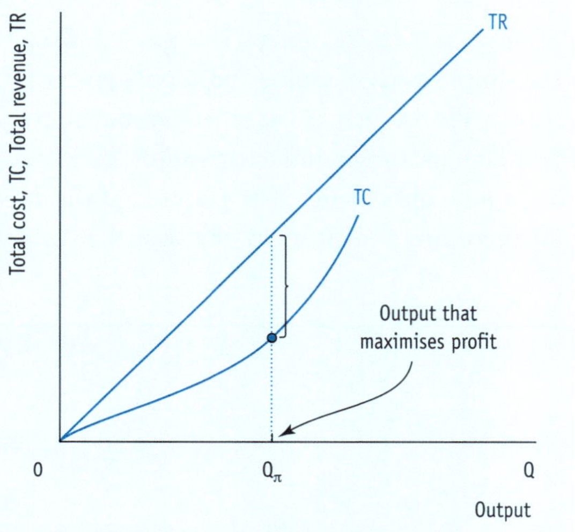

Figure 9.1 **Profit maximising output for the firm in perfect competition**

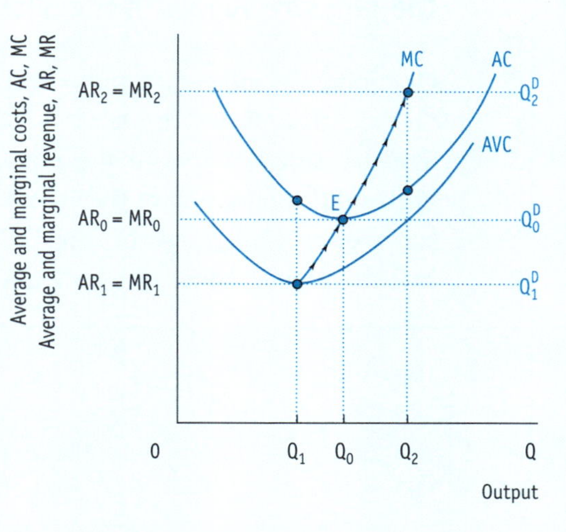

Figure 9.2 **The short-run response of the competitive firm to a change in demand**

If for some reason demand were to fall from Q_0^D to Q_1^D, then the average revenue the firm receives will be less than its average (total) cost. The firm will therefore be making a loss. Since average revenue equals average variable cost and, given an irreversible decision about the level of capital stock in the short-run, the firm will produce the output level Q_1 in the figure. The firm will continue in production provided that demand does not fall below the level Q_1^D. Below this level of demand, the firm's average revenue is less than its average variable cost and it would be adding to its losses if it produced anything.

If demand rises above the level Q_0^D the firm will respond by increasing its output. At the level of demand given by the demand curve Q_2^D, for example, output will be Q_2. We can similarly associate other output levels with other levels of demand above Q_0^D. The short-run supply curve of the firm in perfect competition is therefore obtained from equating average (or marginal) revenue with marginal cost above the minimum point on the average variable cost curve.

It should be clear that this is not sustainable in the long-run. If the firm is making a loss it will be driven out of business. On the other hand, if the firm's average revenue is above its average cost then it will be making above normal profits. Normal profits simply refers to the profit level that is just sufficient to the keep the incumbent firms in the industry, but is not high enough to attract new entrants. A situation in which the existing firms were making abnormal or economic profits would attract new producers into the industry. To look more closely at the long-run adjustments we will now examine the interaction of supply and demand at the level of the industry.

The industry supply in the short-run

Obtaining the industry supply curve involves the simple step of adding the supply curves of all the (identical) firms. In Figure 9.3, there is a representative firm in the left-hand panel and the industry supply curve in the right-hand panel. The short-run industry supply curve is the horizontal summation of the supply curves for the individual firms. For example, if the supply curve of the individual firm is $Q^S = 10P$, and there are 100 firms in the industry then the industry supply curve is simply $Q^S_{IND} = 1000P$.

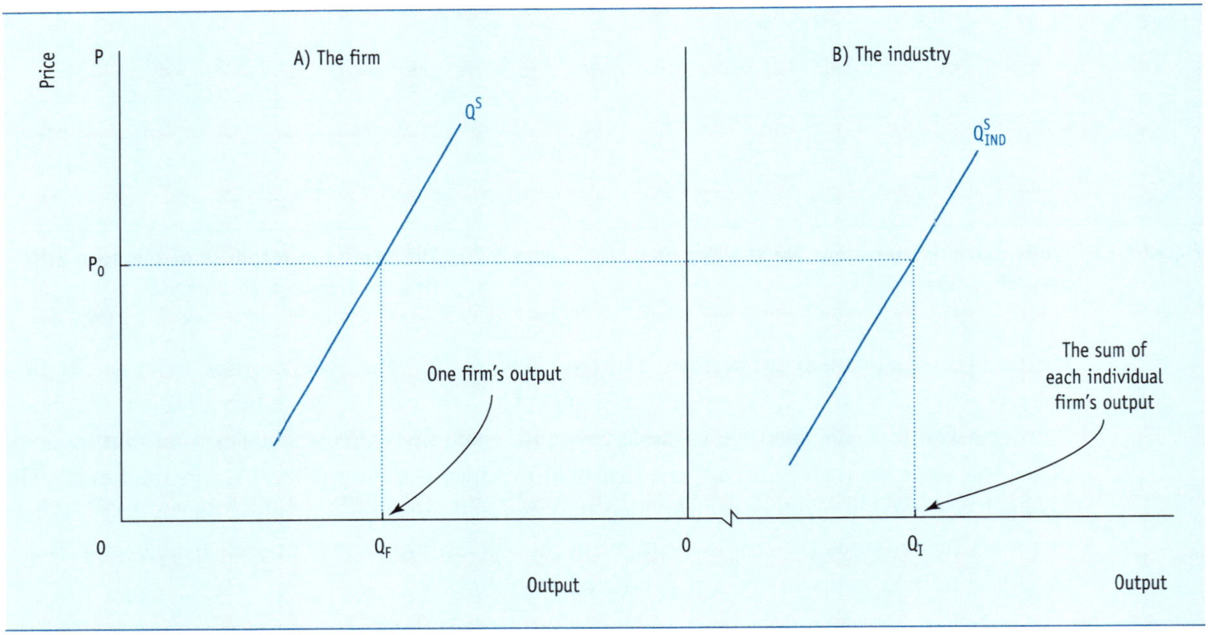

Figure 9.3 The firm and industry supply curve

Equilibrium in the short-run

In Figure 9.4, the firm's demand is initially given by AR_0 in the left hand panel. The profit-maximising firm will produce at the point where the price it receives is equal to its short-run marginal costs, and as drawn it is making economic profits. The industry position is shown in the right-hand panel where the level of industry demand and supply results in the market price, P_0, which generates the profits for the firm.[4]

These profits play a key role in the adjustment from a short-run to a long-run equilibrium, as they attract new firms into the market. The new entrants increase supply and reduce the

4 Of course, the firm need not necessarily be making profits, as we saw when discussing the firm's supply curve the firm could be loss-making in the short-run.

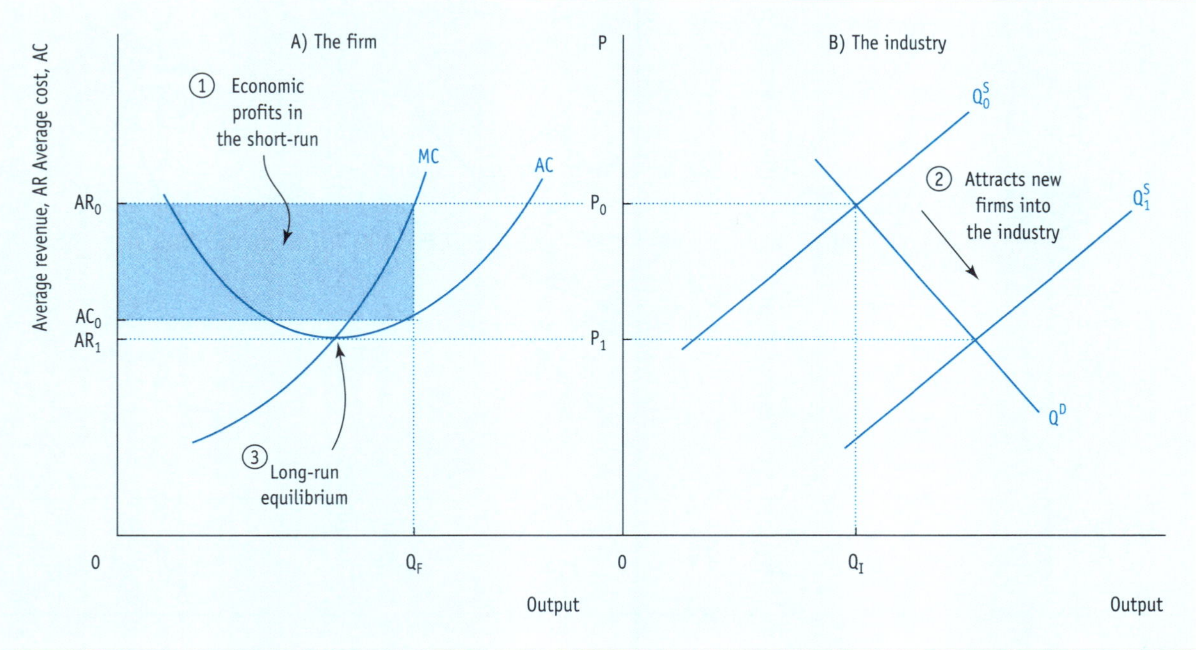

Figure 9.4 **Short-run equilibrium in a competitive industry**

market price, from P_0 to P_1. The impact that this has on the incumbent firm is shown in the left-hand panel by the fall in the firm's demand curve; in the long-run the firm makes normal profits.[5]

The long-run equilibrium position of the competitive firm illustrated in Figure 9.4 has two desirable properties. It produces at the minimum point of its average cost curve, what is known as productive efficiency. It also produces at an output that is allocatively efficient, that is where the price is equal to the marginal cost. The monetary valuation on the last unit of the good purchased by consumers, the price, is equal to the cost of the resources utilised in producing it, that is the marginal cost of production.

The industry supply in the long-run

The short-run supply curve for the industry is drawn as upward sloping in Figure 9.4, representing increasing costs as output expands. In the long-run, the particular shape for the industry supply curve will depend on what happens to factor prices when output increases (we will be assuming constant returns to scale). In principle, the supply curve could be upward

5 This may appear to be a self-defeating exercise for the firms who have to make the decision whether or not to enter the industry: if they do they make only normal profits in the long-run. However in the short-run a new entrant can still make profits and this may provide a justification for entry.

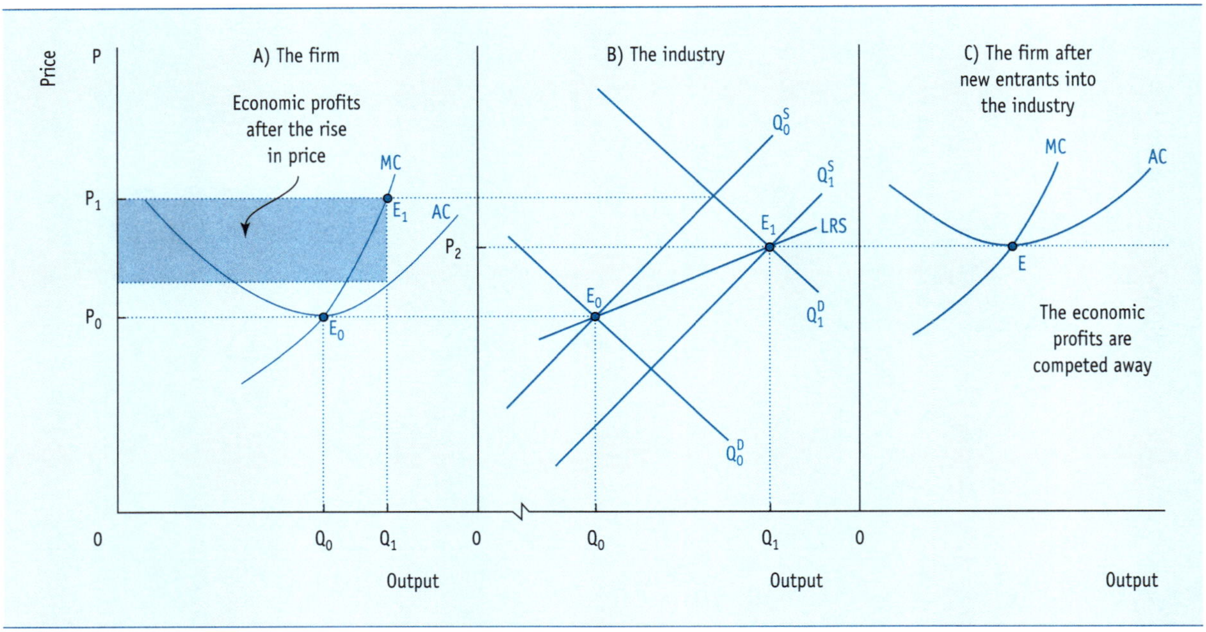

Figure 9.5 **An increasing cost industry**

sloping, horizontal or downward sloping, just depending on what applies in a particular industry. We will discuss each of these three cases in turn.

Figure 9.5, panel A shows the position of the competitive firm in equilibrium, producing at the industry price of P_0. The industry output is shown as Q_0 in panel B. Suppose an increase in demand for the product occurs shifting the industry demand curve from Q_0^D to Q_1^D, causing the market price to rise to P_1. The output of existing firms in the industry rises from Q_0 to Q_1 as shown in panel A, who then make the economic profits shown by the shaded area.

As mentioned above, economic profits encourage new entrants into the industry and the short-run supply curve moves to the right, from Q_0^S to Q_1^S as shown in panel B. The new entrants increase the demand for factor inputs, and if factor prices rise as a result, the new (long-run) equilibrium price is higher than the initial price, P_0. This possibility is shown as P_2 in panel B and the position of the individual firm in long-run equilibrium is shown in panel C. This analysis gives us two points on the long-run industry supply curve, LRS, which are (P_0, Q_0) and (P_2, Q_1). We can then form the supply curve by imagining a range of possible shifts in demand and joining up the associated points; given that the price of factor inputs rise as output expands the LRS will slope upwards.

In the case of the constant cost industry, what differs is that following an increase in demand the price of factor inputs does not change. The increase in demand again causes the price to rise to P_1 and incumbent firms will again be making economic profits as shown in Figure 9.6

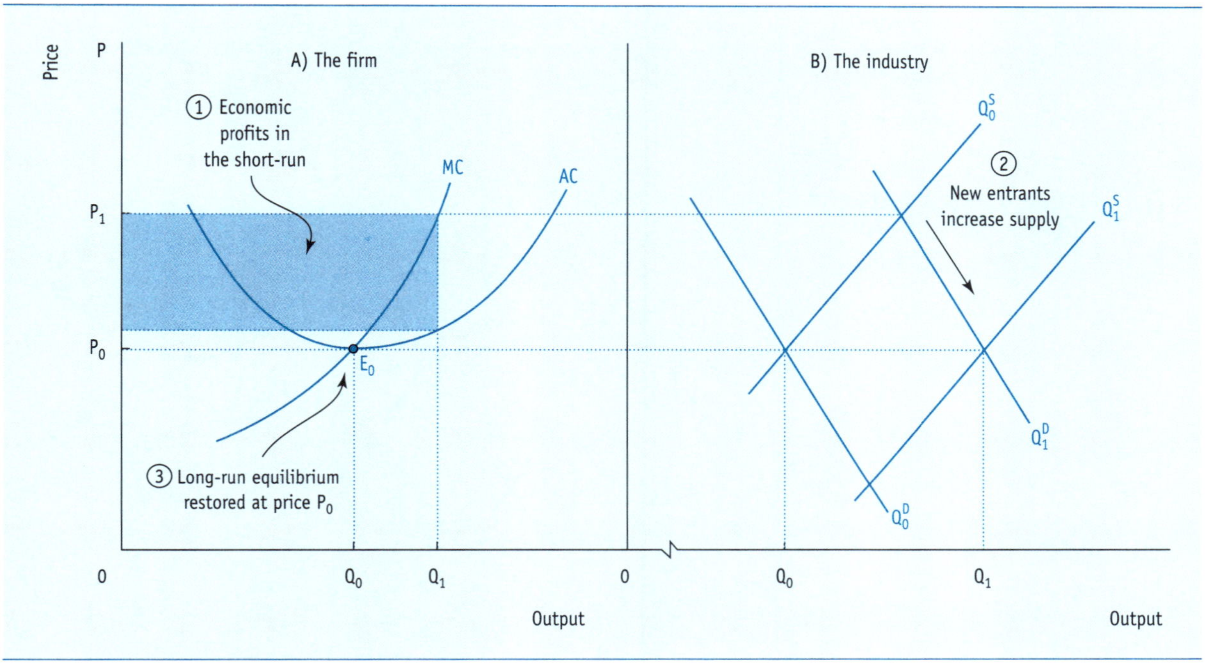

Figure 9.6 **The constant cost industry**

panel A. However, in this case when new entrants increase supply the initial equilibrium price, P_0, is restored. The long-run supply curve, again formed from considering a range of shifts in demand, is horizontal.

Finally, the third case is that of a decreasing cost industry which is illustrated in Figure 9.7. Here the new entrants have the effect of reducing the price of factor inputs, and so the shift in the short-run supply curve shown in panel B leads to a fall in the market price to below the initial equilibrium. The long-run supply curve is formed in the same way as the other cases but is now downward-sloping.

The supply elasticity

The way that the industry supply responds to changes in price is summarised by the supply elasticity. It is

$$\frac{\text{\% Change in quantity supplied}}{\text{\% Change in price}}$$

The value of this elasticity will clearly vary in the short and long-run.

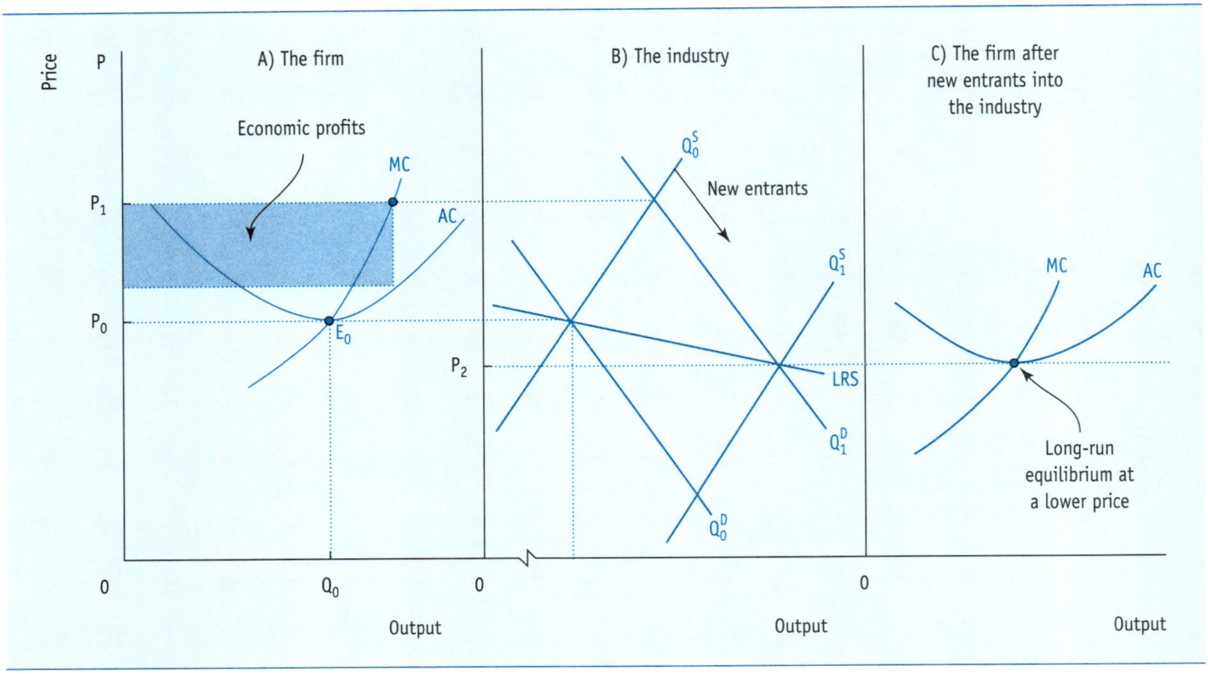

Figure 9.7 A decreasing cost industry

Consumer and producer surplus

Figure 9.8 illustrates the concepts of consumer and producer surplus. Consumer surplus is simply the difference between what the individual pays at the market price and what he or she would be willing to pay as indicated by their demand curve. When we aggregate this across all individuals, the area under the demand curve bound by FEP_0 shows the entire consumer surplus from the consumption level Q_0.

The counterpart for the firm is known as producer surplus. In a competitive market, the price received by each firm is P_0. Below this price the supply curve gives what the firm would be prepared to produce at particular prices. The area of the triangle GEP_0 in Figure 9.8 gives the amount of producer surplus.

Producer surplus is also equal to the difference between the firm's total revenue and its total variable costs. This follows from the fact that the supply curve is obtained from aggregating the marginal cost curves of all firms in the industry. The amount of producer surplus is therefore related to, but is not the same as, the profit made by the firms in the industry. The difference between them is total fixed costs.

Consumer surplus and producer surplus are measures of the aggregate welfare benefits from a competitive market. The neo-classical approach is to assume representative individual

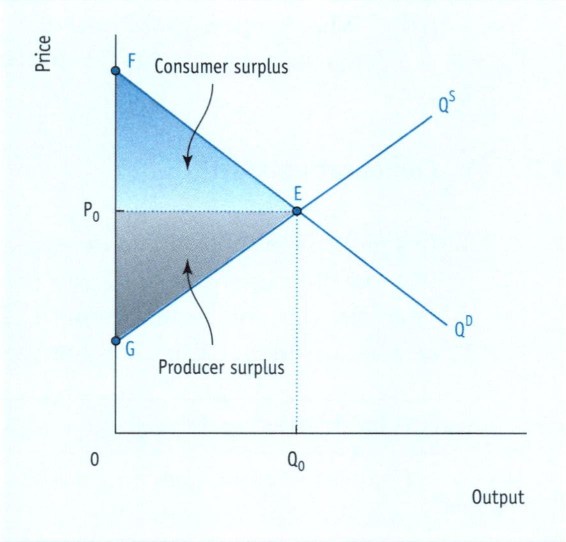

Figure 9.8 **Consumer surplus and producer surplus**

consumers and producers, and use the measures of consumer and producer benefits as *the* measures of welfare. The usefulness of this is something we will return to later in this chapter.

Questions

Q1 A perfectly competitive firm faces a market price of 50 per unit and has a total cost function

$$TC = 10 + 5Q^2$$

(I) Sketch the firm's average cost and marginal cost curves. What is the firm's profit maximising level of output? What is the profit level?

(II) If the government imposes a tax of 10 per unit of output what happens to the firm's output and profit level?

(III) If fixed costs increased to 25 what happens to firm's output and profits?

Q2 The industry demand for a product by made by firms in a perfectly competitive industry is given by

$$Q^D = 100{,}000 - 20{,}000P$$

(I) If there are 1000 identical firms in the industry, and the equilibrium price is 3, how much does each firm produce?

(II) If the demand rises to $Q^D = 160{,}000 - 20{,}000P$ what happens to the equilibrium price in the short run? How many firms will there be in the industry after the increase in demand?

(III) What happens to the level of consumer surplus after the change in demand? How would the answer vary if $Q^D = 160{,}000 - 40{,}000P$?

9.2 Comparative statics

In Chapter 7, we introduced the neo-classical idea of the firm as a 'black box'. We noted there that one of its uses is to study how the firm responds to changes in its external environment. In principle, this could come from a change in any of the (exogenous) variables that affect demand or supply. Table 9.1 indicates a number of the possibilities.

Factors affecting demand	Factors affecting supply
Changes in consumers' incomes	Change in the firm's technology, i.e. a change in the production function
Changes in the price (or the expected price) of a substitute or a complement	Changes in the price of a factor input including the imposition of a tax
Changes in the preferences of consumers	A change in the number of firms

Table 9.1 Variables affecting demand or supply

This is not an exhaustive list. Our concern here is mainly with supply, so we will analyse the response of the firm to the imposition of two different types of tax.

A lump-sum tax on a firm

We need to distinguish between a lump-sum or poll tax, which does not vary with the firm's output, and a per unit tax which does. The analysis of a lump sum tax is relatively straightforward, as it is, in effect, one type of addition to the firm's fixed costs. Figure 9.9 panel A shows the firm's price initially as P_0, and its output as Q_0. At this point the firm is just making normal profits. The imposition of a lump sum tax shifts up the firm's average cost curve from AC_0 to AC_1 but, since there is no change to the firm's marginal costs, there will be no change to the output of the firm in the short-run.[6]

If firms differ in terms of their efficiency, in the long-run the least efficient will be forced to leave the industry. This is represented by the industry supply curve in panel B shifting from Q_0^S to Q_1^S, and the industry output contracting from Q_0 to Q_1. The equilibrium price rises from P_0 to P_1, although the exact outcome does, of course, depend on the shape of the long-run

6 As long as average revenue remains above average variable cost.

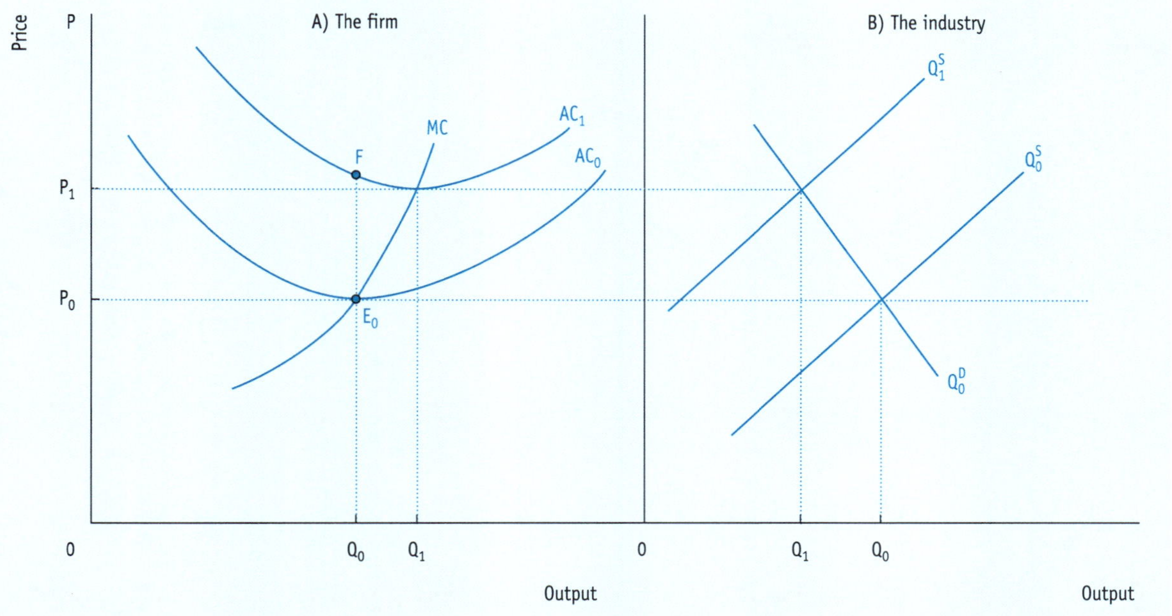

Figure 9.9 **The effect of a lump sum tax**

industry supply curve. The consequence of this at the industry level is fewer firms and lower output, although the output of each individual firm would be higher, as shown by the difference in output level for the individual firm in panel A.

The effect of a per unit tax

The overall effect of a per unit tax is not so clear-cut. The tax will raise the marginal cost of production for the firm by the extent of the tax. In Figure 9.10, this is shown by the marginal cost curve of the individual firm shifting up from MC_0 to MC_1.[7] The profit maximising firm equates marginal revenue and marginal cost, and so its output level is reduced in the short-run, from Q_0 to Q_1 as shown in panel A. At the level of the industry, assuming increasing long-run costs, the price will rise and output will fall. However, the firm's optimal output level could increase or decrease, depending on the relative magnitude of the shifts of the average and marginal cost curves. As drawn in Figure 9.10, the firm's output level is lower in the long-run.

Tax incidence

It is important to appreciate the distinction between the formal and effective incidence of a tax. For example, in the case of the airline industry, there is a tax levied in the form of a fixed

7 It will also raise average variable costs.

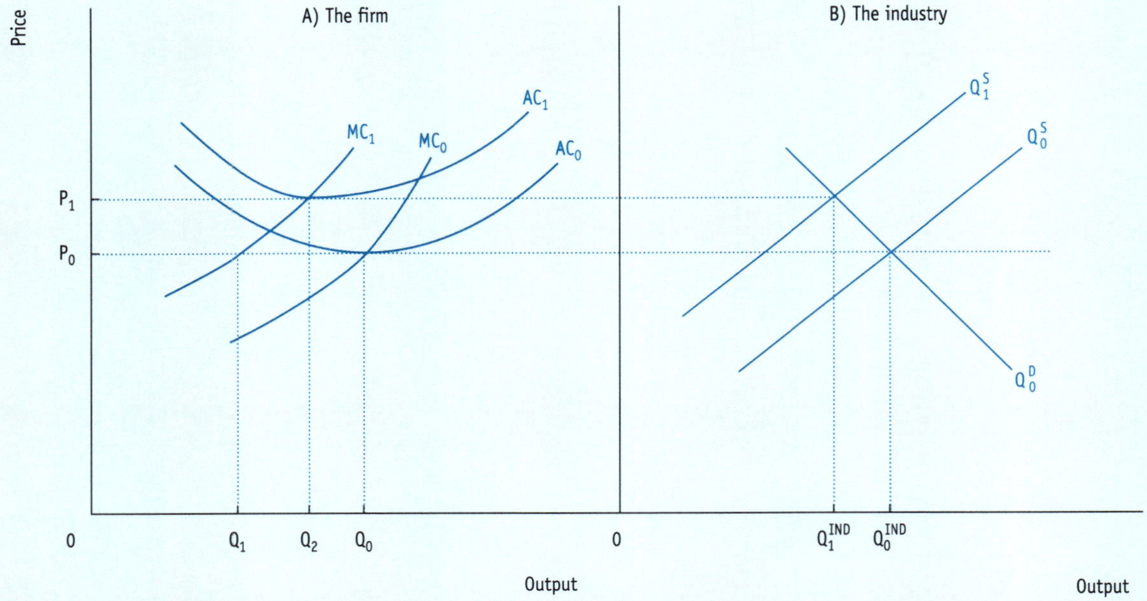

Figure 9.10 The imposition of a per unit tax

charge per passenger. In terms of our analysis, the effect of this, as illustrated in Figure 9.11, is to shift up the industry supply curve from Q_0^S to Q_1^S, with the result of increase in price from P_0 to P_1.

Who pays the tax? The amount of the tax is given by the vertical distance between the two supply curves, which is greater than the increase in equilibrium price. In the figure the tax per passenger is shown by the vertical distance E_1G and the increase in price paid is E_1F. This means that a part of the tax is paid by the airlines in the form of lower revenue received per passenger, shown by the distance FG in the figure. Notionally, the tax is paid by the airline, but effectively the incidence of the tax is shared with passengers. Given the shift in the supply curve, the exact proportion of the tax paid by the two parties will depend on the elasticity of demand: the less elastic demand is, the higher the proportion paid by passengers.

Questions

Q3 A firm has the following cost and revenue structures:

$$AC = 20Q^{-1} + 21 - 5Q + Q^2$$

Where AC is the firm's average total cost and Q is the quantity produced.

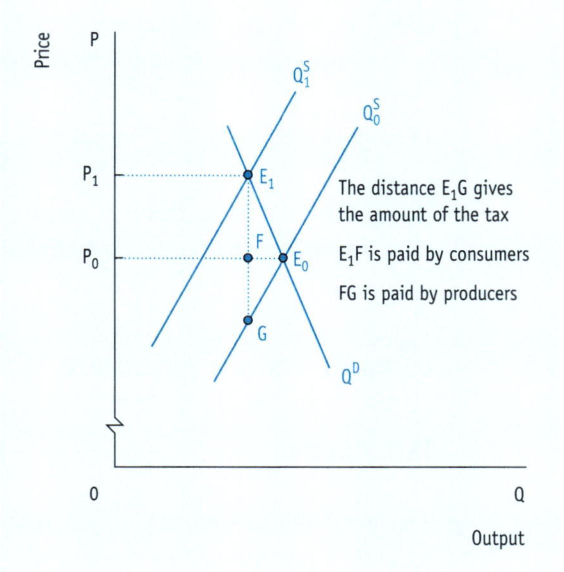

Figure 9.11 Tax incidence

Its demand function is

$$Q^D = 102 - 2P$$

where P is the price charged.

(I) Find the output, price and profit levels if the firm maximises profits.
(II) What is the firm's response to the imposition of a lump-sum tax of 120?
(III) What is its response to the imposition of a tax of 18 per unit of output instead of the lump-sum tax? How would the firm respond if both taxes were imposed?

Q4 The market demand and supply for chocolate biscuits is as follows

$$Q^S = -10 + 5P$$

and

$$Q^D = 20 - P$$

(I) What is the equilibrium price and quantity? Calculate the areas representing consumer and producer surplus.
(II) Suppose the government imposes a lump-sum tax of 1 on the industry, what effect does this have on the equilibrium outcome? What happens to the sum of consumer and producer surplus, i.e. 'the total economic surplus'?

(III) How much of the tax is paid by the producers and how much by the consumers? Suppose the demand curve was $Q^D = 22 - 2P$, how does your answer change?

Q5 Distinguish between the formal and effective incidence of a tax when

(I) Demand is perfectly elastic/inelastic
(II) Supply is perfectly elastic/inelastic.

9.3 European and UK agriculture

Introduction

The agricultural industry forms the starting point in the human food chain and its fundamental importance is obvious. The analysis of agricultural markets raises a series of issues relating to the balance of producer and consumer interests. It also raises the question of what role (if any) there is for government intervention in agricultural markets. In this section, we will use the analytical background we have developed to inform our discussion of these issues.

The agricultural industry in Europe has many of the features that would be expected of a competitive industry: a large number of small farms, unrestricted entry and exit from the industry and considered broadly, an homogeneous product. There is, of course, large variation in the size, and type, of farms across the EU, and in turn the overall importance of agriculture in each member state. For example, in Greece around one in five of employees in the working population are engaged in agriculture, whereas in the UK it is around one in 50. Table 9.2 gives details of the differences between the other member states.

There are nearly eight million farms in the EU. The UK stands out in that the average farm size is much larger than elsewhere, around twice the size of farms in France, for example. The final two rows in Table 9.2 shows the huge difference in farm sizes in Europe and the US.

There has been a long-term growth in the size of farms in the UK which, by European standards, are efficient. In terms of our analysis, the changing production methods that have been associated with this growth, such as mechanisation and the increasing use of pesticides and fertilisers, would be represented by falling input costs. What this means in principle is illustrated in Figure 9.12. The introduction of new technology lowers the average and marginal cost curves of the individual farm, leading eventually to lower prices and larger farm sizes. The individual producer that initially produces an output level of Q_0 at a price of P_0, in the long-run produces an output of Q_1 at a price of P_1. Given that farms vary in terms of their efficiency, the least efficient go out of business (or are taken over by other farms).

Country	Number of farms ('000's)	Average size (hectare)	% Employees of the working population	% GDP
Austria	267	12.9	7.3	1.1
Belgium	76	17.7	2.7	1.3
Denmark	74	37.0	4.4	3.6
Germany	606	28.1	3.3	1.5
Greece	819	4.3	20.4	7.3
Finland	192	14	7.7	1.1
France	801	35.1	4.9	2.0
Ireland	159	26.9	11.1	4.8
Italy	2,488	5.9	7.5	2.7
Luxembourg	3	42.3	3.7	0.9
Netherlands	120	16.8	3.7	2.9
Portugal	489	8.1	11.5	2.0
Spain	1,384	17.9	9.3	3.0
Sweden	92	36.5	3.0	0.4
United Kingdom	244	67.1	2.1	1.0
EU 15	7,815	16.4	5.3	1.7
US	2,073	206.7	6.4	1.8

Table 9.2 **The importance of European agriculture**
Source: European Commission (1996).

A combination of a low price elasticity of demand for foodstuffs and the changes in production methods has historically led governments in the industrialised countries to support farm incomes.[8] This has been done in a number of ways, including direct intervention to affect farm prices. Since the UK joined the then European Economic Community in 1973, it has been done principally via a system of tariffs on imported produce and price floors for the produce from European countries. Chart 9.1 shows the long-term trend in real food prices in the UK. What

8 Intervention has also been motivated by other factors including a strategic need for agricultural produce after the end of the Second World War, and the continuing influence of the farmers' lobbies in some EU member states.

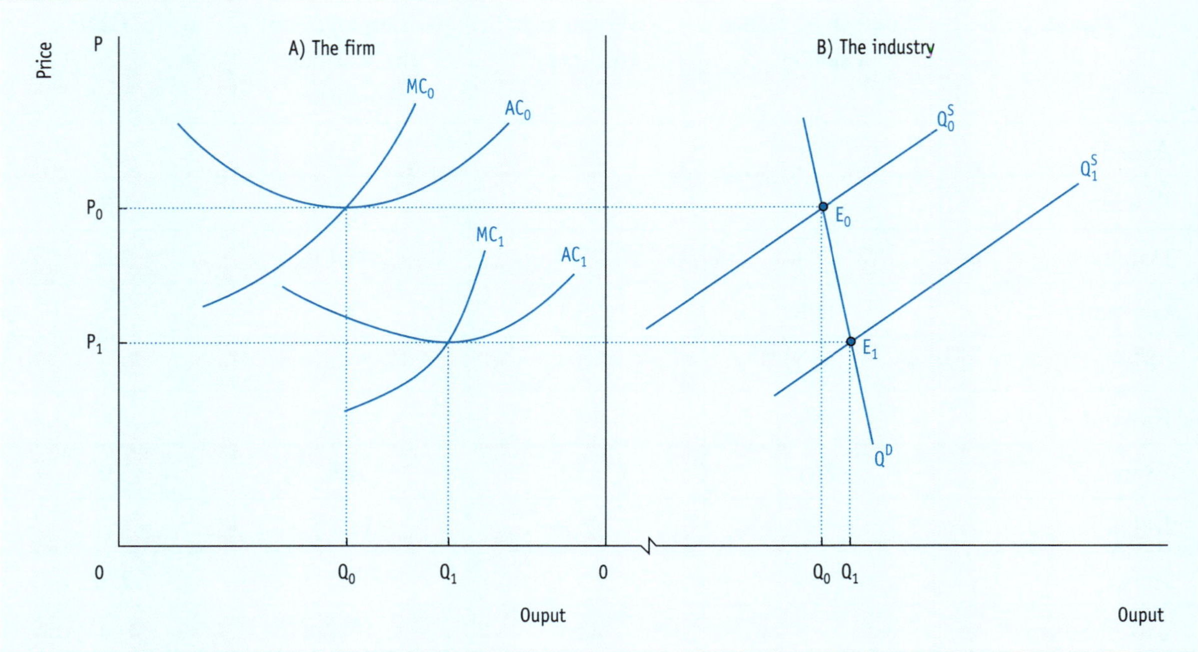

Figure 9.12 A fall in agricultural costs of production

stands out is the absence of any fall in food prices paid by the consumer, which is in sharp contrast to the analysis of what would have happened in the absence of government intervention. Broadly, the effect of government policy has been to prevent food prices from falling.[9]

Chart 9.2 shows the change in the index of food prices since 1948. There have been two periods of relatively sharp price increases; one at the end of a period of rationing after the Second World War, the second after joining the Common Agricultural Policy (CAP) of the EU. The period since the late 1970s has broadly been one of declining food prices. These price movements lead us to policy questions about the balance of interests between consumers and producers, and in turn to the operation of the CAP.

The CAP

The Treaty of Rome which established the then EEC in 1957 set out the objectives of the CAP as

(I) To increase agricultural productivity by promoting technical progress and by ensuring the rational development of agricultural production and the optimum utilisation of the factors of production, in particular labour.

9 To be sure, there is a distinction between the 'farm-gate' price of agricultural produce and the price paid by consumers (which includes the costs of distribution and retailing for example).

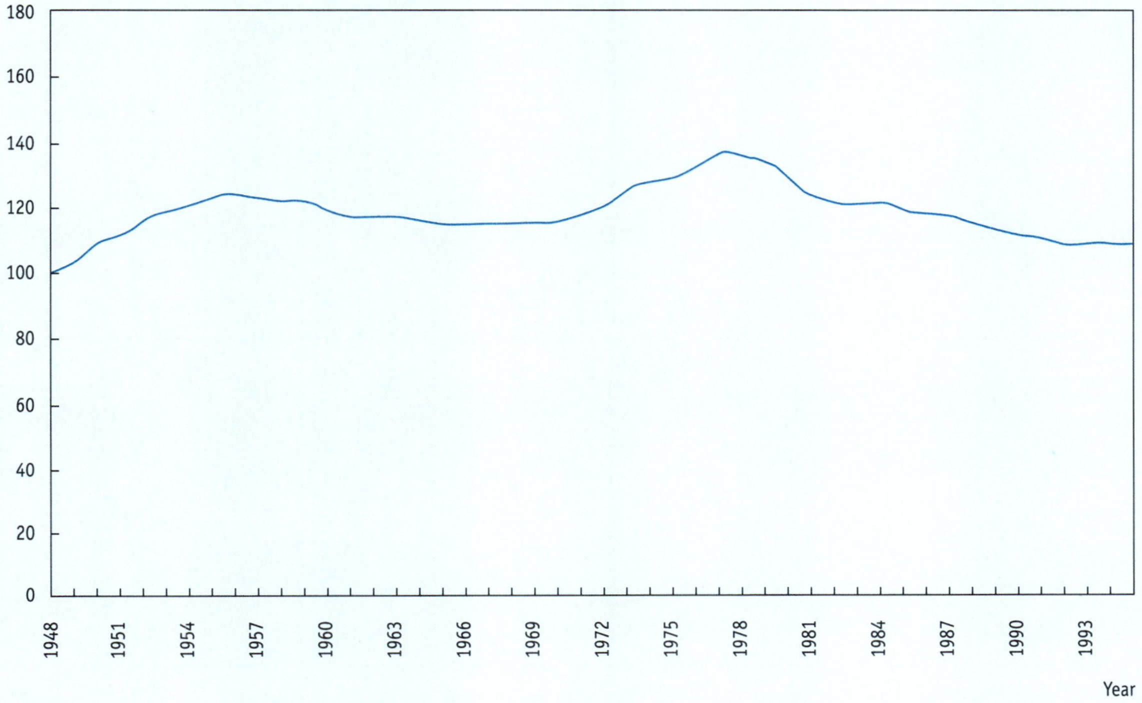

Chart 9.1 Index of real food prices
Source: Economic Trends.

(II) To ensure a fair standard of living for the agricultural community, in particular by increasing the individual earnings of persons engaged in agriculture.
(III) To stabilise markets.
(IV) To assure the availability of supplies.
(V) To ensure that supplies reach consumers at reasonable prices.

Alternatively, the CAP can be thought of in terms of the three principles of (I) a single market, (II) community preference and (III) financial solidarity. The first of these principles, the single market, means here simply the free movement of agricultural produce between the member states of the (now) EU, without distortions in the form of subsidies from domestic governments or other barriers to trade. A single market also requires common prices, and the details of the CAP's operation are designed to this end.[10] Community preference refers essentially to the need for protection from low-priced imports from the world market, which arises from the relatively high costs of production in member states. Finally, the CAP is based on sharing the costs of operating the system of supports between the member states, hence the

10 The operation of the CAP has involved its own monetary system.

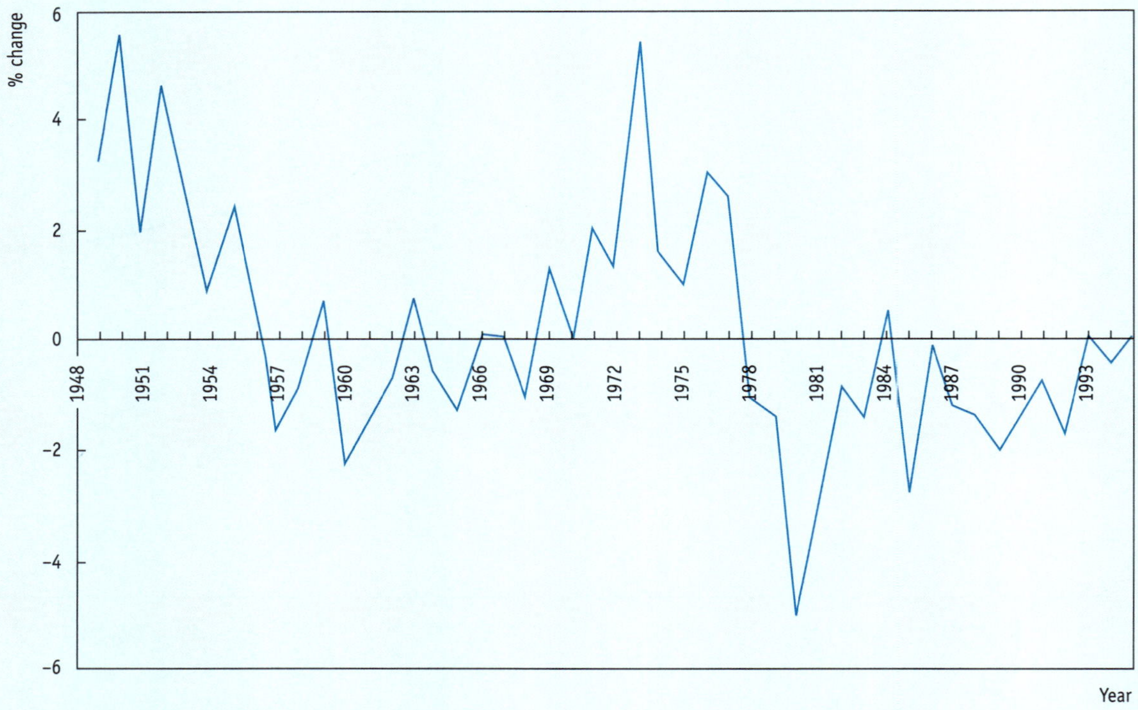

Chart 9.2 Index of change in real food prices
Source: Economic Trends.

principle of financial solidarity. A specially created EU organisation, The European Agricultural Guidance and Guarantee Fund (EAGGF) finances the intervention policies of the CAP.[11]

The operation of the system can seem rather involved with different details for different produce, but Figure 9.13 reduces it to its main essentials. At the top of the figure is the target price, negotiated annually by the Council of Agricultural Ministers. It is the price where the product concerned is in shortest supply in Europe, and is used to form a point of reference for calculating the intervention price.

The world price for agricultural produce is typically below the EU price. Chart 9.3 shows this for a range of farm products. A variable import levy was therefore charged on non-European produce to maintain EU prices; the amount of the levy varied so that imported produce would be no less than the target price once transport costs had been covered. This is shown in Figure 9.14, where the difference between the world price plus the import levy and the target price

11 This organisation is often referred as FEOGA, which are the initials when written in the French language.

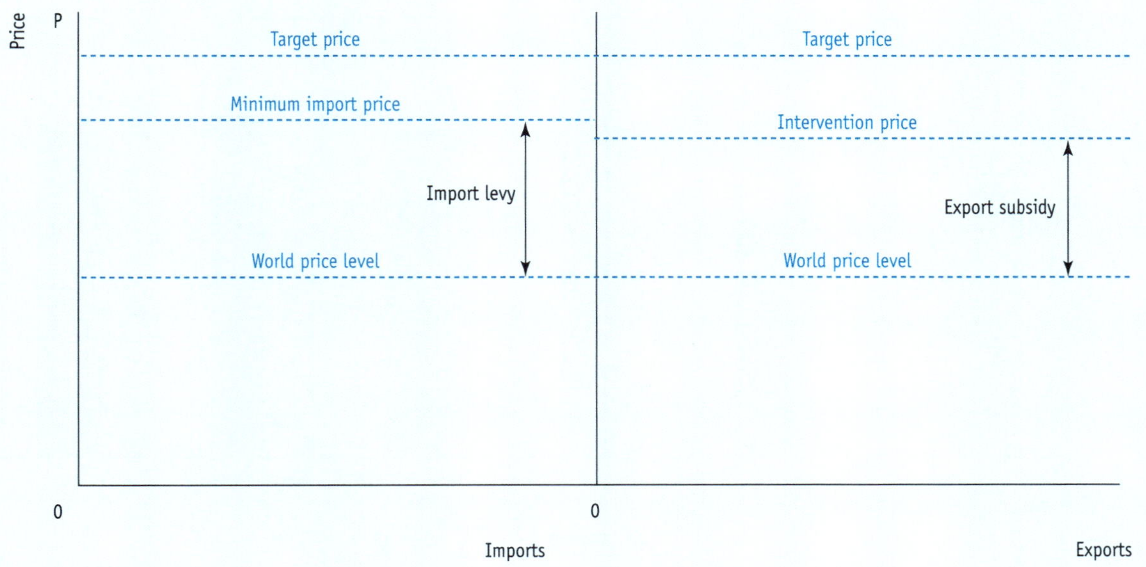

Figure 9.13 The CAP

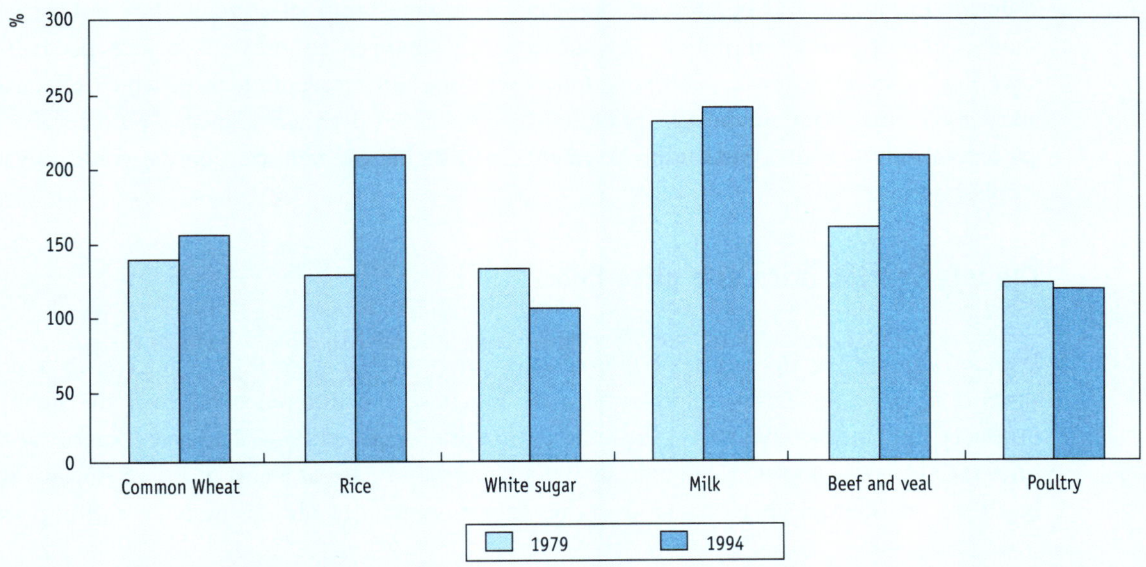

Chart 9.3 EU prices as a % of world market price

Source: Ritson (1997).

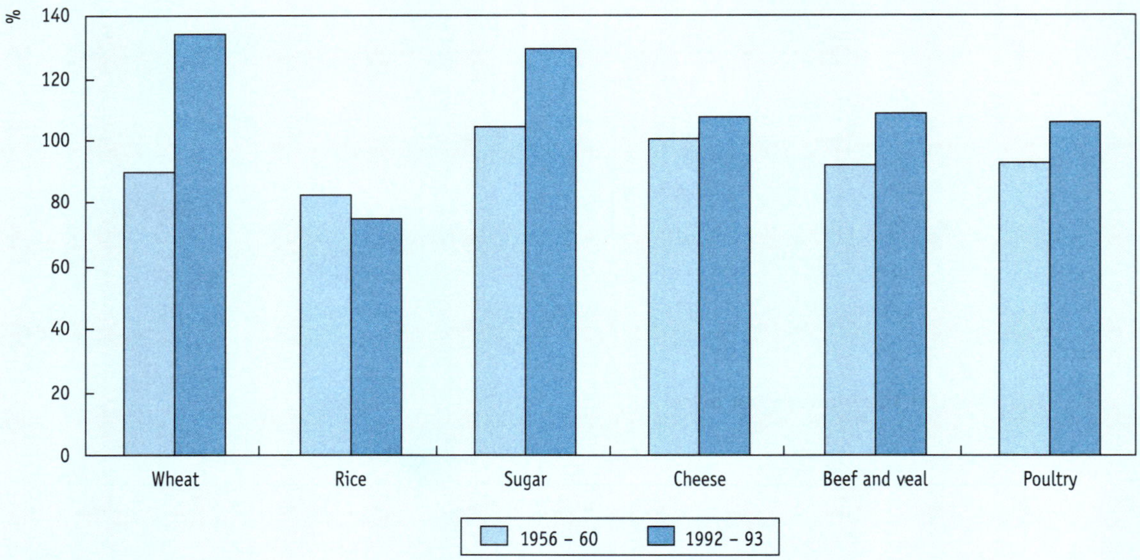

Chart 9.4 **% self-sufficiency within EU**

Source: Ritson (1997).

allows for these transport (and distribution) costs. Over time, this generous system of price supports meant the EU became self-sufficient in a wide range of commodities as Chart 9.4 shows. The operation of policy was subsequently changed to prevent surplus production lowering community prices. This was done by setting an intervention price which effectively acted as a price floor; if the EU price fell below this level either farmers would receive an export subsidy (called a restitution payment), or official intervention boards would buy the surplus output.

The intervention price as a price floor

We can analyse the operation of intervention prices with Figure 9.14. Under such a price support system, the intervention authorities purchase the difference between the quantity produced, and market demand at the intervention price, marked P_{INT}. The excess supply at this price is $Q_{INT} - Q_0$, and this is bought by the intervention board at a cost of $P_{INT} * (Q_{INT} - Q_0)$. In effect, the board adds its demand to the market demand to obtain the intervention price.

In welfare terms, this points to the transfer of resources between consumer and producer relative to the free market outcome. This transfer comes in the form of the higher price paid for food purchased — P_{INT} rather than P_E — and also a lower quantity consumed Q_0 rather than Q_E. This welfare change can be measured by (I) the loss of consumer surplus, which is

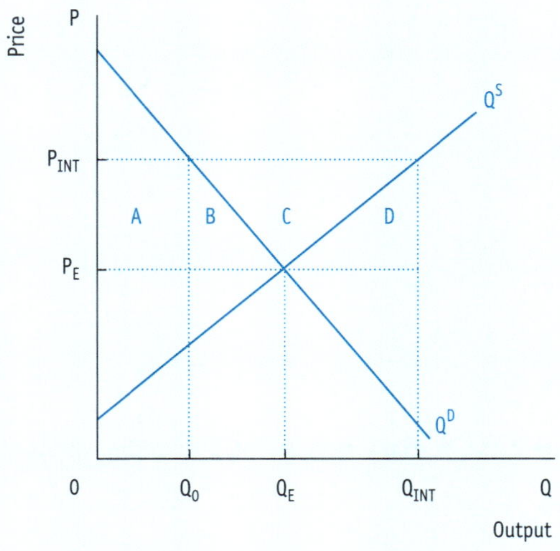

Figure 9.14 The effect of the intervention price

equal to A + B, and (II) the benefit to producers of the higher price and the larger quantity sold so that producer surplus increases by A + B + C.

To evaluate this system of price support, we also need to take account of the taxes necessary to pay for the intervention, storage and potential loss from eventual disposal of the produce. The intervention agency buys the quantity $Q_{INT} - Q_0$ at the intervention price P_{INT}. In general, this expenditure is potentially large depending on the price elasticities of supply and demand, the technical standards that are required by the intervention agency and the particular level at which P_{INT} happens to be set. This cost to the EU can be reduced by disposal on the world market, but, given that European agriculture is relatively high-cost, the cost of intervention in the form of higher taxation is likely to be large. It is worth noting that the most efficient way of redistributing income from consumers to producers would be simply to give farmers a lump-sum payment equal to the area A + B + C.

Reforming the CAP

Dairy quotas

A combination of higher food prices than outside the EU, production surpluses and escalating budgetary costs has lead to reforms to the CAP. We will start with the introduction of production quotas limits that were first imposed on EU dairy producers in 1984. At the time the policy was implemented EU dairy prices were substantially higher than world prices, which is illustrated in Figure 9.15 by the initial intervention price, P_0^{INT} and the world price P_W.[12]

12 The discussion in this section draws on Coleman and Roberts (1997).

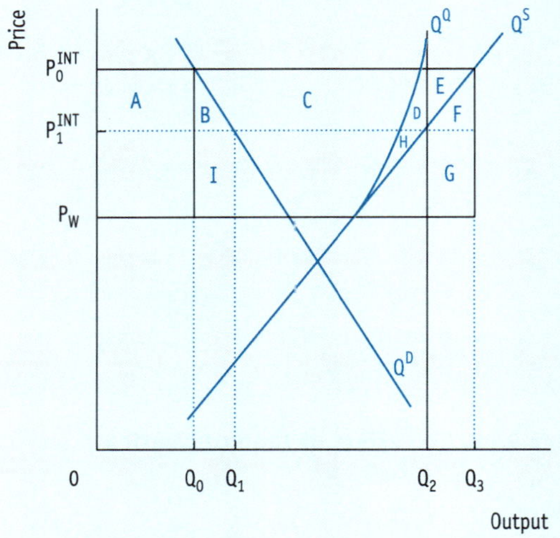

Figure 9.15 Welfare analysis of production quotas

Given that the price supports for dairy producers were leading to large surpluses, the most straightforward policy response to reduce surpluses would have been to lower the intervention price. In the figure, we represent this by the intervention price set at P_1^{INT}.

The effect of doing this is to increase the quantity demanded from Q_0 to Q_1 and to reduce the quantity supplied from Q_3 to Q_2. The welfare effects are shown by the increase in consumer surplus represented by the area A + B and the reduction in producer surplus of the area A + B + C + D + E. The budgetary cost falls from $(P_0^{INT} - P_W) * (Q_3 - Q_0)$ to $(P_1^{INT} - P_W) * (Q_2 - Q_1)$, which as marked on the figure is represented by the area B + C + D + E + F + G + I. This gives an overall welfare gain since the increase in consumer surplus and reduction in budgetary cost is greater than the reduction in producer surplus. The difference is given by B + F + G + I.

To compare the policy of having a fixed quota with the reduction in intervention price, we will assume that the quota is set at the Q_2, which represents the same output level as that after the reduction in price support. The supply curve now becomes Q^Q. Why the particular shape for the supply curve? It follows from the method by which the quotas were allocated. They were given on the basis of historic production levels rather than on the basis of efficiency, so some high cost, inefficient production was retained and some low cost production was lost. The new supply curve as a result of enforcing the quota is therefore steeper.

The introduction of a quota has no direct effect on the price paid by consumers, which is still at its initial level of P_0^{INT}, so there is no change in consumer surplus. The reduction in producer surplus is shown by the areas E + D + H. The areas D + H can, in principle, be recovered by establishing a market for quotas, which would allow low-cost producers to buy quotas from those with high costs. In which case, the loss of producer surplus is limited to the area E. The overall welfare gain from quotas is therefore the budgetary saving of E + F + G less the loss of producer surplus which is given by E. This net gain of F + G is less than that associated with a reduction in price support (by the area B + I).

Why introduce quotas rather than reduce support prices? A reduction in support prices would retain a perfectly elastic demand curve from the producers' point of view, albeit at a lower average and marginal revenue. It can be argued that this would have provided an incentive to lower unit costs. More generally we can conclude that the introduction of quotas was a politically sensitive response to the issue of over-production. We can also note that the policy decision gave no weight to consumers' interests in the form of lower prices.

MacSharry Reforms

Following the 'Uruguay Round' of the GATT negotiations, the CAP was subjected to major reform in 1992/93 which became known as the 'MacSharry Reforms' after the then Agricultural Commissioner of the EU. The need to reach some form of agreement with the United States over the level of farm support in Europe led to reductions in support prices, although farmers are compensated by direct income payments. This represented a partial move in the direction that our analysis in relation to Figure 9.14 suggested would be the most efficient way of maintaining farm incomes.

Land set-aside policies

One of the reforms introduced to curb high levels of EU output was a policy of 'land set-aside' for cereal farms (taking land out of production). The essence of this policy is that the farmer has to decide whether to (I) use all the land on the farm and receive the lower price support for the output or (II) comply with the set-aside requirements and be eligible for compensation payments for doing so.[13]

The decision that the farmer has to make depends on the market price of cereals and the yields obtainable on the land cultivated. When market prices are high, the opportunity cost of participating in the scheme is high, even for high-cost producers; as cereal prices fall so does the opportunity cost, even for those on low-cost, efficient farms. We can think of a market price level where the farmer is indifferent between participating in the scheme and not; which we will refer to as an 'indifference price'. At the indifference price, the profit level is the same whether the farmer takes land out of production or whether the land is cultivated.

13 The compensation payment was intended to be a fixed amount, although it was increased in the years after the reform was introduced.

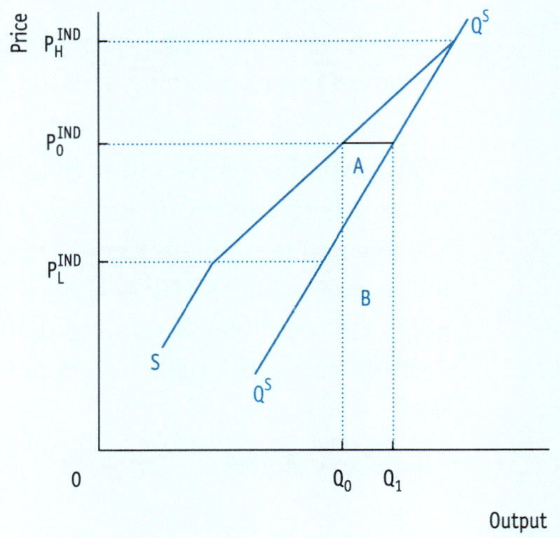

Figure 9.16 Land set-aside policies

Since not all farms are of identical efficiency there will be a range of indifference prices, with low-cost efficient farms having lower indifference prices than high-cost farms. This is illustrated in Figure 9.16, where the indifference price is shown on the vertical axis. P_H^{IND} and P_L^{IND} represent the highest and lowest indifference prices to reflect variations in farm efficiency levels. Above the highest indifference price, all farms utilise their entire land for cereal production. As the indifference price falls, the least efficient take some of their land out of production and the supply curve S Q^S becomes relevant. At P_0^{IND} for example, supply is reduced from Q_0 to Q_1, as the price falls further more farms opt for the set-aside scheme and production declines further, until we reach the lowest indifference price where even the most efficient opt to take (some) land out of production.

If the intervention price is set equal to P_0^{IND}, then given that the scheme is voluntary, we can assume that the reduction in output would only take place if there were no overall loss of producer surplus. The value of the compensation payments must, therefore, be at least equal to the area A in Figure 9.16. The success or otherwise of such a policy is tied up with a number of details. A given % reduction in the area of land for cultivation does not necessarily lead to the same % reduction in output for a number of reasons. These include farmers making more intensive use of inputs on the land that is cultivated, the set-aside of the least-productive land and other means. The shift in the supply curve may, therefore, be less than the analysis in relation to Figure 9.16 suggests it would be.

Concluding comment

The extent of the support that commodities receive varies across agricultural sectors. Traditionally cereal production has been the most generously supported, while some types of produce — potatoes, for example — have not been supported at all. We saw in Chapter 2 that the weighting that food and catering gets in the Retail Price Index is close to 20%, although this masks considerable variation between different groups. Expenditure on food is a much higher proportion of total expenditure for particular groups, such as families on low-incomes and students, for example. Expenditure on food is also much higher in some member states; in Greece and Portugal, the figure is around twice the figure mentioned above.

In distributional terms the CAP has been criticised because it involves a transfer of resources from the poorest consumers to the most prosperous agricultural producers. The principal beneficiaries have been the cereal farmers, which in European terms tends to favour the member states in the north at the expense of those in the south. Within the UK, this favours the larger, more prosperous producers in East Anglia and other parts of Eastern England.

Questions

Q6 Given the supply curve for cereals under a voluntary set-aside scheme

(I) If there is a reduction in the intervention price draw a diagram to show the reduction in producer surplus.
(II) What is the effect on consumer surplus? What is the overall welfare gain?
(III) Suppose that the world price rises as a result of declining EU export subsidies, but remains below the EU intervention price, what difference does it make to your answer to (II)?

Q7 Suppose that the EU was to support agriculture by a means of price subsidy equal to the difference between the world price and the (higher) European costs of production.

(I) Show diagrammatically the effect on the level of consumer and producer surplus.
(II) What is the cost to the intervention agency? How does the welfare outcome differ from a system of intervention prices?

Mathematical appendix

The firm's supply in the short-run

We can approach this as follows, first note that the firm's total costs can be broken down into the sum of (total) fixed costs and (total) variable costs.

$$TC = TFC + TVC$$

Given our definition of profits we have

$$\pi = PQ - TFC - TVC$$

Where P is the price charged, Q is the level of output. If the firm produces nothing at all, Q = 0, then

$$\pi = -TFC$$

The firm will only produce a positive level of output if

$$\pi > -TFC$$

To obtain the supply function, we will start with the relationship between the profit function and the firm's demand for its inputs. The firm's profits are a function of its output, $\pi(Q)$, and its output is a function of its inputs represented by the production function, $Q = F(K,L)$. The profit function

$$\pi(Q) = TR(Q) - TC(Q)$$

can therefore be written as

$$\pi(K,L) = PF(K,L) - rK - wL$$

which shows that the profit-maximising firm's decision becomes a matter of choosing an appropriate level of capital and labour input. The first-order conditions are

$$\frac{\delta\pi}{\delta K} = P\frac{\delta F}{\delta K} - r = 0$$

$$\frac{\delta\pi}{\delta L} = P\frac{\delta F}{\delta L} - w = 0$$

which can then be solved for factor demands

$$K = F(P,r,w)$$
$$L = F(P,r,w)$$

And a supply function

$$Q^S = Q(P,r,w)$$

An example. Suppose the production function is

$$Q = 100K^{0.25}\,L^{0.25}$$

Given $\pi(K,L) = PF(K,L) - rK - wL$, the first-order conditions are

$$\frac{\delta\pi}{\delta K} = 25PK^{-0.75}L^{0.25} - r = 0 \Rightarrow 25PK^{-0.75}L^{0.25} = r$$

$$\frac{\delta\pi}{\delta L} = 25PK^{0.25}L^{-0.75} - w = 0 \Rightarrow 25PK^{0.25}L^{-0.75} = w$$

These two conditions imply that

$$\frac{K}{L} = \frac{w}{r}$$

So that

$$L = \left(\frac{r}{w}\right)K \quad \text{and} \quad K = \left(\frac{w}{r}\right)L$$

Substituting these two expressions into the first-order conditions gives

$$25PK^{-0.75}\left(\frac{r}{w}\right)^{0.25}K^{0.25} = r$$

which solves for

$$K = \frac{(25P)^2}{r^{1.5}\,w^{0.5}}$$

and

$$25P\left(\frac{w}{r}\right)^{0.25}L^{0.25}L^{-0.75} = w$$

which solves for

$$L = \frac{(25P)^2}{r^{0.5}\,w^{1.5}}$$

Finally substitution of the expressions for K and L into the production function solves for

$$Q = \frac{2{,}500P}{r^{0.5}\,w^{0.5}}$$

If, for example, r = w = 5 then

$$Q^S = 500P$$

The market supply function (short-run)

This is simply the sum of all the supply functions of the individual firms in the industry.

$$Q^S_{IND} = \sum_i Q_i = Q(P,r,w)$$

To continue with the example of the firm's supply function if there are 100 firms in the industry then

$$Q^S_{IND} = 50{,}000P$$

Summary

1 The firm in a perfectly competitive market is a price taker. In the short-run, it may make economic profits or losses. It will cease production, however, if the market price falls below its average variable costs.

2 The industry supply curve in the short-run is simply the summation of the marginal cost curves of all the firms (above the point of their average variable cost curves). The short-run industry supply curve will, therefore, slope upwards, providing that the firms are identical and that there are diminishing returns to a variable factor.

3 The long-run industry supply curve is formed by examining the effect of an expansion in industry demand. If factor prices rise, the long-run supply curve will be upward sloping to reflect an increasing cost industry. If factor prices remain constant, the long-run industry supply curve will be horizontal. Finally, if factor prices fall, the industry supply curve will be downward-sloping.

4 The competitive model can be used as a point of reference for examining the operation of actual industries. It is also a benchmark for analysing other market structures.

5 Welfare analysis of competitive markets uses the ideas of consumer and producer surplus. These are, however, both measures of aggregate welfare based on the idea of a representative individual, or firm, which avoids considerations of equity.

6 The agricultural industry has a number of the features of the competitive model. It also has a number of particular features, which include a tendency toward a low price elasticity of demand for its products and also long-term increases in production efficiency through the adoption of mechanisation and the use of pesticides. These two features mean that agricultural prices, and farm incomes, could be expected to fall in the absence of government intervention.

7 In an attempt to provide a stable supply of food, the UK government, and the governments of many other countries, have traditionally intervened to transfer resources from consumers to producers. This can take the form of producer subsidies, price floors and import tariffs.

8 The detail of policy remains controversial, partly arising from the transfer from producers to consumers, but also because of who the beneficiaries within each group are. Higher food prices affect those on lower incomes disproportionately. The coverage of agricultural produce under the CAP is not even, and so the support given to different types of farms varies.

End of chapter questions

Q8 Assume a decreasing cost competitive industry. What happens to the price and output of the industry if demand rises from an increase in consumer's incomes? What does your answer depend on?

Q9 Given the production function

$$Q = K^{0.5}L^{0.5}$$

and that a firm receives a price, P for its output, and pays a price of 10 for both factor inputs

(I) What is the short-run supply function of the firm?
(II) If there are 100 firms in the industry, what is the industry supply curve?
(III) How would your answers differ if the firm's production function was $Q = KL$?

Q10 A restaurant charges an average of £12 per head to each of its diners, the average variable cost of serving a meal is £14 and it has fixed costs of £10,000 per annum. The restaurant knows that there will be 6,000 diners throughout the year.

(I) Should it remain open in the short-run?

The owners decided to make a decision based on a time horizon of two years. They thought that there was an 80–20 chance that the economy would boom in a year's time. In a boom they could charge an average of £20 per head and they would have 10,000 customers during the year. If the economy didn't boom they would have the same demand and have to charge the same price per head as in year 1.

(II) What should the restaurant owners do if the costs of retraining staff after a shut-down are £3,000? What if they are £8,000? What are you assuming about the risk-preferences of the owners? Assume a discount rate of 8%.

Q11 What are the effects of introducing a minimum wage on the sum of consumer and producer surplus? What kind of other information would you need to evaluate whether it was desirable or not?

Q12 Suppose the government imposed a rent ceiling, what is the effect on the total economic surplus? Is such a policy desirable?

Q13 Professional football clubs operate in a competitive industry. The annual football report by the accountants Deloitte and Touche (1998) will give you some idea of how many are chronic loss-makers in the year you are reading this question. Why don't large numbers of clubs go out of business?

References and suggested further reading

The discussion of principles in this chapter is covered widely in other textbooks. Colman and Roberts give a readable account of the economics of the CAP.

Colman, D. and Roberts, D. (1997), 'Economics of the CAP in Transition' in Artis, M.J. and Lee, N. (eds), *The Economics of the European Union*, 2nd edition, Oxford University Press.

Deloitte and Touche (1998), 'Deloitte and Touche Annual Review of Football Finance'.

Earl, P.E. (1995), *Microeconomics for Business and Marketing*, Edward Elgar.

Office for National Statistics (various issues) Economic Trends.

European Commission (1996), *The Agricultural Situation in the European Union: 1996 Report*.

Nicholson, W. (1995), *Microeconomic Theory: Basic Principles and Extensions*, 6th edition, The Dryden Press.

Ritson, C. and Harvey, D. (1997) (eds), *The Common Agricultural Policy*, Wallingford CAB.

Varian, H.R. (1996), *Intermediate Microeconomics, A Modern Approach*, 4th edition, W.W. Norton & Co.

10 Monopoly and Market Power

Key ideas and material

Welfare analysis of monopoly, pricing with market power: price discrimination, two-part tariffs, bundling; regulation

Introduction

A monopoly is an industry in which there is a single producer of a good or service. A monopolist faces a downward-sloping demand curve and recognises that it can choose its output so that it exerts some influence over the price it charges. Pure monopoly — literally only one seller — is rare. There are many markets in which there is competition among a few firms who can exert some monopoly power. The behaviour of firms in such a market situation can become complicated if they behave strategically, something that is discussed in Chapter 11.

The outline of this chapter is as follows. Section 1 discusses the price and output of a 'pure' monopoly and contrasts the outcome with that in a competitive market. Unlike the competitive equilibrium discussed in Chapter 9, the monopolist will produce an output level that is neither allocatively nor productively efficient.

Section 2 analyses a range of pricing policies practiced by firms who can exert some market power. Here, we will discuss the practice of price discrimination and the charging of two part-tariffs. We will also look at the purpose of bundling goods and the role of advertising. This use of market power can lead to extending, or qualifying, the criticisms made of the welfare outcome of a pure monopoly.

In Section 3, we introduce regulation as one way governments may set out limit the adverse welfare effects of monopolies. This will take us on to the subject of regulation and competition in the utility industries, a discussion continued in more detail in Chapter 12.

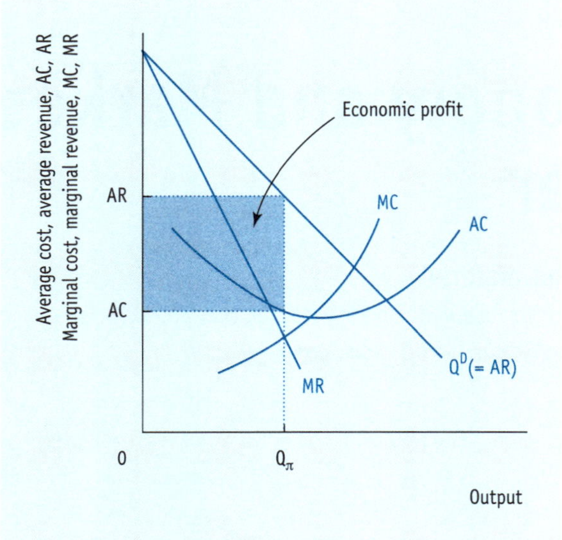

Figure 10.1 **The monopolist's price and output decision**

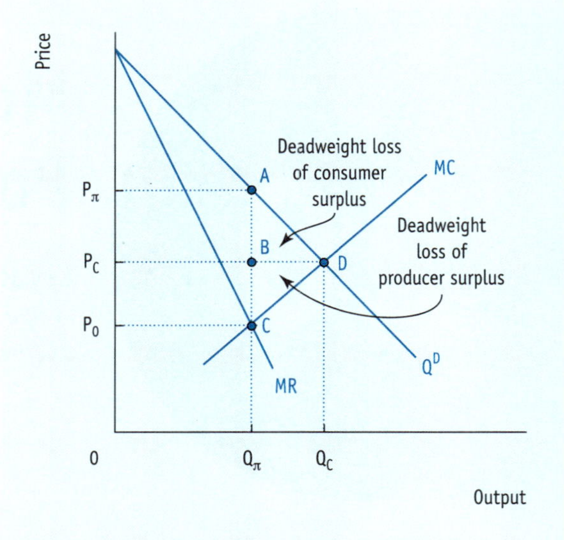

Figure 10.2 **Welfare analysis of a monopoly**

10.1 The welfare analysis of a monopoly

A monopolist is a firm that acts as the only supplier to the market. A profit-maximising monopolist can therefore be a price-setter, if it has knowledge of the demand conditions that it faces. The profit-maximising output for a monopolist, as illustrated in Figure 10.1, is Q_π. At this output level average revenue is above average cost and the firm is making economic profits, shown by the shaded rectangle equal to the area $(AR-AC) * (OQ_\pi)$ in the figure. As was the case with the analysis of the firm in competition, a reduction in output will result in total revenue falling by more than total cost, so the profits of the firm will be lower. In Figure 10.1 the marginal revenue curve lies above the marginal cost curve to the left of Q_π, so the firm can make higher profits by continuing to expand its output. An increase in output above Q_π will also lead to a fall in profits, as the firm's marginal costs are greater than its marginal revenue beyond that point.

This market structure is sometimes called pure monopoly and the welfare analysis of the price-quantity decision conventionally takes the outcome of a competitive industry as a point of comparison. A monopoly charges a higher price and will supply less than would a competitive industry. This is illustrated in Figure 10.2, where the average and marginal revenue curves of the monopolist are drawn as before and (for convenience) marginal costs are drawn as a linear function of output.[1] If we assume that the cost structures of the monopoly and the competitive industry are the same, then the marginal cost curve, MC, is the competitive industry's supply curve as well.

1 It is convenient for the discussion of deadweight losses.

In Figure 10.2, the monopolist's price and output is given by the combination P_π Q_π, that for the competitive industry is given by P_C, Q_C. In addition to charging a higher price and supplying less, the monopolist reduces consumer surplus relative to the competitive outcome. Consumer surplus, the difference between what consumers would be prepared to pay, and what they do pay, falls by the area $P_\pi ADP_C$, as the price rises from P_C to P_π. Producer surplus, the difference between the market price received and the price at which (in this case) the monopolist would be prepared to supply a particular output level, increases by the area $P_C P_\pi AB$ less what is known as the deadweight loss, represented by the triangle BCD.

This deadweight loss arises because of the contraction in output by the monopolist (there is a lower output over which the difference between the market price and the firm's marginal cost is added up). Since consumers buy less, there is also a deadweight loss of consumer surplus equal to the triangle ABD. Overall there is a £ for £ transfer of consumer surplus to producers equal to the area $P_C P_\pi AB$, and a total deadweight loss represented by the area ACD. The monopoly outcome in general is neither allocatively nor productively efficient.

This welfare analysis points to the benefits of a competitive market structure over a monopoly. The remainder of this chapter will consider the basis for this proposition. In the remainder of this section we will analyse the sources of monopoly profits in more detail.

Monopoly and demand elasticity

To start with, the relation between the price charged by a monopolist and the elasticity of demand for its product: the monopolist will produce where the demand is elastic. The elasticity of demand decreases as we move down a linear demand curve, and it is not difficult to see why the monopolist will produce where the demand for its product is elastic.

At the point where the MR schedule intersects the horizontal axis, total revenue will be constant. When total revenue for the firm is not changing we know that total expenditure by consumers will be unchanging as well, so the price elasticity of demand is equal to (minus) one as shown in Figure 10.3A.[2] In the extreme case where the marginal costs of the firm are zero, the intersection of the MR schedule with the horizontal axis gives the output that the monopolist will produce. Marginal costs will more typically be positive, in which case the monopolist will be producing at a point that is further up the demand curve. Starting at some such point, a falling price is associated with positive marginal revenue and higher total revenue. Demand is therefore elastic.[3]

---

2 This ignores the possibility of taxes or subsidies.

3 This conclusion depends on the assumption that the monopolist faces a linear demand curve.

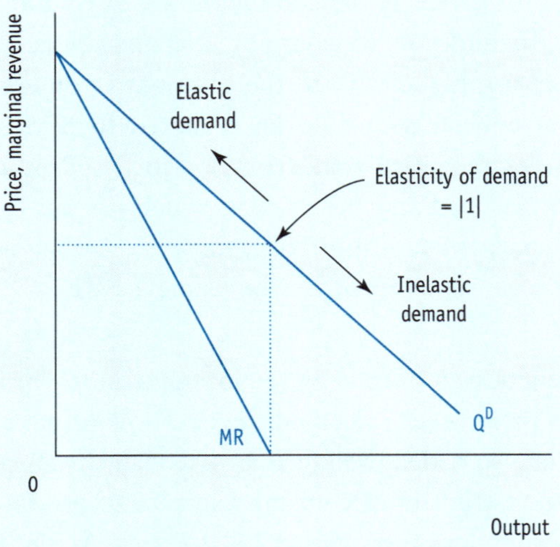

Figure 10.3A A monopolist will typically produce where demand is elastic

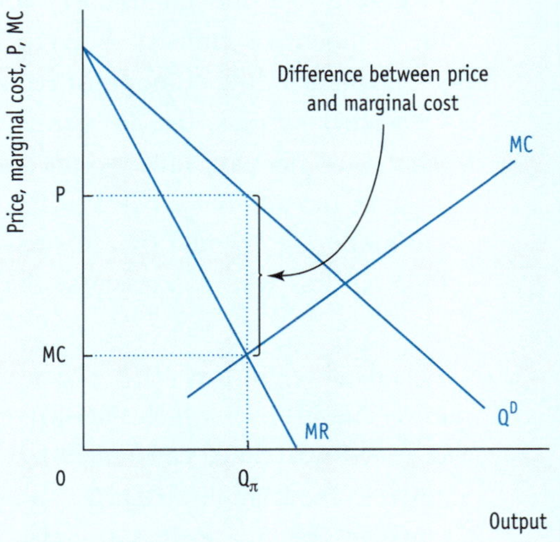

Figure 10.3B The monopolist's mark-up of price over marginal costs

Lerner index

The difference between the price charged by the monopolist and the associated marginal cost, is the basis of one measure of monopoly power known as the Lerner index. It is simply

$$(P - MC)/P$$

The index takes values that lie between 0 and 1. If the firm sets its price equal to marginal cost, the index takes a value of 0. This is what happens in a competitive industry, as we saw in Chapter 9. The greater the difference between price and marginal cost (as a proportion of the price), the greater the value of the index and the greater the monopoly power as measured by this index. Figure 10.3B illustrates; the more elastic the demand curve, Q^D, the smaller the proportionate mark-up of price over marginal cost.

Monopoly profits

The Lerner index is one measure of monopoly power, and to be clear it is consistent with a range of profit levels that a monopolist might obtain. The profits the monopolist earns in the long-run depends on the relation between the price charged and its associated average cost. A given mark-up of price over marginal cost could mean the firm making monopoly profits, or it not doing so, as is illustrated in Figure 10.4. This shows two monopolies, with the same degree of monopoly power as measured by the Lerner index. When average costs are given by AC_0

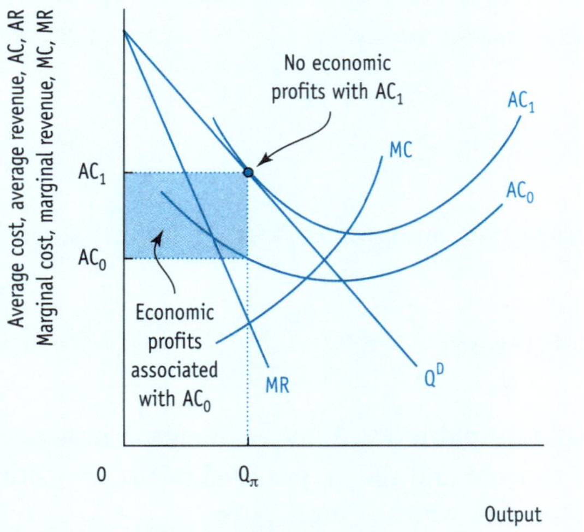

Figure 10.4 **Monopoly profits varying with average costs output**

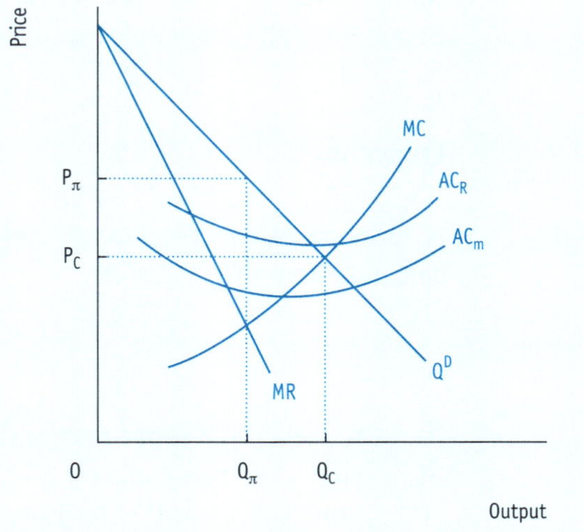

Figure 10.5 **Pre-emptive price-cutting by a monopolist**

the firm makes economic profits as shown in the figure, when average costs are given by AC_1 there are no economic profits. The variation in profit levels obtained by a monopolist will depend on changing demand conditions as well, but the existence of a monopoly is not synonymous with long-run profits.

Barriers to entry

The source of monopoly power lies in barriers to entry, the nature of which varies depending on the particular industry. The control over gold mines in South Africa by the DeBeers company is one much quoted example. Barriers can come from the technology of production, or be a legal creation. The existence of scale economies, i.e. declining average costs of production over the range of market demand is one of the major technical barriers leading to 'natural monopoly'. This was the way the public utilities were seen in the UK and other industrialised nations for an extended period after the Second World War. Legally-created monopolies can arise from patents, or the award of an exclusive franchise to service a market for a specified period.

We saw above that the existence of monopoly does not necessarily mean that it makes a profit, although, if it does, this clearly provides an incentive for other firms to enter the industry. When a monopolist has cost advantages it may engage in pre-emptive price cutting to deter its would be competitors and, in effect, create a barrier to entry. The analysis of this is illustrated in Figure 10.5. The average cost curves of the monopolist and a potential rival are labelled AC_M and AC_R respectively. As drawn, the average cost of the would-be rival is higher than that of the incumbent firm. The price-cutting monopolist can therefore lower the price it charges from P_π to P_C and would force out a rival if it did enter the industry. As drawn in Figure 10.5, the monopolist would still make economic profits.

Questions

Q1 A monopolist can produce at constant average and marginal cost of 25. Given a market demand curve of

$$Q = 100 - P$$

(I) Calculate the profit maximising price and output levels. What is the profit level made?
(II) How does this compare with the price charged and the output level of the competitive firm? Calculate the deadweight loss associated with the monopoly.

Q2 Why there is no supply curve for a monopolist?

10.2 Pricing with market power

In this section, we will broaden the discussion to include pricing policies by firms who exert some monopoly power, i.e. to those that have at least some ability to control the price that is charged for their product. We will start with the idea of price discrimination, which refers to a situation in which different consumers are charged different prices for the same good. Traditionally, three types (or 'degrees') of price discrimination are distinguished following the classification put forward by A.C. Pigou.

Pigou's three degrees of price discrimination

First degree

First degree price discrimination occurs where consumers are charged the maximum they are willing to pay. Referring to Figure 10.6, if a firm supplying Q_0 charged a single price to all its consumers, its revenue would be OP_0EQ_0. If it was able to charge a separate price to each consumer, it could increase its revenue by the amount shown by the area AEP_0. To do this it would, as stated, have to be able to charge each individual consumer the maximum he, or she, was willing to pay. The additional revenue received by the firm from each individual unit of the good sold is then simply the price it charges for it. Perfect price discrimination an extreme case, in which there is a direct transfer of the entire consumer surplus to the producer. The extent of the gain to the firm depends on the slope of the demand curve; a steeper demand curve passing through point E in Figure 10.6 for instance would mean a larger gain.

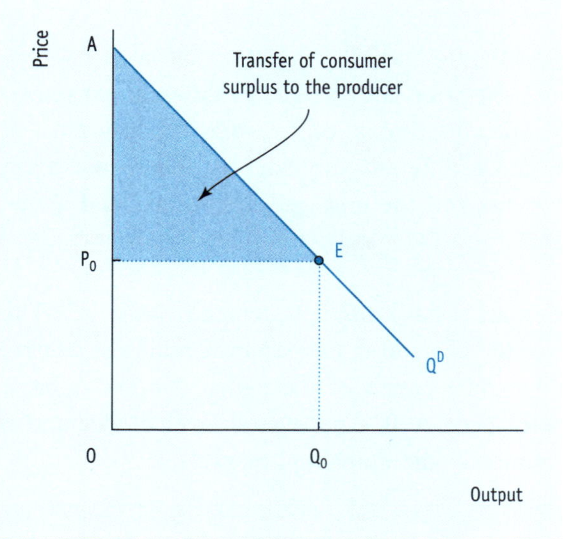

Figure 10.6 **First degree price discrimination**

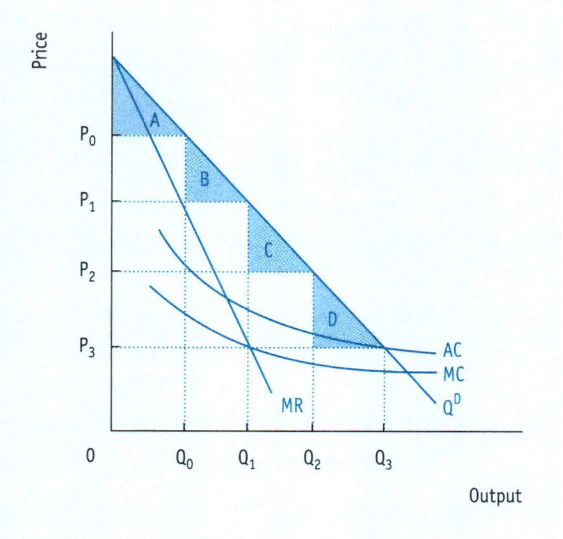

Figure 10.7 **Second degree price discrimination**

In practice, there are various situations where firms may charge several different prices based on their estimates of their customers' reservation prices. Some professionals such as accountants, doctors and lawyers may charge a higher price to those on higher incomes. Cab drivers arriving at and leaving airports may also charge a range of fares, just depending on who their passenger(s) happen to be. However, even for those who have the aid of a computer system to administer the details of a pricing policy; the analysis of first degree price discrimination is really best thought of as a point of reference.

Second degree

This refers to situations where firms charge different prices to consumers for different quantities of a good or service. Examples of this kind of pricing are the charges by utilities (water, electricity and others) in some countries, where consumers pay less per unit as consumption increases. In Figure 10.7 the firm charges a price P_0 for the output Q_0 and a lower price, P_1, for the next block of output and so on. The firm expands output until the point where price equals average cost, which is to the point Q_3 in the figure.

This kind of pricing policy involves a higher level of output than does the single pricing policy, which would be Q_1 in the figure. If there are scale economies then block pricing may encourage the expansion of output and consumer surplus may be increased as a result. In Figure 10.7, consumer surplus is given by the area A + B + C + D. Whether this is more than if a single price is charged depends on whether the area C + D is larger than the area $(P_0 - P_1)OQ_0$. In general, consumer surplus may or may not be higher than that if a single price was charged.

Third degree

Third degree price discrimination occurs if different prices are charged to different consumers in different markets. In order for this type of price discrimination to work, the firm must be able to identify, and keep separate, two or more different sub-markets. There are many examples where this occurs: discounts for students and the unwaged at concerts and shops, airlines who offer special deals and so on.

It is also necessary that the consumers in each market have different demand elasticities. This is illustrated simply in Figure 10.8, which shows the demand in two separate markets, referred to as markets A and B, in the left hand and middle panels of the figure. Market A has a relatively inelastic demand by comparison with market B. The overall level of demand is shown on the right and is the sum of the demands in the individual markets

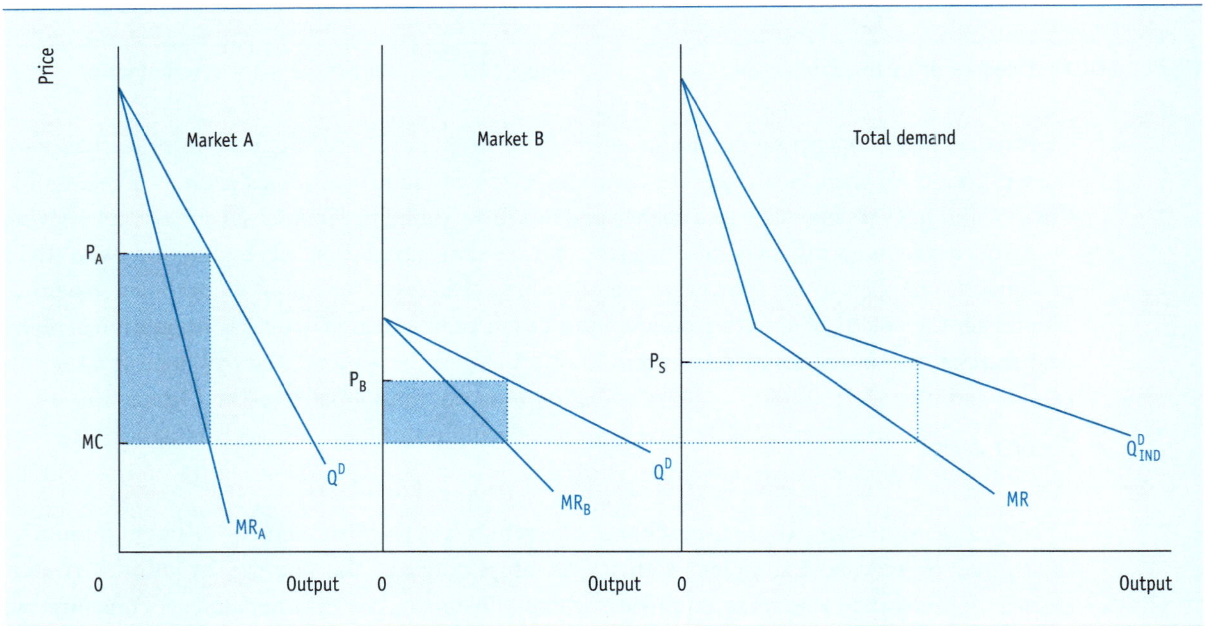

Figure 10.8 Third degree price discrimination

For the sake of simplicity the marginal cost of one extra unit of output in both markets is assumed to be constant. The profit-maximising firm will equate marginal revenue with marginal cost in both markets, if marginal revenue differed across the submarkets the monopolist could re-allocate its output and increase its profit. It will charge a higher price to the group of consumers with a lower price elasticity of demand and a greater willingness to pay. This is shown by the price P_A charged to those in market A, which is above that which they would pay if there was single price, shown as P_S in the right panel. Conversely, a lower price, P_B, is charged to those with a higher price elasticity of demand in market B.

The profit from the two separate markets is shown by the shaded area (and is greater than that if a single price is charged to the whole market). Some consumers gain, while others lose. Price discrimination can bring more individuals to the market than if a single price was charged, and consequently, the welfare assessment depends on distributional considerations as well as efficiency criteria.

Air fares and price discrimination

The airline industry is a good example of where the idea of price discrimination can help us understand the typical pricing policy. We will take Virgin as an example, but their price structure is broadly similar to many other carriers. Table 10.1 gives some fares advertised by the airline for flights from London in 1999.

	New York (one way)	Los Angeles (return)	Tokyo (return)
Economy	311	439	900
Upper Class	3,009	4,949	4,248

Table 10.1 Virgin air fares 1999 £
Source: Virgin (1999).

The division of passengers into economy and upper class forms of travel is suggestive of third degree price discrimination. The fare differentials across the Atlantic vary by factors of ten to twelve and this is a different order of magnitude to that illustrated in Figure 10.8. The impression given by Table 10.2 is that Virgin's pricing policy is based on the identification of sub-markets with very different price elasticities of demand. Plainly, a part of this can be attributed to cost differences: larger seats, better food, preferential treatment and so on in Upper Class.

Economy (21 Day Apex)	311
Economy (14 Day Apex)	334
Economy (7 Day Apex)	341
Premium economy	1,093
Mid Class	351
Upper Class	3,309

Table 10.2 Air fares London to New York 1999 £
Source: Virgin (1999).

However, there are few, if any, cost differences within a particular class of travel. In practice there are many more different types of ticket within a particular class of travel. Table 10.2 gives a basic breakdown for London to New York.

The differences between these fares is determined principally by the time when the passenger makes the booking and certain other restrictions such as a requirement to stay a Saturday night (to dissuade business people from travelling on an economy ticket) and the scope for rescheduling the time of travel.

Table 10.3 gives a total of just six separate published fare categories. There are a wide range of discounts available within categories for children and senior citizens. There are also different fares charged to airline staff (and their friends/relatives), passengers who are frequent-flyers, people who have booked holidays through the airline and those who purchased 'consolidated' tickets from agents. In practice on many flights there are likely to be several dozen different fares paid.

The amount of detail involved points to the success of what airlines call 'yield management'. It also bears out the problematic nature of the welfare assessment of price discrimination. Some individuals are brought into the market that would not otherwise travel and there may be some cross-subsidisation of the fares in different classes of travel.[4]

Two-part tariffs

A two-part tariff shares the objective of price discrimination in that it aims to transfer consumer surplus to the producer. It involves charging a fixed fee to use the product or service, and then a uniform price for each unit consumed. This is typical of the pricing of car rental companies, for example.

The high volume users who are paying a lower price per unit cannot be allowed to re-sell to those who are lower volume users. Given this, the problem for the firm is to decide how to set the fixed charge or entry fee and how to set the usage charge. One approach would be to set the usage charge equal to marginal cost and set the fixed charge equal to the amount of consumers surplus. As a simple piece of analysis if all the consumers had identical demand curves (which were known to the firm) then it would be possible to capture the entire consumers surplus. In terms of Figure 10.6, the output level would be Q_0 and the area $OAEQ_0$ would represent the revenue for the firm.

More realistically, different consumers will have different demands. Figure 10.9A shows the case when there are two separate demands from two individuals (they could also be thought of

4 It may also be that the costs of upper class travel are passed onto final prices (and are, in part, paid by those travelling economy).

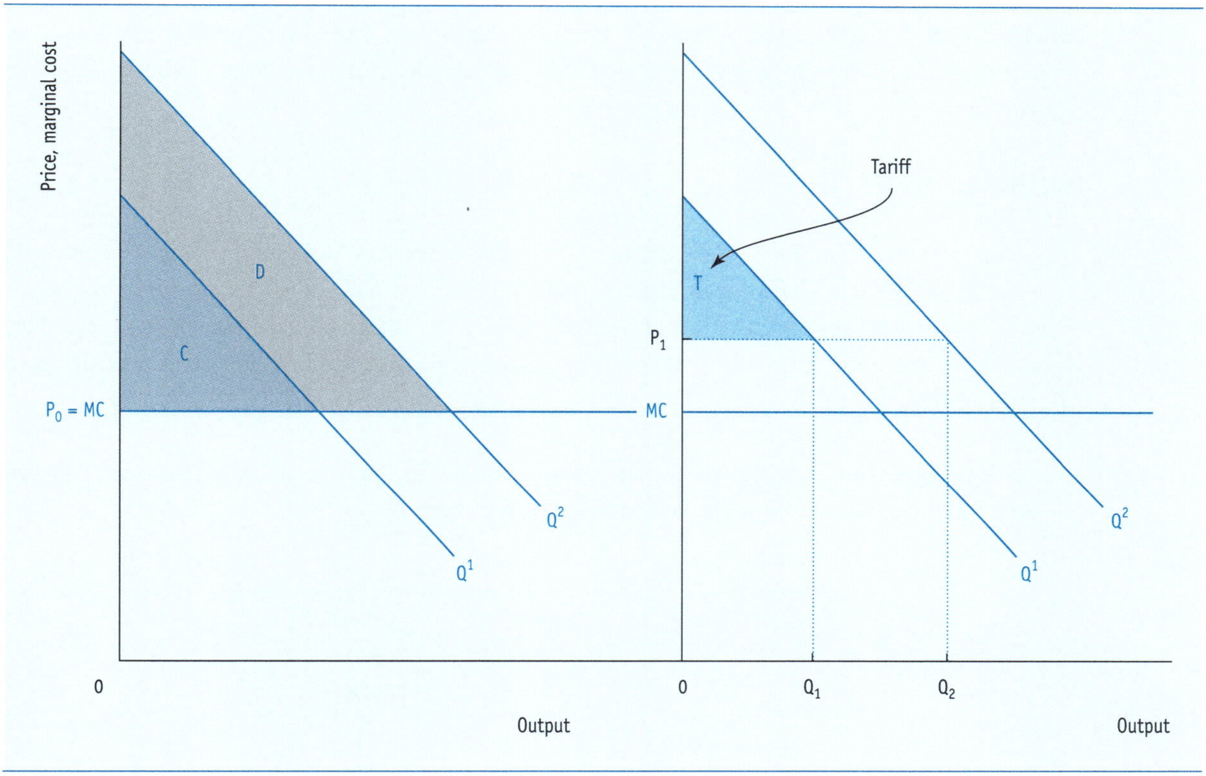

Figure 10.9A **Two-part tariff**

Figure 10.9B **Two-part tariff**

as two separate groups of consumers). If the firm sets a price equal to marginal cost, then the shaded area C is the highest fixed fee it could charge the first individual. Doing this would leave the second individual with consumer surplus equal to the area marked D.

The firm can only set one fixed charge; but if it raises its usage charge above the marginal cost of production, the additional revenue from the second person can lead to higher profits overall.

Figure 10.9B illustrates this. The firm charges the price P_1 and sets a tariff equal to the shaded area, marked T. The firm's profit from charging P_1 is twice the tariff, $2 * T$, plus the firm's profit per unit multiplied by the amount it sells, i.e. $(P_1 - MC) * (OQ_1 + OQ_2)$. This is greater than twice the area marked C in Figure 10.9A.

In practice, most firms face a range of demand from consumers and there is no simple formula for working out an optimal two-part tariff. The lower the fixed fee, or entry charge, the lower the profit it generates; on the other hand the lower the fixed charge the larger the number of consumers, so the higher the revenue from the usage charge. This points to some form of iteration in setting the charge levels to determine what maximises profit. One variant on this is where the entry fee entitles the user to a certain number of free units, for example a certain number of free calls with a mobile phone. This allows the firm to charge a higher entry fee without losing as many low-use consumers.

Bundling

This refers to the bundling of individual products or services that might otherwise be sold separately. There are many examples of this practice, the sale of software suites (a word-processor, spreadsheet and database together), selling two films on one video and so on. This can make sense when consumers have different demands and the firm is not in a position to price discriminate.

As an example, Table 10.3 gives the reservation prices for two (equal-sized) groups of consumers for the purchase of a spreadsheet and a database.

	Group 1 (reservation price)	Group 2 (reservation price)
Spreadsheet	£150	£100
Database	£100	£150

Table 10.3 An illustration of bundling

The first group of consumers has a higher reservation price for the spreadsheet; the second group a higher reservation price for the database. If they were sold separately the firm could only charge £100 for each programme, without losing sales to one or other group. If they were sold together, then both groups would be willing to pay £250 for both programmes.

In Figure 10.10A, the reservation prices of consumers are shown on the two axes. Suppose the prices charged for each of the two goods are P_S and P_W. Since consumers only buy a particular good if the price at which it is sold is less than their reservation price, this gives us four quadrants where individuals buy neither, buy both or buy one or the other of the software packages.

When the two goods are bundled, but are not available separately, consumers are left with the alternatives of buying both, or neither. The consumer will only buy if the bundled price is less than the sum of his, or her, reservation prices. This is shown in Figure 10.10B, where P_B is the bundled price. The effectiveness of bundling will depend on what the bundled price is, and what the consumers' reservation prices are. Generally, bundling will be more effective when

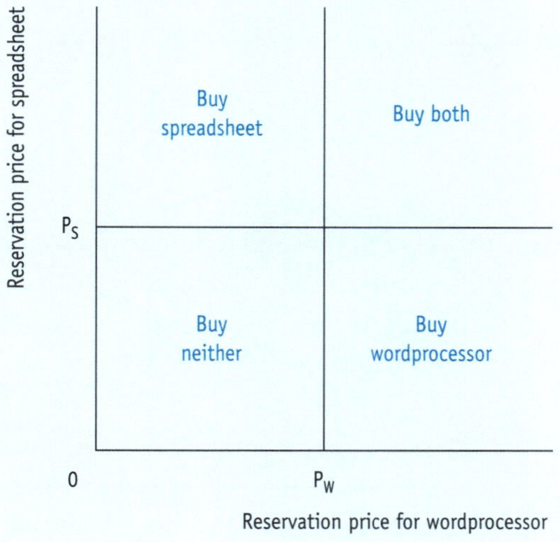

Figure 10.10A Consumption decisions when goods are sold separately

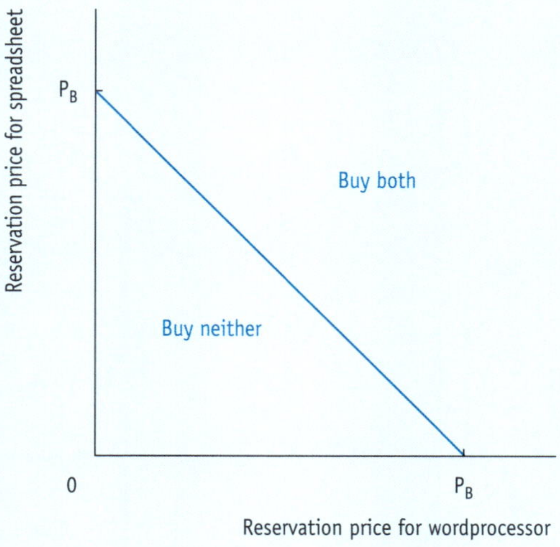

Figure 10.10B Consumpion decisions when goods are sold together

the demands for the two goods are highly correlated,[5] that is when individuals who have a high reservation price for one good have a low reservation price for the other good.

Monopolistic competition

The analysis in Section 1 discussed a monopoly industry as one where there was a single supplier to the market. In principle, this is fine, but it leaves open the detail of what it is the single supplier of. In practice, there is a degree of substitutability for the products of many firms. Monopolistic competition is the name given to a market structure in which there are many firms, each one facing a downward-sloping demand curve. On a spectrum of market structures it lies between the model of competition and the idea of a pure monopoly. In monopolistic competition the goods of different firms are seen as differing in some way by consumers (although they do not actually have to be different). Figure 10.11 depicts the (long-run) equilibrium position of the firm in this market structure. Like a monopoly, the price it charges is above the marginal cost of production and so is above what it would be in a competitive industry. Its output is also lower, although free entry and exit generates competition and this means that the firm produces where average revenue and average cost are equal.

Advertising

The effect of successful advertising in this type of market is illustrated in Figure 10.12. The demand curve for the firm's product shifts out to the right, from Q_0^D to Q_1^D and the costs of

5 Negatively correlated, of course.

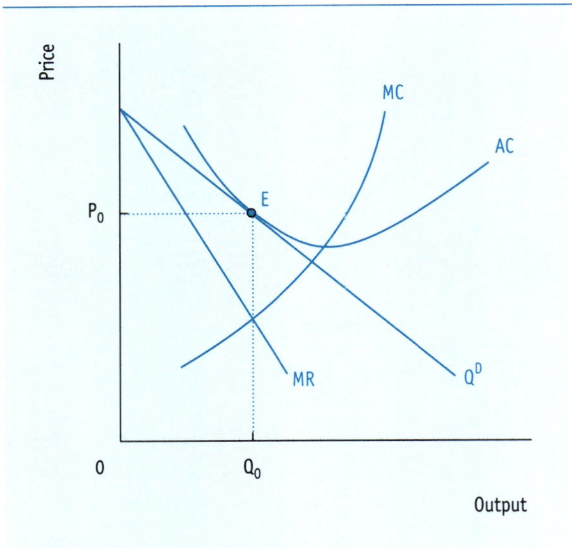

Figure 10.11 **Monopolistically competitive firm in long-run equilibrium**

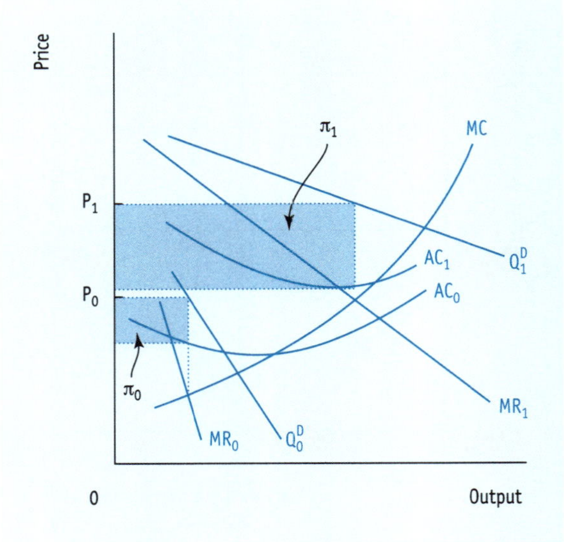

Figure 10.12 **The effect of a successful advertising campaign**

advertising raise the average cost curve of the firm from AC_0 to AC_1.[6] This leads to an increase in output and a higher price, at least in the short-run. The firm is clearly better off with (successful) advertising as profits rise from the area marked Π_0 to Π_1. How much advertising expenditure is optimal from the firm's viewpoint? The answer to this, in principle, is that the firm should increase its expenditure on advertising until the point that marginal revenue is equal to the full marginal cost of doing so (the cost of advertising and the additional costs of production associated with the additional sales).

A more general assessment of the effect advertising on welfare is problematic. If the firm experiences declining average costs then the effect can be to increase demand and output at the level of the firm and to lower the price charged.

Questions

Q3 A small village shop is the single supplier of jam doughnuts to its residents, for which there are two consumers. Ray would be prepared to pay 60 pence for the first doughnut consumed, 40 pence for a second and nothing for any more. Ruth would be prepared to pay 60 pence for the first doughnut and 20 pence for a second one. The average and marginal cost of production is 10 pence per doughnut.

6 In overall terms, advertising expenditure accounts for between 1.5–2% of GDP in the UK, which is broadly the same order of magnitude as the agricultural output discussed in Chapter 9.

(I) If the supplier knew the willingness to pay of the two individuals, how much additional revenue could be obtained by comparison with the situation in which a single price is charged?

(II) Suppose the supplier offers to sell doughnuts at 60 pence each or two for £1, what would the revenue be to the supplier and what would be the consumers surplus?

Q4 The table below gives what four consumers would be prepared to pay for a spreadsheet and a database.

	Individual 1	**Individual 2**	**Individual 3**	**Individual 4**
Spreadsheet	£150	£100	£125	£135
Database	£100	£150	£130	£145

(I) If all four individuals were to remain in the market what would be the highest price that could be charged if the two goods were bundled?

(II) What is the difference in revenue to the firm by comparison with selling the two packages separately?

(III) Suppose the reservation price for individual 1 for the database was £30, what difference, if any, would it make to your answers to (I) and (II)?

Q5 After an advertising campaign the firm we met in Q1 faces the demand curve

$$Q = 150 - 0.5P$$

(I) What is the new the profit level if the costs of advertising are ignored?

(II) At what level of expenditure would the campaign be unprofitable to the firm?

10.3 Monopoly and price regulation

The analysis of Section 1 suggested that there was a welfare loss associated with monopoly. One possible policy response by governments is regulation in some form. In general terms regulation involves a government agency restricting the activity of firms (restrictions that may have statutory force). A set of rules on pricing is one example. Figure 10.13A illustrates the principle in the simple case of a price ceiling. The demand and marginal revenue curves in the absence of regulation are shown as Q^D and MR respectively. A price ceiling could lead to marginal cost pricing if it was set at P_C in the figure. The output level and the price charged

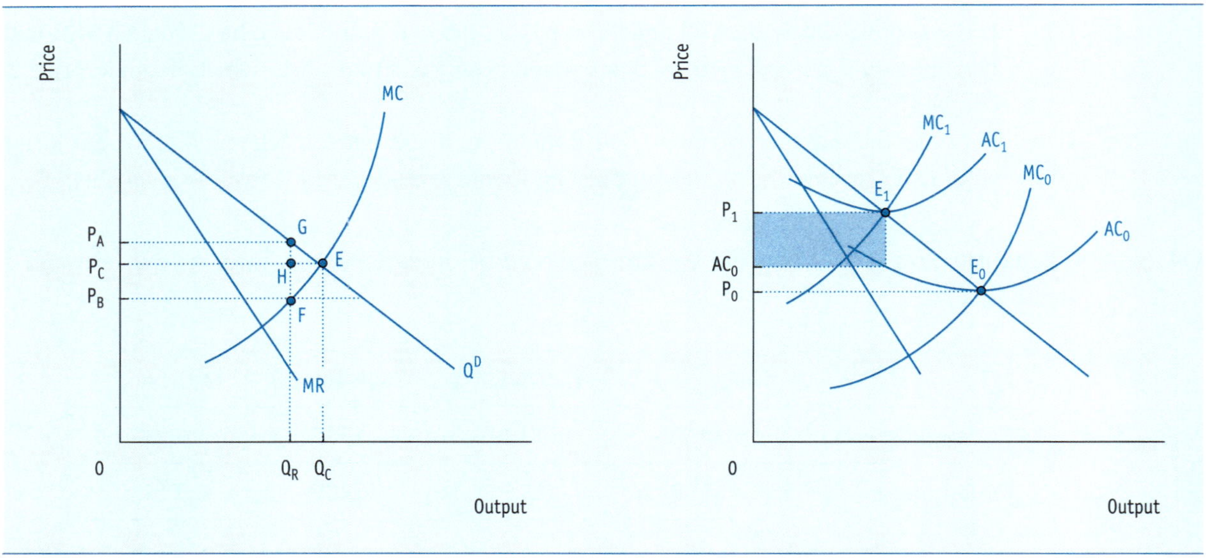

Figure 10.13A **Price regulation of a monopoly**

Figure 10.13B **Regulation of monopoly when there is asymmetric information**

would then be the same as in the case of a competitive industry and there would be no welfare loss.

If the price is set below the competitive level, for example at P_B in the figure, then the equilibrium will be at point F, with output Q_R. The area EFG gives the welfare loss, although this is less than what it would be in the case of an unregulated industry. In the case where the price ceiling is set above the competitive level but is below the unregulated price, for example P_A as shown in the figure, the output level will again be less than the competitive market.

The regulator is often likely to be uncertain about the costs the monopolist may face. If all that the regulator has is a range of estimated costs, and there is a requirement to ensure that production takes place, then the regulator may have to set price equal to the high estimate of costs allowing economic profits if it is an overestimate.

This (potential) dilemma facing the regulator is illustrated in Figure 10.13B where, to simplify there are just two estimates of the monopolist's costs: AC_0 and MC_0 represent the low estimates, AC_1 and MC_1 the high estimates. The regulator does not know which estimate is accurate. In order to ensure production the regulator has to set the price at P_1, since, in this case, to base the price on the low estimate of costs would involve losses if the firm were actually high-cost (and would put the firm out of business). The welfare effects of this are adverse if AC_0 and MC_0 are the actual costs; there is a reduction in consumer surplus given by the area $E_0E_1P_1P_0$, part of which is a deadweight loss, part a transfer to the producer. The shaded area represents the economic profits made by the firm.

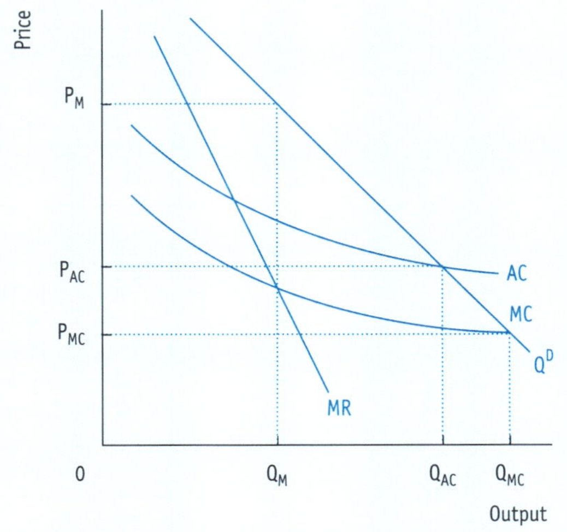

Figure 10.14 Price regulation for a natural monopoly

Privatisation and regulation

The case of a firm with declining average and marginal costs over its entire output range, what is sometimes referred to as a natural monopoly, is illustrated in Figure 10.14. This kind of cost structure is more relevant to the former nationalised utilities in the UK, for whom prior to privatisation, policy involved setting prices equal to both marginal and average costs at various points in time. We will look briefly at both.

With marginal cost pricing is illustrated in Figure 10.14. The monopolist charges P_{MC} and produces output Q_{MC} as marked in Figure 10.14. The monopolist will make losses at this point, since long-run average cost, exceeds average revenue.[7] This is (obviously) an allocatively efficient outcome, and on distributional grounds the prices paid by low income households for 'necessities' such as gas, water and electricity were less than if they had been provided by a profit-maximising enterprise. However, the practical operation of this was at times rather problematic given the 'lumpy' nature of investment decisions, which periodically produced sharp increases in marginal costs. Another criticism that was made of marginal cost pricing, was the absence of an incentive for managers to control costs.

Average cost pricing was another way of attempting to induce an increase in output. In terms of Figure 10.14, the price is determined by the intersection of the demand and average cost curves, giving price and output level P_{AC}, Q_{AC}. The firm will be making normal profits, which

7 The shortfall was often met by general taxation.

Amersham	1982
British Airports Authority	1987
British Airways	1987
British Energy	1996
British Gas	1986
British Petroleum	1987
British Rail	1996
British Steel	1988
British Telecom	1984–91
Britoil	1982–5
Cable & Wireless	1981–83
Enterprise Oil	1984
Jaguar	1984
National Power/PowerGen	1991–5
Regional electricity companies	1990
Rolls Royce	1987
Water companies	1989

Table 10.4 Privatisation in the UK

can be interpreted as the firm earning a fair rate of return on the capital employed. Again, this can be problematic in that it may lead to accommodating to rising costs.

In the UK and elsewhere in the 1980s and 1990s there has been a programme of privatising the formerly state-run industries. The complete list is a long one; Table 10.4 indicates the diversity of firms that have been involved.

One policy development that has occurred since privatisation has been the move to introduce competition into the privatised utilities, including those that were previously thought of as 'natural monopolies'. A general trend is to define the natural monopoly element in an industry, subject it to regulation, and then attempt to introduce competition elsewhere. For example, in the electricity, gas and railway industries, the networks — the wires, pipes and track — are taken as naturally monopolistic, but the supply of services have been opened up to competition.

The regulators in these industries have wide-ranging responsibilities for the level of both 'access' as well as final prices.[8] The problems of asymmetric information are potentially serious where there is limited cost data, and the price caps that the regulator sets also have to balance the interests of the final consumer against the need to encourage new entrants into the industry. The merits of regulation and competition is something that we return to in more detail in Chapter 12.

Question

Q6 If the regulator was to set the price equal to the average cost what is the effect on the incentives for the firm to operate efficiently and to engage in R&D to promote future innovation? Are there ways in which the regulator can set the price to encourage efficiency?

8 The service supplier pays the access price for using the network. The final price is that paid by the consumer.

Mathematical appendix

Price and elasticity of demand

Given that total revenue, TR, is price times quantity, PQ, then by the product rule we have

$$\text{MR} = \frac{\text{dTR}}{\text{dQ}} = \frac{\text{PdQ}}{\text{dQ}} + \frac{\text{QdP}}{\text{dQ}}$$

$$= \text{P} + \text{Q(dP/dQ)}$$

which can be written as

$$= \text{P}[1 + ((\text{Q/P})/(\text{dP/dQ}))]$$

The point elasticity of demand is

$$\varepsilon = \frac{\text{dQ}}{\text{dP}} \cdot \frac{\text{P}}{\text{Q}}$$

which is the reciprocal of the second term in the [ ] brackets. The relation between MR and the elasticity of demand is therefore

$$\text{MR} = \text{P}\left[1 + \left(\tfrac{1}{\varepsilon}\right)\right]$$

The price-discriminating monopolist

The third degree price discrimination case involves equating the marginal revenue the firm receives in its separate sub-markets and hence varying the price charged inversely with the elasticity of demand. We saw above the relation between marginal revenue, price and elasticity. Equating MR_1 and MR_2 therefore means

$$\text{MR}_1 = \text{P}_1\left[1 + \frac{1}{\varepsilon_1}\right] = \text{MR}_2 = \text{P}_2\left[1 + \frac{1}{\varepsilon_2}\right]$$

Hence, for $\text{MR}_1 = \text{MR}_2$, given a more inelastic demand in market 1 means that $\text{P}_1 > \text{P}_2$.

Summary

1 A monopolist is a single producer in an industry. The analysis of a monopolist assumes that it sets out to maximise profits, this leads to a higher price and a lower output than there would be with a competitive industry.

2 The simple analysis of a monopoly is that it is undesirable from a welfare point of view, partly because of the so-called 'deadweight' losses. To this can be added the need to assess the distributional impact on prices.

3 There are a range of pricing policies that monopolies, and other firms with the ability to control the price of their output pursue. These include price discrimination, two-part tariffs and bundling. The welfare effects depend on the detail of each case.

4 Following Pigou's classification there are three degrees of price discrimination. The first degree assumes that the firm knows individual willingness to pay and can therefore extract the entire consumer surplus. The second degree is concerned with charging different prices for different quantities of the good or service consumed. This may or may not decrease consumer surplus overall. Third degree relates to charging different prices to different consumers in different sub-markets. With second and third degree price discrimination some consumers may gain while others lose.

5 Two-part tariffs have the same objective as price discrimination from the point of view of the firm: they are ways of obtaining consumer surplus and increasing revenue. This kind of charging involves a fixed fee to extract some of the consumer surplus, and a usage charge set above the marginal cost of production.

6 Bundling refers to selling individual goods together. It is another way in which a firm with market power can obtain consumer surplus, when the demands of different individuals for two goods are negatively correlated.

7 It is also possible for governments to try and reduce the adverse welfare consequences of a monopoly by some form of regulation. The task of regulating industries creates difficulties with asymmetries of information between the incumbent firm, and the regulator, particularly about costs. The task of the regulator is unavoidably controversial at times, as (s)he has to balance the interests of incumbent producer, the need to encourage new entrants and the interests of the final consumer.

End of chapter questions

Q7 A profit-maximising firm produces a single product that is sold in two totally separated markets whose demand structures are as follows:

$$\text{Market A: } Q_A = 24 - 0.6P_A$$

$$\text{Market B: } Q_B = 48 - P_B$$

Average costs are

$$AC = 10 + 47Q^{-1}$$

(I) What is the price and quantity sold in each market and what is the overall level of profits if the firm charges different prices in each market?

(II) How does the answer differ if the firm charges a single price?

(III) If the demand in Market A drops to $12 - 0.4P_B$, what would be the response of the price discriminating firm?

Q8 A price discriminating monopolist sells its output in two markets for which the demand curves are

$$Q_A = 60 - P_A$$

for the first market, and for the second

$$Q_B = 180 - 4P_B$$

(I) Assuming that the monopolist can produce whatever level of output it wants to at a cost of 10 per unit, what are the prices charged in the two markets and what is the overall level of profits?

(II) Calculate the level of consumer surplus when the firm charges different prices in the two markets. How does it differ from when the monopolist charges a single price?

Q9 A monopolist faces a demand curve of

$$Q = 15 - P$$

and constant marginal cost of 3

(I) What is the profit maximising price and output?

(II) If the government imposes a price ceiling of $P = 6$ what difference does it make to the monopolist's decisions about price and output? What effect does it have on the monopolist's profits? What happens to the degree of monopoly power?

Q10 A monopolist can separate the demand for its product into two submarkets where the demand curves are

$$Q_A = 180 - 3P_A$$

and

$$Q_B = 96 - 2.4P_B$$

(I) If the monopolist's marginal cost per unit is 6, what is the level of consumer surplus in the two markets?

(II) Suppose the monopolist charged a two-part tariff with the fixed charge equal to the consumer surplus in market B. What would be the total profits earned?

(III) How does the level of profit from a two-part tariff compare with charging a single price and with third degree price discrimination?

Q11 A retailer has the options of selling certain film videos separately, or as a bundle. There are equal numbers of consumers in three groups and their reservation prices are given below

Film	Group 1	Group 2	Group 3
Summer blockbuster	£13	£8	£24
Cartoon	£9	£14	£6

Which strategy is the most profitable and why?

References and suggested further reading

The discussion of principles is covered widely in other textbooks. Pindyck and Rubinfeld is good on bundling and extends the discussion of price discrimination. Earl provides some observations on the price-quantity-profit exercises such as those included in the questions here.

Earl, P.E. (1995), *Microeconomics for Business and Marketing*, Edward Edgar.

Nicholson, W. (1995), *Microeconomic Theory: Basic Principles and Extensions*, 6th edition, The Dryden Press.

Pindyck, R.S. and Rubinfeld, D.L. (1998), *Microeconomics*, 4th edition, Prentice Hall.

Varian, H.R. (1996), *Intermediate Microeconomics, A Modern Approach*, 4th edition, W.W. Norton & Co.

11 Models of Oligopoly

Key ideas and material

Cartels and price leadership, Cournot, Bertrand and Stackelberg models, a game theory approach

Introduction

Oligopoly is a market structure that involves a small number of firms. What is fundamentally different about the analysis of this type of market is that firms take strategic decisions; that is they take some account of their rivals' likely reaction to the decisions they make about price, output and other variables. An oligopolist therefore recognises the impact that they have on the price and output of the other firms in the industry.

This chapter discusses different models that emphasise various aspects of a firm's behaviour in an oligopolistic market. We can distinguish between models where firms compete with each other in determining price and output levels, and those where they agree to co-operate. In Section 1, we will analyse models in which firms collude directly in the form of a cartel, or tacitly by some form of price leadership.

A key question is what the strategic variable is in the decision-making of firms. In Section 2, we analyse the traditional models of oligopoly developed by Cournot, Bertrand and Stackelberg. Although developed over 100 years ago, these models were pathbreaking developments in the analysis of the interdependencies of firms' decisions. In the Cournot (and Stackelberg) models the strategic variable is the level of output, in the Bertrand model it is price. The Cournot model may be more relevant in industries where firms have capacity constraints set by lead-in times for production, for example with the building of out-of-town supermarkets. There are other markets where firms pre-announce their prices and compete on the basis of price, mail-order catalogues for example, and here the Bertrand model may be more relevant

The traditional models are best seen as building blocks. In practice, firms make repeated decisions about price and output levels. A nice way of analysing a whole range of decisions about price, output, advertising, and also the role of commitment and reputation, is with game theory and this is an approach we introduce in Section 3.

11.1 Cartels and price leadership

This section covers the analysis of firms who collude to set price and output levels. We will consider first cartels, which although illegal in many countries can, and do, operate on an international basis. The best known cartel is probably that of the oil-producing and exporting countries (OPEC), which has been successful over an extended period in raising prices way above what they would otherwise have been. However the operation of a cartel can be problematic as the analysis will show.

Cartels

Figure 11.1 illustrates a two firm oligopoly, or duopoly, where the producers collude to restrict output and raise price. For simplicity, we will assume that they face the same demand and cost conditions.[1] At an industry level, shown in the right hand panel of the figure, the marginal cost curves of the two firms have been summed to give the industry marginal cost schedule, MC_{IND}. The industry demand curve, Q^D_{IND}, and its associated marginal revenue curve are also shown. Profit-maximisation at the industry level requires the two firms to act as if they were a monopoly; this means equating marginal revenue with marginal cost and producing at output level Q_{IND}, charging a price P_0.

This leaves the question of how the two firms decide who is going to produce what share of the agreed output level. Given the demand and the costs they face, each will have a quota of one half of the total output. This is shown in the left and middle panels where the output levels of Firm 1 and Firm 2 are identical and are shown as Q^1_0 and Q^2_0. When viewed at the level of the individual firm this is not a stable situation. Once the industry price is fixed, from the firm's point of view this price will also be its marginal revenue. The marginal revenue of both firms is above their respective marginal costs; they are left with an incentive to try and increase their output beyond that given from the cartel quota.

While from the viewpoint of an individual producer a higher level of profit could be obtained by producing more, doing so would have the effect of undermining the agreed industry output which produced the incentive in the first place. A question that arises is why some cartels may be successful, while others are not. To be successful the producers collectively must be able to

1 For the purposes of the analysis the two firms are identical.

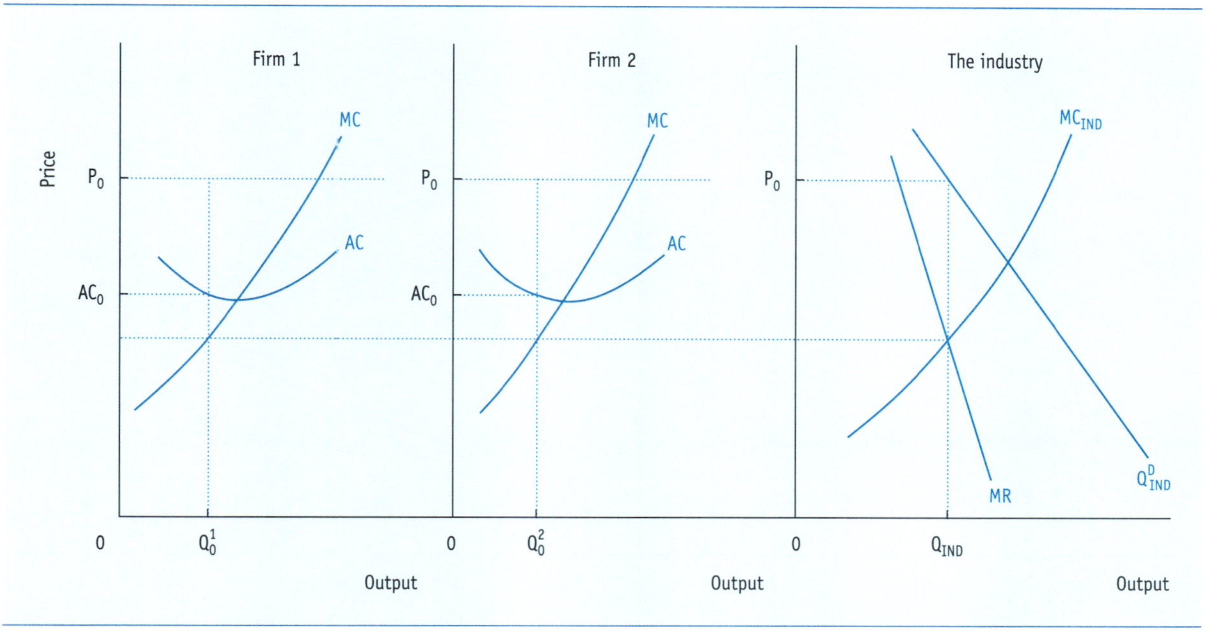

Figure 11.1 A cartel

exert some monopoly power: if the potential gains are great there is a greater chance of an agreement among the cartel members. This may be a part of the explanation as to why OPEC has been successful, while CIPEC for example, a cartel of four copper-producing countries (Chile, Peru, Zaire and Zambia) has not. CIPEC also struggled because the member countries produced less than a half of the world's copper, because the members only had modest cost advantages over the other suppliers of copper and because the (short-run) demand for copper is much more elastic than that for oil.

Price leadership

Tacit collusion between firms to set prices can take a variety of forms. There may, for example, be one dominant firm who acts as a price leader, whom other firms in the industry follow. The main features of the dominant firm model are illustrated in Figure 11.2. Q^D_{IND} is the industry demand curve and Q^S_{FOL} is the supply curve of the firms who follow the dominant firm. At the price P_0 the demand for the industry's output can be met entirely by the smaller firms. When the price is below P_1 these firms supply nothing. As the price falls between P_0 and P_1, we obtain the demand curve for the dominant firm, Q^D_{DOM}, as the difference between the industry demand and the supply of the other firms. When the price falls below P_1 the demand curve of the dominant firm is the industry demand curve.

A dominant firm can emerge because it has significant cost advantages. In Figure 11.2, the marginal revenue and marginal cost curves of the dominant firm are MR_{DOM} and MC_{DOM}.

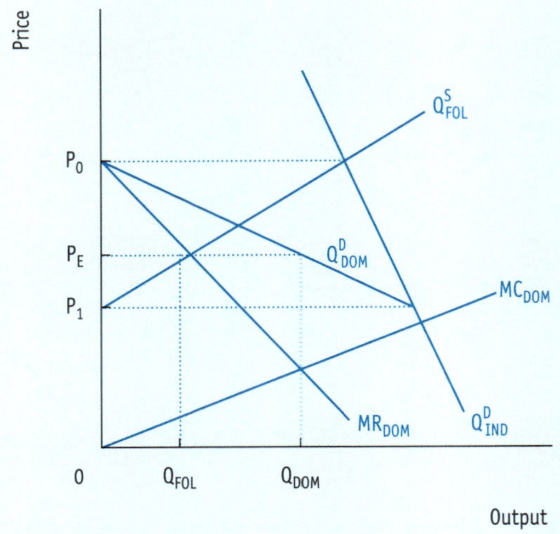

Figure 11.2 Dominant firm and price leadership

The profit-maximising output for the dominant firm is Q_{DOM} who charges a price P_E. At this price the rest of the industry combined produces Q_{FOL}, which together with the output from the dominant firm meets the total industry demand.

Question

Q1 Using the dominant firm model to analyse the operation of cartels

(I) How would you measure the monopoly power of a cartel?

(II) Show why the elasticity of demand for a commodity, and cost differentials between cartel members and other producers, are important to the operation of a cartel.

11.2 Traditional models of oligopoly

The Cournot model with costless production

We will begin our discussion of the Cournot model by assuming that there are two profit-maximising firms. The key behavioural assumption of the model is that each firm assumes that the output level of the other, rival, firm will not change when it is deciding how much to produce. For simplicity, we will assume that the two firms face identical linear demand functions and that production is costless.[2]

2 Cournot's original model was based on production from mineral springs and assumed costless production.

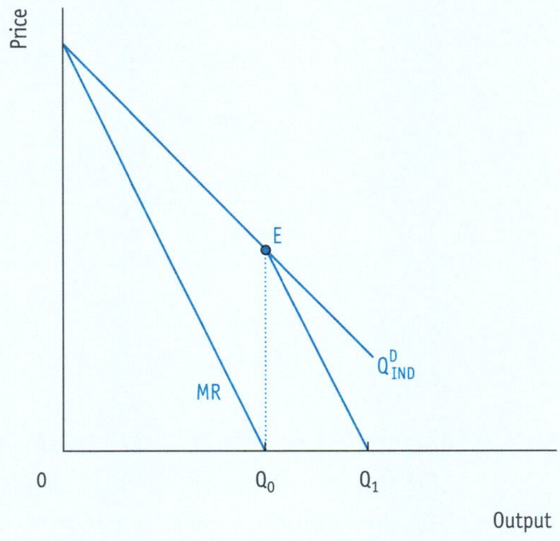

Figure 11.3 The Cournot model (costless production)

In Figure 11.3, the demand curve for the industry is shown by Q^D_{IND}, with its associated marginal revenue curve, MR. The nature of the Cournot model can be explained by assuming that one firm enters production before the other. We will refer to it as Firm 1. This means that it initially faces the entire industry demand. Being a profit-maximiser, it will equate marginal revenue with marginal cost (which is zero by assumption). Production will therefore expand to the point where marginal revenue is zero. In the figure, this is shown by the marginal revenue curve cutting the horizontal axis at output level Q_0, which is equal to half of the industry demand at a price of zero.

Now let the other firm, Firm 2, enter into production. It will take the output Q_0 of the first firm as given, and so only the part of the industry demand below point E is relevant to its output decision. In terms of Figure 11.3, this means that the vertical axis has, in effect, been shifted rightwards to the point Q_0 as far as Firm 2 is concerned. The output of the second firm will also expand to the point where its marginal revenue is zero. It will therefore produce output equal to the distance $Q_1 - Q_0$, which is one-quarter of the industry demand.

This is not an equilibrium in the Cournot model, since the output of Firm 1 was based on an assumption of a zero output level by Firm 2. Given that its rival is now producing a quarter of the industry demand, Firm 1 will re-adjust its output level, treating the new output level by Firm 2 as fixed. Firm 1 will treat the industry demand curve as having shifted to the right and it will now produce one half of three-quarters of the industry demand, or three-eighth's of the total. This new output level for the first firm will, of course, have further repercussions for the second firm. The process of adjustment and readjustment is shown in Table 11.1

The process involves the output of Firm 1 decreasing while that of Firm 2 increases. The output levels of the two firms will adjust until each firm produces one-third of the market

	Firm 1 output (Q^1)	Firm 2 output (Q^2)
Stage 1	1/2 (given $Q^2 = 0$)	0
Stage 2	1/2	1/4 (given $Q^1 = 1/2$)
Stage 3	3/8 (given $Q^2 = 1/4$)	1/4
Stage 4	3/8	5/16 (given $Q^1 = 3/8$)
Stage 5	11/32 (given $Q^2 = 5/16$)	5/16

Table 11.1 Share of industry demand in Cournot duopoly

output. When Firm 1 is producing one-third of the industry output, Firm 2 faces the industry demand less that part already produced by Firm 1. It is therefore faced with two-thirds of the industry demand of which it produces a half, giving Firm 2 one-third of industry output as well. Given the output level of Firm 2, Firm 1 will continue producing one-third of the market demand, giving us an equilibrium. Both firms react to the output decisions of each other in a mutually consistent manner. The level of output will not change, without changes to cost, or demand, conditions.

The Cournot model can be extended to incorporate more than two firms. It can be shown that as the number of firms increases the output of the industry will approach that of a competitive market.[3] The share of total market demand for each firm is $1/(n + 1)$ where n is the number of firms in the industry. As we have seen, if there are two firms this results in 1/3rd of industry output for each firm, 2/3rds of total demand. If there are ten firms, each would produce 1/11th of industry output and collectively they would produce 10/11ths of the output of a competitive industry.

Isoprofit curves and reaction functions

To include costs of production we will introduce isoprofit curves and derive the firms' reaction functions from them to determine the model's equilibrium. Isoprofit curves for Firm 1 are shown in Figure 11.4A. These show different levels of output by Firm 1 and Firm 2 that yield a given level of profit to Firm 1. To understand why the isoprofit curves take the shape they do, start at point A on IP_0. At this point Firm 1 is producing Q_0^1 and Firm 2 is producing Q_0^2. If we move further up IP_0 then both firms will be producing more between points A and B, so total industry output is expanding. As industry output expands the market price falls, but, providing demand is elastic, this increase in output will mean an increase in total revenue for the industry. It follows that initially rising output levels are consistent with Firm 1 maintaining its given profit level. Beyond a certain point, marked B on IP_0, Firm 1 can only increase its output at the

3 This is taken up in the exercises at the end of the chapter.

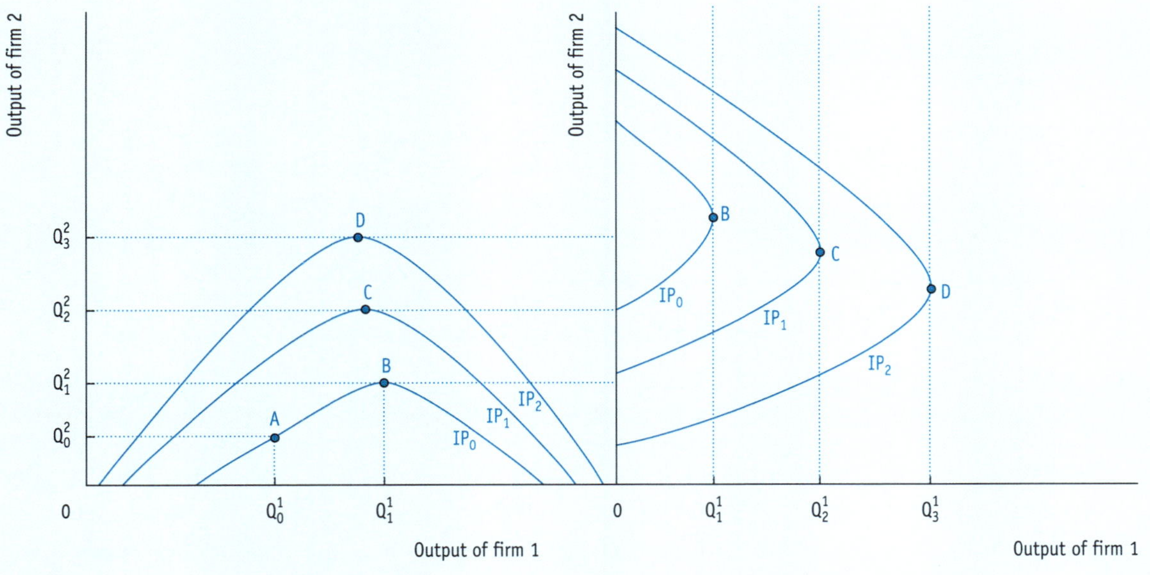

Figure 11.4A Isoprofit map for Firm 1

Figure 11.4B Isoprofit map for Firm 2

expense of Firm 2, if the profit of Firm 1 is to remain unchanged. The explanation for this may be due to either rising unit costs and/or falling elasticity of demand beyond the output level marked Q_1^1.

The higher the isoprofit curve the lower the level of profit for Firm 1. To see why, start at point B on IP_0 in Figure 11.4A. If Firm 2 expands its output level above Q_1^2, then given an unchanged output level by Firm 1 the market price will fall, as will the revenue and profits of Firm 1. The isoprofit curve IP_0 therefore represents a higher profit level for Firm 1, than does IP_1, which represents a higher profit level than IP_2.

For a given output level of Firm 2, there is a particular output by Firm 1 that will maximise its profits. As the output of Firm 2 varies there is therefore a series of profit-maximising output levels for Firm 1. In Figure 11.4A, these points are illustrated by the tangency's of the horizontal lines associated with the output of Firm 2 at Q_1^2, Q_2^2, Q_3^2 and the isoprofit curves IP_0, IP_1 and IP_2. These are the lowest possible isoprofit curves (representing profit maximisation) for Firm 1, consistent with each of the three output levels of Firm 2.

We can construct isoprofit curves for Firm 2 in a similar fashion by combining different levels of output by the two firms that yield the same profit to Firm 2. These isoprofit curves are drawn relative to the vertical axis as shown in Figure 11.4B.

The isoprofit curves are a step towards deriving reaction curves for the two firms. We have seen that given the output level of its rival, there is a particular level of output that will

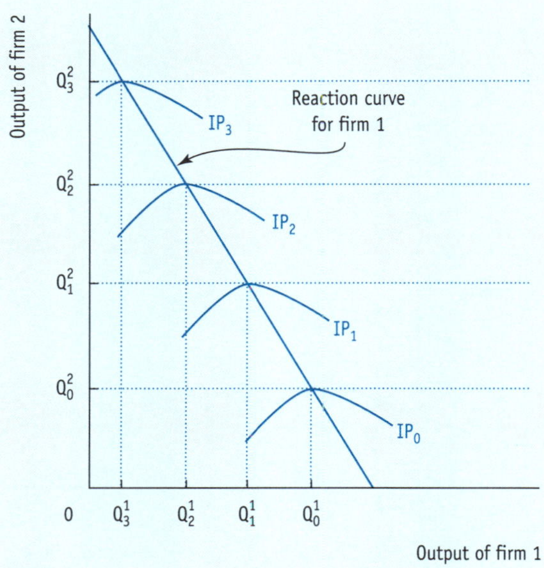

Figure 11.5A **Reaction curve for Firm 1**

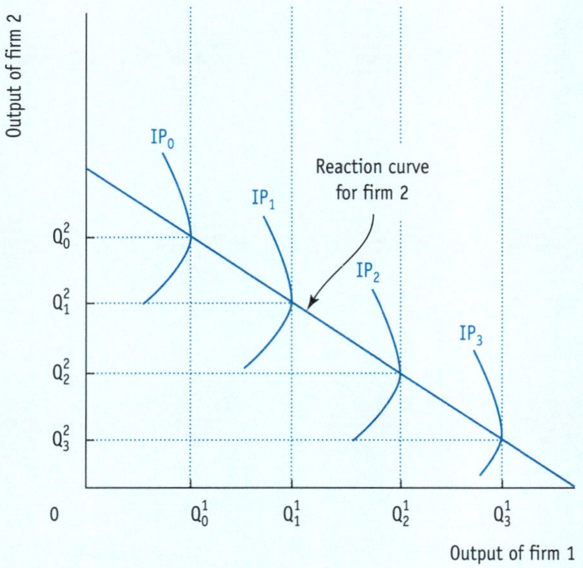

Figure 11.5B **Reaction curve for Firm 2**

maximise a firm's profits. At different levels of output of Firm 2, there will be a series of output levels of Firm 1 that maximise profits for Firm 1. In Figure 11.5A, we have shown four such points; given an output of Q^2_0 by Firm 2 for example, Firm 1 will produce Q^1_0. Similarly, with the other points marked. The locus of all these points joined together gives us the reaction curve for Firm 1, which tells us how much Firm 1 produces given the output of Firm 2. Likewise we can obtain a reaction curve for Firm 2 as shown in Figure 11.5B.

The equilibrium in the Cournot model occurs where the two reaction curves intersect, marked as point E in Figure 11.6. The equilibrium is stable providing that Firm 1's reaction curve is steeper than that of Firm 2. If we start at point F in the figure, where the output of Firm 1 is higher than its equilibrium value and the output of Firm 2 is lower, the adjustment process will lead to equilibrium. Given Firm 1's output at F, Firm 2 will increase its output as indicated by its reaction function, taking us to point G. Given this new output level for Firm 2, Firm 1 will contract its output since it expects the output of Firm 2 to remain that associated with the point G. This takes us to point H. Further iterations lead to the equilibrium outcome at point E.

This process is essentially what we analysed earlier in the tabulation of adjustment to equilibrium (when we assumed zero costs). Plainly, we could also have started from a point such as A, where Firm 1 is producing less than its equilibrium output and Firm 2 is producing more, and would still have converged to equilibrium. The Cournot model is a useful aid for analysing

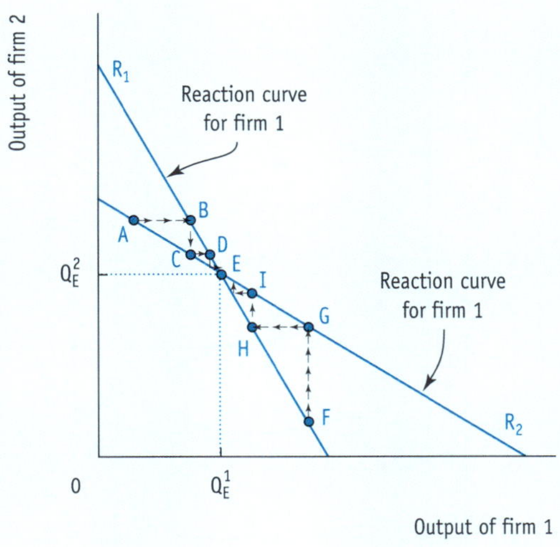

Figure 11.6 Equilibrium in the Cournot model

the interdependency of the decision-making. It does have some rather obvious limitations: price rather than output may be the strategic variable in decision-making and the behavioural assumption that each firm expects the output of its rival to be fixed is rather mechanical. These two points we will take up in the discussion of the Bertrand and Stackelberg models.

Bertrand's duopoly model

The model of oligopoly developed by Bertrand assumes that the strategic variable of the firm's decision-making is price. Both firms set the price of their output so as to maximise their profits, given some expected price charged by the rival firm. The behavioural assumption is analogous to that of the Cournot model: both firms expect that the rival will keep their price constant when it decides what price to charge. For simplicity, we will also take it that both firms face the same (constant) average and marginal costs.

In Bertrand's model, each isoprofit curve shows differing combinations of prices charged by the two firms that yield the same level of profit to one of the firms. In Figure 11.7A, there are four such isoprofit curves for Firm 1. Why the particular shape of the isoprofit curves in this model? Starting at point A on IP_0, as Firm 2 lowers its price, initially Firm 1 can reduce its price to maintain the demand for its product and its profit level. Beyond a certain point, marked as B in the figure, Firm 1's revenue and profits would be reduced if Firm 2 reduced its price any further. Hence a turning point at B on IP_0, and the convex shape of the isoprofit curves. In the Bertrand model higher isoprofit curves are associated with higher profit levels. Starting point B, if Firm 1's price remains unchanged while that of Firm 2 increased, the demand for Firm 1's output would rise, as would its profits.

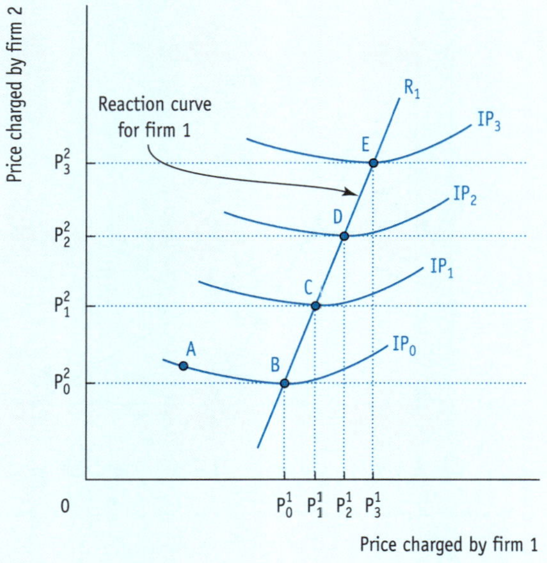

Figure 11.7A **Bertrand model reaction curve for Firm 1**

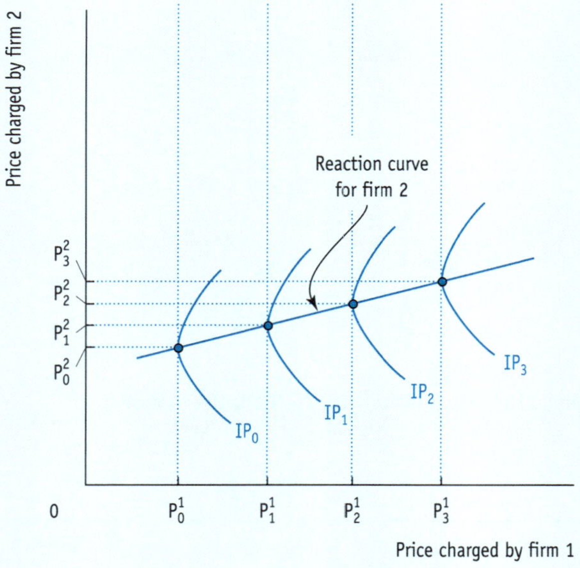

Figure 11.7B **Reaction curve for Firm 2**

In a similar way to the discussion of the Cournot model, given a particular price for Firm 2 we can establish a particular price charged by Firm 1 that maximises its profits. Diagrammatically this is represented by the highest possible attainable isoprofit curve of Firm 1; as we vary the price charged by Firm 2 in Figure 11.7A from P_0^2 to P_3^2 we obtain the points of tangency, marked as B, C, D and E. These four points lie on the reaction curve for Firm 1 and by considering other prices charged by Firm 2 we can again trace out the entire reaction curve.[4] Likewise for Firm 2, a reaction curve can be traced out by joining up the points that give Firm 2 the profit-maximising price level for each price charged by Firm 1. This is illustrated in Figure 11.7B.

Equilibrium in the Bertrand model is given by the point of intersection of the two reaction curves, point E in Figure 11.8. We have (again) drawn the reaction curve for Firm 1 more steeply than that for Firm 2. Given this, if we start at a point such as A on the reaction curve of Firm 2, where both firms are charging prices above the equilibrium, the iterative adjustment process will lead to point E, the equilibrium price. A similar convergence process would apply if we started at prices below the equilibrium. In equilibrium, given our earlier assumption about both firms having the same constant costs, both firms will be charging the same price.

4 The positive slope of the reaction function reflects the fact that by increasing its price by less than that of Firm 2, Firm 1 can increase its profits.

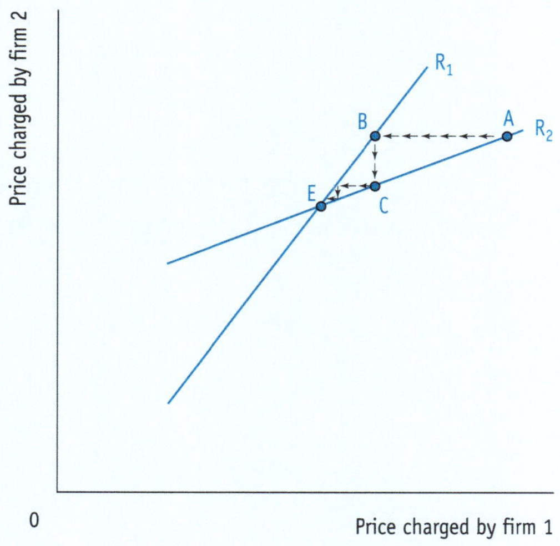

Figure 11.8 **Equilibrium in the Bertrand model**

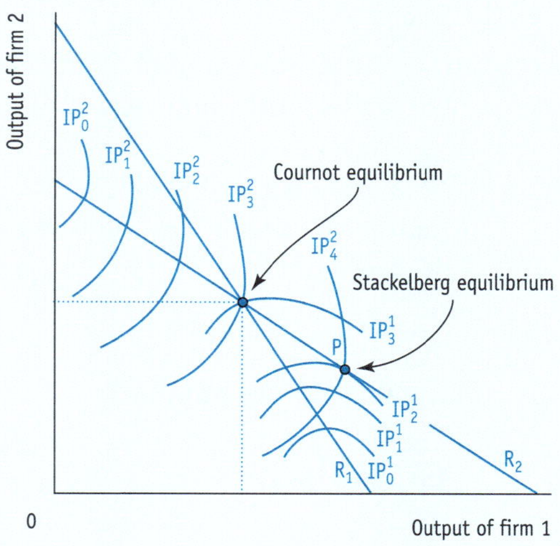

Figure 11.9 **The Stackleberg model**

The Stackelberg model

This model of duopoly is an extension of the Cournot model. In the Stackelberg model, one of the two duopolists follows the earlier assumption of taking the output level of the rival firm as constant. The second duopolist, the leader, recognises the behaviour of this firm, the 'follower' and decides to use this knowledge to its advantage. This it does by incorporating the known reaction of the follower firm into its output decision.

In Figure 11.9, the two reaction curves drawn are those of the two firms in the Cournot model. We will assume here that Firm 1 is the leader in the model. Firm 1 therefore assumes that its rival will follow its reaction curve, R_2, as drawn in the diagram. Firm 1 will then choose to maximise its profits given the reaction curve of Firm 2, i.e. at point P, where there is a tangency between R_2 and IP_2^1. This is of advantage to the leader firm as it involves a higher level of profit than in the simple Cournot model, since a lower isoprofit curve means a higher profit for Firm 1. The follower in the Stackelberg model, represented by Firm 2 here, is clearly a loser. The isoprofit curve it attains at point P is further away from the vertical axis indicating lower profit levels than in the Cournot equilibrium.

Questions

Q2 What factors determine the relative slopes of the reaction curves for the two firms in the Cournot model of duopoly?

Q3 What would be the effect in the Bertrand model if

(I) The two firms sell a differentiated product
(II) One of the firms had a cost advantage?

Q4 With reference to Figure 11.9 where would the equilibrium outcome be if Firm 2 were the leader and Firm 1 was the follower? What would be the outcome if both firms tried to be 'leader'?

11.3 A game theory approach

Introduction

In the first two sections of this chapter, we saw that the interdependence of decision-making in oligopolistic markets raises awkward questions about what kind of decisions firms make, even if they are fully informed about the demand and cost conditions that they face. Game theory offers another approach to strategic decision-making and this section introduces some of the ideas involved.

We will be dealing with games involving only two 'players' who will represent two firms. These two players follow certain moves, or strategies, which, for example, might be to engage in an advertising campaign or to introduce a new brand of product. In the games that firms play, they may decide to co-operate with each other or they may not, depending on whether firms can enter contracts that bind them to joint strategies. The examples that follow will be dealing mainly with situations where there is no co-operation.

Payoff matrices and dominant strategies

In the first example, we will assume that the profits that each firm earns are known and depend simply on the pricing policies that the two firms adopt.[5] We will suppose there are just two alternative strategies: charging a high price or charging a low price.

Table 11.2 shows the payoff, or profit, for the alternative strategies of the two firms. If both firms decide to charge a high price they will both make a profit of £1,000. This is shown in the Table by the top left entry of £1,000; £1,000. The first figure refers to the profit of Firm 1, the second to the profit of Firm 2. If Firm 1 priced high, while Firm 2 priced low then the relevant cell is £500; £1,500 and so on.

Each combination of strategies pursued by the two firms has a payoff associated with it as

5 We are assuming again that the two firms are identical in terms of their demand and cost conditions.

		FIRM 2	
		High price	**Low price**
FIRM 1	**High price**	£1,000; £1,000	£500; £1,500
	Low price	£1,500; £500	£750; £750

Table 11.2 Payoff matrix with a dominant strategy

shown in the payoff matrix. If both firms maximise profits and believe that their rival also acts to maximise profits, what strategy should they follow? Looked at from the interests of Firm 1, if it follows a high price strategy it will make a profit of either £1,000 or £500 depending on the strategy of Firm 2. If it follows a low price strategy it makes either £1,500 or £750 again depending on its rival's strategy. Whether Firm 2 charges high or low, it will make a higher profit by charging a low price: £1,500 rather than £1,000, or £750 rather than £500, depending on whether Firm 2 charges a high or a low price.

In this case, Firm 1 has what is called a dominant strategy. It should charge a low price because it will make a higher profit from doing so no matter what strategy Firm 2 adopts. The payoff matrix in this example is symmetric, so Firm 2 also has the same dominant strategy. If it charges a low price, its profits will be either £1,500 or £750 depending on Firm 1's strategy; if it charges a high price its profit levels will drop to either £1,000 or £500. In this particular example we have a unique equilibrium. Although both firms have a dominant strategy, it does not follow that they maximise profits. Both firms could make a higher profit if they agreed that they both charge a high price.

Nash equilibrium

A Nash equilibrium arises if the strategy each firm chooses to maximise their payoff depends on the strategy of their opponent. As an example, Table 11.3 gives the payoff matrix for two rival holiday companies, who intend to expand their businesses by offering additional vacations, to either Florence or to Monaco.

Neither has a dominant strategy: if Firm 1 offers holidays in Florence it will make a profit of £1,000 or £2,000 depending on whether Firm 2 goes to Florence or Monaco. If Firm 1 goes to Monaco it will earn either £2,000 or £1,000 again depending on where its rival goes. Similarly for Firm 2. They both make higher profits if they offer holidays to different destinations and the best course of action either firm can take depends on the decision of its rival.

A Nash equilibrium occurs when neither firm wants to change its behaviour. When they are opening up different routes their payoffs are greater than when they don't, and neither has an incentive to change if this is what they do. In Table 11.3, a Nash equilibrium occurs when

		FIRM 2	
		Florence	**Monaco**
FIRM 1	**Florence**	£1,000; £1,000	£2,000; £2,000
	Monaco	£2,000; £2,000	£1,000; £1,000

Table 11.3 Payoff matrix with a Nash equilibrium

Firm 1 offers holidays in Florence and Firm 2 trips to Monaco. In general, there may be more than one Nash equilibrium, which is the case with this example.[6]

Repeated games

The discussion of decision-making by firms has so far been limited to a one-off situation. In practice, decisions about price, output and other variables are repeated periodically and, sometimes with great frequency. How does this alter the strategies that firms pursue and the likely outcome of the game?

The payoff matrix in Table 11.4 gives the profits per period that two producers can earn if they enter into a cartel agreement. If both firms follow their dominant strategy and produce a high level of output, they will each make a profit of £750. Both can make a higher level of profits if they agree to restrict output, but clearly given the figures in the Table both have an incentive to cheat on the agreement.[7]

In a repeated game, a firm can modify its strategy from one period to the next, and it can also respond to changes in the strategy of the other firm. One possible strategy that a firm might follow is 'tit for tat'. Suppose the two producers collude and restrict output, from the viewpoint of Firm 1 it will start off by producing a low output, keeping to the agreement until Firm 2 cheats. The tit-for-tat response of Firm 1 to a decision to cheat by Firm 2 is to respond in the next period by increasing its output as well.

The rationale behind this is that a one-period increase in profits from £1,000 to £2,000 is followed by a succession of periods in which the cheating firm (who increased production) is penalised by a lower profit of £750. If both firms think that their rival is following a tit-for-tat strategy the anticipation of a lower profit stream may prevent cheating. The value of this strategy depends on both firms knowing each other are following such a strategy (or at least

6 This leaves open which of the two outcomes would be the equilibrium. There are also games for which there is no Nash equilibrium, a point taken up in the questions.

7 The structure of this problem is an extension of the Prisoner's Dilemma, which is concerned with a one-off decision.

		FIRM 2 Low output	FIRM 2 High output
FIRM 1	Low output	£1,000; £1,000	£0; £2,000
	High output	£2,000; £0	£750; £750

Table 11.4 Payoff matrix for a repeated game

that they might be following it). It is also sensitive to the size of the reward from cheating on the agreement, something that depends on how long the firms think they will be playing this game.

Sequential games

In a sequential game, one firm makes a move, and its rival has to decide how to react to the move. This can lead to a major advantage in moving first, as we shall see. Table 11.5 is a modified version of the earlier example of the alternative strategies available to the two tour operators. To illustrate the potential importance of moving first, the present game assumes that trips to Monaco are more profitable than those to Florence.

		FIRM 2 Florence	FIRM 2 Monaco
FIRM 1	Florence	£0; £0	£1,000; £3,000
	Monaco	£3,000; £1,000	£500; £500

Table 11.5 Payoff matrix for a sequential game

As before firms make a lower profit if they both open up trips to the same destination. Suppose that Firm 1 is in a position to move first, it will choose the more profitable Monaco. Given it is in a position to anticipate the decision of its rival, it knows that Firm 2 will respond with trips to Florence, since that is the best that Firm 2 can do.

Another way of looking at the (given) outcomes from a sequential game is with the extensive form of the game, which is a kind of decision tree. Table 11.6 is an example. It is clear that once its rival decided to open a route to Monaco, Firm 2 will make a higher profit by going to Florence. The 'first-mover' advantage lies in anticipating the response of its rival, and effectively presenting it with a fait accompli. The advantage of moving first in this game is

— Florence £1,000

— Monaco — FIRM 2

— Monaco £500

FIRM 1

— Florence £0

— Florence — FIRM 2

— Monaco £1,000

Table 11.6 Extensive form of a sequential game

clear, but it applies to other situations as well. For example, it may be possible to deter entry into an industry by potential competitors, or to persuade incumbent firms to leave an industry by adopting an aggressive pricing policy.

An important question is how a particular firm might obtain the advantage of moving first. This can depend on a mixture of the speed of operations within firms and also their strategic commitments. In the example, both companies have an incentive to commit themselves by operating on the profitable route. To be successful, the rival firm has to be convinced that the commitment is genuine, which might take the form of an expensive advertising campaign, or the acceptance of advance bookings, which are the kind of decisions that would put a firm's reputation at stake.

Questions

Q5

		FIRM 2	
		Low output	High output
FIRM 1	Low output	£1,500; £800	£2,500; £200
	High output	–£500; £1,400	£1,400; £1,500

(I) Does either firm have a dominant strategy?

(II) Suppose that both firms adopt the low-risk strategy of 'maximin', that is they adopt the strategy which pays the highest of the low payoffs. What would the outcome be?

(III) If Firm 1 has first-mover advantage what would the outcome be? Would it be different if Firm 2 was able to move first?

Q6 This question is based on an adaptation of Table 11.4 in the text.

		FIRM 2	
		Low output	**High output**
FIRM 1	**Low output**	£1,000; £1,000	£0; £5,000
	High output	£5,000; £0	£750; £750

The payoff matrix here gives the monthly profit for the two alternative output levels. The firms initially enter a collusive agreement.

(I) What is the cartel outcome and what are the additional profits over the dominant strategy equilibrium?

(II) Suppose Firm 2 decides to cheat and produce a high level of output, and that Firm 1 responds on a tit-for-tat basis the following month. What happens to the profits of the two firms over a time horizon of twelve months?

(III) How long does it take for Firm 2 to lose out as a result of its decision to cheat?

(IV) Is a tit-for-tat strategy credible in this particular game? If you were Firm 1 what strategy would you adopt?

Mathematical appendix

The Cournot model

The industry price depends on the level of output of the industry

$$P = F(Q) = F(Q_1 + Q_2)$$

Where Q is the industry output, Q_1, Q_2 are the output levels of the two firms. In this appendix the subscripts 1,2 refer to the two firms (in the text we used both super-and subscripts to refer to the firms and particular levels of output). The profit functions of the two firms are

$$\pi_1 = F(Q_1 + Q_2)\,Q_1 - C(Q_1)$$

$$\pi_2 = F(Q_1 + Q_2)\,Q_2 - C(Q_2)$$

The Cournot model assumes that each firm determines its output, given the level of output it expects from its rival. Profits for the two firms will be maximised where

$$\frac{\delta \pi_1}{\delta Q_1} = 0$$

and

$$\frac{\delta \pi_2}{\delta Q_2} = 0$$

Re-arranging the first-order conditions will give expressions of the form

$$Q_1 = F(Q_2)$$

and

$$Q_2 = F(Q_1)$$

from which we obtain the reaction functions of the two firms, and can then solve to find the equilibrium output of the two firms.

An example

Suppose there is a linear demand function for the industry's output

$$P = 100 - Q$$

and that there are two firms, both of which have constant average and marginal costs

$$AC = MC = 10$$

The profit function of Firm 1 can be written as

$$\pi_1 = TR_1 - TC_1$$
$$= (100 - Q)\,Q_1 - 10Q_1$$

Writing industry output as the sum of the firms' output and expanding the bracket gives

$$\pi_1 = 100Q_1 - Q_1^2 - Q_1Q_2 - 10Q_1$$

The first-order condition for profit-maximisation is

$$\frac{\delta\pi_1}{\delta Q_1} = 100 - 2Q_1 - Q_2 - 10 = 0 \Rightarrow 2Q_1 = 90 - Q_2$$

so that the reaction function for Firm 1 is

$$R_1{:}Q_1 = 45 - \tfrac{1}{2}Q_2$$

The reaction function for Firm 2 can be obtained the same way and is

$$R_2{:}Q_2 = 45 - \tfrac{1}{2}Q_1$$

This gives us two equations in two unknowns. Solving for Q_1 we have

$$Q_1 = 45 - \tfrac{1}{2}[45 - \tfrac{1}{2}Q_1]$$

which gives $Q_1 = 30$. Given an identical reaction function the equilibrium output of Firm 2 will also be 30. The industry output is 60 and the industry price, found by substituting the output figure into the demand function, is 40 in this case.

This outcome can be usefully compared with that for a competitive industry and that for a monopoly. In a competitive industry, the individual firm produces where the price equals the marginal cost, giving an output of 90. Given the industry demand function, total and marginal revenue are

$$TR = 100Q - Q^2$$

$$MR = \frac{dTR}{dQ} = 100 - 2Q$$

The equilibrium output for the monopolist is found by equating marginal revenue and marginal cost, so here we get

$$100 - 2Q = 10$$

giving an output of 45 and a price of 55.

The range of outcomes are shown below:

	Competition	Cournot (duopoly)	Monopoly
Price	10	40	45
Output	90	60	55

The industry output in the Cournot model will vary depending on the number of firms in the industry. In general the output will be $n/(n+1)$ of the competitive output. In this example, $n=2$, so it is two-thirds, as shown in the table. If the number of firms in the Cournot model rose to 5, the industry output would rise to 75 and so on.

The Bertrand model: an example

Suppose the demand functions for the two firms in a duopoly are given by

$$Q_1 = 100 - 10P_1 + P_2$$

and

$$Q_2 = 100 - 10P_2 + P_1$$

where P_1 and P_2 refer to the prices charged for their output by both Firm 1 and Firm 2 respectively.

Both firms determine their price on the basis that they expect the price charged by its rival to be fixed. For simplicity we will assume that both firms have fixed costs of 50, and no variable costs. The profit functions can then be written as:

$$\pi_1 = TR_1 - TC_1 = P_1[100 - 10P_1 + P_2] - 50$$

and

$$\pi_2 = TR_2 - TC_2 = P_2[100 - 10P_2 + P_1] - 50$$

Multiplying out the bracket and collecting up terms

$$\pi_1 = 100P_1 - 10P_1^2 + P_1P_2 - 50$$

and

$$\pi_2 = 100P_2 - 10P_2^2 + P_2P_1 - 50$$

The first-order conditions for profit-maximisation are

$$\frac{\delta\pi_1}{\delta P_1} = 100 - 20P_1 + P_2 = 0$$

$$\frac{\delta\pi_2}{\delta P_2} = 100 - 20P_2 + P_1 = 0$$

from which we can obtain the reaction functions for Firm 1 and Firm 2

$$R_1 : P_1 = 5 + \frac{1}{20} P_2$$

$$R_2 : P_2 = 5 + \frac{1}{20} P_1$$

which solve for an equilibrium price of 5.26 for both firms.

The Stackelberg model: an example

The key to solving for equilibrium output in the Stackelberg model is to recognise that the leader firm knows the reaction of its follower. To continue with the same functions used in the Cournot model, Firm 1 knows R_2.

$$Q_2 = 45 - ½Q_1$$

The profit function for Firm 1 obtained in the Cournot model were

$$\pi_1 = 100Q_1 - Q_1^2 - Q_1Q_2 - 10Q_1$$

Given its knowledge of the other firm's reaction function, we can write

$$\begin{aligned}\pi_1 &= 90Q_1 - Q_1^2 - Q_1[45 - \tfrac{1}{2}Q_1] \\ &= 90Q_1 - Q_1^2 - 45Q_1 + \tfrac{1}{2}Q_1^2 \\ &= 45Q_1 - \tfrac{1}{2}Q_1^2\end{aligned}$$

The first-order condition is

$$\frac{\delta\pi_1}{\delta Q_1} = 45 - Q_1 = 0$$

which solves for $Q_1 = 45$, and after substitution into the reaction function for Firm 2 gives $Q_2 = 22.5$.

Summary

1 An oligopolistic industry is one with a small number of firms. The key feature of such an industry is the interdependence of the decision-making by firms. This leads to different models of firm behaviour based on alternative assumptions.

2 There is an important distinction between situations in which the firms in the industry collude and when they compete. Cartels are illegal in many countries, although a number have operated on an 'international basis', of which the best known is probably OPEC.

3 The Cournot model assumes that firms are rivals. The key behavioural assumption of the model is that each firm decides what level of output to produce, given the expectation of an unchanged output by its rival(s). Equilibrium occurs where the output decisions of firms are mutually consistent with one another.

4 The Bertrand model is similar except that it assumes firms compete on the basis of price. This model suggests that when firms compete on price, rather than output, an industry with a small number of firms may still lead to a competitive equilibrium. This conclusion is, however, sensitive to some rather particular assumptions.

5 The Stackelberg model is an example of a leader-follower model. The leader firm can exploit knowledge of the way the follower will react to its decisions. This will give the leader firm a higher level of output and profit.

6 A more modern approach to analysing oligopoly is with the use of game theory. In the language of game theory, individual firms are players and decisions about alternative possibilities are known as strategies.

7 A dominant strategy is one in which a player, or firm, does best following one course of action, no matter what the strategy adopted by rival(s). A Nash equilibrium is one in which the players are doing the best they can given the strategy of their rival(s).

8 The analysis of repeated and sequential games are useful in understanding business decision-making, as they emphasise the role of reputation and the potential advantage of moving first.

End of chapter questions

Q7 An industry demand curve for a particular product is given by

$$P = 40 - 2Q$$

The marginal cost of production for all firms in the industry is

$$MC = 10$$

(I) What is the Cournot equilibrium output and price when there are two firms?
(II) What difference would it make if the costs of production of one of the firms rose to 20?
(III) What is the Stackelberg equilibrium output for the leader and follower firms given demand and cost conditions in (I) above?

Q8 Suppose there are three firms in the Cournot model, all with the same demand and cost conditions. The industry demand is

$$P = 200 - 10Q$$

The marginal cost of production is

$$MC = 5$$

(I) What is the total revenue function for Firm 1 in this industry? What is its profit function?
(II) Given that their demand and cost conditions are identical, what is the relation between the output of Firm 1 and that of the other firms in the industry?
(III) What is the output level of Firm 1 in equilibrium and what is the industry output?
(IV) If there are n firms in the industry, show why each firm produces $1/(n + 1)$ of the industry output.

Q9 Given industry demand of

$$P = 40 - 5Q$$

and marginal costs for all firms of

$$MC = 6$$

(I) What is the industry output and price in the Stackelberg model when there are two firms?
(II) If the follower firm experiences an increase in costs to 10 per unit, how does the answer to (I) change?

Q10 Suppose that the demand curves of a two-firm oligopoly are given by

$$Q_1 = 30 - 5P_1 + 2P_2$$

and

$$Q_2 = 30 - 5P_1 + 2P_2$$

and that both face fixed costs of 20 and have zero variable costs.

(I) Obtain the reaction functions in the Bertrand model.
(II) What is the equilibrium price and output? What is the level of profit made by both firms?
(III) Suppose the costs of Firm 1 rose to 100, what happens to its price and output, and what happens to the industry output? What is the profit made by Firm 2?

Q11 This question deals with how incumbent firms who are in a monopoly position might try to deter others from entering the industry. Firm 1 is in the monopoly position, Firm 2 is the potential entrant who has to invest £60mn in plant and machinery before it can start operating. The payoff matrix gives the profits in £mn of each firm depending on what course of action it follows.

		FIRM 2 (potential entrant)	
		Enters	**Does not enter**
FIRM 1 (incumbent)	**High price**	100; 40	200; 0
	Low price	50; –10	75; 0

(I) If the incumbent threatened to cut its price and expand output if a new firm entered the industry would the threat be a credible deterrent to entry?
(II) Suppose the incumbent firm invested a further £60mn in plant and equipment while Firm 2 was making the decision to enter or not, how would this change the payoff matrix? How does it affect the credibility of announcements by the monopolist to enter into price competition if Firm 2 enters the industry?
(III) If the game was repeated many times how would it affect the incumbent's incentive to cut prices if a new firm did enter the industry?

Q12 The games considered in the text are examples of what are known as 'pure strategies', which dealt with specific moves such as charge a high price or a low price and so on. This question introduces the idea of 'mixed strategies'. Suppose there are two individuals who play a game where they both reveal a penny coin. If both pennies show the same face the first individual wins a £1, if they show a different face the second person wins. The payoff matrix is given below

		Individual 2	
		Head	Tails
Individual 1	Head	1; –1	–1; 1
	Tails	–1; 1	1; –1

(I) Is there a Nash equilibrium (in pure strategies) for either player in this game?

(II) Suppose individual 1 decides to toss the penny to determine whether to play heads or tails, what is the expected payoff from this strategy?

(III) Given that individual 1 follows this strategy what is the best strategy for the second player?

Q13 Two holiday companies are considering whether to offer packages to one of Antigua, Barbados, or Bermuda. The payoff matrix shows the profitability of the destinations to the two companies in £mn. Assume that the two firms make their decisions simultaneously.

		Firm 2		
		Antigua	Barbados	Bermuda
Firm 1	Antigua	–5,000; –5,000	0; 7,500	2,000; 10,000
	Barbados	7,500; 0	–7,500; –7,500	–3,000; 6,000
	Bermuda	10,000; 2,000	6,000; –3,000	–8,000; –8,000

(I) Are there Nash equilibria?

(II) If both firms adopted a maximin strategy what will be their decisions?

References and suggested further reading

The material of this chapter is covered at greater length in other texts. Earl puts the simpler models of price rigidity into historical context. Moschandreas discusses business strategy in oligopolistic markets and presents some evidence on 'the impressively large number of illegal price-fixing agreements' (MM) in the UK and other parts of the world. Romp contains a chapter that develops the analysis of game theory in relation to the three traditional models discussed here.

Earl, P.E. (1995), *Microeconomics for Business and Marketing*, Edward Elgar.

Moschandreas, M. (1994), *Business Economics*, Routledge.

Nicholson, W. (1995), *Microeconomic Theory, Basic Principles and Extensions*, 6th edition, The Dryden Press

Romp, G. (1997), *Game Theory*, Oxford University Press.

Varian, H.R. (1996), *Intermediate Microeconomics, A Modern Approach*, 4th edition, W.W. Norton & Co.

12

Competition and Regulation Policy

Key ideas and material

Competition policy, regulation of utility industries, introduction of competition into utilities, the welfare effects of tariff changes

Introduction

The message from the previous chapters in this part of the book was that a competitive market structure yields welfare benefits that other types of market structure do not. In simple terms, competition leads to more being produced at a lower price. The competitive outcome also maximises the sum of consumer and producer surplus. Given this, we come to the question whether government policy can, by some means, promote competition and its associated welfare benefits.

This chapter looks at government policy towards both competition and regulation, mainly in relation to the utility industries. In the UK and many other countries there has been an extensive programme of privatisation; what were at one time seen as natural monopolies have been transferred into private ownership, subjected to (in the UK) independent price regulation, and are increasingly being opened up to competition. In broad terms policy has divided up monopolies into those areas where competition is possible: the provision of train services or gas supplies for example, and to regulate what remains — the rail track network or gas pipes.

The overall welfare assessment is however not straightforward for a number of reasons. These include issues relating to managerial incentives in some of the privatised companies and those that arise with changes to the price tariffs charged to consumers. The objective of maximising social welfare is not generally viewed as simply a matter of maximising consumer and producer surplus; distributional considerations are important as well.

The outline of this chapter is as follows. Section 1 provides background on the context for competition policy. Section 2 discusses the price regulation of the utility industries since the time of their privatisation in the UK. This leads us to awkward questions about information asymmetries between the regulated and the regulators, which impact on the incentives of the utilities to cut costs. In Section 3, we discuss in some detail the ways in which competition has been introduced and where the limits to policy may be.

12.1 Competition policy

Broadly, the purpose of competition policy is to promote the efficient working of the market. In Chapter 9, we introduced the model of perfect competition, which is the idealised form of market structure that is often used as a benchmark for judging actual industries. The analysis of perfect competition showed that in the long-run there would be an optimal allocation of resources: firms produce at the minimum point on their average cost curves and charge a price equal to the marginal costs of production. This outcome can be viewed as social desirable to the extent that sum of producer and consumer surplus is maximised.

This contrasts with the analysis of a monopoly. The firm does not produce at the minimum point on its average cost curve and there are deadweight losses associated with the contraction in output relative to the competitive outcome. As we noted in Chapter 10, the idealised version of monopoly is also rare; in many instances firms have some degree of monopoly power and the welfare conclusions drawn will then depend on the details of a firm's operation.

This linkage between market structure and firm performance has been influential in the development of policy in the UK since the Second World War. As we have discussed in earlier chapters, this analysis simplifies by treating firms as a black box that just convert inputs into outputs. In practice, the relationship between market structure and economic efficiency is not straightforwardly one-way. Firms develop because of the transactions costs associated with the market place and may establish a dominant position because they have cost advantages. Economic efficiency is one determinant of market structure, although the power and influence of a dominant firm can lead to practices that run against the public interest.

A monopoly may increase its spending on various forms of non-price competition (advertising, product proliferation) with the intention of removing competitive pressures. The combination of economic profits and a desire to avoid the risks associated with Research and Development expenditure may mean that over time there is less innovation and that the costs of production are above what they would otherwise be.

A dominant firm may therefore develop because of efficiency considerations, or from legal protection which create barriers to entry, or by collusion or a merger. This can create a policy dilemma. Figure 12.1 illustrates the position in a competitive industry where average and marginal costs are assumed (for simplicity) to be constant. The output level is given by Q_C and

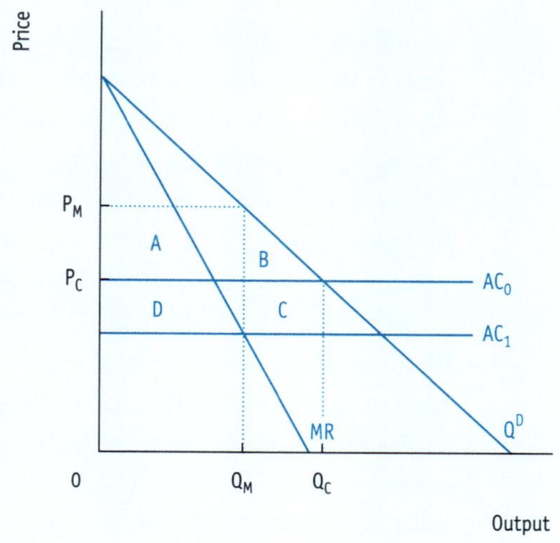

Figure 12.1 The trade-off between allocative and productive efficiency

each firm charges a price P_C. By contrast, if efficiency gains lead to a monopoly industry, the outcome is the output level Q_M and the price charged is P_M.

Is such a move against the public interest? The answer to this question depends on what idea of social welfare is adopted. If this is taken to be the sum of consumer and producer surplus, then consumer surplus would be reduced by the sum of areas A (the rectangle) and B. Producer surplus increases by the area A + D, which arises from the lower costs of production and also the transfer of consumer surplus. This leaves us with the deadweight loss triangle B that does not represent a benefit to the producers. Whether or not there has been an improvement in social welfare would therefore depend on the relative size of the areas marked B and D in Figure 12.1.[1]

UK and EU policy

UK policy has evolved pragmatically since the end of the Second World War. The Monopolies and Restrictive Practices Act of 1948 set up a commission to investigate any industry that might be acting against the public interest. The Monopolies and Mergers Act of 1965 extended powers to investigate mergers and gave the commission its present-day name: the Monopolies and Mergers Commission, MMC.[2] Competition policy in the 1990s derives much of its legal force from the Fair Trading Act of 1973, which set up the Office of Fair Trading, the OFT, whose role it is monitor anti-competitive practice and refer any cases to the MMC.

1 A conclusion that would need to be modified if a greater weight was given to one or other group.

2 The Commission had been divested of its role to investigate restrictive practices by this time.

The MMC decides whether any cases referred to it are against the public interest.[3] This it does on a case by case basis and its work can be viewed as a matter of balancing the gains from scale economies against the costs associated with the absence of competition. The legislative framework does not therefore rule out the existence of monopolies per se. Over time the emphasis of policy has changed. During the 1980s free market theories were influential in policy-making and the 1980 Competition Act allowed for the referral of all firms to the MMC, not just monopolies. More broadly, there was a move away from state involvement in production with the extensive programme of privatisation noted in Chapter 10.

Competition policy also has to be seen in a European context. The main aim of EU policy has been to promote trade between member states and is geared to prohibiting restrictive agreements and practices as outlined in Articles 85 and 86 of the Treaty of Rome. EU legislation is mainly concerned with firms that trade between member states. Articles 92–94 ban aid by national governments which distorts or threatens to distort intra-Community trade.[4] In 1990, the European Commission Merger Regulation came into force. It covers mergers where world wide sales exceed 5 billion ECU, where the EU sales of least two of the companies involved exceed 250mn ECU and where at least one of the companies conducts no more than two-thirds of its EU business in one member state. In practical terms, this means that a small percentage of mergers are affected by the regulations. By 1996 only five mergers had been prohibited.

Individual member states within the EU have a long tradition of pursuing some form of competition policy, although the details at the national level vary. In Germany, for example, the 1957 Act against Restraints on Competition made any form of cartel or price-fixing arrangement illegal. In 1989 the Act was amended to protect the interests of small firms by giving them exemptions. The balance of German policy shifted and the emphasis is different from the UK, where the concern is with market structure. The enforcement of the law is simpler in that it does not require weighing efficiency criteria with anti-competitive behaviour. France also has a long tradition of anti-monopoly legislation, but this is not the case in all member states.

There are also differences between EU members in the way that the competition is viewed and this is reflected in different national policies. In some countries, competition is viewed more as process rather than as a static outcome (which is essentially the perspective given by the model of perfect competition). This leads to the idea of a firm being competitive if it has cost advantages that other firms do not have, and can gain market share as a result. It contrasts with the static view suggesting that a firm is more competitive the less market power it has and this divergence of views generally makes the task of developing EU competition policy more problematic.

---

3 The 1973 Act defines a monopoly as a market share of 25% or more.

4 There are exceptions for regional aid and some forms of development subisidies.

US policy

In the United States, what are known as antitrust laws exist to promote competition and prohibit actions that restrain or that are likely to restrain it. The Sherman Act of 1890 makes price-fixing illegal and prohibits other forms of action that restrict trade. This includes the possibility of implicit collusion in pricing where one firm's prices follow those of another regardless of market conditions (known as parallel pricing). Price discrimination is also illegal if it reduces competition and is against the interest of the consumer.[5]

Questions

Q1 An early study in the 1920s of the welfare loss associated with monopoly by Harberger produced a figure of 0.1% of US national income. In effect, the study attempted to measure area B in Figure 12.1.

(I) What kind of information would you need to have to make an estimate of this welfare loss?
(II) A later study by Cowling and Mueller of US and UK firms in the 1960s argued that advertising expenditure increased costs and was socially wasteful. How would you modify Figure 12.1 to accommodate this argument and how would the social costs of monopoly be represented?
(III) Are there any other costs of monopoly that should be included in assessing welfare loss?

Q2 In Figure 12.1 what is the impact on welfare of the area C and why?

12.2 Regulation of the privatised industries

The privatisation of previously state-owned industries has been a major policy development in the UK and other industrialised countries in the 1980s and 1990s. The advocates of the policy point to the advantages of product market competition on prices and greater consumer choice. Increased efficiency was to be obtained by providing appropriate work incentives for managers and (initially) widening share-ownership in the privatised companies.

The term privatisation covers a range of activities, including the economic regulation of privatised monopolies.[6] In the UK, the gas, rail, telecommunications, electricity and water

5 The Clayton Act, as amended by the Robinson-Patman Act (1936).

6 It is also associated with the contracting out of some public services and the joint public-private sector finance of some capital projects among other things.

industries have all been subjected to various forms of price regulation to prevent exploitation of a dominant market position. These utilities are also referred to as network industries as they are characterised by a network of pipes, rails and wires that would seem to make them natural monopolies.

The regulation of such industries has a number of possible targets. These include obtaining available scale economies and encouraging productive efficiency and ensuring a certain level of service provision (and also minimising the costs of regulation). To this end, price-control, or price-cap, regulation has been adopted in the UK. Regulation has therefore been designed 'to mimic the competitive market by setting prices to price-taking utilities' (Helm, 1994). Table 12.1 gives the details for the industries mentioned since privatisation.

The price-capping formula restricts the annual percentage increase in prices to whatever the rate of inflation is, as measured by the RPI, plus or minus adjustments given by X, Y and K factors. The first of these, the X-factor, relates to the expected productivity gains which are passed on to the final consumer. The Y-factor allows for unavoidable cost increases, such as rises in fuel costs for electricity generation. It is adjusted by the regulator to reflect actual changes in costs. The K-factor is particular to the water industry, and covers the costs of environmental improvements that are imposed on the industry by other regulatory bodies, or by the EU.

The UK system enables the industry regulator to judge the merits of individual industries and it is intended to provide incentives for the incumbent firms to cut costs and be as efficient as possible. If the incumbent firms can reduce costs by more than the X factor, then, in principle, they can retain the benefit.[7] In the early years of regulation, the price-cap set tended to underestimate the potential for cost reductions, and so the X-factor was lower than might have been appropriate. This has led to increases in the size of the X-factor as shown for telecommunications, gas and electricity in the table. The X-factors have also been changed with greater frequency than was initially planned (originally the intention was to keep them constant for five years). This, it could be argued, undermined the incentive to cut costs.[8]

The regulators try to mimic the price-setting process of a market. As we saw in Chapter 10, there is a question of how independent the available information is to the regulators. The utilities may have some (monopoly) control over information and have an incentive to

7 If they do not reduce costs by the given factor they will be loss making.

8 Intervention by regulators within the five-year period has also taken the form of requiring service enhancements and increased investment, without compensating price increases. Generally, this process is known as regulatory-chiselling.

Industry	Regulatory body	Parts regulated	Formula	Parts unregulated
Telecoms (British Telecom, Mercury, Cable Operators)	Office of Telecommunications (OFTEL)	Switched calls and line rentals	RPI-3 (1984–9) RPI-4.5 (1989–91) RPI-6.25 (1991–93) RPI-7.5 (1993–98) RPI-4.5 (1997–2000)	Payphone calls, telex, leased lines
British Gas/Transo, independents	Office of Gas Supply, (OFGAS)	Gas supplied to domestic users. Pipeline charges from Transco to suppliers	Supply: RPI-2+Y (1987–92) RPI-5+Y (1992–97), RPI-4+Y^2 Pipeline Charges: RPI-5 (1995–7), RPI-6.5 (1997–2001)	Price of gas supplied to industrial and commercial users. All supply from 1998, Connection charges and appliance sales
Electricity: generators (National Power, Powergen, Nuclear Electric) distributors (regional companies) Grid: National Grid Company	Office of Electricity Regulation (OFFER)	Prices for transmission, distribution and supply	Distribution: RPI-0 to 2.5+Y (1990–5), RPI-11 to 17+Y (1995/6) RPI-10 to 13+Y (1996/7), RPI-3+Y (1997–2000) Supply: RPI-0+Y (1991–4) , RPI-2+Y (1994–8)	Supply to customers consuming more than .1 of megawatt since 1994
Water (29 water and sewage companies)	Office of Water Services (OFWAT)	Standard domestic and non-domestic supply	RPI+Y+K (1989–94), RPI+1 (1995–2005)	Bulk water supplies to other users, water infrastructure charges
Railways: Railtrack and the train operating companies	Office of the Rail Regulator (ORR) Office of Passenger Rail Franchising (OPRAF)	Charges by Railtrack to the train operating companies	RPI-8 (1995/96), RPI-2 (1996–2001)	Charges by rail companies

Table 12.1 Price regulation of privatised utilities
Source: Sloman (1997).

overstate expected costs and understate demand. If the price is set too high incumbent firms make monopoly profits; if they are set too low firms will under-invest and may go out of business. Since a pure monopoly is rare, the regulators have sources of information from elsewhere, including what is sometimes referred to as 'yardstick information' from other utilities, and evidence from cost trends elsewhere in the economy.

There is also the question of whether regulators will necessarily do what they are supposed to do. They may have the opportunity to pursue their own interests, rather than social objectives implied by the efficient operation of the market. Since the work of the regulator involves becoming familiar with the detailed operation of an industry, there is a danger that his or her position may be compromised.

Questions

Q3 A privatised company which supplies water has a total cost curve

$$TC = 15 + 5Q$$

And faces a demand curve

$$P = 25 - 2Q$$

(I) If the regulator insists on charging a price equal to the marginal cost of production what would be the price-output decision and what would the profit level of the firm be?

(II) Show why a two-tier pricing structure could be advantageous in this situation.

Q4 If a regulator can set price equal to average costs does this necessarily eliminate the dead-weight loss associated with monopoly output?

12.3 Competition in the utility industries

One policy development that has occurred since privatisation has been the move to introduce competition into the utilities, including those that were previously thought of as 'natural monopolies'. A general trend has been to define the natural monopoly element in an industry, subject it to regulation, and then attempt to introduce competition elsewhere. In the electricity, gas and railway industries, the network — the wires, pipes and track — is taken as naturally monopolistic, but the supply of services on the network are opened to competition. We will start this section with some background and then look at the scope for introducing competition in the rail and water industries. The chapter concludes with a welfare analysis of tariff changes on different households.

The incumbent utilities were vertically integrated firms.[9] In the case of gas, for example, this involved the 'upstream' exploration business, which was distinct from the operation of the

9 Vertical integration refers to a firm that is involved in a multi-stage production process (from extraction to distribution depending on the industry). In many industries, the extent of vertical integration is open since the activities could, in principle, be undertaken by a number of different firms (government owned or not).

pipeline network and the 'downstream' supply business. The introduction of competition therefore needed to take account of the possibility of the incumbent firms cross-subsidising the part of the business subject to competition. In the case of rail privatisation, the response was a vertically separated industry.[10] Railtrack are responsible for the operation of the track, but cannot operate train services: train-operating companies compete for the right to run services.

The introduction of competition can take a number of different forms, depending on the nature and the structure of the industry. In the case of gas, for example, entry into the market for industrial users was encouraged by a large reduction in the cost of transportation. This has lead to a large reduction in the share of the market that previously went to the incumbent firm as Chart 12.1 shows.

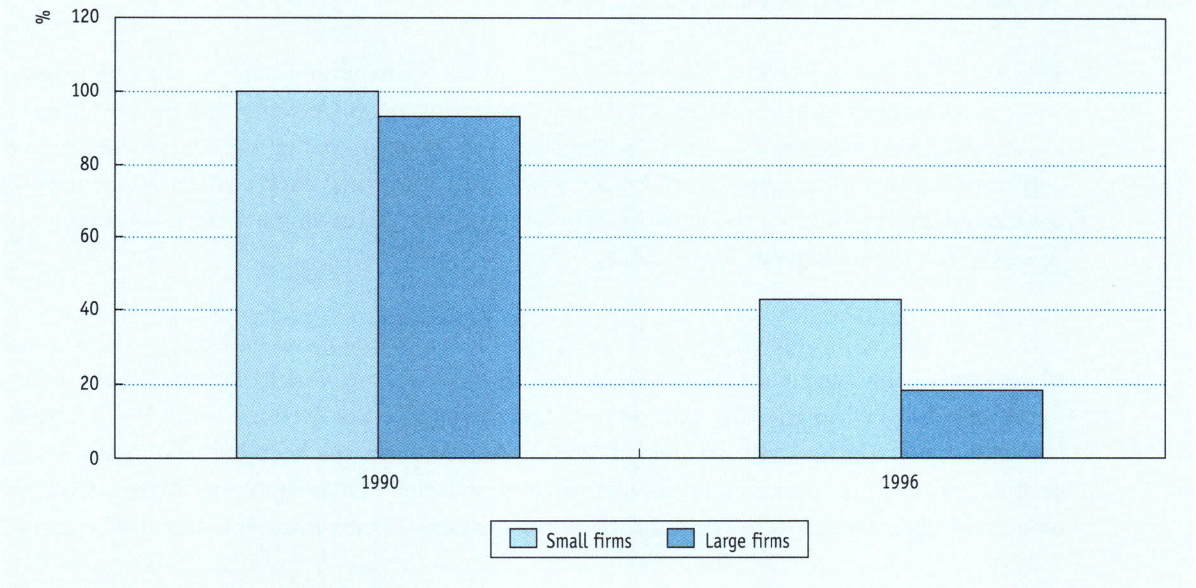

Chart 12.1 British Gas market share 1990–96
Source: Waddams Price (1997)

One way in which competition might be introduced is with franchise bidding. The argument put forward by Demsetz suggests holding an auction and awarding the franchise to the bidder offering to charge consumers the lowest price. However, changing costs and demand conditions means that, in practice, the franchises (or concessions) are only given for a particular period of time, or alternatively, that the franchise is subject to some form of general regulation.

10 Also in the electricity privatisation where there are two networks: the National Grid and local distribution networks operated by the regional companies.

Regulators in the utility industries also have wide-ranging responsibilities for the level of 'access' prices (the prices charged for use of the network by the downstream firms). One pricing rule for competition over networks is the Efficient Component Pricing Rule (ECPR), originally developed by Baumol. Table 12.2 gives an example concerning a (vertically-integrated) incumbent firm offering a rail service between three towns, A, B and C.

	Marginal cost of route AB	Marginal cost of route BC	Joint cost	Access price	Price
Incumbent	10	10	30		50
Efficient entrant		9		40	49
Inefficient firm		11		40	51

Table 12.2 An example of the efficient component pricing rule

Suppose a new entrant wants to develop a rival rail service between towns A and C, but has to pay the incumbent firm for its service between towns A and B. Assume that the costs for the incumbent are as follows: a constant marginal cost of 10 for operating the routes from A to B, and from B and C; and also that there is a joint cost (or average fixed cost) of 30 incurred by the incumbent for running the network. The average cost of running a service between towns A and C for the incumbent is therefore 50.[11]

The ECPR states that the correct access price to charge for the route between towns A and B is the sum of the marginal cost for the route, and also the network cost, which here gives a figure of 40. If a firm entering the industry has marginal costs over the route BC which are below those of the incumbent, then it can profitably enter the industry and undercut the existing price. If a prospective competitor has marginal costs that are higher than the incumbent then an access price of 40 will deter inefficient firms from entering the industry.

In other words, the pricing rule states that the new entrant should be charged the full cost of providing access to the competitive part of the network. The full cost is defined to include the marginal cost of access and loss of profit. The incumbent preserves its profits, and competition benefits consumers, if new entrants can charge lower prices (in which case the incumbent firm can withdraw from the market as it will be compensated by the access price).

This is open to the comment that it allows the incumbent firm to retain whatever economic profits it was making and it could be viewed as an upper limit to the access price that should be charged. Plainly, the lower limit is set by the marginal cost of giving access to the network.

11 This example draws on Klein (1998).

The costs of operating the network could be included in a two-part tariff, with the fixed fee covering the capital costs and a variable payment, to cover the short-run cost of access.

Competition in the rail industry

The railway industry has a number of characteristics that set it apart from other network industries like gas or electricity. Rail services have a number of highly competitive substitutes for both freight and passenger transport, which has led to a long-term decline in the market share of the industry as Table 12.3 shows.

	Passenger Kilometres	Freight tonne Kilometres
1957	17	37
1967	9	17
1977	7	12
1987	7	9
1997	5	6

Table 12.3 Market share of the railway industry %
Source: Transport Statistics (1998).

This decline is a pattern repeated throughout the industrialised economies. Generally, the rail industry in the UK is characterised by elastic demand for most routes and, in practice, the operation of the rail system requires subsidy from central government. In the UK, the 1993 Railways Act split the infrastructure of the industry from the business of operating a train service, breaking the tradition of a vertically integrated industry. The justification given for this was that it would promote competition among the would-be providers of rail services.

The structure created involves 25 separate passenger train operating companies, with the rolling-stock owned by three competing leasing companies (ROSCOs). Although these leasing companies are in a near monopoly position, the intention was to minimise the barriers to entry for the prospective providers of passenger services, by reducing the amount of capital required. The 25 train-operating companies were established by means of franchise bidding. As mentioned, this is in principle a way of generating competition between the would-be suppliers of a service to a monopoly industry. It should meet the interests of consumers who pay fares to the most efficient operators.

In practice, in the context of the railways there were a large number of details that had to be resolved. There was no prior experience of making these decisions and this meant that the bidders were able to exert some influence on the regulator about the prospects for competition on particular routes. The development of future competition is likely to be limited to a small number of routes where there is more than one line, for example from London to Birmingham, or where the franchises overlap, such as London to Gatwick Airport.[12]

To ensure sufficient interest in companies to take on the task of providing passenger services, the regulator was involved in the 'moderation of competition'. In effect existing operators were given protection from competitors until 1999. Some operators are given protection over the period of the franchise in the interests of new investment. For example, on the route from London along stations on the West Coast Main Line, franchisees are given protection for the full 15 years of the franchise, providing the investment in a new fleet of tilting-trains goes ahead.

Given this background, the issue of mergers and franchisees coming under common control is sensitive. There are a total of 13 different enterprises involved in providing services; although the bus company, National Express, controls five out of a total of 25 franchises. This leads to the awkward question of whether horizontal integration between a train operating company and a bus company is in the public interest because it offers a better transport system to the public, or whether it is against it because of the potential loss of competition. Issues of this kind are again a matter of detail.[13]

Competition in the water industry

The water industry is as good example as any of what at one time was thought of as a natural monopoly. Ten regional water and sewerage companies (WaSCs) supply service in the UK after privatisation. There is plainly no need to duplicate the network of water mains and sewers, although, even in this industry, policy has been designed to facilitate competition.[14] Cowan (1998) lists a number of different types of competition that could be applied. These are

(I) *Yardstick competition.* For example, suppose there are two geographically separated companies: the price that one firm is allowed to charge is related to the unit cost of the other firm. This gives the first firm an incentive to be efficient, which in turn, will result in a lower price allowed to the second firm.

(II) *Franchising of services.* As we saw, this has been adopted in the UK for rail services and is used in the water industry in France. In England and Wales, this would be rather

---

12 There is more scope for competition in pricing and the provision of various 'value-added' services (at seat trolley-service, free magazines etc).

13 The benefits once associated with common ownership could be obtained through a contract between two private sector firms.

14 Any new parts of the network could be operated by competitors to the incumbent firms.

problematic since the franchisees are expected to undertake a substantial programme of investment.

(III) *Contracting-out of particular aspects of the companies work*, such as information technology and maintenance services.

(IV) *Product market competition*. With gas, electricity and the railways, there is competition in supply on 'naturally monopolistic' networks, something that could be adopted in the water industry as well (although without a national water grid, companies could only compete at a regional level).

The prospects for water competition may be rather limited, but the regulator of the industry has been able to exert some leverage over the ten companies. OFWAT publishes a wide range of data on capital investment programmes and financial performance, and, generally, has been able to promote a climate in which managers see themselves as competing in a league table.

It is also a climate in which senior company executives devote resources to managing their relationship with the industry regulator. In general terms, the performance of senior management can affect company profitability by reducing 'regulatory risk'. By developing good working relations with the regulator there is less chance of an adverse outcome from the water companies viewpoint in negotiations over the price-cap formula.

The privatised water companies have been heavily criticised in the 1990s for what some see as opportunistic behaviour on the part of their management. Given that the water companies are largely regional monopoly suppliers of water, and that they were protected from take-over for the first five years after privatisation, there was certainly potential for the top figures to act in a self-interested manner.

The performance of the water companies is assessed in terms of their profitability and there is a question to what extent the financial incentives to managers support the interests of shareholders. Privatisation gave senior managers the discretion to design their own reward packages, which, unsurprisingly, lead to an increase in the salaries and bonuses paid as Table 12.4 shows.[15]

The senior management of water companies now follow the recommendations of the Cadbury Committee. All the companies have remuneration committees that are charged with ensuring a fair reward for the executive directors. While this may be procedurally more satisfactory than an arrangement where the executives sit on a committee to decide their own remuneration, it does not necessarily justify the level of pay awarded.

15 And also changes to the ways in which they were paid as performance related bonuses and share options were added to remuneration packages.

	Chairman Nov. 1989 Highest paid director 1990	1994
Anglian		
Chairman	44	101
Highest paid director	77	169
Northumbrian		
Chairman	37	54
Highest paid director	50	135
North-West		
Chairman	61	338
Highest paid director	97	338
Severn Trent		
Chairman	49	174
Highest paid director	108	218
Southern		
Chairman	44	169
Highest paid director	59	169
South West		
Chairman	51	112
Highest paid director	78	130
Thames		
Chairman	49	104
Highest paid director	157	247
Welsh		
Chairman	44	99
Highest paid director	82	139
Wessex		
Chairman	41	177
Highest paid director	55	177
Yorkshire		
Chairman	55	156
Highest paid director	75	156

Table 12.4 **Salaries and bonuses of chairmen and highest paid directors (£000s)**
Source: Ogden (1997).

Those more sympathetic to the position of senior management point to the effect of strategic decision-making on the reduction of costs as a way of increasing profits. The possibility of diversifying into, for example, water-related consultancy activities overseas or water-waste management (which may lie outside the sphere of influence of the regulator) are also ways in which corporate strategy can affect the share prices and profits.

The welfare effects of tariff changes on the cost of living

The regulators of the utility industries have a responsibility to protect the interests of consumers. In the main, this is done, as we have seen, by the system of price caps which gives an overall average figure for price increases allowed. The regulators also have a secondary duty to the interests of particular groups: those of pensionable age and in the case of water and electricity supply, to those living in rural areas.

One response of incumbent firms to competition has been the practice of 'price rebalancing'. Before privatisation the state-run industries charged uniform prices that ignored cost differences arising from, for example, peaks in demand. In areas such as telecommunications and energy line rentals and standing charges were set below cost with the difference being recovered through higher usage charges.

The threat of competition has led to differential pricing by incumbent firms. As pointed out in a study by Waddams Price and Hancock (1998), this has led to British Telecom, for example, increasing line rentals by 7% in real terms over the period 1984–96, while the average cost of calls has fallen by 40%. In the case of British Gas, the price rebalancing has taken the form of charging different prices to those who pay by different methods. Table 12.5 gives the details of how household gas tariffs have changed over the period 1994–98.

Changes of this sort impact on some households more than others since expenditure on gas supply (and the other utilities) is a higher proportion of income for those on low incomes and low income households are less likely to pay by direct debit. How much have individual consumers in different types of household gained and lost as a result of the introduction of

	Standing charge (£ p.a.)			Running rate (p/kwh)		
	Quarterly credit	Direct debit	Prepayment meter	Quarterly credit	Direct debit	Prepayment meter
Dec. 1994	62	62	67	77	77	76
Jan. 1998	75	39	63	67	61	66

Table 12.5 **Index of real residential gas tariffs (1984=100)**
Source: Waddams Price and Hancock (1998).

competition? To answer this question, we will return to the analysis of price changes on consumer welfare and equivalent and compensating variation measures we introduced in Chapter 2.

To measure the impact on individual households, Waddams Price and Hancock took the difference between the prices charged in 1996 and the time when the utilities were privatised, multiplied by the individual consumption levels of the utility services. Figure 12.2 illustrates. P_0 and P_1 represent, for a particular utility industry, the price charged at privatisation and in 1996. Q^D represents the uncompensated demand curve and there are two compensated demand curves, Q_P^D and Q_{96}^D, representing the individual's utility (satisfaction) levels at the time of privatisation and in 1996. X_0 and X_1 are the levels of consumption.

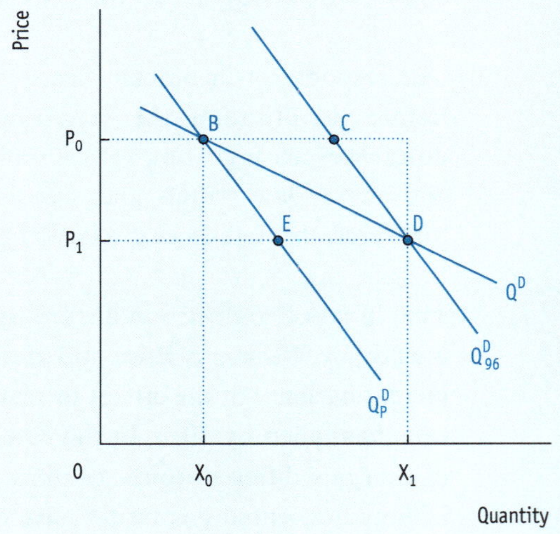

Figure 12.2 Welfare measures of price changes

We saw in Chapter 2 that the compensating variation of a price change is the amount of income that would return an individual to the original utility (satisfaction) level after a relative price change. It can also be represented by the area under the compensated demand curve going through the original price. The compensating variation of the price change in Figure 12.2 is therefore the area bound by P_0BEP_1. The equivalent variation is the amount of money we would need to give an individual to increase utility as much as does the fall in price. It is the area under the compensated demand curve going through the new price. This is the area bound by P_0CDP_1 in the figure. Consumer surplus as discussed in Chapter 9 is given by the area P_0BDP_1 and lies between these two measures.

The survey data that was available to the authors related to the years 1991–93, so the recorded consumption levels were between X_0 and X_1. The actual or empirical welfare measure therefore approximated the consumer surplus measure. Estimates of the impact of price changes

(£ Pa 1996 Prices)		
Households	**Aggregate gain**	**Price rebalancing**
All	240	0
Deviations from average		
Pensioner households	–60	–13
On disability benefit	–3	–3
On income support	–10	+2
Top 20% of income distribution	+41	+6

Table 12.6 **Real gains and losses since privatisation**
Source: Adapted from Waddams Price and Hancock (1998).

arising from the early years of competition (and the threat of it) on different households are given in Table 12.6.

The first column shows the total gains from price reductions since the time of privatisation in the gas, electricity and telecoms industries for different types of household. The overall gain in 1996 prices, from these three industries is given in the first row. There are some differences between pensioner households and those on the highest incomes. The numbers given are a partial measure of the effects of privatisation given that, in the case of water, prices have gone up. There is also a general methodological issue that we do not know what would have been the case in the absence of privatisation; some of the falling prices could plausibly be attributed to the new introduction of new technology that would have occurred under any ownership structure.

The second column of the table shows the rebalancing effect. Over all households, this is, of course, zero. A similar pattern applies in that some of the more vulnerable households lose and the more prosperous households gain. The amounts shown in the table are for broad categories of household, in individual cases the sums involved could be much greater. The overall sums as of 1996 are plainly small, although the growing impact of competition could magnify the amounts in the future.

Question

Q5 (I) In relation to Figure 12.2, what is the Laspeyres (base-weighted) measure of the change in consumer welfare following the price change? What is the Paasche (current-weighted) measure?

(II) What is the relation between these two measures and the measures discussed in the text?

(III) Waddams Price and Hancock suggest that when there is full competition, the price-rebalancing effect might be four to ten times the size of the figures in Table 12.6. How could those who were adversely affected be compensated?

Summary

1 Competition policy is concerned with promoting the efficient operation of the market in all sectors of the economy. Competition is often thought of in terms of product market competition (although the scope of policy also relates to competition in factor markets as well). There are some significant differences between EU member states in terms of their approaches to competition policy at the national level and this can make the implementation of EU policy difficult.

2 In the 1980s and 1990s, there was an extensive programme of privatisation in the UK and elsewhere. This has led to the establishment of industry regulators for the privatised utilities. The main form of regulation has been overall price caps. These were intended to encourage efficient competition and set the price increases allowed below the rate of inflation for the gas, electricity and telecoms industries. In practice, the regulators often understated the potential productivity gains and had to change the price-formula more often than had been initially anticipated.

3 Policy towards the privatised utilities in the UK has extended from regulation to the introduction of competition in some areas. At one time, entire industries were viewed as 'natural monopolies'. Since privatisation, the boundaries of where competition is seen as possible have changed. Broadly, the approach has been to introduce competition for the provision of services and to regulate the companies that operate the physical networks of pipes and rails.

4 The nature of the competition that has been introduced varies from industry to industry. Franchise bidding was the way that competition was introduced in the rail industry in the UK and the water industry in France. This can be problematic when the franchise is for a limited period and there is a need for a substantial programme of investment.

5 The welfare assessment depends on both efficiency and equity criteria. Previously, state-run industries charged uniform prices that ignored cost differences. Rentals and standing charges were below cost and the difference was recovered through higher usage charges. This practice favoured low-users such as pensioners. The introduction of competition has changed this; those at the top of the income distribution have gained as a result, while some vulnerable groups have lost out.

End of chapter questions

Q6 Many large retail chains can exert considerable buyer power. Should pricing policies which discriminate in favour of large firms be prohibited?

Q7 What justification could be put forward for executive share option schemes in the case of (I) gas, (II) rail and (III) the water industry?

Q8 In the UK, the physical infrastructure of the water system is old; the asset base of the industry is around 10% of the replacement cost. Should prices charged by the industry reflect average or marginal costs?

Q9 A utility company has a production function of the form

$$Q = 100KL$$

The price of its output is 10 and the factor prices are both 5.

(I) Obtain an expression for the rate of return on capital.

(II) Suppose that the return on capital is constrained by a regulator to be some value. Set up the Lagrangian for the firm's decision-making. Assuming that the value of the Lagrange multiplier lies between 0 and 1, what happens to the amount of capital and labour the firm hires by comparison with when there is no regulation?

References and suggested further reading

The chapter by Young and Metcalfe gives extended background on the historical and legal framework for competition policy within the EU. The book edited by Helm and Jenkinson includes a more developed discussion of many of the issues discussed in Sections 3 and 4. There are separate chapters on individual industries.

Cowling, K. and Mueller, D.C. (1978), 'The Social Costs of Monopoly Power', *Economic Journal*, **88**.

Helm, D. (1994), 'British Utility Regulation: Theory, Practice, and Reform', *Oxford Review of Economic Policy*, **10**.

Helm, D. and Jenkinson, T. (eds) (1998), *Competition in Regulated Industries*, Oxford University Press.

Klein, M. (1998), 'Network Industries' in Helm, D. and Jenkinson, T. (eds), *Competition in Regulated Industries*, Oxford University Press.

Ogden, S. (1997), 'Corporate Governance in the Privatised Utilities: The Case of the Water Industry' in Keasey, K., Thompson, S. and Wright, M. (eds), *Corporate Governance: Economic and Financial Issues*, Oxford University Press.

Sloman, J. (1997), *Economics*, 3rd edition, Prentice Hall.

Waddams Price, C. (1997), 'Competition and Regulation in the UK Gas Industry', *Oxford Review of Economic Policy*, 13, 1.

Waddams Price, C. and Hancock, R. (1998), 'Distributional Effects of Liberalising UK Residential Utility Markets', *Fiscal Studies*, **19**.

Department of the Environment and Regions (1998), 'Transport Statistics'.

Young, D. and Metcalfe, S. (1997), 'Competition Policy' in Artis, M.J. and Lee, N. (eds), *The Economics of the European Union*, 2nd edition, Oxford University Press.

Analysis of Factor Markets

13 Factor Markets

Key ideas and material

Neo-classical theory of factor markets, investment criteria of firms, changes in the distribution of wages, the distribution of factor income

Introduction

This chapter begins our discussion of factor markets. We start simply in Section 1 with neo-classical analysis of both competitive and monopolistic market structures. The discussion will concentrate on the labour market, although this kind of analysis can be adapted in a straightforward way to examine the markets for both land and capital as well. In Section 2, we take account of the durability of the firm's capital input and look at the role of investment appraisal techniques. In an uncertain environment, we will see that the conventional criteria need to be modified to take account of the option value of the firm's investment.

The conventional neo-classical analysis is concerned with homogeneous factor inputs. The relevance of this may be questionable when, for example, there has been a lengthy period of increasing wage inequality, such as that experienced in the UK and the US in the 1980s and 1990s. In the labour market the difference between skilled and unskilled labour, and the changing pattern of relative demand, is also important. However, the experience in the UK and the US has not been repeated everywhere and, in Section 3, we start our discussion of why this might be so. Some of the issues and policy questions are looked at in more detail in Chapter 14. The distribution of income between factors of production is taken up in Section 4, where we discuss its relation to the distribution of income between households.

13.1 Neo-classical theory

The neo-classical analysis of factor markets sets out to explain how the prices and employment levels of the factors of production are determined. The analysis presented here is primarily concerned with factor demand in alternative market structures. The demand for a factor input is a derived demand from the good or service it produces, which leads us to make a broad distinction between demand in competitive and monopolistic product markets. In principle, a firm may also be faced with either a competitive or a monopsonistic factor input market, giving a total of four different combinations of market structures.

The role of the firm in this context is that of an intermediary between the preferences of consumers which creates the demand for the goods and services, and the factor inputs which combine to produce them. This type of analysis can be adapted to examine the market for land, labour or capital, although we will confine our explicit discussion in this section to the case of the labour market. We will start at the level of the firm before moving on to questions of how demand is aggregated across firms, and industries, to give total market demand.

Short-run analysis of the labour market

A competitive labour market is one in which there are a large number of buyers and sellers of the labour input. In this type of market structure, the decisions taken by individual firms relating to the demand for labour, or by individual workers relating to its supply, will have no effect on the wage rate. Both buyers and sellers act as price takers.

To understand what determines the demand for labour by an individual firm we will go back to the idea of a production function. The first two columns of Table 13.1 give the example of a short-run production function that we first encountered in Chapter 7. The level of capital is assumed to be fixed, and the level of output varies with the level of labour input as shown. This can be seen in the third column which shows the associated marginal physical product of labour, MPL, which increases until the numbers employed reach three, then declines and eventually becomes negative.

The decision that the firm has to make is how much labour to hire. The decision rule in factor markets is similar to that for product markets: the firm will find it profitable to hire another unit of labour as long as the additional revenue from doing so exceeds the additional cost. The additional revenue to the firm from hiring the extra unit of labour is known as the value of the marginal product, VMP, when it sells its output in a perfectly competitive market; it is known as the marginal revenue product, MRP, when it faces a downward-sloping demand curve. When we are dealing with competitive factor input markets, the VMP and MRP schedules are in effect labour demand schedules.[1]

The difference between the VMP and the MRP is shown in Table 13.1. In this example, the firm in a perfectly competitive industry can sell all of its output at a price of £10. The VMP

1 This is, of course, subject to the firm's shut-down condition that average revenue is not less than average variable cost (in the short-run), and not less than average total cost (in the long-run). In the context of factor markets, a firm will not hire a factor if its average revenue product is less than the factor payment divided by the firm's product price.

L	Q	MPL	Price £	VMP £	Price £	MRP £
			Perfect competition		Monopolistic market	
1	6	6	10	60	10	60
2	13	7	10	70	9	57
3	21	8	10	80	8	49
4	28	7	10	70	7	22
5	34	6	10	60	6	16
6	39	5	10	50	5	–9
7	42	3	10	30	4	–7
8	40	–2	10	–20	3	–68

Table 13.1 **The firm's production function: VMP and MRP**

shown in the fifth column is then calculated straightforwardly as the individual worker's marginal physical product multiplied by the price charged, so giving the contribution of each worker to the firm's revenue.

The MRP is the counterpart in a monopolistic product market. When a firm hires an additional worker, we have to take account of the inverse relation between price and quantity demanded on the additional revenue that a firm receives. For example, when the output increases from 6 units to 13, the price paid for it falls from £10 per unit to £9. The additional revenue from hiring a second unit of labour is therefore 13 * £9 – 6 * £10 = £57. This is evidently less than the VMP of £70. It is also £6 less than MPL * Price for the second worker, which is 7 * £9 = £63. This is because revenue from the sale of the output of the first worker declines; a price of only £9, not £10, for the first 6 units of output.

Figure 13.1 illustrates the general relation between VMP and the MRP schedules. Assuming that the marginal product of labour eventually decreases as the employment of labour increases, then both schedules will be downward sloping. The VMP schedule, showing the additional revenue from an extra unit of labour employed in the competitive market, is above the MRP schedule. The vertical distance between them is determined by the slope of the demand curve the firm faces in the product market.

Short-run equilibrium

The employment level in a particular market will, of course, also depend on labour supply as well. In a perfectly competitive market, the firm can hire as much labour as it wants to at the

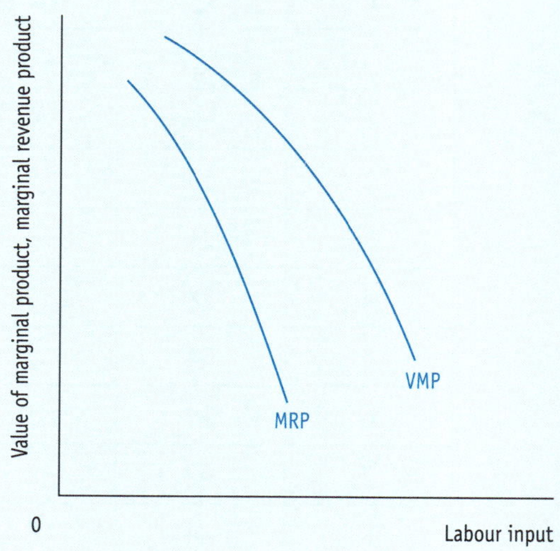

Figure 13.1 The VMP and MRP schedules

going wage rate. This is illustrated in Figure 13.2A where the going wage rate is marked as W_0. When the firm operates in both competitive factor and product markets the level of employment is L_0. At this point, the profit-maximising firm has hired labour up to the point where the additional revenue it generates is equal to the additional cost. In the case where the firm faces a downward-sloping demand curve in the product market, the firm equates the wage rate and the marginal revenue product of the last worker employed. In Figure 13.2A, the employment level is L_1; the firm hires less labour at the market wage rate than it would do under competitive market conditions. This follows from the nature of the product demand it faces, since each extra unit of labour employed generates less additional revenue than it would in a competitive market.

It may be that the firm faces a monopsonistic labour market, where it is the sole buyer of labour. In this case, the firm has to increase the wage paid as it hires additional labour, so that the marginal cost of labour rises as the level of labour employed rises. This is shown in Figure 13.2B where the MC_L curve lies above the AC_L curve. Again, there are two possible equilibrium outcomes, depending on the nature of the product market the firm faces. In a competitive market, the decision-rule leads the firm to employment level L_0 as shown in the figure. However, the average payment to the labour input, the wage rate, is given by the point on the AC_L schedule associated with an employment level of L_0. The worker is paid a wage rate of W_0, which is less than his or her VMP.

In the case where the firm faces a downward-sloping demand curve in the product market, the wage is W_1 and the employment level is L_1. This point gives a lower wage rate and a lower employment level than any of the other combinations of market structures. The equilibrium conditions that determine the level of employment are summarised in Table 13.2.

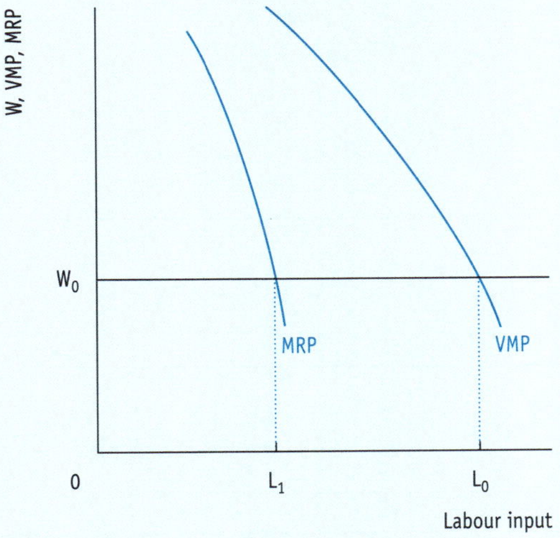

Figure 13.2A **Labour employment levels in a competitive factor market**

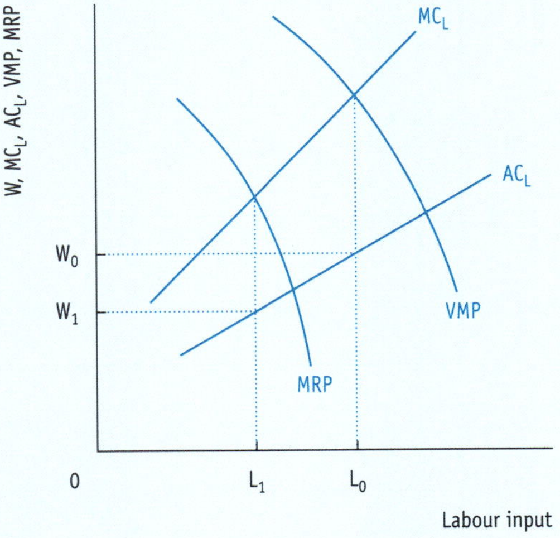

Figure 13.2B **Labour employment levels in a monopsonistic factor market**

	Product market	
Factor market	Perfectly competitive	Monopsonistic
Perfectly competitive	W = VMP	W = MRP
Monopsonistic	MC_L = VMP	MC_L = MRP

Table 13.2 **Equilibrium conditions in different market structures**

The firm's demand for labour in the long-run

To avoid repetition, we will explicitly discuss the case where the firm faces a downward-sloping demand curve in its output market. To keep the analysis simple, we will also confine ourselves to only two factor inputs: capital and labour. In the long-run, both factors of production are variable, and so to analyse the demand for one factor we need to take account of its interrelation with the other factor.

For example, suppose there was an increase in the supply of labour in a competitive factor market because, for example, of demographic change. Labour is available at a wage rate where previously it was not. In Figure 13.3 panel A the firm can hire whatever quantity of labour it wants at W_1, rather than W_0. The additional revenue from hiring an extra unit of labour now exceeds the additional cost at the original employment level, L_0. The firm will therefore increase its employment of labour, to L_1 as shown in the figure.

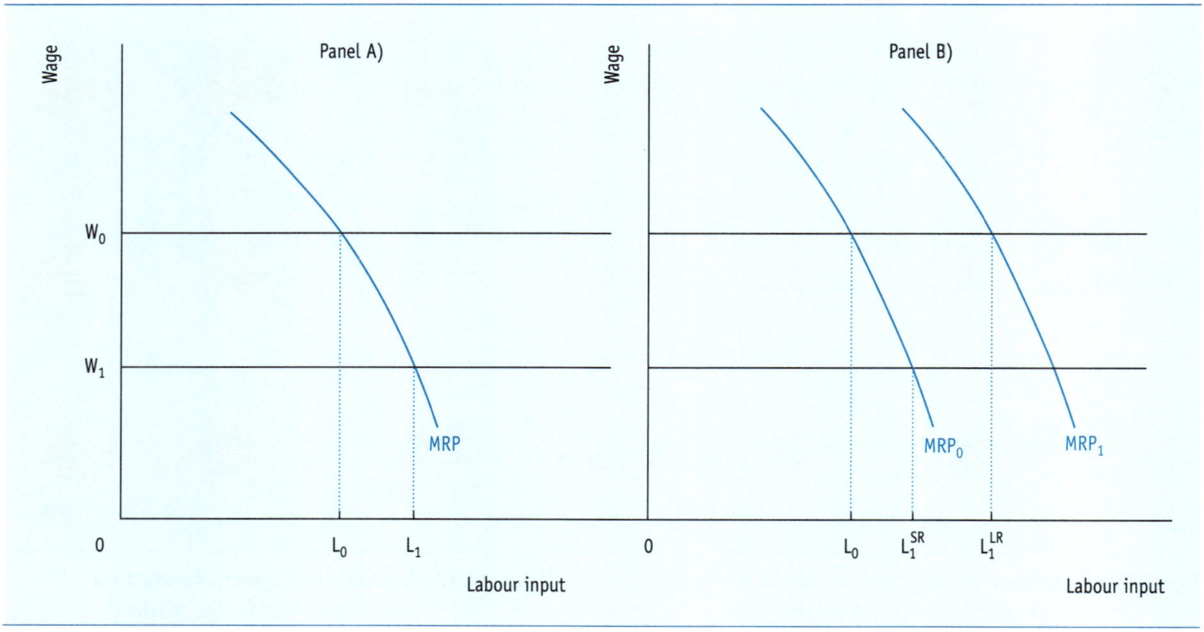

Figure 13.3 **The effect of a fall in the wage rate**

In the long-run, the fall in the wage rate will affect both capital and labour inputs. Figure 13.3 panel B shows the effect of this on the MRP curve for labour. The fall in the wage rate means it is profitable for the firm to expand its level of output, and so the demand for both factors of production rises.[2] The larger capital stock employed will increase the marginal product of labour and the MRP curve shifts out to the right, from MRP_0 to MRP_1 as shown in the figure. The effect of the increase in output is to increase the employment of labour to L_1^{LR} in the figure, which clearly exceeds the employment level associated the movement along MRP_0 schedule to L_1^{SR}. The effect of a lower wage on the demand for labour at the level of the firm therefore depends on the change in the capital stock. So far, what we have seen suggests that the demand for labour by the firm should be more elastic in the long-run.

Market demand for labour in the short-run

To determine the industry demand for labour we need to take into account the effect of the change in the factor price on the industry output and price. When there is a fall in the wage rate paid, the industry as a whole will hire more labour. In turn, this will lead to higher industry output and a lower product price (since we are concerned with the case where demand is not perfectly price elastic). In Figure 13.4 panel A, this fall in the product price shifts the MRP of labour schedule of the firm inward, from MRP_0 to MRP_1. The consequence of this is that the firm will hire less labour than it would have done if the product price had not fallen.

2 It is possible that a factor is 'inferior' but we assume this not to be the case here.

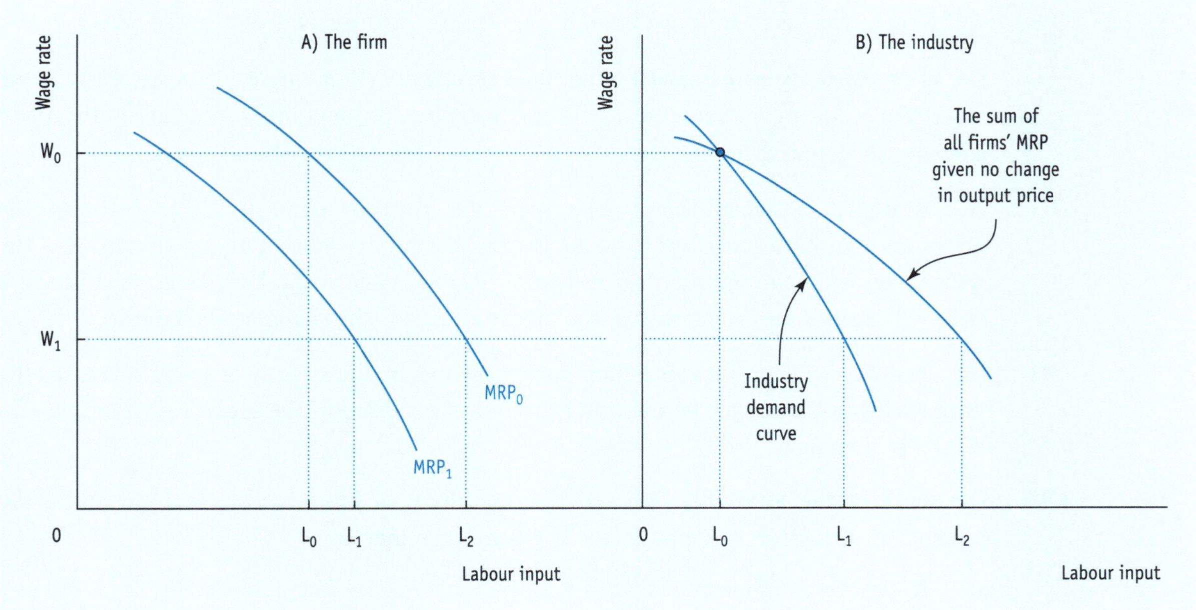

Figure 13.4 Industry demand for labour

Figure 13.4 panel B shows the summed firm demand curves and the industry demand curve. The industry curve is drawn more steeply — demand is less elastic — when we allow for the effect of output price variations on the demand for the factor input. The aggregation from the demand by one industry to the market demand for labour across all industries is then simply a matter of summation. This, of course, implicitly assumes that the level of capital does not change, that is we are dealing with the short-run.

If we allow capital to vary in this analysis, then the industry demand for labour in the long-run may be either more or less elastic than it is in the short-run. As the wage rate falls, there are two effects on the MRP for labour shown in Figures 13.3 and 13.4. There is the effect of the fall in the wage rate on the capital stock, shifting the firm's MRP schedule out to the right. There is also the effect on the output price which shifts the individual firm's MRP schedule inward, making the industry demand curve for labour steeper and hence less elastic. The net effect depends on which one of these two influences dominates. In principle, the long-run industry and market demand curves could be more or less elastic than their short-run counterparts.

The elasticity of factor demand

The elasticity of factor demand typically plays a prominent role in the neo-classical analysis of factor markets. We will conclude this section by looking at a number of influences on the price elasticity of demand for labour. The importance of this will be looked at in the next chapter, when we discuss the possible effect of a statutory minimum wage on employment.

Broadly, the own price elasticity of demand for a factor will depend on the following.[3]

(I) **The price elasticity of demand for the final product**. For example, if an increase in the wage rate leads to an increase in the price of the product, then the larger the price elasticity of demand for the product, the greater the fall in labour demand.

(II) **The elasticity of substitution.**[4] The (constant output) elasticity of substitution is measured by the percentage change in the capital to labour ratio, divided by the percentage change in the factor price ratio. If labour and capital are close substitutes, a given increase in the wage rate has a larger effect on the demand for labour.

(III) **The elasticity of supply of the other factor inputs**. In the case of a wage increase, the more elastic is the supply of the other factors of production the greater is the reduction in labour demand.

(IV) **The share of the total cost**. The greater the share of labour costs in total costs, the greater the reduction in demand for a given wage increase.

Questions

Q1 A firm faces the short-run production given in the first two columns.

L	Q	APL	MPL	P	VMP	Price	ARP	MRP
				Perfect competition		Monopolistic market		
1	10			5		20		
2	30			5		18		
3	60			5		16		
4	100			5		14		
5	140			5		12		
6	170			5		10		
7	190			5		8		
8	200			5		6		

3 This set of factors originates from the work of Hicks and Marshall.

4 This was introduced in Chapter 7.

(I) Calculate the average and marginal products of labour and their associated revenue products.

(II) Suppose there is a perfectly elastic supply curve for labour at a wage of 60. What is the level of employment in the two different types of market?

Q2 In a competitive market economy, the supply of a particular type of labour is given by

$$Q_L^S = 5W$$

and the demand for labour is given by

$$Q_L^D = 210 - W$$

Where W is the wage rate.

(I) What is the equilibrium wage rate and level of employment?

(II) What is the difference between the wages the workforce receive and what they would be prepared to work for, i.e. what is their economic rent?

(III) If the supply of labour is controlled by a monopsonistic union whose aim is to maximise the economic rent of its members what happens to the level of employment and the wage rate paid?

Q3 In 1970, the record transfer fee for a footballer in the UK was £200,000. In 1996, it was £15mn. The general increase in the (RPI measure) of the price level over this period was approximately 680%. Can this increase in the transfer fee paid be explained by changing marginal revenue products? If so, how?

13.2 Investment criteria of firms

In simple neo-classical analysis, the demand for capital can be treated in the same way as the demand for the other factors of production. Analysing the demand for capital per period is sometimes appropriate, for example with decisions to hire office space or lease machinery. However, in many instances firms are concerned with one-off decisions.

Capital is, of course, a durable asset and the analysis of Section 1 needs to be modified to take account of this fact. Investment in building new plant or undertaking research and development (R&D) will typically have effects on the revenues of a firm over a period of time as capacity is increased, or as new products are introduced.[5] This leads to the question of how a firm might assess the viability of an investment. What we will do here is look at two techniques

5 The return to an investment can of course also take the form of reduced costs over time.

for investment appraisal that firms can (and do) use: the net present value (NPV) and the internal rate of return (IRR) of an investment project.[6]

It is worth noting at the outset that in practice a major part of the work in evaluating an investment project is obtaining appropriate data. When, for example, the product market structure is oligopolistic, the firm needs to take account the likely response of other firms to a change in its capacity. A firm will need estimates of both the costs of the project and the future revenue levels that it will generate. When this data is available, appraisal techniques can then be used to determine whether a project is viable.

As a first step, we will begin by discussing the NPV and IRR criteria, on the assumption that the costs and future revenues of a project are known with certainty. We will then analyse more realistic cases where there is uncertainty surrounding both the costs of the project and the revenue stream. This will lead us to the importance of timing in such decisions, and the not-so-obvious value that can be placed on the opportunity to defer an investment.[7]

Present values

We discussed discounting future streams of income in the two-period model of Chapter 4. As a reminder, the sum of £1 this year can earn an interest payment and so will be worth £1(1 + r) next year, where r is the rate of interest. It follows that £1(1 + r) next year has a present value, PV, of £1 this year and so the sum of £1 next year has a PV of £1/(1 + r) this year; the rate of interest, r, being referred to as the rate of discount. The process of discounting can be extended to a greater number of periods. A £1 in two years time is worth £1/(1 + r) next year. The PV this year of £1/(1 + r) next year is £1/(1 + r) of that sum, which is £1/$(1 + r)^2$. The PV of £1 in three years time will be £1/$(1 + r)^3$ and so on.

The PV of a given income stream therefore depends on what the rate of discount is, and how far into the future the payment will be received. This can vary enormously, as Table 13.3 illustrates. For example, the PV of £1 received in five years time discounted at a rate of 10% is 62 pence, received twenty years into the future it is only 15 pence.[8]

Net present value criterion for investment decisions

For simplicity, we will assume initially that all of the cost of the investment occurs immediately, that the income stream it generates occurs in the future, and that the rate of discount is

6 In practice they tend to be used by large firms, small firms often rely on simple rule-of-thumb payback rules.

7 Following Dixit and Pindyck (1994).

8 Again, we are referring to the real rate of interest.

Interest rate	1 Year	2 Years	5 Years	20 Years
2%	0.98	0.96	0.91	0.67
5%	0.95	0.91	0.78	0.38
10%	0.91	0.83	0.62	0.15

Table 13.3 PV of £1 for selected discount rates and time periods

a constant over the period concerned. The net present value, NPV, of the project is the PV of the income stream $Y_1 \ldots Y_N$ less the initial outlay, C. The NPV criterion for a project can be expressed algebraically as invest if

$$NPV = Y_1/(1 + r) + \ldots Y_N/(1 + r)^N - C > 0.$$

In words, the firm should invest in a project as long as the NPV from doing so is positive. We saw that the decision rule in Section 1 was that the firm should hire labour as long as the additional revenue generated from doing so was greater than the additional cost. The rule in this context is similar: as long as the NPV is positive, the addition to the firm's revenues is greater than the addition to its costs.

However, using this rule is not quite as straightforward as it may initially seem. The relative profitability of alternative investment projects can be sensitive to the rate of discount chosen. Suppose a firm has just two alternative investments with the same initial cost outlay and with the revenue streams shown in Table 13.4.

	Year 0 (this year)	Year 1	Year 2
Revenue stream 1	£2,000	£2,000	£0
Revenue stream 2	£300	£2,000	£2,000

Table 13.4 Present values of alternative revenue streams

Which revenue stream has the higher PV? At a discount rate of 0% payment stream 2 is greater since, in effect, the PV involves just adding the cash sums in each case. Given a cost outlay of up £4,000 both projects would be profitable. Above a cost of £4,000, there is a range of cost levels where the project associated with revenue stream 2 is profitable, whereas the other project is not.

At a discount rate of 10%, the PV of revenue stream 1 is £3,818, for stream 2 it is only £3,771. There will be a range of cost levels where only the project associated with revenue stream 1 is profitable. Given alternative investment opportunities the chosen discount rate is potentially important in determining which project(s), if any, are viable.[9]

The internal rate of return

This is a second method of appraising alternative investments. The IRR is the rate of return at which the PV of the income stream from an investment is equal to the PV of the cost. In other words, it is the rate of return on a project that yields a NPV of zero.

The decision rule for the firm is to invest if the cost of borrowing is less than the IRR. This may appear to be a similar decision rule to the NPV criteria, although again its use is not necessarily straightforward. In certain types of investment, a firm may incur costs both at the outset of the project and also at its termination. For example, cleanup costs after years of dumping waste occur in some industries. In such cases the IRR criterion can return multiple solutions, as the example in Table 13.5 shows.

	Year 0 (this year)	Year 1	Year 2
Costs	£5,000	£0	£36,000
Revenues	£0	£36,000	£0

Table 13.5 IRR giving a multiple solution

There are two rates of interest where the IRR of this project is equal to zero, r = 20% and r = 500%. A straight application of the IRR criteria does not make sense since, at interest rates below 20%, the NPV of this investment is negative.

Uncertainty

The discussion above assumed that the benefits and costs of an investment were known with certainty. In practice, this is often not so. We will now discuss how to incorporate uncertainty into investment appraisal. At the outset, you might think that the effect of an uncertain environment is to reduce the number of investment projects that firms undertake. We will see here that this need not always be the case.

We have noted that one aspect of investment in plant, machinery and other capital goods is the durability of these types of asset. The one-off decisions that are taken to invest are often irreversible. When the future value of the investment is uncertain, this irreversibility generates

9 In principle, the firm should use a discount rate that reflects the opportunity cost of the investment outlay.

an opportunity cost: the cost of not deferring the decision, and obtaining more information about the future profitability of the project. Some examples of this follow.

Uncertainty about revenue

Suppose that a firm is considering an investment in a new machine at a cost of £6,000 and also suppose that the firm will not know the price of the product it sells (and hence its revenue stream) until next year. All that it knows this year is that there is a 50% chance that the revenue stream will be £1,000 per year, and a 50% chance that it will be £500. Should the firm invest this year when the revenue stream is not known, or should it defer its decision until next year?

We will assume for simplicity that the firm receives the stream of payments, whether £1,000 or £500, in perpetuity. This does not affect the analysis and we can use the neat fact that the PV of £1 received into the future forever, discounted at a rate of r, is simply £1/r.[10] The expected income stream is 0.5 * £1,000 + 0.5 * £500 = £750. Assuming a discount rate of 10%, the NPV criterion gives us

$$\text{NPV} = £7{,}500 - £6{,}000 = £1{,}500$$

and points to the firm taking the decision to invest this year. The alternative decision open to the firm is to wait, and only invest if the revenue stream is £1,000 per annum, as the NPV figure is negative if it is £500. This gives the following

$$\text{NPV} = 0.5[£10{,}000 - £5{,}455] = £2{,}273$$

since the investment cost next year discounted to this year is £5,455. The difference between the PV of the revenue stream and the cost outlay is then weighted by the probability that the revenue stream is £1,000 per year. We can therefore conclude that it might be preferable to delay.

The difference between the two NPV calculations can also be thought of as how much a firm would pay for an investment decision that is flexible, that is, one that can be delayed until next year. In this case it is £2,273 – £1,500 = £773. Alternatively, we could ask what investment cost the firm would be willing to incur to take the flexible investment. In this example, the firm would have a higher NPV with an investment cost of up to £7,700.[11]

10 Why this is so is given the mathematical appendix. It is simpler (less tedious) to assume that the stream of payments is made in perpetuity than for a long period of time. As we saw in Table 13.3, payments received many years into the future add relatively little to the present value of an income stream.

11 There is an analogy between the decision to invest and a call option in financial markets. The firm has the right (which it can choose to exercise if it pleases) to make an investment.

Uncertainty about cost

Cost uncertainty can also be important with, for example, large building projects or with projects that involve large R&D expenditure. One type of cost uncertainty is that over the price of the raw material and labour inputs, which varies over the duration of the business cycle and also with changes in government policy. This can have a similar effect to the uncertainty over the future payoff from the investment, in that there may be an opportunity cost associated with not waiting for new information.

Continuing with the previous example, suppose the cost of the investment is known to be £6,000 this year, but next year there is a 50–50 chance the cost will rise to £9,000 or fall to £3,000. To simplify, we will now assume that the revenue stream is known to be £750 per year. If the firm invests this year the project has a NPV of £1,500. If the firm takes the decision to delay until next year, it will not invest if the cost rises to £9,000, as the NPV will be negative. If the investment cost falls, the NPV is

$$\text{NPV} = 0.5[£7{,}500 - £2{,}727] = £2{,}386$$

which is higher than if the decision is taken to invest in the current year, pointing to the firm delaying the decision.

Another source of cost uncertainty is not knowing the exact length of time and cost of completing a project. Suppose, for example, that the firm knows it faces an initial expense of £3,500, with a 50% chance that a further £10,000 may be needed to complete the project in the current year. The expected cost of the project is now £3,500 + 0.5 * £10,000 = £8,500 giving a negative NPV.

However, this ignores the value of the information from completing the first phase of the project. The firm has the option to abandon the project if it chooses to do so. The appropriate calculation of the NPV in this case is –£3,500 + 0.5 * £7,500 = £250, suggesting that the investment would be profitable. Uncertainty over the cost of an investment can therefore affect the decision to invest either way; there may be an incentive for the firm to invest if it is a way of settling cost uncertainty.

Uncertainty about interest rates

Suppose now the interest rate this year is 10% but that there is a 50–50 chance it will either rise or fall by 5% next year (at which rate it will remain). The expected rate of interest is therefore 10%, which is the same as this year's known rate of interest. What effect does this have on the firm's decision-making? A payment stream of £750 in perpetuity gives a present value of £7,500 as we know from the earlier examples. The expected value of the perpetuity in the uncertain case is 0.5 * (£750/0.05) + 0.5 * (£750/0.15) = £10,000 which makes the investment more attractive, other things being equal.

However, interest rate uncertainty also has a second effect, as there is a return to deferring a decision to see whether interest rates rise or fall. This works rather like the uncertainty associated with the revenue stream from the investment that we considered before. The NPV in our example with known interest rates is £1,500, with uncertainty over rates it is £4,000, given a known cost of £6,000 for the project. If the firm waits until next year before making a decision, it will not invest if interest rates rise to 15%. If interest rates were to fall the NPV calculation is

$$\text{NPV} = 0.5[\pounds750/0.05 - \pounds6{,}000/1.05] = \pounds4{,}643$$

which is higher than if the firm invests immediately. The timing of an investment is therefore sensitive to the volatility of interest rates; the greater the volatility the greater the incentive to delay a decision.

Questions

Q4 A firm is considering two alternative investment projects that have the revenue streams given below.

	Year 0	Year 1	Year 2
Revenue stream 1	£6,000	£0	£12,000
Revenue stream 2	£3,000	£14,500	£0

(I) Which stream has the higher PV when the rate of discount is 0% and when it is 10%?

(II) Suppose the cost of the project is incurred at the outset and is known to be £14,000. Are either of the projects profitable for the firm to undertake if the rate of discount is 25%?

Q5 A firm is considering an investment in a new computer costing £10,000 this year, which it expects to reduce its operating costs in the future. However, all that it knows now is that there is a 50-50 chance that costs per annum will fall by either £1,500 or by £750 in the future.

(I) Assuming a discount rate of 10%, and that the reduced costs will be sustained in perpetuity, what is the NPV of the investment if it is made this year?

(II) If there is a 90% probability that costs will fall by £1,750 and a 10% probability that they don't fall at all, should the firm invest this year?

(III) Suppose that in addition to the cost of the computer the firm also faces the cost of training staff to use it over the following year. There is a 75% chance that this is £1,000 and 25% chance that it is £10,000. What should the firm do if it is certain that the reduction in other operating costs is £1,125 per annum?

13.3 The changing structure of wages

The simple neo-classical analysis assumes that inputs of a factor are homogeneous. This allows for substitution between factors, but assumes away the possibility of within-factor substitution. In the UK, and elsewhere, where the labour force is heterogeneous in terms of its skills and experience, there is obviously scope for substitution between different types of labour. Changes in the demand and supply of particular types of labour can have a large effect on structure of the wage distribution, and are an important part of understanding wage and employment levels.

In this section, we will look briefly at some of the key features of changes to the employment structure and the distribution of wages. Table 13.6 gives details on the employment structure in the UK in 1979 and 1993. Table 13.7 present evidence of the experience of wage inequality in selected OECD countries over the period 1973–95.

The changes in the structure of employment are evident from Table 13.6. There has been a sizeable reduction in the employment share of those without qualifications, and a greater fall in the share of those who are union members. The proportion of two-adult households with two earners has increased, as has that of two-adult households with no earners. Overall, there has been a movement away from the once stereotypical idea of a male-breadwinner.

Changes in the distribution of earnings are summarised in Table 13.7. The 90/10 percentile earnings ratio shown here is just one simple way of summarising the degree of wage dispersion. The numerator gives the earnings of the individual at the 90th percentile of the distribution (the point where only 10% of the workforce earn more). The denominator corresponds to the point in the distribution where only 10% earn less. This ratio, therefore, gives one measure of the degree of inequality between the low and the high earners. For example, in the distribution of male earnings in the UK in 1973, the individual at the 90th percentile earned 2.5 times as much as the person at the 10th percentile point and so on.

Broadly, the table indicates a greater degree of dispersion in the pattern of earnings in the US than in either Europe or Japan. What is also clear is that the degree of inequality in the UK increased markedly and to a lesser extent in the other English-speaking countries over the period covered. This was an experience not shared elsewhere.

	1979	1993
Employment shares: those with		
Degree or higher qualification	0.06	0.08 (1991)
Intermediate qualification	0.44	0.55 (1991)
No qualifications	0.50	0.37 (1991)
Manufacturing sector	0.30	0.20
Union members	0.53	0.35
Among two-adult households		
No earners	0.04	0.10
Single earners	0.43	0.28
Two earners	0.53	0.62

Table 13.6 **Changes in employment structure in the UK**
Source: Machin (1996).

	1970s	1990s
	Men/women	**Men/women**
Australia	2.00/1.78 (1976)	2.38/2.05
Canada	3.21/3.09	3.77/4.01 (1994)
France	3.23/2.65	3.21/2.51 (1990)
Germany	2.40/2.64 (1983)	2.24/2.26 (1993)
Japan	2.59/2.22 (1979)	2.77/2.24 (1994)
Sweden	2.07/1.87	2.15/1.82 (1991)
UK	2.50/2.57	3.61/3.33
US	4.71/4.19 (1975)	5.56/4.86 (1992)

Table 13.7 **90/10 percentile of earnings ratio in OECD countries 1973–95**
Source: Low Pay Commission (1998), which gives details of data definitions.

Explanations for the patterns of wage inequality

How can we explain the trends in the structure of wages? A modified supply and demand diagram may help. To simplify, suppose the workforce consisted of just two groups: the skilled and the unskilled. On the vertical axis of Figure 13.5, we have the ratio of wage rate paid to the skilled workers relative to that paid to the unskilled (W_S/W_U). Similarly, on the horizontal axis, we measure the relative employment level of the two groups (L_S/L_U). We have the conventional, downward-sloping demand curve, as a lower relative wage paid to skilled labour increases the demand for it. Conversely, the upward-sloping supply curve reflects rising (relative) numbers of skilled workers as their (relative) wage rises.

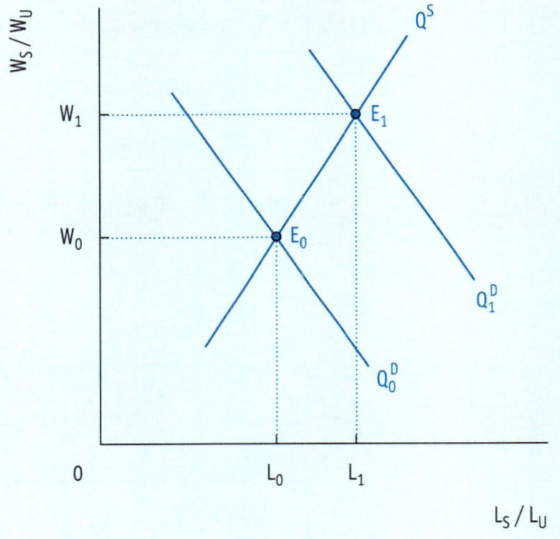

Figure 13.5 Changes in the relative demand for labour types

The data in Tables 13.6 and 13.7 show both higher relative wages, and a greater share of employment, for the skilled workforce in the UK. We can note here that this has happened in spite of the increasing share of the labour force with some form of educational qualification which, in terms of Figure 13.5, would be represented by an outward shift of the supply curve and a decline in the W_S/W_U ratio. The data covers a period of 15–20 years and will, of course, reflect various influences on both supply and the demand. However, the data can be explained simply with an outward shift in the demand curve in Figure 13.5. So the search for an explanation leads us to ask what may have made such a shift in demand the dominant influence.

A number of explanations have been advanced for it. They include the growing internationalisation of production, which may have led to a decline in the demand for unskilled labour in industries making tradable goods. The effect of this would be to lead to a greater number of unskilled workers seeking work in domestic industries, depressing relative wages. However, this explanation alone does not account for the evidence which suggested inequality grew in the UK and US, but not, for example, in France or Germany. A second explanation that has been put forward cites the effect of skilled-biased technological change. The widespread use of computers in already highly paid occupations, and the growing use of robotics in assembly lines, are put forward as examples of this process.

The international variation in wage inequality suggests that there may also be particular explanations in each country for the patterns observed. This leads us to the importance of institutional features and policy variations. A part of the explanation could be the failure of the education and training system in some countries such as the UK — at least in the short term — to provide unskilled workers with the skills necessary to meet labour market demands. Secondly, policy in the 1980s and 1990s in the UK was geared to promoting competitiveness, something which has been associated with the decline of unionism and the phasing out of wages councils which set statutory minimum wage rates in particular industries or occupations.

It remains an open question whether or not this pattern of change to the wage structure will continue. To the extent that other OECD countries follow Anglo-American labour market policies, then we may see a pattern of increasing inequality of earnings in those countries as well. Changes to policy in the UK may mean the pattern of increasing inequality does not continue. The role of education and training and the arguments concerning the impact of a national minimum wage are subjects we return to in detail in the next chapter.

Question

Q6 What would you expect the effect of a national minimum wage to be on the demand for skilled workers? Can you say what the effect would be on the wage differential?

13.4 The distribution of factor income

In this section, we will discuss what determines the distribution of income between the factors of production, what is sometimes referred to as the functional distribution of income. At the outset, however, it is important to recognise the distinction between this and the distribution of income between individual households, which is the subject of Chapter 18. Historically, the division of income into wages, profits and rent broadly corresponded to the income shares of workers, capitalists and landowners. At the end of the 20th century, the distribution of income is more diffuse and large numbers of individuals receive some combination of employment income, investment income and social security benefits.

In simple neo-classical analysis, we imagine an economy which consists of a single profit-maximising firm whose output is determined by an aggregate production function $Q = F(K, L)$, which is sold at a market price, P. Q, K and L are the output and capital and labour inputs as before. Given just two homogeneous factor inputs which are in fixed supply, the share of total income that goes to labour will be wL/PQ and that for capital will be rK/PQ, where w and r are the factor prices. Assuming further that the firm acts as if it were in a competitive market, it will continue to employ both factors to the point where the value of their respective marginal products is equal to their factor prices.

We can, therefore, express the share of labour income as

$$\frac{wL}{PQ} = \frac{P^*MPL^*L}{PQ} = \frac{MPL^*L}{Q}$$

and likewise that for capital as

$$\frac{rK}{PQ} = \frac{P^*MPK^*K}{PQ} = \frac{MPK^*K}{Q}$$

Over a period of time, factor shares would also depend on how the supply of the factor inputs change.[12] The elasticity of substitution is one way of summarising how relative shares change as input proportions change. If this equals 1, for example, the factor input ratio (K/L) changes in the same proportion as the factor price ratio, which we will express here as r/w. A 10% increase in the factor price ratio is associated with a 10% decrease in the factor input ratio. The factor prices, and factor inputs, change in equal proportion but in opposite directions so that the factor income shares are unchanged. If there is an increase in the factor price ratio, the share of profits will increase if the elasticity of substitution is less than one, and conversely will fall if it is greater than one.

This kind of analysis at least has the advantage of keeping the discussion, of what is a very large subject in a manageable form. It does not involve the description of an actual economy and several aspects of it have been the subject of heated debate.[13] This does not mean that such a structure is without its uses: the assumption of a perfectly competitive output market, for example, can be relaxed to allow for a degree of monopoly power. We saw in Section 1 that the decision rule for the firm then becomes w = MRP, where the MRP of labour is some proportion less than the VMP. It follows that the relative share of national income going to the suppliers of labour will be lower by whatever this proportion happens to be. These two alternative assumptions about market structure can then, in principle at least, be tested by comparing the predictions from a particular production function against data on factor shares.

12 This is not so if it the aggregate production function is a Cobb-Douglas function.

13 Blaug (1992) discusses the theoretical problems in some detail.

Factor shares: empirical evidence

The UK National Accounts (the 'Blue Book') provides a breakdown of gross domestic product (GDP). The data for 1995 is given in Table 13.8 from a study by Ryan (1996). To adjust the published data to a form that relates to the Hicksian definition of income, capital consumption is subtracted from GDP, and net property income from abroad, (NPIA), is added to it. National income can then be divided into employment, self-employment and investment shares.

Income component	£bn	% Share of income
Employment	377.8	
Self-employment	67.7	
Trading surplus of companies	91.0	
Rent	62.8	
Trading surpluses (of public corporations, general government)	4.6	
Gross domestic product NPIA, capital consumption, net national income	604.2	**100%**
Employment income	377.8	62.5
Self-employment income	67.2	11.1
Investment income	159	26.4

Table 13.8 **1995 GDP breakdown into income shares**
Source: Ryan (1996).

The analysis above was concerned with the breakdown of factor income into the shares going to labour and capital. Table 13.8 gives a three-way classification, and the question arises as to if, and how, we might sensibly assign self-employment income to the labour and capital shares. The self-employed cover a very wide range of occupations — occasional window-cleaners and partners in successful law firms — and accurate data on their incomes is difficult to obtain. Most of the methods used in studies of factor income shares include much, if not all, self-employed income in with the share going to labour income.

The variations in factor shares over time is one part of the explanation of the changing pattern of inequality between households. The study by Ryan (1996) suggests that the shares have varied quite widely over the twenty-year period from the mid 1970s. The share of employment income, for example, was found to vary by some 10% between peak and trough. The share of investment-related income in the mid-1990s was around twice what it had been at the post World War II low of under 9% in 1974.

The combination of the growing wage inequality looked at in Section 3, and the increase in the investment income share, might be taken as evidence that the distribution of household income has become more unequal. However changes in the factor shares are only one part of the background. In principle, an increase in the share of investment income could be associated with an increase or a decrease in the overall level of inequality. There is also a need to take account of, for example, the redistributive role of the government budget, which affects individual incomes by providing some form of cash benefits and/or levying some form of direct tax. The important question of equity between households is pursued in detail in Chapter 18.

Question

Q7 An economy consists of 100 competitive firms all of whom face the same production function

$$Q = 100L^{0.75}K^{0.25}$$

They sell their output at price, P. The owners of the labour input are paid w, the owners of the capital input are paid r.

(I) Show that the distribution of factor income is split between labour and capital on the basis of the technology of production.

(II) If the factor price ratio doubles what can you say about the distribution of factor payments?

(III) What difference does it make to the distribution of factor payments if the production function was $Q = 100L^{0.5}K^{0.5}$?

Mathematical appendix

The PV of a £1 in perpetuity can be written as

$$£1/(1 + r) + £1/(1 + r)^2 + £1/(1 + r)^3 + \ldots$$

which we will refer to as P. It follows that

$$P\,(1 + r) = £1 + £1/(1 + r) + £1/(1 + r)^2 + \ldots$$

So that $P\,(1 + r) = £1 + P$, from which it follows that $rP = £1$ and $P = £1/r$.

Summary

1 Factor demands are derived from the demand for the good or service of the firm. The short-run analysis of factor demands follows on from the analysis of the short-run production function that was discussed in Chapter 7.

2 It will be profitable for a firm to continue to hire additional units of a factor as long as the additional revenue from doing so is greater than the additional cost.

3 The level of employment of a factor depends on the nature of the firm's product market because it affects the revenue it receives. The additional revenue if employment is increased will be greater if the firm faces perfectly elastic demand for its product, than if it does not. If the demand curve for its product or service slopes down, then the additional revenue from an extra unit employed has to take account of the effect of a falling price on the revenue from the existing units.

4 Investment appraisal techniques include those that involve the net present value, NPV, and/or internal rate of return, IRR, of a project. If the costs and revenues of an investment project are known with certainty, and the NPV of a project is positive, it will be profitable for a firm to undertake the investment.

5 When there is uncertainty about the future revenue stream or costs of a project, the NPV rule needs to be modified. Investment decisions can be irreversible, and in an uncertain environment it may advantageous for a firm to defer a decision in order to acquire new information. The effect of uncertainty on investment decisions is however not necessarily negative.

6 A major feature of the labour market in the 1980s and 1990s has been the changing structure of wages. Broadly there has been greater inequality in the English-speaking economies than in other OECD countries over this period. This pattern may be at least partly a consequence of policy toward labour market institutions by national governments.

7 The neo-classical analysis gives us a starting point in understanding the distribution of income. The factor distribution of income is determined by the technical properties of the production function. This was more relevant when the economy could be plausibly broken down into landlords, bourgeois entrepreneurs and the workers.

8 At the end of the 20th century, the links between the factor distribution of income and the distribution of income between households are not straightforward. There are large differences between individual earnings. But many who supply labour also own capital and so receive income from more than one source.

End of chapter questions

Q8 Sleepy-days minicabs has the following short-run production function

$$Q = 6L - L^2$$

Where Q is its output in terms of the number of trips per hour, L is its labour input.

(I) What is the marginal product of labour for this firm? At what point does the slope of the production function turn negative?

(II) Draw the firm's demand curve for labour if the market price of all journeys is £5.

(III) If the wage rate paid is £4 per hour how many drivers would the firm hire? What is labour's share of the firm's total revenue?

Q9 A monopolist has the following demand function

$$P = 200 - 4Q^D$$

Its production function is

$$Q = 10L$$

The factor cost is £3 per hour.

(I) How much of the factor of production will the monopolist employ and what is its level of output?

(II) How would the answers to (I) differ if the industry were competitive?

Q10 A firm produces 100 plastic chairs hourly with a Cobb-Douglas production $Q = KL$

Capital input K	Labour input L	Output	Total cost	Total cost
			Wage rate = 2 Rental rate = 8	Wage rate = 8 Rental rate = 2
25	4	100		
20	5	100		
10	10	100		
5	20	100		
4	25	100		

(I) What is the elasticity of substitution when the factor price ratio changes from that in the fourth column to that in the fifth?

(II) If the firm's output was to double then what would happen to the elasticity of substitution for this production function?

Q11 An investment project costs £750,000 initially and a further £500,000 in a year's time. The capital equipment has a scrap value of £100,000 after five years. The revenue stream generated is £350,000 per annum for the five-year horizon. Assume a discount rate of 8%

(I) What is the payback period for the investment?

(II) Should the project go ahead by the NPV and IRR criterion?

Q12 A UK firm is considering an investment in new equipment but faces uncertainty about real interest rates. Suppose that it knows that the additional revenue stream will be £25,000 per annum in perpetuity and that there is a 90–10 chance that $r = 3\%$ or $r = 9\%$ depending on the success of the euro.

(I) What is the difference between the additional revenue stream when interest rates are uncertain and when they are known to be 6% with certainty?

(II) Suppose the cost of the equipment was £500,000 what would you advise the firm to do?

(III) If there was a 75–25 chance that $r = 4\%$ or $r = 10\%$ what difference would it make to your answer to part (II)?

Q13 If a firm faced limits on the amount it could borrow would it be better to evaluate its investment projects by

(I) the difference between the (discounted) benefits and costs, the NPV criterion,

or

(II) its profitability index which gives the ratio of the benefits to costs?

References and suggested further reading

Estrin and Laidler gives a fuller discussion of the neo-classical analysis of factor demands. Blaug offers critical comment on this type of analysis. Dixit and Pindyck Chapter 2 is a source of examples of how uncertainty affects investment, and discusses the analogy with option pricing. Most of the rest of the book is aimed at more advanced study. The article by Machin on wage inequality is generally accessible. The issues of relating the data from the national income accounts to factor income shares are discussed in more detail in the article by Ryan, and in the chapter by Atkinson.

Atkinson, A.B. (1996), 'Seeking to explain the distribution of income' in Hills, J. (ed.), *New Inequalities*, Cambridge University Press.

Blaug, M. (1992), *The Methodology of Economics*, Cambridge University Press.

Dixit, A. and Pindyck, R. (1994), *Investment Under Uncertainty*, Princeton University Press.

Estrin, S. and Laidler, D. (1995), *Introduction to Microeconomics*, 4th edition. Harvester Wheatsheaf.

Gosling, A., Machin, S. and Meghir, C. (1996), 'What has happened to the wages of men since 1966?' in Hills, J. (ed.), *New Inequalities*, Cambridge University Press.

Low Pay Commission (1998), 'The National Minimum Wage, First Report of the Low Pay Commission'.

Machin, S. (1996), 'Wage Inequality in the UK', *Oxford Review of Economic Policy*, **12**, No. 1.

Nicholson, W. (1995), *Microeconomic Theory, Basic Principles and Extensions*, 6th edition, The Dryden Press.

Ryan, P. (1996), 'Factor Shares and Inequality in the UK', *Oxford Review of Economic Policy*, **12**, No. 1.

Varian, H.R. (1996), *Intermediate Microeconomics, A Modern Approach*, 4th edition, W.W. Norton & Co.

14

The Labour Market

Key ideas and material

Screening and signalling, efficiency wage models, a national minimum wage

Introduction

In this chapter, we are going to look at some of the institutional features and government policies that explain the structure of wage differentials. We will start by looking at the role that educational qualifications play in the labour market. In Chapter 4, we discussed education in terms of its impact on human capital. This is one explanation of why the wage or salary paid to an individual will vary over time and, in turn, why wage levels between individuals will vary at a particular point in time.

An alternative view is that education acts as a signal of high productivity. The analysis of this is discussed in Section 1. This recognises that labour is heterogeneous and that employers make decisions on the basis of the abilities and characteristics of individuals, in a market characterised by asymmetric information. The analysis provides useful insights, although the empirical evidence about factors affecting educational attainment shows the process to be complex.

The idea that individuals differ in terms of their productivity takes us on to models of efficiency wages in Section 2. These models provide another perspective on observed wage differentials; the common idea being that the quality of the workforce employed by firms depends on the wage rate they offer. This raises the possibility that a firm can increase both its employment levels and profits by paying its workforce higher wages and in turn points to variation between firms as a source of wage inequality.

Finally, in this chapter, we look at statutory wage floors and consider the impact of a national minimum wage, NMW, in the UK. Policy variations over time may be important in explaining changes in the extent of low pay. The UK operated a system of wage floors for some industries until the early 1990's and the introduction of a national minimum can be seen as one way of trying to compress the distribution of earnings. In Section 3, we discuss the consequences of a NMW for employment levels, pay differentials and also investment in training and education.

14.1 Screening and signalling in the labour market

The analysis of this section assumes that workers differ in terms of their productivity. Individuals know how productive they are but their (prospective) employers do not prior to a hiring decision. Given this asymmetry of information, if employers could not screen workers, and workers could not signal their productivity, all would be paid the same wage based on the average productivity level. This creates an incentive for those with high productivity to signal this fact, and one way that they might do this is by educational attainment. If high and low productivity workers were to face differential costs in obtaining a given level of education then, in principle, employers can treat education as a signal from those with high productivity. The differences in wage levels paid will then reflect productivity differences.

Employers can attempt to find out the productivity level of prospective workers by using education as a screen in the labour market. Suppose the workforce is divided into just two groups with equal numbers of individuals, who differ only in terms of their productivity. Those in the first group, Group 1, we will assume have an average and marginal product of 100 per annum; for the second group, Group 2, we will assume an average and marginal product of 200. The average product of the workforce is therefore 150. For simplicity, we will suppose that firms operate in a competitive environment and sell their product for £100 per unit. The revenue expected from the low productivity group is then £100 * 100 = £10,000, which is clearly one-half that of the high productivity group.

In a world of perfect information, individuals could be identified and would be paid according to the value of their marginal product, VMP. This is illustrated in Figure 14.1, where on the vertical axis we measure the wage rate, and on the horizontal axis we measure the level of education, E. In this context, it would make sense to interpret the level of education as being the number of years in post-compulsory education (or, alternatively, the number of years in higher education). To examine the role played by education we will simplify further and assume that it does not affect individual productivity directly and that it does not provide any personal benefit.

The preferences of the individual worker can then be represented by an indifference curve. Utility in this context depends on the wage received net of the cost of obtaining a particular

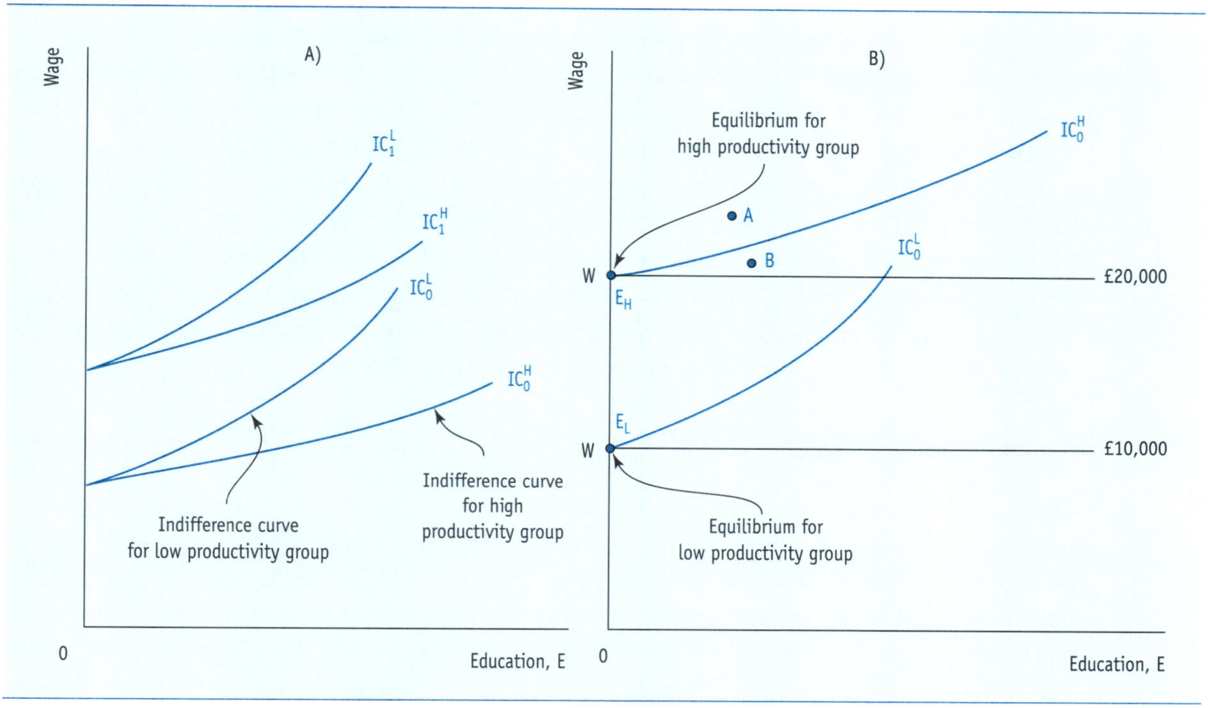

Figure 14.1 Screening and wage-education choices (symmetric information)

level of education. The cost of acquiring education is assumed to be greater for those in Group 1, the low productivity group. The costs here include those associated with book purchases, maintenance and the opportunities foregone by not working. They are obviously greater the longer the time taken to obtain a particular qualification, so that the cost is greater for those with low productivity.

The differential costs of obtaining a given education level are reflected in the slopes of the indifference curves for the two types of worker. In Figure 14.1A, a high productivity worker has a flatter indifference curve than a member of the low productivity group. This is because the cost of acquiring a given level of education is less and so a smaller increase in wages is required to maintain a given level of utility as the level of education rises.

When the two groups of workers can be distinguished, the horizontal lines at W = £10,000 and W = £20,000 in Figure 14.1B show the wages paid. These wage rates would yield normal profits in a long-run competitive equilibrium. At these wages, the workers are paid their VMP; if the wage were less then firms would make abnormal profits, if the wage were higher they would make losses. In the first case the demand for labour would expand and wages would increase; in the second case, if the losses made by a firm persisted it would eventually go out of business.

If a competitive firm knew which productivity group individuals belonged to, then given our assumptions about the role of education, the equilibrium point for both groups occurs where E = 0 in Figure 14.1B. At these points, individuals in both groups attain the maximum possible utility consistent with firms who employ them making normal profits. For the high productivity group, E_H is the point of equilibrium, where the indifference curve IC_0^H intersects the W = £20,000 line. At point A, for example, utility for the individual would be higher but his or her employer would be making losses. At point B, an individual could move onto a higher indifference curve, by opting for a combination involving a lower level of education and a lower wage. A similar line of argument can be used to justify the equilibrium for the individuals in the low productivity group (E = 0, w = £10,000) at E_L.

Asymmetric information

The problem that the firm has is that it does not know directly which group any particular individual belongs to. However, it may be possible for employers to vary the wage in accordance with the education level of the two groups, if only the high productivity group finds it worthwhile to obtain the necessary education. In analytical terms this is a question of whether there is a separating equilibrium, that is whether or not there is an outcome where individuals in the two groups self-select on the basis of their productivity.

For example, suppose employers offer to pay a wage of £10,000 to those with education level E = 0, and £20,000 to those with the qualification from E = 3. This may result in a separating equilibrium, if, only the high productivity workers find E = 3 worthwhile. The outcome depends on the cost of acquiring education, which again is reflected in the indifference curves of both groups. As illustrated in Figure 14.2 panel A, the high-productivity workers would be willing to obtain more than E = 3 for a wage of £20,000. The most education the low-productivity group are willing to undertake is E = 2. To obtain a higher level of education would make this group worse off than at E = 0 as the indifference curve of the low ability group that would pass through E = 3 is below IC_0^L.

In Figure 14.2 panel B, we have an equilibrium where the two groups are separated with education levels E = 0 and E = 3 respectively. Those with high productivity obtain the utility associated with the indifference curve marked IC_1^H, which passes through point E in Figure 14.2 panel B. As drawn in the figure, the high productivity workers are on a higher indifference curve than they would be if all workers were paid on the basis of the average product, i.e. £15,000.

Signalling

Signalling and screening are closely related ideas. Signalling in the labour market relates to the decisions made by individual workers about how much education to attain in advance of receiving job offers from employers. The beliefs of employers about how then to interpret the

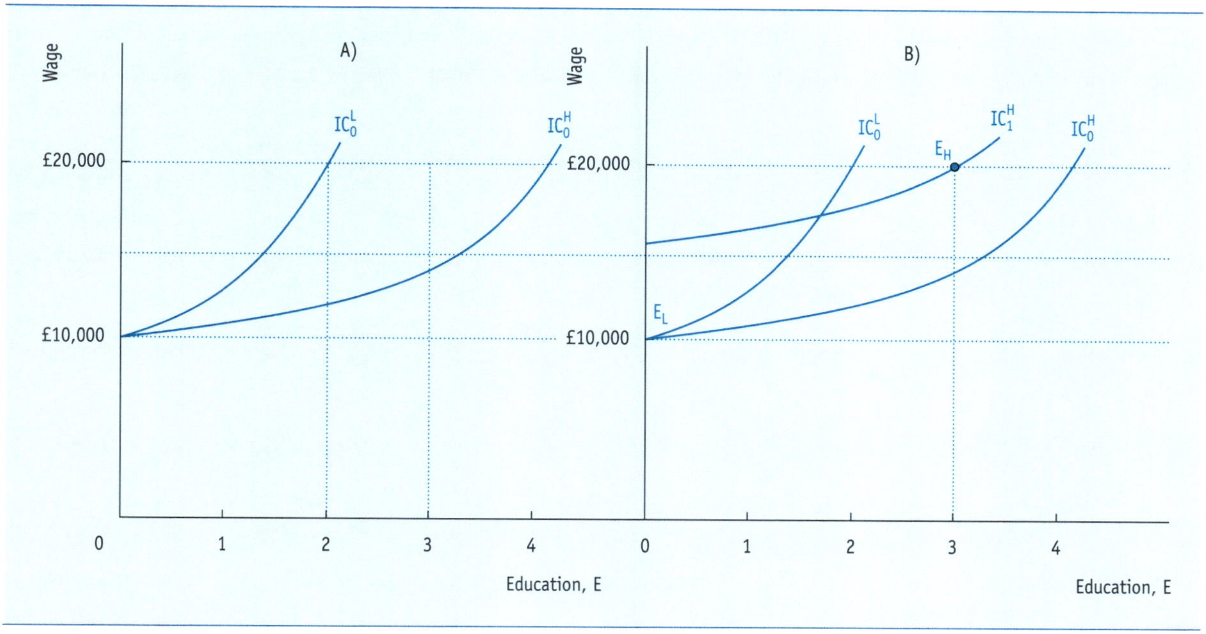

Figure 14.2 Screening

signals are important: in equilibrium their prior beliefs about the productivity of individual workers must be consistent with their experience.

To see what this means, suppose that employers believe that any worker with a qualification from, say one year of post-compulsory education, is in the high productivity group, and offer to pay such individuals on the basis that their productivity level is 200. In Figure 14.3 panel A such a wage-education combination is shown at point D. As drawn in the figure, both high and low productivity workers would obtain the necessary education, rather than choose w = £10,000 and E = 0. Individual workers in both groups would be able to move onto higher indifference curves at point D.

Point D, therefore, will not be a point of equilibrium. If both groups of workers do acquire one year of (post-compulsory) education, employers will come to realise that not all of them are members of the more productive group. The experience of employers would not be consistent with their prior belief that all such workers have a productivity of 200. If workers in both groups obtain educational level E = 1 then all that employers would be willing to pay is £15,000. This is point F in Figure 14.3 panel A, where the wages paid are equal to the VMP of each worker.

However, a lower level of education than that at E = 1 would also lead to the same outcome with w = £15,000, but would allow both groups of workers to attain higher utility levels. The highest possible indifference curves for the two groups are associated with the point associated

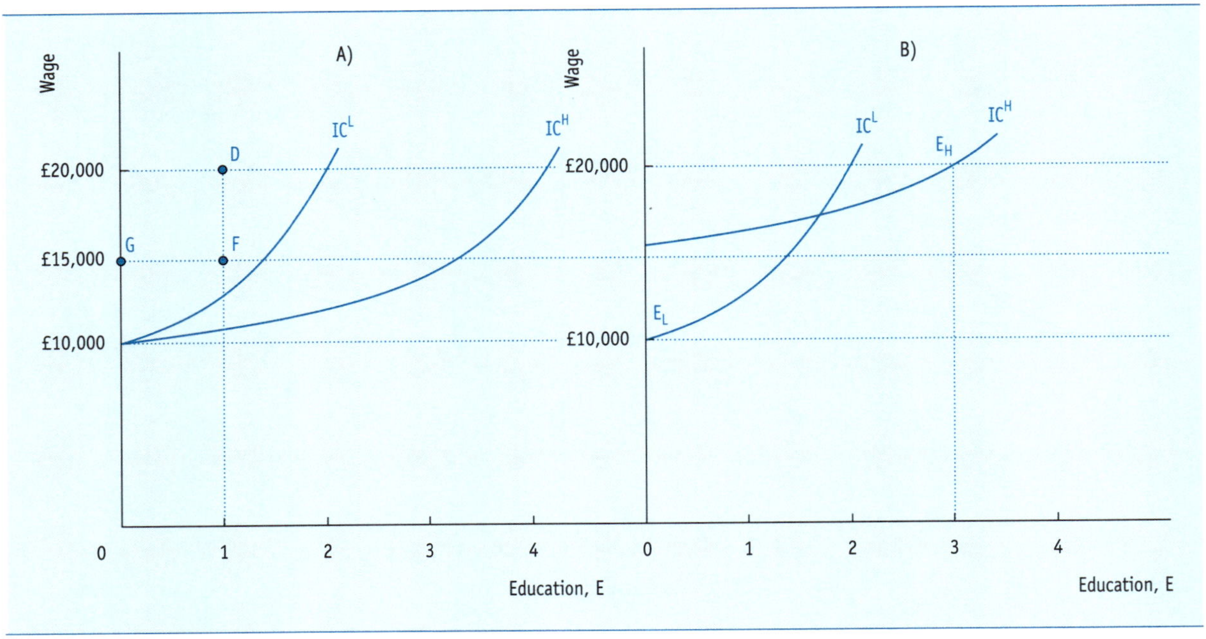

Figure 14.3 Signalling and wage-education choices

with W = £15,000 and E = 0, point G. This is an equilibrium point, though clearly it is not one in which education serves a useful signalling function.

Suppose, however, that employers believe that anyone with (the qualifications from) three years of post-compulsory education is a high productivity worker. A separating equilibrium that does not conflict with the beliefs of employers is shown in Figure 14.3 panel B. Given the employers' beliefs, a Group 1 worker will choose w = £10,000, E = 0. A Group 2 worker will choose w = £20,000, E = 3. The employers' experience of the productivity of individual workers will then confirm their prior beliefs.

Empirical evidence

The idea that educational levels perform the role of a signal is a plausible one, although the influences on an individual's education are many and not all of them are linked to individual productivity. Tables 14.1 and 14.2 present estimates of the marginal effect of a number of variables on educational attainment taken from the study by Blundell *et al.* (1997). This was a study of the experiences of a group of individuals from birth in 1958 to 1991 in the UK using data from the National Child Development Survey, the NCDS. The individuals were interviewed at five different points over the 33 year period, which yielded considerable detail on the backgrounds and characteristics of those who went onto study for a degree qualification. At the time these individuals entered into higher education the main entry qualification was two (or more) 'A' levels.

The list of variables in both tables may appear lengthy. The tables show the marginal effect of each factor listed on the probability of obtaining a particular qualification.[1] The maths and reading ability variables measure the effect relative to those who are in the bottom 20%. So, for example, a boy in the top quintile in maths ability tests at the age of 7 was 16% more likely to be educated to 'A' level standard, than was a boy in the bottom quintile. For a girl the corresponding effect was estimated to be 20%.

Broadly, the maths and reading ability test variables might be taken as attempts to measure 'innate' ability.[2] The tables also show the effect of other variables reflecting the family background in terms of such factors as parental educational levels, and the type of school that an individual attended. Plainly, there is a wide range of influences on the probability of an individual being educated to 'A' level standard. How close the relation is between innate individual ability — productivity in terms of our analytical discussion — and obtaining an 'A' level is an open question from the evidence in the Table 14.1

Table 14.2 shows the marginal effects on the probability of obtaining a degree. These are generally smaller, although maths and reading ability at the age of seven were again found to be a positive influence on the likelihood of graduating.[4] However, measures relating to family income such as attending a private school, and measures relating to social backgrounds, such as high levels of parental education and parents in professional occupations, were also found to exert positive influences. Generally, we can conclude that as a signal a graduate level of education reflects a mixture of influences, of which ability is only one.[5]

The links between ability, educational attainment and wage levels are in practice difficult to determine, partly because of the number of influences on the educational attainment of individuals. The Blundell study does provide clear evidence that both men and women with higher education receive higher wages: at age 33 around 21% higher for men and about twice that figure for women. These estimated returns vary, however, with the number of other factors that enter into the equation determining wage levels (that is with the number of controls used). This was particularly so for men, with the 'raw' returns being reduced to 12% in some estimates.[6]

---

1 There are a number of questions of econometric detail discussed in the original study, but which lie outside the subject matter of this book.

2 Whether or not they actually do this or whether this is all that is being measured is a separate matter, which we will not pursue here.

3 This refers to the number of older siblings.

4 Also on the likelihood of obtaining a higher degree.

5 There are some differences between men and women, details of which are given in the original study.

6 The controls were influences in Tables 14.1 and 14.2 and some others as well.

Individual variables		Marginal effect	
		Men	Women
Maths ability tests aged 7:	Top quintile	0.16	0.20
	4th quintile	0.09	0.11
	3rd quintile	0.08	0.12
Reading ability tests aged 7:	Top quintile	0.34	0.32
	4th quintile	0.27	0.25
	3rd quintile	0.15	0.15
	2nd quintile	0.07	0.09
	No. of siblings	–0.02	–0.02[3]
Region 1974:	London	0.04	0.03
	Scotland	0.14	0.26
Less than 1 week off school 1974		0.08	0.09
School type 1974:	Grammar	0.26	0.25
	Private	0.39	0.20
Family background variables:	Father's years of education	0.03	0.02
	Mother's years of education	0.02	0.04
Adverse financial situation 1969/74		–0.04	–0.06

Table 14.1 Factors affecting the probability of getting 'A' levels
Source: Blundell et al. (1997).

Questions

Q1 Suppose the labour force is divided into two groups of workers of equal numbers, Group 1 with an average and marginal product of 100, Group 2 with an average and marginal product of 200. In a competitive market firms sell their product at £25 per unit. Assume that education is less costly for Group 2 than for Group 1

(I) Is the separating equilibrium, where the individuals are paid the value of their marginal products, necessarily a Nash equilibrium?

(II) How would the analysis change if the number of workers in Group 1 were 70% of the total workforce?

Individual variables		Marginal effect	
		Men	Women
Maths ability tests aged 7:	Top quintile	0.03	0.05
	4th quintile	0.02	0.04
Reading ability tests aged 7:	Top quintile	0.03	0.04
	4th quintile	0.02	0.02
	No. of siblings	–0.01	–0.01
Region 1974:	London	0.02	0.01
	Scotland	0.00	–0.05
Father in a professional occupation		0.02	0.01
School type 1974:	Grammar	0.01	0.04
	Private	0.01	0.04
Family background variables:	Father's years of education	0.01	0.05
	Mother's years of education	0.00	0.01
Adverse financial situation 1969/74		–0.04	–0.03

Table 14.2 Factors affecting attainment in higher education
Source: Blundell et al. (1997).

Q2 The study by Blundell et al (1997) quoted in the text also found that

(I) there were few important wage differences between those taking different subjects a higher education level.

(II) those who entered higher education but failed to obtain any qualification had lower wages than those who did not enter higher education at all.

Do you consider these findings to be consistent with higher education as a signalling device?

14.2 Efficiency wages

In this section we will discuss efficiency wage models. The general idea of these models is that firms recognise that the wage paid is related to the quality of the workforce. A low wage

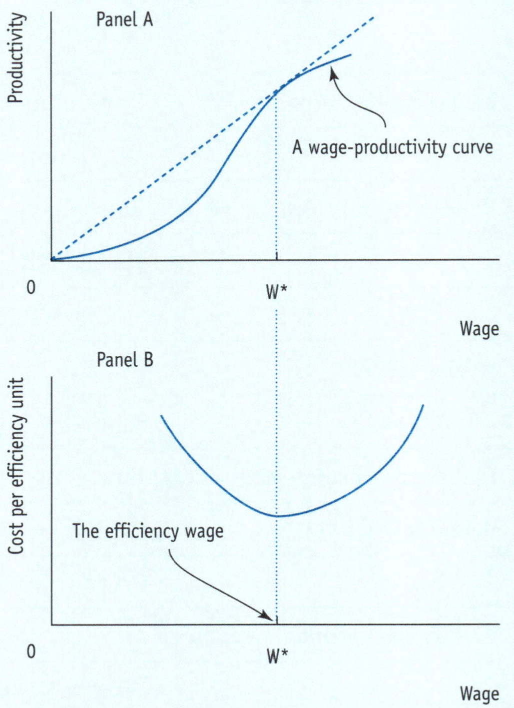

Figure 14.4 Efficiency wages

worker therefore does not necessarily mean a low cost worker and it may be efficient for firms to pay above the (neo-classical) equilibrium wage rate.

When a firm faces a market with an excess supply of labour, the conventional neo-classical analysis suggests that market equilibrium will be restored by individuals offering to work at a lower wage rate. However, if employers believe that there is a relation between an individual's productivity and the wage rate at which he or she is prepared to work they may not hire these workers. Whether or not it is worthwhile from the point of the view of the firm depends on how productive these workers are, and in turn the impact on the firm's costs.

In Figure 14.4 panel A, we have drawn a wage-productivity curve, which gives the relation between the productivity of an individual worker and his or her wage rate. As drawn, productivity rises more quickly than the wage rate as the curve approaches W*, at wage rates above W* it rises more slowly. In panel B, we have the relation between the cost per efficiency unit, and the wage rate paid to the firm's workforce. The cost per efficiency unit is simply the cost per unit of labour service rather than per unit of labour input. Intuitively, it reflects what people do in work rather than how many of them there are. The relation depicted is derived from the wage productivity curve in panel A; where there are increasing returns the cost per efficiency unit is declining, where it reaches a minimum we have what is known as the efficiency wage. The existence of a wage-productivity relationship is not a new idea in economics, and there are a number of alternative explanations for it. We will now look at two of them.[7]

The shirking model

This is a model that is based on the idea that some workers may shirk — choose to not work very hard — for the firm that hires them. This may happen if monitoring the productive effort of the workforce is costly, and/or is not fully effective. In such a situation, individuals who shirk may continue to be paid by the firm.[8] Firms have an incentive to pay workers above the market equilibrium wage to give them an incentive not to shirk. If the wage premium is high enough, the cost of losing a job to an individual if caught, will be high enough to deter him or her from shirking. The lowest wage level at which no shirking occurs is the efficiency wage.

This is illustrated in Figure 14.5. If firms pay the neo-classical market-clearing wage, W_N, the employment level is given by L_N. In the analysis of a competitive market, if an individual is caught shirking they could be re-employed at the same wage rate. The prospect of losing a job offers no deterrent against the temptation to shirk. If a single firm paid a wage above the market-clearing equilibrium, individuals working for the firm would have an incentive not to lose their jobs, as no other employer would pay them as much. If all firms paid above the market-clearing equilibrium, they would still have an incentive not to shirk because they face the risk of a period of unemployment.

The no-shirking constraint, NSC, in Figure 14.5, shows the wage that firms have to pay to persuade workers not to shirk at different levels of unemployment. The wage increases as the level of unemployment falls. This is because at lower levels of unemployment the cost to the shirker is less in terms of the probability of a period of unemployment or the duration of any spell is less. The efficiency wage is shown in Figure 14.5 by the intersection of the demand for labour and the no-shirking constraint. This gives a wage rate W_E, which is above the neo-classical wage rate W_N. The employment level, L_E, is a lower by the amount $L_N - L_E$ over the neo-classical equilibrium.[9]

Labour turnover

The costs of labour turnover are another reason why firms may minimise costs per unit of labour service if they pay efficiency wages. If workers quit their jobs, firms spend time and

7 We are concerned with applications relating to the industrialised countries. In the context of developing countries, models of efficiency wages point to the link between productivity and nutrition; a higher wage may enable workers to eat better and work more effectively.

8 In analytical terms this is again a situation of asymmetric information.

9 The labour supply schedule here represents aggregate labour supply, which is why it is drawn as a vertical line.

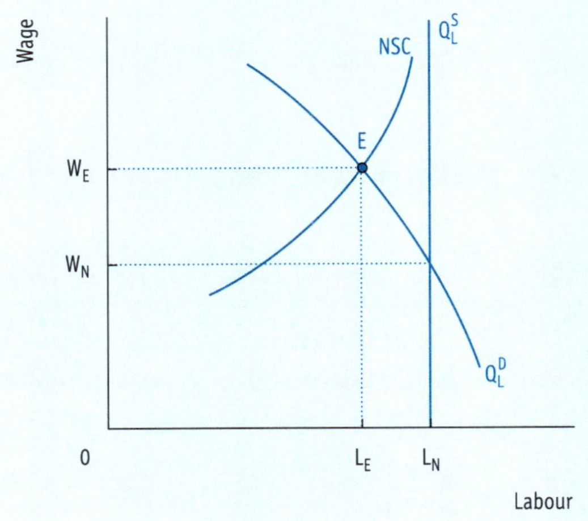

Figure 14.5 The shirking model

other resources hiring and training new members of staff. The greater the quit rate the greater will be these turnover costs. If a firm pays a wage rate above the market-clearing rate, then both the rate of labour turnover and its unit costs may be lower.

There is some empirical evidence to support this idea. A study by Dearden *et al.* (1997) looked at what types of individual received different kinds of employer-provided training and the effect it had on labour mobility. The study used data from both the Labour Force Survey, the LFS, and the NCDS. Table 14.3A shows details of the amount of training provided.[10]

The LFS gives a higher figure for training for both men and women. In the LFS, training includes only that undertaken in the four weeks prior to the survey; in the NCDS it refers to that given in the previous three months. The data from the NCDS covered the 10-year period to 1991, in the LFS it covered the period 1992–94. The survey figures shown, therefore, reflect a mixture of sampling variability, different data definitions and a changing macroeconomic environment.

It is important to make a distinction between employer-funded and other types of training. For men, the study found that those who received employer-funded training were less likely to move between jobs in the following year. Table 14.3B shows the effect of different training types (using the NCDS data set) on labour mobility.

The interpretation of the statistical information in this table is similar to that for obtaining qualifications as discussed in Section 1. The columns give the marginal effect from completing

10 It also clearly shows the variability between different sources of data.

	Men		Women	
	LFS	**NCDS**	**LFS**	**NCDS**
Any training	14.6%	8.2%	15.6%	7.1%
— Employer funded	8.6%	6.9%	8.1%	4.9%
— Other training	6.0%	3.5%	7.5%	2.2%

Table 14.3A Incidence of training
Source: Dearden et al. (1997).

	Marginal effect	
Type of training	**Men**	**Women**
Any training	–0.01	0.006
Employer-funded	–0.029	0.002
Other	0.025	0.012

Table 14.3B The effect of training on mobility
Source: Dearden et al. (1997).

the training given on the probability of moving jobs within a year. So, for example, the estimated effect of any form of training is to reduce the probability of a male worker moving job the following year by 1%, according to the estimates in this study.[11] The reduction is greater for those men who were given training financed by their employer. Conversely, those men who had undertaken other types of work-related training, particularly training which led to a qualification, had a higher probability of moving between jobs.

None of the estimates for women shown in the third column are statistically significant, although the authors did find, not surprisingly, that those taking vocational qualifications were much more likely to be moving jobs. They estimated marginal effects of between 3–5% depending on the level of the qualification.

Chart 14.1 shows the relation between employees in the UK who were looking for a different (or additional) paid job in 1997 and their rate of pay. As you would expect, this shows an inverse relation between wage rates and those seeking alternative employment. Again this chart suggests that higher wages might reduce turnover costs, and this is something that we will return to in the next section in the particular context of a national minimum wage.

11 It reduced the probability of moving to 14.7%.

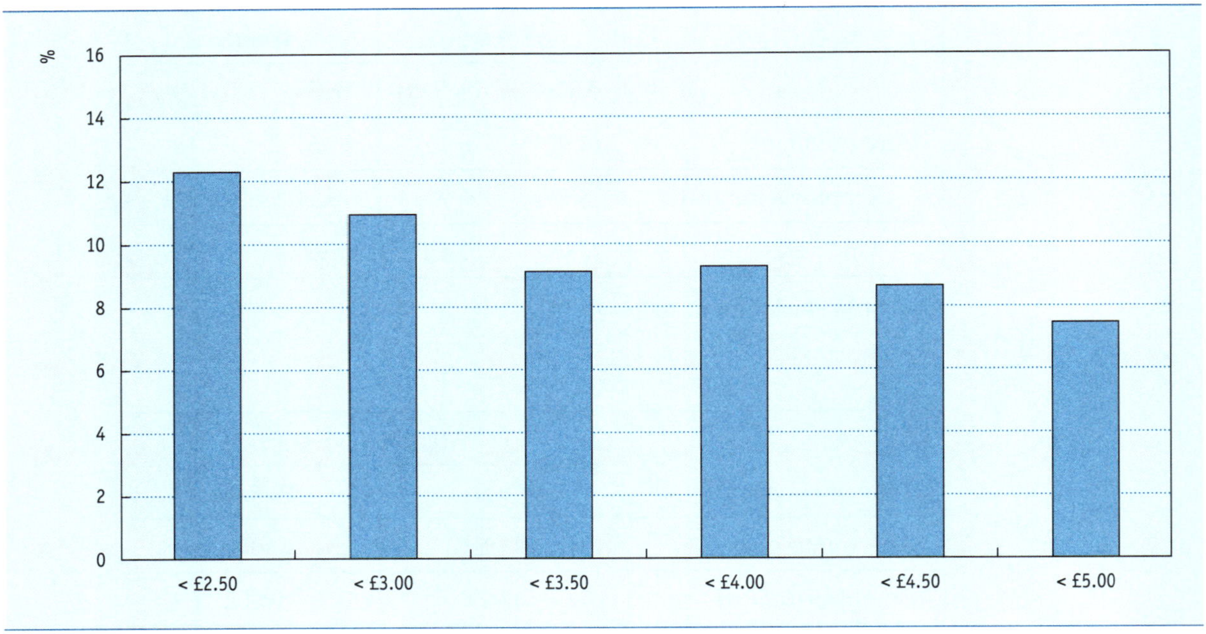

Chart 14.1 % of employees looking for alternative employment in the UK 1997
Source: Low Pay Commission (1998).

Question

Q3 In the shirking model what would be the effect of

(I) a rise in the detection rate of those who shirk
(II) a rise in the level of unemployment benefit
(III) a rise in the probability of being made redundant (whether the individual shirks or not)

on the efficiency wage?

14.3 A national minimum wage

In this section, we turn our attention to the subject of a statutory wage floor. Table 14.4 gives some background on how widespread a minimum wage is among OECD countries and also how long they have been in operation.

As was mentioned in the introduction to this chapter, the UK had a system of wage floors, operated by wages councils, for some industries until the early 1990s. A national minimum wage, NMW, is due to be introduced in 1999 for the first time, and this section will

Country	Year a minimum wage was established
Australia	1966 (in some form since 1907)
Belgium	1975
Canada	Women 1918–1930, men 1930s–1950s
France	1950 (1970 in its current form)
Greece	1953 (1990 in its current form)
Holland	1968
Japan	1959 (1968 in its current form)
New Zealand	1945 (1983 in its current form)
Portugal	1974
Spain	1963 (1976 in its current form)
United States	1938

Table 14.4 Minimum wages in OECD countries
Source: Low Pay Commission (1998).

concentrate on its potential impact. We will begin by reviewing the arguments about the effect that a NMW would have, in principle, on employment levels in both competitive and monopsonistic markets.

A competitive market

The conventional analysis of introducing a minimum wage in a competitive market suggests that it causes involuntary unemployment among low-paid workers, although it raises the wage paid to those that remain in work. Figure 14.6A illustrates this where the industry supply of labour is given by Q_L^S, the industry demand by Q_L^D and the free market equilibrium is given by point E. The equilibrium wage rate is W_E and the employment level is L_E. In low-skilled, low paid occupations a minimum wage, W_{MIN}, will be above the free market wage level, W_E; this causes a reduction in the demand for labour and with it a reduction in employment. In the figure this is shown by the distance $L_E - L_{MIN}$.

Those workers who are the least productive, those with a VMP less than the minimum wage the firm would no longer employ. The amount of unemployment that arises will be determined by the extent to which the minimum wage lies above W_E, and by the elasticity of the labour supply and demand. The greater the elasticities, the greater the reduction in employment and

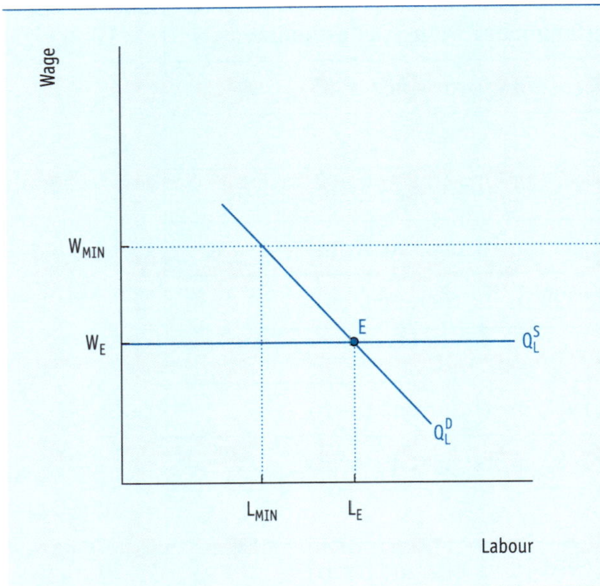

Figure 14.6A A minimum wage in a competitive market

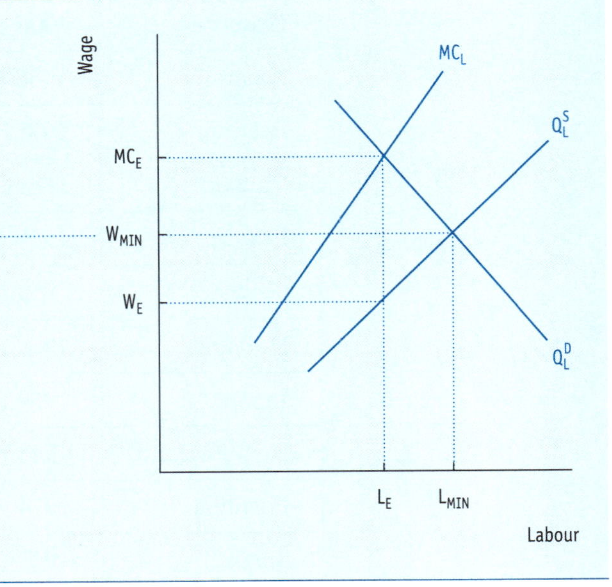

Figure 14.6B A minimum wage in a monopsonistic market

with it the greater the resulting unemployment. The conclusion is that if the labour market for the low-skilled is competitive, the effect on employment levels may be large.[12]

This is the static, one-period analysis of competitive markets. The demand for labour as drawn in Figure 14.6A is for a given level of other factor prices. In the long-run, if the impact of a minimum wage is felt widely in other industries, then the demand for a substitute factor will rise. A rise the price of labour could therefore cause some firms to change their methods of production, substituting capital for labour. A more capital-intensive method of production may then increase the marginal revenue product of the labour employed, and consequently lessen the effect on employment.

A monopsonistic market

The general conclusion that the introduction of a minimum wage would increase unemployment may, in principle, be reversed when we consider the analysis in the context of a monopsonistic employer. In Figure 14.6B, we show the situation in such an industry. The MC_L curve represents the marginal cost of labour in the absence of a minimum wage. It slopes upward as the firm is the single buyer of labour and therefore faces the entire industry supply. It has to pay more for each additional unit of labour so that MC_L lies above Q_L^S (which gives the average cost of labour or the wage rate paid). The intersection of the industry demand with the

12 Although some may work in ways not covered by a statutory minimum.

marginal cost of labour determines the employment level L_E, and the individual worker is paid a wage, W_E, which is less than his or her marginal revenue product.

The introduction of a minimum wage means that no labour will be supplied below whatever that wage happens to be, marked as W_{MIN} in the figure. The marginal cost of labour schedule is now constant at W_{MIN} until it meets the supply curve. There are therefore a range of wage levels between W_E and MC_E in Figure 14.6B that would lead to more, not less, employment than L_E. The minimum wage that would lead to the largest increase in employment is W_{MIN} in Figure 14.6B. As with the competitive model, the size of the impact on employment depends on the elasticities of labour supply and labour demand.

In principle, the effect on employment depends on whether the model of competition or that of monopsony offers a better approximation to the operation of actual markets. Both models indicate that if a minimum wage is set above a certain level, above W_E in Figure 14.6A and above MC_E in Figure 14.6B, it would cause a reduction in employment. What the analysis of a monopsony suggests is that there is a range of rates over which the minimum wage can be set where there will be non-negative effects on employment.

This simple analysis ignores variations in productivity that may exist between firms. These may arise because of differences in the firm's capital stock, or from variations in work effort or labour turnover or for other reasons. Dickens *et al.* (1994) discuss the situation in which firms face the same labour supply schedule, but the marginal revenue productivity of labour varies between firms. They classify a firm as being in one of three regimes, referred to as (i) the unconstrained regime, (ii) the supply-constrained regime and (iii) the demand-constrained regime.

The unconstrained regime reflects the situation in which the MRP schedule gives a wage level above the minimum wage. In this case, the minimum wage has no effect, as shown by the wage associated with $MRPL_3$ in Figure 14.7. The supply-constrained regime reflects the situation where the firm pays its workforce the minimum rate, employing all the workers that are willing to work at this wage rate. This would be the case if the marginal revenue product of a firm's workforce was given by $MRPL_2$, for example. Without a minimum wage, the wage rate paid would be W_2 and the employment level would be L_2. For firms in this situation, there is a higher level of employment with a minimum wage. The third type of regime, demand-constrained, is where the MRP of the firm is so low that it is not optimal for the firm to employ all those who want to work at the minimum wage rate. This is represented by $MRPL_1$.

The analysis above suggests that there may be employment falls in firms with low levels of productivity, but that there is a range of productivity for firms where the employment level may increase. In principle, the overall effect on employment of a minimum wage will depend on the numbers in each regime.

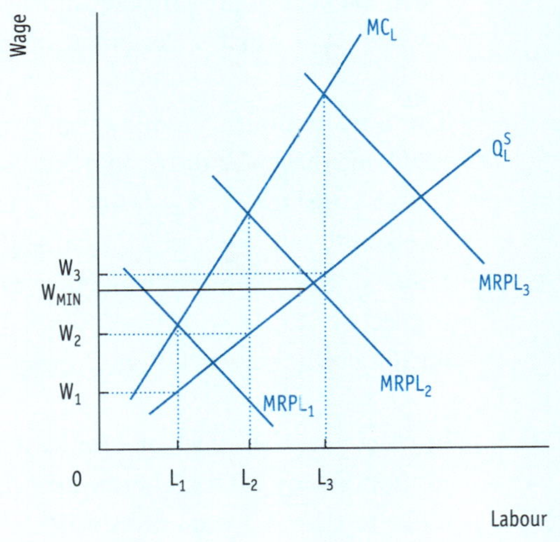

Figure 14.7 Inter-firm variations in productivity

Empirical evidence

In the UK context, a lot of attention has been given to the impact that a minimum wage would have on employment levels. In 1997, the British government set up a low pay commission, the LPC, to advise it on the rate for the national minimum (and what, if any, exemptions there should be).[13]

The simple theoretical analysis points to the sensitivity of the level at which a minimum wage is set when discussing its effect on employment. Those in favour of a NMW as a way of reducing wage inequality tend to discuss the rate in terms of a low-pay threshold, such as a half or two-thirds of (male) median earnings. What this means as a wage rate per hour varies considerably depending on the exact definition of the wage and also on the particular data source used to make the estimate. For example, taking the threshold as one half male median earnings, would have meant a NMW of £3.50 per hour, in April 1996 prices. A low-pay threshold of two-thirds of male median earnings would have meant a NMW of £4.80 per hour.[14]

Table 14.5 shows one estimate of the numbers of individuals earning less than £3.50 per hour in 1997 on a male/female break down and a full-time/part-time basis.

The table gives an estimate of the numbers based on the LFS; if there had been a NMW of £3.50 per hour in 1997 the data in the table suggests around 2.75mn individuals would have seen an increase in pay. There are however two main data sources for providing estimates

13 The LPC report can be downloaded free. Details are given at the end of the chapter.

14 Fernie and Metcalf (1996).

('000s)	
Male full-time	656
Male part-time	265
Female full-time	630
Female part-time	1219

Table 14.5 Estimated number of employees earning less than £3.50 per hour in 1997
Source: Low Pay Commission (1998).

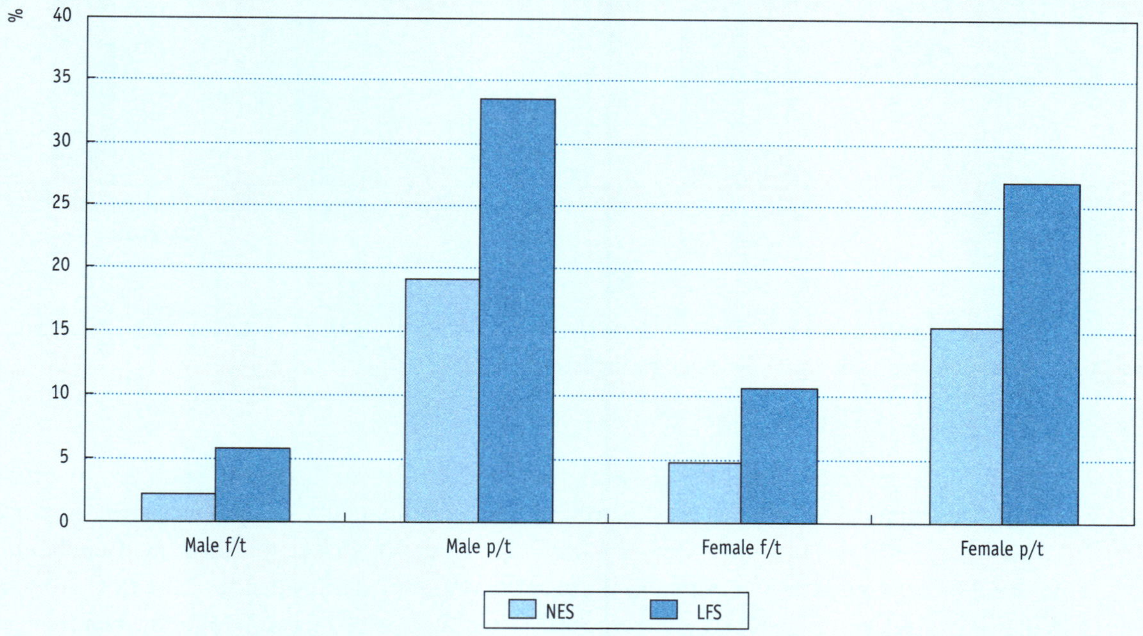

Chart 14.2 Estimates of % earning less than £3.50 per hour in 1997
Source: Low Pay Commission (1998).

of the numbers in low pay; the other is the New Earnings Survey and the estimates of the earnings distribution differ considerably between them. Chart 14.2 shows by how much.

The evidence is consistent to the extent that there were more female than male full-time employees than men earning less than £3.50 and that a higher proportion of the much smaller overall number of men in part-time work also earned less than this hourly rate. Chart 14.3 shows that the evidence is consistent in terms of which industries have the greatest concentrations of low paid workers, but again there are sizeable variations about the percentages affected.

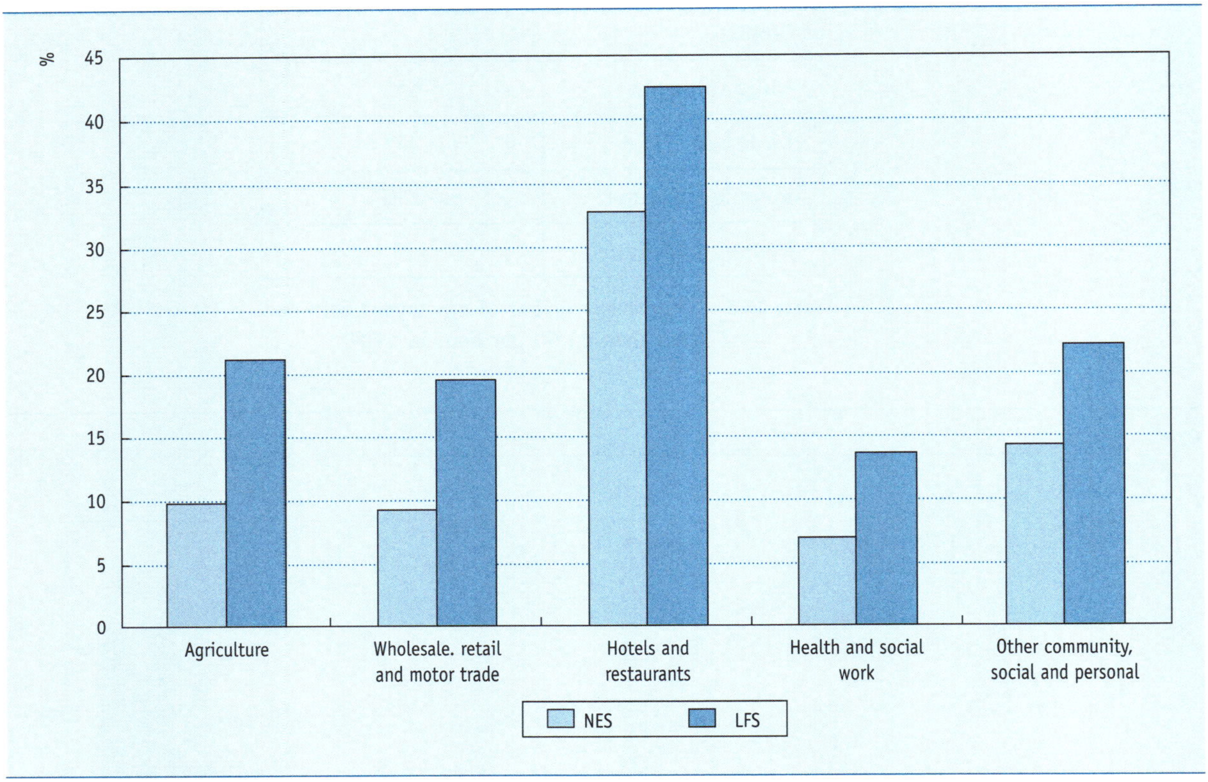

Chart 14.3 **% Earning less than £3.50 per hour by industry in 1997**
Source: Low Pay Commission (1998).

These differences led the LPC to work with the Office for National Statistics to provide adjusted estimates of the earnings distribution. The estimated % of the number of employees below certain thresholds are given in Chart 14.4, where it is clear that how many individuals would be affected is very sensitive to the exact NMW rate. The evidence of the LPC suggested that the direct cost of a NMW on the overall wage bill (in 1997 prices) doubles when the figure rises from around £3.50 to £4.25.

As to the groups of the workforce who would be affected, Table 14.6 provides some detail on this from a report by Fernie and Metcalf.[15]

The information in Table 14.6 provides an estimate of those who would be affected at one point in time. The extent of pay mobility is also relevant here, that is, the extent to which individuals move up and down the earnings distribution over their working lives. If there were no pay mobility at all, a proportion of all individuals would be on low pay for the entirety of

15 These are the characteristics of those with less than half median hourly earnings of full-time adult employees (both men and women).

Chart 14.4 Estimated % of employees below earnings threshold 1997
Source: Low Pay Commission (1998).

their working life and, at the other extreme, it is possible that all individuals have an equal period of time in a low paid job. Gosling *et al.* (1997) found that at one point in time 7% of employed men and 28% of employed women would be paid a NMW, if it was set at the one-half male median earnings threshold. Over a three-year time horizon, the effect of employment and wage mobility would mean 12% of men and over 40% of women would be affected. The experience of some individuals of moving between low paid employment and unemployment, known as churning, means that a NMW affects larger numbers than it would appear to do at any one particular time.

The effect of an NMW on employment

As we have seen, the simple analysis of the impact of a minimum wage leaves open the effect on the level of employment. The impact of an NMW may, of course, vary over time, so that introducing it in the 1990s might have different effects than if it had been introduced in the 1980s, or the 1970s. This could arise from changing wage and employment levels in particular industries over time, or because the firms who would be affected experience a change in the nature of the product market for their good or service.

It should be clear that assessing the effect of an NMW is not straightforward. An appreciation of the data sources, and descriptive information on which types of individuals, or which groups

Characteristic	Male	Female
All	8	24
Years of post compulsory education		
0	11	36
1–3	8	22
4+	3	9
Age		
18–20	43	46
21–25	12	22
26–35	6	20
36+	4	25
Race		
White	8	25
Non-white	12	13
Workplace		
Union recognition		
Yes	4	11
No	13	37
Industry		
Agriculture	30	35
Distribution, hotels and catering	20	44
Manufacturing	5	21
Banking and finance	3	10

Table 14.6 Percentage low paid by different groups
Source: Fernie and Metcalf (1996).

in the workforce would be affected, can only take us so far. We need to know what the effect of introducing an NMW would be, other things being equal. In principle, what we require is a controlled experiment in order to estimate its effects on employment (and other variables). Given the absence of such, we are left looking for some kind of substitute counterfactual.

In the context of the UK, one possibility is to look at the experience of the wages councils. Table 14.7 summarises the large number of studies that either examined the effect of wages councils on all the industries covered, or in some studies the effect in individual sectors.

Author	Sample	Definition of statutory minimum wage (SMW)	Elasticity of employment with respect to pay
Kaufman (1989)	1971–79, All wage council sectors.	Real SMW, i.e. SMW/product price	–0.06
Bazen (1990)	1968–93. 16 Industries (SIC)	% of male median pay.	–0.60
Dickens, Machin and Manning (1994)	1978–92. 12 Wages Councils	(SMW/Average) by sector	+0.15 to +0.54
Morgan *et al.* (1985)	1950–81 Clothing Industry	Real product SMW	–0.27
Canning and Tarling (1985)	1950–81 Clothing Industry	Real SMW, i.e. SMW/RPI	–0.05
Lund *et al.* (1982)	1960–80 Agriculture	Real product SMW	+0.03 to +0.45
Dickens *et al.* (1995)	Agriculture 1954–91	SMW/Average	+0.1 to +0.2
Machin and Manning (1994)	1979–90 10 Wages Councils	SMW/Average	Catering +0.99 Retail +0.60 Clothing +0.27 Hairdressing –0.45

Table 14.7 Impact of wages councils on employment
Source: Fernie and Metcalf (1996).

The studies listed in the table are all econometric investigations. This kind of investigation typically defines a wage variable that measures the effect of the wages council, which is then regressed on employment (together with other relevant variables). The model's coefficient on the wage variable is the basis for the estimated elasticity given in the fourth column in the table.

The studies can be divided into those that covered time periods up to 1980, and those that cover a later period. In the first group, the elasticity of employment with respect to pay is usually negative. To take the study of Bazen as an example, the estimated elasticity of employment with respect to pay is -0.60, so that a 10% increase in pay would result in a 6% reduction in employment in the industries covered. However, there are estimated elasticities for studies covering periods after 1980 (before in agriculture) which are positive, indicating an increase in pay would result in an increase in employment.

These findings might be taken as evidence that the monopsony model was more appropriate than the competitive one in the sectors covered by the study. However, as we have seen elsewhere, empirical evidence is often not conclusive. For example, it is difficult to know, a priori, what the length of time is between a change in the wage level and its full effect on employment. How long is the long-run? The positive elasticities could also be a statistical artefact from the estimated model. If, for instance, the wage variable was increased at a time when employment was rising then the econometric models may have reversed the direction of causation.

A study by Dickens and Manning (1995) examined the effects of the abolition of the wages councils after 1993. They set out to find whether the abolition of a system, that might have kept wage levels above the free market, had led to lower wages and higher employment levels. This does not give us a counterfactual as such, but does ask whether there is evidence to support a particular view of what might otherwise have been. They found that in the years after 1993, wages rose less quickly in some of the larger industries covered by the former wage councils — such as clothing, catering and retail — than they did in other industries. The effects on employment are again not easy to assess for the reasons mentioned. On a one-year time horizon, the share of employment in the industries mentioned was virtually unchanged: the numbers in employment rose from 2.444 million to 2.461 million, a rise of seventeen thousand. The empirical work on the employment impact of introducing a minimum wage evidently presents problems of interpretation. Although in the 1990s the balance of the evidence seems to have shifted away from those who argued that a NMW would necessarily have large negative consequences.

An NMW and pay differentials

What the impact of an NMW is on pay differentials is also an important issue. It is a subject that was considered in some detail by the LPC who looked at a range of evidence. If a firm's internal pay hierarchy is pyramid-shaped, the pressure to restore differentials may be great and the impact on the total wage bill could be important. However, this type of structure may be less typical than was once the case.[16]

Changes to pay bargaining arrangements also suggest that the response of those not directly affected may be limited. The coverage of trade unions has diminished as we have seen, and in many cases now bargain at an enterprise level, rather than on a national basis. As expressed by UNISON's evidence to the LPC

> 'in general, a minimum wage is unlikely to jack up differentials — in part because low-paid workers are often separated by contract or bargaining unit from others'.

---

16 The analysis of changing relative demands for skilled and unskilled labour in Chapter 13 suggests a diamond shape might be more appropriate for many firms.

Plainly, the effect on differentials will vary between industries. In the catering industry, for example, the effect may be more readily absorbed in increased prices as firms pass on higher costs to consumers. In clothing, and textiles, where suppliers face international competition, the effect on employment is likely to be greater. Given the distribution of low pay that we saw in Chart 14.3, some industries may experience a sizeable increase in their costs, which could lead to a growing concentration of activity in larger firms

An NMW and training levels

Another area of interest is the impact of an NMW on education and training levels. Would an NMW lead to a better trained, more productive workforce? In principle, firms could react to a minimum wage by additional training. This is an area where the age of the worker is important as Table 14.8 shows.

Age	Percentage in lowest 10% of wage earners
16–17	65
18–20	37
21–25	11

Table 14.8 Probability of low pay by worker age
Source: LPC (1998).

Around two-thirds of those aged 16–17 in employment are in the bottom decile of the wage distribution, a percentage figure that drops dramatically with age. The view taken by the LPC was that, given the importance of training to young workers and their concentration in some industries (hotel and catering for instance), those aged 16–18 should be excluded from the NMW, and those aged 18–20 should be paid at a lower rate.

Concluding comment

We have in this chapter seen the importance of differences in the abilities and characteristics of individuals in determining the distribution of wages. In analytical terms, this heterogeneity leads to problems of asymmetric information, which can be resolved by particular institutional mechanisms. The analysis of data on a range of subjects, such as the role of educational qualifications and the employment impact of an NMW shows that theoretical models we have discussed provide partial, though useful, insights. An understanding of data sources and data analysis helps to fill out the picture on what is and what is not known about the structure of wages.

Questions

Q4 Given the following market for labour.

$$Q_L^S = 9 + w$$

$$Q_L^D = 14 - w$$

Q_L^S Q_L^D are labour supply and labour demand, w is the wage rate per hour.

(I) What is the free market equilibrium wage and employment level?

(II) If the government imposed a minimum wage of £3 per hour what is the employment level? What is the level of unemployment? What would the effect be if the minimum wage were set at £4?

(III) What is the elasticity of employment with respect to wages paid between £3–4 per hour?

(IV) Suppose that the labour demand schedule is given by $Ld = 10 - w$, what would the elasticity of employment with respect to wages paid be?

Q5 A profit-maximising fast food outlet makes profits of £40 per hour employing 20 staff at £3 per hour prior to the introduction of a minimum wage. A statutory hourly minimum of £4 is introduced reducing profits to £20 per hour. Is it possible that employment in this profit-maximising firm will increase after the minimum is imposed, and if so, how?

Q6 Suppose the government decides to introduce an NMW and the labour market consists of two sectors. In the covered sector workers receive the NMW, in the uncovered sector they do not (because the activities are excluded or are not reported). Assuming that all workers have the same level of skill:

(I) What is the effect of the NMW on the wage rate and employment level if the market for labour is competitive?

(II) What is the effect on wage rates and employment levels if the covered sector is monopsonistic and the uncovered sector is competitive?

Summary

1 This chapter analyses why wage levels vary between individuals who differ in terms of their abilities, backgrounds and characteristics.

2 There are two views of the role played by education in determining wage levels. One view is that it raises the productivity of the individual directly. This is the human capital approach. A second view is that education is less costly to acquire for more capable individuals, who therefore use it as a signal to send to prospective employers.

3 In practice, the level of educational attainment of most individuals reflects a mixture of influences, some of which may be related to innate ability, some of which are not.

4 The quality of the workforce that a firm hires may depend on the wage rate paid. This is summarised by a wage-productivity relationship. A low-paid worker is not necessarily a low-cost worker to the firm, if he or she shirks on the job, or if there is a high labour turnover among the low-paid. This may lead firms to pay efficiency wages, which are above the competitive equilibrium rates.

5 A minimum wage above the free market equilibrium will create unemployment if the market is competitive. The extent of the unemployment will depend on the elasticity of demand and the elasticity of supply of labour for any given minimum rate. If the labour market is monopsonistic, it is possible that a minimum wage could raise, lower or have no effect on employment.

6 One way of trying to assess the effects of a national minimum wage in the UK is to look at the experience of the wages councils, which used to set minimum wages for individual industries (agriculture, clothing, retail and so on). Broadly the evidence from studies that have estimated employment-wage elasticities suggests that they may have changed over the period from the 1960s and 1970s through to the 1990s.

End of chapter questions

Q7 In the analysis of signalling the workforce is collectively worse off by the cost of signalling. Who gains from the process?

Q8 What is the rate for the NMW in the UK? Suppose the government had taken a figure based on a half male-median earnings in 1996 (£3.50) and increased it in line with (I) the Retail Price Index and (II) the Average Earnings Index, what would the rate be in the year you are reading this question?

Q9 The data in the table below give international minimum wage rates in terms of £ (cash amounts at purchasing power parity) and as a percentage of full-time median earnings.

Country	Rate (December 1997 £)	% Median earnings (mid-1997)
Australia	4.77	54
Belgium	4.56	50
Canada	3.80	40
France	3.97	57
Holland	2.41	49
Japan	4.27	31
New Zealand	3.18	46
Portugal	1.65	—
Spain	2.10	32
United States	3.67	38

The Low Pay Commission described the introduction of an NMW as a 'journey into uncharted waters' How useful do you think international comparisons would be in determining the minimum rate?

Q10 Should young-workers be exempted from a NMW?

Q11 In Chapter 3, we introduced the role of in-work benefits as a means of encouraging labour supply. This question asks to you study the interaction of the in-work benefit, the Working Family Tax Credit and the NMW.

Carol, a single parent with a 4 year-old son earned £3 per hour (in 1998/9 prices) in a job where she worked for 30 hours per week. She paid no income tax, but did pay 10% of her earnings above £64 per week in National Insurance Contributions.

(I) What was her net income?

For convenience, the structure of the WFTC is shown again in the table.

Basic tax credit	£48.80
Tax credit for each child aged 0–11	£14.85
" 11–16	£20.45
" 16–18	£25.40
30 hours credit	£10.80
Taper (percentage withdrawn)	55%

(II) What is her entitlement to WFTC? What is her total net income if she also receives Child Benefit of £13.95?

(III) Suppose now that the government introduces an NMW at a hourly rate of £3.60, what is the effect on her net income and her marginal tax rate? At what income level would she cease to be entitled to WFTC?

References and suggested further reading

Hillier provides a more theoretical discussion on the analysis of problems of asymmetric information. There are accessible summaries to the Blundell *et al.* and Dearden (1997) surveys available on the IFS web page, http//www.ifs.org.uk. Fernie and Metcalf have a helpful discussion on the likely impact of a NMW. Kennan provides a readable discussion of the work of Card and Krueger, albeit with a primarily US focus.

The Low Pay Commission Report of 1998 can be downloaded free from their website, http://www.lowpay.gov.uk and the treasury's website, http://www.hm-treasury.gov.uk is also useful for uptodate briefing on labour market incentives and reforms.

Blundell, R., Dearden, L., Goodman, A. and Reed, H. (1997), *Higher Education, Employment and Earnings in Britain*, Institute for Fiscal Studies, London.

Card, D.E. and Krueger, A.B. (1995), *Myth and Measurement: The New Economics of the Minimum Wage*, Princeton University Press, Princeton.

Dearden, L., Machin, S., Reed, H. and Wilkinson, D. (1997), *Labour Turnover and Work-Related Training*, Institute for Fiscal Studies, London.

Dickens, R., Machin, S. and Manning, A. (1994), 'Minimum Wages and Employment', *International Journal of Manpower*, **15**, 2/3.

Dickens, R. and Manning A. (1995), 'After Wages Councils' *New Economy*.

Employment Policy Institute (1996), 'Employers and a National Minimum Wage', *Economic Report*, **10**, No. 8.

Fernie, S. and Metcalf, D. (1996), *Low Pay and Minimum Wages: The British Evidence*, Centre for Economic Performance, LSE.

Gosling, A., Johnson, P., McCrae, J. and Paull, G. (1997), *The Dynamics of Low Pay and Unemployment in Early 1990s Britain*, Institute for Fiscal Studies, London.

Hillier, B. (1997), *The Economics of Asymmetric Information*, Macmillan.

Kennan, J. (1995), 'The Elusive Effects of Minimum Wages', *Journal of Economic Literature*, **33**.

Low Pay Commission (1998), *'The National Minimum Wage: First Report of the Low Pay Commission'*.

Machin, S. and Manning, A. (1994), 'The Effects of Minimum Wages on Wage Dispersion and Employment', *Industrial and Labour Relations Review*, **47**, 2, January.

Stiglitz, J.E. (1987), 'The Causes and Consequences of the Dependence of Quality on Price', *Journal of Economic Literature*, **25**.

15 Capital Markets and Investment by Firms

Key ideas and material

Capital structure and the cost of capital, asymmetric information and rationing of finance, empirical evidence on investment finance

Introduction

In this chapter, we will look more closely at the determinants of investment by firms. The neo-classical model of the demand for capital assumes that firms operate in a perfect capital market where they can borrow freely at the market rate of interest. That kind of analysis is primarily concerned with externally financed investment, borrowing from a bank for example, and led to the decision rule that firms should invest in a project as long as the present value of the associated revenue stream was greater than the cost.

We begin this chapter by looking in more detail at what affects the cost of financing an investment and consider whether there is a relationship between the cost of finance and the way in which it is obtained. This is the subject matter of Section 1. The investment decisions of firms may also depend on the availability of different types of finance. It is possible that a firm cannot obtain external debt finance and has to rely on generating funds internally through retained profits. In Section 2, we analyse the effect that asymmetric information in market for credit. We will look at the problem of (adverse) selection and the impact it has on the willingness of banks to provide loan finance. As with the discussion of efficiency wages in the previous chapter, this is another area in which the market price in the neo-classical framework may not operate to equate supply and demand.

Section 3 looks at some empirical evidence. We will make international comparisons between the so-called market-based system of which the UK and the US are given as examples, and the bank-based system associated with Germany and Japan. This is important if one system is more effective than another in funding investment projects. Although the discussion in this section points to a range of institutional and policy influences on the investment levels of firms.

15.1 The cost of capital and the firm's capital structure

In neo-classical analysis, the marginal revenue product of capital is equated to its rental rate to determine the firm's demand. We saw in Chapter 13 the need to discount the revenue streams from individual projects and we also discussed the impact of uncertainty on the timing of decisions. However, this discussion effectively assumed that investment projects were financed by external sources. In this section we will look at the firm's capital structure and the effect it has on the firm's cost of capital and investment decisions.

The cost of capital

The cost of capital relates to the costs of obtaining plant, equipment and other types of capital goods and can be expressed as

$$C = p(r + \delta - g)$$

where C is the cost of capital, p is the price of a unit of capital, r is the rate of interest, δ is the rate of depreciation and g is the rate at which the price of capital goods increases. The firm's decision-making is, therefore, related to the interest cost of borrowing, the rate of depreciation and variations in the price of capital goods. The effect of an increase in the first two is clearly to increase the cost of capital; the effect of a general increase in the price of capital goods works in the opposite direction.[1]

However, this refers to the cost of external finance (which may or may not be available) and it may differ from the cost of internally generated finance. This distinction between the two sources of finance brings us to the capital structure of firms.

The capital structure of firms

The capital structure of the firm refers to financial considerations, and more particularly to its level of debt and equity; the ratio of debt to equity gives what is known as the gearing ratio.[2]

1 The cost of capital is also referred to as the user cost of capital. The definition here ignores the existence of taxes and inflation. Refinements to allow for the tax treatment of interest payments, for example, can be made quite straightforwardly and are discussed under the tax shield below.

2 The capital structure forms a part of the firm's financial structure (which includes current liabilities and a detailed breakdown of its stock-holdings).

The cost of investing in physical capital will therefore depend on the capital structure of the firm, if the cost of finance from different sources varies. In principle, if there were a perfect capital market the rate of interest would be the same to both borrowers and savers. At its simplest, the returns to different types of assets would be equalised and so a firm raising funds for an investment project would pay the same to both a lender and a provider of equity.

In practice, capital markets are not perfect and the rate of return differs between assets. The cost of capital to a firm is, therefore, likely to vary depending on how much equity and how much debt finance is involved. What is sometimes called the traditional approach takes a weighted average of the cost of each source of finance.

Figure 15.1 shows the cost of capital in relation to the firm's gearing ratio following the traditional approach. As drawn in the figure, the cost of capital financed by equity is higher than the cost of debt finance. This is because it has a greater risk attached to it, given that debt payments have a prior call on a firm's revenues. A simple example in Table 15.1A illustrates this point.

Figure 15.1 The cost of capital and the gearing ratio (traditional approach)

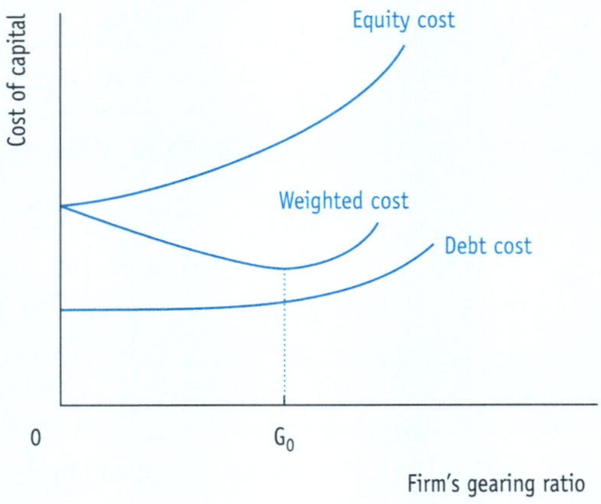

The firm has capital of £1mn, which we assume generates revenues of £150,000 per period. The rate of interest on borrowings is assumed to be 10%. Given the ratio of debt to equity shown in the second row, £50,000 is paid in debt interest. Those who lend to the firm are therefore sure of their return provided the firm's revenue is at least £50,000. The holders of equity in the situation shown in the table receive a return of 20%, but this return is clearly sensitive to the firm's revenue stream.

Suppose, for example, the firm's revenues were to double to £300,000 the return on equity would increase from 20% to 50%; if the revenues were to fall by half, the return on equity would

Capital	£1mn
Debt/equity ratio	50/50
Revenues	£150,000
Debt interest paid	£50,000
Return net of debt interest	£100,000
Return on equity	20%

Table 15.1A An example of a firm's capital structure

	Firm 1	Firm 2
Capital	£1mn	£1mn
Debt/equity ratio	50/50	90/10
Revenues	£250,000	£250,000
Debt interest paid	£50,000	£90,000
Return net of debt interest	£200,000	£160,000
Return on equity	40%	160%

Table 15.1B Gearing and the cost of equity finance

drop to 5%. The variation in the return on equity is evidently greater than the variation in the firm's revenues. The degree of risk to the providers of equity finance also rises when a firm's gearing ratio is higher. Table 15.1B gives an example.

The two firms have the same capital stock and generate the same revenues, but differ in terms of their gearing ratios. If, for example, both firms' revenue was 25% of the capital employed, the return on equity for Firm 1 would be 40% while that for Firm 2 would be 160%.

As revenues vary, the return on equity varies more for those with holdings in the more highly-geared firm. If, for example, the revenues of both firms fell to 10% of the capital employed, then the return to equity would be 10% for both firms. As there is a higher financial risk in holding equity in a more highly geared firm, other things being equal, the cost of equity finance will increase as the gearing ratio rises. This is what is shown in Figure 15.1. The higher the cost of equity to a firm, the greater the risk to those who lend to it and so as a firm gears up eventually the cost of debt will rise as well.

Figure 15.1 therefore shows the cost of finance from both sources increasing as the gearing ratio rises beyond a certain point. When the firm has no debt, the cost of capital is simply the cost of equity; this shown in the figure by the point of intersection on the vertical axis of the equity cost and weighted cost curves. As the proportion of debt increases relative to equity, the weighted average of the cost of debt and equity finance falls. The cost of capital falls up to the capital structure associated with the point marked G_0 in Figure 15.1. Beyond this point, the rising proportion of debt in the firm's capital structure leads to an overall increase in the cost of capital.

Modigliani-Miller

Given a perfect capital market and the absence of taxes, Modigliani and Miller (MM) argued that the cost of capital is independent of the firm's capital structure.

The essence of the proposition is illustrated in Figure 15.2. We saw above that debt finance is less risky to lenders than is equity so as the gearing ratio rises the cost of capital declines, other things being equal. However, we also saw before that an increase in the gearing ratio lead to an increase in the required return of those who provide equity finance. The firm's optimum capital structure will be where, at the margin, the increasing cost of equity finance is offset by the decreasing cost of debt finance. Overall, the cost of capital to the firm remains constant.

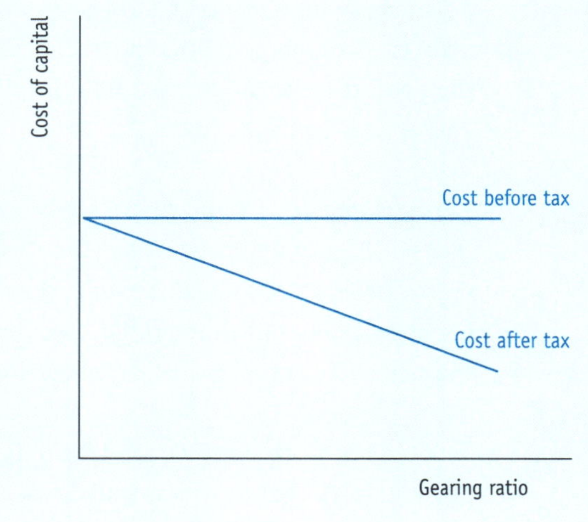

Figure 15.2 **The Modigliani-Miller argument**

The introduction of taxation alters this conclusion. If interest payments can be offset against tax, the cost of borrowing is reduced by a factor that depends on the (corporate) tax rate. A firm's tax bill will decline as the gearing ratio rises, and so the firm's net of tax returns per share will increase. It follows that as the debt to equity ratio rises, the shareholders' risk is limited by the effect of taxation on debt interest. This is known as the tax shield and as a result the required rate of return of shareholders is lowered.

Agency costs

The capital structure may also be important because of the different agency costs in raising debt and equity finance. We saw in Chapter 8 that a firm's management, acting as agents, may not necessarily follow the interests of the principals, the firm's shareholders. This led us to analyse executive share options as a way of aligning the interests of both parties. The existence of such work incentives is one reason for thinking that the firm's capital structure might affect the cost of capital.

Management may be inclined to award themselves generous perquisites and may shift the objectives of the firm in their own interests. Shareholders can attempt to monitor the behaviour of managers by auditing procedures but these can be costly, as can be the so-called 'bonding costs' which relate to expenditures by management to convince equity holders that they do act in accord with their interests.

Agency costs also bring us to problems that arise from asymmetries of information. There may be problems with hidden action if the lender is unable to observe what investment decision the firm makes until after loan finance has been given. For example, the managers of a firm may be tempted to invest in a very risky project with a large payoff, particularly if the firm is struggling. If the project is successful, the principal beneficiary will be the firm. If the project fails, the limited liability of the owners and/or managers of the firm means that the lender will bear the loss.

Lenders can try to anticipate such problems by including particular clauses in contracts with firms. These may concern the level of dividend paid that the holders of equity award themselves or, they may also require that a firm does not sell certain assets. There are, however, limits to the detail that can be specified in advance, and they clearly have to be consistent with the need for managers of organisations to act in a flexible and timely way.

The cost of both equity and debt may therefore vary with a firm's gearing ratio because of the agency costs that are incurred. Jensen and Meckling suggested a general relationship between agency costs and the firm's gearing ratio, which is depicted in Figure 15.3. This shows the agency cost of debt rising as the gearing ratio rises because of the incentives it presents to managers to undertake more risky investment projects. This cost will clearly reach an upper limit when the gearing ratio is at a maximum.

Conversely, the agency costs of equity will be at their greatest when all the firm's finance comes from outside equity, and reaches a minimum when the gearing ratio is at a maximum. Beyond

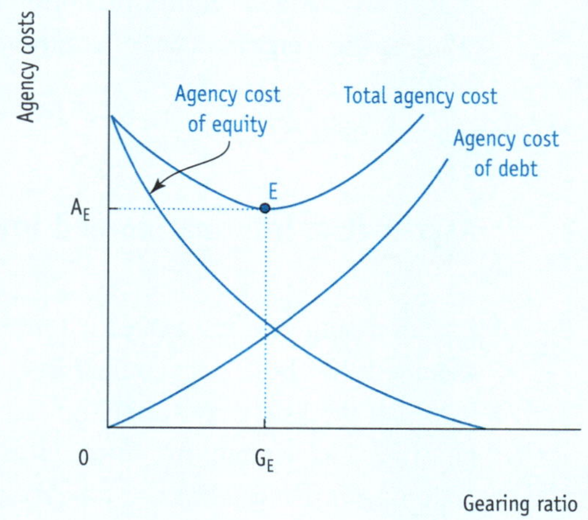

Figure 15.3 Agency costs and capital structure

a certain point, the marginal agency cost of debt exceeds the marginal agency cost of equity and 'the result of this is the generally observed phenomenon of the simultaneous use of both outside debt and equity' (Jensen and Meckling (1976)). This is illustrated in Figure 15.3 where the minimum agency cost occurs at point E, with agency costs, A_E, and a gearing ratio G_E.

Questions

Q1 Given the following capital structure of two firms

	Firm 1	**Firm 2**
Capital	£100,000	£100,000
Gearing (debt/equity)	60/40	40/60
Revenues	£25,000	£25,000
Return net of debt interest		
Return on equity		

(I) Assuming the rate of interest to be 10%, what are the return on debt interest and the return on equity for the two firms?

(II) What would you expect to happen to the return on equity for the two firms if the revenues of the two firms were to double? What would happen if they fell by a half?

(III) Suppose the interest paid on debt can be offset against a tax and that the tax rate is 20%. What happens to the return on equity in the answers to (I) and (II) above?

Q2 A firm with a debt equity ration of 1:4 faces a cost of debt of 6% and a cost of equity of 8%. What is the weighted cost of capital if the firm pays no tax on its debt? What is it if the tax rate is 20%?

15.2 Asymmetric information and investment finance

In discussing the impact of alternative methods of finance on the cost of capital we have assumed that both debt and equity is available to the firm. We will now analyse circumstances in which the firm may simply not be able to obtain debt finance for an investment project. It is possible that asymmetric information in the market for investment finance may lead to credit rationing, arising from the adverse selection problem.[3]

An increase in the rate of interest may affect the pool of applicants for a bank loan, as those firms seeking a loan at higher rates are conveying information to the lender that they are not able to obtain finance elsewhere. A higher proportion of firms seeking a loan may then be at the risk of default; so from the viewpoint of the lender the expected return on a loan may fall as the rate of interest rises. Firms with a low risk of default may be unable to obtain debt finance at a rate of interest at which banks would otherwise be prepared to lend to them.

There is a parallel with the analysis of efficiency wages in that quality again depends on price. The rate of interest acts as a selection mechanism for the lenders of capital to distinguish between the quality of different types of loan in terms of their riskiness, and in turn, the expected payoff. It is, therefore, possible (again) that in equilibrium quantity supplied does not equal quantity demanded. The rest of this section analyses this possibility in more detail.[4]

Credit rationing

Suppose that a firm is considering an investment with a cost of £10,000. It knows it will receive either a gross return of £15,000 with some probability, p, or alternatively that it will simply make enough to cover the initial outlay, with a probability of $1-p$. If, for example, the probability of the investment being successful is 0.5, then the expected return (or the expected revenue) to the firm is simply

$$E(R) = 0.5 * £15{,}000 + 0.5 * £10{,}000 = £12{,}500.$$

---

3 We first discussed adverse selection in the market for household insurance in Chapter 5.

4 This section draws much from Hillier (1997).

In words, the expected return to the firm of the investment project is a weighted average of the gross return when the project is successful and the initial outlay. In this case, it gives a figure of £12,500. To simplify, we will assume here that the firm knows the expected return on all the investments it considers, and further suppose that it has to borrow to raise all the funds for the investment.

The form of the contract between the firm and the bank that we will assume here is referred to as the standard debt contract.[5] This is a contract in which the borrower repays the sum borrowed and, but only if the investment is successful, an interest payment on the debt. If, for example, the interest rate charged on the loan was 12% then the outcomes are shown in the payoff matrix below.

	Successful investment	**Unsuccessful investment**
Gross return	£15,000	£10,000
Bank receives	£11,200	£10,000
Firm retains	£3,800	£0

Table 15.2 Payoff matrix for standard debt contract

In this case, the firm's expected profit from borrowing to finance a project is simply the gross return if successful, less the repayment, weighted by the probability of the investment being a success. In our example, this gives 0.5 * £3,800 = £1,900. The higher the interest rate on the loan, the greater the gross return needed for a positive expected profit. If, for example, the rate of interest charged by the bank was 100%, the gross return on the investment would need to rise to £20,000 plus £1 in order to make the expected profit positive. Rather obviously, the firm will wish to borrow from the bank as long as it expects to make a profit from doing so.[6]

The expected rate of return for the bank is simply the rate of interest charged, weighted by the probability that the investment it finances is successful. In the example, this is 0.5 * 12% = 6%. We will assume here that the bank is risk-neutral, and importantly that although it knows the expected return across projects, it does not know the probability of success on any individual investment. This leaves the bank with a selection problem in terms of which individual project it decides to finance.

In order to analyse this problem, we will assume that there are only two broad types of investment, both of which have the same expected return. We will take it that both types have

5 The use of the term standard here is a rather particular one, the rationale for it is taken up later.

6 Formally, this is known as the participation constraint of the firm.

an initial outlay of £10,000, which the firm recovers if the project is not successful. The two project types have different probabilities of a successful outcome and also different gross returns. For Type 1 projects, we will assume a 75% probability of being successful with a gross return of £13,333.33. Type 2 projects are as given before — a 50–50 chance of providing a gross return of £15,000. The expected return on both types of project is therefore £12,500.

Firms will choose to invest when the gross return is greater than the capital sum borrowed, plus the interest charged on it. Given that we are confining ourselves to projects with the same expected return, £12,500 in this case, the larger the gross return the smaller the probability that the investment will be successful. The interest rate in this situation acts as a selection mechanism to determine which firms decide to apply for a loan, and which do not. In our example, firms with the first type of project make a profit if the rate of interest charged on the bank loan is less than 33.3%, but drop out of the market when it exceeds this level. Firms with the second type of project make a profit as long as the rate of interest charged is less than 50%, but then drop out of the market when rates rise above it.

As the interest rate rises the firms with the less risky investments — those with a higher probability of being successful — are the first to drop out of the market. This is illustrated in Figure 15.4, which gives the demand curve for loans. In this instance, it is a step function; at interest rates up to 33.3% firms with both types of projects will be seeking a loan, at interest rates above 33.3% up to 50% only firms with the second type of project will apply.

Turning to the supply of loans, we will for simplicity treat banks as costless organisations that operate in a competitive market. In equilibrium, the deposit rate that they pay to suppliers of funds will equal the expected rate of return from making loans to firms. As indicated, the

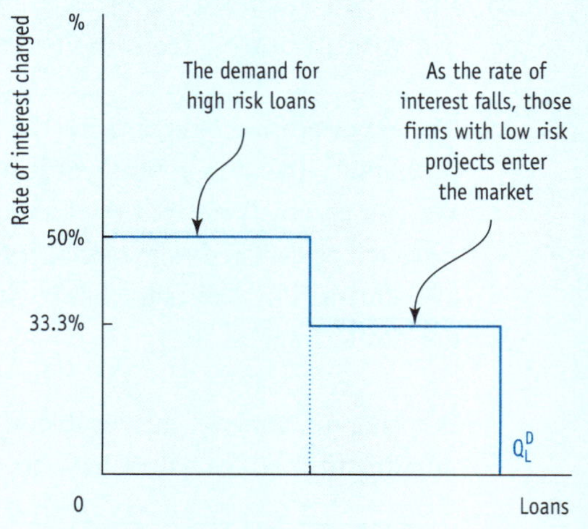

Figure 15.4 The demand for loans

expected rate of return to a bank differs from the rate charged on loans because some loans are not successful (and under the standard debt contract they would receive no interest). An increase in the rate of interest has the obvious effect that it increases the interest received on any given successful investment. Since it also acts a selection mechanism, firms that are more likely to be successful will withdraw from the market as the rate of interest increases, raising the possibility that the expected return to the bank may fall.

Equilibrium in the loan market

We are now in a position to examine the outcome in the market for bank loans. Figure 15.5A shows the relationship between the expected return to the bank and the rate of interest it charges. Type 1 projects give a higher expected return at any rate of interest charged, since this type of project has a greater probability of being successful. The line marked I_1 represents the relation for Type 1 projects and therefore lies above I_2, which represents the relation for Type 2 projects.

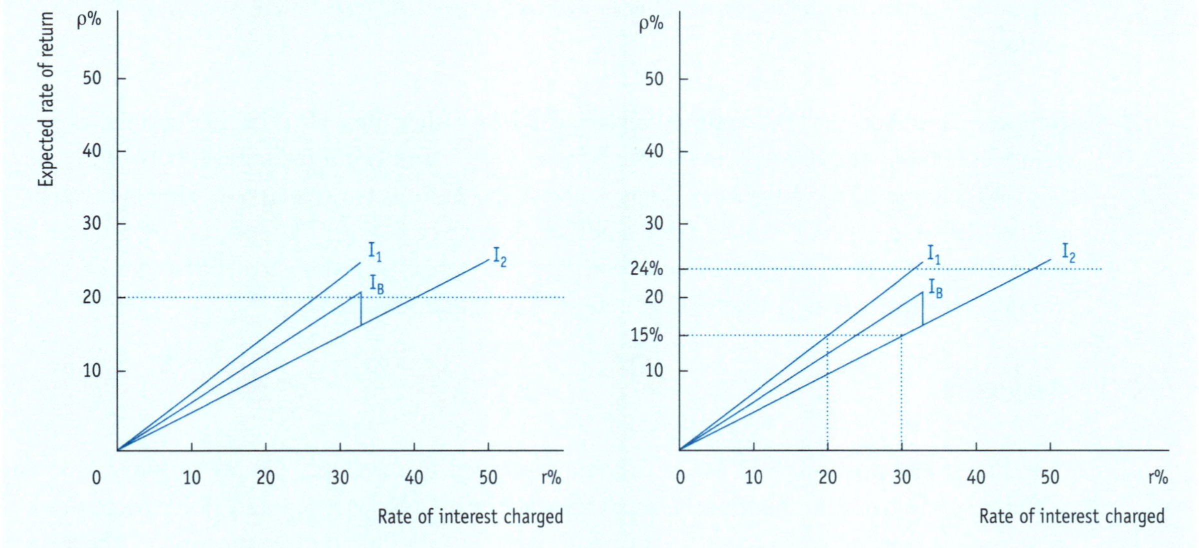

Figure 15.5A The relationship between the rate of interest charged and the expected rate of return to the bank

Figure 15.5B The selection problem

The I_1 line does not go beyond a rate of interest charged of 33.3% because, above that level firms with this type of project do not seek loan finance. The point at which this happens for firms with Type 2 loans is at an interest rate of 50%. The line I_B gives the expected return for the bank at given rates of interest; if there were equal numbers of the two types of projects then it would lie halfway between I_1 and I_2 until $r = 33.3\%$. This is how it is drawn in the figure.

The I_B line shows a positive relation between the expected rate of return and the rate of interest charged on loans until the latter reaches 33.3%. At this point, the expected rate of return to the lender is approximately 20.8%. As the rate of interest charged rises to 33.4% and the Type 1 projects drop out of the market, the expected rate of return drops to approximately 16.7%. This is shown by the vertical section of the I_B line. The positive relation then resumes until the rate of interest charged is 50%, the I_B and I_2 lines coincide above $r = 33.3\%$.

If the lender can distinguish between the two types of loan, then to obtain a return of 15%, for example, the bank would need to charge Type 1 projects 20% and Type 2 projects 30%. This is shown in Figure 15.5B by the intersection of the horizontal line associated at $\rho = 15\%$ with the two lines I_1 and I_2. When the bank cannot distinguish between the two types of project, it has to charge a common rate of interest of 24%. Why 24%? This gives $\rho = 15\%$ since there is a 75% chance that the bank gets a rate of interest of 24% from the firms with Type 1 projects, and a 50% chance they get 24% from those with Type 2 projects. Given that we have assumed equal proportions of firms with each project type, this gives us the expected return of 15% from the common rate of interest of 24%. Firms with Type 1 projects pay a higher rate of interest than when the bank can distinguish between project types and effectively subsidise the Type 2 projects.

Suppose, however, that the required return was 24% rather than 15%. In this case the expected return lies above the broken part of the I_B line. If the bank could distinguish between projects it would charge 32% and 48% to Type 1 and Type 2 projects respectively. However, when it cannot tell one type of project from another, it cannot charge a single rate of interest and finance both types of project. A common rate of interest to firms with both types of project would drive those with a low risk of default out of the market.

Rationing

To analyse the possibility of credit rationing we need to develop a supply of loans schedule, which is done from the relation between the rate of interest charged and the expected rate of return discussed above. Figure 15.6A re-draws this relation. If deposits rise as the rate of interest paid to depositors rises, the supply of loans will be as drawn in Figure 15.6B. The horizontal segment in the supply curve showing a fall in the supply of loans corresponds to the vertical segment in the ρ–r relation drawn in the previous figure. As the interest rate charged rises, above 33.3% in our example, the expected return to the bank falls, as does the rate of interest paid to depositors. Hence the fall in the supply of loans.

In Figure 15.7, we bring together the supply and demand schedules for loans that we have developed. To illustrate the possibility of credit rationing in our example, we will now make the assumption that the number of firms with Type 1 projects is small in relation to the total

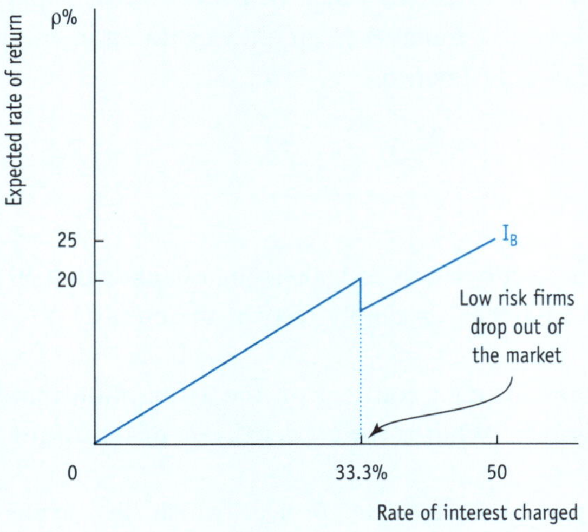

Figure 15.6A **The ρ–r relationship**

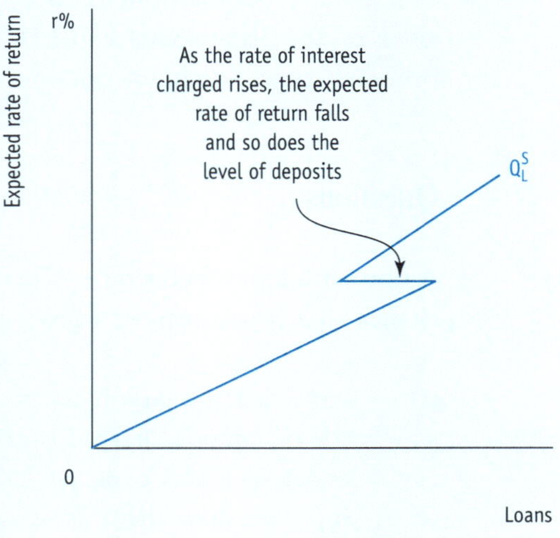

Figure 15.6B **The supply of loans schedule**

Figure 15.7 **Rationing in the credit market**

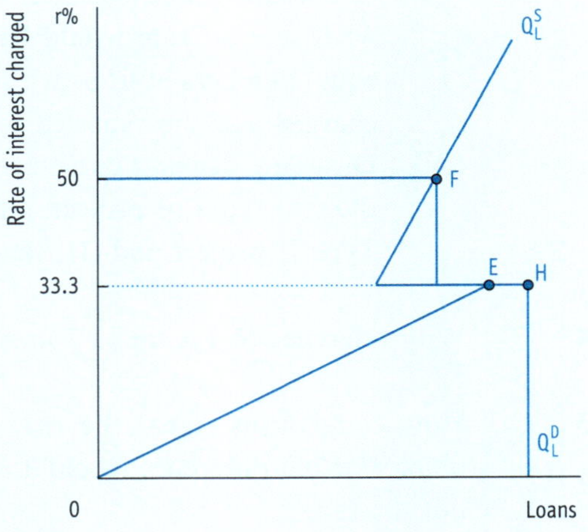

number of firms. This means that the demand function for loans has a much longer horizontal segment at r = 50% and this is how it is drawn in Figure 15.7.

In the figure, the supply and demand for loans are equal to one another at point F. However point E will be the competitive market equilibrium because there is a higher supply of loans than at point F, and a higher rate of interest is paid to depositors. At the rate of interest where the horizontal segments of the supply and demand schedules coincide, it is apparent that demand exceeds supply. The equilibrium point, therefore, implies rationing the availability of debt finance between prospective borrowers. The extent to which demand exceeds supply is given by the distance marked EH. Some firms will be unable to go ahead with an investment project because it cannot obtain the necessary debt finance.

Questions

Q3 A firm with a particular type of investment project borrows £50,000 from a bank with a 50–50 chance that it will receive a gross return of £100,000, or simply recover the outlay.

(I) Construct the payoff matrix for a standard debt contract on the assumption that the rate of interest charged on the loan is 20%. What is the expected rate of return for the lender with this contract?

(II) Suppose that there is a second type of investment project which the lender is considering where the firm borrows £50,000 and there is a 90-10 chance that it will receive a gross return of £77,777, or simply recover the initial outlay. What is the expected return on lending to the firm with the second type of investment project?

(III) At what interest rates would firms from the two types of investment project be willing to borrow from the lender? In order for the lender to obtain an expected return of 20% what interest rate would have to be charged to the two types of investment (assume equal numbers of firms with each)? What is the relationship between the rate of interest charged and the expected return to the lender?

(IV) Draw the demand curve for loans on the assumption that there are equal numbers of the two types of project, and (I) that there is a 75%–25% split between a Type I and Type II project and (II) that there is 90%–10% split.

Q4 With reference to Figure 15.7 in what circumstances would there be no credit rationing?

Q5 How could firms signal the riskiness of their investment project to the suppliers of loan finance? What difference would it make if the expected returns of the investment projects were not the same?

15.3 Empirical evidence

The first two sections have pointed to the firm's capital structure, and the possibility of credit rationing as influences on the investment decisions made by firms. The analysis suggested in a general way that there may be a difference between the cost of capital that is raised internally and that which is raised from external sources. The presence of asymmetric information, costly monitoring of the behaviour of agents and other difficulties make internal and external funds imperfect substitutes.

In this section, we will consider some of the empirical evidence on the determinants of firm's investment decisions. We begin by looking at international evidence on the sources of finance for fixed investment (plant and machines). The globalisation of financial markets has reduced the cost differences in obtaining some types of finance, although institutional features of individual countries remain important.

One distinction that is sometimes made is between the so-called 'market-based' system of the UK/US and the 'bank-based' systems of continental Europe and Japan. Table 15.3A gives some details on the sources of investment finance for these countries.

	United States	United Kingdom	Japan	Germany
Internal finance	96.1	93.3	69.9	80
Bank finance	11.1	14.6	26.8	10.8
Bond finance	15.4	4.2	3.9	–1.4
New equity	–7.6	–4.6	3.5	0.2

Table 15.3A Financing of fixed investment 1970–94
Source: Bond and Jenkinson (1996).[7]

The data in Table 15.3A relates to the financing of new investment. In the UK, and the US, there is heavy reliance on internal finance for new fixed investment; whether this is a result of problems in the system of external finance, or simply due to a lack of demand for investment finance is an open question on this evidence. It is also clear that bank financing is more important in Japan than elsewhere, including Germany.[8] In Japan, more than a quarter of new fixed investment was financed by the issue of bank debt or in the form of bonds.

In addition to data on finance for new investment, the gearing ratio of companies will inform how the capital stock has been financed. Table 15.3B shows (balance sheet) measures of company gearing for 1991.

The evidence of the two data sources should be broadly consistent since, in principle, the (physical) capital stock of firms is the accumulation of past investment decisions. Given the varying importance of debt-finance we should expect to see the highest gearing ratio in Japan and the lowest ratio in Germany. Table 15.3B broadly confirms this.

7 German figures are until 1992. The figures do not add up to 100 as some categories of finance such as trade credit and capital transfers are omitted.

8 The importance of bank lending in Japan declined from over 40% to under 20% over the period.

9 The numbers are sensitive to the particular method of measuring the gearing ratio. In addition to the book value which the numbers in Table 15.3B show, there is also a market valuation. This makes a large difference to the figure for Japan, which would then be 28% rather than 49% on this method.

(Balance Sheet)				
	United States	**United Kingdom**	**Japan**	**Germany**
Book value	45	19	49	10

Table 15.3B Measures of gearing 1991
Source: Rajan and Zingales (1995).[9]

The evidence points to the dominant role played by internal finance in the UK, US and Germany. Banks play a proportionally much smaller role in providing investment finance and on the time horizon of a quarter of a century the equity markets in the UK and the US actually made a negative contribution to investment finance.[10] The evidence on Japan provides some basis for thinking of it as a bank-based system.

Internal finance is fundamentally the re-investment of shareholders' money on their behalf by the management of the firm. The desirability of this hinges on the effectiveness of management investment decisions, and in turn, the way in which investors monitor managers. This is an area where practice varies between countries. The hostile take-over of one company by another has been almost unknown in Germany and Japan, but (at least the threat of it is) widespread in the US and the UK. It is certainly possible that a constant threat of a hostile take-over is likely to encourage short-term decision-making and that this may be at the expense of long-term investments.

The study by Prowse, from which Table 15.4 is taken, gives the background on a long-view. There has been some reduction in the number of hostile takeovers in the US by the end of the 1990s. In the UK, there is little monitoring by banks, little or no cross-monitoring between companies and the ownership of assets by institutional investors is highly dispersed.[11] This leads to a low threat of challenge to the incumbent management. The exercise of corporate control is largely via the threat of the take-over market. The extent to which this influences investment decisions is another open question: if managers do not expect to benefit the level of investment may be reduced. If there is inflexibility on the level of dividend payout required then this may worsen the problems with obtaining external sources of finance.

Other influences

A source of information on the factors affecting investment in the UK is the CBI Industrial Trends Survey. This is a quarterly survey of between 1,200 and 1,500 firms and asks them to

10 These figures are aggregates. Overall the negative numbers are partly the result of takeover and merger activity. If a firm uses its cash flow to buy the equity of another company and issues no additional equity, this will produce a negative figure for equity.

11 Evidence for this was presented in Chapter 8.

Mechanism	United States	United Kingdom	Japan	Germany
Board independence/power over management	Little	Little	Little formally More influence informally through President's Club	Greatest
Importance of pay/ performance in top management compensation package	Small	Small	Less	Important for owner-managed firms
Frequency of hostile take-overs	Frequent	Frequent	Virtually non-existent	Virtually non-existent

Table 15.4 Importance of corporate control mechanisms
Source: Prowse (1994).

report what limits their investment spending. Table 15.5 gives the results of this survey over the period 1985–96.

The two factors that were most often mentioned are an inadequate net return on the investment, and the uncertainty over demand. The cost of finance was mentioned directly by a much smaller percentage though the importance given to the rate of return does suggest that firms take account of both interest rates and tax rates.

	1985–90	1991–6	1985–96
Inadequate net return	44.8	43.8	44.3
Uncertainty about demand	36.5	52.2	44.3
Shortage of internal finance	19.5	23.8	21.7
Cost of finance	11.8	6.7	9.3
Inability to raise external finance	1.7	3.3	2.5
Labour shortages	6.0	5.0	5.5

Table 15.5 Factors limiting UK investment 1985–96 (%)
Source: Bond and Jenkinson (1996).[12]

12 The firms are asked 'what factors are likely to limit (wholly or partly) your capital expenditure authorisations over the next months?' Clearly the numbers in each column do not have to add up to 100%.

Conclusion

The simple neo-classical analysis of factor markets emphasises the role of the (rental) cost of capital in the context of a perfect capital market. This is a very limited view of the nature of investment decisions taken by firms in the UK and in other industrialised countries. In this chapter, we have broadened the discussion to take account of alternative sources of investment finance.

We have analysed the possibility that the rate of interest will not equate the supply and demand for loans, when the market is characterised by asymmetries of information between lender and borrower. The empirical evidence points to a range of institutional and policy factors that are important to varying degrees in OECD countries. Whether there is a problem with under-investment among UK firms remains a moot point. The sceptics of the Anglo-American system point to the potential conflict between the need for making short-term profits and the needs for long-term investments. On a long view, the share of GDP going to investment in gross fixed capital formation in the UK and the US, and to a lesser degree the other Western European countries, is lower than in Japan. These differences may or may not matter. Some of the issues relating to this subject are taken up in the question that follows.

Question

Q6 The levels of investment as a share of GDP in Germany, Japan the UK and the US are given below.

	Germany	Japan	UK	US
1960–93 gross fixed capital formation	22.4	31.3	18.1	18.4
GFCF: machinery and equipment	8.7	12.4	8.4	7.6
1980–93 gross fixed capital formation	20.5	29.7	17.3	18.2
GFCF: machinery and equipment	8.6	11.5	8.0	8.0

(I) These figures are taken from OECD Historical Statistics (1995). They include investment expenditure by both the public and private sectors. Do you think that from the viewpoint of analysing the level of investment that this is an appropriate measure?

(II) Are there any reasons why the data in the table may not give a good guide to the level of investment in the countries mentioned?

(III) Would it make more sense to measure the rate of growth of capital stock, rather than relate investment to the level of output? If so, why?

(IV) In the UK, the level of investment in manufacturing has been lower than in other OECD countries. Does this matter, or are there plausible explanations for why it does not?

Summary

1 The simple neo-classical model of investment assumes that firms can borrow freely in a perfect capital market. At its simplest, firms invest up to the point where the cost of borrowing equals the marginal revenue product of capital.

2 A firm's capital structure is concerned with the level of debt and equity. A higher ratio of debt to equity is referred to as a higher gearing ratio. A starting point for analysis of the firm's investment decisions is whether or not the cost of capital varies with the gearing ratio. The traditional approach, which involves simply taking a weighted average of the cost of debt and equity, suggests that it does.

3 An alternative point of view was put forward by Modigliani and Miller who argued that the firm's capital structure would be irrelevant to the cost of capital in a perfect capital market. In their analysis, the rising cost of equity when the gearing ratio rises is exactly offset by the lower cost of debt finance.

4 More recent ideas of economists have stressed the importance of asymmetries of information. The analysis of Section 2 showed that when the rate of interest indicates the 'quality' of a loan to the lender, i.e. its riskiness, it is possible that there may be credit rationing in equilibrium.

5 The analysis of this chapter suggests that for some firms the cost of external finance is greater than that of internal finance. An increase in the rate of interest will therefore work through several channels. It will have its impact on the cost of capital viewed straightforwardly; it will also lead to an increase in the cost differential between internal and external finance.

6 The empirical evidence suggests that investment by Japanese firms in the recent past relied more on banks as a source of finance than was the case in the US, or Europe (at least as far as Germany and the UK is concerned). This may be a part of the explanation for the different levels of investment in OECD countries.

End of chapter questions

Q7 What do the investment criteria discussed in Chapter 13 assume about the availability of finance for investment?

Q8 Write out an equation for the cost of capital such as that in Section 1 to allow for the differential cost of debt and equity finance and differential tax treatment. If you were running a small business, would increasing the size of your mortgage be a good way of raising finance for investment?

Q9 Is the cost of capital to a mutually-owned financial intermediary less than that for an organisation with PLC status?

Q10 This question and the next one cover the background to the standard debt contract on which the analysis of Section 2 was based. You will need to read Hillier (1997) Chapter 3 before attempting this question.

The cost of an investment project is £10,000 and the return is uniformly distributed between £10,000 and £30,000. The bank cannot observe the actual project return without monitoring the firm at a cost of £3,000.

(I) What is the expected return on an individual project?

(II) Suppose the bank decides to offer a contract to fund the project for 90% of whatever the project yields, what is its expected return? What is the problem with this? What is the expected return to the bank after allowing for monitoring costs?

(III) What rate of interest would the suppliers of funds have to receive to ensure that the banks breakeven? Assume that, as in Section 2, they are costless organisations

Q11 (I) What is the maximum payoff to a bank when it offers a contract such as that in Q4 and monitors the firm's return?

(II) What project return would give the bank the same return when it does not monitor the firm?

(III) If the firm knows this critical value for the project return how would you expect it to adjust its behaviour? What contract can the bank offer the entrepreneurs without affecting payments to the bank? What are the gains to the parties involved?

(IV) If the banks engaged in competition how could they improve the terms available to the firms?

References and suggested further reading

The text by Hillier presents a more formal theoretical analysis of the role of asymmetric information in the market for investment finance. The survey article by Stiglitz draws parallels between the analysis of labour market and credit markets. Bond and Jenkinson provide a readable survey of empirical evidence.

Bond, S. and Jenkinson, T. (1996), 'The Assessment: Investment Performance and Policy', *Oxford Review of Economic Policy*, **12**, 2.

Hillier, B. (1997), *The Economics of Asymmetric Information*, Macmillan.

Jensen, M.C. and Meckling, W.H. (1976), 'Theory of the Firm: Managerial Behaviour, Agency Costs and Ownership Structure', *Journal of Financial Economics*, **3**, pp 305–60.

Modigliani, F. and Miller, M.H. (1958), 'The Cost of Capital, Corporation Finance and the Theory of Investment', *American Economic Review*, **48**.

Moschandreas, M. (1994), *Business Economics*, Routledge.

OECD: Organisation for Economic Co-operation and Development (1995), *Economic Outlook, Historical Statistics 1960–93*, Paris.

Prowse, S. (1994), 'Corporate Governance in an International Perspective', *BIS Economic Papers*, Basle.

Rajan, R.G. and Zingales, L. (1995), 'What do we know about Capital Structure? Some Evidence from International Data', *Journal of Finance*, **50**(5).

Stiglitz, J.E. (1987), 'The Causes and Consequences of the Dependence of Quality on Price', *Journal of Economic Literature*, **25**.

General Equilibrium and Social Welfare

16 General Equilibrium Analysis

Key ideas and material

Simple general equilibrium models, general equilibrium including production, social welfare analysis, the role of the state

Introduction

Parts 1–3 of this book have been concerned with what is known as partial equilibrium analysis. This deals with individual markets in isolation, ignoring the interdependencies between them. However, the links between markets can be large and important. For example, with the introduction of digital technology on televised sport, in partial equilibrium analysis the effect would be analysed simply in terms of the television market alone. The changes in television clearly have direct consequences for the market for live sport and in the related (factor) markets for players, agents and managers and in the market(s) for other types of entertainment.

General equilibrium analysis takes account of the inter-relationships between markets. We will begin this chapter with a simple example in Section 1, using the familiar supply-demand framework by way of an introduction. We then examine in some detail the role of exchange between individuals and the price mechanism in a market economy. In Section 2, we subsequently develop the analysis in a more complete model of the economy.

This leads us to the large question of whether a system of competitive markets will lead to socially desirable allocations of the available goods and services. We will begin to discuss questions of social welfare in Section 3 and particular issues are taken up in the following chapters. Chapter 17 deals with externalities, which can be viewed as one type of market failure; Chapter 18 addresses issues of equity between individual households.

16.1 A simple general equilibrium model

We will begin with a simple example to illustrate the need for general equilibrium analysis. Figures 16.1A and 16.1B show the markets for travel from London to Paris by air and by rail respectively. The initial point of equilibrium is shown as E_0, with OQ_0 passengers travelling both ways.[1]

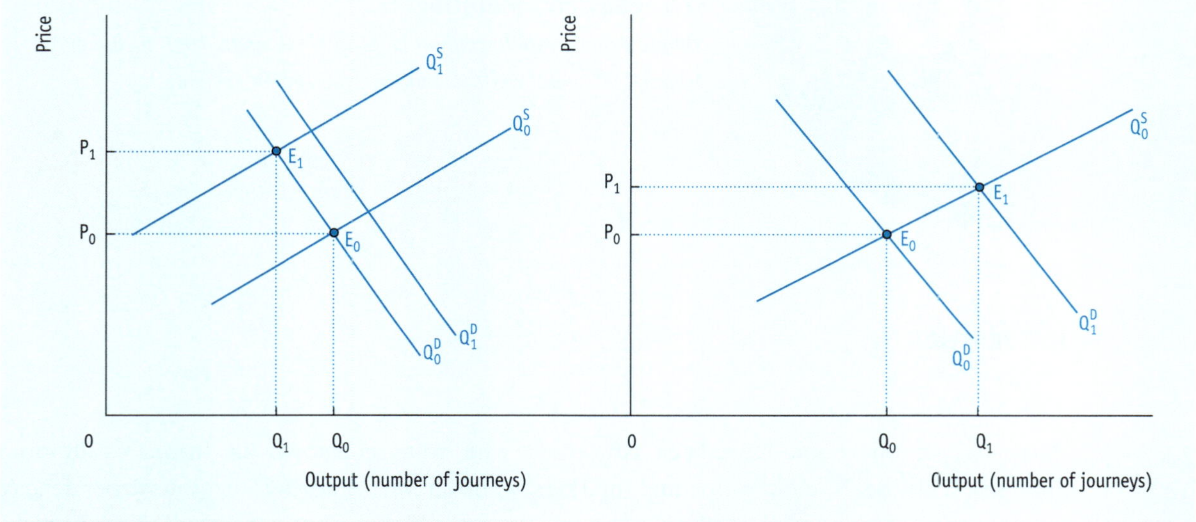

Figure 16.1A The market for air travel **Figure 16.1B The market for train travel**

Suppose the government was to impose an airport tax. In Figure 16.1A, the effect of this is to shift the supply curve from Q_0^S to Q_1^S, reflecting the increased cost of travel by air. Given conventionally shaped supply and demand curves, the price of air travel will rise, from P_0 to P_1 as shown, and the number of journeys contracts to Q_1. In partial equilibrium analysis, this piece of comparative statics is the end of the matter as far as the market for air travel is concerned.

Here, we will allow for the repercussions in the market for train travel. The rise in the price of air travel will increase the demand for train travel, other things being equal. This is shown by the shift in the demand curve for rail travel out to Q_1^D in Figure 16.1B, with new equilibrium price P_1 as shown. The price has risen in both markets, but the numbers travelling by rail have risen; by how many will depend on the cross-price elasticity of demand between the two forms of transport.

1 In practice, there are, of course, detailed pricing structures for travel by both air and rail. The background to this was discussed in Chapter 10.

The demand for air travel is, of course, drawn for a given price of train travel. Now the price of rail journeys has increased, there will be a rightward shift in the demand curve for air travel in Figure 16.1A from Q_0^D to Q_1^D as drawn. These interactions will continue, depending on the elasticities of supply and demand in the individual markets, and also the cross-price elasticity of demand. The extent of these subsequent shifts in demand will then determine the new equilibrium outcome. In general equilibrium, the prices in both markets will ensure that supply equals demand in both markets. Following a price rise, a partial equilibrium analysis will tend to understate the rise in the equilibrium price when the two goods are substitutes.

An exchange economy: the Edgeworth box

In order to look at the nature of general equilibrium analysis in more detail we will go back to the fundamentals of exchange between individuals. To begin with, a simple model that only involves consumption decisions, known as an exchange economy. We will confine ourselves to a model with two individuals and two goods; the two individuals we will refer to as Catherine and David, who live quite happily trading quantities of bagels and whisky. To help with the analysis we will use a box diagram, such as that in Figure 16.2, known as an Edgeworth box.[2]

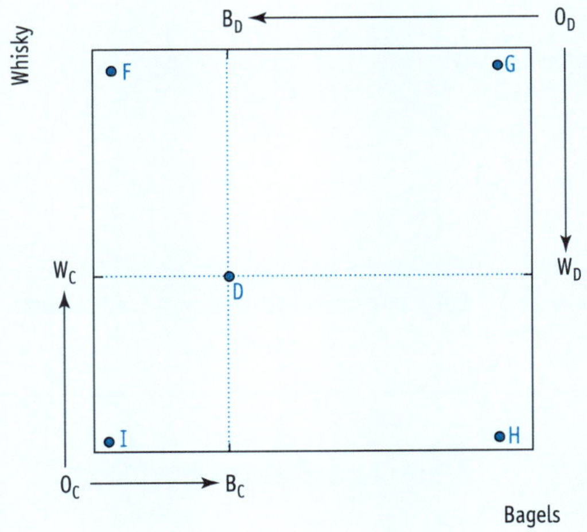

Figure 16.2 The Edgeworth box

In the absence of production, the individuals are given endowments of the two goods, the quantities of which are measured on the axes in Figure 16.2. Catherine is shown with the south-west corner as her point of reference, with David's position shown with reference to the north-east. Any point in the box represents a particular allocation of the two goods. For

2 We introduced this type of diagram in the discussion of work incentives in Chapter 8.

example, point D gives O_cB_c of bagels and O_cW_c of whisky to Catherine. The remainder goes to David. Point D is, of course, completely arbitrary; we could have chosen any other point in the box as the endowment point for the two individuals. Clearly, there would be different distributional implications; at point F for example, Catherine has nearly all of the whisky and David has nearly all of the bagels. At point H, the proportion of the two goods that each individual has is reversed. At point G, in the north-east corner, Catherine has nearly all of both goods. At a point such as I, in the south-east corner, it is David that has nearly all of both goods.

The next step is to introduce the preferences of the two individuals. Figure 16.3 shows the indifference maps of the two individuals drawn in an Edgeworth box. We will again be assuming that the two goods are substitutes, and that the preferences of the two individuals can be represented by indifference curves that are convex to their respective origins. For Catherine, indifference curves moving away from the south-west origin represent higher levels of utility. For David, higher utility levels are associated with moving towards it.

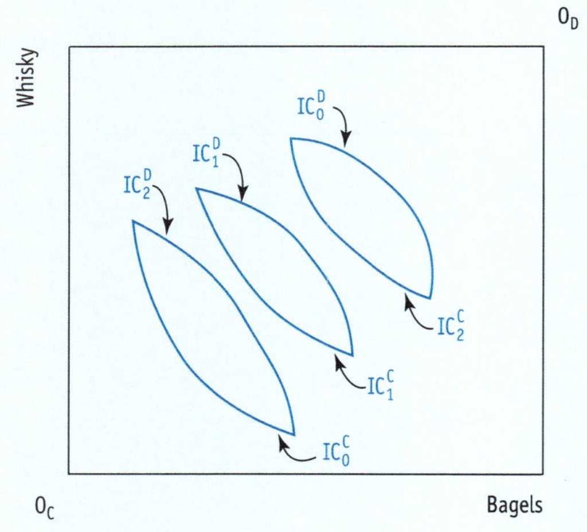

Figure 16.3 **Consumer preferences in an Edgeworth box**

Trade and Pareto-optimality

To see why trade might take place look at Figure 16.4. The endowment point D is on the indifference curve IC_0^C for Catherine, IC_0^D for David. Catherine is on the steep part of her indifference curve, so her marginal rate of substitution of whisky for bagels is relatively high. She has a relatively large endowment of whisky, and would be willing to trade relatively large amounts of the drink for some additional food. David is on a relatively flat part of his indifference curve, and his marginal rate of substitution of whisky for bagels is relatively low. His willingness to exchange drink for bagels is less than is that of Catherine at the endowment point.

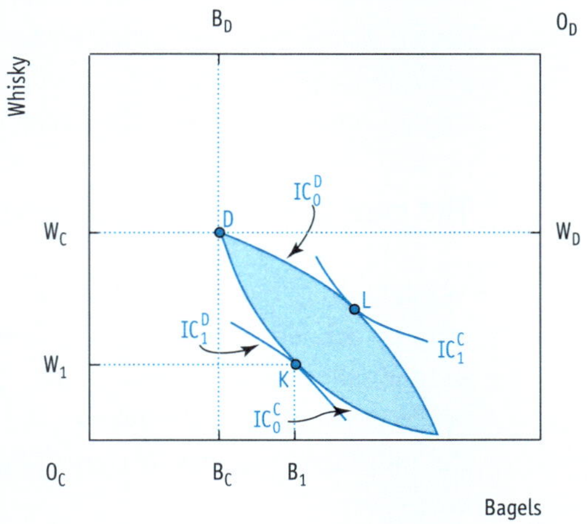

Figure 16.4 **The region of mutual advantage**

This particular initial allocation that they have been given is not optimal. Either, or both, of them could obtain a higher level of satisfaction by trading, Catherine by exchanging whisky for bagels and David by doing the opposite. The area that is bound by the two indifference curves that meet at point D gives us a region of mutual advantage and with it the opportunity for beneficial trade. Any allocation in the shaded area would be better than point D, and would constitute a Pareto-improvement. What this means is that it would be possible to make one individual better off without making another worse off. For example, by exchanging W_C–W_1 of whisky for B_1–B_C of bagels Catherine would remain on the same indifference curve IC^C_0 and move round from point D to point K. She would, by definition, be no worse off at point K than she is at point D. David, who makes the opposite exchange, then moves onto the higher indifference curve IC^D_1. In this case, all the benefit from trade goes to David. The alternative extreme starting at point D would be to move to point L, where David would remain on IC^D_0 and Catherine would be the sole beneficiary from trade. It should be clear that both individuals would become better off by moving to a point somewhere in the shaded area.

Points K and L are examples of Pareto-optimal outcomes. At these points, it is not possible to make one person better off without making another worse off. At a point of Pareto-optimality, the marginal rate of substitution between the two goods is the same for both individuals; diagrammatically, the indifference curves are tangential.[3] The gains from trade are exhausted; if the rate at which both individuals would be willing to exchange whisky for bagels is the same they are not able to trade to advantage.

At points such as K or L in Figure 16.4, it is only possible to make one individual better off at the expense of the other. A re-allocation of the two goods that moves one individual onto a

3 In a more general model, the marginal rates of substitution of all individuals would be the same.

higher indifference curve can only be at the expense of the other individual. For example, David would be made better off by moving to a point to the south-west of point K. This could only be done by moving Catherine onto an indifference curve below IC_0^C. A similar argument applies with Catherine being made better off at points to the north-east of point L.

The core and the contract curve

We can safely reason that neither individual will voluntarily choose a level of utility lower than that associated with point D, their endowment point. The indifference curves for the two individuals that pass through this point therefore give us the boundary for possible Pareto-optimal outcomes. In principle, we can think of a whole series of points of tangency between the indifference curves within the region of mutual advantage. This is called the core of the economy.

The logic of the analysis would apply equally well if we had started from any other endowment point such as those marked in Figure 16.2 (or any other point in the Edgeworth box). In principle, there are a large number of initial allocations that can produce an outcome consistent with Pareto-optimality. Pareto-optimal allocations are therefore not unique. In Figure 16.5, we have drawn a contract curve, which is just a curve that joins all Pareto-optimal allocations. For clarity, the Figure explicitly includes just four such allocations marked as A, B, C, and D but in principle it is possible to think of many of such outcomes between O_C and O_D.

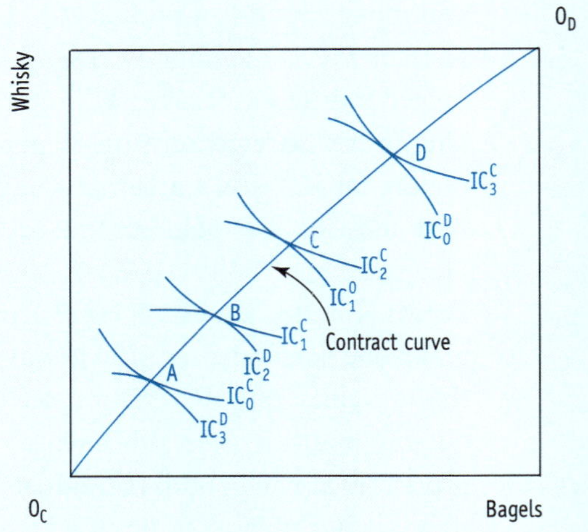

Figure 16.5 The contract curve in an exchange economy

This leaves open the question of how the goods are re-allocated between the individuals if the endowment point is not a point of Pareto-optimality. In terms of Figure 16.4, what is it that determines where the individuals move to within the region of mutual advantage? The general answer to this question is that it is determined by the price mechanism, which is what we now come to.

The role of the price mechanism

In Figure 16.6, the line P_I represents the prices of the two goods. The slope of the price line reflects one particular (arbitrarily chosen) price ratio. A steeper slope than that drawn could arise from either a rise in the price of a bagel, or a fall in the price of whisky, or both. A flatter slope would arise from any of the opposite movements.

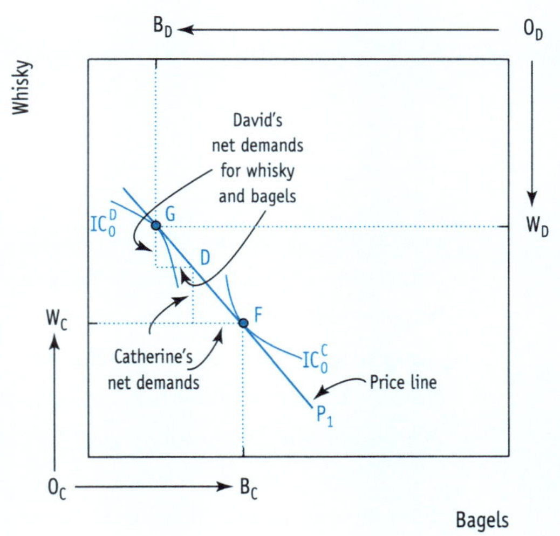

Figure 16.6 The price mechanism

The price line passes through the endowment point D. At this price ratio, the indifference curves for the two individuals that maximise their utilities are given by IC_0^C and IC_0^D respectively. These are tangential to the price line at points F and G. Catherine would prefer to consume more bagels and less whisky than is given by her initial allocation at point D. The same is true for David. We therefore have an excess demand for bagels and an excess supply of whisky at this price ratio.

In more formal language, the gross (or total) demand for the two goods by Catherine is O_CB_C, OW_C. This is the sum of her endowments of the two goods plus the net (or excess) demands for them. A similar breakdown applies to David. Given the relative price of P_I, the gross demand from the two individuals for bagels is greater than the total supply (measured by the length of the horizontal axis). The gross demand for whisky is less than its total supply measured along the vertical axis.

The price mechanism in a competitive market economy will adjust the relative prices of the two goods, raising the price of bagels and lowering that of whisky, until a point of equilibrium

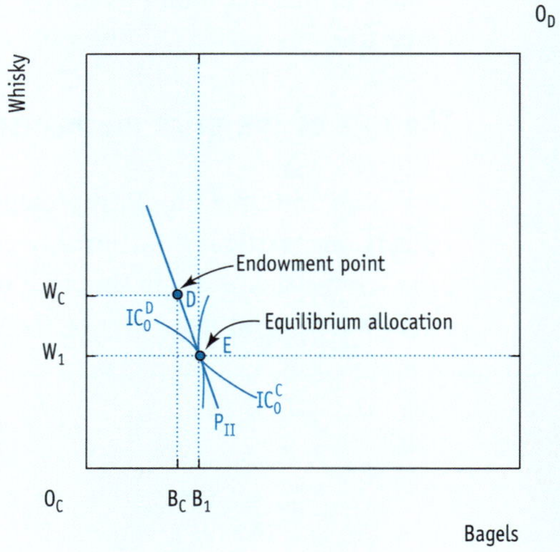

Figure 16.7 Equilibrium in the exchange economy

is reached in both markets. Figure 16.7 shows such equilibrium at point E. The slope of the price line, P_{II}, is, therefore, steeper than in the previous figure, reflecting the rise in the price of bagels relative to the price of whisky. At the equilibrium price ratio, individuals have traded to maximise their respective utilities and we have a Pareto-improvement on the endowment point. At the equilibrium point, the marginal rate of substitution, MRS, between the two goods for the two individuals are equal, and are also equal to the price ratio implied by P_{II}.

This simple model describes the economy in terms of individual endowments and individual preferences, from which we can obtain individual supply and demands at various price levels. In principle, the individual functions can then be aggregated across all individuals. If relative prices are adjusted until supply and demand balance in all markets, then there is a state of general equilibrium. Individual pursuit of private interest — utility maximising behaviour by consumers — leads to economic equilibrium.

It is, however, important to distinguish between the conditions for an economy to be in general equilibrium, and its associated welfare properties, and the questions of how, and if, an economy moves towards such a state. The approach in a number of textbooks is to first analyse the conditions and properties of competitive general equilibrium, and then consider departures from the assumptions on which it depends. In this text, we have already considered why in the case of factor markets, for example, asymmetries of information may mean that the price mechanism does not adjust to equate demand and supply.

The question about how the right set of prices can be found if the economy does not happen to generate them is a difficult one. There is an inconsistency in the analysis of this chapter; in a competitive market all individuals act as price takers, yet the analysis is based on changing relative prices to eliminate excess demand. How, therefore, do relative prices adjust if everyone takes them as a given? Discussions of the process sometimes resort to 'as if' statements, and sometimes make use of the idea of a fictitious 'auctioneer' who ensures that the equilibrium prices can be obtained and that trading can take place. This idea of an acutioneer originates from the workings of commodity markets and the stock market in Paris in the 19th century, and is associated with the work of the theorist Walras.[4]

In the context of our model, this auctioneer 'announces' the (relative) price of the two goods, and the two individuals respond with their demands for the two goods. There is then an iterative process that eventually leads to the equilibrium prices for the two goods.[5] Clearly, this is no description of the workings of a modern economy, but more generally the question arises as to whether the model is sufficiently good at explaining the operation of economies for it to be useful. This question produces a wide range of opinions, and we will expand on a number of the issues in this chapter and the two that follow. In the remaining sections in this chapter, we will elaborate on the competitive model, and discus some departures from it. Before we do so, we will briefly discuss the experience of Local Exchange Trading Systems, known as LETS.

Local Exchange Trading Systems

The LETS system has grown in popularity in the UK and by the mid-1990s there were over 400 groups operating, with similar forms of organisation in other parts of Europe and worldwide. LETS operate multilateral trades in goods and services that vary widely just depending on the local community they operate in. The goods and services traded include, for example, alternative health therapies, the provision of organic foods as well as relatively mundane household chores (ironing, cleaning, etc.) and more specialised services such as language tuition.

In those LETS where commodities are exchanged that have been produced within the mainstream economy, we can view them as a sort of exchange economy. The mainstream economy, in a sense, delivers the endowments of the goods to the individuals who trade. Trading takes place with its own form of currency or tokens, the names of which often relate to the local area. For example, the Canterbury LETS operates with tales, in Reading they trade in readies and in Bristol they trade in thanks (a token). Unlike our model of the exchange economy, trade takes place at rates of exchange determined through bilateral negotiation between individuals. There is no mechanism to ensure the rate negotiated will generate an equilibrium rate within a local organisation.

---

4 These kinds of markets have some particular features. Financial markets are often concerned with relatively small numbers of individuals trading standardised, second-hand goods (assets) in very large quantities. Many other markets are concerned with large numbers of individuals trading new goods in relatively small individual exchanges.

5 In the context of our two-good model, when there is an equilibrium price in one market, equilibrium in the second market follows directly.

Questions

Q1 Suppose the price of rail travel on the London–Paris route is reduced following a reduction in costs. Rework the general equilibrium analysis of the markets for rail and air travel. Does it suggest a larger or a smaller change in the equilibrium price than if the market for rail travel had been considered in isolation? What determines the amount of the change in the equilibrium price?

Q2 If two individuals gain from trade is the new allocation of goods necessarily optimal?

Q3 Maggie is a professional therapist and Dave is a professional gardener. They form a two-person Local Exchange Trading System. Maggie offers three hours of aromatherapy and Dave three hours of gardening services.

(I) Draw an Edgeworth box and mark the endowment point.

(II) Assuming that Maggie's utility only increases with gardening services and Dave's increases only with aromatherapy, draw in their respective indifference maps. Being idealistic at first, Maggie agrees to exchange one-hour of her services for one hour of gardening work; a rate of exchange Dave is pleased to accept. Draw in the price line. Where would the equilibrium outcome be?

(III) Dave leaves the locality to be replaced Henry who offers to take her dog for a walk. Maggie decides to negotiate at the rate of half an hour of aromatherapy for every hour of dog walking, which Henry agrees to. On the basis that she still offers three hours of her time to the LETS draw the new Edgeworth box. What is the slope of the new price line and where would the new equilibrium point be if Henry's utility function only depended on the hours of aromatheraphy?

16.2 General equilibrium with production

We will now build on the analysis of Section 1 by introducing two industries that employ two factors of production, capital and labour, to produce the two goods that Catherine and David consume. Figure 16.8 shows a production box diagram. In this case, the two axes represent the total supplies of the factor inputs available to the two industries, and a point in the box shows different combinations of capital and labour that are available for the production of bagels and whisky.[6]

The output of bagels is shown with reference to the south-west, that of whisky with reference to the north-east. Given the production functions for the two goods, we can draw in isoquants

---

6 The production of bagels and whisky clearly requires more than just capital and labour but we are ignoring this for simplicity.

associated with the outputs. In Figure 16.8, the isoquants marked Q_0^B, Q_1^B, Q_2^B show increasing numbers of bagels, and likewise Q_0^W, Q_1^W, Q_2^W represent increasing output from the whisky industry. The figure shows three points of tangency, which represent situations where increasing the output of one good necessarily means reducing the output of the other. For example, a move from E to F involves a greater number of bagels, a lower output of whisky; a move from E to G means the opposite.

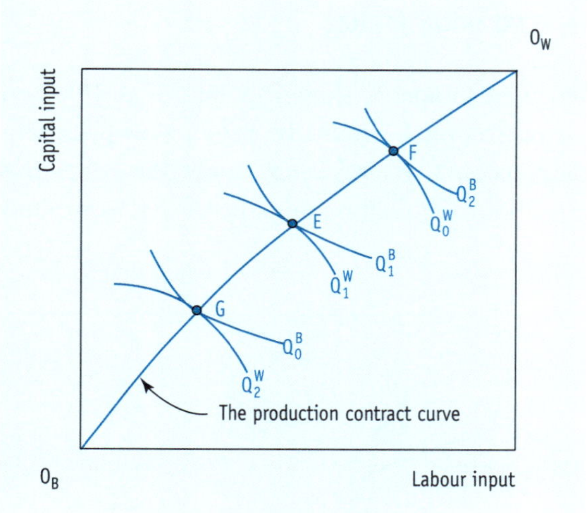

Figure 16.8 **The production box diagram**

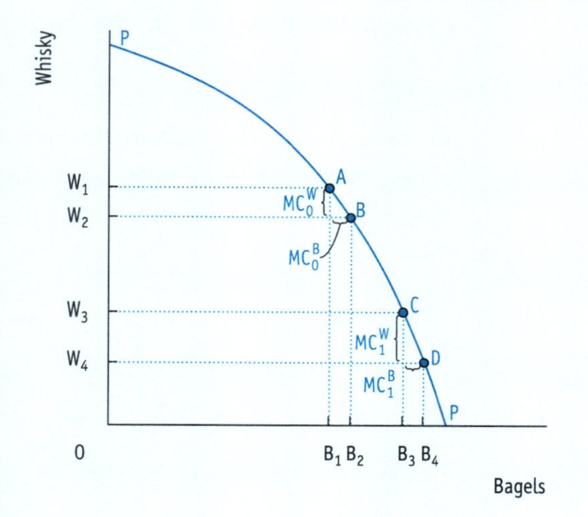

Figure 16.9 **The production possibility curve**

The curve that joins up all such points of tangency is known as the production contract curve. In Figure 16.8, this is drawn as a line from O_B to O_W. At all points on this contract curve, the marginal rate of technical substitution between the two factors of production in the two industries will be equal. Analogously to the exchange economy, at a point off the curve, it would be possible to increase the output of at least one of the goods without reducing the output of the other. The contract curve, therefore, shows the combinations of output which are technically efficient.

The next step is to recast the production contract curve as a production possibility curve (or frontier), and this is done in Figure 16.9. The curve shows the maximum possible combinations of bagels and whisky, given the factor supplies and the state of technology. The curve slopes down for the obvious reason that an increase in the output of one industry means reductions in the output of the other. The shape of the curve — concave to the origin — reflects an increasing marginal cost of one industry's output in terms of the marginal cost of the other industry.

For example, as we move from point A to point B, the marginal cost of the producing B_2 bagels rather than B_1 is the reduction in whisky, MC_0^W. The move from point C to point D further down gives the same additional output of bagels but a much greater reduction in the quantity of whisky than before, shown by MC_1^W. As the economy becomes increasingly specialised in one industry, the rate at which it gives up the (potential) output of the other increases. The ratio of the marginal costs gives what is known as the marginal rate of transformation, MRT. This varies between moving from A to B, and from point C to D and, in general, it is given by the (negative of the) slope of the production possibility curve.

General equilibrium in the two consumer-two good model

General equilibrium in the two consumer-two good model is shown in Figure 16.10 where we have drawn the Edgeworth box developed in Section 1 within the production possibility curve. We are now in position to analyse simultaneously the decisions about the goods that individuals choose, together with the decisions about the factor inputs necessary to produce them.

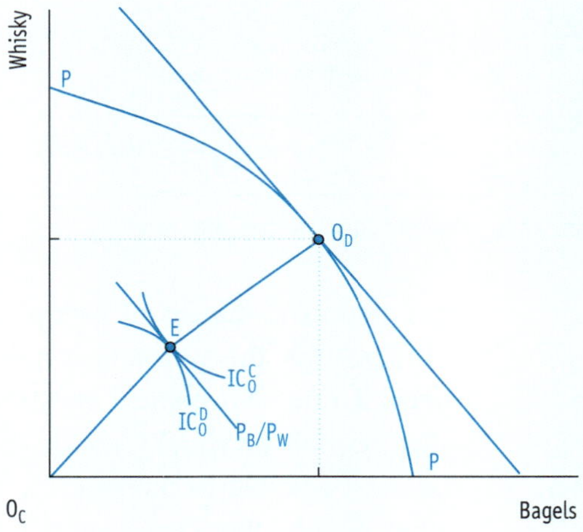

Figure 16.10 Equilibrium in the two consumer-two good model

All that we are concerned with here are the conditions that will lead to a Pareto-efficient outcome. Such an outcome must be on the contract curve within the Edgeworth box, since if it was not it would be possible to make one or both consumer(s) better off. For there to be a Pareto-efficient outcome, it must also be that the MRT between the two goods is equal to the MRS of the two consumers. Why? Suppose the MRT was equal to 1, and that the MRS between whisky and bagels for Catherine was 1/2. This would mean that she would be prepared to exchange two bagels for one whisky (however measured). Given that it would be possible to produce an extra two units of whisky for the extra two bagels, Catherine could be made better off without making David any worse off. It is, therefore, possible to make Pareto-improvements to any allocation where the MRS and the MRT are not equal.

To see the general equilibrium outcome in Figure 16.10, start with the point marked O_D on the production possibility curve. This gives us the north-east point of reference for the Edgeworth box. Assuming that firms operate in competitive industries, it follows that their output price will equal the marginal costs of production and so, in turn, the MRT will equal the price ratio. The economy will be in equilibrium when this price ratio is consistent with a point of equilibrium for the two consumers, which we know will happen somewhere along the (consumption) contract curve inside the Edgeworth box. This is illustrated in Figure 16.10 at point E, where — in words — the marginal rate of transformation in production is equal to the marginal rate of substitution in consumption and are both equal to the price ratio. This gives us a Pareto-efficient outcome. Symbolically, we have

$$MRT_{WB} = MRS_{WB} = P_B/P_W.$$

It should be appreciated that not all of the points on the contract curve O_CO_D will be consistent with a Pareto-efficient outcome. A point on the curve only represents equality of the MRS between the two consumers, nothing more. If the MRS differs from the MRT, then we do not have a point of general competitive equilibrium, since then it would be possible for at least one individual to become better off without affecting any other person, as we discussed before.

In this model, the consumers also supply the capital and labour used to make the goods. Given the point O_D on the PP curve, there is a particular point on the contract curve in the production box that is associated with it. The slope of the isoquants gives the ratio of the marginal physical products of the two factors.[7] Assuming competitive conditions, then labour gets paid the same rate in both industries, as do those who supply capital. At the point of equilibrium, the ratio of the marginal physical products in the two industries is the same as is the ratio of factor payments. Since factor payments are completely distributed in the competitive economy, the distribution of factor supplies between individuals generates a particular distribution of income so that the two consumers can reach the general equilibrium outcome shown in Figure 16.10.

In general, there are likely to be a large number of such equilibrium outcomes.[8] This follows from the possibility of there being other points on the consumption contract curve where the price ratio equals the MRT. The analysis also took a particular point on the production possibility curve, which was one of a large number that could have been chosen. One way of illustrating these alternative Pareto-efficient outcomes is with a utility possibilities frontier, UU, such as that drawn in Figure 16.11. This shows the highest level of utility Catherine can

7 This draws on the discussion of Chapters 7 and 14.

8 An infinitely large number.

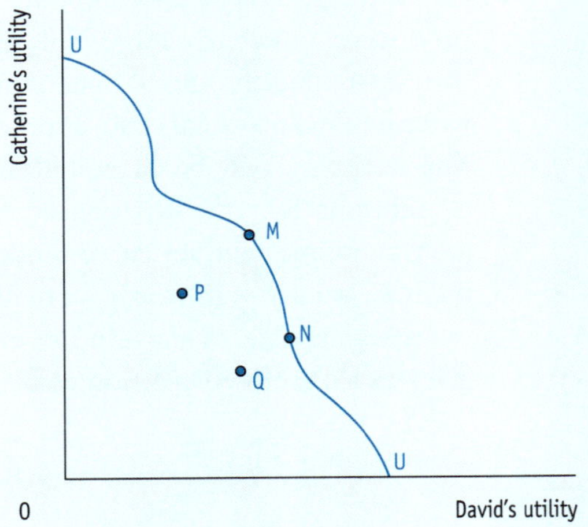

Figure 16.11 The utilities possibility frontier

obtain, given David's utility level (and vice versa). Points M and N on the frontier therefore represent two of the possible Pareto-efficient outcomes.

This gives us one way of deciding whether a re-allocation of resources between individuals is desirable. A move from point P to M in Figure 16.11 is clearly desirable by the Pareto-criterion in that both individuals have been made better off. Anywhere to the north-east of point P would be a Pareto-improvement on the initial allocation.

Plainly, this does not cover reallocations in which one individual gains and another loses; a move from point P to point N, for example in Figure 16.11. One alternative criterion, proposed by Kaldor is that the reallocation should go ahead if the individual who gains could (potentially) compensate the person who loses, and still have a net gain overall.

Questions

Q4 If there were increasing returns to scale in the whisky industry and constant returns to scale in the production of bagels what shape would the production possibility frontier be? If the returns to scale were the other way around what shape would it be? How would such changes affect the production contract curve?

Q5 In a certain cool country there are only two industries: film-making and finance. The government decides to subsidise film-making, while the price of financial services remains at its competitive market level. Assuming that the economy was initially in a state of Pareto-efficient general equilibrium, what would be the effect of introducing the subsidy?

Q6 Draw a utility possibilities frontier. For an allocation to be equitable must it be efficient?

Q7 A certain large football club wants to enlarge its ground capacity by 15,000. However, the ground is situated in the middle of a densely populated area, and the development could only go ahead by knocking down some terraced properties. These currently house elderly residents, some of whom have lived in them all of their lives. Should the proposed redevelopment go ahead?

16.3 Social welfare analysis

Two fundamental theorems

The previous section dealt the conditions that are necessary for a Pareto-efficient outcome in a market economy. There are two fundamental theorems of welfare economics associated with such an allocation of resources. The first states that any equilibrium in a competitive market economy is Pareto-efficient; so that the allocation will be somewhere along the utility possibilities frontier. This is an important argument since it provides a foundation for welfare arguments that favour (competitive) market economies.

The criteria of Pareto-efficiency does not address issues of equity, either in terms of the endowments of goods in the exchange economy, or factor supplies when we include production. It does not address issues of equity in an equilibrium allocation. The second welfare theorem has some bearing on this issue. It states that any (feasible) equilibrium allocation can be generated by a competitive market economy. The words can be are central as it requires the initial allocation, or endowment, to be consistent with the desired outcome. To obtain the endowment point consistent with the desired outcome needs distributional policies which might, for example, be lump-sum income transfers. In principle, the second theorem detaches questions of equity from those of efficiency, and suggests that to achieve a particular equity goal it is not necessary to sacrifice the criterion of Pareto-efficiency.

Social welfare functions

There are many allocations that are Pareto-efficient, and there remains the question of what criteria we might use to decide which, if any, of these outcomes is to be preferred. To this end we can think in terms of a social welfare function, which is one way we might aggregate the preferences of individuals into some form of social preference. As a simple example, in the two-person model we can postulate that social welfare depends on the utilities of the individuals

$$\mathrm{SWF} = F(U_C, U_D)$$

where U_C is the utility of Catherine and U_D is David's utility.

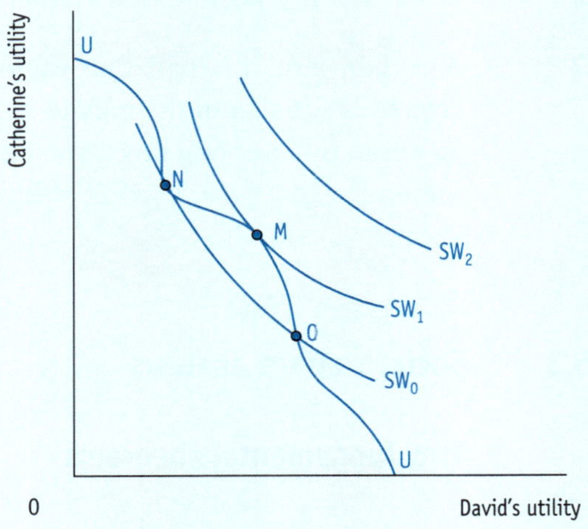

Figure 16.12 A social welfare function

This kind of function is sometimes referred to as a utilitarian type of social welfare function. It assumes that social welfare increases as the utility of each individual increases. Figure 16.12 shows social indifference curves for the two-consumer model, marked as SW_0, SW_1 and SW_2. In this context, each indifference curve shows different combinations of the utility of the two individuals that yields the same level of social welfare. A decrease in Catherine's utility has to be compensated for by an increase in David's to maintain a given level of social welfare, and vice versa. Social indifference curves further away from the origin represent higher welfare levels. In Figure 16.12, point M gives the social optimum.

However, this has some rather obvious limitations. There is a question of whether it is possible to aggregate individual preferences and, if so, how? If it does make sense to think in terms of a social welfare function, there remains the open question of what form it takes. We could, in principle, have drawn other social welfare functions that would have produced other outcomes as socially optimal. We have, in effect, moved the question from which point on the utility possibilities frontier to which type of social welfare function is optimal. There are many alternative types of social welfare function: for example, a Benthamite welfare function is simply the sum of the individual utilities. A variation of this is the weighted sum of utilities welfare function, where, clearly, the weights need not be equal. A third type of utility function is the Rawlsian social welfare function, which states that the social welfare of an allocation depends crucially on how it affects the least well-off member of the society.

Voting

One obvious possibility for deciding on preferences is some kind of majority voting. If a majority of individuals prefer one allocation to another, it could be taken as the socially

Catherine	David	Elle
X	Z	Y
Y	X	Z
Z	Y	X

Table 16.1 **Simple majority voting**

preferred outcome. This is, however, not straightforward. For example, suppose there are three alternative allocations of goods that we will refer to as X, Y and Z, in a three-person world.

Catherine and David prefer allocation X to Y, Catherine and Elle prefer allocation Y to Z. David and Elle prefer allocation Z to X. We have majorities in favour of X over Y, Y over Z and Z over X. Given that their preferences are intransitive, there is no best allocation arrived at by simple majority voting. The outcome would depend on the order in which the vote is taken.

One alternative to simple majority voting is to aggregate the preferences of individuals by rank-order voting. Individual preferences are ranked and the numbers 1, 2, 3, assigned to first, second and third choice. The sum of the scores for each allocation is used to determine the social preference. For example, suppose initially that only two of the alternative allocations were available, X and Y. Given the preferences shown in Table 16.2, allocation X would be given a score of 2 by Catherine, and a score of 1 by David. The other allocation would reverse these individual scores and the outcome of the voting would be a tie. The introduction of a third allocation, Z, over which the two individuals have to determine their preferences means that allocation X has a combined rank score of 3, and is to be preferred to Y with a score of 4 (and allocation Z with a score of 5). In determining social preferences, the rank ordering is therefore sensitive to the introduction of additional allocations.

It is plainly problematic to aggregate individual preferences and we now come to Arrow's Impossibility Theorem.

Rank score	Catherine	David
1	Y	X
2	X	Z
3	Z	Y

Table 16.2 **Rank order voting**

Arrow's Impossibility Theorem

This theorem is concerned with whether it is possible to fairly rank alternative 'social states' so that they represent individual preferences. If

(I) Individual preferences are complete and the social preference ranks all alternative states.

(II) The ranking of preferences is transitive, that is the preferences of individuals result in social preferences with the same properties.

(III) All individuals have a particular preference between two allocations X and Y, then the social preferences rank X ahead of Y.

(IV) Preferences between allocations do not depend on how they rank other allocations. That is if a new alternative becomes available this does not affect the ranking of alternative states.

Then all social rankings are the rankings of just one individual; i.e. it's a dictatorship. The theorem highlights the difficult nature of aggregating individual preferences into some form of social welfare function. Clearly, social preferences do get expressed in democracies and we will return to a number of matters relating to this.

The role of the state

The analysis so far has been concerned with the benefits of a competitive market economy, and the conditions necessary to obtain them. A competitive market in its idealised form is, of course, simply an abstraction. In practice, government involvement in western economies is often widespread, although the degree and the nature of involvement varies between the US/Japan and Europe. In the UK, for example, in recent years the government has accounted for around 40% of all spending in the economy.

Why is there such large-scale government involvement in the economy? In broad terms, answers given to this include the aim of trying to achieve a more efficient market outcome than would otherwise be, and also a more socially acceptable distribution of well being.[9] The discussion of the remainder of this section, and the next two chapters, will directly address the role of government intervention in relation to both economic efficiency and equity. We will begin here by discussing what kind of government intervention is appropriate to meet the

9 We have, in earlier chapters, already discussed the nature of government intervention in some areas such as the labour market and in competition policy to give two examples.

efficiency objective, starting with what is known as the theory of the second-best. The discussion of public goods then gives us a second departure from the criteria of Pareto-efficiency. In Chapters 17 and 18, we address the role of government more broadly in relation to the environment and achieving a socially acceptable distribution of income.

Second best

There are many reasons why the allocation of resources in an economy may not be Pareto-efficient. For example, monopolies do not equate price and marginal cost, and policy interventions to tax, or subsidise, certain goods and services will also lead to departures from general competitive equilibrium.

In the context of our simple model with two individuals, and two industries, we can illustrate the effect of this with a modification of Figure 16.10. Suppose there is a tax imposed on the production of bagels, when hitherto there had been none. This has the effect of increasing the price ratio P_B/P_W, which now exceeds the ratio of the marginal costs of production. In Figure 16.13, the slope of the price ratio which the consumers face exceeds the marginal costs of production at point O_D on the production possibility curve. The two consumers are giving up more whisky for bagels at the prevailing market prices, than is necessary given the MRT.

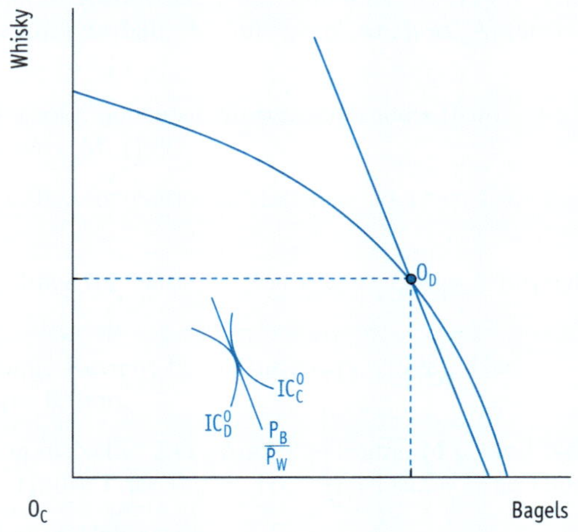

Figure 16.13 A tax on bagels

Departures from marginal cost pricing lead to departures from a Pareto-efficient allocation of resources. Starting from a position where some goods are taxed, or given subsidies, a question that we might ask is whether other goods should be taxed as well? The theory of the second best tells us that if a first best, or Pareto-efficient, outcome is not attainable, then it may be less inefficient to create other divergences between price and marginal cost on efficiency grounds.

In our example, the efficiency loss from the bagel tax can be offset by a tax on whisky at a rate that restores the equality between the price ratio that consumers face and the ratio of the marginal costs of production at point O_D. This is, of course, a rather obvious point in the two-good model. When there are many goods to consider, it suggests that the efficiency consequences of imposing a tax need to be evaluated by examining the effects in all related markets. In principle, this is a potentially very large undertaking given that indirect taxes alone account for between 8–10% of household income and are imposed on a very wide range of consumer goods.[10]

Public goods

These are goods that can be classified by two characteristics, non-excludability and non-diminishability in consumption. What this means is, firstly, that my consumption of a good does not prevent your consumption of it, or that of anyone else. Secondly, that my consumption or yours does not reduce the quantity of it available for anyone else. Standard examples include public street-lighting and certain services, such as those provided by the armed forces. Once a public good is provided, the marginal cost of others consuming it is zero and in this public goods differ from, say, the consumption of a cola drink.

The question to be asked here is whether a market economy will produce the efficient level of public goods. For a public good, the total demand for it is found by the vertical summation of the demand curve of individuals, which differs from a private good where total demand is found from the horizontal summation. Why the difference? With a public good the quantity is fixed — the number of streetlights, for example, is taken as a given — and we can add up the demand of individuals by seeing how much they would be willing to pay.[11]

To determine the level of efficient public good provision, we equate the marginal benefit with the marginal cost and Figure 16.14 illustrates this. For simplicity, we have two individuals whose demand curves are shown in panels A and B. The individual demands are summed into the market demand schedule shown in panel C of the figure. The point of intersection on the vertical axis in panel C is therefore the vertical sum of the points of intersection in panels A and B. The output level Q_0 is the point at which the first individual would not be willing to pay anything more for additional provision, and this produces a kink in the demand curve in panel C.

The efficient output occurs at the point where price equal marginal cost. This is shown in panel C of Figure 16.14 by the intersection of the demand (marginal benefit) curve and the

10 Office for National Statistics (1998).

11 In the case of a private good, we are obtaining the different quantities individuals can buy at a given price (see Chapter 1).

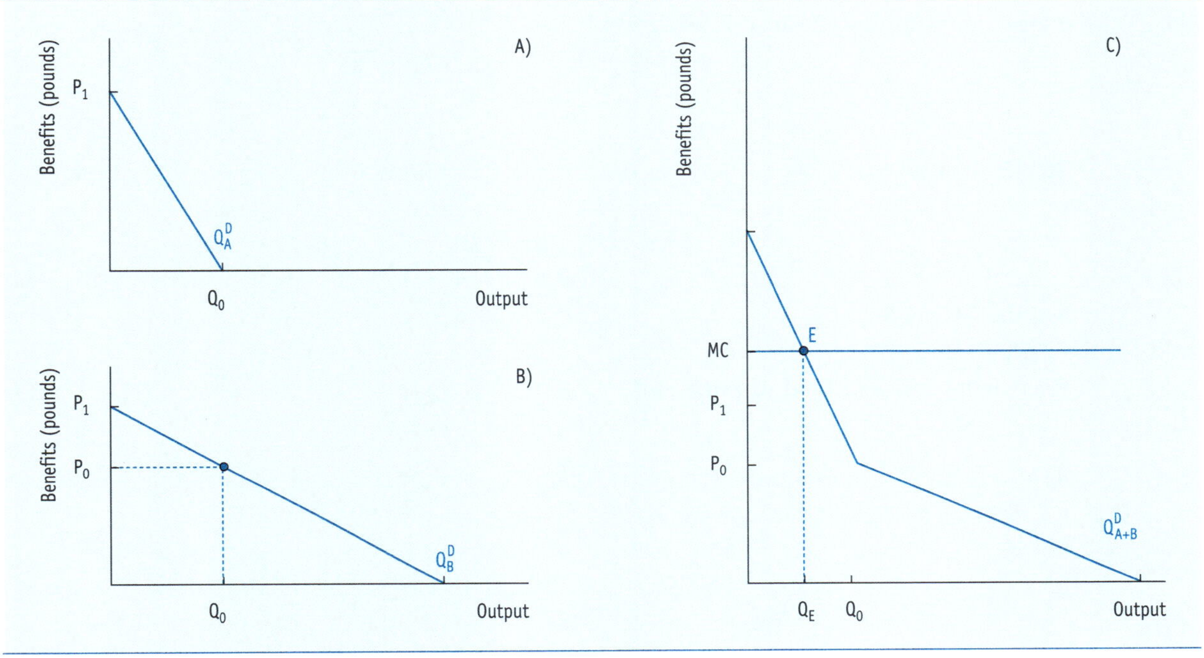

Figure 16.14 Demand for public goods

marginal cost curve, marked as MC. The efficient level of provision is Q_E, despite the fact that the MC of production is greater than the price that either individual alone would be prepared to pay for any of the good.

In practice, it should be appreciated that the classification of a public good is often a matter of degree. For example, a walk down Oxford Street in London at 9 o'clock in a February morning is not the same as walking along it at 6 o'clock in the evening, a week before Christmas. In the second case, the non-excludability condition generally holds, but non-diminishability (or non-rivalness) typically does not.

Questions

Q8 Which of the following would you classify as public goods:

(I) A public service television broadcaster.
(II) Royal Parks in London (Hyde Park, Regents Park and others).
(III) Royal Botanic Gardens at Kew in London (where you pay an entrance fee).
(IV) Your local reference library.
(V) The British Library?

Q9 Kerry's demand curve for a public good is

$$Q^D = 24 - P$$

Jerry's demand is

$$Q^D = 16 - 2P$$

and the MC is 8.

What is the efficient level of provision?

Summary

1 General equilibrium analysis is concerned with the interactions between markets.

2 A starting point is a two-person exchange economy, which can be illustrated with an Edgeworth box. This is a way of representing the total available goods and the allocation of them between the individuals. If the marginal rate of substitution of one good for the other differs between the individuals, then there are potentially gains from trade. In other words it is possible to make a Pareto-improvement.

3 A Pareto-optimal outcome is one in which it is not possible to make one person better off, without making someone else worse off. The marginal rate of substitution between the two goods for the two consumers will be equal to each other, and also equal to the price ratio. Such an allocation of goods is not unique. The locus of all the Pareto-optimal allocations is known as the contract curve.

4 The Edgeworth box diagram can be adapted to present production within the economy. The total supplies of the two factors are measured on the respective axis of the box. The contract curve can be readily redrawn as the production possibility frontier.

5 Given a particular point on the production possibility frontier, competitive general equilibrium can be presented by drawing the Edgeworth box within it. Equilibrium occurs where the ratio of the marginal rate of technical substitution between the two factors equals the factor price ratio, which equals the price ratio of the two goods, which equals the marginal rate of substitution of the two individuals ('marginal everything equals marginal everything else').

6 The First Welfare Theorem states that any equilibrium in a competitive market economy is Pareto-efficient. The Second Welfare Theorem states that (under certain conditions) that every Pareto-efficient outcome can be achieved as a competitive market equilibrium. Broadly, this suggests that efficiency objectives can be separated from equity considerations.

7 There are many reasons why, in practice, the allocation of resources in an economy may not be Pareto-efficient. These include non-competitive market structures, taxes and subsidies which may be imposed for reasons of equity. The market may also fail to produce certain types of goods such as public goods.

End of chapter questions

Q10 Kate and Tony inhabit an exchange economy where they eat apples and chocolate bars. Kate's utility function is

$$U_K = AC$$

Tony's preferences are given by

$$U_T = \min\{A, C\}$$

(I) What are the demand functions for chocolate bars for Kate and Tony?

Kate's endowment is no apples and eight chocolate bars and Tony's endowment is 16 apples and four bars of chocolate.

(II) Let the price of apples equal 1 and the price of chocolate bars be P_2. Write out equations for Kate and Tony that give their endowments of the two goods.
(III) Obtain the sum of Kate and Tony's demand for chocolate in terms of the price of chocolate alone.
(IV) What is the price of chocolate that equates its supply and demand? What are their respective consumption levels of apples and chocolate?
(V) Where does the contract curve lie in the Edgeworth box and why?

Q11 In a two-person LETS Fiona offers four hours of classical guitar tuition and Phil offers 10 hours of painting. Fiona's utility function is given by

$$U_F = 3P$$

Where P is the number of hours of painting, and Phil's utility is given by

$$U_P = 2G$$

Where G is the number of hours of guitar tuition

(I) Sketch the indifference maps of the two individuals in an Edgeworth box.
(II) Where would the equilibrium outcome be?
(III) Suppose that Phil's preferences were given by the utility function

$$U_P = \min\{P, G\}$$

What would be his consumption level of the two commodities?

Q12 Suppose the utility possibilities frontier in the two-person model was given by the relation

$$U_C + 2U_D = 100$$

(I) Draw the frontier. If social preferences were represented by the welfare function

$$SWF = U_C\ U_D$$

What is the point where the function would be maximised? What are the utility levels of the two individuals?

(II) Suppose the welfare function was based on the idea of maximising the utility of the best off member of society, where would utility be maximised on the frontier?

(III) What form would you expect the social welfare function to be if it reflected the Rawlsian criteria? At what point on the utility frontier would welfare be?

(IV) How would your answers to (I)–(III) differ if the utilities possibility frontier was given by $2U_C + 2U_D = 200$?

Q13 In the partial equilibrium framework of Chapter 9, we noted that welfare depended on the sum of consumer and producer surplus. Welfare was maximised when the sum of these surpluses were maximised. The analysis of Section 2 in this chapter showed that there could be an infinite number of Pareto-efficient outcomes. Are these two pieces of analysis inconsistent?

References and suggested further reading

The material of this chapter is often covered in several chapters in other textbooks. There are good discussions of the main principles in each of Estrin and Laidler, Nicholson and Varian. Earl gives some critical discussion of co-ordination mechanisms. Croall gives more details on the background and the experience of LETS in the UK in the 1990's.

Croall, J. (1997), *Lets Act Locally*, Gulbenkian Foundation.

Earl, P.E. (1995), *Microeconomics for Business and Marketing*, Edward Elgar.

Estrin, S. and Laidler, D. (1995), *Introduction to Microeconomics*, 4th edition, Harvester Wheatsheaf.

Nicholson, W. (1995), *Microeconomic Theory, Basic Principles and Extensions*, 6th edition, The Dryden Press.

Office for National Statistics (1998), *Economic Trends*.

Varian, H.R. (1996), *Intermediate Microeconomics, A Modern Approach*, 4th edition, W.W. Norton & Co.

17 Externalities and the Environment

Key ideas and material

Externalities, global environmental problems, road transport and the environment

Introduction

The analysis in Chapter 16 was primarily concerned with the conditions in which a market economy will allocate resources efficiently. We are now going to develop this discussion by looking at externalities. An externality is simply an action taken by an individual, or a firm, which affects others in ways not connected with the price mechanism. They are one important reason why market economies do not produce Pareto-efficient outcomes. A simple example of an externality is smoking; the smoker's pleasure directly reduces the quality of the air available to others nearby. In this case, the externality relates to consumption and its impact is negative, but it is sensible to think of externalities as being widespread. They can have either positive or negative effects, arise through consumption or productions decisions, and be felt locally or globally.

A market system in which individuals pursue their private interests will not take account of externalities.[1] The level of consumption and production will be inefficient in that the marginal benefit will not be equal to marginal cost for the last unit consumed (or produced). This leads to the question of whether private sector institutions will devise arrangements that correct the resulting inefficiencies, or whether some form of state intervention will lead to a more efficient outcome.

In Section 1 of this chapter, we discuss the nature of externalities in detail. We will examine the Coase theorem which suggests that where externalities do exist, the parties involved have an incentive to bargain and that the market system can still lead to an efficient outcome. We

1 Unless, of course, it was in their interests to do so.

will however also discuss various forms of regulation, and the potential role for taxes and subsidies in correcting market distortions.[2]

Environmental concerns have become very prominent in the 1990s. Section 2 deals with the large question of global warming and what policy responses may be appropriate by national governments. We will discuss the seemingly ill-fated attempts of the European Union to introduce a carbon-energy tax, which will show why the interplay of efficiency and equity considerations can be important. Finally, in Section 3 we look at the external costs of private road transport and discuss a number of possible policy responses by government.

17.1 Externalities

At the outset, we should be clear about the difference between actions that affect others through the price mechanism and those that do not. The general equilibrium analysis of Chapter 16 suggested that there are potentially large changes in the distribution of income that can arise from changing relative demands for a good. For example, in the case of travel between London and Paris, the introduction of a rail link reduces the demand for cross-channel ferry services, other things being equal. A straight application of the supply and demand analysis suggests that the price of ferry services will fall. In turn, the incomes of those connected with ferries will fall if some individuals are laid off, or the profits of the ferry companies decline. The change in the distribution of income in this case takes place through the market mechanism via a relative price adjustment. In terms of the analysis, changing travel patterns, and the fall in the relative price of ferry services, does not prevent the economy from moving from one Pareto-efficient allocation to another.

The distribution of income and welfare can of course also be affected for reasons unrelated to the price mechanism. An obvious example is the widespread effect of pollution, the problems of which have been exacerbated by the long-term increase in car ownership. Exhaust emissions adversely affect the health of (among others) those with respiratory complaints; a group that includes disproportionate numbers of children under the age of 5 and pregnant women. The private cost of motoring ignores this kind of cost and so constitutes a negative consumption externality.

A production externality

We will begin our analysis with the case of a negative production externality. Figure 17.1A illustrates the position of a competitive firm and Figure 17.1B shows the position of the

2 Taxes designed to correct market inefficiencies that arise from externalities are known as Pigouvian taxes, after A.C. Pigou, who put forward the idea in 1920.

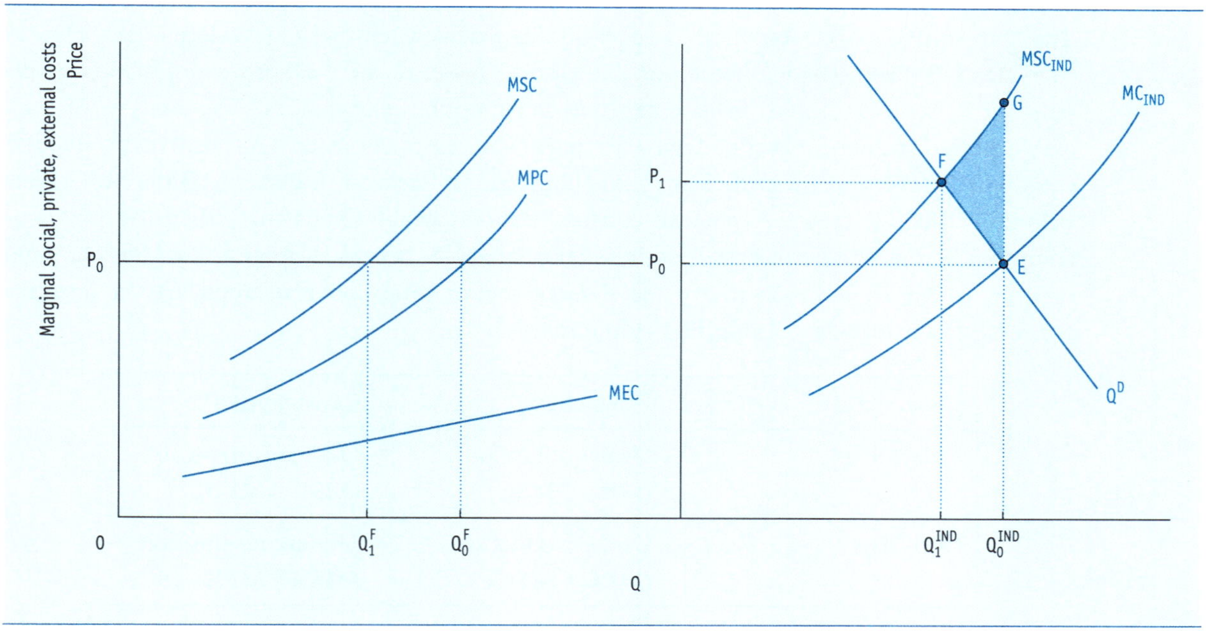

Figure 17.1A Production externality (firm) **Figure 17.1B Production externality (industry)**

industry in which it operates. The industry price when there are no externalities, P_0, is that given by the intersection of the market demand curve and the industry supply curve. Suppose the firm is responsible for emitting some type of harmful pollutant(s) into the environment. We can represent this by the marginal external cost schedule, labelled MEC in Figure 17.1A. This shows the additional environmental cost to others from an additional unit of output, and is assumed to rise as the firm's output rises.

The addition of the marginal external cost to the firm's marginal private cost, MPC, gives the marginal social cost, MSC. The marginal cost of production to the firm therefore understates the marginal cost to society. The vertical distance between the MPC and the MSC schedules in Figure 17.1A illustrates this. If the external cost of this one firm is typical of others in the industry, then the MSC for the industry will lie above the supply curve and this case is what is assumed in drawing Figure 17.1B.

The socially-efficient level of output is determined by the intersection of the MSC_{IND} curve and the industry demand curve, Q^D. This is given by Q_1^{IND} in Figure 17.1B where the associated price is P_1. The private decisions of individual firms, which ignore the social costs of pollution, leads to an inefficiently high level of production. For the individual firm this is shown by the distance $Q_0^F - Q_1^F$ in Figure 17.1A. For the industry, the extent of the oversupply is given by $Q_0^{IND} - Q_1^{IND}$ in Figure 17.1B. The welfare cost of the (industry) inefficiency is given by the area EFG. This measures for each unit of overproduction, the difference between the marginal social cost and the marginal benefit as represented by the market demand curve.

The competitive market outcome is generally inefficient when there are externalities. Figures 17.1A and B illustrate one of the possible cases. There are three others: a production externality that is positive, and positive/negative consumption externalities. The analysis of each case follows straightforwardly from the particular case discussed. A positive production externality leads to inefficiently low production, since in terms of Figure 17.1B the MSC_{IND} is below the MC_{IND} curve. A positive consumption externality leads to inefficiently low consumption of the good concerned, as the marginal social benefit is greater than the marginal private benefit as represented by the demand curve. The converse applies to a negative consumption externality. Table 17.1 summarises.

Externality	Production	Consumption
Negative	Overproduction (MPC < MSC)	Overconsumption (MSB < MPB)
Positive	Underproduction (MPC > MSC)	Underconsumption (MSB > MPB)

Table 17.1 Externalities in consumption and production

Responses to externalities: the Coase theorem

There are several alternative responses to externalities, some of which require government action, some of which do not. We will start by considering the argument that the market can still provide the efficient solution when there are externalities, which leads us to the Coase theorem.

To understand the main point of this theorem, we can think of an externality as something that arises from a 'missing' market. To keeps things simple, suppose that a production externality involves just two parties: a firm that is responsible for pollution and a second firm, a theme park, which is affected by it. The firm that pollutes the environment is using up clean air, which we can think of as a commodity like any other. If there were a market for clean air, then by conventional economic reasoning there would be a market price where (private) marginal benefit was equated with (private) marginal cost.

Without a market for clean air, the polluting firm is in the position where it can take its price as zero. The market system will not lead to efficient use of this resource as no one 'owns' clean air, and there are, therefore, no sellers or buyers. It can be argued that it is this absence of ownership rights that is the cause of the inefficient outcome.

If the polluting firm held the ownership rights they could, in principle, charge the theme park for the benefits of clean air. It would give the polluter an incentive not to 'over-pollute' because they would otherwise lose the payments from the theme park. Conversely, if the firm that operated the theme park owned the right to clean air, they could charge the polluter, who would then have to incorporate this charge into its costs of production. The logic of this argument is that the problems caused by externalities can be dealt with by putting resources into private ownership.

Suppose that the polluter is given ownership rights, it will base its output decisions at the margin on the compensation payment from the theme park and its loss of profit as output declines. If the compensation payments are greater than the reduction in profits, the firm has an incentive to reduce its output. Using Figure 17.1A to illustrate this point, the extent of the damage by the polluting firm is represented by the difference between the MSC and MPC schedules. This tells us the maximum amount the theme park would be prepared to pay to the polluter to reduce its output, and therefore gives the size of the compensation payments it would be willing to make. The loss in profit as output changes is simply the difference between the firm's marginal revenue and (private) marginal cost schedule.

At output levels below Q_1^F in the figure, it is evident that the compensation payment is less than the additional profit from increasing output. The compensation the theme park would be willing to offer is not sufficient to stop the polluting firm from expanding its output. At output levels above Q_1^F, the reverse is true and the firm can be given compensation large enough not to expand its output any further. In principle, if the polluter was given ownership rights, and there were no bargaining costs, the parties affected could agree to produce at the socially optimal output.

Alternatively, suppose that the theme park has a right to clean air. The question now becomes how much the polluting firm would be prepared to pay to it for permission to pollute. The answer to this is that the affected party accepts additional pollution levels as long as the compensation exceeds the damage done. The polluter finds it worthwhile to pay for the opportunity to produce more providing the additional cost of doing so is less than the additional revenue. In this case, the polluter would pay the theme park the difference between the MSC and MPC schedules. The polluter will again have an incentive to expand output up to Q_1^F, but not beyond. We again get the conclusion that the private market system will lead to the economically efficient output level.

There will be an efficient outcome providing that one or other party is given ownership rights. Who has the rights is obviously important in terms of the distribution of welfare but, in principle, the Coase theorem leads to separating issues that relate to economic efficiency from those that relate to equity. This analysis does, of course, assume away bargaining costs. In practice, externalities can involve millions of individuals across the globe and co-ordination of bargaining can be highly problematic. A part of these costs may be due to the free-rider problem. This occurs when, for individuals there is an incentive not to get involved, but to rely on the efforts of others to negotiate on their behalf without incurring any time or effort. If all individuals did this there would, of course, be no negotiation and no benefits.

Government intervention: regulation

In practice, governments do intervene to deal with environmental problems that arise, in part because of the absence of well-defined property rights and missing markets as discussed. Broadly, we can distinguish between regulation in the form of emissions standards, used to control various chemical processes and waste incineration for example, and taxes and subsidies. We will start with regulation.

Emissions standards and fees

Figure 17.2 illustrates the ways that emissions standards or fees might work. The horizontal axis of the figure measures the level of pollution emitted by a firm. The MSC curve again measures the marginal social cost of the firm's output. Suppose that the firm can reduce the level of pollution it is responsible for by the use of anti-pollution measures. The additional cost that the firm incurs from doing this is shown by the marginal cost of abatement curve, labelled MCA in the figure. The MCA curve is drawn on the assumption that the cost of successive reductions in emissions rise (given that the level of abatement is read from right to left in this figure).

By conventional reasoning, the efficient level of emissions is E_F in Figure 17.2, where MSC = MCA. A lower level of abatement expenditure would leave emissions above the level E_F; at the margin the cost of abating pollution is less than the social costs it imposes, and so the optimal level of abatement expenditure is always higher until we reach point E_F. Conversely, with a level of abatement higher than E_F. A zero level of pollution is therefore not optimal.

Both an emissions standard and an emissions fee could achieve an efficient outcome. A standard is a legally binding (quantity) limit on the level of emissions. In principle, this could be set at the level E_F in the Figure. A firm could then be discouraged from higher levels of emissions by financial penalties, or by legal redress. A fee is an amount the firm has to pay on each unit of the pollutant(s) emitted. In Figure 17.2 if this were set at F_F, it would achieve the same outcome as would an emissions standard.

This kind of analysis is rather simple. The impact of standards and fees differs when, for example, regulation policy has to be devised on the basis of incomplete information. In general, a regulator is not likely to be completely informed about differences in production methods. Figure 17.3 illustrates the case where the marginal cost of abatement differs between firms. The level of abatement is again read from right to left, i.e. as a reduction in emissions. Suppose there were just two firms, and that the MCA for Firm 1 is greater than that for Firm 2. This is shown

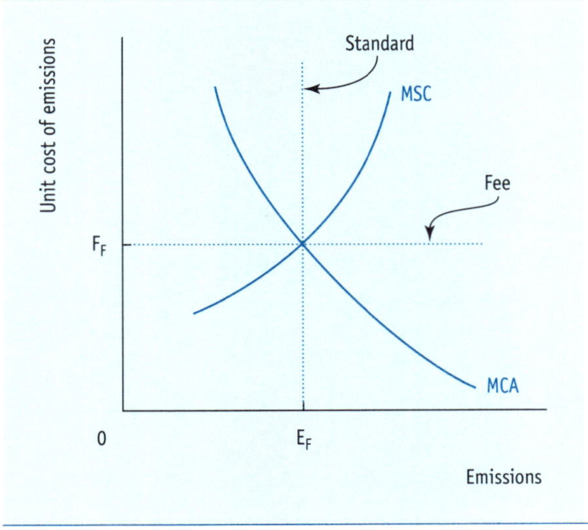

Figure 17.2 Emissions standards and fees

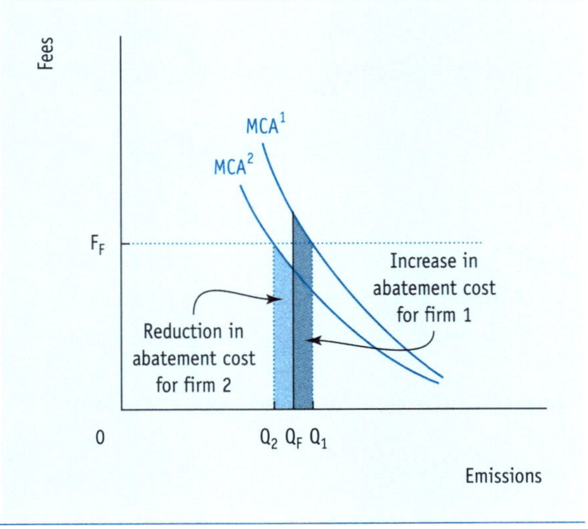

Figure 17.3 The case for an emissions fee

in Figure 17.3 by the respective positions of the two MCA schedules. If the regulator wanted to reduce the level of emissions to an average of Q_F per firm, the least cost way of doing this is for Firm 1 to reduce its emissions to Q_1 and for Firm 2 to reduce its emissions to Q_2. With this outcome, the marginal cost of abatement for the two firms is equal, and we have the most efficient way of obtaining a given reduction in the level of pollution.[3]

If both firms have to reduce their level of emissions to Q_F, the additional cost for Firm 1 is greater than the reduction in cost for Firm 2. This outcome is not therefore cost minimising; the same reduction in pollution could be efficiently achieved by setting an emissions fee equal to F_F. The charging of fees has the attraction that, in principle, they create an incentive for firms to introduce more environmentally friendly production techniques. A fee would be appropriate when all firms have to be judged by the same emissions criteria.

There are other circumstances where it may be preferable to adopt an emissions standard. In Figure 17.4 the efficient fee level is F_F, but suppose, because of incomplete information, the regulator has to set the fee below the efficient level at say F_0, then the welfare cost is large. In the figure, it is equal to the are EFG. A similar margin for error in terms of setting a standard produces a smaller social cost, in the figure it is given by the area EHI.

Emissions permits

An alternative to the use of either standards or fees is the use of transferable emissions permits. In the United States, for example, a Clean Air Act gives firms the legal right to emit a

3 This assumes that the MSC schedules of the two firms are the same.

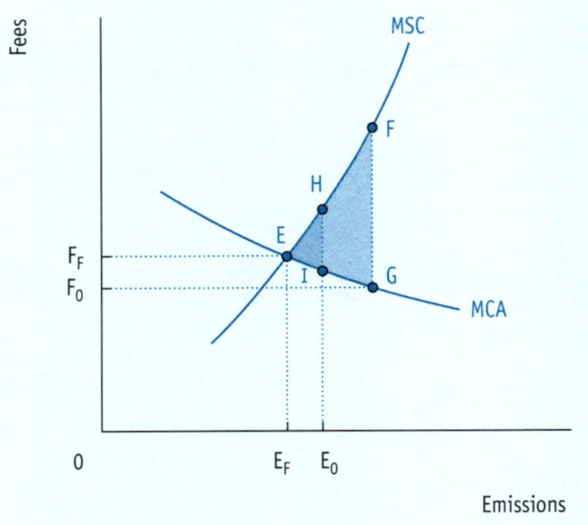

Figure 17.4 The case for an emissions standard

certain level of sulphur dioxide. A permit specifies a particular level of emissions. These can be traded, leaving firms with the option of purchasing a permit or adopting production methods that reduce emissions. Those that find the later expensive will therefore have an incentive to buy the permits.

In principle, a competitive market could be established for such permits, effectively creating a market for externalities: in equilibrium the price of an emissions permit would equal the marginal cost of abatement. Whatever the level of emissions determined by the regulator, the outcome would be achieved with the minimum cost.

Pigouvian taxes

One possible government response toward firms responsible for pollution is to raise the price of the firm's output by means of a tax. A Pigouvian tax is a tax levied on each unit of the firm's output, so that the amount the firm pays in tax equals the marginal external cost at the (socially) efficient level of output. In practice, this is not straightforward since it requires that the government has knowledge about the types and quantities of various pollutants, how they are used in production and what effect they have.[4] Figure 17.5A illustrates the effect of imposing a per unit tax to correct a negative externality. A tax equal to the difference between the MSC and MPC schedules at the output Q_1^F will lead to the Pareto-efficient output level. The revenue received from the tax is equal to $(MSC_1 - MPC_1) * O Q_1^F$ as shown by the shaded area in the figure, which may or may not be greater than the external cost. However, in principle, it could (at least partly) pay for the external damage. Given that we have allowed for an increasing marginal external cost function, a per unit tax that equals the

4 We will discuss the practicalities of these issues when discussing the particular case of road transport in Section 3.

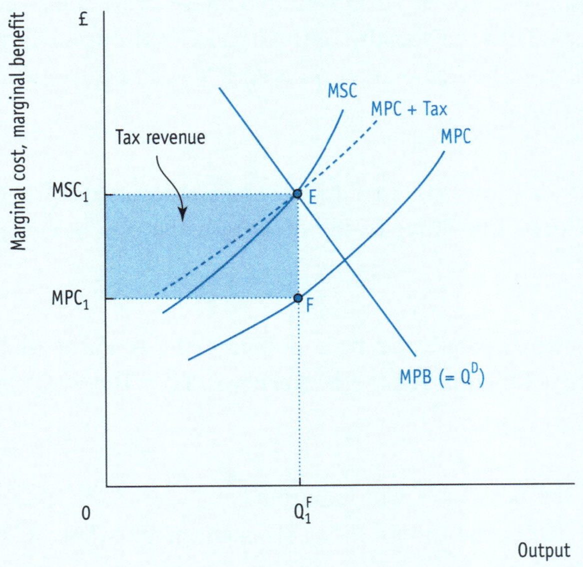

Figure 17.5A A Pigouvian tax

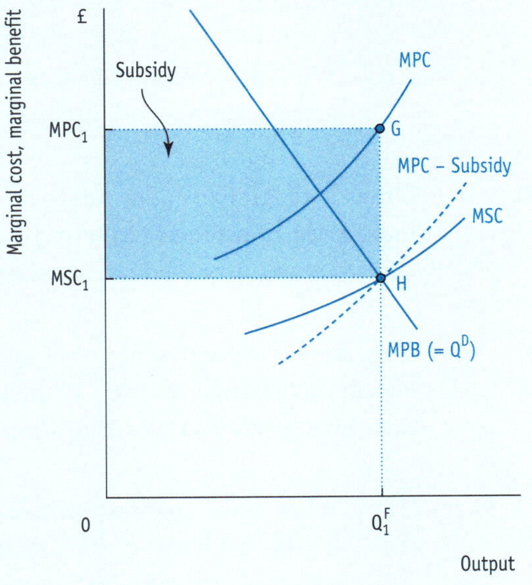

Figure 17.5B A subsidy

marginal external cost at QF_1, will be either an under- or an overestimate of the damage at other output levels.[5]

In the case of a positive production externality the relation between the MSC and MPC schedules is reversed and this is what is shown in Figure 17.5B. The market outcome is inefficient as the marginal private benefit measured by the demand curve equals the MSC at Q_1^F. Too little is produced and consumed. The government could again intervene, this time by providing a subsidy equal to GH in the figure. Consumers would then only pay the MSC of production. The cost to the government of the subsidy is given by $(MPC_1 - MSC_1) * O\,Q_1^F$. A per unit subsidy is of course only optimal at Q_1^F if the marginal external benefits rise as output rises. The subsidy would also need to be financed; at least a part of which could come from those who benefit from the externality.

Questions

Q1 The demand for the product of a competitive industry is $Q^D = 140 - P$ and the industry supply is given by $Q^S = -100 + P$, where Q is expressed in thousands of tonnes and P is in £.

(I) Obtain the free market equilibrium price and output level.

5 The Pareto-efficient output therefore requires that the government know the marginal external cost function.

(II) Suppose that the industry is responsible for environmental damage with social cost equal to 0.5 per unit of output. Calculate the socially optimal price and output levels.

(III) What is the welfare loss associated with the free market outcome? What tax level would achieve the socially optimal output level?

Q2 Draw a diagram similar to Figure 17.2 to show the cost to the firm associated with the imposition of a fee at the level F_F. How does this differ to the firm from the cost associated with adhering to an emissions standard?

Q3 A beekeeper operates near an apple orchard, where the bees pollinate the orchard to the benefit of the apple-grower. If the total cost function for the beekeeper is $TC = 100 + 2Q^2$ and each hive yields £24 worth of honey,

(I) What is the number of hives that the beekeeper will maintain?

(II) If the orchard owner saves £8 from the pollination of each hive, what is the economically efficient number of hives?

17.2 Externalities and the global environment

In this section, we will look at the global environmental picture and discuss a number of issues relating to common property resources, by which we simply mean a valuable asset to which all are given free access. The atmosphere and the oceans are examples of common property resources.

The co-ordination and implementation of policy raises some particular questions in an international context. There is no world government that can effect socially desirable outcomes when there are externalities and enforcement of policy agreements may be difficult because of free rider problems. There may also be problems that arise with the use of market-based instruments, if they result in large changes in prices and have a large effect on the (global) distribution of income.

There are international institutions such as the United Nations Environment Programme which have been mandated to co-ordinate environmental protection efforts. These institutions, however, have to respect the sovereignty of national governments and so international policy relies primarily on agreement. Where there is no agreement, policy is likely to be frustrated, as with the experience of the International Whaling Commission, for example. The Commission has found that attempts to introduce bans or prohibitions against killing some whales have been resisted by the countries affected.

Global warming

While the scientific basis of predictions of global warming remains uncertain, the conceivable damage from this phenomenon by the middle of the 21st century is huge. Table 17.2 presents a breakdown of the emissions that are thought by many scientists to be responsible, the so-called greenhouse gases.[6]

Gas	Source
Carbon dioxide	Generated by burning forests, fossil fuels
Chlorofluoro-carbons (CFC's)	Used in refrigerators and air conditioning systems
Methane	Generated by rotting vegetation
Nitrous oxides	Generated by the breakdown of fertilisers

Table 17.2 A breakdown of greenhouse gases by source
Source: European Economy (1992).

The policy questions posed by global warming are difficult and the approach taken by the European Union has for the most part been cautious. In the 1990s, it has set targets to stabilise, or reduce, the emissions of CO_2 gases in particular. The progress made between 1990 and 1995 within the EU is shown in Chart 17.1, which shows a modest overall reduction, although there is considerable variation between member states.

EU policy involves a range of measures, including an energy-carbon tax and increases in annual vehicle licence duties.[7] The use of energy-carbon taxes, and taxes on motoring, to meet environmental objectives are interesting because they link efficiency and equity issues. The proposed EU carbon tax was intended to be a tax on the carbon content of coal, oil and gas. The idea was to tax non-renewable forms of energy such as nuclear power at one rate, but to levy a higher rate on coal, oil and gas providing an incentive to switch to other forms of energy. In principle, a tax on carbon has an advantage over value based taxes, such as VAT, in that it is less affected by variations in coal or oil prices. Denmark, Finland and Austria do have carbon taxes, but attempts by the EU to introduce one generally have been delayed and frustrated.

There have been a number of studies of the effect of introducing a carbon-energy tax on the distribution of income. One simulation exercise by Symons, Proops and Gay found that a tax

6 But not all scientists.

7 Also a range of voluntary and regulatory measures aimed at promoting energy conservation.

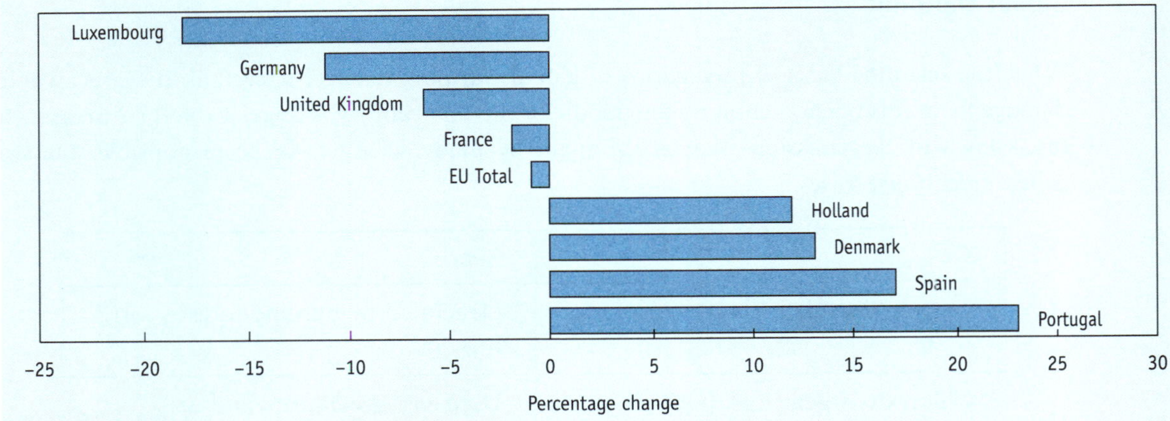

Chart 17.1 Changes in CO_2 emissions in EU 1990–95
Source: Transport Statistics (various).

which set out to reduce CO_2 emissions by 20% had a severely regressive effect, that is the proportion of the income paid in tax was highest at the bottom end of the distribution of income. Achieving such a reduction in emissions levels would, of course, raise tax revenue which, in turn, could be used to raise the level of social security benefits paid to those affected. However, the consequence of a revenue-neutral reform in terms of the government's finances would be to limit the reduction in demand; for instance, the effect of such a package in the simulation was to halve the amount by which $C0_2$ emissions were reduced.

International co-operation

The deforestation of the Amazon rain forests is a good example of what is called a uni-directional externality. The forests play a globally important role in the preservation of biological diversity; burning the forests for cattle ranching, or hydroelectric schemes, puts a large number of species in danger of extinction. The forests also absorb carbon dioxide. With no global government, the rights to generate these externalities are, in effect, vested in the Brazilian government.

Game theory analyses may help in understanding the nature of the problems this creates for international policy-making.[8] For simplicity, we will examine the problems of co-ordinating policy in a two-country model where each country emits a certain level of pollution. Country 1's pollution affects both countries, whereas that generated in country 2 is restricted to its own borders. Both are able to invest in costly abatement technology, or make costly changes to government policy, which reduce emissions levels.

8 The discussion here draws on Romp (1997).

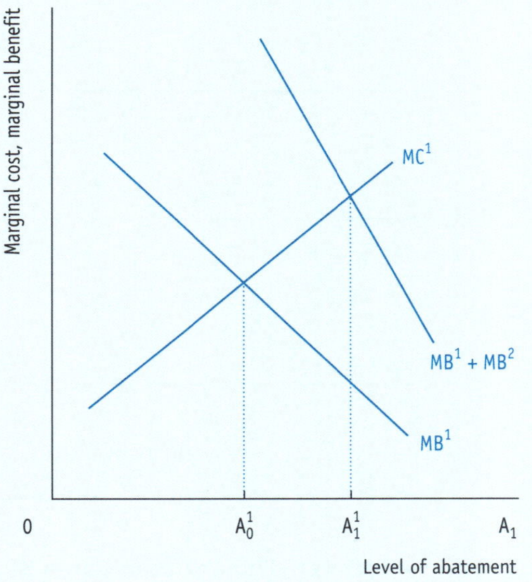

Figure 17.6A **A unidirectional externality: country 1's position**

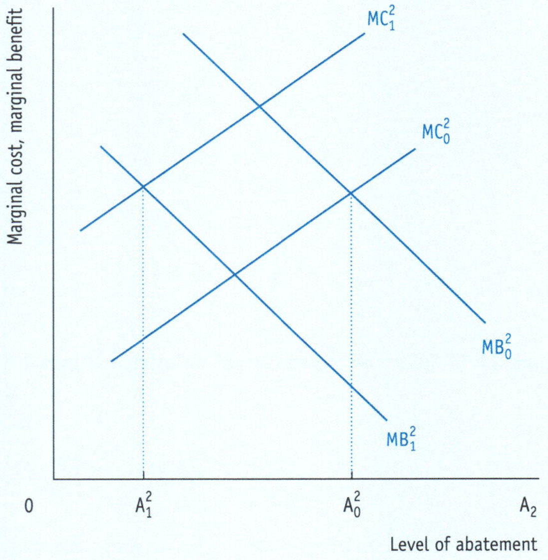

Figure 17.6B **Country 2's position**

In a non co-operative game, each country determines the level of abatement that maximises its own social welfare. A reduction in pollution increases welfare, so, applying the decision-making discussed in Section 1, both countries will equate the marginal benefits and marginal costs of abatement measures. This is illustrated in Figures 17.6A and 17.6B, which shows the marginal benefit and the marginal cost schedules, MB and MC, for both countries.[9] Country 1 equates its marginal benefit schedule, MB^1 with that for its marginal cost, MC^1, giving an abatement level of A_0^1. The corresponding level of abatement for country 2 is A_0^2.

The reaction functions of the two countries are shown in Figure 17.7. The benefits and costs for country 1 are independent of the pollution level in country 2 and whatever abatement measures that country 2 adopts. It follows that country 1's reaction function R_0^1 is horizontal in the figure. From the perspective of country 2, its benefits and costs will be dependent on emission levels in country 1. If country 1 were to reduce its emissions, it would mean less pollution in country 2. In turn, this would reduce the marginal benefit and increase the marginal cost of abatement for country 2, so leading to a reduction in its abatement measures. It follows that the reaction curve of that country will be downward sloping in Figure 17.7.

A move down the reaction function of country 2, R^2, is associated with a lower level of welfare for that country as it reflects a higher level of abatement. In a non co-operative game, the

9 These schedules again assume that the marginal benefit falls and the marginal cost rises as the level of abatement rises.

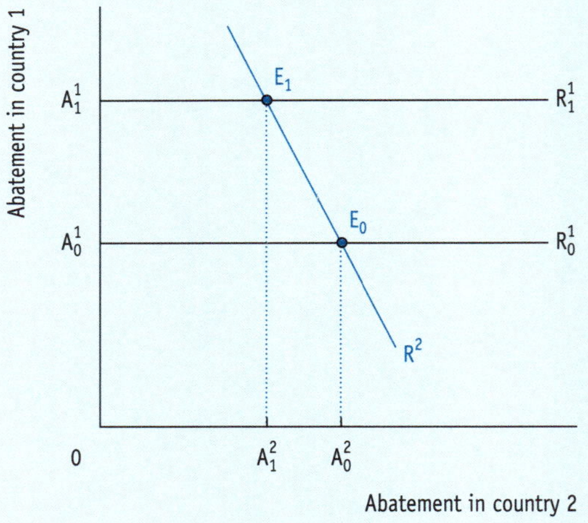

Figure 17.7 Reaction functions of countries 1 and 2

equilibrium point is E_0 where the two reaction functions intersect. The abatement level of the two countries are just those that equate their own national benefits and costs. In the language of game theory, we have a Nash equilibrium.

In a co-operative game, the countries would maximise their joint social welfare. For country 2, this means no changes in its actions. Country 1 would now set the sum of the marginal benefits in both countries equal to its marginal cost of abatement. In Figure 17.6A, this is shown by the intersection of the schedule labelled $MB^1 + MB^2$ with the marginal cost schedule, MC^1. Its optimal abatement level is now A_1^1; in Figure 17.7 there is a new equilibrium at point at E_1. The response of country 2 is to reduce its abatement to A_1^2 as the marginal benefit of abatement falls and the marginal cost rises. Country 2 has been made better off at the expense of country 1 in the process of maximising joint welfare.

It is possible, in principle, to reach a co-operative outcome without changing the assumption that each country acts in its own interest by introducing what are called side payments. In the context of the two-country model, this would involve payments from country 2 to country 1, although this kind of arrangement does not usually happen in practice. Negotiations between countries on environmental problems tend to be based on the principle of a right to an unpolluted environment, sometimes referred to as as the Polluter Pays Principle (PPP).

Global environmental problems, of course, require multilateral agreements rather than bilateral ones, and are therefore likely to encounter the free rider problem. The game theory analysis of environmental protection is not therefore particularly encouraging in terms of the welfare outcomes it points to. However, with common property resources, the analysis of repeated games may be more appropriate. Given the choice of the co-operative and non co-operative strategies, there may be tacit agreement between the parties and the equilibrium outcome could be the co-operative strategy. The analysis also assumes a rather simplified set of objectives for both parties. The welfare objective of each country may be, in part at least, guided by some (moral) principle that it should take account of the effect of its decisions on other countries.

Question

Q4 Two individuals live in separate flats in a converted house. They both place a monetary value of £1,000 on clean air but the cost of an air purification system is £1,500. If one individual does decide to pay for it, there is no way that the other can be prevented from receiving the benefits.

(I) Construct a pay-off matrix for the two individuals. What is the dominant strategy equilibrium?

(II) What (side) payment would be necessary for a Pareto-improvement on the dominant strategy equilibrium?

17.3 Road transport and the environment

In this section, we will discuss the growth of private car usage, the external costs that are imposed on others and the possible responses of government to remedy the market inefficiency that arises. There has been a long-term trend towards individual car use. In the mid-1950s, under a quarter of all UK households had a car, by the 1990s, two households in three owned a least one vehicle and around a quarter have two vehicles or more. The trends in passenger transport are shown in Chart 17.2. As incomes have grown and social organisation changed the number of bus journeys made has fallen dramatically. Changing social structure, which is projected to increase the number of single person households, is likely to lead to a further increase in the demand for private cars in the 21st century.

Simple economic theory suggests that individual car users will make decisions based on their private costs and benefits.[10] Private motoring costs do not include the social cost of air and noise pollution. Repairs and additional maintenance of roads become necessary as traffic volumes increase, and there are considerable costs of traffic congestion in some urban areas. There are also the costs associated with accidents.

10 This assumes that individuals base their decision on a narrow view of financial criteria, though some individuals may take into account environmental concerns.

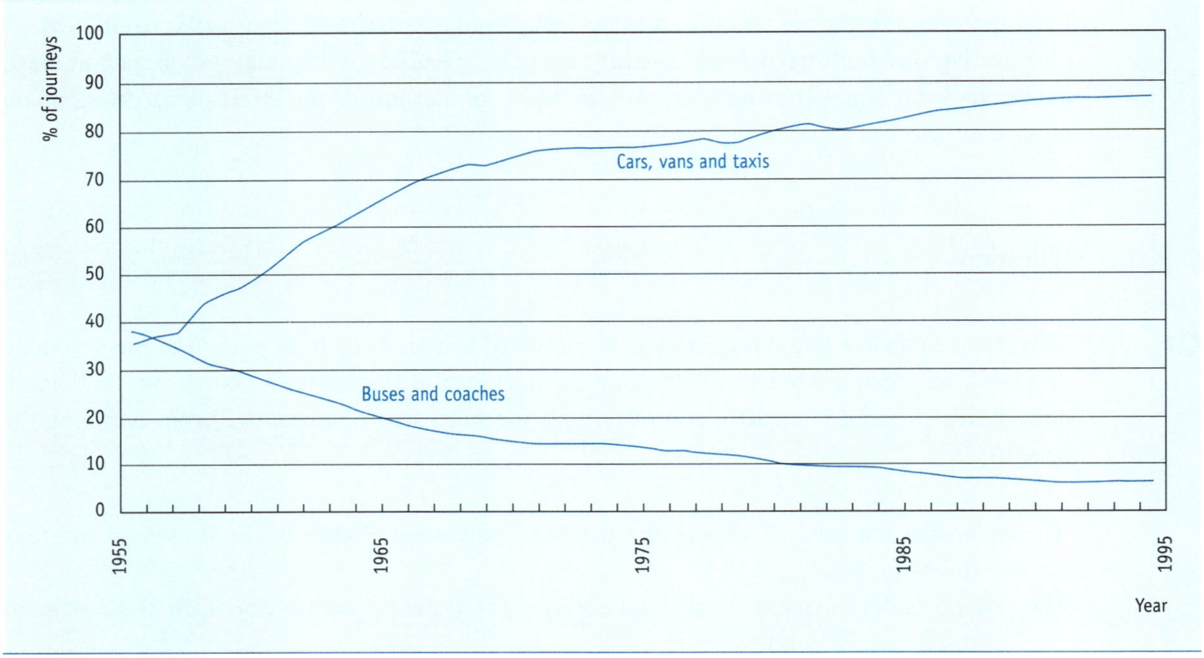

Chart 17.2 Passenger transport by mode 1955–96
Source: Transport Statistics (1998).

Our discussion of principle suggested that to deal with the problem road users should pay the true social cost of their journeys. How this might be done? We will concentrate here on the environmental externalities of pollution and congestion, but we can note that awkward questions of measurement arise with the other types of social cost. The cost of an accident externality, for example, arises when an increase in the number of road vehicles increases the probability of someone being in an accident. This leads to additional health-care costs, but the overall figure depends very much on how the loss (or the saving) of a life is valued. Possible approaches to this question include surveys of the willingness to pay, WTP, of individuals, and estimates based on the earnings foregone of the accident victim.[11]

Taxing pollution

Road users are responsible for emissions of harmful pollutants such as oxides of nitrogen and carbon dioxide. Traffic in the 1990s accounted for well over a half of the total of the first of these and around a quarter of the second. Carbon dioxide emissions have fallen in the UK overall in the last 25 years, although emissions from road transport have almost doubled.[12]

11 Estimates of the cost of accidents are also based on a link between traffic volumes and the risk of accident, the extent of which is open to some doubt as it may be that driver behaviour adjusts as the volume of traffic increases.

12 Future trends will be sensitive to the rate of technical improvements, the level of emissions of nitrogen oxide have been falling and technical improvements may continue this trend.

From a policy perspective, it is desirable to try and control the level of emissions as directly as possible, either by quantity controls or by imposing a tax. The government may not be able to measure (or accurately estimate) the emissions of private cars, which it needs to do if it is to impose a Pigouvian tax. Nor is the government well informed about the reaction of individual motorists to the introduction of a tax. However, rather than take the ideal outcome as the target, policy can still pragmatically set a tax rate that would reduce pollution below what it would otherwise have been. To some extent, the uncertainty surrounding the appropriate level of tax, and the subsequent behavioural response of motorists, can be reduced by adjustments to the rate of tax over time.

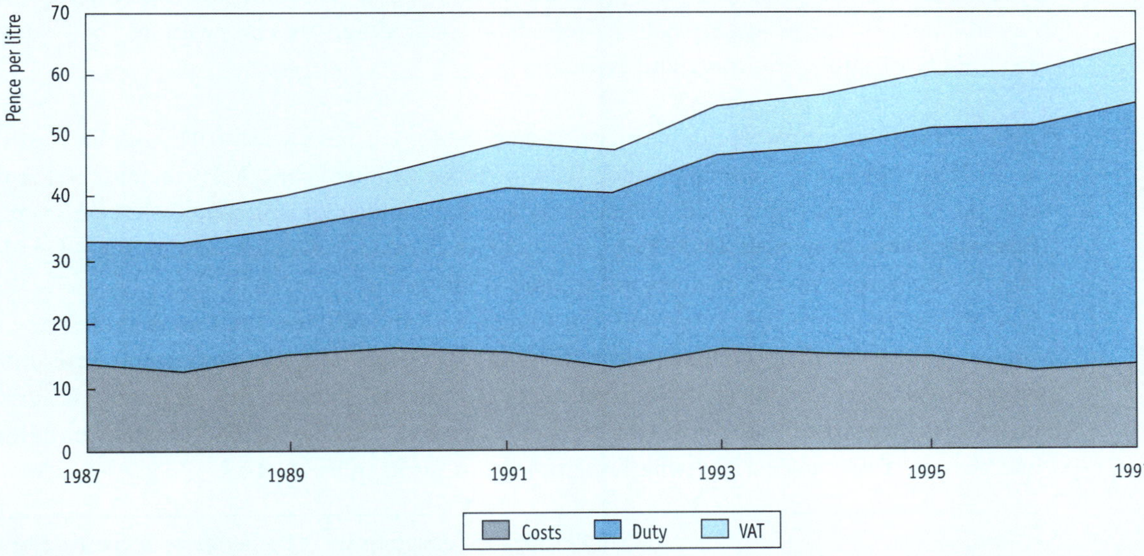

Chart 17.3 **Tax and petrol prices 1987–97**
Source: Transport Statistics (various).

Taxation may also have some advantages over regulation in the long run. It may provide incentives to introduce cheaper methods of abatement because the level of pollution is charged per unit. This is less likely to happen if all that is required is compliance with some minimum standard. In the UK, there are two main taxes levied on private motorists: road fuel taxes and Vehicle Excise Duty, VED. Excise duty on car fuel is an indirect way of trying to achieve the same end as a Pigouvian tax since, broadly, there is a link from fuel consumption levels to carbon dioxide emissions and global warming. It can be argued, therefore, that a fuel tax is an appropriate way of taxing this externality. To this end UK governments have embarked on a policy of substantial real increases in fuel duties. Chart 17.3 shows the trend in petrol prices and tax levels over the period 1987–97 in the UK.

Distributional impact of fuel duty

A tax change is one practical way of trying to improve economic efficiency. However, as was mentioned in connection with an energy-carbon tax, this kind of policy response will have an impact on the distribution of individual welfare as well. To gauge the impact of such a policy requires an estimate of the behavioural response of motorists, and more particularly how the demand for fuel varies between households.

A study by Blow and Crawford (1997) estimated a model of car usage that was used for analysis of the (compensated) demand responses to policy changes. Using data from the National Travel Survey, the key relation they estimated was that between car mileage done per household and the price per mile. This estimate is given a number of controls (or other determinants of car mileage) such as household income and its composition, the cost and availability of public transport and so on.

Their estimate of the own-price elasticity of demand for car miles was –0.41, with an elasticity of –0.48 for single car households and –0.20 for those with two cars. A 1% increase in the real cost per mile of driving would therefore reduce the number of miles by 0.48% on average. Generally, two-car households have higher incomes than do those with one household, and so may be less responsive to changes in the cost of motoring.[13]

This was then used to simulate the effects of tax changes on the demand for car miles. Simulations were done to analyse the effect of a 4.5% real increase in fuel prices and a 30% increase (as a proxy for the effect of 6 years' increases). The estimated reduction in mileage and the effect on the cost of living for motorists is given in Table 17.3.

	Weekly mileage reduction		**% increase in the cost of living (car owners)**	
Duty increase	4.5%	30%	4.5%	30%
All car owners	2.6	16.4	0.25	1.6
One-car households	3.1	19.2	0.28	1.7
Two-car households	1.4	8.8	0.19	1.2
Company cars	2.9	18.5	0.26	1.6

Table 17.3 Effects of increase in road duty
Source: Blow and Crawford (1997).

13 The average income elasticity of demand was estimated at 0.20.

For example, the average effect on all car owners of a 4.5% increase in fuel duty is estimated to be to reduce weekly motoring by 2.6 miles. The cumulative effect over a period of six years is, however, estimated to be over 800 miles per year on average, with a greater impact on single car households. The effect on the cost-of-living indices for households with cars are shown in the third and fourth columns. This gives the estimate of what increase in income would restore the pre-tax change level of welfare.[14]

The effect on the distribution of income of such a policy change is rather mixed since the poorest households tend not to own a car, and are not directly affected. Their cost of living may fall if they external costs of motorists are reduced. For those that do own a car, the study found that the poorest tenth will face an estimated increase in their cost-of-living of over 2%. For those in the richest tenth it was estimated to be less than 1%.

Congestion costs

As mentioned, pollution costs are only one type of social cost associated with private motoring. Another important external cost is that which arises from increased journey times when traffic volumes increase. For congestion costs, what we require is an estimate of the total amount of extra time taken by all other vehicles as the traffic volume increases per vehicle: the marginal congestion cost, MCC, of an extra vehicle.[15] As you would expect, congestion costs vary enormously between rural/urban areas and between peak/off-peak times, as the estimates given in Table 17.4 indicate.

The table shows a congestion cost of around 4.2 pence per passenger car unit per kilometre, PCUkm, one measure of the amount of traffic). In 1993, the total figure for PCUkm was 456bn, giving an overall figure for congestion costs of £19bn in 1993 prices.

Designing an appropriate policy response to congestion costs may be more problematic than it is with pollution costs. The evidence in the table suggests that private motorists are significantly undercharged for road use, particularly at peak times in urban areas. Raising the price of motoring in an appropriate way is a difficult exercise simply because the costs vary so enormously. A fuel tax is a very imprecise instrument. In some European countries, charges such as motorway tolls are made for road use. However, in the UK, with a large number of motorway junctions particularly in, and around, cities, tolls may be rather impractical in many cases.[16]

14 In terms of the discussion of Chapter 2, this is the compensating variation required.

15 The marginal cost of the additional trip increases with traffic volume and is above the average cost. To the extent that motorists base their journeys on the average cost, traffic volumes are too high because the marginal private benefit is less than the marginal social cost.

16 The development of technology may make electronic tagging of vehicles practical in the future. The driver can then be charged for the distance travelled.

	MCCp/PCUkm
Motorway	0.32
Urban central peak	44.74
Urban central off-peak	35.95
Non-central peak	19.51
Non-central off-peak	10.75
Small town peak	8.47
Small town off-peak	5.17
Other urban	0.08
Rural dual carriageway	0.06
Other trunk and principal	0.23
Other rural	0.06
Average	**4.18**

Table 17.4 **Costs of congestion in Britain 1993**
Source: Newbery (1993).

Reducing the cost of public transport to obtain a second-best solution is not without its difficulties either. A congestion charge of 44 pence per km would be needed at peak times in urban centres (1993 prices) and a higher figure for some roads where traffic is particularly slow. It would be difficult to reduce the cost of public transport by this order, although increases in subsidy levels may be a part of overall policy.

Questions

Q5 How would you go about measuring the opportunity cost of lost time through travel congestion?

Q6 An effective system of road pricing should (I) relate the charges to the amount of road use by the motorist; (II) vary between peak and off-peak times; and (III) be known in advance by individuals. Are there any schemes that meet these criteria?

Summary

1 An externality is an action taken by an individual or firm which affects others in ways not connected to the price mechanism. Externalities are important because they suggest that a market economy may not lead to a Pareto-efficient outcome.

2 Consumption externalities drive a wedge between the marginal private benefit, measured by the demand curve, and the marginal social benefit. Production externalities drive a wedge between marginal private costs and marginal social cost. With a positive consumption externality the private benefit is less than the social benefit. If it is negative, then the opposite is the case. A negative production externality means that the marginal social cost is greater than the private cost; with a positive externality it is the other way around.

3 There are a number of possible responses to the problems caused by externalities. Coases' theorem suggests that bargaining between the parties involved could, in principle, lead to the socially efficient level of output without intervention by government. This theorem does not take account of bargaining costs (and the potential for the free rider problem).

4 A central authority may intervene to regulate harmful pollutants. Emissions can be reduced by the introduction of standards or fees, or by establishing a market for tradable permits. However, a non-zero level of emissions may be economically efficient.

5 Governments may intervene to impose taxes or to provide subsidies. This can also lead to socially efficient levels of production or consumption. This takes no account of administrative costs and the information needed about the external costs or benefits.

6 Common property resources such as the oceans or the atmosphere raise particular problems of international co-ordination. The use of game theory offers some insights into the problems that arise.

7 In practice, while the use of taxes for environmental purposes may increase efficiency, there will also be important effects on the distribution of income if the change in tax rates is large. This can make the introduction of certain taxes difficult, energy-carbon taxes are a case in point.

8 There has been a long-term increase in demand for private car travel. This creates a number of externalities from congestion, pollution and road damage from road users.

9 The use of road fuel duties in the UK has been partly motivated by environmental concerns. The British government in the 1990s committed itself to a series of large increases in fuel duty over a period of 6 years. The estimates of one model suggests that the own-price elasticity of

demand for car miles is around –0.48. The cumulative effect of a 30% increase in the price of fuel is estimated to be a reduction of around 800 miles per year for the average motorist.

10 Policy responses to the congestion costs of motoring are problematic because of the very wide variation in costs at different times and in different places. Road tolls are practicable on cost grounds in some countries, but not in others. Subsidising public transport would be one way of changing the relative prices that motorists face.

End of chapter questions

Q7 Ralph and Rowena live in a university residence where there are two goods: wine and music. Ralph likes very loud music, Rowena does not. Assume that when music is played both individuals have to listen to it. They sleep for 8 hours a night and are given eight glasses of wine each.

(I) Draw a box diagram in which hours of music are measured on the vertical axis and the amount of wine is measured on the horizontal axis. Ralph's utility function is

$$U_{RA} = W + M$$

and Rowena's utility function is

$$U_{RO} = W - M$$

Where W represents the number of glasses of wine and M is the number of hours of music at high volume. Sketch in some indifference curves for the two individuals.

(II) Suppose there is a policy not to have to listen to another person's music. Where is the endowment point? Can both individuals be made better off by trading?

(III) If there was a policy that allowed anyone to play their music at whatever volume they wished where would the endowment point be? Is a Pareto-improvement on this endowment point possible?

Q8 Show diagrammatically the welfare costs associated with positive and negative consumption externalities.

Q9 Two separate industries have marginal abatement cost schedules given by $MCA_I = 100 - 5Q$ and $MCA_{II} = 60 - Q$ respectively, where Q measure the emissions of a pollutant.

(I) The marginal social cost of pollution in the first industry is given by the function $MSC_I = 20Q$, in the second industry it is $MSC_{II} = 5Q$. What is the socially optimal level of pollution in each industry?

(II) What is the least cost solution to obtain the socially optimal pollution level?

Q10 Would it be possible to achieve a 20% reduction in $C0_2$ emissions in the UK by the year 2010 without reducing use of private motor transport? If so, how?

Q11 Is a fifth terminal at Heathrow Airport desirable?

References and suggested further reading

An alternative discussion of principles is provided in all the main microeconomics textbooks listed before. Lee provides a readable overview of the changing context of environmental policy in the EU. The study by Blow and Crawford gives a lot of empirical background on private motoring costs and the effects of higher fuel taxes. Button gives more detail on the background to the material in Section 3.

Barrett, S. (1996), 'The Problem of Global Environmental Protection', in Jenkinson, T. (ed.) *Readings in Microeconomics*, Oxford University Press.

Blow, L. and Crawford, I. (1997), *The Distributional Effects of Taxes on Private Motoring*, Institute for Fiscal Studies, London.

British Lung Foundation (1998), *Transport and Pollution: The Health Costs.*

Button, K.J. (1993), *Transport Economics*, Edward Elgar.

Department of the Environment (1996), *Digest of Environmental Statistics.*

European Economy (1992), 'The Climate Challenge, Economic Aspects of the Community's Strategy for Limiting CO_2 Emissions', **51**, May.

Lee, N. (1997), 'Environmental Policy' in Artis, M.J. and Lee, N. (eds), The *Economics of the European Union*, 2nd edition, Oxford.

Newbery, D.M. (1996), 'Pricing and Congestion: Economic Principles Relevant to Pricing Roads' in Jenkinson, T. (ed.) *Readings in Microeconomics*, Oxford University Press.

Romp, G. (1997), *Game Theory*, Oxford University Press.

Symons, E., Proops, J. and Gay, P. (1994), 'Carbon taxes, consumer demand and carbon dioxide emissions: a simulation analysis for the UK', *Fiscal Studies*, **15**, 2.

18 The Distribution of Income

Key ideas and material

Measurement questions, inequality trends, poverty and income dynamics

Introduction

The analysis of general equilibrium presented in Chapter 16 was primarily concerned with economic efficiency. We introduced there two fundamental theorems of welfare economics. The first theorem implied that in a simple model of a competitive economy the allocation of resources would be somewhere on the utilities possibility frontier. The second theorem tells us that, in principle at least, questions of efficiency and equity can be separated. A competitive market economy can produce any Pareto-efficient distribution between individuals provided that the endowment of resources is appropriate. This points to lump sum income transfers as a means of redistribution, rather than taxes and subsidies which affect relative prices and could therefore reduce economic efficiency.

This kind of analysis is a starting point. It leaves wide open a range of questions, of both fact and principle, which are important in a discussion of social welfare. What is the endowment of resources between individuals? Should we be concerned with an individual's resources at a particular point in time, or over his or her lifetime? Is it appropriate to aggregate individuals into family units or households? In practice, how and why do governments set about redistributing resources? The discussion of these issues is begun in Section 1, which looks at some conceptual questions and a number of issues of measurement.

Changes in the distribution of resources between individuals over time can lead to a range of social problems. If some individuals are drawn into problems related to the misuse of drugs, or if long spells of unemployment creates difficulties for some in making the transition back to work, this may subsequently impose economic costs on the majority of the population. The degree of income mobility is therefore important: what proportion of those with the least resources remain in that situation over time? Of those that move up the income distribution, do they have any individual characteristics, or are there particular circumstances which differentiate them from those who don't? These questions are introduced in Section 2, and explored in more detail in Section 3.

Section 3 also discusses the important subject of poverty. A first step is simply to clarify the distinction between absolute and relative poverty. The extent and importance of poverty is a controversial subject and, in this section, we will point to the importance of careful data analysis in estimating the extent of poverty in the UK and elsewhere.

18.1 Measurement questions

The distribution of income or expenditure?

In Chapter 4, we analysed the life-cycle model, which predicted that individuals adjust their consumption to their lifetime income. Broadly, the message was that in the early and late stages of their lifecycle, individuals go through periods when expenditure exceeds income. This might be while paying for a period of study for example, or to maintain consumption when they are no longer working. These periods were financed by savings during the individual's working life. The life-cycle theory, therefore, points to expenditure rather than income as a measure of individual welfare at a given point in time. In principle, if all individuals had the same lifetime resources at their disposal, the simplest version of the theory predicts that all would have the same lifetime consumption levels. We would nevertheless observe variations in incomes simply because individuals would be at different stages of their lifecycles.

The model discussed was based on a number of simplifying assumptions which, in practice, are not met. Capital markets are not perfect: it is not always easy to borrow against future labour income, and sometimes it is not possible at all. The empirical evidence discussed in that chapter suggested that people do not conform to the behavioural assumptions of the simplified model. Those in retirement with financial and housing assets do not always run them down to zero, in part because individuals face uncertainty about both the timing, and the amount, of future needs.

However, basing an assessment of social welfare over the (complete) lifecycle of individuals would be a gargantuan, impractical task. To keep the discussion manageable, we will take a year as the time horizon in much of what follows. This, of course, leaves the question of looking at income or expenditure (or both), which is important because the statistical picture of inequality can be quite sensitive to which is used. Many empirical studies use income because of the availability of data, and what follows here draws on a number of them. We will therefore be mainly concerned with the distribution of income.

Statistical measures: the Lorenz curve and the Gini coefficient

In principle, we want to be able to describe the levels of income received by each individual in an economy. In the UK, for example, there are around 40 million adults so what is required is a combination of a (large) survey of data on individual incomes, and also a way of summarising the information. The surveys of data we will come to below. Summarising information on incomes can be done very simply by, for example, tabulating income levels by percentiles of the population. An alternative often used by economists is to draw a Lorenz curve, and compute an associated statistic, the Gini coefficient.[1]

A Lorenz curve shows the share of total or national income going to a particular percentage of the population. In Figure 18.1A, we measure the population on the horizontal axis ordered from those with the lowest income on the left, to those with the highest income on the right. We can then mark off proportions: those with incomes in the lowest 20%, those in the next 20% and so on. On the vertical axis is measured the shares of total income, ordered from 0% at the bottom to 100% at the top.

We can now draw a Lorenz curve. To take one extreme case, suppose everybody had the same income, then the curve is a line of complete equality as drawn in the figure. Those with the 'lowest' 20% of incomes receive the same income share — 20% — as those with the 'highest' 20% of incomes. In Figure 18.1A, we have marked points on the horizontal axis at each 20% of the population. Reading the associated points on the vertical axis gives exactly the same proportion of income at each point. Each individual within each percentile range will get the same income as any other individual in any other percentile range.

At the other extreme end of the possibilities is a distribution in which one individual received all income and no one else received anything. In this situation, the Lorenz curve would coincide with the two axes. This is shown starkly in Figure 18.1B.

The Gini coefficient is a statistical measure of inequality and summarises the information represented by the Lorenz curve in one number. The coefficient can be measured by the area between the Lorenz curve and the diagonal divided by the total area under the diagonal.

This number associated with this ratio therefore lies between 0 and 1. When there is complete equality, the Lorenz curve is the diagonal so the measure gives a value of 0. This is the case shown in Figure 18.1A. At the other extreme where one individual receives all the income, the area between the Lorenz curve and the diagonal is equal to the area under the diagonal, and

1 This statistic is often used in official publications and academic studies on the distribution of income.

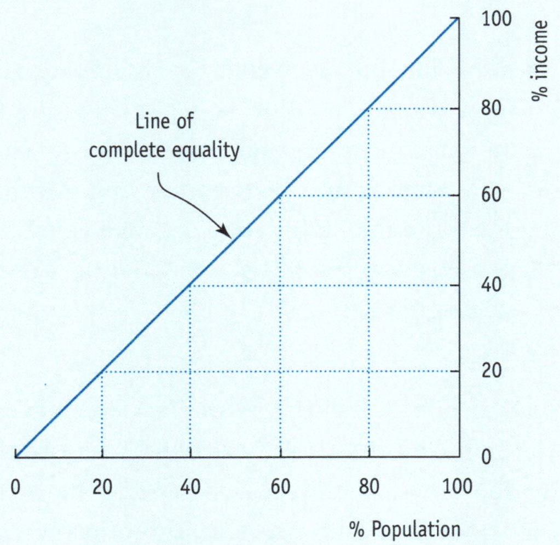

Figure 18.1A **The Lorenz curve (complete equality)**

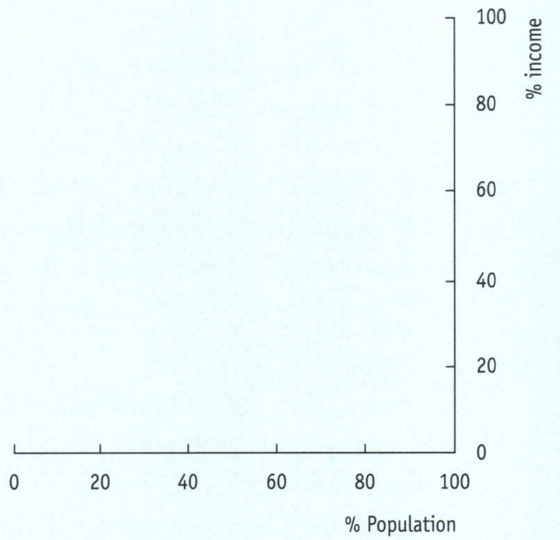

Figure 18.1B **The Lorenz curve (complete inequality)**

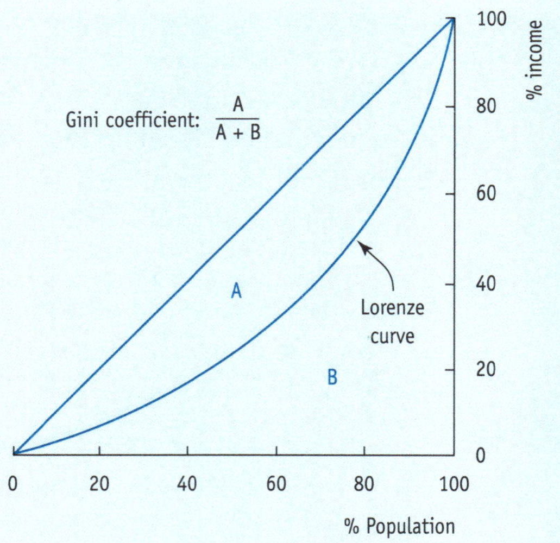

Figure 18.1C **The Lorenz curve and the Gini coefficient**

hence the Gini coefficient takes the value of 1. This is what is shown in Figure 18.1B. A more realistic example is shown in Figure 18.1C where the Lorenz curve lies between the diagonal and the axes. The Gini coefficient is simply the ratio A/(A + B).

A simple numerical example may help with understanding the Gini. Table 18.1 gives incomes for a hypothetical economy with four individuals.

Individual	1	2	3	4
Income	30	65	80	145

Table 18.1 Incomes in a hypothetical economy

Algebraically, the Gini coefficient can be expressed as

$$G = (2/n^2\bar{Y})\sum i(Y_i - \bar{Y})$$

In our example n = 4 and $\bar{Y}$ = 80, so

$$G = (2/1280)[1(30 - 80) + 2(65 - 80) + 3(80 - 80) + 4(145 - 80)]$$

which gives a Gini coefficient of 0.28.

If, for example, all the incomes were equal, then the deviation of each individual's income from the mean income would be zero and each term inside the [ ] brackets would be zero. The overall measure would then be zero as well.

Data issues

Information on household incomes in the UK comes from large government surveys, including the Family Expenditure Survey, the FES and the British Household Panel Survey, the BHPS.[2] In the discussion that follows, the data includes incomes going to each household from employment and/or self-employment, from investments and from transfer payments. It should be noted that this does not correspond to a definition of income in the Hicksian sense discussed in Chapter 1.[3]

Given the available data sources, and the particular measures of income that it gives, there is a question whether we should look at income before, or after, income tax and National Insurance contributions have been deducted. To the extent that living standards are dependent on what goods and services an individual can buy, then income after the deduction of direct taxes makes sense. There is also the question of whether income should be measured before, or after, allowing for housing costs. This can be important when looking at the position of those on low incomes. For example, when housing costs rise, those in receipt of Housing Benefit will experience a rise household incomes (before housing costs) when there may have been no change in individual living standards.

2 In future, income data will be taken from the Family Resources Survey in government publications.

3 To approximate such a measure of income we would need to add capital gains in the period concerned. There are also questions relating to the treatment of home-production (child-care, DIY, etc.) and the receipt of fringe benefits.

The unit of analysis and equivalence scales

The distribution of income can be presented by household unit or by family unit or by individual. In practice, there is some sharing of resources within households and within families, most obviously where there are children who typically have small amounts of income or none at all. The precise degree of sharing between adults is an open question, although it may be influenced by the amount of income each individual receives. On pragmatic grounds, given the absence of detailed information about this, data is typically presented by household (which implicitly assumes that there is equal sharing within households).

Empirical studies often make an adjustment to allow for households of different sizes. It can be argued that, for example, a household consisting of a married couple, with three children and an income of £400 per week, has a different standard of living to a single person with the same income. Put another way, the single individual will require a lower weekly income than would the family to have a given standard of living.[4]

Comparisons of living standards between household units that are of different sizes can be made on the basis of what are called equivalised incomes. Equivalised income is simply the actual income that a household receives adjusted for its size. The adjustment factors are formed from a set of equivalence scales. One particular set of equivalence scales, those devised by McClements, are often used in empirical studies and are given in Table 18.2.

A single person household with an income of £61 per week would have the same equivalised income, as a married couple with £100, and a married couple with two children aged 5 and an actual income of £142 per week. The equivalised income of all three groups would be £100 per week. It should be apparent that the use of equivalence scales can lead to a re-ordering of individual households within the distribution of income. If the single person had an actual income of £65 per week in this example, his or her equivalised income would be the highest although measured by actual income it would be the lowest.

The distribution of income in the UK

Table 18.3 shows the average income per household in 1996–97 in the UK.

The data in the table shows original, gross and disposable income by quintiles for the year 1996–97. Original income includes income from employment, self-employment and from investments. Looking across the top row, it is not surprising to find that this is very unevenly

4 It can also be argued that it is not sensible to try and measure the differences between households with and without children, because the presence of children adds to the utility of the household that has them.

Household member	
Head	0.61
Spouse of head	0.39
Second adult	0.46
Third adult	0.42
Subsequent adults	0.36
Dependants aged 0–1	0.09
2–4	0.18
5–7	0.21
8–10	0.23
11–12	0.25
13–15	0.27
16+	0.36

Table 18.2 **McClements equivalence scales**
Source: McClements (1977).

Average income per household £	Bottom quintile	2nd	3rd	4th	Top	All
Original income	1,409	5,280	13,353	24,098	48,330	18,494
Gross income	5,519	10,205	16,856	26,190	49,684	21,690
Disposable income	4,947	8,973	13,892	20,795	38,377	17,397

Table 18.3 **The distribution of income in the UK 1996–97**
Source: Office for National Statistics (1998).

distributed as the data reflects the position of those in work and those who are not. The average income of those in the bottom 20% of the distribution — on this income measure — was £1,409 in 1996/97. Those in the top quintile received more than 30 times as much on average. The income share going to the bottom quintile was 1.5%, to the top quintile it was over 50%.

The second row shows gross income, which adds government cash benefits such as the state pension to those who have retired and means tested benefits such as Income Support and Housing Benefit to those on low incomes. The effect of this is to raise the income figure for all parts of the distribution, but in proportionate terms it clearly does most for the bottom two quintiles.[5] The income of the bottom quintile rises by a factor of more than three, that of the second quintile by a factor of around two. Disposable income is gross income less direct taxes (and council tax). A first look at the impact of direct taxes on household incomes shows a limited degree of progressivity: disposable income is around 90% of gross income for the bottom quintile, around 77% for the top quintile.

The distribution of incomes in Table 18.3 reflects the distribution of household sizes. Table 18.4 presents the same data using the McClements equivalence scales.[6]

Ranked by equivalised income (£)						
Average income per household	**Bottom quintile**	**2nd**	**3rd**	**4th**	**Top**	**All**
Original income	2,310	6,450	14,710	24,220	44,780	18,490
Gross income	7,080	11,250	18,070	26,180	45,870	21,690
Disposable income	6,360	9,810	14,890	20,770	35,150	17,400
Numbers in each household	2.4	2.3	2.5	2.5	2.3	2.4

Table 18.4 The distribution of household income 1996–97
Source: Office for National Statistics (1998).

The use of the equivalence scales has compressed the distribution of all three income measures in terms of the range of incomes. The ratio of disposable/gross income has fallen slightly for the top quintile. The income share of the bottom 20% has risen while that of the top 20% has fallen.

Finally, it should be borne in mind that the data in both tables understate the dispersion of incomes. This is partly because the figures given are the mean incomes of those in the bottom and top quintile group. There will be some individuals with negative incomes, such as the self-employed with loss-making businesses, and some others with very high incomes, which is not evident from the way the data is presented. It is also partly because surveys of the household population such as the FES do not adequately sample the rich; nor do they include some of the poorest individuals such as the homeless sleeping rough, or living in hostels.

5 The comparatively modest increase in incomes for those in the top quintile can be attributed to universal child benefit.

6 The income figures are still the actual incomes people received. To present the equivalised rather than the actual incomes in the Table would be a reasonable alternative.

Changes in the distribution of income over time

A large official source of data on the distribution of income in the UK is the Department of Social Security's Households Below Average Income (HBAI). For example, the 1997 publication provides data on the distribution of income from 1979 through to 1994/95. Over this period, real incomes grew on average by around 40% although, as you might expect, this average masks wide variation. Incomes at the top on average rose by 60% and more, those in the bottom 10% rose by only 10%. If the income measure taken is that after housing costs, then the incomes of those in the bottom decile fell over this period.

However, the degree of inequality fell somewhat in the early to mid 1990s. Over the period 1991/92 to 1994/95, the poorest groups began to do somewhat better; HBAI data showed that incomes in the bottom quintile grew more quickly than they did in any other part of the distribution. The income share at the bottom rose slightly, while at the top it fell.

Chart 18.1 shows what happened to the Gini Coefficient over the period 1977–96 for the distribution of disposable income.[7] It is apparent from the chart that the distribution of income became markedly more unequal during the 1980s in the UK, but that the Gini statistic stopped increasing in the early-mid 1990s.[8]

Questions

Q1 In a particular economy there are 4 individuals who have the same lifetime opportunities. Their ages are 25, 50, 59 and 75 respectively. Each individual works for 40 years between the ages of 20 and 60, and then lives 20 years in retirement. They each have an annual income of £30,000 while in work and follow the simple lifecycle theory to smooth their consumption levels.

(I) What is the range and the variance of the income distribution and what is the Gini coefficient?

(II) If the incomes of the individuals double in real terms over time has inequality of incomes increased? What happens to the measures you calculated in (I)?

(III) Does the distribution of income appear more or less unequal than the distribution of consumption or wealth?

---

7 Equivalised disposable income.

8 The trend of increasing inequality was particularly strong in the UK, but it was also discernible in other English-speaking countries, including Australia, New Zealand and the United States. This pattern was also evident in Sweden, though it was less pronounced than in the UK. In France and Italy, inequality fell over the period.

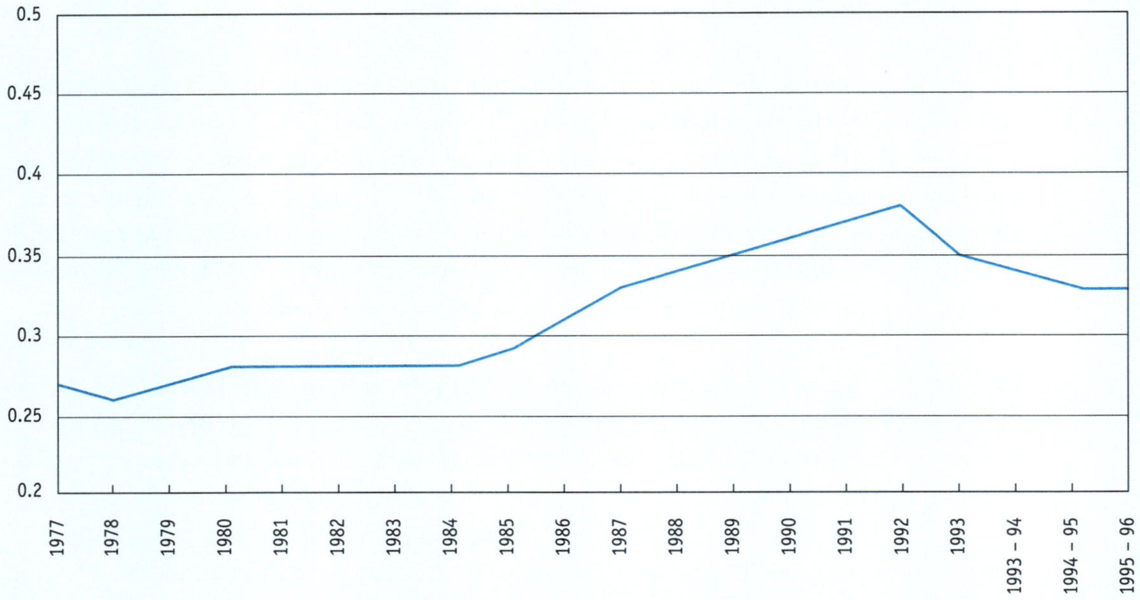

Chart 18.1 **Gini statistics 1977–96**
Source: Office for National Statistics (1998).

Q2 A government decides to follow an egalitarian policy and reduces the tax rate paid by those on low incomes and increases it for those at the top of the income scale. What would you expect to happen to the position of the Lorenz curve? What, if anything, can you say about the change to the distribution of income if the old and new Lorenz curve cross at some point after a policy change?

18.2 Inequality trends

The next question we will look at is whether variation in overall inequality over time matters. One way of starting to answer this question is to break down the overall changes into the changes attributed to inequality of earnings, investment income and so on. In Chapter 13, we saw the trend of increasing wage inequality in the 1980s and 1990s in some countries and this type of analysis extends this to look at the dispersion of all income sources. A second way of accounting for the changing pattern is to break down inequality by family groups. This would allow us to see whether there were some that did particularly well or particularly badly.

Decomposition of inequality by income source

Table 18.5 gives the breakdown of income inequality by income source taken from a study by Goodman *et al.* (1997). The statistical measure used to do this is half the squared coefficient of

	1961–63	1976–78	1991–93
Half the square of the CV * 1000: overall income inequality	137	101	280
Inequality arising from:			
(I) Earnings	100	88	177
(II) Social security	–11	–15	–21
(III) Self-employment income	29	19	67
(IV) Private pensions	2	3	12
(V) Investment income	17	7	42

Table 18.5 Income inequality in the UK by income source
Source: Goodman et al. (1997). The statistic has been scaled up by a factor of 1000 for ease of reading.

variation.[9] Why use this statistic, rather than one of the others above? The answer lies with the fact that it is 'additively decomposable'. What this means is that we can break down the overall measure of inequality into the inequality arising from each income component.

The first row shows that inequality was lower in the mid-late 1970s than in the early 1960s but that it had grown rapidly by the early 1990s. This is broadly in line with the evidence from the Gini coefficient given in Section 1.[10] The first column gives the break down of income inequality for the years 1961–63. For overall income, the half the square of the coefficient of variation was 137. 73% of this statistical measure of inequality could be accounted for by the inequality in earnings, i.e. (100/137)*100. The negative numbers in the second row reflect the fact that social security payments decline as total income rises, so that in the absence of social security the overall level of inequality would have been higher.[11] The inequality in self-employment income, private pensions and investment income is shown in the other rows.

The relative contribution to overall inequality of each income component depends on three factors. These are

(I) Within-source inequality. The more unequal the distribution of each income component the larger its contribution.

(II) The share of the income source in total income. The larger this is the greater the contribution to the overall measure.

9 The squared coefficient of variation is the variance of the distribution divided by the square of the mean.

10 It also shows that it is problematic to quantify by how much inequality rose in a single number.

11 The differences between original and gross income in Tables 18.2 and 18.3 also make this point for the year 1996/7.

(III) The correlation of the income source to total income. A positive correlation with total income, which there is with income from employment and self-employment, investments and pensions, the higher the coefficient of variation. A negative correlation reduces the value of the index, as is shown by the effect of social security payments. The more strongly correlated is the component part, the larger the contribution it makes.

Earnings count for well over a half of all household income for the period covered by the study and plainly variations in the distribution of earnings are an important part of the overall picture. Although both overall income inequality and the inequality of earnings increased between the late 1970s and the early 1990s, the relative contribution of earnings to the overall picture declined, from 87% for the period 1976–78 to only 63% during 1991–93. This was because of the declining share of earnings in household income, which more than offset the increase in inequality of earned income.

The evidence in Table 18.5 shows that when inequality was falling, social security played an increasingly important part.[12] During the 1980s, general benefit levels were uprated over time only in line with prices, rather than with earnings. Other things being equal, this has the effect of widening the differences between those on benefit and the rest of the population during periods of economic (and hence earnings) growth. The table shows the decline in the relative importance of social security payments as an equalising factor. The remaining three income sources all grew in importance, reflecting the growing number of people who became reliant on self-employment income in the 1980s, a growing number of retired (and semi-retired) who had income from private pensions and a general increase in the numbers with investment income.

Decomposition by family type

The purpose of this kind of decomposition is to account for the trend in inequality in terms of changing demography. Table 18.6 gives some details.

The statistical measure used for this table is the Mean Log Deviation (MLD). The reason for using another measure is that it provides a neat decomposition of overall inequality into that which can be attributed to differences between family groups, and that which comes from within particular groups.

The change in measured inequality is broadly in line with the other summary statistics. The first row gives the overall figure. The second row gives the inequality due to that between family groups; if the mean income levels of all six groups were identical, this figure would be

12 Social security income is the largest source of income after earnings, and it is the share of these payments in total income that makes it important.

Mean Log Deviation × 1,000	1961–63	1976–78	1991–93
Total inequality	116	98	187
— Between family types	12	14	19
— Within family types	104	84	168
(I) Married pensioners	9	5	11
(II) Single pensioner	9	5	8
(III) Couple with children	43	39	72
(IV) Couple without children	22	18	39
(V) Single with children	3	3	6
(VI) Single without children	18	14	33

Table 18.6 **Break down of inequality by family type**
Source: Goodman et al. (1997).

zero. The within-group inequality is shown in the third row; this would return a figure of zero if all married pensioners had the same (mean) income, all single pensioners had the same income and so on.

It is evident from the table that on this break down most inequality can be attributed to variation within, rather than between, family types. The fall and rise in inequality over the period is largely a reflection of the experiences of those of working age, although it is clear that inequality rose within all family types.

Income mobility

Finally, in this section, we will introduce some evidence on income mobility. In principle, each individual could spend an equal amount of time at a given point in the distribution of income before moving up (or down) the scale over his or her lifecycle. If there is a high level of income mobility, the policy implications for income redistribution of observing inequality at one point in time may be limited. Conversely, if there is little or no mobility. Table 18.7 gives some detail on the experience of those who were in the bottom 10% of the income distribution in 1991, and what had happened to them by 1995.

The table shows that 36% of those in the bottom 10% of the income distribution were in the bottom 10% in 1995, that 22% of them were in the next decile up and so on. Nearly two-thirds of those at the bottom of the distribution in 1991 had moved up the scale by 1995. There are a number of details to bear in mind when looking at these figures. First there is a question as to what is considered to be a 'low income' from a welfare point of view. This issue is taken up in detail in the next section, but we can note here that the appearance of mobility decreases, if the

Position in 1991	Position in 1995					
	% Bottom decile	% 2nd decile	% 3rd decile	% 4th decile	% 5th decile	% Top half
Bottom decile	36	22	13	7	5	17
Bottom two deciles		53	16	10	6	15
Bottom three deciles		61		13	9	15

Table 18.7 Income mobility 1991–95
Source: Department of Social Security (1997).

bottom two or three deciles of the distribution are taken as the reference point. In the latter case, 61% of those who were in the bottom three deciles were in the bottom three deciles in 1995. Second, there is a question of how many moves are temporary and how many are not. How many individuals move up for a period, but then return to the bottom of the distribution? This leads to the question of how, if at all, the characteristics of those who move up the income distribution on a permanent basis differ from those who do not. We will take these questions up in more detail in the discussion of poverty in the next section.

Questions

Q3 One line of criticism about the break down of the income distribution presented in this section is that it takes no account of changes in the amount of leisure. For example, in the 1990s unemployment was generally higher than in the mid-1970s, when in turn, it was higher than in the early 1960s. There has also been a long-term reduction in the length of the average working week. Does this mean that using the distribution of income as a measure of welfare is systematically misleading?

Q4 Do you think that the assumption of equal sharing of resources within a household is justified? If not, what impact would you expect allowing for differences to make?

18.3 Poverty

In this section, we will focus our attention on the bottom end of the income scale, and look at the extent and nature of poverty. As a first step, we need to be clear what is (or can be) meant by poverty. There are various ways of defining poverty and, as we shall see, the data on low incomes needs careful interpretation before reaching conclusions about how many individuals are in a state of poverty.

Broadly, we need to make a distinction between absolute and relative poverty. The pioneering studies of Rowntree, at the turn of the 20th century, developed an approach in which poverty means not having income sufficient to buy a nutritionally adequate diet. This approach is problematic in practice because there is no single food intake that equates with subsistence. Poverty can also be defined in relative as well as absolute terms. As economies grow over time, living standards rise generally and perceptions about what constitutes a state of poverty change. The level of social security payments could be taken as an indicator of poverty, although this means that policies to raise the living standards of the poor would, ironically, increase the numbers measured as being in poverty.[13] An alternative is to take an income level that is some proportion of the national average.

Estimates of the numbers in poverty: the HBAI data

In empirical studies, one of the key numbers is a simple headcount of those who are deemed to be in poverty. Plainly, estimates of this number will depend on exactly what yardstick measure is used and which year(s) the estimates refer to. The HBAI publication presents estimates of the numbers below certain percentages of mean income since 1979, and this can be taken to reflect the idea of relative poverty. A rise in the numbers below a certain % of mean income over time would then indicate an increase in the numbers in poverty in relative terms.

This leaves open the question of what the % mean income figure should be. The European Union, in making cross-national comparisons, often takes a figure of 50% of the mean. Pragmatically, the HBAI publishes numbers below 40,50 and 60% on measures of income both before and after housing costs. The details for 1992/93 are given in Chart 18.2. The overall figure is plainly very sensitive to the % of the mean that is taken. The total number of individuals is increased by a factor of more than three by moving the yardstick from 40% of the mean income (before housing costs) to 60% (income after housing costs). However, it does not follow from using this measure that there will always be some individuals in poverty. If the distribution of income became sufficiently compressed then it is possible that no one would live in a family with an income below 40 (or 50 or 60)% of average income.

Low income dynamics

The problems that individuals face are likely to increase the longer the time they spend in a state of low income. Income dynamics at low levels of income are therefore important. We saw in Section 2 that there was certainly some movement away from the bottom over a period of years; however, the data in Table 18.7 was based on 'snapshots' of individuals' disposable incomes, in 1991 and in 1995. This leaves open their experience in the intervening years. For example, the HBAI publication reported that 6% of those in the bottom decile of the income

13 A policy that reduced the level of benefits paid would have the effect of reducing the numbers measured as being in poverty.

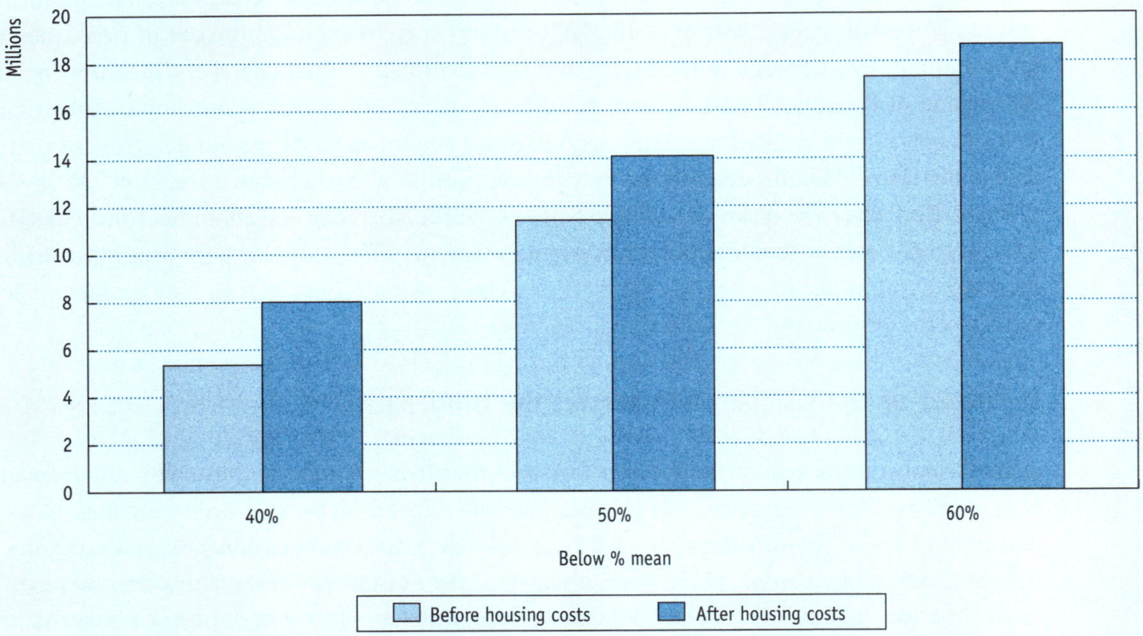

Chart 18.2 **Numbers with incomes below % mean in the UK 1992/93**
Source: Department of Social Security (1997).

distribution in 1991 remained there for the entire 5-year period covered by the table and that 12% of those in the bottom three deciles remained in the bottom three deciles.

A study by Jarvis and Jenkins sheds some further light on this by examining low-income exit and re-entry rates.

Duration		Low income exit rate	Percentage of cohort with low income
Year 1	Start		100
	End	0.50	
Year 2	Start		50
	End	0.38	
Year 3	Start		32
	End		

Table 18.8 **Low income exit rates**
Source: Jarvis and Jenkins (1997).

The definition of low income used in making the estimates in Table 18.8 are incomes in the bottom two deciles of the distribution. Starting with year 1 of the BHPS survey, 1991, one-half left a state of low income as defined, leaving the remainder on low incomes the following year. At the end of the second year the low income exit rate of 0.38 reduced this figure to only 32%.

The study also calculated re-entry rates; the re-entry rate after one year not on low income was 0.30, so that after one-year out of the bottom two deciles 30% restarted a second period on low income. After a two-year period nearly a half, some 47% re-entered another period of low income.

This turnover of those on low incomes points to the importance of the social security system in stabilising incomes of many more individuals than would appear in a headcount at a particular point in time. The benefit system is also particularly important to those who are persistently poor, a group that includes pensioners many of whom will continue to be reliant on state benefits.

The HBAI data again gives useful background on the persistently poor (those who were in the bottom three deciles for all five years from 1991–95 were taken as being in a state of persistently low income).[14] Charts 18.3A–18.3D provides a detailed break down of those in this situation and the numbers in the population as a whole. Broadly,

(I) Pensioners were represented disproportionately among those who were persistently poor.

(II) Those households who were fully employed were a much smaller fraction than the numbers in the total population.

(III) Twice the percentage in the bottom three deciles had no educational qualifications compared to the overall population.

(IV) More than a half of those in permanently on low income were living in some form of social housing compared to under a quarter in the population as a whole.

Concluding comment

The point of departure for this chapter was a simple model of general equilibrium in competitive markets. The analysis of competitive markets is often concerned with considerations of efficiency, rather than equity and the purpose of this chapter has been to redress this

14 The data in the charts relates to the individual characteristics in 1991, some of which (family type, tenure, education) will of course have changed over the period.

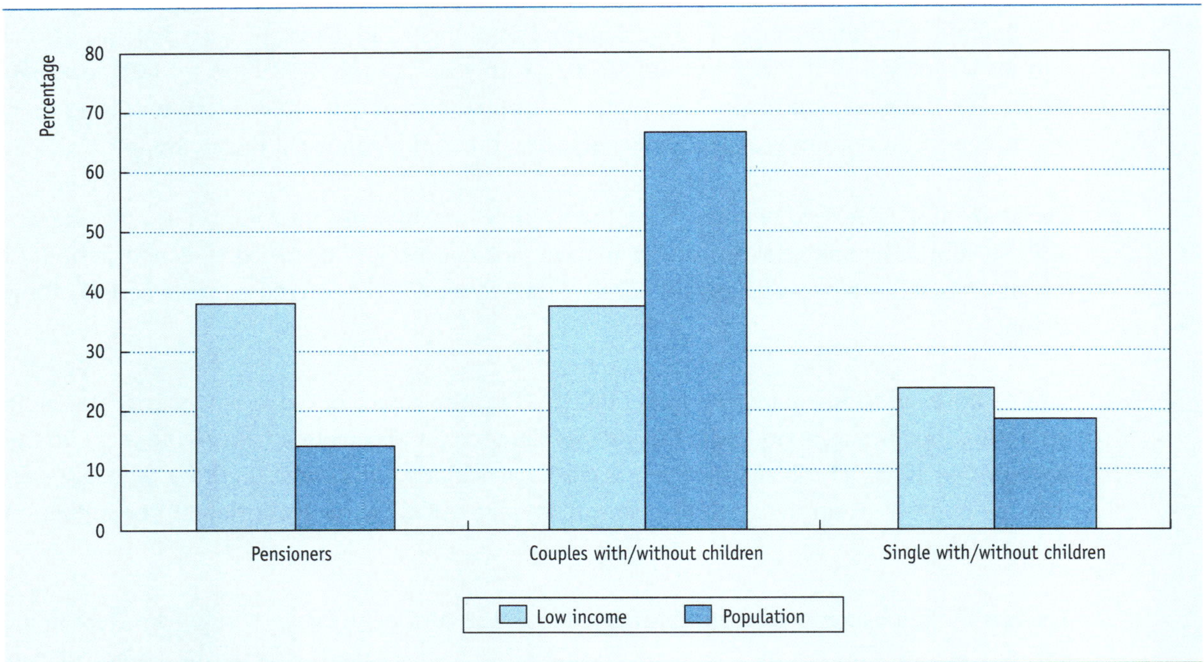

Chart 18.3A Family types of those on low incomes 1991–95
Source: Department of Social Security (1997).

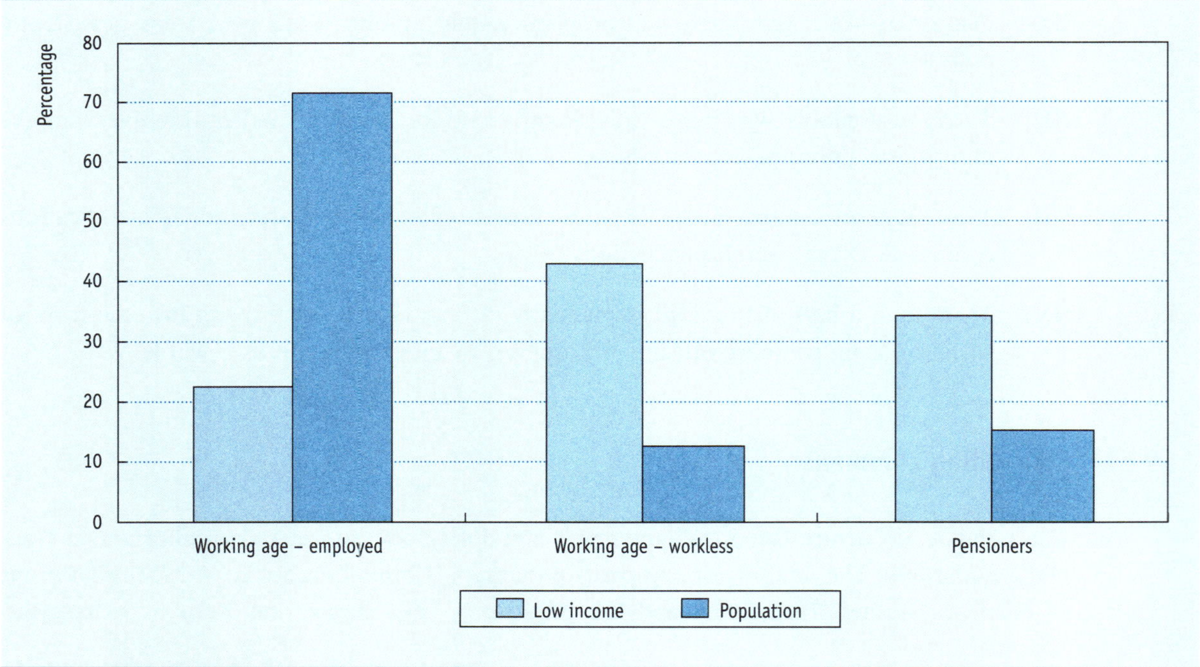

Chart 18.3B Employment position of those on low incomes 1991–95
Source: Department of Social Security (1997).

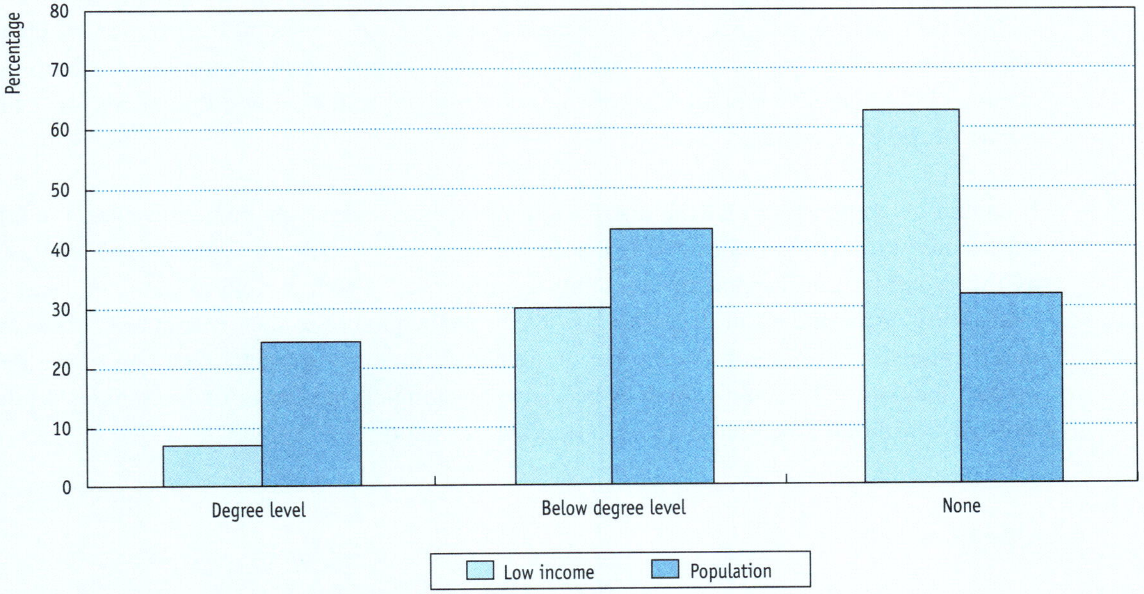

Chart 18.3C **Education of those on low incomes 1991–95**

Source: Department of Social Security (1997).

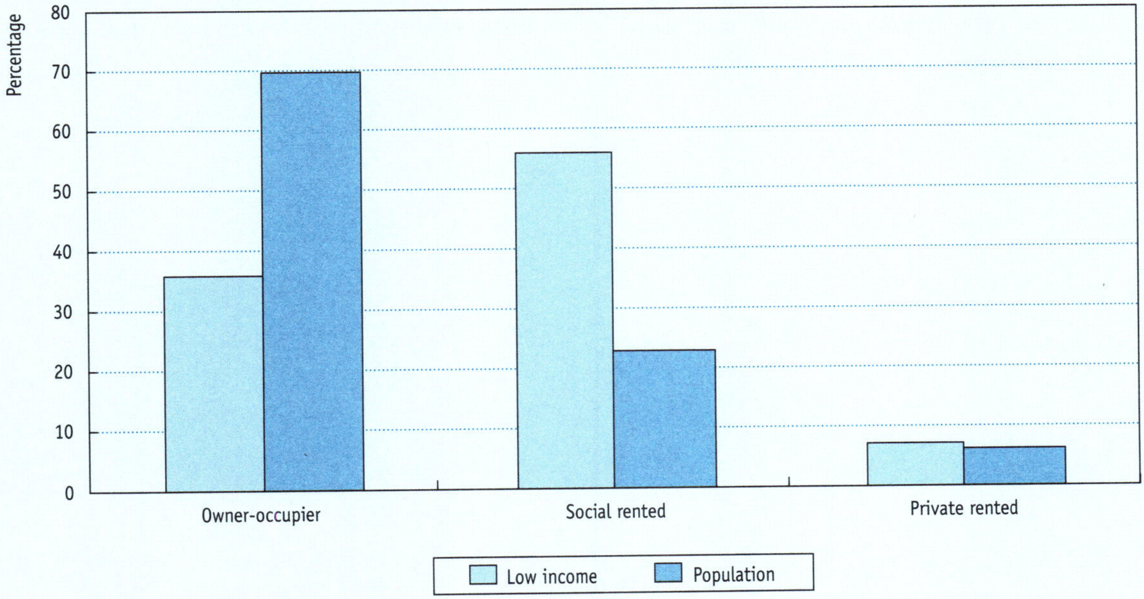

Chart 18.3D **Housing tenure of those on low incomes 1991–95**

Source: Department of Social Security (1997).

balance. We have seen a mixture of tools of analysis, and data, that sheds some light on the distribution of resources between individuals in the UK. An unequal distribution of income does not necessarily mean that the judgement on social welfare in a competitive economy is adverse. Life-cycle factors, and in a growing economy, the influence of different cohorts will be a part of the explanation.

It should be appreciated that the distribution of income varies over time. However, the UK's experience in the 1980s and early 1990s seems to have been a rather singular one at least as far as the extent of the increase in inequality is concerned. From a welfare point of view, the availability of panel data in the 1990s has filled out the picture of the experience of those who find themselves in a state of low income. A significant minority spent the first half of the 1990s on low incomes. These individuals were disproportionately members of households without work and without educational qualifications of any kind.

Questions

Q5 If a government wanted to increase in work-benefits as a means of encouraging those with few skills and family commitments into work would it be better to (I) increase the basic WFTC; or (II) lower the taper of 55%? Why? (Figures for WFTC are given in Chapter 3.)

Q6 What do you understand by the term 'social exclusion'? Given that a disproportionate number of pensioners are among those classified as being persistently on low income, what would be an appropriate policy response?

Summary

1 The standard of living of an individual is a difficult concept to measure. The lifecycle model suggests that consumption rather than income may be a better proxy for individual well being.

2 Empirical work concerned with distributional analysis tends to concentrate on measures of income. This may be weekly or annual income depending on the purpose of the study. Income over a shorter period of time is appropriate for studies of poverty, for example. The measure used is sometimes dictated by the form of the available data.

3 There are a large number of alternative measures of inequality. The Gini coefficient is one of the most widely used and is easily related to a Lorenz curve. More detailed analyses which breakdown overall inequality by different income sources, or by that between and within particular subgroups require other statistical measures. Two such measures are one half the square root of the coefficient of variation, and the mean log deviation, both of which are additively decomposable.

4 A number of reasons have been put forward to account for the rise in income inequality in the UK. The inequality in earnings is a large part of the story because it is the largest component of income overall. Other factors were also relevant including a declining role for social security provision and the increasing importance of self-employment and investment income.

5 Poverty is multifaceted and therefore difficult to measure precisely. In the UK, the government publishes data on the number and type of households below average income (HBAI). The numbers who are on 'low incomes' can be very sensitive to the exact percentage of average income, and also whether the measure of income is before or after housing costs.

6 The availability of panel data, such as that from the British Household Panel Study, has added to what is known about the experience of individuals over a period of time. This is a development from the 'snapshot' which is provided by cross-section data such as the Family Expenditure Survey.

7 The BHPS shows that a significant number of individuals remained on low incomes throughout the period 1991–95. The social security system has an important role to play for these individuals, but it is also important to a large number of individuals who move up the distribution for a time but then move back down.

End of chapter questions

Q7 In a particular four person economy the incomes per annum of the individuals were as follows

Student £4,000, Policeman £18,000, Doctor £40,000, Pensioner £40,000.

(I) What is the Gini coefficient for this income distribution?

(II) Suppose that the student and policeman are single individuals, that the doctor is married with two children aged 6 and 15, and that the pensioner is also married. Use the McClements equivalence scales to calculate an equivalent income measure for each household. What happens to the rank ordering of each household?

(III) What is the Gini coefficient measure of inequality for this distribution of equivalent income? Is this a better measure of income inequality than the figure based on the unadjusted incomes?

Q8 Should governments set official poverty targets? Would they help to eradicate poverty?

Q9 In a hypothetical economy of four individuals, individuals I and II are workers, while individuals III and IV are not. The incomes of the four individuals are £300, £400, £190, and £85 per week respectively. The MLD statistic is

$$I = (1/n)\sum_{i=1}^{n} \log(\bar{y}/y_i)$$

where $\bar{y}$ is the mean income

(I) What is the MLD statistic for this economy?

(II) 15 years later the same individuals have income £400, £500, £180, and £150 per week. Has inequality increased or decreased?

(III) The statistic can be 'decomposed' into the inequality within group and that between groups

$$I = \sum (n_k/n)I_k + \sum(n_k/n)\log(\bar{y}/\bar{y}_k)$$

Where k refers to each of the subgroups.

What does the decomposition of this statistic tell you?

Q10 In Chapter 2, we introduced the essentials of an income tax system. This question asks you to examine the impact of a negative income tax (or equivalently a minimum income system). With an income tax when an individual's income exceeds the tax threshold, tax is paid at a given rate. With a negative income tax any shortfall is multiplied by the tax rate and given to the individual.

(I) If the individual tax allowance was £6,000 and the tax rate was 25% how much would the individual receive if he or she had no other sources of income? Graph the relation between an individual's income from £0 to £20,000.

(II) What is the average and marginal rate of tax in the negative income tax scheme in (I) above?

(III) If the tax rate was 25% and the tax credit to be given to each individual was £4,000 what would the individual tax allowance have to be? Alternatively, if the tax allowance were constrained to be £6,000 what would the tax rate have to be?

(IV) Does it follow that a negative income tax system is undesirable?

References and suggested further reading

Data on the distribution of income is published annually in Economic Trends, by the Office for National Statistics. The HBAI publication presents many detailed tabulations of the distribution of income over time. It also has a section on income dynamics. Goodman *et al.* (1997), which Section 2 draws on contains a lot of additional detail. A technical and sophisticated discussion of measurement issues is given in Cowell. The Joseph Rowntree Foundation funds a series of research programmes and produces reports which are good on the policy issues.

Cowell, F.A. (1995), *Measuring Inequality*, LSE Handbooks in Economics, 2nd edition, Prentice Hall.

Department of Social Security (1997), *Households Below Average Income: A Statistical Analysis 1979–1994/5*.

Goodman, A., Johnson, P. and Webb, S. (1997), *Inequality in the UK*, Oxford University Press.

Hills, J. (1998), *Income and Wealth: The Latest Evidence*, Joseph Rowntree Foundation.

Jarvis, S. and Jenkins, S.P. (1997) 'Low income dynamics in 1990's Britain', *Fiscal Studies*, **18**, 2.

McClements, L. (1977), 'Equivalence scales for children', *Journal of Public Economics*, **8**.

Office for National Statistics (1998), *Economic Trends*.

Office for National Statistics (1998), *Transport Statistics*.

Appendix

Answers to Selected Questions

Chapter 1

Q1 His marginal rate of substitution between chips and watching games will increase during the course of a season.

Q2 Pasta is a 'good', but pollution is a 'bad'. To maintain a given level of utility requires more of the good to compensate for the bad. Her indifference curves will therefore slope upwards.

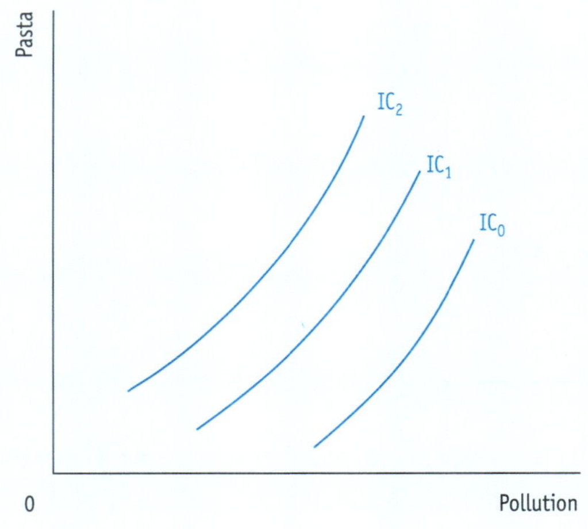

Figure A.1

Q3 L-shaped indifference curves would be appropriate if additional 4-packs do not generate disutility.

Q4

I:	Karen satiated	in neither good.
II:	"	in water.
III:	"	in both goods.
IV:	"	in shortbread.

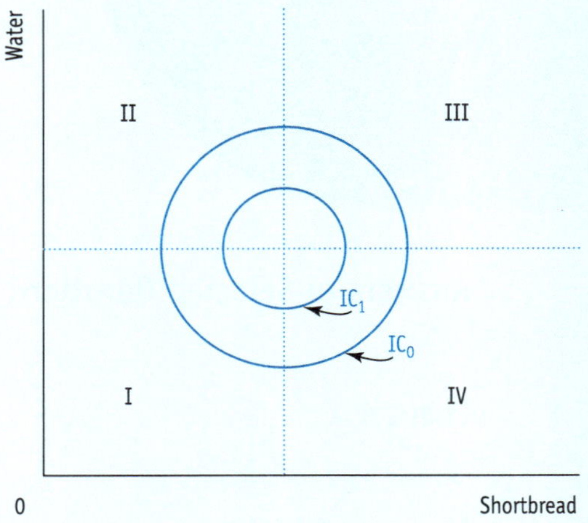

Figure A.2

Q5 The slope of the budget line is –0.5.

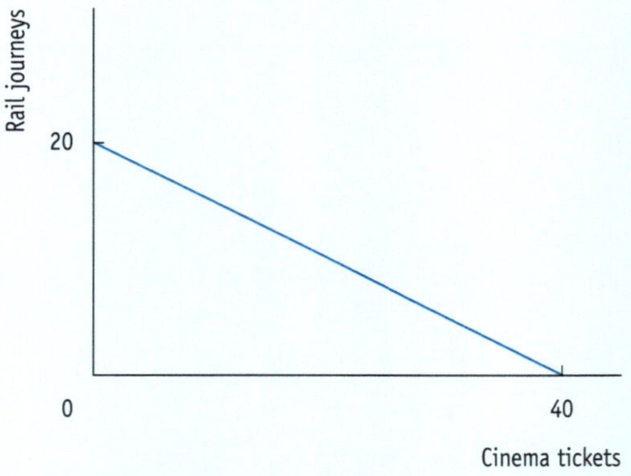

Figure A.3

I: A parallel shift out of the budget constraint.

II: A pivot round the point cinema tickets = 40. The new point of intersection on the vertical axis is where rail journeys = 16.

III: A parallel shift inwards of the budget constraint so that it is half the distance from the origin.

IV: No change.

Q7 The compensated demand curve measures the substitution effect of a price change. A negative income effect for an inferior good means that it is flatter. The uncompensated demand curve for a Giffen good slopes up while the compensated demand curve slopes down.

Q12 A utility function that attaches a higher number to greater quantities of X and Y will preserve the original representation of preferences.

(I) U = 5XY

X	Y	U = 5XY	X	Y	U = 5XY
25	4	500	50	8	2,000
20	5	500	40	10	2,000
10	10	500	20	20	2,000
5	20	500	10	40	2,000
4	25	500	8	50	2,000

(II) U = –5XY

X	Y	U = –5XY	X	Y	U = –5XY
25	4	–500	50	8	–2,000
20	5	–500	40	10	–2,000
10	10	–500	20	20	–2,000
5	20	–500	10	40	–2,000
4	25	–500	8	50	–2,000

(III) $U = (-5XY)^2$

X	Y	$U = (-5XY)^2$	X	Y	$U = (-5XY)^2$
25	4	250,000	50	8	4mn
20	5	250,000	40	10	4mn
10	10	250,000	20	20	4mn
5	20	250,000	10	40	4mn
4	25	250,000	8	50	4mn

(IV) $U = (-5XY)^3$

X	Y	$U = (-5XY)^3$	X	Y	$U = (-5XY)^3$
25	4	–125mn	50	8	–8bn
20	5	–125mn	40	10	–8bn
10	10	–125mn	20	20	–8bn
5	20	–125mn	10	40	–8bn
4	25	–125mn	8	50	–8bn

(I) and (III) do, (II) and (IV) do not.

Q13 The Lagrangian is

$$V = X^{0.25} Y^{0.75} + \lambda[300 - 2X - 6Y]$$

The first-order conditions are

$$V_X = 0.25X^{-0.75} Y^{0.75} - 2\lambda = 0 \qquad \text{(i)}$$

$$V_Y = 0.75X^{0.25} Y^{-0.25} - 6\lambda = 0 \qquad \text{(ii)}$$

$$V_\lambda = 300 - 2X - 6Y = 0 \qquad \text{(iii)}$$

Dividing (i) by (ii) and re-arranging we obtain

$$\frac{0.25Y}{0.75X} = \frac{2}{6} \Rightarrow Y = X$$

The optimal values for Y, X can be found by substituting Y = X into (iii). This gives

$$300 - 8X = 0$$
$$300 - 8Y = 0$$

Giving equilibrium values of X = Y = 37.5 To obtain the demand functions for X and Y, re-arrange the budget constraint

$$Y = \frac{M}{Py} - \frac{Px}{Py}X$$

Since Y = X

$$Y + \frac{Px}{Py}Y = \frac{M}{Py}$$

$$Y\left(1 + \frac{Px}{Py}\right) = \frac{M}{Py}$$

$$Y = \frac{M}{Px + Py}$$

For X

$$X = \frac{M}{Px} - \frac{Py}{Px}Y$$

Substitute X = Y

$$X\left(1 + \frac{Py}{Px}\right) = \frac{M}{Px}$$

$$X = \frac{M}{Px + Py}$$

Q15 The marginal rate of substitution of good Y for good X is equal to the price ratio. At this point the rate at which the individual is willing to give Y for X is just equal to the rate at which they can be exchanged given market prices.

Yes, when there is a corner solution for the example.

Chapter 2

Q2 (I) Her mortgage interest payments without MITR, would be £2,000*0.6 = £120 per annum. With MITR, the £120 acts as an offset against tax. This gives a reduction of £36 in interest payments.

(II) A mortgage of £57,000 and an interest rate of 10% mean an annual interest payment of £5,700. If MITR had been available, the interest saving would be £5,700*0.2 = £1,140.

(III) With a £30,000 ceiling and a tax rate of 15p in the £, the interest reduction is £450. This is £690 less than in (II).

Q4 (I) In year 0 the index is 100. Since the weighting for good 2 is 0 in the base period, a base-weighted index does not change in either period 1 or 2.

(II) The chain-weighted index does not change between period 0 and 1. The weights from period 1 are:

Good 1	£100/£130 = 0.769
Good 2	£30/£130 = 0.231

Applying these weights to the change in prices, we get

$$0.769*0\% + 0.231*-33.3\% = -7.69\%$$

The chain-weighted index for period 2 is therefore 92.31.

Q7 (I) 7.3%

(II) £368.70

(III) The interest paid on the mortgage, assuming tax relief as with (I), would be £2,190. To this should be added the opportunity cost of the deposit, making £2,558.70 in all. The capital gain over this particular 4-year period was £32,801. Interest rates were not constant over the period and the capital gain is given in nominal terms, but plainly the cost of housing was negative given the magnitude of the capital gain.

(IV) With a mortgage of £62,051 and an effective interest rate of 7.3% the interest paid is £4,529.75. A 10% deposit on the average price of property would have been £6,894.60, so the opportunity cost with a bank rate of 6% is £413.67. There was also a (nominal) capital loss of £6,491 over 4 years.

Chapter 3

Q2 There is a parallel shift up in the non-labour income line. The earned income budget line is now twice as steep.

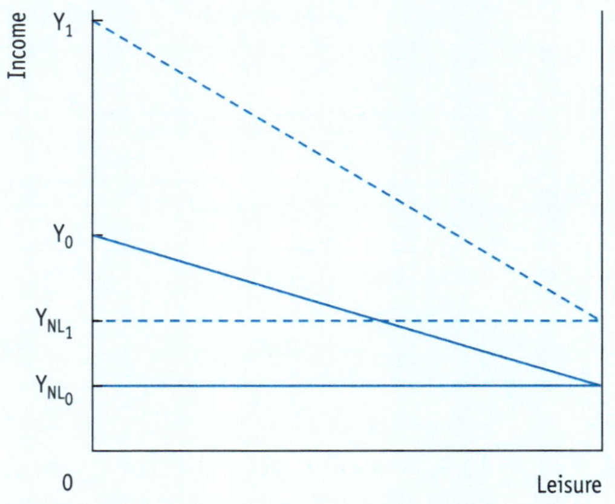

Figure A.4

Q8 Her earnings £120 and her Housing Benefit needs allowance is £61.40 + £19.80 = £81.20. Her excess income is £120 – £81.20 = £38.80, so her Housing Benefit would be £50 – .65*£38.80 = £24.78 (subject to rounding).

(I) If her earnings rose by £40 she would get no Housing Benefit.

(II) The marginal rate of benefit withdrawal on £10 is 65%
on £100 is 24.78%
(ignoring all other taxes and benefits).

(IV) An increase of 20% would raise Penny's rent to £60. The benefit calculation is now

$$£60 - 0.65*£38.80 = £34.78$$

Q15 (I) The needs allowance is £75.20 + £10.55 + 2*£16.45 + £24.10 = £142.75. With earnings of £160, excess income is £17.25 and Housing Benefit is £43.79 (without rounding). At earnings of £200 excess income is £57.25, which with a taper of 65p in the £ reduces HB to £17.79 (without rounding).

(ii) If the government disregards the first £25 of earnings, then with a total earnings figure of £200, excess income is £32.25 and HB is £34.04 (again without rounding).

Chapter 4

Q1 Very steep indifference curves represent a relatively high willingness to exchange future consumption for consumption in the present. Very flat curves represent the opposite.

Q3

Interest rate	Inflation rate	Real rate of interest	
		Approximately	Exactly
5%	3%	2%	1.94%
16%	6%	10%	9.43%
15%	25%	–10%	–8.00%
60%	200%	–140%	–46.6%

Q4 In terms of Figure 4.6 for example, the effect of the tax-exemption is to rotate the budget constraint above point D upwards. The effect on a saver is ambiguous because of the wealth and substitution effects. If the individual were neither borrower nor saver the outcome would depend on the slope of the indifference curve (i.e. his or her preferences).

Chapter 5

Q1 The expected value of his income is £14,000. The cost of actuarially fair insurance is £6,000. The cost of fair insurance to an individual with the same income prospects and a probability of being unemployed of 5% is £600. If the probability of unemployment is 75%, the cost of fair insurance is £9,000.

Q5 An L-shaped indifference curve represent infinitely risk-averse preferences.

Q6 The slope of the budget line for the high-risk group is –4, that for the low-risk group is –0.25.

Chapter 6

Q3 (I) The standard deviation before the tax is imposed is 500. After it is imposed it is 375.

(II) The imposition of the tax reduces the degree of risk associated with holding asset X. Those with risk-averse preferences are therefore more likely to hold a risky asset.

Q7 2%, 3%, 4.6%.

Chapter 7

Q6

Capital, K	Capital, L	Output, Q	Total Cost
18	2	36	100
9	4	36	65
6	6	36	60
4	9	36	65
2	18	36	100

(I) 6 units of capital and labour.

(II) If 6 units of capital is given, then in the short-run the firm will require 12 units of labour. The total cost is 90.

(III) The total cost in the long run is 84.85.

(IV) The unit (average cost) in the short-run changes from

$$\frac{60}{36} \text{ to } \frac{90}{72}, \text{ and in the long run to } \frac{84.85}{72}$$

(V) If demand increased so that the input levels treble then output rises to 324 and the total costs are 180. Unit costs are therefore 180/324. There are increasing returns to scale over the entire range of possible output. In principle, this suggests that a monopoly is the most efficient way of organising production.

Q15 $Q = 7K^{0.5}\ L^{0.5}$ and $w = 1 \quad r = 4$

(I) The Lagrangian is

$$V = 7K^{0.5}\ L^{0.5} + \lambda[200 - 4K - L]$$

With first-order conditions

$$V_L = 3.5\ K^{0.5}\ L^{-0.5} - \lambda = 0 \qquad \text{(i)}$$

$$V_K = 3.5\ K^{-0.5}\ L^{0.5} - 4\lambda = 0 \qquad \text{(ii)}$$

$$V_\lambda = 200 - 4K - L = 0 \qquad \text{(iii)}$$

$$\text{(i)} \div \text{(ii) implies that } \frac{K}{L} = \frac{1}{4} \text{ or } 4K = L$$

Substituting this relation into (iii) gives

$$2L = 200 \text{ so } L = 100,\ K = 25$$

and

$$Q = 7(25)^{0.5}\,(100)^{0.5} = 350$$

(II) The Lagrangian is now

$$V = L + 4K + \lambda[100 - 7K^{0.5}L^{0.5}]$$

With first-order conditions

$$V_L = 1 - 3.5K^{0.5}\,L^{-0.5} = 0 \qquad \text{(i)}$$

$$V_K = 4 - 3.5K^{-0.5}\,L^{0.5} = 0 \qquad \text{(ii)}$$

$$V_\lambda = 100 - 7K^{0.5}\,L^{0.5} = 0 \qquad \text{(iii)}$$

(i), (ii) again imply that 4K = L

Substitution into (iii)

$$100 - 7K^{0.5}(4K)^{0.5} = 0$$

giving

$$K = \frac{100}{14} = 7.14$$

and

$$100 - 7\left(\frac{L}{4}\right)^{0.5} L^{0.5} = 0 \Rightarrow L = \frac{200}{7} = 28.57$$

so the minimum cost is

$$wL + rK = \frac{200}{7} + \frac{400}{14} = \frac{400}{7} = 57.14$$

(III) To obtain the factor demands, re-arrange the expression for total costs

$$TC = wL + rK$$

$$K = \frac{TC}{r} - \frac{w}{r}L$$

In equilibrium

$$\frac{K}{L} = \frac{w}{r} \Rightarrow L = \frac{r}{w}K$$

$$K = \frac{TC}{r} - \left(\frac{w}{r}\right)\left(\frac{r}{w}\right)K$$

$$\Rightarrow K^D = \frac{TC}{2r} \text{ and } L^D = \frac{TC}{2w}$$

Chapter 8

Q1 $ATC = 16 \div Q + 4Q$

$Q = 12 - ½p$

(I) The firm's profit can be written as

$$\Pi = TR - TC$$

Total revenue is

$$TR = PQ$$

Given

$$½p = 12 - Q \Rightarrow P = 24 - 2Q$$

so

$$TR = 24Q - 2Q^2$$

$$TC = 16 + 4Q^2$$

$$\Pi = -6Q^2 + 24Q - 16$$

The first-order condition is

$$\frac{d\pi}{dQ} = -12Q + 24 = 0 \Rightarrow Q = 2$$

and

$$\frac{d^2\pi}{dQ^2} = -12 < 0$$

so the second-order condition is also satisfied.

Substitution gives

$$P = 20,\ TR = 40,\ \Pi = -24 + 48 - 16 = 8$$

(II) $\Pi = -6Q^2 + 24Q - 16 = 2$

so

$$-6Q^2 + 24Q - 18 = 0$$

Divide both sides by –6 and factorising gives

$$Q^2 - 4Q + 3 = 0$$

$$(Q-1)(Q-3) = 0$$

So if $Q = 1$, $P = 22$ and $TR = 22$

$Q = 3$, $P = 18$ and $TR = 54$

So the revenue maximising firm produces more and charges a lower price than does the profit-maximising firm.

Chapter 9

Q3 $AC = 20Q^{-1} + 21 - 5Q + Q^2$

$Q^D = 102 - 2P$

(I) Profits can be written as

$$\Pi = TR - TC$$

To obtain TR

$$2P = 102 - Q$$

$$P = 51 - \tfrac{1}{2}Q$$

$$TR = 51Q - \tfrac{1}{2}Q^2$$

To obtain TC

$$TC = AC^*Q$$
$$= 20 + 21Q - 5Q^2 + Q^3$$

So

$$\Pi = [51Q - ½Q^2] - [20 + 21Q - 5Q^2 + Q^3]$$
$$= -Q^3 + 4½Q^2 + 30Q - 20$$

The first-order condition is

$$\frac{d\pi}{dQ} = -3Q^2 + 9Q + 30 = 0$$

To solve for Q, simplify by dividing both sides by –3. This gives

$$Q^2 - 3Q - 10 = 0$$

which factorises as

$$(Q + 2)(Q - 5) = 0$$

giving an output level of 5.

The firm's price is therefore

$$P = 51 - ½(5) = 48.5$$

and the profit is

$$\Pi = -5^3 + 4½(5)^2 + 30(5) - 20$$
$$= -125 + 112.5 + 150 - 20 = 117.5$$

To ensure a maximum the second-order condition needs to be met. We have

$$\frac{d^2\pi}{dQ^2} = -6Q + 9 < 0, \text{ given } Q = 5$$

and so the second-order condition is satisfied.

(II) The imposition of a lump-sum tax of 120. The profit function now becomes

$$\Pi = -Q^3 + 4.5Q^2 + 30Q - 140$$

which will again solve for Q = 5 and P = 48.5. The profit is now –2.5 so that in the long-run the firm will close.

Chapter 10

Q2 In the model of competition we varied the level of demand and 'traced-out' a supply curve. Since the monopolist faces the entire market demand, there is only one point on a supply-curve (where MR = MC).

Chapter 11

Q5
(I) Firm 1 has a dominant strategy, which is to produce a low level of output.
(II) Both firms will produce a low output.
(III) With first-mover advantage for firm 1, both will produce a low level of output. If firm 2 moves first, they will both produce a high level of output.

Chapter 12

Q3
(I) If the regulator insists on charging a price equal to the firm's marginal cost then P = MC = 5. Given this the firm makes a loss of 15.

Chapter 13

Q1
(I)

L	Q	APL	MPL	P	VMP	P	ARP	MRP
				Perfect competition		Monopolistic market		
1	10	10	10	5	50	20	200	200
2	30	15	20	5	100	18	270	340
3	60	20	30	5	150	16	320	420
4	100	25	40	5	200	14	350	440
5	140	28	40	5	200	12	336	280
6	170	28.3	30	5	150	10	283.3	20
7	190	27.1	20	5	100	8	217.1	–180
8	200	25	10	5	50	6	150	–320

(II) An employment level of 7 in the perfectly competitive market, 5 in the monopolistic market.

Q4 (I) With a rate of discount of 0% the PV of revenue stream 1 is £18,000, that of revenue stream 2 is £17,500 when the rate of discount is 10%

PV of revenue stream 1: $\pounds 6,000 + \dfrac{\pounds 12,000}{1.21}$

$= \pounds 15{,}917$

PV of revenue stream 2: $\pounds 3,000 + \dfrac{\pounds 14,500}{1.1}$

$= \pounds 16{,}181$

Revenue stream 1 has a higher PV when r = 0%, revenue stream 2 is higher when r = 10%.

(II) Cost = £14,500

PV of revenue stream 1: $\pounds 6,000 + \dfrac{\pounds 12,000}{1.5625}$

$= \pounds 13{,}680$

PV of revenue stream 2: $\pounds 3,000 + \dfrac{\pounds 14,000}{1.25}$

$= \pounds 14{,}600$

The second project is profitable.

Q5 (I) The expected reduction in operating costs

$$0.5 \times \pounds 1{,}500 + 0.5 \times \pounds 750 = \pounds 1.125$$

The NPV calculation is

$$\text{NPV} = \left[\frac{\pounds 1,125}{0.1} - \pounds 10,000\right] = \pounds 1,250$$

(II) The expected reduction in costs is

$$0.9 \times \pounds 1{,}750 + 0.1 \times \pounds 0 = \pounds 1{,}575$$

Yes, since

$$\text{NPV} = \left[\frac{£1,575}{0.1} - £10,000\right] = £5,750$$

(III) $$\text{NPV} = 0.75\left[\frac{£1,125}{0.1} - £11,000\right] + 0.25\left[\frac{£1,125}{0.1} - £20,000\right]$$

$$= 0.75 * £250 + 0.25 * -£8750$$

The NPV is negative and by this criteria the investment is not worthwhile.

Q8 (I) $Q = 6L - L^2$

$$\text{MPL} = \frac{dQ}{dL} = 6 - 2L$$

The slope of the production function reaches a maximum when MPL = 0, so $6 - 2L = 0$ implies that this point occurs when L = 3. With labour input above this level, the slope of the function turns negative.

(III) At a wage of £4 the firm would hire 3 workers. Labour's share of total revenue is 0.27.

Chapter 14

Q4 (I) The wage is £2.50, the employment level is 11.5.

(II) Employment (given by the labour demand function) is 11, the level of unemployment is 1. With a minimum wage set at £4, the employment level is 10 and the unemployment is 3.

(III) The elasticity is –0.27.

(IV) The elasticity would be –0.43.

Chapter 15

Q1 (I)

	FIRM 1	FIRM 2
Capital	£100,000	£100,000
Gearing (debt/equity)	60/40	40/60
Revenues	£25,000	£25,000
Return net of debt interest	£19,000	£21,000
Return on equity	47.5%	35%

(II) Revenues of £50,000

Firm 1:	Return net of debt interest	£44,000
	Return on equity	110%
Firm 2:	Return net of debt interest	£46,000
	Return on equity	76.7%

Revenues of £12,500

Firm 1:	Return on equity	16.25%
Firm 2:	"	14.2%

Q2 (III) The payoff matrix with a standard debt contract is

	Successful investment	**Unsuccessful investment**
Gross return	£100,000	£50,000
Bank receives	£60,000	£50,000
Firm retains	£40,000	0

The firm's participation constraint that it expects to make a profit is satisfied. The expected rate of return to the lender is

$$E(R) = 0.5 \times 20\% + 0.5 \times 0\% = 10\%$$

(III) The second type of project has a higher probability of success and so yields a greater expected return to the lender at any given rate of interest charged. Firms with type 2 would borrow if the interest rate were less than 55.55%; firms with type 1 projects would be prepared to borrow until interest rates reached 100%.

Chapter 16

Q2 Individuals can gain from trade without the resulting allocation being (Pareto-) optimal.

Q6 It is not necessary for an allocation to be efficient in order that it is equitable.

Chapter 17

Q3 (I) The marginal cost to the beekeeper is found by differentiating the total cost function. This gives $MC = 4Q$. Marginal revenue is found by differentiating total revenue (which itself is obtained by multiplying the average revenue by quantity). This gives $MR = 24$. The profit-maximising beekeeper will maintain 6 hives.

(II) The marginal social benefit, MSB, of the hives is the sum of the marginal revenue to the beekeeper and the benefit to the apple-grower. The MSB is therefore 32 and the socially-optimal number of hives is 8. The free-market solution results in under-production (there are too few hives maintained).

Chapter 18

Q2 Other things equal this would move the Lorenz curve in towards the diagonal, as the distribution of income becomes more equal. If the new and old Lorenz curves cross after a policy change, we cannot unambiguously say whether the distribution is more or less equal. Whether such a change is desirable is a value judgement and would depend on which groups/individuals are affected.

Index

Acknowledgements

The Publisher would like to thank the following who have kindly given permission for the use of copyright material.

Page 4	Chart 1.1	Economic Trends 1997, Office for National Statistics © Crown Copyright 1999
Page 4	Table 1.1	Economic Trends 1997, Office for National Statistics © Crown Copyright 1999
Page 26	Table 1.4	Reproduced by permission of Routledge, from Simmons, R. (1996), The Demand for English League Football: A Club Level Analysis, Applied Economics, Vol. 28
Page 39	Table 2.1	Reproduced by permission of Council of Mortgage Lenders from Maclennan, D. and Stephens, M. (1997)
Page 45	Table 2.2	Economic Trends 1998, Office for National Statistics © Crown Copyright 1999
Page 47	Table 2.3	Economic Trends 1998, Office for National Statistics © Crown Copyright 1999
Page 47	Table 2.4	National Institute Economic Review, from Oulton, N. (1998), The Implications of the Boskin Report
Page 54	Table 2.7	Reproduced by permission of Nellis, J.G., from Flemming, M.C. and Nellis, J.G. (1984), The Halifax House Price Index: Technical Details, The Halifax
Page 55	Table 2.8	Reproduced by permission of Halifax plc
Page 56	Chart 2.1	Reproduced by permission of Halifax plc
Page 67	Table 3.1	Office for National Statistics © Crown Copyright 1999 from Social Trends 1998
Page 73	Charts 3.1A and 3.1B	TUC 1997 from Students at Work, TUC Labour Market Report
Page 74	Table 3.2	National Union of Students

Page 79	Table 3.6	HM Treasury © Crown Copyright 1999, from Taylor, M. (1998), The Modernisation of Britains Tax and Benefit System No. 3
Page 80	Chart 3.2	Office for National Statistics © Crown Copyright 1999, from Annual Abstract of Statistics
Page 83	Table 3.7	Policy Studies Institute from Blundell, R.W. (1994), Work incentives and labour supply in the UK, in Bryson, A. and McKay, S. (eds) Is it worth working?
Page 103	Table 4.4	Office for National Statistics © Crown Copyright 1999 from Social Trends 1998
Page 107	Table 4.5	Reproduced by permission of Institute of Fiscal Studies from Banks, Dilnot and Tanner (1997), Taxing Household Saving, IFS Commentary No. 66
Page 108	Table 4.6	Reproduced by permission of Institute of Fiscal Studies
Page 110	Chart 4.1	Office for National Statistics © Crown Copyright 1999, from Inland Revenue Statistics 1997
Page 125	Table 5.1	Association of British Insurers (1993), Insurance Statistics Yearbook 1983–93
Page 133	Table 5.2	Reproduced by permission of Institute of Fiscal Studies, from Gosling, A., Johnson, P., McCrae, J. and Paull, G. (1997), The Dynamics of Low Pay and Unemployment in Early 1990s Britain
Page 134	Table 5.3	Reproduced by permission of Institute of Fiscal Studies, from Gosling, A., Johnson, P., McCrae, J. and Paull, G. (1997), The Dynamics of Low Pay and Unemployment in Early 1990s Britain
Page 150	Chart 6.1	Office for National Statistics © Crown Copyright 1999, from Financial Statistics 1997
Page 151	Table 6.4	Reproduced by permission of Institute of Fiscal Studies
Page 152	Table 6.5	Reproduced by permission of Institute of Fiscal Studies, from Banks, J. and Tanner, S. (1996), Savings and Wealth in the UK
Page 154	Chart 6.2	Council of Mortgage Lenders, from Maclennan, D. and Stephens, M. (1997), EMU and the UK Housing and Mortgage Markets
Page 155	Chart 6.3	Reproduced by permission of Halifax plc
Page 156	Table 6.6	Reproduced by permission of Halifax plc
Page 157	Chart 6.4	Council of Mortgage Lenders, from Thomas, R. (1996), Negative Equity: Outlook and Effects
Page 158	Table 6.7	Council of Mortgage Lenders, from Maclennan, D. and Stephens, M. (1997), EMU and the UK Housing and Mortgage Markets
Page 159	Table 6.8	Office for National Statistics © Crown Copyright 1999, from Financial Statistics, various years
Page 167	Table 7.1	© Times 1998. Reproduced by permission of HarperCollins Publishers Ltd
Page 201	Chart 8.1	Office for National Statistics © Crown Copyright 1999, from Financial Statistics 1996
Page 202	Chart 8.2	Economic Policy, from Franks, J. and Mayer, C. (1990), Corporate Ownership and Corporate Control

Page 202	Table 8.2	Reproduced by permission of Blackwell Publishers UK, from Leech, D. and Leahy, J. (1991), Ownership Structure Control Type Classifications and the Performance of Large British Companies, Economic Journal, 409, pp 1418–37
Page 206	Table 8.3	W. Hornby (1995), The Theory of the Firm Revisited, Management Decision, Vol. 33, published by MCB
Page 208	Table 8.4a and Table 8.4B	BIS Economic Papers, Basle, S. Prowse (1994), Corporate Governance in an International Perspective
Page 216	Table 8.6	© A. Bruce, from Bruce, A. and Buck, T. (1997), Executive Reward and Corporate Governance
Page 241	Table 9.2	EC (1996), The Agricultural Situation in the European Union 1996 Report
Page 243	Chart 9.1	Office for National Statistics © Crown Copyright 1999, from Economic Trends
Page 244	Chart 9.2	Office for National Statistics © Crown Copyright 1999, from Economic Trends
Page 245	Chart 9.3	Ritson, C. and Harvey, D.R. (1997), The Common Agricultural Policy, 2nd edition, published by CAB International
Page 246	Chart 9.4	Reproduced by permission of CAB
Page 267	Tables 10.1 and 10.2	Our thanks to Virgin for quoting their fares by telephone
Page 317	Table 12.1	© Pearson Education, Sloman, J. (1997), Economics, 3rd edition, Prentice Hall
Page 319	Chart 12.1	Reproduced by permission of British Gas
Page 321	Table 12.3	Dept of Environment & Regions © Crown Copyright 1999, from Transport Statistics 1998
Page 324	Table 12.4	Ogden, S. (1997), Corporate Governance in the Privatised Utilities, in Keasey, K., Thompson, S. and Wright, M. (eds) Corporate Governance, published by Oxford University Press
Page 325	Table 12.5	Reproduced by permission of Institute of Fiscal Studies, from Waddams Price, C. and Hancock, R. (1998), Distributional Effects of Liberalising UK Residential Utility Markets, Fiscal Studies 19
Page 327	Table 12.6	Reproduced by permission of Institute of Fiscal Studies
Page 351	Table 13.6	Taken from Oxford Review of Economic Policy, Vol. 12, No. 1, 1996, 'Wage Inequality in the UK' by Machin, S., Table 8. Reproduced by permission of Oxford University Press
Page 351	Table 13.7	Low Pay Commission 1998, Office for National Statistics © Crown Copyright 1999 from The National Minimum Wage, First Report of the Low Pay Commission
Page 355	Table 13.8	Taken from Oxford Review of Economic Policy, Vol. 12, No. 1, 1996, Factor Shares and Inequality in The UK, by Ryan, P. Reproduced by permission of Oxford University Press
Page 375	Table 14.3A	Reproduced by permission of Institute of Fiscal Studies from Dearden, L., Machin, S., Reed, H. and Wilkinson, D. (1997), Labour Turnover and Work Related Training

Page 376	Chart 14.1	Low Pay Commission 1998, Office for National Statistics © Crown Copyright 1999 from The National Minimum Wage: First Report of the Low Pay Commission
Page 377	Table 14.4	Low Pay Commission 1998, Office for National Statistics © Crown Copyright 1999
Page 381	Table 14.5 and Chart 14.2	Low Pay Commission 1998, Office for National Statistics © Crown Copyright 1999
Page 382	Chart 14.3	Low Pay Commission 1998, Office for National Statistics © Crown Copyright 1999
Page 383	Chart 14.4	Low Pay Commission 1998, Office for National Statistics © Crown Copyright 1999
Page 384	Table 14.6	Fernie, S. and Metcalf, D. (1996), Low Pay and Minimum Wages: The British Evidence, published by Centre for Economic Performance
Page 385	Table 14.7	Fernie, S. and Metcalf, D. (1996), Low Pay and Minimum Wages: The British Evidence, published by Centre for Economic Performance
Page 387	Table 14.8	Low Pay Commission 1998, Office for National Statistics © Crown Copyright 1999, from The National Minimum Wage: First Report of the Low Pay Commission
Page 407	Table 15.3A	Taken from Oxford Review of Economic Policy, Vol. 12, No. 2, 1996, The Assessment: Investment Performance and Policy, Bond, S. and Jenkinson, T., Tables 5 & 7. Reproduced by permission of Oxford University Press
Page 408	Table 15.3B	Rajan, R.G. and Zingales, L. (1995), What do we know about Capital Structure?, Journal of Finance, Vol. 50/5, published by Blackwell
Page 409	Table 15.4	Prowse, S. (1994), Corporate Governance in an International Perspective BIS Economic Papers, Basle
Page 409	Table 15.5	Bond, S. and Jenkinson, T. (1996), 'The Assessment: Investment Performance and Policy', Oxford Review of Economic Policy, Vol. 12, published by Oxford University Press
Page 453	Table 17.2	European Economy (1992), The Climate Challenge, Economic Aspects of the Communitys Strategy for Limiting CO_2 Emissions, Vol. 51 May
Page 454	Chart 17.1	Transport Statistics 1998, Dept of Environment & Region © Crown Copyright 1999
Page 458	Chart 17.2	Transport Statistics 1998, Dept of Environment & Region © Crown Copyright 1999
Page 459	Chart 17.3	Transport Statistics 1998, Dept of Environment & Region © Crown Copyright 1999
Page 460	Table 17.3	Reproduced by permission of Institute of Fiscal Studies, from Blow, L. and Crawford, I. (1997), The Distributional Effects of Taxes on Private Motoring
Page 462	Table 17.4	Newbery, D.M. (1993), Pricing and Congestion, in Jenkinson, T. (ed.) Readings in Microeconomics, published by Oxford University Press
Page 473	Table 18.2	McClements, L. (1977), Equivalence Scales for Children, Journal of Public Economics, Vol. 8

Page 473	Table 18.3	Economic Trends 1998, Office for National Statistics © Crown Copyright 1999
Page 474	Table 18.4	Economic Trends 1998, Office for National Statistics © Crown Copyright 1999
Page 476	Chart 18.1	Economic Trends 1998, Office for National Statistics © Crown Copyright 1999
Page 477	Table 18.5	Reproduced by permission of Institute of Fiscal Studies, from Goodman, A., Johnson, P. and Webb, S. (1997), Low Income Dynamics in 1990s Britain, Fiscal Studies, Vol. 18/2
Page 477	Table 18.6	Goodman, A., Johnson, P. and Webb, S. (1997), Inequality in the UK, published by Oxford University Press
Page 480	Table 18.7	Dept of Social Security © Crown Copyright 1999, from Households Below Average Income A Statistical Analysis 1979–1994/5
Page 482	Chart 18.2	Dept of Social Security 1997 © Crown Copyright 1999
Page 482	Table 18.8	Reproduced by permission of Institute of Fiscal Studies, from Jarvis, S. and Jenkins, S.P. (1997), Low Income Dynamics in 1990s Britain, Fiscal Studies, Vol. 18/2
Page 484	Charts 18.3A and 18.3B	Dept of Social Security 1997 © Crown Copyright 1999
Page 485	Charts 18.3C and 18.3D	Dept of Social Security 1997 © Crown Copyright 1999

The Publisher has attempted to contact all that permissions are required from. They would welcome hearing from any copyright holders whom it has not been possible to contact.